T0396893

CAMBRIDGE
UNIVERSITY PRESS

University Printing House, Cambridge CB2 8BS, United Kingdom

Cambridge University Press is part of the University of Cambridge.

It furthers the University's mission by disseminating knowledge in the pursuit of education, learning and research at the highest international levels of excellence.

www.cambridge.org
Information on this title: www.cambridge.org/9781107034006

First published 2014

A catalogue record for this publication is available from the British Library

Library of Congress Cataloguing in Publication data
Intellectual property at the edge : the contested contours of IP / [edited by] Rochelle Cooper Dreyfuss, Jane C. Ginsburg.
pages cm. – (Cambridge intellectual property and information law ; 22)
ISBN 978-1-107-03400-6 (Hardback)
1. Intellectual property–European Union countries. I. Dreyfuss, Rochelle Cooper, 1947– editor of compilation. II. Ginsburg, Jane C., editor of compilation.
KJE2636.I5725 2014
346.404′8–dc23 2013040416

ISBN 978-1-107-03400-6 Hardback

Intellectual Property at the Edge

The Contested Contours of IP

Edited by

Rochelle Cooper Dreyfuss and Jane C. Ginsburg

Intellectual Property at the Edge

Intellectual Property at the Edge addresses both newly formed intellectual property rights and those which have lurked on the fringes, unadmitted to the established IP canon. It provides a basis for studying and discussing the history of these emerging rights as well as their relationship to new technological opportunities and to the changing importance of innovation and creative production in the global economy. In addition to addressing the scope of new rights, it also focuses on new limitations to patent, copyright and trademark rights that spring from similar changes. All of these developments are examined comparatively: for each new development, scholars in two jurisdictions analyze the evolving legal norm. In several instances, the first of the paired authors writes from the perspective of the legal system in which the doctrine emerged, and the second addresses its reception in his or her jurisdiction.

ROCHELLE COOPER DREYFUSS is the Pauline Newman Professor of Law and Co-director of the Engelberg Center on Innovation Law and Policy at New York University School of Law. Her research interests include international and domestic intellectual property law as well as civil procedure.

JANE C. GINSBURG is the Morton L. Janklow Professor of Literary and Artistic Property Law at Columbia University School of Law, where she is also Faculty Director of the Kernochan Center for Law, Media and the Arts. She teaches legal methods, copyright law and trademarks law.

Cambridge Intellectual Property and Information Law

As its economic potential has rapidly expanded, intellectual property has become a subject of front-rank legal importance. *Cambridge Intellectual Property and Information Law* is a series of monograph studies of major current issues in intellectual property. Each volume contains a mix of international, European, comparative and national law, making this a highly significant series for practitioners, judges and academic researchers in many countries.

A list of books in the series can be found at the end of this volume.

Contents

Figures

Tables

Contributors

STEFAN BECHTOLD Stefan Bechtold is Professor of Intellectual Property at ETH Zurich, Switzerland. His research interests include intellectual property, law and technology, telecommunications law, and antitrust law, as well as law and economics.

BARTON BEEBE Barton Beebe is the John M. Desmarais Professor of Intellectual Property Law at New York University School of Law and Co-Director of the Engelberg Center on Innovation Law and Policy.

LIONEL BENTLY Lionel Bently is Herchel Smith Professor of Intellectual Property law and Director of the Centre for Intellectual Property and Information Law in the Faculty of Law at the University of Cambridge. He is a professorial fellow at Emmanuel College, Cambridge.

GRAEME B. DINWOODIE Graeme B. Dinwoodie is the Professor of Intellectual Property and Information Technology Law at the University of Oxford, and Director of the Oxford Intellectual Property Research Centre. Prior to taking up the IP Chair at Oxford in 2009, he taught at Chicago-Kent College of Law, the University of Pennsylvania School of Law and the University of Cincinnati College of Law, and from 2005 to 2009 held a Chair in Intellectual Property Law at Queen Mary University of London. From 2011 to 2013, he was the President of the International Association for the Advancement of Teaching and Research in Intellectual Property.

STACEY L. DOGAN Stacey Dogan teaches property and intellectual property law at Boston University School of Law. Her research focuses on trademark, copyright, and right of publicity law, with an emphasis on the challenges wrought by digital media and the Internet.

ROCHELLE C. DREYFUSS Rochelle Cooper Dreyfuss is Pauline Newman Professor of Law at New York University School of Law and Co-director of the Engelberg Center on Innovation Law and Policy. Her teaching and scholarship largely focus on national and international patent law and civil procedure. She currently serves on the National Academies of Science's Committee on Science, Technology, and Law. With Jane Ginsburg, she edited *Intellectual Property Stories* (2005), which inspired this volume.

SÉVERINE DUSOLLIER Séverine Dusollier is Professor of Intellectual Property Law at the University of Namur (Belgium) and Head of the Research Center in Information, Law and Society (CRIDS), which is one of the oldest and biggest research centers in information technologies and law. Séverine Dusollier has carried out research on several European and national projects and drafted reports for the World Intellectual Property Organization (WIPO), the Council of Europe, UNESCO and the European Commission, and has published extensively in copyright, IP rights and IT law matters. Her current research includes digital rights management (DRM), copyright enforcement on the Internet, intellectual commons and open source, interoperability and IP, public domain, copyright exceptions, and competition law and IP.

SUSY FRANKEL Susy Frankel is a Professor of Law at Victoria University of Wellington and Director of the New Zealand Centre of International Economic Law. She is Chair of the Copyright Tribunal (NZ). She has published extensively on international intellectual property law and policy, and particularly intellectual property's relationship with trade law and the protection of indigenous peoples' traditional knowledge.

JEANNE C. FROMER Jeanne C. Fromer is a Professor of Law at New York University School of Law. Professor Fromer previously served as a law clerk to Justice David Souter of the US Supreme Court and to Judge Robert Sack of the US Court of Appeals for the Second Circuit. She also worked at Hale and Dorr LLP (now WilmerHale) as an intellectual property attorney. She earned her B.A. in Computer Science from Barnard College, Columbia University; S.M. in Electrical Engineering and Computer Science from the Massachusetts Institute of Technology; and J.D. from Harvard Law School.

DEV S. GANGJEE Dr. Dev Gangjee is presently a university lecturer in intellectual property at the Law Faculty of Oxford University. Prior to this, he was a senior lecturer in law at the London School of Economics. His research focuses broadly on IP, but with a special emphasis on branding and trademarks, Geographical Indications and copyright law. Additional research interests include the history and political economy of IP, collective and open innovation, and the interface between IP and theories of development.

DANIEL GERVAIS Daniel Gervais is the Professor of Law at Vanderbilt University Law School and Director of the Vanderbilt Intellectual Property Program, where he also serves as Faculty Director of the Master's Program. He is Editor-in-Chief of the peer-reviewed *Journal of World Intellectual Property* and editor of www.tripsagreement.net. In 2012, he became the first law professor in North America elected to the Academy of Europe. Before he joined the Academy, Professor Gervais was successively Legal Officer at the GATT (now World Trade Organization); Head of Section at the World Intellectual Property Organization (WIPO); and Vice President, International, of Massachusetts-based Copyright Clearance Center, Inc. (CCC). Professor Gervais studied computer science and law at McGill University and the University of Montreal, where he also obtained LL.B. and LL.M. degrees, and received several awards.

JANE C. GINSBURG Jane C. Ginsburg is the Morton L. Janklow Professor of Literary and Artistic Property Law at Columbia University School of Law, and Faculty Director of its Kernochan Center for Law, Media and the Arts. She teaches legal methods, copyright law and trademarks law, and is the author or co-author of casebooks on all three subjects. In addition to co-editing *Intellectual Property Stories* (2005) with Rochelle Dreyfuss, she was a co-reporter with Rochelle Dreyfuss and Professor François Dessemontet for the American Law Institute project on *Intellectual Property: Principles Governing Jurisdiction, Choice of Law and Judgments in Transnational Disputes* (2008).

C. SCOTT HEMPHILL Scott Hemphill is Professor of Law at Columbia Law School, where his research examines the balance between innovation and competition set by antitrust law, intellectual property and other forms of regulation. From 2011 to 2012, Professor Hemphill served as Chief of the Antitrust Bureau, in the Office of the New York State Attorney General. He holds a J.D. and Ph.D. in economics, both from Stanford University, and is a graduate of Harvard and the London School of Economics, where he studied as a Fulbright Scholar.

RT HON. SIR ROBIN JACOB Sir Robin Jacob is Hugh Laddie Professor of Intellectual Property Law and Director of the Institute of Brand and Innovation Law, University College London. A member of the Intellectual Property Bar from 1967 to 1993, Robin Jacob was appointed to the Bench in 1993, when he was a designated Patent Judge. From 1997 to 2001 he was Supervising Chancery Judge for Birmingham,

Bristol and Cardiff. He was appointed a Lord Justice of Appeal in October 2003. He formally retired from the Court of Appeal in May 2011 but continues to sit from time to time in that court. In addition, he sometimes acts as an arbitrator, mediator or expert witness on English or European law, and lectures in the UK and abroad. He writes extensively on all forms of intellectual property.

ANNETTE KUR Professor Kur is a senior member of research staff and Head of Unit at the Max Planck Institute for Intellectual Property and Competition Law. She is affiliated professor at the University of Stockholm and honorary professor at the University of Munich.

DAVID LEFRANC David Lefranc is a French lawyer specializing in intellectual property. He obtained his doctorate in law in 2003. His thesis, under the direction of Professor Henri-Jacques Lucas, addressed the legal consequences of fame in copyright and trademark law and rights of personality. Following six years of university teaching, David Lefranc became an *avocat* and founded Laropoin legal office. He continues his research through the publication of numerous articles. He is also a lecturer at EDHEC Business School and at the universities of Nantes and Douai, France.

JOSEPH P. LIU Joseph P. Liu is a professor of law at Boston College Law School, where he writes and teaches in the areas of copyright, trademark, property and Internet law. His main area of academic research is on the impact of digital technology on copyright law and markets, with a particular focus on how digital technology is changing the way individuals interact with copyrighted works.

JUSTINE PILA Justine Pila is Fellow and Director of Studies (Law) at St Catherine's College, Oxford University, University Lecturer in Intellectual Property Law at the Oxford University Faculty of Law, and Research Fellow at the Oxford Institute of European and Comparative Law (IECL).

CAROL M. ROSE Carol M. Rose is Lohse Professor at the James E. Rogers College of Law, University of Arizona and Gordon Bradford Tweedy Professor (Emerita) at Yale Law School. Her publications include several books and numerous articles on traditional and modern property regimes, natural resource and environmental law, and intellectual property. Her work has been translated into several languages and published in a number of countries, and she has enjoyed many honors, including membership in the American Academy of Arts and Sciences.

TED SICHELMAN Ted Sichelman is a Professor of Law at the University of San Diego School of Law, where he teaches and writes in the areas of intellectual property, law and entrepreneurship, empirical legal studies, law and economics, and computational legal studies. Previously, he was an intellectual property attorney at Heller Ehrman and Irell & Manella, and a law clerk for the Honorable A. Wallace Tashima of the Ninth Circuit Court of Appeals. Before becoming a lawyer, he founded and ran a venture-backed software company.

KATHERINE J. STRANDBURG Katherine Strandburg is Alfred B. Engelberg Professor of Law at New York University School of Law. Her research and teaching focus on patent law and information privacy law. Current projects include an institutional theory of patentable subject matter, studies of medical innovation by physicians and its relationship to patenting, and a study of an NIH initiative to promote collaborative research into rare diseases. Professor Strandburg graduated from the University of Chicago Law School with high honors in 1995 and served as a law clerk to the Honorable Richard D. Cudahy of the US Court of Appeals for the Seventh Circuit. Prior to her legal career, Professor Strandburg was a Ph.D. research physicist at Argonne National Laboratory.

JEANNIE SUK Jeannie Suk is Professor of Law at Harvard Law School. She has been a Guggenheim Fellow and a fellow of the MacDowell Colony, and named one of the Best Lawyers under forty by the National Asian Pacific American Bar Association. She has given Congressional testimony on law and innovation in the fashion industry.

REBECCA TUSHNET Rebecca Tushnet is a professor at the Georgetown University Law Center. She clerked for Associate Justice David H. Souter on the Supreme Court and practiced intellectual property law before beginning teaching. Her publications on copyright, trademark, advertising law, and related issues are available at https://tushnet.wordpress.com/writings/. She helped found the Organization for Transformative Works, a non-profit dedicated to supporting and promoting fanworks, and currently volunteers on its legal committee.

SILKE VON LEWINSKI Silke von Lewinski, Adj. Prof. Dr., tenured at Max Planck Institute for Intellectual Property and Competition Law (Munich), specializes in international and European copyright law and in IP and folklore. She has been copyright expert to the European Commission and to governments of Eastern and Central European and former Soviet Union countries, and member of EC and German delegations, respectively, at World Intellectual Property

Organization (WIPO) Diplomatic Conferences in 1996, 2000, 2012 and 2013. She has frequently been visiting professor at many universities worldwide, and among numerous publications are the books *International Copyright Law and Policy* (2008) and (as editor) *Indigenous Heritage and Intellectual Property: Genetic Resources, Traditional Knowledge and Folklore* (2004, 2nd edn., 2008; Chinese edn., 2011).

Editors' Preface

In 2005 we edited *Intellectual Property Stories*, a book recounting the seminal cases in traditional intellectual property law in the United States. By examining the contemporary socio-economic conditions and the human "backstory" to the leading nineteenth- and twentieth-century cases in copyright, patent and trademarks, the book attempted to uncover the factors that led courts to structure the law as we find it in the twenty-first century in the United States. *Intellectual Property at the Edge* is both more forward-looking and more geographically encompassing. It addresses intellectual property rights that are either newly forming or, if of older vintage, had nonetheless lurked on the fringes, unadmitted to the established canon. The emergence of these rights reflects new technological opportunities as well as the increasing dependence of the economies of developed and many developing countries on innovation. Their appearance calls for a fresh look at history and an analysis of their impact on creativity.

Significantly, emerging norms do not pertain only to rights holders. As intellectual property law develops, the public's interest, in the form of new limitations on longstanding rights as well as concomitant curbs on new aspirants, also claims attention. A book about the *Contested Contours of IP* necessarily confronts the contending demands of creators for new or increased coverage and of users (whether other creators, commercial competitors or their audience) for freedom to innovate or to enjoy the fruits of intellectual endeavors. Thus, in addition to addressing the scope of new rights, this book focuses its last chapters on emerging limitations on patent, copyright and trademarks.

Because the growing prominence of new forms of intellectual property rights and limitations is a global phenomenon, we chose to examine these developments comparatively. Accordingly, for each new development, we asked scholars in two jurisdictions to describe the evolving legal norm and to consider the extent to which the development responded only to internal conditions, or instead was influenced by legal evolution elsewhere. In several instances, the first of the paired authors writes from the perspective of the legal system in which the doctrine emerged, and the second addresses its reception in his or her jurisdiction.

Intellectual property rights also evolve in the broader context of property rights in general. While rights in intangibles may seem more susceptible to expansion (or contraction), the phenomenon of changed contours is not unique to intellectual property. The book therefore begins with an introduction by Carol Rose, a scholar of real property, who has written extensively about how such changes occur in property regimes more generally. Like Professor Rose, many of the other contributors to this volume enjoy long-established international reputations. However, as seems appropriate to a work about emerging IP norms, several authors are emerging IP scholars whose international standing we hope this book enhances.

We would particularly like to thank Nicole Arzt for all her excellent assistance.

ROCHELLE COOPER DREYFUSS
JANE GINSBURG
June 2013

Table of Cases

Australia

National Research Development Corporation (NRDC) v. Commissioner of Patents (1959) 102 C.L.R. 252 345n7

Stevens v. Kabushiki Kaisha Sony Computer Entertainment [2005] HCA 58 (6 October 2005) 261n37

Belgium

Anvers (9e ch.), 28 February 2002, *Auteurs & Media*, 2002 258n21

Civ. Namur, 7 January 2004, *R.D.T.I.*, October 2005 259n26

Corr. Charleroi, 23 October 2003, no 2626 258n21

Corr. Charleroi, 23 October 2003, no 68.L7.343/02 259–60n27

Corr. Gand, 23 April 2008, no 68.98.1806/07/FS1 259–60n27

Corr. Gand, 23 April 2008, no 2008/1322 258n21

Mons, 4 May 2007, no 135 H 04 258n21, 259–60n27

Canada

Dairy Bureau of Canada v. Annable Foods Ltd (1993) 46 CPR (3d) 289 (British Columbia SC) 309 130n1, 141n49

Institut National des Appellations d'Origine des Vins et Eaux-de-Vie v. Andre Wines Ltd (1990) 30 CPR (3d) 279 (Ontario CA) aff'g (1987) 16 CPR (3d) 385 (Ontario HCJ), leave to appeal refused [1991] 1 S.C.R. x (note) 130n1, 141n49

Institut National des Appellations d'Origine des Vins et Eaux-de-Vie v. Andres Wines Ltd 14 CIPR 138, 40 DLR (4th) 239 (1987) (Ontario CA) 106n5

European Union

Finland

France

Germany

Hong Kong

India

Italy

Netherlands

New Zealand

South Africa

Spain

United Kingdom

United States

Introduction: A real property lawyer cautiously inspects the edges of intellectual property

Carol M. Rose

No one should take this title in the wrong way: that's a "real" property lawyer in the sense of real estate, not in the sense of actuality – realty, not reality. I believe the editors of this volume thought that they themselves knew too much about intellectual property to see the perplexities that could obscure the path for uninitiated readers. And so, for the Introduction, the editors sought out someone who knows something about ordinary property, but not so much about intellectual property. Lucky me! Thanks to their request, I have had the great pleasure of going through these very enlightening essays about the emerging and sometimes ongoing issues in this area, really one of the most dynamic fields in all of property law. But I can only hope that my relative unfamiliarity with specifically *intellectual* property enables me to feel at one with other less expert readers. For the readers who are more like me, I hope this brief introductory essay can point out some of the common themes and some of the oddities that these chapters address, and in some cases connect those themes and oddities to current theoretical trends in other areas of property law.[1]

I will begin with a question that runs through most of the chapters and commentaries in this book: What is intellectual property

[1] Just to reassure the forgetful or uninitiated even further, here is a quick and very conventional primer on the main regimes of IP: *Copyright* protects artistic and authorial productions, but it has considerable leeway for peripheral copying; its protection also lasts a long time, but not forever – now usually the life of the author plus someone else's life after that. *Trademark* protects distinctive brands, symbols and slogans that identify the sources of commercial products; trademarks too allow some exceptions, but they can last indefinitely, so long as they are in use. *Patents* give very strong protection to useful inventions, but they generally only last twenty years. Besides, patents take some effort and expense to get, and they require the inventor to tell others how to make and use the invention, even if those others are not supposed to do so until the patent expires. *Trade secrets*, on the other hand, allow inventors to hold on to their secrets indefinitely (like trademark), but a trade secret gives no protection if someone else figures out how an invention works.

supposed to be doing? After that, I will take up some versions of the "edge" and what several of these chapters mean by the edges of intellectual property. After that, I will run through a *mélange* of other themes that readers may find in these chapters – certainly not an exclusive list, but one that generally bounces off other ideas in property law.

So, to begin with the most fundamental question.

What is it all about?

Silke von Lewinski (Chapter 10),[2] commenting on the differences between traditional knowledge protections and conventional commercial copyright, observes that both copyright and protection of traditional knowledge aim to control uses of intellectual endeavors. Indeed, without too much of a stretch, one might say the same about the rest of intellectual property (IP) as well. But to what end? Are IP protections supposed to encourage innovation, by preventing others from free-riding on original work for some appropriate period of time, and (at least in the case of trademark) by protecting quality and staving off consumer error? Those are the conventional rationales, and if true, the underlying innovation-incentivizing goal ought to benefit the public and give a good reason for the public's recognition and enforcement of IP claims. But von Lewinski's comments also suggest that these and other conventional IP rationales seem rather mismatched with the reasons for protecting the creative productions of traditional peoples, including the Maori haka performance works described by Susy Frankel (Chapter 9). For many such works, the object is not to innovate at all, but rather to reaffirm the identity and continuity of the community and the community's place in the larger universe; indeed one might think that innovative (aka mistaken) performance may cause grievous cosmic disarray.

But even within the many more conventionally familiar types of IP, like patent or copyright, aid to innovation may be a sideshow, and the real object of protection may lie somewhere else. For example, might the idea of IP protection be simply to help businesses repress rivals, whether or not innovation is involved? Some of the chapters in this book suggest this rather questionable objective, notably the regional wine makers' claims against others' use of the name "Spanish Champagne"

[2] In this as in other references to the authors in this book, I will use brief names together with the chapter locations of the authors' contributions.

(Gangjee, Chapter 5). Alternatively, as the the Rt Hon. Robin Jacob (Chapter 20) rather tartly but interestingly suggests about copyright in particular, might a good deal of IP protection be aimed at protecting *amour propre*?

If *amour propre* is a matter of dignity, then some topics in these chapters answer Jacob's comment affirmatively, because a number of dignitary claims – some more sympathetic than others – do surface in these chapters. Traditional cultural expressions, like those of the Maori haka performances (Frankel, Chapter 9), would appear to raise quite sympathetic dignitary claims indeed, as traditional peoples try to impose a respectful treatment on outsiders. On the other hand, Stacey Dogan (Chapter 1) describes how baseball cards in gum packages initiated a right to personal celebrity, but seemingly with little purpose other than to make certain that celebrity images could be hawked for exclusive advertising deals. The French, perhaps not surprisingly, have taken a somewhat more limited and one might even say more *dignified* approach to celebrity protection (Lefranc, Chapter 2), in which celebrity is not so readily bought and sold. Perhaps this reflects a greater Continental concern for "moral rights" and personality protection than has been the case for the bubblegum-snapping commercial cousins across the Atlantic.

But coming back to *amour propre*, it is hard to see what motivation other than affronted dignity would drive the early twentieth-century makers of the "Odol" brand of mouthwash to object to the use of "Odol" by a cutlery manufacturer (Beebe, Chapter 3), unless perhaps there was an unspoken rivalry about some other personal hygiene matter, like nail clippers. Indeed, subsequent developments of the trademark dilution concept after *Odol*, in both America and Europe, suggest motivations mixing possessiveness with a sense of *lèse majesté* on the part of commercial kingpins (Beebe, Chapter 3; Dinwoodie, Chapter 4). Another kind of dignitary claim appears in the actions of the optical surgeon who took out a patent on a surgical method, because, he said, he felt disrespected by professional insiders (Strandburg, Chapter 15), although this surgeon did seem to have some monopoly profits in mind as well. And speaking of mixing dignity with money, there is always the much-lampooned but ever-defended Barbie (Tushnet, Chapter 19): is it *amour propre* or innovation or simply monopoly profit that induces Mattel to threaten to sue the purveyors of Barbie-like whip-wielding "dungeondolls"? Or perhaps do all three motivations conjoin, under the rubric of reputation? And should the rest of us care? With that question in mind, let us turn to another set of common themes: edges.

What is all this about edges? What is in and what is out of IP, or, the edge of the cliff

The title to this book has to bring a certain smug smile to the lips of lawyers who deal in real property. Try as they might, scholars dealing in more ethereal forms of property cannot seem to escape metaphors that refer to the brute physicality of real things. An *edge* smacks of real estate and other tangibles: the edge of a cliff, or the edge of a field – the border between something and nothing on the one hand; or on the other hand, the border between one crop and another. The edge of the knife suggests a different kind of edge: "edgy" in the sense of cutting, critical, hard to manage. All three of those metaphors of the edge show up in these chapters. But I will start with the cliff.

Several topics in the book seem so close to the edge of IP that they threaten to fall off the cliff altogether. Fashion is one of those cliff-toppling topics (Hemphill and Suk, Chapter 7; Kur, Chapter 8) – too artistic and too ephemeral for patent, too functional for copyright, in effect straddling the copyright/patent divide without belonging to either. But the chapters on geographical designations for wines (Gangjee, Chapter 5), protections of traditional knowledge (Frankel, Chapter 9), and surgeons' methods for medical procedures (Strandburg, Chapter 15) also present scenarios that fit only very uncomfortably into the usual rubrics of IP. The fit is uncomfortable for surgical procedures because of the surgeons' own vehement professional objections to proprietary claims on medical procedures. It is uncomfortable for wine makers' geographical designations – and indigenous cultural expressions too – at least in part because the identities of the rights holders are somewhat uncertain. Who is in, and who is out of the rights-holding group? Who qualifies for membership; and who gets to define the qualifying activities?

Some scholars think that such issues are manageable through evolving concepts in more traditional IP; Gervais (Chapter 6), for example, thinks that trademark can deal with demands for geographical designations. On the other hand, Frankel (Chapter 9) proposes a quite different way to manage indigenous people's traditional knowledge, allocating control to traditional guardians. In the fashion industry, Hemphill and Suk (Chapter 7) describe the 1930s upscale designers' elaborate organization to ward off copyists, suggesting that a given industry might try to organize itself to come up with its own crypto-property rights. By the way, this organization sounds much like the diamond merchants' and cotton traders' organizations that Lisa Bernstein has described in detail elsewhere, except that industry self-organization in those trades appears to have been considerably more robust than was the case for the 1930s fashionistas.[3]

The larger point is that cliff-hangers like these regularly emerge to raise institutional issues for IP law. Should the cliff-hangers have their own IP rubrics, known in this area as *sui generis* regimes? Or might they manage to squeeze into standard IP categories? Or should they escape from formal IP and design their own institutional norms? Those are the issues that emerge when the edge means the edge of the entire IP cliff.

But there are other edges in this book as well.

The edge of the field: The borders between different IP domains

Several of the chapters in this book describe the ways that the boundaries can blur between different areas of IP – and what happens when they do. Lionel Bently (Chapter 14) describes an early example, where the purveyors of an eighteenth-century medical concoction received a patent early on, but then claimed trade secrecy many years later. Here the blurring occurred in a context in which legislators and courts themselves had not yet really figured out the boundaries between these types of protections. But another example came decades later, when the boundaries should have been clearer to all concerned. Jeanne Fromer (Chapter 13) describes a case in which the inventor of an industrial pump got the protection of a patent for a time, but then managed to tack on the advantages of trade secrecy – confidentiality and indefinite duration – to what looked suspiciously like the same invention whose patent protection had expired. Similarly, Rebecca Tushnet (Chapter 19) tells of the way that the producers of the very famous Barbie have endeavored to use both copyright and trademark for their notorious dolls, maneuvering between these regimes to try to take advantage of the most protective features of each.

As the last two examples suggest, blurring the boundaries can enable inventors and authors alike to expand the protection of their work beyond what either regime alone would accord them. In more conventional property, there is a similar pattern that has been noticed in some less-developed countries, where traditional landed property arrangements have been only partially displaced by modernist titling regimes. In that context, as Daniel Fitzpatrick has described, clever and

[3] Lisa Bernstein, "Private Commercial Law in the Cotton Industry: Creating Cooperation Through Rules, Norms, and Institutions," 99 *Mich. L. Rev.* 1724 (2001); Lisa Bernstein, "Opting Out of the Legal System: Extralegal Contractual Relations in the Diamond Industry," 21 *J. Legal Stud.* 115 (1992).

powerful players can shift back and forth to claim more than either regime alone would have given them.[4] There too, a blurring that begins in simple confusion can take a more purposeful and aggrandizing turn. Which brings me to yet another edge.

The edge of the knife: Stilettos and blunderbusses in IP-land

"Edgy" can mean something cutting and critical, and parody is one of the edges in that sense. Parody requires some copying of the target to get the target in view (and then stick in the stiletto), but in so doing, parody becomes particularly transgressive to the holders of IP rights. Not only is the parodist copying the song or the slogan, but she is poking fun at it. The IP rights holders know it, and as Robin Jacob illustrates (Chapter 20), they can work themselves into quite a huff about parody, sometimes to the point of making themselves look ridiculous.

Parody needles the trademark or creative work on purpose, but some other transgressive types just want to have fun – without paying for it, of course. In his chapter, Joseph Liu (Chapter 11) suggests the great lengths to which hackers will go to watch an encrypted television show or play a time-restricted video game, sneaking through the cracks in anti-circumvention "digital rights management" (DRM) code to do so; while Séverine Dusollier (Chapter 12) points to the difficulties that computer gamers cause for European IP law when, say, they tinker with PlayStation software in order play games outside the PlayStation empire.

These chapters suggest that transgression and defense establish a peculiar kind of thrust and parry between transgressors and IP rights holders. The fight begins when the transgressors take a jab at IP-protected material, but then it goes on: The rights holders defend themselves so aggressively as to overreach the protections that they would have under IP itself. For example, US copyright law allows exceptions for parodies under the rubric of "fair use," with rather less regard than the Europeans have for authors' fusty "moral rights" (Jacob, Chapter 20). Nevertheless, Mattel scares off would-be parodists everywhere by mixing and matching trademark and copyright claims, claiming more protections than would be available under either copyright or trademark alone (Tushnet, Chapter 19).[5] Trademark dilution – i.e., knocking-off someone else's

[4] Daniel Fitzpatrick, "Evolution and Chaos in Property Rights Systems: The Third World Tragedy of Contested Access," 115 *Yale L. J.* 996 (2006).

[5] This kind of mix and match could backfire, though. See Jane C. Ginsburg, *Of Mutant Copyrights, Mangled Trademarks, and Barbie's Beneficence: The Influence of Copyright on*

famous brand to publicize some other kind of product altogether – often rings of parody too, and of the major brands' reactions to parody.[6] The early case of Odol mouthwash/cutlery looked all very serious, but "Greatest Snow on Earth" was Utah's little joke at Barnum & Bailey's expense.[7] Barnum & Bailey lost in court, but they and other famous brands won over Congress, which soon armed them with the blunderbuss of dilution protection, safeguarding marks far beyond the traditional idea of fending off imitation by competitors (Beebe, Chapter 3; Dinwoodie, Chapter 4).

Liu and Dusollier's contributions on "Paracopyright" (Chapter 11, Chapter 12) describe an eerily similar pattern of thrust and aggressive parry when it comes to technological restraints on copying: The technology of DRM does not always outsmart the transgressive gamers and other hackers, and in order to fend them off, holders of IP rights call on legislation to punish those who would sneak through technological protections. But once having attained this goal, the rights holders then find a pleasant surprise: they can stretch the new legislative language to protect matters considerably beyond the scope of IP – for example, stopping players who figure out ways to "cheat" at computer games. Cheating may be undesirable to the game manufacturers, but it is hard to say it is a copyright violation in itself.

By the way, several chapters suggest something that I will take up shortly again: what may be a persistent difference between the European and American approaches. In this area of overreaching, the European model seems to use *ex ante* legislation to crack down on rights holders' overextension of IP, while the Americans do so *ex post*, through the judiciary. But both efforts may be haunted by the specter of contracts, in which the parties determine their rights outside the ambit of public legislation, either through direct agreement, as described by Dusollier (Chapter 12), or through producer-imposed "shrinkwrap" contracts that

Trademark Law, in Trademark Law and Theory: A Handbook of Contemporary Research 481 (Graeme B. Dinwoodie & Mark D. Janis eds., Edward Elgar, Cheltenham, UK, 2008) (describing how the copyright "fair use" defense has infiltrated some trademark law).

[6] One of my personal favorite examples is the former Anchorage rock band known as Mr. Whitekeys and the Fabulous Spamtones. Hormel, the maker of the meat product Spam, was not amused. See Mike Dunham, "'Whale Fat' Comes Back," *Anchorage Daily News*, September 11, 2011 (mentioning Hormel's objections to the use of the name Spamtones). Even better known is Hormel's unsuccessful suit against Jim Henson's company for a Muppet movie character named "Spa'am," described in the case as "the high priest of a tribe of wild boars that worships Miss Piggy as its Queen Sha Ka La Ka La." *Hormel Foods Corp. v. Jim Henson Productions, Inc.*, 73 F.3d 497 (2d Cir. 1996).

[7] *Ringling Bros.-Barnum & Bailey Combined Shows, Inc. v. Utah Div. of Travel Development*, 170 F.3d 449 (4th Cir. 1999), certiorari denied 528 U.S. 923 (1999).

have been much discussed in the context of software licensing.[8] Contracts like these raise a further question about IP: Is the law of IP a ceiling as well as a floor on rights holders' claims? And is there something about the history of IP rights that drives in the direction of overprotection?

Morals and the evolution of rights

Conventional property rights are often discussed in evolutionary terms. Blackstone has a little potted story about the evolution of property rights at the beginning of his exhaustive (and exhausting) discussion of the common law of property, and much the same story is told by modern economists and "free market environmentalists." The story, very roughly, is that property rights systems cost something to create and maintain, but that they will evolve when it is worth the cost and effort.[9]

Several of the contributions in this book, however, suggest a somewhat different and rather surprising element in the opening stages of evolving property rights, at least in the IP world: moralisms. Barton Beebe (Chapter 3) discusses the 1924 German decision protecting the Odol brand of mouthwash as an opening salvo in the still-controversial concept of trademark dilution. But the *Odol* decision reads as if the judge was more concerned about the copycat cutlery company's bad manners than about any legal rights that the mouthwash firm might have had. Similarly, in Jeanne Fromer's description of *Tabor v. Hoffman* (Chapter 13), where the issue was the copying of a boiler-maker's construction patterns, the judges seemed more concerned about the copyist's bad behavior than about the pattern maker's legal rights under trade secret law. The early twentieth-century *Haelen* case, according baseball celebrities a hitherto unknown "right of publicity," focused on celebrities' "bruised feelings" and the corresponding unjust enrichment to the unauthorized user (Dogan, Chapter 1). Much more recently, in cases testing new statutory DRM protections, it may be significant that the entering wedges to extending DRM beyond copyright were instances where decryption devices permitted owners to receive broadcast signals without paying for them (Liu, Chapter 11).

All this creates some interesting possibilities about the evolution of property rights. Property is supposed to be good "against the world," but

[8] See, e.g., Mark A. Lemley, "Intellectual Property and Shrinkwrap Licenses," 68 *So. Cal. L. Rev.* 1239 (1995) (querying whether sellers of software can "opt out" of intellectual property).

[9] For some variations on this story, see Carol M. Rose, "Property as Storytelling: Perspectives from Game Theory, Narrative Theory, Feminist Theory," 2 *Yale J. Law & Humanities* 37 (1990).

could it be that when property rights are at early stages, more attention focuses on unseemly behavior by some of the pushier non-owners from out there in the "world"? Only later, as conflicts and pressures grow, does one seem to find closer attention to the content and validity of the right itself, as in the case of trademark dilution and, more recently, DRM protection; and even then, the moral ire lingers on. Graeme Dinwoodie (Chapter 4) notes that a 2009 British case about perfume packaging expressed some moralisms about knock-offs that echo the old *Odol* case (Chapter 3). The question then becomes whether the early moralisms can set us on a course of overbroad protection, where moral aggravation eclipses reconsideration and readjustment of the property right.

Institutional design: *Ex ante* vs. ex *post*, rules vs. standards, and similar issues

The possible pitfalls of evolution raise more questions about institutional design. Moralisms may push IP rights in the early stages in the direction of overly broad definitions, but there also may be other factors that undermine a legal system's ability to strike the right balance about new kinds of innovations – factors like the "hindsight bias" that makes innovation seem obvious after the fact, and that perhaps might work in the direction of under-protection rather than overprotection.[10] On the one hand, the DRM discussions (Liu, Chapter 11; Dusollier, Chapter 12) suggest that it is all too easy to overreact to the need to safeguard what look like important innovations, and to create protections that sweep up activities considerably beyond whatever it was that called for protection in the first place. On the other hand, however, Ted Sichelman's discussion of the 1948 *Funk* case (Chapter 17), with the majority's dismissive attitude toward mixtures of biological materials, strongly reinforces the idea that it is easy to make light of genuine innovation.

But then, what to do? One possible route is to focus on potential overreaching, and to take a tightfisted approach to creating new IP rights at the outset, and only later follow up with rigorous and tailored protective systems. In the conventional property/contract literature, one might call this the "rules" approach. On the other hand, Sichelman is more concerned about the problem of under-recognition of innovations, and takes what one might call the "standards" line. On this view, precisely because of the difficulty of assessing innovation, legislatures and courts

[10] Jeffrey J. Rachlinski, "A Positive Psychological Theory of Judging in Hindsight," 65 *U. Chi. L. Rev.* 571 (1998).

should set up IP regimes as loose and expansive at the outset, but subject to *ex post* revision as the scope of the innovation comes into focus.

Incidentally, in this area of institutional design, readers may notice a trace of a difference between European and American thinking about IP – or more generally civil law and common law approaches. One notices several instances in which commentators suggest that the European approach is more sparing about recognizing IP rights in new areas – Lefranc (Chapter 2), for example, notes that the French have been slow to acknowledge rights in the emerging areas of celebrity or publicity, and thereafter they have made the right more personal and less subject to exclusive rights for commercial purposes. In a different area, Justine Pila (Chapter 18) insists on a European view that there be some "there there" of patentable subject matter – unlike Sichelman's loosey-goosey anything-goes view of what counts as a patentable *subject* up front, but with strict post hoc reins on the *scope* of the patent right. Similarly, Stefan Bechtold's contribution (Chapter 16) notes that European legislation takes the more precise – and more restrictive – path of banning patents on medical procedures, as opposed to the looser American approach that allows potential patents of these procedures, but excuses doctors from patent liability. Moreover, in keeping with the civil law tradition, the European approach is more apt to take the form of *ex ante* formal legislation, as in the case of the French legislation about parody, whereas the American IP system tends to dump all such questions on the courts for *ex post* assessment (Jacob, Chapter 20).

One should not make too much of these differences; as Graeme Dinwoodie (Chapter 4) notes about US and European conceptions of trademark dilution, there is considerable dialog between systems in many areas of IP. But if there are differences, it will be interesting to see whether or how they play out in areas that now thoroughly stretch IP, like protections for indigenous traditional knowledge. One might expect the European approach to proceed with caution but then look for *sui generis* codes, while the common law jurisdictions might be more likely to let judges tinker with existing IP regimes post hoc, or perhaps to give the issues to a special commission for case-by-case resolution, as with New Zealand's Waitangi Tribunal's resolutions on the Maori haka (Frankel, Chapter 9).

And still more institutional design: The social structure of innovation

IP discussions often tell a standard story that is very familiar in conventional property theory. The story is that property rights produce good things for a reason: These rights induce their holders to put effort, investment, and careful management into the assets they own, because property rights allow one to reap what one sows. But anyone with even a passing knowledge of IP has to realize that IP is under fire in some quarters, on the ground that creative productivity requires *less* property protection rather than *more*, or at least that creativity emerges from social structures that differ from the standard market structures of individual property rights with contractual transfers. There has been much discussion of these issues already – all those disquisitions on Shakespeare's theater group or the multiple contributions to open source software.[11] IP, Jamie Boyle complains, is fixed on the "romantic" individual author or inventor, the lone genius who is falsely supposed to act as the fount of creativity.[12]

While none of the chapters here take up the whole "copyleft" enterprise of attacking IP root and branch, several do offer interesting perspectives on the social structure of innovation, and how and whether formal IP plays a role. Some of these perspectives focus on group-based efforts to encourage and protect innovation. The American fashion designers of the 1930s could not really rely on IP protection, which at best could have come up with something like the short-term "hot news" protections that the courts created for news gathering organizations; so instead they created their own very elaborate administrative structure to protect their fashion products, basically borrowing early New Deal ideas of cartelized industrial organization (Hemphill and Suk, Chapter 7). Unfortunately for the designers, their self-made protections succumbed to internal quarrels, transactions costs, and antitrust scrutiny; they barely outlasted the New Deal's more general experiment with economic corporatism.

Katherine Strandburg's (Chapter 15) discussion of the "user innovator" surgeons suggests a different model of group-based self-organization for innovation, one that is less formal and that relies more on social and professional norms, but that appears to be considerably more durable. Strandburg's user innovators are rather like the cohorts of scientists that Robert Merges has described elsewhere in the context of patent pooling among innovators: They share information among themselves, and they take their rewards not only from their pooled information but also from prestige accorded by other insiders to the most innovative

[11] Mark Rose, *Authors and Owners: The Invention of Copyright* (Harvard University Press, Cambridge, Mass., 1993); Yochai Benkler, "Nicely Sharing: On Sharable Goods and the Emergence of Sharing as a Modality of Economic Production," 114 *Yale L. J.* 273 (2004).

[12] James Boyle, *Shamans, Software and Spleens: Law and the Construction of the Information Society* (Harvard University Press, Cambridge, Mass., 1996).

contributors.[13] In this context, an exclusive individual patent is disruptive, as was the case with Dr. Pallin's abortive attempt to force his fellow ophthalmological surgeons to accept his patent rights on a particular mode of incision. Even Dr. Pallin backed down in the face of the increasingly organized outrage from other members of the user innovator group.

Strandburg draws a very evocative contrast to medical *devices*, which require the participation of outsiders like engineers, who are not subject to the whole normative reward system of the user innovators; hence the special reward system of patent is not so objectionable. But this contrast suggests further extension. One intriguing possibility is that the user innovators' additions are generally incremental improvements on business-as-usual, but that major innovations of any kind are sharper departures, and they are just as likely to come from outsiders. Dava Sobel's wonderful book *Longitude* comes to mind: To the shock of disdainful eighteenth-century astronomical insiders, the great innovation for calculating longitude was the use of timepieces rather than stars.[14] Insider approbation was obviously not an appropriate reward for the man the astronomers thought a mere tinker. Outsiders like that need special incentives rather than the chummy prestige enjoyed among insiders. In the case of longitude, the special reward was a prize, but formal IP might help to fill the bill too; as Jeanne Fromer notes (Chapter 13), patent law is democratic; and in another context, Rebecca Tushnet has said much the same of copyright, albeit with some qualifications.[15]

The potential importance of outsider contributions links IP to some discussions in the conventional property world too, especially to some recent criticism of the work of Elinor Ostrom and her colleagues. Ostrom's school has rediscovered and celebrated resource management in community-based property regimes, and quite appropriately so; but some critics think those communities are not necessarily very egalitarian or open-minded, and their hierarchical character can stifle innovation.[16]

[13] Robert P. Merges, "Property Rights Theory and the Commons: The Case of Scientific Research," 13 *Social Phil. & Pol'y* 145 (1996).

[14] Dava Sobel, *Longitude: The True Story of a Lone Genius Who Solved the Greatest Scientific Problem of his Time* (Walker, New York, 1995).

[15] Rebecca Tushnet, "Copyright as a Model for Free Speech Law: What Copyright Has in Common with Anti-Pornography Laws, Campaign Finance Reform, and Telecommunications Regulation," 42 *B. C. L. Rev.* 1 (2000).

[16] Elinor Ostrom, *Governing the Commons* (Cambridge University Press, New York, 1990); Brigham Daniels, "Emerging Commons and Tragic Institutions," 37 *Envtl. L.* 515 (2007); Hanoch Dagan & Michael A. Heller, "The Liberal Commons," 110 *Yale L. J.* 549 (2001); for these and other discussions of the impact of Ostrom's work, see Carol M. Rose, "Ostrom and the Lawyers: The Impact of *Governing the Commons* on the American Legal Academy," 5 *Intl. J. of the Commons* 28 (2011).

The larger points are these: First, formal IP may not really serve well for incremental innovation, which probably does dominate human innovation overall.[17] Incremental innovation is hugely important, and it may well depend on the organization of social groups with appropriate social norms. Some organizations do not work out well (the fashion designers), but some do (the user innovator surgeons). It is important to study those groups to see why some work and some do not.

But second, the big creative breakthroughs may often come from outside the user innovator social box. Insider approval is unlikely to incentivize that sort of change. In this respect, perhaps the major role of IP is to celebrate and reward the weird and the wonderful, and dare one say it, the romantic author or inventor.

★★★

And so, Reader, these are some of the themes that a real property lawyer (i.e., a lawyer of real property) sees in these very provocative chapters about the edges of IP. But you and other readers will see other edges and other themes as well. I guarantee it.

[17] See J. H. Reichman, "Of Green Tulips and Legal Kudzu: Repackaging Rights in Subpatentable Innovation," 53 *Vand. L. Rev.* 1743 (2000) (discussing the prevalence of small-scale innovation).

Part I

Right of publicity

1 *Haelan Laboratories v. Topps Chewing Gum*: Publicity as a legal right

Stacey L. Dogan

Most scholars and courts credit *Haelan Laboratories, Inc. v. Topps Chewing Gum, Inc.*[1] with ushering in the modern right of publicity in the United States.[2] In *Haelan*, the Second Circuit Court of Appeals recognized an alienable legal right in the value of a celebrity image.[3] In particular, the court held that baseball players could sell to one party the exclusive right to use their images on baseball cards. It is not that celebrities lacked legal rights pre-*Haelan*. They could object to many uses of their name or likeness to advertise products, and had at least some cognizable privacy rights as well. But before *Haelan*, these legal rights focused largely on avoiding harm to the celebrity; no court had recognized celebrity images as legal rights that could be sold to the highest bidder. Since *Haelan*, this sale of celebrity has become ubiquitous. Although publicity interests had long floated around the edges of intellectual property, *Haelan* marked their debut as full-fledged intellectual property rights.

Evolution of the right

Given the magnitude of its impact, *Haelan* was a remarkably terse decision – skimpy in its discussion of precedent, short on normative

[1] 202 F.2d 866 (2d Cir. 1953).

[2] *See, e.g.*, J. Gordon Hylton, "Baseball Cards and the Birth of the Right of Publicity: The Curious Case of *Haelan Laboratories v. Topps Chewing Gum*," 12 *Marq. Sports L. Rev.* 273 (2001).

[3] 202 F.2d at 868. In a recent article, Jennifer Rothman takes issue with the notion that the right of publicity is alienable. *See* Jennifer E. Rothman, "The Inalienable Right of Publicity," 101 *Geo. L. J.* 185 (2012). She points to examples such as bankruptcy and divorce proceedings, in which courts have often refused to order involuntary transfers of the right. The fact that the law places some limits on the right's alienability, however, does not mean that it is *in*alienable. *Haelan* established the right of publicity as an economic interest that celebrities could transfer to third parties who could then sue for infringement of the right. In that sense, the right of publicity became generally alienable, despite courts' willingness to limit the transfer of the right in certain circumstances.

rationale, and utterly lacking in an examination of potential consequences. Together with the court's sweeping definition of its new legal right, these shortcomings have created a sort of rogue intellectual property right, lacking internal limits and disciplined only by the intervention of the First Amendment. Scholars and even some judges have lamented this state of affairs, but their worries have done little to curb the legal right's persistent expansion.[4]

How did this lawsuit between competing chewing gum manufacturers bring about such a revolution in the law's treatment of celebrity identity? In my view, two features of the *Haelan* opinion interacted to produce a particularly unwieldy form of legal right. First, the *Haelan* court deliberately abandoned a harms-based approach to celebrity publicity rights in favor of an approach centered on unjust enrichment. In doing so, the court paved the way for a presumption of celebrities' entitlement to every cent of commercial value conferred by the use of their identities, without regard to whether the use caused them any reputational or personal harm. Second, because the Second Circuit considered only the perceived equities of the parties before it, the court failed to take into account the broader social consequences of recognizing or denying the right in any particular case. Unlike other forms of intellectual property, which have doctrinal tools for considering positive externalities created by a defendant's use, the right of publicity defined in *Haelan* has no such escape valve.[5] As a result, courts considering right of publicity claims have no

[4] *E.g.*, Michael Madow, "Private Ownership of Public Image: Popular Culture and Publicity Rights," 81 *Calif. L. Rev.* 127 (1993); Stacey L. Dogan & Mark A. Lemley, "What the Right of Publicity Can Learn from Trademark Law," 58 *Stan. L. Rev.* 1161 (2006); Mark P. McKenna, "The Right of Publicity and Autonomous Self-Definition," 67 *U. Pitt. L. Rev.* 225, 288–89 (2005). For judicial perspectives, see *White v. Samsung Elecs. Am., Inc.*, 989 F.2d 1512 (1993) (Kozinski J., dissenting from denial of rehearing *en banc*); *Cardtoons, L.C. v. Major League Baseball Players Ass'n*, 95 F.3d 959 (10th Cir. 1996).

[5] Copyright, for example, has numerous limiting doctrines, including the idea/expression dichotomy, merger, the substantial similarity requirement, and fair use. *E.g.*, 17 U.S.C. §102(b) (denying copyright protection to ideas, methods, and processes); *Nichols v. Universal Pictures Corp.*, 45 F.2d 119, 121 (2d Cir. 1930) (articulating idea/expression dichotomy); *Knitwaves, Inc. v. Lollytogs Ltd*, 71 F.3d 996, 1002 (2d Cir. 1995) ("where we compare products that contain both protectible and unprotectible elements, ... we must attempt to extract the unprotectible elements from our consideration and ask whether the *protectible elements, standing alone*, are substantially similar"); *Morrissey v. Procter & Gamble Co.*, 379 F.2d 675, 678 (1st Cir. 1967) (merger: "[w]hen the uncopyrightable subject matter is very narrow, so that 'the topic necessarily requires,' if not only one form of expression, at best only a limited number, to permit copyrighting would mean that a party or parties, by copyrighting a mere handful of forms, could exhaust all possibilities of future use of the substance") (internal citations omitted). Trademark's functionality and fair use doctrines, among others, offer similar protections in trademark law. *E.g.*, *TrafFix Devices, Inc. v. Marketing Displays, Inc.*, 532

mechanism for vindicating the interests of the public, except to rely on the slippery protection offered by the First Amendment.[6] And parties considering the unauthorized use of a celebrity identity – whether through art, entertainment, or tongue-in-cheek advertisements – proceed at considerable risk.

Of the many strands of *Haelan*'s legacy, one of the most profound has been the extension of publicity rights to the use of a celebrity image *as* a product or *in* a product, rather than the use of such an image to advertise some unrelated product. *Haelan* itself involved a sort of blending of these two types of use: The baseball cards were packaged with chewing gum and clearly intended to enhance gum sales, but baseball fans surely viewed the cards as a part of the product they were buying, rather than an advertisement for a piece of chewing gum. By finding a publicity right violation under those facts, *Haelan* invited celebrities to complain any time that the use of their name, image, or other identifying attributes enhanced the appeal of a product sold to consumers.

And complain they have. From Tiger Woods,[7] to Joe Namath,[8] and from the Three Stooges[9] to college athletes,[10] celebrities have objected to the sale of products that depict them or describe them or even evoke them. The celebrities, moreover, have had a plausible doctrinal basis for each of these claims. Because the right of publicity focuses on benefit to the unauthorized user rather than harm to the celebrity, it was not laughable when Tiger Woods sued an artist who sold prints based on a painting of his image,[11] when Arnold Schwarzenegger objected to

U.S. 32–33 (2001) (functionality); 15 U.S.C. § 1115(b)(4) (allowing unauthorized "use, otherwise than as a mark, of the party's individual name in his own business, or of the individual name of anyone in privity with such party, or of a term or device which is descriptive of and used fairly and in good faith only to describe the goods or services of such party, or their geographic origin"); *Toyota Motor Sales, U.S.A., Inc. v. Tabari*, 610 F.3d 1171, 1175–76 (9th Cir. 2010) (noting that "nominative fair use" doctrine protects parties who use trademark to refer to trademark holder).

[6] *Cf.* Zachary C. Bolitho, "When Fantasy Meets the Courtroom: An Examination of the Intellectual Property Issues Surrounding the Burgeoning Fantasy Sports Industry," 67 *Ohio St. L. J.* 911, 943 (2006) (noting the "black hole that has become freedom of speech jurisprudence"); Thomas F. Cotter & Irina Y. Dmitrieva, "Integrating the Right of Publicity with First Amendment and Copyright Preemption Analysis," 33 *Colum. J. L. & Arts* 165, 173 (2010) (noting that a "set of problems centers on the relationship between the right of publicity and the First Amendment").

[7] *ETW Corp. v. Jireh Publ'g, Inc.*, 332 F.3d 915 (6th Cir. 2003).

[8] *Namath v. Sports Illustrated*, 80 Misc. 2d 531 (N.Y.S. 1975).

[9] *Comedy III Prod., Inc. v. New Line Cinema*, 200 F.3d 593 (9th Cir. 2000).

[10] *O'Bannon v. Nat'l Collegiate Athletic Ass'n*, No. C 09-1967 CW, 2010 WL 445190, at *1 (N.D. Cal. Feb. 8, 2010).

[11] *See ETW Corp.*, 332 F.3d at 918.

bobble-head dolls poking fun at him,[12] or when the baseball players' union sought to stop the use of players' batting averages by a fantasy sports service.[13] Toys, t-shirts, video games, movies, even paintings – virtually anything that evokes a celebrity without permission – invite a cease and desist letter or, worse, a legal complaint. And while courts often rule in favor of the defendant on First Amendment grounds, they do so by applying murky legal standards that offer little certainty or comfort to parties thinking about selling a product that draws upon a celebrity identity.[14]

Perhaps all of this expansion was inevitable. Perhaps a court or legislature that fully considered all relevant interests would have given celebrities broad veto power over products that evoke them.[15] But given the stakes, it is at least unsettling to realize that publicity rights find their roots in a scant opinion that rested on an instinct that celebrities "would feel sorely deprived" if they were not given rights in their images.

Haelan v. Topps

Haelan v. Topps arose out of a dispute between dueling chewing gum manufacturers over the use of players' images on baseball cards packaged with the manufacturers' gum.[16] The use of baseball cards as an enticement to buy food products was not new, but prior to the mid-twentieth century, food sellers had not generally obtained or enforced exclusive contracts with their players.[17] Beginning in 1948, however, the Bowman Gum Company – the predecessor to the plaintiff in the suit – started entering into exclusive agreements with players. Under these contracts, players agreed not to allow any other gum sellers to offer baseball cards

[12] See David S. Welkowitz & Tyler T. Ochoa, "The Terminator as Eraser: How Arnold Schwarzenegger Used the Right of Publicity to Terminate Non-Defamatory Political Speech," 45 *Santa Clara L. Rev.* 651, 652 (2005).

[13] *C.B.C. Distrib. & Mktg., Inc. v. Major League Baseball Advanced Media, L.P.*, 505 F.3d 818 (8th Cir. 2007).

[14] *See* Marshall Leaffer, "The Right of Publicity: A Comparative Perspective," 70 *Alb. L. Rev.* 1357, 1363 (2007) (describing the courts' approach to balancing right of publicity interests against the First Amendment as "disordered and incoherent").

[15] *See generally* Roberta Rosenthall Kwall, "Is Independence Day Dawning for the Right of Publicity?," 17 *U. C. Davis L. Rev.* 191, 192 (1983) (arguing that "the right of publicity should be construed expansively so that every person and her heirs and grantees can rely upon it to prevent the commercial exploitation of any personal attribute capable of public recognition").

[16] For an engaging account of the history of baseball cards, the chewing gum industry, and the history of the *Haelan* litigation, *see* Hylton, "Baseball Cards and the Birth of the Right of Publicity," *supra* note 2.

[17] *See ibid.* at 275 (tracing the use of cards to sell tobacco to the late 1800s, and the use in connection with candy to 1908).

with their pictures. And, despite a shaky start, by 1951 Bowman's strategy was paying off: the company earned nearly a million dollars in revenues from its baseball card/chewing gum combination.[18]

Topps – which later grew to dominate the market for baseball cards[19] – was at the time a bold upstart. Aware of Bowman's exclusive contracts with the players for cards packaged with chewing gum, Topps initially offered its baseball cards with candy rather than gum.[20] When Bowman responded by broadening the scope of its contracts, however, Topps abandoned its efforts to avoid the contracts and went into direct competition with Bowman, selling cards packaged with gum. Topps – often through third parties – had obtained a license from each featured player to use his image, but these licenses directly conflicted with the exclusive arrangement that many of the players had with Bowman. Topps undoubtedly knew that its sales would trigger a lawsuit, but it had a credible defense: because Bowman's contracts were with the players, not Topps, only the players could face liability in the event of a breach. And while Bowman (now Haelan[21]) had a plausible claim for tortious interference with contract, Topps itself had not dealt directly with some of the players, but had acquired the license from third parties.[22] According to Topps, the players may have breached their contract with Bowman, and the third parties may have induced that breach, but Topps itself had done nothing wrong. In particular, Topps argued that the players had no transferable legal right to the publicity value of their photographs; any right they had under New York law was a personal, non-alienable one that they waived by licensing their rights to Topps.[23]

Topps had plenty of support for its argument against the assignability of the players' rights. Before the *Haelan* case, it was generally understood

[18] *Ibid.* at 281.

[19] *See generally Topps Chewing Gum, Inc. v. Fleer Corp.*, 799 F.2d 851, 852 (2d Cir. 1986) (noting, in antitrust action against Topps, that Topps "has become the undisputed leader of the baseball card business, having obtained exclusive licenses from virtually every person now playing baseball in the major leagues").

[20] The early contracts between Bowman and the players gave Bowman the exclusive right to use player images with gum, but did not apply to other candy products. *See* Hylton, "Baseball Cards and the Birth of the Right of Publicity," *supra* note 2, at 281.

[21] Haelan had purchased Bowman after all of the contracts were entered, but prior to the lawsuit; the suit was brought in Haelan's name. *See* Hylton, "Baseball Cards and the Birth of the Right of Publicity," *supra* note 2, at 283.

[22] In related litigation, Haelan prevailed on a tortious interference claim against Topps. *See Haelan Labs, Inc. v. Topps Chewing Gum, Co.*, 112 F. Supp. 904, 910–11 (E.D.N.Y. 1953).

[23] 202 F.2d at 868 (noting Topps' argument "that none of plaintiff's contracts created more than a release of liability, because a man has no legal interest in the publication of his picture other than his right of privacy, i.e., a personal and non-assignable right not to have his feelings hurt by such a publication").

that the law protected against use of people's names or images to protect them against *harm* that could result from such exposure. The type of harm varied depending on the identity of the individual and the nature of the use. Private parties, for example, were thought to suffer invasions of privacy from unwanted exposure.[24] Celebrities or other public figures, on the other hand, did not have the same privacy expectations, but they could suffer reputational harm from the unauthorized use of their name on product endorsements.[25] In either case, however, the law stepped in to prevent an injury – not to avoid an unjust enrichment.[26] Haelan sought to extend the law to situations involving no proven harm to the celebrity, but some economic benefit to someone using the celebrity's identity without permission.

The court's response to this argument about privacy versus publicity rights was the great innovation of *Haelan*. In two short paragraphs, the court reconceived both the purpose and the nature of a celebrity's right to control use of his image. The court flatly rejected Topps' claim that the right sounded only in privacy:

> A majority of this court rejects this contention. We think that, in addition to and independent of that right of privacy (which in New York derives from the statute), a man has a right in the publicity value of his photograph, i.e., the right to grant the exclusive privilege of publishing his picture, and that such a grant may validly be made "in gross," i.e., without an accompanying transfer of a business or of anything else. Whether it be labeled a "property" right is

[24] *See Pavesich v. New England Life Ins. Co.*, 122 Ga. 190, 50 S.E. 68 (1905) (invoking right of privacy in private individual's false endorsement claim); N.Y. Civ. Rights Law §§ 50, 51 (creating criminal and civil liability for the use "for advertising purposes, or for the purposes of trade, the name, portrait or picture of any living person" without consent). The New York privacy statute was passed in response to a court's refusal to enjoin the use of a private individual's image on an advertisement for sale of flour. *See* Leonard A. Wohl, "The Right of Publicity and Vocal Larceny: Sounding Off on Sound-Alikes," 57 *Fordham L. Rev.* 445, 447 n.28 (1988), and N.Y. Civ. Rights Law §§ 50–51 (McKinney 1976); *see generally Roberson v. Rochester Folding Box Co.*, 171 N.Y. 538, 64 N.E. 442 (1902) (rejecting invasion of privacy claim by young woman pictured on flour advertisements).

[25] False endorsements could sometimes hurt the celebrity's reputation directly, by associating her with an unsavory or low quality product; more generally, however, false statements of endorsement took away the celebrity's ability to control her associational choices. *See* McKenna, "The Right of Publicity and Autonomous Self-Definition," *supra* note 4 at 225, 288–89.

[26] Admittedly, some decisions before *Haelan* used property-like language in discussing the right of publicity. *See, e.g., Edison v. Edison Polyform Mfg. Co.*, 67 A. 392, 393–94 (N.J. Ch. 1907) (enjoining firm from falsely suggesting that Thomas Edison endorsed its product, and invoking both property-based and harms-oriented reasoning). But because these prior cases all involved suits by the individual whose identity was used without permission – and because they also involved allegations of harm – none established the right as something that could be transferred to a third party.

immaterial; for here, as often elsewhere, the tag "property" simply symbolizes the fact that courts enforce a claim which has pecuniary worth.[27]

To defend this new legal right, the court relied primarily on intuition:

This right might be called a "right of publicity." For it is common knowledge that many prominent persons (especially actors and ball-players), far from having their feelings bruised through public exposure of their likenesses, would feel sorely deprived if they no longer received money for authorizing advertisements, popularizing their countenances, displayed in newspapers, magazines, busses, trains and subways. This right of publicity would usually yield them no benefit unless it could be made the subject of an exclusive grant which barred any other advertiser from using their pictures.[28]

The court, in other words, recognized a right in celebrities in large part because celebrities expected the right and would feel "deprived" by its absence. And the right that it created was no longer a personal one, but an alienable one that could be transferred like any commodity.[29]

Two features of the *Haelan* opinion combined to create a right with few internal limits. First, by defining the right of publicity by reference to celebrities' rights to *capture benefits* associated with use of their images, the court abandoned any requirement that the use of the celebrity identity harm the celebrity's person or reputation in some way. The court thus endorsed an unjust-enrichment-based right of publicity that gave celebrities rights in any "money" acquired through use of their images. The court essentially validated celebrities' sense of entitlement to any economic value that their celebrity status might confer to another party's product or service. Second, because the court failed to consider the effect of this publicity right on anyone except the parties directly involved, it precluded inquiry into the positive social benefits that might result from unauthorized use of celebrity image – or, for that matter, negative consequences that might result from commodifying identity in this way.[30] In the baseball card context itself, for example, one could argue that the

[27] 202 F.2d at 868.

[28] *Ibid.* While the court was undoubtedly correct that celebrities could make more money by selling an exclusive license, the notion that non-exclusive licenses could confer "no benefit" was counter-factual. Celebrities had, for many years, made money from licensing their identity for use in advertising and products. *See generally* Rothman, "The Inalienable Right," *supra* note 3, at 194.

[29] *But see ibid., passim* (contending that the right of publicity is not freely alienable, at least in certain circumstances).

[30] *See generally* Rothman, "The Inalienable Right," *supra* note 3, at 193. "Despite the claim that the right of publicity was the only way to protect the economic and dignitary interests of performers, athletes, and others, the assignability of publicity rights largely promotes the interests of publicity-holders, sometimes at the expense of identity-holders," i.e., the celebrities themselves.

existence of exclusive contracts created a non-competitive market dominated by a single firm; both consumers and, possibly, the ball players themselves may have benefited from greater competition.[31] But the right of publicity defined in *Haelan* eschewed any inquiry into these effects.

Celebrity image in relationship to advertisements and products

The right of publicity since *Haelan* has stretched in multiple directions, but it has retained the core unjust-enrichment impulse reflected in the Second Circuit's original opinion. As a result, it has been challenging for courts to articulate meaningful internal limits on the right; instead, they have turned to the First Amendment to do the heavy lifting. This constitutional turn has, among other things, contributed to a dichotomy between two different uses of celebrity identity: the use of celebrity images to advertise some unrelated product, on the one hand, and those involving the use of celebrity as a feature of a product, on the other.

The first uses – pure advertising uses – are routinely resolved in favor of the celebrity, in large part because they fall into the disfavored class of commercial speech.[32] Even advertisements that parody, comment upon, or transform the celebrity image consistently run afoul of the celebrity's publicity rights.[33]

Uses of celebrity identity within a product, however, find a more mixed reception. Because of the breadth of the right as defined by most

[31] Topps, for example, paid the players substantially more for its non-exclusive license than Bowman paid them for its exclusive right. *See* Hylton, "Baseball Cards and the Birth of the Right of Publicity," *supra* note 2, at 283. While Topps may well have been paying a premium to encourage the ballplayers to break their contracts, it is equally plausible that Bowman was taking advantage of its dominant position, and that competition among buyers of ballplayers' images would have led to higher fees to players. *Cf. ibid.* at 293 (noting that real competition in the baseball card market did not emerge until the 1980s, "and only then through the diligent efforts of the Major League Baseball Players' Association to increase the income of its members by breaking Topps' grip on the market"); *see generally* Roger G. Noll, "'Buyer Power' and Economic Policy," 72 *Antitrust L. J.* 589 (2005) (discussing economics and law of monopsony, in which a single buyer dominates a market).

[32] Commercial speech is defined as "speech that does no more than propose a commercial transaction." *See United States v. United Foods, Inc.*, 533 U.S. 405, 409 (2001). Advertisements – whose purpose is to induce a purchase – are a prototypical example of commercial speech.

[33] *See, e.g., White v. Samsung Elecs. Am., Inc.*, 971 F.2d 1395 (9th Cir. 1992) at 1395 (dismissing argument that parody in advertisement could enjoy First Amendment protection); *Abdul-Jabbar v. General Motors Corp.*, 85 F.3d 407, 416 (9th Cir. 1996) (use of "newsworthy" player statistics not protected because defendant "used the information in the context of an automobile advertisement, not in a news or sports account").

state laws, courts often find the right of publicity presumptively violated when a defendant sells a product incorporating celebrity identity.[34] But because non-advertising uses merit stronger protection under the First Amendment, courts generally engage in some balancing between the interests of the speaker (i.e., the seller of the product) and those of the celebrity. These balancing tests have brought considerable uncertainty over the scope of publicity rights, particularly for products that use celebrity identity in novel ways.

Celebrity as advertisement

As discussed above, well before *Haelan* courts had condemned the unauthorized use of celebrity names and images in product advertising.[35] Most of these opinions rested on some theory of harm to the celebrity,[36] to the public,[37] or both.[38] Post-*Haelan*, inquiry into harm was

[34] *E.g.*, *C.B.C. Distrib. & Mktg., Inc.*, 505 F.3d at 822–23 (finding Missouri right of publicity violated by fantasy sports league's use of baseball player names and statistics, but concluding that First Amendment protected the use); *Cardtoons, L.C.*, 95 F.3d at 968 (holding that parody baseball cards violated players' right of publicity under Oklahoma law, but relying on First Amendment to rule in favor of defendants). There are exceptions, such as news reporting, *e.g.*, FLA. STAT. § 540.08(4)(a) (right of publicity does not apply to "[t]he publication, printing, display, or use of the name or likeness of any person in any newspaper, magazine, book, news broadcast or telecast, or other news medium or publication as part of any bona fide news report or presentation having a current and legitimate public interest and where such name or likeness is not used for advertising purposes"); CAL. CIV. CODE § 3344(d) (West 2012) (exempting use "in connection with any news, public affairs, or sports broadcast or account, or any political campaign"). Apart from news or informational uses, however, courts tend to find a violation and leave it to the First Amendment to define external limits on the right.

[35] Private figures, too, had a right to prevent use of their name or likeness in advertising, though the right reflected privacy concerns that differed at least somewhat from the interests of celebrities. *See, e.g.*, *Pavesich*, 122 Ga. 190 (allowing claim by private individual against life insurance company that used his likeness without permission to suggest that he endorsed their product).

[36] *Fairfield v. Amer. Photographic Equip. Co.*, 138 Cal. App. 2d 82, 86, 291 P.2d 194, 197 (Cal. Ct. App. 1955) (recognizing privacy violation in advertisement that falsely described prominent lawyer as satisfied customer: "The right of privacy concerns one's own peace of mind . . . The injury is mental and subjective. It impairs the mental peace and comfort of the person."). *Compare O'Brien v. Pabst Sales Co.*, 124 F.2d 167, 169–70 (5th Cir. 1941) (denying claim by famous college athlete that use of his image on beer calendar infringed his privacy rights, based in part on lack of injury, reasoning that "nothing in it could be legitimately or reasonably construed as falsely stating that he used, endorsed, or recommended the use of Pabst's beer").

[37] *See, e.g.*, *Foster-Milburn Co. v. Chinn*, 134 Ky. 424, 120 S.W. 364, 366 (1909) ("It is a fraud on the public to publish indorsements of public men in publications of this character which are not genuine.").

[38] *Cf. Edison*, 67 A. at 393–94 (enjoining firm from falsely suggesting that Thomas Edison endorsed its product, and invoking both property-based and harms-oriented reasoning).

unnecessary.[39] If celebrities own the full commercial value of their likeness, then *any* use that captures some of that value would violate their rights, absent some speech-related justification. And advertisements, as commercial speech, get little shield from the First Amendment. As a practical matter, then, virtually every use of celebrity name or image for purposes of advertising an unrelated product is unlawful.[40]

As courts have grown increasingly wedded to the unjust-enrichment impulse, moreover, many have extended the right beyond names and images to other symbols that call the celebrity to mind. From look-alikes,[41] to sound-alikes[42] and from catch phrases[43] to robots,[44] advertisements and product promotions that evoke the image of a celebrity have been found to violate the modern publicity right.[45] Admittedly, some of these cases would have fitted comfortably into a pre-*Haelan* world, because they involved a concern over reputational and other harms that can result from false suggestions of endorsement.[46] But

[39] *See generally Cardtoons, L.C.*, 95 F.3d at 967–68 (noting that right of publicity applies to uses of name and likeness even in the absence of any confusion as to endorsement).

[40] A different rule applies to advertisements of expressive products that make legitimate use of the celebrity identity. *See, e.g., Booth v. Curtis Publ'g Co.*, 15 A.D.2d 343, 223 N.Y.S.2d 737 (N.Y. App. Div. 1962) ("it suffices here that so long as the reproduction was used to illustrate the quality and content of the periodical in which it originally appeared, the statute was not violated, albeit the reproduction appeared in other media for purposes of advertising the periodical").

[41] *E.g., Motschenbacher v. R.J. Reynolds Tobacco Co.*, 498 F.2d 821 (9th Cir. 1974) (finding right of publicity violation in advertisement featuring slightly altered picture of famous driver's race car, because public would recognize race car and assume that plaintiff was driver).

[42] *E.g., Waits v. Frito-Lay, Inc.*, 978 F.2d 1093 (9th Cir. 1992) (upholding jury verdict finding a right of publicity violation based on use of sound-alike in radio advertisement); *Midler v. Ford Motor Co.*, 849 F.2d 460 (9th Cir. 1988).

[43] *E.g., Carson v. Here's Johnny Portable Toilets, Inc.*, 698 F.2d 831 (6th Cir. 1983) (enjoining "Here's Johnny" as name for portable toilet because the name evokes Johnny Carson).

[44] *E.g. White*, 971 F.2d at 1395 (finding that a Samsung advertisement depicting a robot on the set of the Wheel of Fortune could be found to have violated the right of publicity of Vanna White, who appears on the show); *Wendt v. Host Int'l., Inc.*, 125 F.3d 806 (9th Cir. 1997) (right of publicity claim against airport bar featuring television characters played by plaintiff actors).

[45] *See generally Landham v. Lewis Galoob Toys, Inc.*, 227 F.3d 619, 624 (6th Cir. 2000) (the right of publicity "is now generally understood to cover anything that suggests the plaintiff's personal identity"); *see also Abdul-Jabbar*, 85 F.3d at 416 (allowing right of publicity claim against advertiser who used player statistics "in the context of an automobile advertisement, not in a news or sports account").

[46] In *Waits*, 978 F.2d at 1104, for example, the plaintiff, singer Tom Waits, was ideologically committed not to sell his performances for use in commercials. The court concluded that he had suffered embarrassment, mental anguish, and reputational injury from a commercial in which a voice imitator crowed about a Frito-Lay product. *See ibid.* ("the jury could have inferred from the evidence that the commercial created a public impression that Waits was a hypocrite for endorsing Doritos").

courts have not conditioned the right of publicity claim on such injury. It is enough that the defendant evokes the celebrity's image; confusion as to endorsement is unnecessary. And thanks to the commercial speech doctrine, even parodies generally do not pass muster if they appear in an advertisement.[47]

Celebrity as product

Although it has undoubtedly contributed to the expansion of celebrity rights with respect to advertisements, *Haelan*'s unjust-enrichment rationale has wreaked special havoc in the context of celebrity-related products. If celebrities own the commercial value of their identities, then it stands to reason that they have cause to complain whenever their image enhances a product's appeal.[48] Unlike advertisements, however, celebrity-oriented products rarely constitute pure commercial speech.[49] As a result, courts cannot simply duck the First Amendment; they must address, head-on, the tension between the right of publicity and speech.

The First Amendment's intervention means that unlike advertisements, the use of celebrity identity *in* a product does not always violate the right of publicity, even in a post-*Haelan* world. *Haelan*'s unjust-enrichment impulse notwithstanding, courts and legislatures have recognized that the First Amendment requires some access to celebrity identity as a tool of expression. Yet finding the right balance has proven surprisingly challenging. In part, this results from the amorphous normative goals of the right of publicity.[50] If the goal were to incentivize

[47] *See White*, 971 F.2d at 1401 ("The difference between a 'parody' and a 'knock-off' is the difference between fun and profit."); *see generally Estate of Fuller v. Maxfield & Oberton Holdings, LLC*, 906 F.Supp. 2d 997, 1006 (N.D. Cal. 2012) (noting complete absence of "authority establishing that there is any First Amendment protection for the use of a celebrity's name, transformed or otherwise, to sell an unrelated product").

[48] The unjust-enrichment impulse has also been harnessed in favor of descendibility of the right. *Cf. Lugosi v. Universal Pictures*, 603 P.2d 425, 446 (1979) (Bird, C.J., dissenting) ("There is no reason why, upon a celebrity's death, advertisers should receive a windfall in the form of freedom to use with impunity the name or likeness of the deceased celebrity who may have worked his or her entire life to attain celebrity status. The financial benefits of that labor should go to the celebrity's heirs.") (quoting Note, "The Right of Publicity Protection for Public Figures and Celebrities," 42 *Brook. L. Rev.* 527, 547 (1976)).

[49] *See Hoffman v. Capital Cities/ABC, Inc.*, 255 F.3d 1180 (9th Cir. 2001) (noting that uses of celebrity identity count as commercial speech only when the identity is used "entirely and directly for the purpose of selling a product"); *Comedy III Prods., Inc. v. Gary Saderup, Inc.*, 25 Cal. 4th 387, 396, 21 P.3d 797, 802 (Cal. 2001) (limiting commercial speech to uses in "an advertisement for or endorsement of a product").

[50] *See generally* Dogan & Lemley, "What the Right of Publicity Can Learn," *supra* note 4; Madow, "Private Ownership of Public Image," *supra* note 4.

the pursuit of celebrity-oriented vocations, courts could evaluate whether a particular use of celebrity identity might interfere with that goal. If the right of publicity aimed to avoid reputational and informational harm that might result from celebrity association with certain products, judges could consider that risk and decide whether it outweighs the speech interests of the defendant in the case at hand. The right of publicity, however, resists this kind of normative classification. Courts defending the right point to an undifferentiated cluster of goals that it purportedly serves, without committing themselves to any single vision.[51] Indeed, if we believe *Haelan*, the goal of the right is simply to reserve to the celebrity all of the fruits associated with her fame. As a result, *any* use of celebrity identity constitutes an affront to the right of publicity's core values; to overcome the right of publicity, defendants must convince the court that their speech is somehow important enough to outweigh the celebrity's interest in capturing the value of her fame.

The celebrity-as-product cases thus reflect a set of assumptions – sometimes express, sometimes implicit – about the relative value of different types of expression. High-value expression can overcome publicity rights, while less favored speech is condemned. In conducting their valuation, courts rely on a combination of intuition, precedent, and custom. The effect is to privilege customary and overt forms of expression, while sometimes devaluing subtle and less traditional uses of celebrity identity.

At one end of the spectrum lie traditional expressive products such as newspapers, books, and movies that offer information, criticism, or commentary about the celebrity. These overtly expressive products reliably defeat right-of-publicity claims. Some states' right-of-publicity statutes explicitly exempt these uses of celebrity identity;[52] in other

[51] *See, e.g.*, *Comedy III Prods.*, 25 Cal. 4th at 400 ("society may recognize, as the Legislature has done here, that a celebrity's heirs and assigns have a legitimate protectible interest in exploiting the value to be obtained from merchandising the celebrity's image, whether that interest be conceived as a kind of natural property right or as an incentive for encouraging creative work"); *White*, 971 F.2d at 1399 ("Considerable energy and ingenuity are expended by those who have achieved celebrity value to exploit it for profit. The law protects the celebrity's sole right to exploit this value whether the celebrity has achieved her fame out of rare ability, dumb luck, or a combination thereof.").

[52] *See, e.g.*, 42 PA. CONS. STAT. ANN. § 8316(e) (2003) (defining "commercial or advertising purposes" to exclude, among other things, any "news report or news presentation having a public interest," "expressive work," or "original work of fine art"); FLA. STAT. ANN. § 540.08(4)(a) (West 2007) (Florida right of publicity does not apply to use in "any newspaper, magazine, book, news broadcast or telecast, or other news medium or publication as part of any bona fide news report or presentation having a current and legitimate public interest and where such name or likeness is not used for advertising purposes"); *cf.* CAL. STAT. ANN. § 3344(d) (exempting news, sports broadcasts, and uses in political campaigns).

states, courts have interpreted the right to exclude news reports and other public-interest uses.[53] Either way, the law protects uses perceived as newsworthy and informational. The protection, moreover, applies even when the celebrity likeness appears not only in the work itself, but also in advertisements for the work. In *Lane v. Random House, Inc.*,[54] for example, an historian objected to the use of his photograph on an advertisement for a book that took issue with his account of the John F. Kennedy assassination. The photograph appeared only in the advertisement and not in the book, but the court found the use legitimate:

> While the newsworthiness privilege may not apply to an advertisement for a non-speech product, it does apply to advertisements for speech products – even those that propose a commercial transaction. Lane's theories about a pivotal and baffling public issue are manifestly newsworthy; serious analyses of his theories are derivatively newsworthy; and an advertisement promoting the sale of a book containing such analyses retains a newsworthiness immunity against a claim of misappropriation.[55]

While the doctrinal vehicle differs from case to case, the outcome of these "expressive commentary" cases is consistent: courts uniformly privilege the use of names and images. Courts appear persuaded that the public interest in access to news and commentary outweighs the celebrity's interest in capturing the full value of her image.

At the other end of the spectrum lie products viewed as pure "celebrity merchandise" – posters, trinkets, and other standalone products featuring the celebrity's unaltered likeness – which are consistently found to violate the right of publicity. Celebrities – or in many cases, their assignees[56] – have a presumptive right to capture the commodity value

[53] In New York, for example, the use of an image violates a celebrity's rights only if it is used "for purposes of trade," a phrase that courts have interpreted to exclude news reporting and commentary. *E.g.*, *Messenger ex rel. Messenger v. Gruner + Jahr Printing and Pub.*, 94 N.Y.2d 436, 727 N.E.2d 549 (2000) ("we have made clear that [New York's privacy statute does] not apply to reports of newsworthy events or matters of the public interest," and "a wide variety of articles on matters of public interest – including those not readily recognized as 'hard news' – are newsworthy").

[54] 985 F. Supp. 141 (D.D.C. 1995).

[55] *Ibid.* at 147; *see also Groden v. Random House, Inc.*, 61 F.3d 1045, 1049–51 (2d Cir. 1995) (finding identical advertisement legitimate use of other conspiracy theorist's image); *Cher v. Forum Int'l, Inc.*, 692 F.2d 634, 639 (9th Cir. 1982) ("Constitutional protection extends to the truthful use of a public figure's name and likeness in advertising which is merely an adjunct of the protected publication and promotes only the protected publication.").

[56] *E.g.*, *Martin Luther King, Jr., Ctr. for Social Change, Inc. v. Am. Heritage Prods., Inc.*, 296 S.E.2d 697 (Ga. 1982) (holding that assignee of Martin Luther King's right of publicity had claim against seller of Martin Luther King bust).

of their celebrity;[57] and most courts deride the notion of merchandise as speech.[58] The design and manufacture of celebrity merchandise undoubtedly entails creative judgment, but courts generally presume that commercial motivations overwhelm expressive ones in cases involving mass-market goods. Nor does the speech analysis in merchandise cases give any weight to audience interests in adopting, embracing, projecting, and re-coding the celebrity image through use. Although scholars have demonstrated the expressive importance of cultural icons to social movements and marginalized groups,[59] courts have yet to consider whether these speech interests might argue in favor of broader access to non-parody celebrity merchandise.[60] True to *Haelan*, the right of publicity

[57] *E.g.*, *ibid.* at 703 ("we hold that the appropriation of another's name and likeness, whether such likeness be for a photograph or sculpture, without consent and for the financial gain of the appropriator is a tort in Georgia. . . ."). Indeed, many right of publicity statutes explicitly give celebrities rights over merchandise. *See, e.g.*, CAL. CIV. CODE § 3344 (West 2012) ("Any person who knowingly uses another's name, voice, signature, photograph, or likeness, in any manner, on or in products, merchandise, or goods, or for purposes of advertising or selling, or soliciting purchases of, products, merchandise, goods or services, without such person's prior consent, . . . shall be liable. . . ."); OKLA. STAT. tit. 12, § 1449(a) (West 2012). Giving celebrities and their heirs the right to prevent merchandise sales may sometimes reflect a moral rights-like impulse against uses that cheapen the celebrity's image. This may well have motivated the court in the Martin Luther King case. *See Martin Luther King, Jr. Ctr. for Social Change*, 296 S.E.2d at 706 (noting plaintiffs' goal "to prevent the exploitation of [Martin Luther King's] likeness in a manner they consider unflattering and unfitting"). As a matter of doctrine, however, these cases turn, not on harm to the celebrity, but on whether the defendant obtained commercial benefit from the use.

[58] *See, e.g.*, *Titan Sports, Inc. v. Comics World Corp.*, 870 F.2d 85, 88 (2d Cir. 1989) ("In contrast to the treatment of newsworthy items, it seems clear that photographs marketed as posters are used for purposes of trade."); *cf. Hicks v. Casablanca Records*, 464 F. Supp. 426, 430 (S.D.N.Y. 1978) ("[M]ore so than posters, bubble gum cards, or some other such 'merchandise', books and movies are vehicles through which ideas and opinions are disseminated and, as such, have enjoyed certain constitutional protections, not generally accorded 'merchandise.'"). Courts give more favorable treatment to merchandise providing commentary. *See, e.g.*, *Cardtoons, L.C.*, 95 F.3d at 969–70 ("we see no principled distinction between speech and merchandise that informs our First Amendment analysis," in a case involving parody baseball cards).

[59] *See, e.g.*, Madow, "Private Ownership of Public Image," *supra* note 4, at 138–47; Rosemary J. Coombe, "Objects of Property and Subjects to Politics: Intellectual Property Laws and Democratic Dialogue," 69 *Tex. L. Rev.* 1853, 1855 (1991) ("Intellectual property laws stifle dialogic practices – preventing us from using the most powerful, prevalent, and accessible cultural forms to express identity, community and difference."); *cf.* Sonia Katyal, "Semiotic Disobedience," 84 *Wash. U. L. Rev.* 489 (2006).

[60] The failure to consider audience interests may not seem surprising, because the defendant in merchandising cases is generally a for-profit enterprise rather than a member of a social movement or marginalized group. But people speak through the greeting cards they send, the posters on their walls, and the t-shirts they wear; audience re-coding often depends critically upon the availability of merchandise sold by commercial actors. *See generally* Madow, "Private Ownership of Public Image," *supra*

inquiry looks only at the parties before the court; if the defendant has no particular expressive goal beyond selling the image as merchandise, then the speech analysis ends. So viewed, merchandise sellers will almost never make the grade.[61]

With "expressive commentary" cases at one end of the spectrum and merchandise at the other, the middle presents the biggest challenge. How should a court treat t-shirts featuring a sketch that celebrates the celebrity, or trading cards that parody her? What about services like fantasy sports leagues, which profit from the use of athlete names and statistics? Or video games that use the celebrity's image in whole or in part? All of these examples involve a product whose value is enhanced by use of the celebrity's identity, and not in a traditional biographic or news-reporting context. *Haelan*'s blunt unjust-enrichment-based approach might well suggest that they violate the right of publicity. But these products also reflect substantial expressive contributions by someone other than the celebrity. Denying the celebrity's claim in these cases would deprive her of at least some of the fruits of her fame; allowing it, on the other hand, would give the celebrity rights over these other parties' productive labors.

The right of publicity's lack of a normative rudder proves especially problematic in these cases, because it offers no coherent value against which to measure the speech interests on the other side. As a result, in cases involving neither pure merchandise nor reporting or commentary, judges have relied upon a hodge-podge of doctrines to determine whether a defendant's use of celebrity identity is fair play or foul.[62] The *Rogers v. Grimaldi* test, for example, allows the use of celebrity names in connection with expressive works unless the name is "wholly unrelated" to the content of the work or is "simply a disguised commercial advertisement for the sale of goods or services."[63] The "transformativeness"

note 4, at 143–44 ("When we buy, exchange, and display cultural commodities" like t-shirts, posters and greeting cards, "we 'are actively contributing to the social circulation' of meanings about the celebrity.") (quoting John Fiske, *Understanding Popular Culture* 174 (Unwin Hyman Ltd, London, 1989)). Consumers' interest in access to such merchandise, however, has not played a role in courts' consideration of right of publicity claims.

[61] *See generally Hilton v. Hallmark Cards*, 599 F.3 894, 910 (9th Cir. 2010) ("[I]t is clear that merely merchandising a celebrity's image without that person's consent, the prevention of which is the core of the right of publicity, does not amount to a transformative use.").

[62] *See Hart v. Elec. Arts, Inc.*, 808 F. Supp. 2d 757, 775 (D.N.J. 2011) ("Courts throughout the United States have utilized up to eight 'balancing' tests that attempt to weigh the First Amendment rights of an author/creator against the right of publicity.").

[63] *Rogers v. Grimaldi*, 875 F.2d 994, 1005 (2d Cir. 1989). Although courts and commentators generally attribute this rule to *Rogers*, it derives from a long line of state court opinions limiting rights of privacy and publicity. *See ibid.* at 1004 (citing *Gigliemi v.*

test asks whether the defendant's use of the celebrity identity is sufficiently transformative to outweigh the celebrity's exclusive interest in exploiting her image.[64] The "predominant use" test asks whether the product "predominantly exploits" the celebrity identity or, instead, has a predominant purpose "to make an expressive comment on or about [the] celebrity..."[65] And the First Amendment balancing test directly balances the celebrity's publicity interests against the perceived speech interests of the defendant.[66] To further complicate matters, courts often equivocate over which doctrine to apply and sometimes utilize several of them in the same opinion.[67] While this approach may well reinforce the court's confidence that it has reached the right outcome in a particular case, it offers little guidance about which standard will prevail in future litigation.

This diverse doctrinal menu, when combined with the subjectivity of the standards as applied, leaves the impression that most cases turn less on doctrine than on judges' personal views about the line between legitimate use and exploitation.[68] Some courts show skepticism about publicity rights and weigh them lightly against speech interests,[69] while

Spelling-Goldberg Productions, 25 Cal.3d 860, 160 Cal. Rptr. 352, 603 P.2d 454, 455 (1979), and *Frosch v. Grosset & Dunlop, Inc.*, 75 A.D.2d 768, 427 N.Y.S.2d 828 (N.Y.A.D. 1980)). New York had, for many decades, applied the standard to its right of privacy statute. *See generally Murray v. N.Y. Magazine Co.*, 27 N.Y.2d 406, 408–09, 267 N.E.2d 256, 258 (1971) ("The law is settled, however, that 'A picture illustrating an article on a matter of public interest is not considered used for the purpose of trade or advertising within the prohibition of the statute ... unless it has no real relationship to the article ... or unless the article is an advertisement in disguise.'") (quoting *Dellesanfdoedro v. Henry Holt & Co.*, 4 A.D.2d 470, 471, 166 N.Y.S.2d 805, 806 (N.Y.A.D. 1957)).

64 *Comedy III Prods.*, 25 Cal. 4th 387.

65 *Doe v. TCI Cablevision*, 110 S.W.3d 363, 374 (Mo. 2003).

66 *E.g.*, *Cardtoons, L.C.*, 95 F.3d at 972 ("This case ... requires us to directly balance the magnitude of the speech restriction against the asserted governmental interest in protecting the intellectual property right."); *Gionfriddo v. Major League Baseball*, 94 Cal. App. 4th 400, 415 (2001).

67 *E.g.*, *ETW Corp.*, 332 F.3d at 915 (analyzing defendant's use under a modified fair-use analysis, as well as a First Amendment balancing test); *Hart*, 808 F. Supp. 2d at 777 (noting preference for transformativeness test over *Rogers* test, but concluding that video game use of athlete identity deserves First Amendment protection under either standard).

68 *Compare, e.g.*, *ETW Corp.*, 332 F.3d at 938 ("After balancing the societal and personal interests embodied in the First Amendment against Woods's property rights, we conclude that the effect of limiting Woods's right of publicity in this case is negligible and significantly outweighed by society's interest in freedom of artistic expression."), with *ibid.* at 960 (Clay J., dissenting) ("[C]ontrary to the majority's conclusion otherwise, it is clear that the prints gain their commercial value by exploiting the fame and celebrity status that Woods has worked to achieve. Under such facts, the right of publicity is not outweighed by the right of free expression.").

69 *E.g.*, *ibid.* at 938 (finding golfer's publicity interests "negligible" in comparison to artist's interest in depicting him in print); *Cardtoons, L.C.*, 95 F.3d at 973–76 (skeptically reviewing various justifications for right of publicity and concluding that "the effect of limiting [plaintiff's] right of publicity in this case is negligible").

others hew to *Haelan* and view any attention-grabbing use of celebrity identity as inherently suspect.[70] As a result, beyond the conventional world of books, movies, and news accounts, sellers of celebrity-oriented products proceed at their peril.

Admittedly, some jurisdictions have crept toward predictability in dealing with certain uses of celebrity identity in products. Most courts allow broad use of celebrity name and likeness for purposes of parody or critique, even when the commentary appears in merchandise.[71] Courts have generally resisted attempts to limit access to facts about celebrities, even when those facts are packaged in commercial products such as fantasy sports leagues.[72] And the "transformativeness" test – at least in jurisdictions that follow it[73] – offers reliable protection to parties who transform a celebrity's appearance and character in a new creative work. Parties that portray a celebrity as "half-human and half-worm," or that manipulate a celebrity's clothing, affect, and general appearance, can escape liability even though the reference to the celebrity might enhance the value of the creative work.[74]

[70] *See, e.g., Doe*, 110 S.W.3d at 374 (concluding that a comic book's "metaphorical reference to [celebrity,] [as] a literary device, has very little literary value compared to its commercial value," and thus violates the right of publicity).

[71] *See, e.g., Cardtoons, L.C.*, 95 F.3d at 972 (finding parody baseball cards protected by First Amendment); *see also Comedy III Prods.*, 25 Cal. 4th at 403 ("[T]he right of publicity cannot, consistent with the First Amendment, be a right to control the celebrity's image by censoring disagreeable portrayals. Once the celebrity thrusts himself or herself forward into the limelight, the First Amendment dictates that the right to comment on, parody, lampoon, and make other expressive uses of the celebrity image must be given broad scope."); *cf. Doe*, 110 S.W.3d at 374 (finding speech interests inadequate to justify use of hockey player's name, when "the use was not a parody or other expressive comment or a fictionalized account of the real Twist").

[72] *E.g., Gionfriddo*, 94 Cal. App. 4th at 411 ("The public has an enduring fascination in the records set by former players and in memorable moments from previous games . . . The records and statistics remain of interest to the public because they provide context that allows fans to better appreciate (or deprecate) today's performances."); *C.B.C. Distrib. & Mktg., Inc.*, 505 F.3d at 823 (allowing use of names and statistics by fantasy sports league; "it would be a strange law that a person would not have a first amendment right to use information that is available to everyone").

[73] The Missouri Supreme Court has rejected both the "transformativeness" test and *Rogers* approach as providing inadequate protection against celebrity exploitation. *See Doe*, 110 S.W.3d at 374. ("Though these tests purport to balance the prospective interests involved, there is no balancing at all – once the use is determined to be expressive, it is protected.")

[74] *Winters v. DC Comics*, 30 Cal. 4th 881, 134 Cal. Rptr. 2d 634, 69 P.3d 473 (2003) (holding that comic books featuring "half-human and half-worm" characters with visual resemblance to plaintiff singers contained sufficient transformative elements to escape liability); *Kirby v. Sega of Am., Inc.*, 144 Cal. App. 4th 47, 50 Cal. Rptr. 3d 607 (Cal. Ct. App. 2006) (video game character sharing some similarities with plaintiff singer, but presented in different context and featuring a number of differences in appearance and habits, found not to violate right of publicity); *cf. No Doubt v. Activision Publ'g, Inc.*, 192

Other product-based uses of celebrity identity, however, continue to perplex the courts. The struggle is particularly acute in cases involving new-media uses of celebrity images, such as video games featuring (relatively) accurate physical portrayals of the celebrity. The "transformativeness" standard is a poor fit for these products, whose creative contributions lie not in manipulation of celebrity image but in presenting faithful depictions in new and creative contexts.[75] Yet more and more courts have invoked that standard in video game and other new-media cases. In *Keller v. Electronic Arts*,[76] for example, a college football player sued the manufacturer of a video game called "NCAA football," for including a quarterback modeled on him.[77] The court applied the "transformativeness" test to rule for the plaintiff, finding the depiction of him non-transformative and refusing to look beyond that depiction to other game elements.[78] In *Hart v. Electronic Arts*,[79] the district court considered the very same video game series, and found the game protected by the First Amendment, largely because the game creators made the athlete's appearance alterable by people playing the game.[80] On appeal, the Third Circuit reversed the judgment, finding the game's faithful depiction of the player non-transformative, and refusing to consider other expressive game features in the mix.[81] A California court reached a similar conclusion in a case involving *Band Hero*, concluding that the video game's use of avatars resembling real-life band members violated their publicity rights, the First Amendment

Cal. App. 4th 1018, 122 Cal. Rptr. 3d 397 (Cal. Ct. App. 2011) (avatars found to violate musicians' right of publicity, given strong physical resemblance to musicians in contrast with "fanciful, creative characters").

[75] *See, e.g.*, David Tan, "Political Recoding of the Contemporary Celebrity and the First Amendment," 2 *Harv. J. Sports & Ent. L.* 1, 25–26 (2011) ("the test is focused on visual transformation which can be overprotective of art and entertainment that contribute little to the discussion of public issues, but underprotective of political speech which may be contextually transformative (because of its recoding) though not visually transformative").

[76] No. C 09-1967 CW, 2010 WL 530108 (N.D. Cal. Feb. 8, 2010).

[77] *Compare, e.g.*, *Hart*, 808 F. Supp. 2d 757 (applying "transformativeness" standard to conclude that video game featuring NCAA college football players did not violate players' right of publicity), with *Keller*, 2010 WL 530108, at *5 (concluding that same video game violated players' right of publicity, and was not sufficiently transformative to merit First Amendment protection).

[78] *See Keller*, 2010 WL 530108, at *5 ("this Court's focus must be on the depiction of Plaintiff in 'NCAA Football,' not the game's other elements").

[79] 808 F. Supp. 2d 757 (D.N.J. 2011).

[80] *Ibid.* at 784–85.

[81] *Hart v. Elec. Arts, Inc.*, 717 F.3d 141, 169 (3d Cir. 2013) ("Decisions applying the Transformative Use Test invariably look to how the *celebrity's identity* is used in or is altered by other aspects of a work. Wholly unrelated elements do not bear on this inquiry.") (emphasis in original).

notwithstanding.[82] The court in *Kirby v. Sega of America*,[83] on the other hand, ruled in favor of a game developer whose character resembled the plaintiff musician; despite many similarities in appearance and behavior, the court found the game character "transformative" because of differences in clothing, mannerisms, body shape, and setting.[84]

If this trend continues, the transformativeness standard will result in a de facto presumption in favor of celebrities in video game cases. Any video game that depicts them with any degree of accuracy will be held to violate their right of publicity. Yet it is curious that courts have applied this legal standard with little consideration of whether it makes sense in the context of a complex creative work like a video game, as opposed to a t-shirt.[85] These new-media cases invite renewed reflection about the purpose of the right of publicity and the value of new forms of speech. Are video games, which allow users to interact with images of the celebrity, more like books (which have generally been protected) or trinkets (which have not)? *Haelan*'s unjust enrichment notwithstanding, many uses of celebrity identity have long escaped the reach of the right of publicity, even when they bring profits to some third party. But apart from critical or parodic uses, courts have failed to articulate just what makes these traditional uses legitimate. Is it because they make us think, or entertain us, or present celebrity images in new and creative ways? Is it enough that they communicate "information, ideas, or expression, beyond proposing a commercial transaction?"[86] Without such guiding principles, courts considering new media often end up woodenly applying governing doctrine without addressing the broader social consequences of recognizing publicity rights in a particular case.

This state of affairs, of course, finds its roots in *Haelan. Haelan* established a basic presumption: If use of a celebrity image adds value to a product, then the celebrity or his assignee has a cause to complain. Not because it would lead to better outcomes, but because celebrities would

[82] *See No Doubt v. Activision Publishing, Inc.*, 122 Cal. Rptr. 3d 397 (Cal. Ct. App. 2011) ("That the avatars can be manipulated to perform at fanciful venues including outer space or to sing songs the real band would object to singing, or that the avatars appear in the context of a videogame that contains many other creative elements, does not transform the avatars into anything other than the exact depictions of No Doubt's members doing exactly what they do as celebrities.").

[83] *Kirby v. Sega of Amer., Inc.*, 50 Cal. Rptr. 3d 607 (Cal. Ct. App. 2006).

[84] *Ibid.* at 616.

[85] The case in which the California Supreme Court first adopted the transformativeness standard involved a t-shirt featuring a sketch of the Three Stooges. *See Comedy III Productions, Inc. v. New Line Cinema*, 200 F.3d 593 (2000).

[86] Bill McGeveran has suggested an exemption from trademark liability for such "communicative works." *See* William McGeveran, "The Trademark Fair Use Reform Act," 90 *B.U. L. Rev.* 2267, 2308 (2010).

feel "sorely deprived" by an alternative rule. Had the court considered broader social questions – such as whether a competitive baseball card market would enhance product diversity, improve access to tools of expression, or lower prices for consumers – it might well have adopted a more nuanced or balanced publicity right. By eschewing inquiry into these issues, the court created a right that yields only to compelling speech interests on the other side. And while critical, political, or informational speech commonly meets that standard, courts seem less persuaded by the expressive value of other entertainment products, such as video games.

This narrow-mindedness has real social consequences. Just as exclusive licenses for baseball cards arguably led to a monopolistic market post-*Haelan*, the prevalence of licensing in the video game context can contribute to a market dominated by a single firm.[87] Electronic Arts – which in recent years has paid the NFL for an exclusive license for player images and team trade dress – has faced antitrust suits charging it with anticompetitive practices and widespread consumer complaints about over-priced and under-innovative products.[88] And while some commentators have argued that certain collectively negotiated exclusive trademark licenses may violate the antitrust laws,[89] no court has yet condemned them.[90] Even if these antitrust claims succeed, moreover,

87 *See generally* Matthew J. Mitten, "From Dallas Cap to American Needle and Beyond: Antitrust Law's Limited Capacity to Stitch Consumer Harm from Professional Sports Club Trademark Monopolies," 86 *Tul. L. Rev.* 901, 913 (2012) (discussing economic effect of sports league control over uniform colors and other trade dress, and noting that "trademarked sports merchandise commands an estimated 46.5% higher premium than similar products").

88 *See Pecover v. Elec. Arts Inc.*, No. C08-02820 (N.D. Cal. filed June 5, 2008). The parties have agreed to settle the case on terms which include Electronic Arts' commitment not to seek exclusive licenses with a number of sports leagues, but notably excluding the NFL. *See Notice of Motion and Motion for Final Approval of Class Action Settlement, Pecover v. Electronic Arts Inc.*, No. 08-cv-02820 CW (filed Jan. 3, 2013); *see generally* The Dude, "Is Electronic Art's Madden a Monopoly?," *Wethegamerz* Feb. 7, 2011, *available at* www.ghostvolta.com/is-electronic-arts-madden-a-monopoly/#/vanilla/discussion/embed/?vanilla_discussion_id=0 ("In business, competition creates two things, and those things are lower prices and product improvement. Electronic Arts' (EA) exclusive NFL license cuts into both.").

89 *E.g.*, Mitten, "From Dallas Cap to American Needle and Beyond", *supra* note 87, at 931 (contending that "league clubs' collective granting of exclusive product licenses should be invalidated under the quick-look rule of reason because this restraint has clear anticompetitive effects that are not necessary to further any procompetitive justifications that enhance consumer welfare").

90 The Supreme Court ruled, in *American Needle, Inc. v. National Football League*, 130 S. Ct. 2201 (2010), that collective licensing by sports leagues should be evaluated under antitrust law's rule of reason, which weighs pro-competitive justifications for restraints of trade against their anticompetitive effects. Because they involve a host of complex economic issues – including market definition and speculative judgment about

they will address only the collective aspects of licensing agreements, involving organizations such as sports leagues, and do not address exclusive licenses executed with individual teams or individual celebrities. As a result, while antitrust laws may ultimately provide a partial counterpoint to the right of publicity, they do not guarantee consumer access to celebrity-related products, nor do they ensure a reasonable price for products that exist. As long as celebrity images have unique value to consumers, products bearing them are likely to remain costly – and sometimes unavailable.

Perhaps it is fair for fans to pay high prices for licensed celebrity products such as video games. Perhaps *Haelan* was right that famous people and their assignees deserve to control the sale of products exploiting their fame. Given the enduring economic and social costs of the unjust-enrichment presumption, however, it is troubling that it arrived through such a blunt and non-reflective opinion as *Haelan*.

Conclusion

Because the right of publicity has no coherent normative objective, the process of balancing celebrity rights against speech interests can appear rudderless and ad hoc. Just as intuition drove the Second Circuit's adoption of the right, so it informs courts' treatment of the right in new and unanticipated contexts. Particularly for products that incorporate celebrity images into an expressive whole, the unjust-enrichment instinct that informed the creation of the right in *Haelan* has led to unpredictable results and significant costs for both creators and consumers.

Given the time that has passed since *Haelan* and its widespread acceptance among state courts and legislatures, it seems unlikely that the right of publicity will ever return to its place at the periphery of intellectual property. Although numerous scholars (including myself) have called for a return to a harms-based approach to publicity rights,[91] neither courts nor legislatures have shown any real interest in abandoning *Haelan*'s benefits-oriented framework.

efficiencies resulting from particular agreements – rule of reason cases "are notoriously difficult for plaintiffs to win." *See* Mark A. Lemley & Christopher R. Leslie, "Categorical Analysis in Antitrust Jurisprudence," 93 *Iowa L. Rev.* 1207, 1260–61 (2008).

[91] *See, e.g.*, Dogan & Lemley, "What the Right of Publicity Can Learn," *supra* note 4 (proposing a trademark-like approach to the right of publicity, focused on harm to the celebrity or to consumers from certain uses of celebrity identity); McKenna, "The Right of Publicity and Autonomous Self-Definition," *supra* note 4 (proposing a right of publicity that protects individuals' right "to control uses of her identity that interfere with her ability to define her own public character").

At the same time, both courts and commentators appear to be recognizing a need for some limits on the right. The theoretical foundations of *Haelan* are woefully underdeveloped in comparison to its cousins at the core of intellectual property. A number of recent courts have taken note of *Haelan*'s weak conceptual footing in deciding whether to condemn particular uses of celebrity identity.[92] From parody to portrait, courts have begun to evaluate whether society's interest in recognizing publicity rights outweighs the First Amendment interests of sellers of celebrity-related products. Until now, these analyses have focused primarily on a speaker's interest in making critical commentary, and have left aside audience and speaker interests in non-critical forms of speech. Even so, they offer a framework for introducing a variety of speech interests into the mix – including, perhaps, consumers' interest in self-expression through access to celebrity merchandise and celebrity-related products. As celebrities assert their rights against an ever-expanding list of products that use or evoke their image, scholars and advocates have an opportunity to demonstrate the ways in which these products reflect or enable speech. *Haelan*'s right of publicity may have failed to anticipate the importance of these broader questions, but perhaps, now that a half-century has passed since *Haelan*, the time has come to examine them. As robust arguments for access meet up against the right of publicity's weak normative justifications, the right of publicity may well return to its rightful place at the fringes of the intellectual property universe.

[92] *E.g.*, *ETW Corp.*, 332 F.3d at 931–38; *Cardtoons, L.C.*, 95 F.3d at 973–76; *cf. White*, 989 F.2d 1512 (Kozinski J., dissenting).

2 Do the French have their own "*Haelan*" case? The *droit à l'image* as an emerging intellectual property right

*David Lefranc**

No need to wait for the answer: French case law has no equivalent to the *Haelan* decision. No court has yet clearly asserted that celebrities "would feel sorely deprived" if they could no longer exploit their fame.[1] As a result, there is no decision laying the foundation for an exclusive right in the market value of celebrity identity. Instead, there are innumerable decisions that in fact apply such a right, without ever explaining why, because French judges are very reluctant to articulate principles and lay down rules. Article 5 of the Civil Code,[2] moreover, formally prohibits French judges from doing so. Nonetheless, a judge-made phenomenon very similar to the "right of publicity" (including its normative shortcomings) can be observed in France. It is therefore worth endeavoring to make a comparison between French and US publicity rights.

French law has long protected privacy, as has US law. But the right was codified only in 1970.[3] Since then article 9 of the Civil Code has provided: "Everyone is entitled to the respect of his private life." There is no other statutory provision, apart from criminal law.[4] Article 9 concerns only privacy. The case law and the commentary nonetheless acknowledge that article 9 indirectly recognizes a right in one's image distinct

* English translation by Jane C. Ginsburg.

[1] *Haelan Laboratories, Inc. v. Topps Chewing Gum, Inc.*, 202 F.2d 866, 868 (2d Cir. 1953): "This right might be called a 'right of publicity'. For it is common knowledge that many prominent persons (especially actors and ball-players), far from having their feelings bruised through public exposure of their likenesses, would feel sorely deprived if they no longer received money for authorizing advertisements, popularizing their countenances, displayed in newspapers, magazines, busses, trains and subways. This right of publicity would usually yield them no money unless it could be made the subject of an exclusive grant which barred any other advertiser from using their pictures."

[2] France, Civil Code, art. 5: "Judges are forbidden to decide cases submitted to them by way of general and regulatory provisions."

[3] Law no 70-643 of July 17, 1970 to reinforce the guarantees of the individual rights of citizens.

[4] Violations concerning privacy: art. 226-1 of the Penal Code; violations concerning one's image: art. 226-8 of the Penal Code; defamation: Law of July 29, 1881 on the freedom of the press.

from privacy rights. The distinction is not at all as clear as that between privacy rights and the "right of publicity" in the US. In fact, article 9 of the Civil Code serves to protect purely moral and personal interests. Sometimes, however, it protects celebrities' commercial interests. It has been said that article 9 was the "matrix" of personality rights.[5] The characterization is very appropriate. Because article 9 is short and of general application, it leaves much liberty to judges. But this freedom is, in fact, too broad for a French judge, who feels real difficulty in recognizing the existence of a right lacking explicit legislative foundation. In cases involving commercial uses of images in particular, the judge is discomfited because article 9 was originally conceived as a moral protection for individuals. The French judge is moreover confronted with a true technical difficulty, because the regulation of the image should be part of a complete legal regime. But the judge's sole tool is the formula "Everyone is entitled to the respect of his private life." One can understand the French judge's unease. That is why it is so enriching to compare the work of French judges with that of Judge Frank in the famous *Haelan* decision.

A French jurist would first note that *Haelan* was decided by a federal court interpreting New York state law. France, however, is not a federal system. It has only one kind of private law tribunal, which interprets French law. It will therefore be difficult to find among French decisions one that plays the same role in the legal order. But the difficulty is not insurmountable.

France is part of the European Union (EU) and therefore is subject to Community law. Community law can either harmonize the laws of the Member States through "Directives," or directly impose uniform law throughout the EU through "Regulations." Special courts interpret Community law, particularly the Court of Justice of the European Union (CJEU). That is why one finds in Europe a situation somewhat similar to that of the US: The fields of Community/Member State competence are divided and there are two kinds of courts. Sometimes the CJEU even interprets the domestic laws of Member States, when Community law refers to them.

Of course, Community law does not govern the whole of the law of the Member States. These preserve their domestic laws in many areas. In particular, rights of personality have never been regulated by the EU legislative or administrative authorities. There is no Directive or Regulation in this field, just as there is no general federal law on the right of

[5] J.-C. Saint-Pau, "L'article 9 du Code civil: matrice des droits de la personnalité?" note on *Cour de cassation*, first civil chamber, decision of July 16, 1998: D. 1999, p. 541.

privacy in the US. But, a bit like the Second Circuit in *Haelan*, the CJEU was recently called upon to decide on the existence of a kind of "right of publicity." This was the *Fiorucci* case.[6]

The *Fiorucci* case

Elio Fiorucci is an Italian fashion designer who became famous in the 1970s. In 1990 he assigned his intellectual property rights to Edwin Co., including trademarks incorporating the Fiorucci name. Later, Fiorucci learned that Edwin Co. had, in 1999, registered a Community trademark in Elio Fiorucci. Recall that a Community trademark grants uniform protection throughout the EU. The Community trademark was established by a 1993 Regulation, which, as we have seen, imposes uniform rules on all EU Member States.[7] Fiorucci believed that Edwin Co. should have obtained his authorization to register the new trademark. He therefore brought a cancellation action before the Community courts.

Fiorucci grounded his claim in the Community Trademark Regulation, which allows for cancellation of the mark if it violates the right to an individual's name or image. Fiorucci contended that by virtue of Italian law, he enjoyed the exclusive right to exploit his name and that this right was part of his "right in his name" in the sense of Community law. In fact, the Regulation specifies that the rights to name and image depend on the domestic law of the Member State at issue:

> A Community trade mark shall also be declared invalid on application to [the Community Trademark Office] or on the basis of a counterclaim in infringement proceedings where the use of such trade mark may be prohibited pursuant to another earlier right, and in particular: (a) a right to a name; (b) a right of personal portrayal; [...] under the Community legislation or national law governing the protection.[8]

Edwin Co. claimed that Community law understands "the right to one's name" to mean only a personal right in a name, that is, an inalienable right not subject to commercial exploitation. Thus the Community Trademark Regulation would not allow cancellation of a mark that affected the commercial value of the celebrity's name, but only an action for moral damage. In *Haelan*, Topps had adopted a similar strategy. It had argued that New York law covered a "right of privacy," and that such

[6] CJEU Grand Chamber, 05/07/2011, case no C-263/09 (available at www.curia.europa.eu).
[7] Council regulation (EC) 207/2009 of 26 February 2009 on the Community trademark, OJEU L 78/1, art. 53(2).
[8] *Ibid.*, art. 53(2).

a right was an inalienable personal right.[9] But Judge Frank nonetheless ruled that "[...] in addition to and independent of that right of privacy, a man has a right in the publicity value of his photograph [....]."

In *Fiorucci*, the CJEU's analysis proceeded in two steps. First, the court observed that Italian law grants celebrities the right to authorize or to prohibit the registration of their names as trademarks.[10] Second, the CJEU interpreted the Community Trademark Regulation. The court ruled that the "right to one's name," which could be asserted against a subsequently registered trademark, protects both commercial and non-commercial interests. Fiorucci could therefore seek the cancellation of the mark registered by Edwin Co. by invoking the right to exploit the commercial value of his name.

The CJEU thus proceeded a bit like Judge Frank. The CJEU, a European court, interpreted Italian law to recognize the existence of a right to exploit celebrities' names. Judge Frank, a federal judge, interpreted New York law in order to recognize the existence of a right of exploitation of celebrity images.

While there are differences between *Haelan* and *Fiorucci*, the two decisions nonetheless are comparable. First, in *Haelan* a federal judge interpreted and applied state law. In *Fiorucci*, the analysis is more complex: a European judge must interpret the law of a Member State in order to apply the Community law which refers back to the national law. There is another difference as well: In *Haelan*, New York judges had not yet enunciated a "right of publicity." In *Fiorucci*, the Italian trademarks statute provided for the special protection of celebrity names:

> If they are well known, the following may be registered as a trade mark by the proprietor, or with the consent of the latter or of the persons referred to in paragraph 1: personal names, signs used in the artistic, literary, scientific, political or sporting fields, the designations and acronyms of events and those of non-profit making bodies and associations, including their characteristic emblems.[11]

In *Fiorucci*, it was easy for the CJEU to recognize a kind of right of publicity because it already existed in Italy. It is also true, and this is

[9] "This statutory right of privacy is personal, not assignable; therefore, plaintiff's contract vested in plaintiff no 'property' right of other legal interest which defendant's conduct invaded. [...] a man has no legal interest in the publication of his picture other than his right of privacy, i.e., a personal and non-assignable right not to have his feelings hurt by such a publication."

[10] "[...] the proprietor of a well-known name is entitled to prevent the use of that name as a trade mark where he maintains that he has not given his consent to registration of that mark."

[11] Italy, Code of Industrial Property, art. 8, §3.

the last distinction with *Haelan*, that the CJEU's decision is not as broadly written as *Haelan*. In particular, the CJEU did not assert that it would be necessary to recognize an exclusive right of exploitation of celebrity identity. The reach of *Fiorucci* is therefore more modest than *Haelan*'s. But its solution could apply to all EU countries which recognize a form of right of publicity. France is one of them.

The *Bordas* case

In France, the commercial exploitation of celebrity is a phenomenon which the *Cour de cassation* (France's highest private law court) had first developed through rights in names. In fact, names are the object of strict regulation. Since the French Revolution, it has been forbidden to French citizens to take a name other than that appearing on the birth certificate. From this prohibition many rules have been developed, including the rule of inalienability of one's name. This legal regime accords well with the nature of the right to one's name, which the French range among "personality rights." These rights are called non-economic, because they protect only a person's moral integrity. But, after the Second World War, courts were increasingly confronted with the commercial use of personal names, and especially of celebrity names. How is it possible to sell one's name to a commercial enterprise if the name is inalienable? A very important 1985 decision of the *Cour de cassation* concerning the rights in the name of the "Bordas" publishing house supplied an answer.[12]

Pierre Bordas was born in southern France in 1913.[13] In 1943, with his brother Henri, he founded in Lyon a company called "Éditions de la France Nouvelle."[14] In 1946, the enterprise was transferred to Paris and took the name of "Éditions Bordas." The early efforts of Pierre Bordas led notably to his publication of surrealists like Philippe Soupault.[15] The enterprise grew and proved particularly successful in the school and university book market, with best-sellers such as the literary anthology *Lagarde et Michard*.[16] The Bordas name became famous. But, following the acquisition of several companies, the banks took control over the company, making Pierre Bordas a minority shareholder. A conflict then erupted with his associates over editorial policy. In 1978 Pierre Bordas resigned from the company[17] and initiated a lawsuit to prohibit "Éditions Bordas" from using his name. The Paris Court of Appeals upheld his

[12] Cass. com. March 12, 1985, appeal no 84-17163: Bulletin civil 1985, IV, no 95, p. 84; JCP G 1985, II, 20040, note Georges Bonet.

[13] P. Bordas, *L'édition est une aventure*, Éditions de Fallois, Paris, 1997, p. 9.

[14] *Ibid.*, at 116. [15] *Ibid.*, at 184. [16] *Ibid.*, at 249. [17] *Ibid.*, at 371.

claim on the ground that he could not assign his name to the business. According to the court, Pierre Bordas merely tolerated the use of his name, but he could at any time revoke this toleration.[18] The Court of Appeals therefore strictly applied the regime of inalienable personality rights.

The *Cour de cassation* reversed the decision. It ruled that the principle of inalienability of one's name merely prevents the selling of one's name to another physical person. This principle does not prohibit contracting with a company, a juridical person, to authorize the commercial use of one's name. The *Cour de cassation*'s decision is especially important because it establishes the validity of such contracts. The bylaws of the 1946 company stipulated that the company would carry out its commercial activities under the Bordas name. As a result, and with his agreement, the name of Pierre Bordas became a "distinctive sign" (akin to a common law trademark). This is not a mere toleration. Pierre Bordas could no longer go back on his authorization, which the court ruled did not violate the rule of the inalienability of one's name. According to the *Cour de cassation*, the "Éditions Bordas" company acquired an incorporeal property right in the Bordas name. Pierre Bordas died in 2000, leaving in his memoirs his account of this famous lawsuit.[19] Ever since this decision, it is established that contracts assigning elements of personality to commercial enterprises are valid.

But *Bordas* does not go as far as *Haelan*. In *Bordas*, the famous publisher attacked his own co-contractant. It is not surprising that the courts would enforce the contract. In *Haelan*, by contrast, the celebrities' co-contractant moved against a third party. It was not clear that the contract concluded between Haelan's predecessor and the baseball players could be applied against Topps. Judge Frank recognized the difficulty:

> [...] under the New York decisions, defendant correctly asserts that any such contract between plaintiff and a ballplayer, in so far as it merely authorized plaintiff to use the player's photograph, created nothing but a release of liability. On that basis, were there no more to the contract, plaintiff would have no actionable claim against defendant.[20]

[18] "Whereas this incorporation in the corporate name of the company of the name 'Bordas,' which, like all patronymics is inalienable and remains the property of its owner and of his family, can only be treated as a mere toleration of the use of his name on the part of Pierre Bordas, a toleration to which he could put an end without thereby abusing his rights so long as he supplied a sufficient justification," CA Paris, November 8, 1984.

[19] J.-L. Douin, "Pierre Bordas. Le fondateur des éditions Bordas," *Le Monde* October 10, 2000. Pierre Bordas' memoirs are titled, *L'édition est une aventure*, *supra* note 13.

[20] 202 F.2d 866 (2d Cir. 1953), §1(b).

In addition, *Bordas* did not articulate the nature of the right which enabled Pierre Bordas to authorize his company in 1946 to make commercial use of his name. *Haelan*, by contrast, affirms the existence of a new right. *Bordas* therefore is not as significant as *Haelan*, but in France it initiated the development of a kind of right of publicity.

The *Ducasse* case

Almost twenty years later, the *Ducasse* decision provided the occasion for the *Cour de cassation* to respond to the question left open by *Bordas*: What is the nature of the right which permits one to authorize the commercial exploitation of one's identity? Born in 1956, Alain Ducasse is a chef honored by the prestigious Michelin Guide. A picture of Alain Ducasse is shown in Figure 2.1. He distinguished himself early on by becoming the chef of the Louis XV restaurant of the Hôtel de Paris in Monaco. Progressively, Ducasse built a gastronomic empire across the world: France, Russia, United Kingdom, China, Japan, the US, etc. His restaurants are located in the most prestigious venues, such as the Eiffel Tower, where he runs the Jules Verne restaurant. In 1998, Alain Ducasse founded the company De

Figure 2.1: Alain Ducasse (© Mickael Vojinovich)

Gustibus, which allowed him to diversify his activities into training and book publishing. But before creating De Gustibus, Ducasse had, in 1991, founded another company, Alain Ducasse Diffusion (ADD); this company was the subject of a lawsuit. The company's objective was to exploit the image of Alain Ducasse through the creation, the production and the commercialization of all kinds of products and other media. In 1993, Alain Ducasse sued ADD, which had, without his authorization, registered French trademarks in "ALAIN DUCASSE DIFFUSION" and "ALAIN DUCASSE MONTE CARLO." Ducasse sought the cancellation of the registrations.

A first judgment in 1995 vindicated Alain Ducasse,[21] but in 2000 ADD prevailed on appeal to the Court of Appeals of Aix-en-Provence.[22] The 1985 *Bordas* decision underlay the judges' determination that Alain Ducasse had authorized ADD to use his name by integrating it into the name and bylaws of the company. The Alain Ducasse name therefore would have become the incorporeal property of ADD. The Court of Appeals thus gave a very broad (indeed, too broad) interpretation to *Bordas*: Once the founder of a company gives it his name, the company can do with it as it wills. According to the decision, ADD could demand "the free exercise of its property rights" in the Alain Ducasse name, notably the power to register the name as a trademark.

The *Cour de cassation* rejected the Court of Appeals' excessive enlargement of the scope of *Bordas*. In its 2003 decision,[23] the court asserted that a celebrity enjoys "property rights" in his name. The court specified that the registration of a celebrity's name as a trademark requires special authorization, even if tacit. In the case of Ducasse, in giving his name to ADD, he did not thereby authorize ADD to register his name as a trademark. *Ducasse* might therefore be considered to have given official birth to property rights in personality. That is, it marks the beginning of an American-style right of publicity. Indeed, French legal commentators immediately drew the comparison. In his analysis of the decision, Professor Grégoire Loiseau wrote that the *Cour de cassation*:

> clearly confirms the entry on the legal scene of property rights in personality. The propertization of these rights is, it is true, a kind of irrepressible forward motion which little by little is taking over all legal systems. North American laws were the first, adopting fifty years ago a *right of publicity* which apprehends the market dimension of personality and confers upon the individual the right to control commercial or advertising uses of the attributes of that personality.[24]

[21] TGI Draguignan, 1st civ. A, September 28, 1995, RG no 93-03382: unpublished.
[22] CA Aix-en-Provence, 2nd ch., April 27, 2000, RG no 96-14438: unpublished.
[23] Cass. com., May 6, 2003, appeal no. 00-18192.
[24] G. Loiseau, "La propriété d'un nom notoire," D. 2003, p. 2228.

In 1995, Professor Loiseau announced this development in his doctoral thesis, which was devoted to comparative law developments in the right of publicity.[25] At the end of the 1990s, one could sense in France that celebrity was in the process of becoming a new object of property. By extraordinary coincidence, the *Ducasse* decision came down seven months before I defended my thesis on *Fame in Private Law*.[26] I had begun the thesis in 1998. It is also as of 2000 that French sociologists began to listen to their American colleagues, who had already long since considered celebrity as an important social phenomenon. Nathalie Heinich drew from American works to write her 2012 book on visibility.[27] The *Ducasse* decision is indeed the fruit of a period which is, in France, a latecomer relative to the US.

Since then, French jurists can affirm that personality rights have a double nature, both moral and economic. With respect to names, images, and private life, there are therefore two autonomous prerogatives: a non-economic right which provides a remedy for harm to one's feelings, and an economic right that allows celebrities to exploit the market value of their identity. *Ducasse* is therefore the French counterpart to *Haelan* for its recognition of the right of commercial exploitation of elements of personality.

Nonetheless, *Ducasse* does not explicitly establish that these economic rights can be applied against third parties. The case concerned only two co-contractants who differed on the interpretation of their agreement. But, from the French point of view, it is clear that the *Cour de cassation* established a true right good against the world. Indeed, its decision aligns with a prior decision in which it had held that the right to control the copying of one's image applies to third parties.[28] The rights to one's name and to one's image are both rights of personality. Thus, it does not matter that Alain Ducasse did not sue a stranger to his contract. The scope of the *Cour de Cassation*'s May 6, 2003 decision thus is comparable to *Haelan*, even if the relations between the parties were different. But there is another French decision whose facts are almost identical to *Haelan*. It concerns the famous French rock star Johnny Hallyday.

[25] G. Loiseau, *Le nom objet d'un contrat*, preface by Jacques Ghestin, LGDJ, Paris, 1998, 401–14.

[26] D. Lefranc, *La renommée en droit privé*, preface by Henri-Jacques Lucas, LGDJ, Paris, 2004.

[27] N. Heinich, *De la visibilité: Excellence et singularité en régime médiatique*, Gallimard, Paris, 2012.

[28] Cass. 2nd civ., February 11, 1999, appeal no 97-10465 – Cass. 2nd civ., June 30, 2004, appeal no 02-19599.

The *Hallyday* case

Jean-Philippe Smet is a popular singer born in 1943. He is known under the pseudonym Johnny Hallyday. He is very famous to the French public, to whom he introduced certain American musical genres in the 1960s: twist, country, blues and especially rock 'n' roll. For many years Hallyday worked with his record producer, Universal Music. But the relationship deteriorated. The singer brought a lawsuit seeking the return of the master tapes of his recordings. The suit lasted from 2003 to 2006, ending with a loss for Hallyday.[29] Since then, Hallyday has worked with Warner Music.

When Johnny Hallyday worked for Universal Music, he entered into a "merchandizing" contract permitting his record producer to exploit his fame. The singer assigned to this producer "the exclusive right to reproduce his image" on a variety of goods, in particular printed products. In exchange, the singer would receive almost $1,000,000 per year. Two years before the separation, Universal Music discovered that a publisher, CJL, was reproducing Johnny Hallyday's image on a calendar without Universal's authorization. Universal sent CJL a cease and desist letter invoking its "status as the exclusive owner of the right to utilize Johnny Hallyday's image for purposes of merchandizing." CJL declined to cease publication because it had properly obtained a third party's authorization to exploit the image. In fact, a photographic agency belonging to the French state had authorized the reproduction of the image pursuant to its copyright rights. But the authorization covered the photograph, not the rights of the person portrayed. Universal therefore sued CJL, putting in evidence the exclusive contract signed by Johnny Hallyday. Universal prevailed before the first instance court; CJL then appealed to the Court of Appeals of Versailles.

CJL elaborated several arguments against its alleged liability. It first observed that the image at issue represented Johnny Hallyday as an actor in the 1963 film *Cherchez l'idole*. In France, CJL contended, an actor's performance is protected by an intellectual property right "neighboring" to copyright, not by personality rights. Thus, by this reasoning, only the movie producer, as the assignee of Hallyday's performance rights, would have had standing to complain of the reproduction of the image. CJL also invoked arguments similar to those of Topps, by contending, on the one hand, that personality rights could not be granted by contract, and, on

[29] Decision of the Court of Appeal, CA Paris, 18th ch. D, April 12, 2005, *Universal Music c/ Jean-Philippe Smet*: Juris-Data no 2005-269722 – Decision of the *Cour de cassation*: Cass. soc. December 20, 2006, appeal no 05-43057, *Jean-Philippe Smet c/ Universal Music*.

the other, that the contract concluded between Hallyday and Universal could not be applied against it. *Hallyday* and *Haelan* thus pose the same question: Can the grantee of exclusive rights in a celebrity image enforce those rights against third parties?

On September 22, 2005, the Versailles Court of Appeals replied in the affirmative,[30] as had Judge Frank fifty years earlier. The decision asserts that "every person holds over his images or the use of his images an exclusive right which permits him to prevent their dissemination without his express and special authorization." Hallyday could therefore grant to his record producer, on an exclusive basis, a general authorization to exploit his image. But the court's statement goes only to the celebrity's own claim against unauthorized third parties. In the absence of case law on the latter point, Universal preferred to sue on a theory of unfair competition rather than claiming to exercise Johnny Hallyday's image rights in his stead. In finding against CJL, the Court of Appeals of Versailles therefore did not so hold on the basis of article 9 of the Civil Code. Liability rested on the tort of unfair competition:

> [...] reproduction of this image in disregard of the rights of which the plaintiff company is the owner by virtue of the exclusive license that was granted to him by Johnny Hallyday constitutes unfair competition.[31]

CJL was therefore held liable for having diverted Universal's customers, and not for having violated Universal's property rights as successor-in-interest to Hallyday's image rights. In *Haelan*, the baseball players' right of publicity was not only transferable, but it was also enforceable by Haelan against Topps. That is a significant reason why the *Hallyday* decision is not equivalent to *Haelan*, even if the practical outcome is the same. Moreover, *Hallyday* is an isolated decision, for we know of no other decisions which find a violation of a grant of exclusive image rights to be an act of unfair competition.

The Court of Appeals of Versailles did not address an important argument that CJL advanced: The calendar publisher emphasized that it was completely unaware of the contract between Universal and Johnny Hallyday. This argument was grounded in article 1165 of the Civil Code, which establishes that a contract has no effect on non-parties. It is true that CJL was not a party to the contract between Johnny Hallyday and Universal. In *Haelan*, Judge Frank did not

[30] CA Versailles, 12th ch., sect. 2, Sept. 22, 2005: Juris-Data no 2005-288-693 – CCE January 2006, no 1, comm. no 4, obs. C. Caron.
[31] *Ibid.*

completely sidestep the problem of Topps' awareness of the ballplayers' grant. Judge Frank clearly posed the elements of a right of publicity claim:

> [. . .] plaintiff, in its capacity as exclusive grantee of a player's "right of publicity," has a valid claim against defendant if defendant used that player's photograph during the term of plaintiff's grant and with knowledge of it.[32]

In *Haelan*, Topps had knowingly violated Haelan's exclusive rights. In *Hallyday*, CJL reproduced an image of the rock-and-roll star without having known of the exclusive contract with Universal. But CJL should have been aware that an authorization was necessary to publish a calendar reproducing the portrait of a star. Every day, the general French public reads in the press numerous stories of lawsuits brought by celebrities. Ignorance of the contract with Universal should not permit CJL to deny its liability, because it certainly wished to exploit the singer's celebrity for its own benefit. According to the Versailles Court of Appeals, a professional publisher like CJL had a duty to inform itself of the rights protecting Hallyday's image. In addition, CJL should have known that a copyright license from the photographer did not necessarily confer an authorization with respect to the image rights of the portrait's subject. When one is a publisher, one ought to cover the legal aspects of one's activity.

What would have happened if the *Cour de cassation*, the highest jurisdiction, had heard an appeal in the case? One can speculate about the outcome on the basis of that court's case law. When the appellate court rendered its decision in 2005, the *Cour de cassation* had already clearly recognized the right to one's image. In 1998, it had held, in two decisions concerning celebrity photographs decided seven months apart, that "everyone has the right to object to the reproduction of his image."[33] Repeating exactly the same formula, the court reaffirmed this result in 2009.[34] Other decisions of the *Cour de cassation* are even more explicit. Some specify that there is no need to allege a violation of one's privacy in order to enforce one's rights in one's image.[35] That means that the right to one's image is indeed distinct from the right to privacy, even if the two rights are grounded in the same text (article 9 of the Civil Code). Particularly by the time of the Versailles court's decision in 2005, the *Cour de cassation* had already affirmed the exclusive nature of the right to

[32] 202 F.2d 866 (2d Cir. 1953), §2[2].
[33] Cass. 1st civ., January 13, 1998, appeal no 95-13694 – Cass. 1st civ., July 16, 1998, appeal no 96-15610.
[34] Cass. 1st civ., September 24, 2009, appeal no 08-11112.
[35] Cass. 1st civ., July 9, 2009, appeal no 07-19758.

one's image.[36] If the right to one's image is exclusive, then third parties should respect it. CJL therefore should have respected it. The publisher would have discovered the existence of the grant if he had taken the trouble to inquire directly of Johnny Hallyday. Moreover, the *Cour de cassation* had already had occasion to recognize the validity of contracts granting rights in celebrity names in the *Bordas* and *Ducasse* cases. That is why, if it had had to render a judgment in the *Hallyday* case, it would probably have reproached CJL for failure to respect the singer's image. The court would have done so because, by grounding its claim in unfair competition law, Universal had cleverly anticipated and avoided the theoretical difficulty: The court would not have had to recognize a grantee's right of publicity, because the debate was not posed in those terms. Even today, the *Cour de cassation* has still not decided a case in which the grantee of image rights is exploiting them in the place of the grantor.

Conclusion

In summary, the 1985 *Bordas* decision admitted the validity of contracts concerning the commercial exploitation of an individual's name. The 2003 *Ducasse* decision established property rights in celebrities' names. The 2005 *Hallyday* decision recognized property rights in one's image. This decision moreover acknowledged that these rights can be granted, and that the grantee can enforce them against third parties. One can therefore assert that French law applies a result similar to the one imposed by Judge Frank in *Haelan*, even if, in France, one speaks not of a "right of publicity" but of property rights in personality, or of unfair competition. Both countries recognize celebrities' power to exercise a monopoly over the commercial exploitation of their identities. Let us now go beyond this comparison and ask two questions: (1) Are property rights in personality governed by a coherent legal regime, and (2) are property rights in personality a new form of intellectual property?

1. *Property rights in personality are not subject to a coherent regime under French law*

The rules respecting names are not the same as those regarding images. As we have seen, the *Ducasse* decision granted the chef protection only because he was famous. The *Cour de cassation* even subsequently

[36] Cass. 2nd civ., February 11, 1999, appeal no 97-10465 – Cass. 2nd civ., June 30, 2004, appeal no 02-19599.

specified that it was necessary to be famous through all of France in order to protect one's name.[37] By contrast, the *Cour de cassation* continues to recognize all persons' exclusive rights over images, whether or not the individual is famous. There is no explanation for this difference in regime. In my opinion, only famous people should be able to monopolize the commercial value of their identity. In fact only the existence of market value can provide a basis for an exclusive right of exploitation. Without fame, there is no economic value to exploit. In this regard, the case law of the *Cour de cassation* is not easy to understand.

The differences in the regimes of rights in names and rights in images do not stop there. In *Ducasse*, the *Cour de cassation* formally recognized the existence of property rights in one's name. By contrast, that court has never recognized the existence of property rights in one's image. It has limited itself to recalling that any reproduction of an individual's image requires that person's authorization. But we do not know if that authorization is based on a personal and moral right or on a property right over exploitation. It is impossible today to answer that question. How can the *Cour de cassation* explain its recognition of a property right in names yet forbear from doing so for images? We have not the slightest idea. This uncertainty explains why, in *Hallyday*, Universal chose to rely on unfair competition rather than claim to exercise the singer's rights over his image by virtue of his transfer of exclusive rights to Universal. French law remains very ambiguous.

2. *Commentators have a tendency to see a new form of intellectual property in property rights in personality, and even a kind of "neighboring right"*[38]

The significance of the assimilation of property rights in personality to intellectual property rights concerns three issues: exceptions to property rights, compensation for their transfer, and proof of violations.

With regard to exceptions, the *Cour de cassation* has frequently recalled that the right to one's image should not violate freedom of expression. For example, the caricature of an individual is permitted if it is done consistently with the "laws of the genre."[39] The right to know also prevails over the right to one's image when the portrait of a

[37] Cass. com. June 24, 2008, *Sté André Beau c/ Beau*, appeal no 07-10756: CCE December 2008, comm. no 133, obs. Christophe Caron; Juris-Data no 2008-044537.

[38] C. Caron, "Un nouveau droit voisin est né: le droit patrimonial sur l'image," obs. ss. CA Versailles, 12th ch., 2nd sect., September 22, 2005: CCE January 2006, no 1, comm. no 4.

[39] Cass. 1st civ., January 13, 1998.

famous person accompanies the report of a current event.[40] From this point of view, the case law is rather clear, even if it recognizes only general exceptions whose contours remain fairly indeterminate (as in the US).

With respect to compensation for transfers, most celebrities wish to obtain remuneration proportionate to the profits of the exploitation of their images (royalties). They reason by analogy from the copyright law, which makes proportional remuneration a legal obligation. In fact, article L. 131-4 of the French Code of intellectual property provides:

> Assignment by the author of the rights in his work may be total or partial. Assignment shall comprise a proportional participation by the author in the revenue from sale or exploitation of the work.

The *Cour de cassation* has unambiguously denied celebrities a right of proportional remuneration when the contract granting rights to exploit their images did not clearly provide for royalties. This is the outcome of a 2008 decision which rejected the application of the Code of intellectual property to contracts granting image rights.[41] That result was confirmed by another decision in 2010.[42] In general, the *Cour de cassation* declines to interfere in assignments or licenses of image rights, agreements which must be freely negotiated and can even be tacit.[43] In the event of the unexpected success of the goods reproducing the image, there is no claim for additional remuneration on the part of the person portrayed.

With respect to the proof of violations of rights of personality, there is no positive law equivalent to the *saisie-contrefaçon*. This is a procedural device that allows the court to order a seizure of goods and premises at the outset of an infringement action in order to conserve evidence. A very recent case illustrates the point. A famous photographer, Irina Ionesco, had taken erotic portraits of her daughter Eva between the ages of 4 and 12. Today, Eva Ionesco is trying to prevent her mother from exploiting the most degrading photographs. Of course, given the ambiguity of French law, we do not know whether Eva Ionesco is complaining of commercial or moral harm. Eva Ionesco initiated the lawsuit at the outset of the promotional campaign for her first film, the autobiographical *My Little Princess*. Moreover, in the early 2000s she had authorized her mother to reproduce certain images in a book titled *Eva: In Praise of*

[40] Cass. 2nd civ., June 30, 2004.
[41] Cass. 1st civ., December 11, 2008, appeal no 07-19494.
[42] Cass. 1st civ., January 28, 2010, appeal no 08-70248.
[43] Cass. 1st civ., November 13, 2008, appeal no 06-16278.

My Daughter. In April 2011, Eva's lawyer arranged for a seizure at the home of Irina Ionesco of a box of negatives labeled "Eva." To effect the seizure, Eva's lawyer acted on the basis of the general law of civil procedure. This law is not well-adapted to the objective pursued, because ordinarily it is not possible to seize the goods of an individual. And indeed, in a judgment of December 17, 2012, the Paris trial court ruled that the seizure was not lawful, because it violated Irina Ionesco's property rights in her negatives.[44] In the case of Eva Ionesco one regrets that there is not a kind of *saisie-contrefaçon* reserved for the gravest kinds of violations of image rights.

If one adopts a theoretical approach, it would be difficult to say that the US right of publicity and the French right to one's image are new intellectual property rights. Normally, intellectual property concerns creations. But a person does not create herself, apart from her style and appearance (though these elements can make up a celebrity's *persona*, and therefore constitute a kind of creation). One becomes embroiled in endless questions of legal philosophy: What is intellectual property? What is personality and what is a person? It is better to take a pragmatic point of view. Exploitation of celebrity is continually evolving. With the collapse of sales of CDs, the music industry is relying increasingly on merchandizing properties: European singers register their names as trademarks; clothing lines are created in their names, etc. The drop-off in attendance at movie theaters is prompting the same developments in the world of cinema. It is becoming more and more urgent to clarify the regime of publicity rights.

In her analysis of *Haelan*, Stacey Dogan regrets that, apart from the First Amendment, appropriate restraints have not developed alongside the growth of the right of publicity, a shortcoming she perceives as a consequence of the inadequate normative and legal foundations for the right. But perhaps it is precisely because the right is still evolving that its frontiers remain insufficiently defined. Were the right recognized as within the core of intellectual property rights, rather than as an outsider on the margins straining to enter, perhaps the requisite limitations would more readily fall into place. An intellectual property right can be subject to significant limitations. Even a very curtailed intellectual property right can have practical utility. French law offers many examples. The neighboring right of the phonograms producer is circumscribed by a very broad compulsory license that disables the producer from preventing

[44] D. Lefranc, "Posséder l'enfance? L'image de l'enfant 'modèle' au piège de l'art et du temps," note ss. TGI Paris, December 17, 2012, *Ionesco c/ Ionesco*: Légipresse February 2013, no 302, pp. 107–115.

the radio broadcasting of the sound recording.[45] The neighboring right of the database producer does not afford it a general exclusive exploitation right. Only substantial extractions of data are subject to unconditional prohibition.[46]

What is certain is that celebrities are exploiting their image rights as if those rights were intellectual property rights. We have seen that the right to one's image is becoming a de facto exclusive exploitation right, akin to copyright. Image rights contracts can provide for royalties, as do copyright contracts. Image rights encounter exceptions in the public interest, as does copyright. Like copyright, the protection of image rights requires conservation of evidence through the *saisie-contrefaçon*. In 2002, I had already contended that personality rights were slowly adopting the same legal regime as that of French copyright law: moral rights and a right of exploitation.[47] US law offers the equivalents in the form of a personal right to privacy and a commercial right of publicity. From my point of view, the right to one's image has become an intellectual property right, because it functions like an intellectual property right. That said, it is not easy to say whether the right of publicity matches any particular model of intellectual property. A French lawyer would be tempted to say that it follows the "droit d'auteur" (i.e. French "copyright") model because personality rights have a double nature, both moral and economic. But celebrity name and image are not perceived by the public as works of authorship. Name and image rather are distinctive signs, akin to trademarks: One recognizes an artist or an athlete through his or her portrait or name, much as one identifies a product with its trade dress or trademark. That is why one may inquire whether trademark law would not furnish a better model for publicity rights, if one day legislation were to be enacted.

That said, trademark law does not offer an ideal model. Indeed, the protection of fame is as problematic in trademark law as it may be with

[45] France, Code of intellectual property law, art. L. 214-1: "Where a phonogram has been published for commercial purposes, neither the performer nor the producer may oppose: 1. its direct communication in a public place where it is not used in an entertainment; 2. its broadcasting or the simultaneous and integral cable distribution of such broadcast. Such uses of phonograms published for commercial purposes shall entitle the performers and producers to remuneration whatever the place of fixation of such phonograms [. . .]."

[46] Art. L. 342-1 CPI: "The producer of a database has the right to prohibit: 1. The extraction, by the permanent or temporary transfer of all or a substantial part, qualitatively or quantitatively, of the contents of a database to another medium, by any means or in any form; 2. The reuse, by making available to the public all or a substantial part, qualitatively or quantitatively, of the contents of a database, in any form whatsoever."

[47] D. Lefranc, "L'auteur et la personne. Libres propos sur les rapports entre le droit d'auteur et les droits de la personnalité," D. 2002, p. 1926.

respect to the right of publicity or to French law rights in one's image. Graeme Dinwoodie's chapter demonstrates how the protection of famous marks against dilution encounters similar difficulties.[48] Some judges are very reticent to extend existing intellectual property monopolies or to create new ones.[49] They fear prohibiting the commercialization of new products that are neither copies nor illicit imitations simply on the ground that the newcomers are profiting from others' fame. Dinwoodie therefore reasons that antidilution protection should depend more on the unfairness of the use, in order to avoid undesirable economic consequences. A similar intuition animates Stacey Dogan's lament that the right of publicity eschews a "harm-based approach." For her, the right of publicity tends to block the availability of new products for which there should be a legitimate market. Both Dinwoodie and Dogan deplore the lack of a coherent legal regime to circumscribe the new property rights in famous marks and celebrity images. Admittedly, a balance remains to be found, but that does not alter the fact that these rights arise within the core of intellectual property, and not at its outer bounds. To say that these rights arise *at the edge of intellectual property* suggests that they are suspect, and do not belong. Perhaps one would encounter fewer theoretical difficulties if one inquired, as a matter of principle, how fame should be protected. One solution might be to cut the umbilical cord that ties the right of publicity to the right of privacy, and the antidilution right to trademark rights. One could then reason freely about what the contours of this new form of intellectual property should be.[50] It would be a small revolution.

For now, neither US nor French law have yet been capable of giving a formal, coherent, legal foundation to this new intellectual property right. Moreover, it is much easier for the legislature to devote its time to literary and artistic works, to trademarks, or to patents, than to celebrities. In France, a law which benefited only celebrities would surely lack political legitimacy, because the French maintain a complicated relationship with their élites. Image rights will probably remain an incomplete right, a half an intellectual property right . . . forever?

[48] See Dinwoodie, Chapter 4 in this volume.
[49] Lefranc, "L'auteur et la personne," *citing* Lord Justice Jacob.
[50] Lefranc, *La renommée en droit privé.*

Part II

Dilution

3 The suppressed misappropriation origins of trademark antidilution law: The Landgericht Elberfeld's *Odol* Opinion and Frank Schechter's "The Rational Basis of Trademark Protection"

Barton Beebe[*]

In September 1924, the Landgericht Elberfeld, a minor German regional trial court just east of Dusseldorf, issued a brief, eight-paragraph decision resolving a dispute between the complainant, the longtime registrant of the nationally famous trademark "Odol" for mouthwash, and the respondent, a recent registrant of the same mark for various steel products.[1] The court found that the "respondent has registered the mark for its steel goods for the obvious purpose of deriving from [the mark's] selling power some advantage in marketing its own products,"[2] and ordered the cancellation of the respondent's registration on the ground that "[i]t is opposed to good morals to appropriate thus the fruits of another's labor in the consciousness that that other will or may thereby be damaged."[3] The dissimilarity of mouthwash and steel products prompted the court to explain:

[*] The original German text of the *Odol* case and a full English translation are available at www.bartonbeebe.com. Thanks to Hendrik van Echten and Matthias Schrader for excellent research assistance.

[1] LG Elberfeld, 14 September 1924, 204 – *Odol* [hereinafter *Odol*]. Neither the complainant nor the respondent is specifically identified in the record of the opinion. *See also* "§ 826 BGB. Der Inhaber einer sehr bekannten Mundwassermarke (Odol) kann verhindern, daß ein Anderer das gleiche Zeichen für andere Waren (Stahlwaren) benutzt," *Juristische Wochenschrift* 502 (1925). The Landgericht Elberfeld was renamed the Landgericht Wuppertal in 1930.

[2] *Odol*, *supra* note 1, at 204 ("Die Beklagte hat sich das Warenzeichen für ihre Stahlwaren in der offenen Absicht eintragen lassen, aus dessen Schlagkraft für die Verbreitung ihrer Waren Nutzen zu ziehen."). The English translation is from Dr. Ludwig Wertheimer, "Broadened Protection of Names and Trade-Marks Under the German Law," 20 *T. M. Bull.* (N. S.) 75, 77 (1925).

[3] *Odol*, *supra* note 1, at 205 ("Es verstößt gegen die guten Sitten, sich die Früchte fremder Arbeit in dieser Weise anzueignen in dem Bewußtsein, daß der andere dadurch geschädigt werde bzw. geschädigt werden könne."). The English translation is from Wertheimer, *supra* note 2, at 77.

> To be sure, the parties, on account of the wholly different goods put out by them are not in actual competition. That, however, is beside the point. The complainant has created a demand for its goods, while employing thereon a word having drawing power, for only through the year[s]-long and extended activity of the complainant was its selling power acquired.[4]

The court reasoned that the complainant thus had "the utmost interest in seeing that its mark is not diluted [*verwässert*]: it would lose in selling power if everyone used it as the designation of his goods."[5] And so, in the seminal *Odol* opinion, whose author remains unknown, the concept of trademark dilution was born.[6]

The herald of a concept at the very edge of trademark law, the *Odol* decision soon made its way to America, and to the pages of the *Harvard Law Review*, and eventually, to the pages of the US Reports. The journey began with the December 1924 issue of the German intellectual property law journal *Gewerblicher Rechtsschutz und Urheberrecht*, which reported the *Odol* decision in full.[7] Four months later, in April 1925, the *Bulletin of the United States Trade-Mark Association* published a two-page discussion and partial translation of the *Odol* case by one Dr. Ludwig Wertheimer.[8] Then, in 1927, came the main event. In that year, the young German-speaking[9] American lawyer Frank Schechter published in the *Harvard Law Review* an article entitled "The Rational Basis of Trademark

[4] *Odol*, *supra* note 1, at 205 ("Freilich stehen die Parteien wegen der gänzlichen Verschiedenheit der von ihnen vertriebenen Waren nicht im Wettbewerb miteinander. Dies tut aber nichts zur Sache. Die Beklagte hat für ihre Ware Reklame gemacht, indem sie sich eines zugkräftigen Wortes bediente, das gerade durch die langjährige und ausgedehnte Tätigkeit der Klägerin allein seine Zugkraft erlangt hatte.") The English translation is from Wertheimer, *supra* note 2, at 77.

[5] *Odol*, *supra* note 1, at 204 ("Die Klägerin hat infolgedessen das größte Interesse daran, daß ihr Zeichen nicht verwässert wird; es würde an Werbekraft einbüßen, wenn jedermann es zur Bezeichnung seiner Waren verwenden würde."). The English translation is from Wertheimer, *supra* note 2, at 77. In this and subsequent quotations from Dr. Wertheimer's translation, I have occasionally added the underlying German in brackets, where appropriate.

[6] For the German context of the *Odol* decision, see Andreas Sattler, "Dilution of Well-Known Trademarks—An Analysis of its Foundations in Germany and the European Union," 3 *Zeitschrift für Geistiges Eigentum/Intellectual Property Journal* 304 (2011). *See also* Michael Lehmann, "Unfair Use of and Damage to the Reputation of Well-Known Marks, Names, and Indications of Source in Germany: Some Aspects of Law and Economics," 17 *IIC* 746 (1986); Amelie Winkhaus, *Der Begriff der Zeichenähnlichkeit beim Sonderschutz bekannter Marken*, 30–31 (Peter Lang, Frankfurt am Main, 2010).

[7] *See Odol*, *supra* note 1, at 204.

[8] *See* Wertheimer, *supra* note 2, at 75.

[9] In an August, 1919 issue of *The New York Times Magazine*, Schechter published a quite humorous and insightful Twainian account of his World War I service as a battalion intelligence officer for the American army in Germany. Frank I. Schechter, "Army of Occupation, Binsfield," *N.Y. Times*, August 13, 1919. He wrote of using "my Columbia University German" while "Proconsul" of twenty-one German villages in 1919. *Ibid.*

Protection"[10] which relied heavily, though cagily, on the *Odol* case, and which would eventually become the most cited law review article ever written on trademark law. The extraordinary influence of Schechter's article and, through it, of the *Odol* case was confirmed in 2003 in the US Supreme Court opinion *Moseley v. V Secret Catalogue, Inc.*[11] The *Moseley* court quoted the thesis of Schechter's article that "the preservation of the uniqueness of a trademark should constitute the only rational basis for its protection,"[12] explained that Schechter "supported his conclusion by referring to a German case protecting the owner of the well-known trademark 'Odol,'"[13] and dutifully quoted in a footnote from Schechter's discussion of the *Odol* case: "The German court 'held that the use of the mark, "Odol" even on non-competing goods was "*gegen die guten Sitten.*"'"[14] Remarkably, the Supreme Court offered no translation of the meaning of the German: "opposed to good morals."

To be sure, the impact of "Rational Basis" has been profound, but it has also been scattered and confused. The article and the conception of trademark dilution that it set forth have generated an enormous amount of scholarly commentary both in the United States and abroad,[15] not to mention two federal antidilution statutes,[16] thirty-eight state antidilution statutes,[17] and numerous foreign antidilution laws.[18] Yet the "dauntingly elusive concept"[19] of dilution remains essentially an enigma. As a leading American commentator attests:

> No part of trademark law that I have encountered in my forty years of teaching and practicing IP law has created so much doctrinal puzzlement and judicial incomprehension as the concept of dilution ... Few can successfully explain it

[10] Frank I. Schechter, "The Rational Basis of Trademark Protection," 40 *Harv. L. Rev.* 813 (1927).

[11] 537 U.S. 418 (2003). [12] *Ibid.* at 429. [13] *Ibid.* [14] *Ibid.* at 429 n. 9.

[15] *See, e.g.*, Laura Bradford, "Emotion, Dilution, and the Trademark Consumer," 23 *Berkeley Tech. L. J.* 1227 (2008); Clarissa Long, "Dilution," 106 *Columbia L. Rev.* 1029 (2006); Sandra L. Rierson, "The Myth and Reality of Dilution," 11 *Duke L. & Tech. Rev.* 212 (2012); Rebecca Tushnet, "Gone in Sixty Milliseconds: Trademark Law and Cognitive Science," 86 *Tex. L. Rev.* 507 (2008).

[16] *See* Federal Trademark Dilution Act of 1995, Pub. L. No. 104-98, 109 Stat. 985 (1996) (codified at 15 U.S.C. § 1125(c)); Trademark Dilution Revision Act of 2006, Pub. L. No. 109-312 (2006) (codified at 15 U.S.C. § 1125(c)).

[17] See generally Caroline Chicoine & Jennifer Visintine, "The Role of State Trademark Dilution Statutes in Light of the Trademark Dilution Revision Act of 2006," 96 *Trademark Rep.* 1195 (2006).

[18] *See generally* Ilanah Simon Fhima, *Trade Mark Dilution in Europe and the United States* (Oxford University Press, 2012); David S. Welkowitz, *Trademark Dilution: Federal, State, and International Law* (Bureau of National Affairs, Washington DC, 2002).

[19] *Ringling Bros.-Barnum & Bailey Circus Combined Shows, Inc. v. Utah Div. of Travel Dev.*, 170 F.3d 449, 451 (4th Cir. 1999).

without encountering stares of incomprehension or worse, nods of understanding which mask and conceal bewilderment and misinterpretation.[20]

If dilution is an enigma, even more so is "Rational Basis." The article has produced a variety of conflicting interpretations of what its author thought dilution was, why he thought we should prevent it, and how he thought we should do so.[21] Indeed, one wonders if even Schechter himself – who died only ten years after publishing "Rational Basis," too young at the age of forty-seven, before he could further develop and clarify his ideas[22] – ever fully understood what he intended when he used the term "dilution."[23] The result is that now nearly a century since the *Odol* case and "Rational Basis," we are still struggling to reach consensus on what exactly the Landgericht Elberfeld and Schechter meant – and, more importantly, what exactly we mean – by trademark dilution.

While the concept of trademark dilution, even in its pure and perfect form, whatever that may be, is no doubt quite subtle, dilution's theoretical elusiveness cannot fully explain why the concept continues so thoroughly to befuddle trademark courts and commentators. This brief essay offers an additional explanation for the mystery surrounding the concept, an explanation grounded not in theory, but in history. It argues that Schechter deliberately sought in "Rational Basis" to obscure the true

[20] J. Thomas McCarthy, "Dilution of a Trademark: European and United States Law Compared," 94 *Trademark Rep.* 1163, 1163 (2004). *See also* Stacey L. Dogan, "What *Is* Dilution Anyway?," 105 *Mich. L. Rev. First Impressions* 103 (2006); Christine Haight Farley, "Why We Are Confused About the Trademark Dilution Law," 16 *Fordham Intell. Prop., Media & Ent. L. J.* 1175 (2006). For a good example of the situation McCarthy describes, see the oral argument in *Moseley*, which consisted essentially of variations on the question of what, if anything, dilution is. Transcript of Oral Argument, *Moseley v. V Secret Catalogue*, 537 U.S. 418 (2003), 2002 WL 31643067.

[21] *See e.g.*, William G. Barber, "A 'Rational' Approach for Analyzing Dilution Claims: The Three Hallmarks of True Trademark Dilution," 33 *AIPLA Q. J.* 25 (2005); Gerard N. Magliocca, "From Ashes to Fire: Trademark and Copyright in Transition," 82 *N. C. L. Rev.* 1009 (2004); Sara Stadler Nelson, "The Wages of Ubiquity in Trademark Law," 88 *Iowa L. Rev.* 731 (2003); Jerre B. Swann, "Dilution Redefined for the Year 2002," 92 *Trademark Rep.* 585, 587 (2002).

[22] *See* Sol M. Stroock, "Memorial of Frank Isaac Schechter," *Assoc. of the Bar of the City of New York: Year Book* 416 (1938). *See also* "Frank Schechter, Lawyer, Dies at 47," *N.Y. Times*, Sept. 27, 1937.

[23] Commentators often state that Schechter himself never used the term dilution. This is not correct. In a 1936 article in the *Columbia Law Review*, Schechter explained how a trademark may be damaged "by the gradual dilution or whittling away of its uniqueness—and hence of its selling power." *See* Frank I. Schechter, "Fog and Fiction in Trade-Mark Protection," 36 *Colum. L. Rev.* 60, 66 (1936) [hereinafter "Fog and Fiction"]. Schechter again used the term in a 1937 article in *Fordham Law Review*: "In [the Odol case] involving the same mark on such far removed articles as mouth-wash and steel ties, the court found that it was the 'dilution' of a mark and the impairment of its selling-power or drawing-power that must be enjoined." *See* Frank I. Schechter, "Trade Morals and Regulation: The American Scene," 6 *Fordham L. Rev.* 190, 204 n. 42 (1937).

nature of the *Odol* case and of antidilution protection, and that even a century later, his effort at obfuscation remains more or less a success, at least in the United States. What Schechter sought to obscure in "Rational Basis" is that the *Odol* case was not, strictly speaking, a trademark case. Rather, it was a misappropriation case that happened to involve a trademark. Schechter sought to suppress this basic truth – that the concept of trademark dilution is essentially a misappropriation concept – in order to sell his proposed doctrinal reforms to an American audience altogether suspicious of misappropriation doctrine and increasingly under the sway of American Legal Realism. A highly sophisticated trademark scholar and New York lawyer, a recent graduate of Columbia Law School, and the son of the great rabbi Solomon Schechter, Frank Schechter very likely understood in 1927 that his thinking – and the *Odol* decision – was in sync with the commercial realities of his time but strangely out of sync with its legal thought. Only nine years earlier, the Supreme Court had handed down its controversial majority opinion in the misappropriation case of *International News Service v. Associated Press*.[24] In separate dissents, which would eventually become part of the canon of American Legal Realism, Justice Holmes and Justice Brandeis both criticized Justice Pitney's majority opinion for the empty formalism and circularity of its finding that the petitioner was "endeavoring to reap where it has not sown."[25] Justice Brandeis in particular expressed concern that courts were ill-equipped to limit the reach of a broad misappropriation rule by which the respondent might "prevent appropriation of the fruits of its labor by another."[26] Schechter needed to disassociate the *Odol* case from the *International News* majority; he needed somehow to clothe his essentially formalist misappropriation doctrine in the guise of legal realism. To do so required a great deal of finesse, or to put it more bluntly, of dissembling, and "Rational Basis" is full of it. As we will see, Schechter went so far as to delete from his lengthy quotation of Dr. Wertheimer's translation of the *Odol* opinion the opinion's central holding, that the respondent sought "to appropriate thus the fruits of another's labor."

Due both to its frequent misdirection and ambiguity and to its emphatic suppression of any suggestion that trademark dilution is a form of misappropriation, "Rational Basis" has remained an altogether open text. It has managed over the years to mean many different things to many different people, all seeking some theoretical means to fill the void left in the absence of misappropriation. As new generations try to decipher what the prophet meant to tell us in "Rational Basis," each

[24] 248 U.S. 215 (1918). [25] *Ibid.* at 239. [26] *Ibid.* at 264 (Brandeis J., dissenting).

reader fastens upon a different passage and takes away a different meaning, and the exegetical debate only intensifies. The result is that "Rational Basis" still remains essentially inscrutable, as does Schechter's concept of dilution, and this very inscrutability has been the source of the article's enduring influence and the concept's enduring fascination. Even now, in the face of ever more scholarly and judicial commentary recognizing that dilution is essentially a form of "free-riding,"[27] and likely one that typically inflicts no substantial harm on the misappropriated mark, the obfuscatory nature of Schechter's text enables the concept of dilution to survive behind a fog of indeterminacy.

In what follows, I first discuss the *Odol* case itself. I then turn to "Rational Basis," its expurgation of the *Odol* case, and its many artful formulations and reformulations of the concept of trademark dilution.

The *Odol* case

The *Odol* case presented the Landgericht Elberfeld with an especially difficult set of facts: The respondent had registered at the German Patent Office a trademark identical to the complainant's widely recognized trademark, but had done so for use on goods unrelated to the complainant's goods. While the complainant used "Odol" in connection with mouthwash, the respondent succeeded in registering "Odol" for steel products such as nail clippers. The difficulty was that the German Trademark Act of 1894[28] would grant relief only if the complainant could show that the respondent's mark was likely to cause consumer confusion as to the true source of the respondent's goods. But because the complainant's and respondent's goods in the *Odol* case were so different and no reasonable connection could be imagined between them, consumers were not likely to be confused as to source. Instead, consumers would likely believe that another company was now also using the "Odol" mark as a designation of source of its own goods. In 1905, the German Supreme Court at Hamburg had considered a similar set of facts in which the complainant had long been using the well-known mark "Kodak" on cameras and the respondent had more recently registered the same mark for use on, among

[27] *See* David J. Franklyn, "Debunking Dilution Doctrine: Toward a Coherent Theory of the Anti-Free-Rider Principle in American Trademark Law," 56 *Hastings L. J.* 117, 117 (2004). *See also* Farley, *supra* note 20, at 1185. For judicial recognition of the free-riding characteristics of trademark dilution, see, for example, *Thane Intern., Inc. v. Trek Bicycle Corp.*, 305 F.3d 894, 911 (9th Cir. 2002), and *Tiffany & Co. v. Tiffany Prods., Inc.*, 147 Misc. 679, 681 (N.Y. Sup. 1932).

[28] Gesetz zum Schutz der Warenbezeichnungen vom 12. Mai 1894, Deutsches Reichsgesetzblatt, Vol. 1894, No. 22, p. 441.

other things, toilets and bath tubs.[29] Because these facts could not support a likelihood of consumer confusion as to source, the Hamburg court refused to order the cancellation of the respondent's registration.[30]

But importantly, the *Odol* court did not analyze the facts before it under trademark law. Instead, it based its decision on two other provisions in German law, neither of which required a showing of consumer confusion. The first was § 826 of the German Civil Code of 1900 (the "BGB"):[31] "Who, in a manner contrary to good morals [*gegen die guten Sitten*], intentionally inflicts damage on another is liable to compensate the other for the damage."[32] The second was § 1 of the Law against Unfair Competition of 1909 (the "UWG"):[33] "Who, in the course of trade, takes actions that impede against good morals [*gegen die guten Sitten*] can be sued for injunctive relief and compensation."[34] In theory and in practice, these two provisions were largely redundant of each other,[35] but § 826 BGB required a showing of intent ("intentionally inflicts damage")[36] while § 1 UWG was understood to require a showing of competition between the parties ("in the course of trade").[37]

The broad provisions of § 826 BGB and § 1 UWG did not formally require anything like a showing by a trademark complainant that its mark was famous, but like a present-day trademark court considering a dilution cause of action, the *Odol* court turned first to the issue of the fame or

[29] RG, 12 December 1905, MuW 1906, 73 – *Kodak*, cited in Ansgar Ohly, "Blaue Kürbiskerne aus der Steiermark," in B. Schenk et al. eds., *Festschrift für Irmgard Griss*, 521, 521–22 (Jan Sramek Verlag, Vienna, 2011).

[30] *See* "The 'Kodak' Litigation in Germany," 19 *T. M. Bull.* (N.S.) 105 (1924). *See also* Ohly, *supra* note 29; "Protecting the Kodak Trade-Mark," 18 *T. M. Bull.* (N. S.) 267 (1923). Interestingly, in a contemporary English case, the court enjoined the defendant's unauthorized use of the mark "Kodak" on bicycles. *See Eastman Photographic Materials Co. v. John Griffith Corp.*, 15 R.P.C. 105 (1898). This led Walter Derenberg to conclude that the concept of dilution "originated in England when the British court protected the trademark 'Kodak' against use on bicycles," and then "further developed" in the *Odol* case. Walter J. Derenberg, "The Problem of Trademark Dilution and the Antidilution Statutes," 44 *Cal. L. Rev.* 439, 448 (1956). See also *Interflora, Inc. & Anor v. Marks & spencer plc & Anor* (C-323/09) [2012] E.T.M.R. 1 at pp AG 51 (CJEU 2011) (discussing the "so-called Kodak doctrine that justifies an extensive scope of protection against confusion of well-known marks").

[31] Bürgerliches Gesetzbuch (1900).

[32] The German is: "Wer in einer gegen die guten Sitten verstoßenden Weise einem anderen vorsätzlich Schaden zufügt, ist dem anderen zum Ersatz des Schadens verpflichtet."

[33] Gesetz gegen den unlauteren Wettbewerb (1909).

[34] The German is "Wer im geschäftlichen Verkehre zu Zwecken des Wettbewerbes Handlungen vornimmt, die gegen die guten Sitten verstoßen, kann auf Unterlassung und Schadensersatz in Anspruch genommen werden."

[35] *See* Rudolf Callmann, *Der unlautere Wettbewerb*, 92–93 (Bensheimer, Mannheim, 1929).

[36] *See* Sattler, *supra* note 6, at 308. [37] *See ibid.* at 311–14.

notoriety of the complainant's mark. Apparently, the court believed that this was a threshold issue and that only famous marks could qualify for the special form of protection the court would eventually set forth. As translated by Dr. Wertheimer, the court found:

> [T]he word "Odol" has become a catchword – a nickname as distinguishing the goods of the complainant, and has attained a good-will superior to that of its former meaning as a trade-mark, so that everyone when he hears or reads the word "Odol," thinks of the complainant's mouth wash. These facts are of the greatest significance to the complainant; its goods have a good reputation, and an article designated with the name "Odol" leads the public to assume that it is of good quality.[38]

Here, in its reference to the strong tendency of the public to link "Odol" with mouthwash and with quality, the *Odol* court anticipated the two specific forms of dilution that US trademark law would eventually recognize: the "blurring" of the link between the plaintiff's mark and the plaintiff's goods and the "tarnishment" of the plaintiff's reputation.[39]

Having established the fame of the "Odol" mark, the court turned to the issues of damage, intent, and moral violation under § 826 BGB and competition between the parties under § 1 UWG. As to damage, the *Odol* court offered a remarkably incisive explanation of what trademark dilution entails: a mark "would lose in selling power if everyone used it as the designation of his goods." This initial appeal to the extreme case, in which many – or all – companies use the same mark and thereby dilute the mark's distinctiveness of any one of those companies, remains a very effective rhetorical strategy in describing to the uninitiated what dilution is.[40] But not "everyone" was using the "Odol" mark, so the court

[38] Wertheimer, *supra* note 2, at 76. The *Odol* court's description of the fame of the "Odol" mark is similar to, and was perhaps influenced by, the opinion of Landgericht Chemnitz in an April 1923 case involving the trademark "4711," used by the complainant for perfume and subsequently by the respondent for luxury goods. *See* "Schutz gegen Verwendung eines Warenzeichens für ungleichartige Waren, LG. Chemnitz, Urt. v. 11. April 1923, 8 Hg 354/22," *Juristische Wochenschrift* 722 (1924) [hereinafter *4711*]. The *4711* court described the fame of the "4711" mark as follows: "If 4711 is used as a mark on a good, everyone who belongs to this consumer population [of those who buy perfume] will automatically first think of the goods of the plaintiff." "Wenn '4711' zur Bezeichnung einer Ware gebraucht wird, so wird jedermann, der diesen Kreisen angehört, unwillkürlich an die Waren der Klägerin zuerst denken." *Ibid.* at 722.

[39] As Marcus Luepke notes, German thinking typically distinguishes between dilution (*Verwässerung*), which is typically equated with blurring, and tarnishment (*Rufschädigung*). *See* Marcus H.H. Luepke, "Taking Unfair Advantage or Diluting a Famous Mark – A 20/20 Perspective on the Differences between U.S. and E.U. Dilution Law," 98 *Trademark Rep.* 789, 793 n. 16.

[40] *Cf.* Rudolf Callmann, *Callmann: Unfair Competition and Trade-Marks* (Callaghan, Chicago, 1950), at 1348 (comparing dilution to a process in which, "[i]f one dealer is allowed to sell the article as he wishes, a thousand may do so, and it would soon be forgotten which get-up is that of the trade-mark owner.").

retreated in the next paragraph of its opinion to "anyone" and to what we would now recognize as the gradual, continuous "death by a thousand cuts"[41] description of dilution: "The respondent must also admit that when anyone calls his goods 'Odol,' the word 'Odol' loses value for the complainant."[42] The *Odol* court wisely made no effort further to quantify this loss in value, thus avoiding one of the most difficult questions in contemporary dilution doctrine: Short of "everyone" using a particular famous mark, how do even multiple unauthorized commercial uses of that mark actually damage the famous mark or its proprietor?

As to intent, the court attributed to the respondent knowledge that its conduct could cause dilution of the "Odol" mark. Here again, the *Odol* court's discussion of what motivated the respondent to use a mark identical to the complainant's is strikingly astute. Dr. Wertheimer translated the court's discussion as follows:

> The respondent has registered the mark for its steel goods for the obvious purpose of deriving from its selling power [*Schlagkraft*] some advantage in marketing its own products. There are of course numerous euphonious words that the respondent could have used as the symbol of its goods; it chose the word "Odol," it was clear, because this mark had acquired an especially favorable prestige [*einen besonders guten Klang*] through the efforts of the complainant. It must further be said, that there is at least a possibility that the complainant may be damaged through its action. In this knowledge the respondent has registered its mark, thus acting at least with far-sighted cunning.[43]

To satisfy § 1 UWG's requirement that there be competition between the parties, the court engaged in a bit of sleight of hand typical of trademark courts of that era both in Germany and the United States.[44] The *Odol* court found competition in a more general sense:

[41] Trademark Dilution Revision Act of 2005: Hearing Before the Subcomm. on Courts, the Internet and Intellectual Property of the H. Comm. on the Judiciary, 109th Cong. 4 (2005) (statement of Rep. Howard L. Berman). *See also* Callmann, *supra* note 40, at 1338 (dilution "is analogous to the situation where the plaintiff's building is demolished because it is carried away stone by stone").

[42] *Odol*, *supra* note 1, at 205. The English translation is from Wertheimer, *supra* note 2, at 77. Compare the language of the Landgericht Chemnitz in its earlier *4711* opinion: "As more firms sell their goods to this consumer population under the '4711' mark, so must the mark lose power." ("Je mehr Firmen ihre Waren unter dem Zeichen '4711' in diesen Verbraucherkreis bringen, um so mehr muβ es an Kraft verlieren."). *4711*, *supra* note 38, at 722. The *4711* court had earlier spoken of the mark's "distinctiveness and advertising appeal" ("Kennzeichnungskraft und Werbekraft"). *Ibid.* The court analyzed the facts before it only under § 826 BGB, which the court held could support an action for the "impairment of the uniqueness and distinctiveness of another company" ("eine Beeinträchtigung der Eigenart und Unterscheidungskraft des fremden Betriebes"). *Ibid.* at 722. It was apparently left to the *Odol* court, however, to refine the concept of and coin the term "dilution."

[43] *Ibid.* [44] *See* Lehmann, *supra* note 6, at 752.

The complaint may also be based on Section 1 of the law against unfair competition, since this legal provision does not impose the condition that the one who offends against good morals in business shall be in competition with the one claiming an injunction and damages, it being sufficient that the defendant encroaches on the business of two competitors. Here, however, complainant's ability to compete with other manufacturers of mouth wash will be impaired if the significance of its mark is lessened.[45]

Thus the court resolved the paradox created, on the one hand, by § 1 UWG's requirement that the parties be in competition, and on the other, by the nature of dilutive conduct, in which a defendant uses the plaintiff's mark in a manner that does not cause consumer confusion as to source, typically because the defendant is not in direct competition with the plaintiff, but rather dilutes more generally the distinctiveness of the mark.[46]

In comparison to its treatment of damage, intent, and competition between the parties, the *Odol* court devoted relatively little attention to the main issue at the core of the *Odol* case: whether the respondent had actually done anything wrong, anything "*gegen die guten Sitten.*" After all, many intentional competitive acts may damage a competitor, such as selling similar goods at a lower price or placing one's store across the street from a competitor's, but not all of them, in fact, very few, are *contra bonos mores*. The moral violation is all the more difficult to establish when the conduct of one company (for example, a manufacturer of digital cameras) damages another company (a manufacturer of photographic film) with whom it is not in direct competition. More to the point, if one company copies the same innovative marketing strategy as another company (for example, an emphasis on minimalist product design), the uniqueness of that marketing strategy will be damaged, as will the company that innovated it, but we do not consider such conduct to be "opposed to good morals." Similarly, the territoriality principle in trademark law permits one company intentionally to copy another company's trademark and use it on goods identical to those of the copied company in any country in which the copied company does not sell its goods, has not registered its mark, and is not well-known.[47] Here again, though such conduct may damage the copied company (for example, by

[45] *Odol*, *supra* note 1, at 205. The English translation is from Wertheimer, *supra* note 2, at 77.

[46] *See* Diethelm Klippel, "Grundfragen des Schutzes gewerblicher Kennzeichen gegen Verwässerungsgefahr," *GRUR* 697, 702–03 (1986).

[47] *See Person's Co. v. Christman*, 900 F.2d 1565 (Fed. Cir. 1990). *See generally* Graeme B. Dinwoodie, "Trademarks and Territory: Detaching Trademark Law from the Nation-State," 41 *Hous. L. Rev.* 885 (2004).

preventing that company from expanding its business), we do not find a violation of good morals. How then was the respondent's conduct in the *Odol* case different? The *Odol* court offered no answer. It simply declared, as quoted above, that "it is opposed to good morals to appropriate thus the fruits of another's labor in the consciousness that that other will or may thereby be damaged." This was the totality of the court's reasoning, never mind that most commercial conduct in a market economy consists, in the abstract, of exactly what the *Odol* respondent was accused of having done.[48]

The *Odol* case thus had all the characteristics – and limitations – of a straightforward misappropriation case, albeit one that involved the misappropriation of a trademark's "selling power." German courts and commentary generally understood the *Odol* case and contemporary cases like it in these terms. To be sure, in 1905, in the *Kodak* case, the German Supreme Court at Hamburg had denied protection on the ground that the complainant had failed to show competition between the parties, likelihood of confusion, or intent by the respondent to inflict damage, even if the respondent's exploitation of the "fruits of another's labor" was "reprehensible from a moral standpoint."[49] But as Rudolf Callmann's 1929 treatise *Der unlautere Wettbewerb* suggests, sentiment quickly changed. Callmann pointed to the 1918 case Bona – Tengelmanns Bona[50] in which, in finding infringement the court never explicitly mentioned a likelihood of consumer confusion, but rather spoke exclusively of, as Callmann put it, "the contrariety to good morals [*Sittenwidrigkeit*] of the deliberate exploitation of the 'drawing power' of the catchphrase 'Bona'."[51] Alfred Rosenthal, another prominent treatise writer of the time, commented on a 1926 case involving the well-known mark "4711" for Eau de Cologne: "What is important is not whether the public will be misled, but whether the work of another is subject to unfair exploitation [*illoyalen Ausnutzung*] through the copying of one of the most well-known marks in the entire German marketplace."[52]

Just as German courts and commentators understood the *Odol* case as a misappropriation case, so American courts and commentators should have as well, particularly in light of its commonalities with the 1918

[48] *See International News Service v. Associated Press*, 248 U.S. 215, 257 (1918) (Brandeis J., dissenting).
[49] Comment by Leo, MuW 1906, 73 (quoted in Ohly, *supra* note 29, at 521–22).
[50] RG, 15 February 1918, MuW 1918, 214 – *Bona – Tengelmanns Bona.*
[51] *Callmann, supra* note 35, at 343.
[52] Alfred Rosenthal, Comment on *4711*, *Juristische Wochenschrift* 105 (1927). Other commentators described other dilution cases in similar terms. *See generally* Callmann, *supra* note 35, at 343–44.

Supreme Court case *International News v. Associated Press*.[53] There, the Supreme Court determined that International News's practice of copying without attribution the Associated Press's news stories (which were not protected by copyright law) violated the Associated Press's "quasi property"[54] rights. As Justice Pitney explained in his opinion for the majority, the Associated Press's news product "has all the attributes of property necessary for determining that a misappropriation of it by a competitor is unfair competition because contrary to good conscience."[55] International News was acting *contra bonos mores* because it was simply free-riding on the Associated Press's work.

> The defendant, by its very act, admits that it is taking material that has been acquired by complainant as the result of organization and the expenditure of labor, skill, and money, and which is salable by complainant for money, and that defendant, in appropriating it and selling it as its own, is endeavoring to reap where it has not sown, and by disposing of it to newspapers that are competitors of complainant's members, is appropriating to itself the harvest of those who have sown.[56]

In defining such conduct as a violation of a property right, albeit a property right only against competitors rather than against the world, Justice Pitney brought his classical formalism to bear on the facts before him, and this particular brand of formalism might have been quite congenial to the *Odol* case and the formation of antidilution protection in the United States. But there were other opinions in *International News*, and Justice Holmes's and Justice Brandeis's dissents represented the newly emerging, if not prevailing, opinion by the mid-1920s, particularly at Columbia Law School, Schechter's intellectual home. It should thus not be surprising that when Schechter eventually addressed the *Odol* case in "Rational Basis," he took such pains, as we will see, to distance it from Justice Pitney's increasingly unfashionable doctrine of misappropriation.

Schechter's revision of the *Odol* case in "Rational Basis"

In "Rational Basis," Schechter shrewdly left his discussion of the *Odol* decision until the final paragraphs of the article. This gave the impression that he merely "supported his conclusion"[57] by reference to the decision

[53] *International News Service v. Associated Press*, 248 U.S. 215, 236 (1918).
[54] *Ibid. See* Shyam Balganesh, "Quasi-Property: Like, But Not Quite Property," 160 *U. Pa. L. Rev.* 1889 (2012).
[55] 248 U.S. at 240. [56] *Ibid.* at 239–40.
[57] *Moseley v. V Secret Catalogue, Inc.*, 537 U.S. 418, 429 (U.S. 2003) ("Schechter supported his conclusion by referring to a German case protecting the owner of the well-known trademark "Odol" for mouthwash from use on various noncompeting steel products.").

when in fact it appears to have inspired his entire concept of trademark dilution, much of his terminology, such as "selling power" (*Werbekraft*) and dilution (*Verwässerung*), and many of his arguments. For example, Schechter followed the *Odol* court's lead in belittling the traditional requirement that for relief to be granted under trademark law, the parties must be in competition, or in US terminology, the goods of both parties must be "related" in some way.[58] He also emphasized that antidilution protection was most appropriate for marks that were, like "Odol," linked to a particular product and level of quality, marks that, in Schechter's words, "have, from the very beginning, been associated in the public mind with a particular product, not with a variety of products, and have created in the public consciousness an impression or symbol of the excellence of the particular product in question."[59] And while the *Odol* court emphasized that there were "numerous euphonious words that the respondent could have used as a symbol of its goods," Schechter defended antidilution protection against the "historical fear of monopoly which has possessed the courts"[60] with a quote from an American trademark case that "[a]ll the rest of infinity is open to defendant."[61]

But for all of his reliance on the *Odol* case and his extensive quotation from Dr. Wertheimer's translation,[62] Schechter omitted one sentence in particular. The penultimate page of "Rational Basis" provides a lengthy block quotation from the Wertheimer translation, but from the middle of that block quotation Schechter excised and replaced with an ellipsis the following sentence, now familiar to us, from the *Odol* opinion: "It is opposed to good morals to appropriate thus the fruits of another's labor in the consciousness that that other will or may thereby be damaged."[63]

Why would Schechter feel compelled to suppress the *Odol* court's core finding, the very foundation of its ruling?[64] Schechter's expurgation of this sentence is consistent with another peculiarity of "Rational Basis." While the *Odol* court did not hesitate to explain why the respondent used the "Odol" mark ("for the obvious purpose of deriving from its selling power some advantage in marketing its own products"), Schechter scrupulously

[58] *See* Schechter, *supra* note 10, at 819–24. [59] *Ibid.* at 829.
[60] *Ibid.* at 833. [61] *Ibid.*
[62] It is not clear if Schechter ever consulted the original German-language *Odol* opinion.
[63] *See* Schechter, *supra* note 10, at 832.
[64] Admittedly, a page earlier, Schechter stated that the Odol court "held that the use of the mark 'Odol' even on non-competing goods was '*gegen die guten Sitten*,' pointing out that, when the public hears or reads the word 'Odol,' it thinks of the complainant's mouth wash, and that an article designated with the name 'Odol' leads the public to assume that it is of good quality." *Ibid.* at 831. But note that Schechter is careful to omit from this quotation the *Odol* court's statement that the respondent "appropriat[ed] thus the fruits of another's labor."

avoided speculating in "Rational Basis" on what motivated defendants to adopt famous marks.[65] Instead, he addressed only the damage such conduct inflicted on those marks.[66] Indeed, he repeatedly sought to focus attention on the mysterious nature of this damage. Schechter's purpose here was the same that motivated his deletion of the *Odol* court's reference to "appropriat [ing] thus the fruits of another's labor": he sought to suppress any link between trademark dilution and misappropriation.

Schechter did so, I suggest, in an attempt to cloak his concept of dilution in the emerging fashion of legal realism. In a recent groundbreaking article (without which this chapter would not have been possible), Robert Bone calls attention to the realist context in which Schechter published "Rational Basis,"[67] but Bone misses, I believe, the essentially duplicitous nature of "Rational Basis." Bone argues that "Schechter was a legal realist"[68] who "proposed dilution in the spirit of legal realism."[69] "Rational Basis" was, says Bone:

> a quintessential legal realist project. Schechter's analysis follows a typical realist format: start by explaining how judges are straining formalistic doctrines to implement underlying policies in a modern setting; then expose the policies beneath the formalisms; and conclude by calling for the elimination of formalisms and for decisions based directly on the policies.[70]

This is certainly a fair description of the surface of "Rational Basis" (including the article's title), and its author may well have been sympathetic with the basic insights of legal realism. As Bone emphasizes, the article repeatedly invoked the "true functions"[71] of the trademark, criticized the failure of courts and commentators "to keep pace with the necessities of trade and the functional development of trademarks,"[72] and lamented that "the proper expansion of trademark law has been hampered by obsolete

[65] As Robert Bone notes, Schechter does speak of "trademark pirates" and "commercial buccaneers." *See* Robert Bone, "Schechter's Ideas in Historical Context and Dilution's Rocky Road," 24 *Santa Clara Computer & High Tech. L. J.* 469, 486 n. 95 (2008) (citing Schechter, *supra* note 10, at 825 and 832). But as Bone recognizes, these references contain no detail on what motivates defendants to engage in dilutive conduct.

[66] *See, e.g.*, Schechter, *supra* note 10, at 825 (describing dilution as "the gradual whittling away or dispersion of the identity and hold upon the public mind of the mark or name by its use upon non-competing goods."); *ibid.* at 827 (describing dilution as the "vitiation of the identity of a mark"); *ibid.* at 831 (describing dilution as occurring when a mark's "uniqueness or singularity is vitiated or impaired by its use upon either related or non-related goods").

[67] *See* Bone, *supra* note 65.

[68] *Ibid.* at 483. *See also ibid.* ("In brief, Schechter was a legal realist – a moderate legal realist, to be sure, but a realist nonetheless.").

[69] *Ibid.* at 471. [70] *Ibid.* at 489.

[71] *See* Bone, *supra* note 65, at 485 (quoting Schechter, *supra* note 10, at 818).

[72] Schechter, *supra* note 10, at 824.

conceptions both as to the function of a trademark and as to the need for its protection."[73] As Bone also notes, Schechter assailed the "cardinal principle that 'there is no property in a trade-mark apart from the business or trade in connection with which it is employed.'"[74] In a characteristically realist line of attack, he criticized the principle as inconsistent with the underlying "consideration of public policy" that motivated it.[75]

Yet for all of Schechter's efforts to speak the new language of the realists, at least one realist reader of "Rational Basis" was not convinced, and for good reason. Buried in a footnote of Schechter's now-forgotten 1936 article "Fog and Fiction in Trademark Law" is his admission that not all had gone as planned with "Rational Basis." Schechter acknowledged that "Rational Basis" had been "fairly roughly handled from the general standpoint of ethics and social utility"[76] by a 1935 article that would go on to become more influential even than "Rational Basis": Felix Cohen's "Transcendental Nonsense and the Functional Approach."[77] "[F]airly roughly handled" was an understatement. One of the leading texts of American legal realism, "Transcendental Nonsense" seemed to reserve special scorn for trademark law, "this homestead law for the English language,"[78] and much of this scorn seemed to be pointed directly at Schechter and his proposal that the use of certain marks be "restricted to a single firm."[79] It is often

[73] Among the article's many references to the "true functions" of a trademark, Schechter singled out the prominent trademark commentator Edward Rogers for "not accurately stat[ing] the function of a trademark today." *See ibid.* at 818. This was a strong accusation in a high-profile journal and could not have endeared Schechter to Rogers, whom others routinely identified as the "Dean of the Trademark Bar." Julius R. Lunsford, Jr., "Foreword," 62 *Trademark Rep.* at iv, iv (1972). A HeinOnline search suggests that in Rogers' thirty-four articles on intellectual property law issues appearing from the years 1902 to, posthumously, 1972, Rogers cited Schechter exactly once, and briefly. *See* Edward S. Rogers, "New Directions in the Law of Unfair Competition," 74 *N. Y. U. L. Rev.* 317, 323 (1940) (citing Schechter's *The Historical Foundations of the Law Relating to Trade-Marks* (Columbia University Press, New York, 1925)). In a hearing before the House Committee on Patents in 1932, Schechter strenuously advocated that Congress establish federal antidilution protection. *See* Trademarks: Hearings Held before the Committee on Patents of the House of Representatives, 72d Cong. 1 (1932) [hereinafter Hearings] (testimony of Frank I. Schechter). At the same hearing, Rogers stated that he saw no need for reform. *See ibid.* at 43 ("I have this feeling that if a situation is pretty good and is getting better perhaps the best thing to do is let it alone.") (testimony of Edward S. Rogers); *ibid.* at 42 ("[T]he courts are dealing with [the problem of non-competing uses of famous marks] pretty adequately"). Rogers' refusal to support Schechter's proposal may help to explain why Congress first established federal antidilution protection only in 1995.

[74] Schechter, *supra* note 10, at 822. [75] *Ibid.*

[76] "Fog and Fiction," *supra* note 23, at 66 n. 14.

[77] Felix Cohen, "Transcendental Nonsense and the Functional Approach," 35 *Colum. L. Rev.* 809 (1935).

[78] *Ibid.* at 817. [79] *Ibid.* at 815.

forgotten that Cohen's famous exposure of the "if value, then right" circularity[80] took the form of an attack on Schechter's proposal for antidilution protection:

> The current legal argument runs: One who by the ingenuity of his advertising or the quality of his product has induced consumer responsiveness to a particular name, symbol, form of packaging, etc., has thereby created a thing of value; a thing of value is property; the creator of property is entitled to protection against third parties who seek to deprive him of his property ... The vicious circle inherent in this reasoning is plain. It purports to base legal protection upon economic value, when, as a matter of actual fact, the economic value of a sales device depends upon the extent to which it will be legally protected.[81]

"According to the recognized authorities on the law of unfair competition," explained Cohen, "courts are not *creating* property, but are merely *recognizing* a pre-existent Something."[82] For Cohen, this was "economic prejudice masquerading in the cloak of legal logic."[83] (In his footnote, Schechter responded: "to this article I shall have occasion to refer later in Part II of this paper."[84] But there would be no part II. Schechter died the next year.)

Cohen correctly identified the fundamental problem with "Rational Basis," the problem that Schechter tried to hide from his realist readers by focusing to such an extent on the damage to the plaintiff's famous mark rather than on the motives of the defendant – on the harm rather than on the misappropriation. The problem is that, as a species of misappropriation, dilution suffers from the same circularity that besets the more general concept of misappropriation. In their dissents in *International News*, both Justice Holmes and Justice Brandeis attacked this circularity in Justice Pitney's majority opinion. Holmes protested that "[p]roperty, a creation of law, does not arise from value."[85] Justice Brandeis focused on the labor theory underlying misappropriation doctrine: "[T]he fact that a product of the mind has cost its producer money and labor, and has a value for which others are willing to pay, is not sufficient to ensure to it this legal attribute of property."[86]

[80] *See generally* Rochelle Dreyfuss, "We Are Symbols and Inhabit Symbols, So Should We Be Paying Rent? Deconstructing the Lanham Act and Rights of Publicity," 20 *Colum.-VLA J. L. & Arts* 123, 142 (1996).

[81] Cohen, *supra* note 77, at 815. [82] *Ibid.* at 815 (italics in original).

[83] *Ibid.* at 817. [84] "Fog and Fiction", *supra* note 23, at 66 n. 14.

[85] *International News Service v. Associated Press*, 248 U.S. 215, 246 (1918) (Holmes J., dissenting). Notably, Justice Holmes had himself embraced exactly this form of "if value, then right" reasoning fifteen years earlier in his opinion for the majority in *Bleistein v. Donaldson Lithographing Co.*, 188 U.S. 239, 252 (U.S. 1903).

[86] 248 U.S. at 250 (Brandeis J., dissenting).

"Transcendental Nonsense" simply brought the spirit of Holmes's and Brandeis's dissents to bear on "Rational Basis."

More revealingly, another of Schechter's contemporary readers, the intellectual property specialist and Heidelberg- and Columbia-educated comparativist John Wolff, explicitly criticized "Rational Basis" as taking *International News* too far, at least for an American audience. In a 1937 article in *Columbia Law Review* comparing American and German trademark law, Wolff expressed his sympathy with Schechter's efforts to protect famous trademarks from dilution,[87] and correctly identified the essentially formalist spirit of Schechter's proposed test for dilution – which would simply ask (1) does the plaintiff's mark qualify for antidilution protection by virtue of its inherent distinctiveness and fame, and (2) is the defendant's mark identical or closely similar to the plaintiff's mark?[88] Wolff recognized Schechter's attempt thus to insulate famous marks from the messy empirical inquiry that attended a likelihood of confusion analysis, but concluded that Schechter's proposal was too radical for American courts:

> What [Schechter], in effect, proposes is to divorce the law from the uncertainties inherent in estimating the state of the public mind and entirely to eliminate the issue of confusion. Yet the American law of unfair competition and trademarks rests firmly on passing off. The very incongruousness of Schechter's theory with the tradition and the fundamental principles of the common law forms the chief obstacle to its general acceptance in this country.[89]

In a footnote, Wolff went to the heart of the matter – and of the *Odol* case. He compared American and German approaches to misappropriation:

> In *International News Service v. Associated Press*, it is true, the copying of news was held unfair competition even in the absence of passing off. But the courts have shown little inclination to apply the principle of this case to other types of

[87] John Wolff, "Non-Competing Goods in Trademark Law," 37 *Colum. L. Rev.* 582, 602 (1937).

[88] *See Ringling Bros.-Barnum & Bailey Circus Combined Shows, Inc. v. Utah Div. of Travel Dev.*, 170 F.3d 449, 457 (4th Cir. 1999) (discussing and collecting cases that take this approach).

[89] Wolff, *supra* note 87, at 602. With respect to the "state of the public mind," Wolff was likely thinking of the following passage from Schechter's book-length history of trademark law: "Any theory of trade-mark protection which ... does not focus the protective function of the court upon the good-will of the owner of the trade-mark, inevitably renders such owner dependent for protection, not so much upon the normal agencies for the creation of good-will, such as the excellence of his product and the appeal of his advertising, as upon the judicial estimate of the state of the public mind. This psychological element is in any event at best an uncertain factor, and 'the so-called ordinary purchaser changes his mental qualities with every judge.'" *See* Schechter, *supra* note 73, at 166. For further elaboration of Wolff's view, see Callmann, *supra* note 40, at 1336.

copying ... There is a far cry from the *International News* case to a general rule making it unlawful for one man to reap the fruits of another's efforts and expenditures.

In Germany, on the other hand, § 1 of the Unfair Competition Statute ... forbids competitive acts *contra bonos mores*. This provision is not limited to cases of passing off. All unethical conduct is embraced within the prohibition. Thus German courts have a much wider latitude than the American courts in enlarging the concept of Unfair Competition. This is why the *Odol* case doctrine, though entirely novel ... has found easy entrance into German law.[90]

Schechter could not have been unaware of this basic difference between American and German approaches to misappropriation. On the contrary, he was likely all too conscious of this difference, which helps to explain why he presented a bowdlerized version of the *Odol* case to his American readers and sought in the process to shift his concept of dilution out of the conceptual field of misappropriation and into trademark law.

The many faces of dilution in "Rational Basis"

Despite the limitations of "Rational Basis" that Cohen and Wolff identified, it is clear that Schechter's concept of dilution survived the initial realist circumstances in which it was born. By 1955, Massachusetts, Illinois, New York, and Georgia had adopted statutory antidilution protection, and in 1965, the United States Trademark Association added an antidilution provision to its Model State Trademark Bill.[91] The European Union wrote antidilution protection into its Trade Marks Directive in 1988,[92] and in 1995, the United States established federal statutory antidilution protection,[93] which it revised in 2006.[94] What is notable about these various forms of statutory antidilution protection is that they define dilution in so many different ways. In many cases, these differences are slight, but in some – for example, in US federal antidilution protection as compared to EU antidilution protection – the differences are quite substantial.

[90] Wolff, *supra* note 87, at 602 n. 98.

[91] *See* Beverly W. Pattishall, "The Dilution Rationale for Trademark – Trade Identity Protection, its Progress and Prospects," 71 *Northwestern U. L. Rev.* 618, 620 (1976) (cited in Bone, *supra* note 65, at 497).

[92] First Council Directive 89/104/EEC, 1989 O.J. (L 40) 1 (EC), repealed and replaced by Parliament and Council Directive 2008/95, 2008 O.J. (L 299) 28, 29 (EC).

[93] Federal Trademark Dilution Act of 1995, Pub. L. No. 104-98, 109 Stat. 985 (1996) (codified at 15 U.S.C. § 1125(c)).

[94] Trademark Dilution Revision Act of 2006, Pub. L. No. 109-312 (2006) (codified at 15 U.S.C. § 1125(c)).

To the extent that Schechter sought in "Rational Basis" to obscure the true nature of trademark dilution, it should not be surprising that so many varying approaches to antidilution protection have developed in the article's wake. Schechter seems deliberately to have defined dilution in a variety of subtly different ways. Sometimes he described dilutive conduct as consisting of the use of a famous mark on goods unrelated to those on which the mark was traditionally used. For example, "[dilution] is the gradual whittling away or dispersion of the identity and hold upon the public mind of the mark or name by its use upon non-competing goods";[95] or, dilution is the "destruction of the uniqueness of a mark by its use on other goods."[96] The harm here was the "dissociation"[97] of the famous mark from the goods with which it was traditionally associated. But then "Rational Basis" also defined dilution as occurring when a mark's "uniqueness or singularity is vitiated or impaired by its use upon either *related or non-related* goods."[98] The harm here, under the rubric of "vitiation,"[99] was the general loss of a mark's uniqueness in the marketplace regardless of its connection to any particular good. Thus Schechter counseled in "Rational Basis" that "the possibility of vitiation of identity of a mark should in itself constitute the basis of relief."[100] On this definition, antidilution protection would promote the "preservation of the uniqueness or individuality of the trademark"[101] in itself. And sometimes it seems that Schechter was trying to split the difference between these two possible – and incommensurate[102] – forms of dilution, as when he spoke of the need to protect famous marks "against vitiation or dissociation from the particular product in connection with which it has been used."[103]

"Rational Basis" could also be quite slippery as to whether dilution involved a blurring of the link between the mark and the good with which it was traditionally used or between the mark and the company that

[95] Schechter, *supra* note 10, at 825. [96] *Ibid.* at 823. [97] *Ibid.* at 825.
[98] *Ibid.* at 831 (emphasis added). [99] *Ibid.* at 825. [100] *Ibid.* at 825.
[101] *Ibid.* at 822.
[102] As between "dissociation" and "vitiation," dissociation is the more easily understood concept, but vitiation is the more fundamental and important concept that subsumes dissociation. This is likely why antidilution doctrine has generally tended towards deemphasizing whether the defendant's goods are related or unrelated to the plaintiff's. *See* Graeme B. Dinwoodie, Chapter 4 in this volume (discussing *Davidoff v. Gofkid* (C-292/00) [2003] E.T.M.R. 42). Dissociation in the unrelated goods scenario is simply one mode of the more general harm of vitiation, which can occur either in related or unrelated goods scenarios. "[V]itiation of identity of a mark" may occur in either scenario in the sense that consumers no longer believe that the mark originates from a single source and conveys a single meaning.
[103] Schechter, *supra* note 10, at 825.

produced the good.[104] For example, Schechter cited the 1926 case *Duro Pump & Manufacturing Co. v. California Cedar Products Co.*[105] as an example of a case where a court ruled in favor of the plaintiff on antidilution grounds. The plaintiff had long been using the mark "Duro" on "pneumatic pressure systems"; the defendant sought registration of the same mark on wall board. Schechter quoted the DC Circuit's opinion: "If the California Cedar Products Company were permitted to use this mark, which has come to represent the Duro Company and its product to the public, other companies likewise might use it, with resultant loss of identity of the Duro Company."[106] It may be that Schechter simply assumed that any given company sold only one product, so that it made little difference whether consumers, upon seeing the "Duro" mark, thought of the good (pneumatic pressure systems) or of the source (Duro Pump & Manufacturing Company). But this assumption left "Rational Basis" and the concept of dilution that it advocated unprepared for the emergence of brands, such as "Virgin," that would identify multiple, unrelated goods, and for the emergence of the licensing of such brands to multiple, unrelated sources. Such practices would eventually give rise both to the problem of "self-blurring"[107] and to the need for a theory of dilution that relies solely on the loss of uniqueness rather than on any kind of blurring of a semantic link between the mark and a good or between the mark and a source.

Finally, Schechter was ultimately non-committal about what kinds of marks should qualify for antidilution protection. He implied in "Rational Basis" that only "arbitrary, coined or fanciful marks"[108] should qualify, and most of his readers have understood him to support this position.[109] And yet this is difficult to square with at least one example he gives in "Rational Basis" of a mark that should receive antidilution protection: the descriptive mark "Rolls-Royce,"[110] which was based on the surnames of Charles Stewart Rolls and Sir Frederick Henry Royce. By the 1930s, it appears that Schechter had moderated his position, if he ever held it in the first place, that antidilution protection should extend only to inherently distinctive marks. In Congressional testimony, he pointed out that

[104] In semiotic terms, Schechter did not specify whether dilution involved the blurring of the link between the signifier (the mark) and the referent (the good to which the mark is affixed), or between the signifier and the signified (the company that produces the good). *See* Barton Beebe, "The Semiotic Analysis of Trademark Law," 51 *UCLA L. Rev.* 621, 645–48 (2004)

[105] 11 F.2d 205 (D.C. Cir. 1926).

[106] *Ibid.* at 206 (quoted by Schechter, *supra* note 10, at 827–28).

[107] *See* Stadler Nelson, *supra* note 21, at 791.

[108] Schechter, *supra* note 10, at 828.

[109] *See, e.g.*, Bone, *supra* note 65, at 477 n. 46.

[110] Schechter, *supra* note 10, at 829.

"I have limited that notion of mine to marks of an arbitrary or fanciful or original nature," but later stated that "*particularly* a unique and fanciful mark such as Odol or Kodak"[111] should receive antidilution protection. In "Fog and Fiction," he returned to this form of qualification when he asserted that dilution could occur "*especially* when the mark is coined or fanciful."[112] Schechter, it appears, would not have been troubled by the extension of antidilution protection to other non-inherently distinctive marks.

Perhaps Schechter simply was not certain what he meant by trademark dilution, be it in the form of "vitiation" or "dissociation" or some combination of the two, which would explain why he offered such a mercurial formulation of the concept and of what should qualify for antidilution protection. Yet as his published work, and particularly his history of trademark law, attests, Schechter was a highly sophisticated lawyer and legal theorist. It seems more probable that just as he sought to disguise the true nature of the *Odol* case, so he sought to invest the concept of trademark dilution with an indeterminacy sufficiently protean to evade, as it has, nearly all attacks leveled against it.

Conclusion: Schechter's (and Callmann's) legacy

Schechter arguably never conceived of "blurring" or "tarnishment" as forms of trademark dilution, nor did he ever use these terms.[113] Yet these conceptualizations of dilution have come to dominate the US approach to antidilution protection. Congress has twice had the opportunity to include a European-style misappropriation cause of action in federal antidilution law and has twice declined to include this "third variant."[114] In the United States, blurring and tarnishment have rushed in to fill the

[111] Hearings, *supra* note 73, at 10 (testimony of Frank I. Schechter) (emphasis supplied).

[112] "Fog and Fiction," *supra* note 23, at 65 (emphasis added).

[113] In 1925, the year that Columbia Law School conferred on Schechter its first doctorate in law, the *Columbia Law Review* published an anonymous case note, "Appropriation of Trade Symbols by Noncompetitors," 25 *Colum. L. Rev.* 199 (1925), parts of which read like an early draft of the thesis of "Rational Basis." The author addressed both the "disparagement" of a mark and the dilution of its uniqueness: "Leaving aside all consideration of the question of disparagement, in the instant case [*Vogue Co. v. Thompson-Hudson Co.*, 300 Fed. 509 (6th Cir. 1924)], the value of the plaintiff's symbol depended in large part upon its uniqueness. Employed in the manner described, it was indicative in the public mind of the plaintiff's magazine. The direct tendency of the defendant's action was to destroy this association." *Ibid.* at 204.

[114] See Dinwoodie, Chapter 4 in this volume. *See also* Barton Beebe, "A Defense of the New Federal Trademark Antidilution Law," 17 *Fordham Intell. Prop. Media & Ent. L. J.* 1143, 1164–65 (2006).

void left by Schechter's suppression of the misappropriation basis of antidilution protection.

It is a strange irony that the German-American treatise writer Rudolf Callmann is largely responsible for the Americans' embrace in the late-century of blurring and tarnishment,[115] terms which Callmann initially took from an anonymous 1964 *Harvard Law Review* note.[116] The irony is that Callmann made no effort in his many publications on dilution to hide the misappropriation basis and rights-in-gross nature of antidilution protection. On the contrary, he openly advocated conceiving of trademark law as a species of property law rather than unfair competition law[117] and candidly stated his belief that when courts held in favor of antidilution plaintiffs, they did so on misappropriation grounds.[118] Yet Callmann – and anti-blurring and anti-tarnishment law – nevertheless benefited from Schechter's initial suppression of the misappropriation origins of the concept of trademark dilution. American courts continue to rule in favor of antidilution plaintiffs, and very likely do so on unstated misappropriation grounds, but so malleable is the doctrine that Schechter left us that they can now do so on Callmann's less formalist, more "functional" – and more "rational" – bases of blurring and tarnishment.

[115] I am indebted to Bone for emphasizing the importance of Callmann to the antidilution story. *See* Bone, *supra* note 63, at 498–501. Callmann was a well-established trademark lawyer and commentator in Germany in the 1920s and 1930s and a founding member of the *Reichsvertretung der deutschen Juden.* A World War I combat veteran, he emigrated to the US in 1936. *See* Christopher Wadlow, "Rudolf Callmann and the Misappropriation Doctrine in the Common Law of Unfair Competition," 7 *Intell. Prop. Q.* 110 (2011).

[116] *See* Note, "Dilution: Trademark Infringement or Will-o'-the-Wisp?," 77 *Harv. L. Rev.* 520, 531 (1964) ("Junior uses may blur a mark's product identification, or they may tarnish the affirmative associations a mark has come to convey."). This appears to be the earliest reference to blurring and tarnishment in trademark commentary. Callmann first cited this Note in Callmann, *supra* note 40, 1965 Cumulative Supplement, at 230. The first reference in a US court opinion to "blurring" as a form of trademark dilution appears to be *James Burrough Limited v. Beef/Eater Restaurants, Inc.*, 272 F.Supp. 489, 493 (D.C.Ga. 1967).

[117] *See, e.g.*, Rudolf Callmann, "Unfair Competition Without Competition?," 95 *U. Pa. L. Rev.* 443 (1947).

[118] *See, e.g.*, 2 Rudolf Callmann, *The Law of Unfair Competition and Trade-Marks* 1338 (Callaghan, Chicago, 1945) (arguing that, in dilution cases, "courts are influenced, consciously or otherwise, by the fact that the defendant is attempting to appropriate values which are properly the plaintiff's.").

4 Dilution as unfair competition: European echoes

Graeme B. Dinwoodie

Introduction

Trademark dilution has long troubled American courts and commentators, as is well recounted by Barton Beebe in his chapter 'The suppressed misappropriation origins of trademark antidilution law'.[1] This anxiety is born of a number of unknowns. Some are theoretical: what is the harm against which the cause of action protects, and why should the law care? Some are doctrinal: which subset of marks warrants this extra layer of protection, and what acts of third parties cause whatever harm is theoretically a problem? Almost all these puzzles are fundamental to an assessment of how the dilution concept has extended the edges of trademark protection.

Beebe suggests that these difficulties can be traced in part to the law review article by Frank Schechter, 'The Rational Basis of Trademark Protection', which appeared in the *Harvard Law Review* in 1927 and is commonly accepted as providing the intellectual foundation for dilution law in the United States.[2] In particular, Beebe argues that (many) conventional readings of 'Rational Basis' miss its essential point: dilution is nothing more than a cause of action for 'misappropriation' of a trademark. As Beebe notes, this truth is beginning to dawn on observers of contemporary American dilution jurisprudence. However, Beebe goes further, suggesting that it was always thus, and points to the 1924 German *Odol* case from which Schechter drew inspiration to highlight his argument.

Moreover, Beebe argues, the conventional accounts of 'Rational Basis' miss the point because Schechter consciously sought to obscure it via elaborate discussion of (inter alia) the 'true functions' of marks in the

[1] 'The suppressed misappropriation origins of trademark antidilution law: The Landgericht Elberfeld's *Odol* opinion and Franck Schechter's "The Rational Basis of Trademark Protection"' (hereafter 'Suppressed Origins'; *see* Chapter 3 of this volume).

[2] *See* Frank I. Schechter, 'The Rational Basis for Trademark Protection', 40 *Harv. L. Rev.* 813 (1927); *Moseley v. V Secret Catalogue, Inc.* 537 U.S. 418, 429 (2003).

marketplace of the day. Thus, what Bob Bone in 2007 saw as the mark of a legal realist,[3] Beebe sees as duplicitous faux-realism by a savvy formalist.[4] And, Beebe suggests, the conscious ambiguity in 'Rational Basis' has been its under-appreciated genius, allowing the article (and the concept) to mean all things to all people, each new exegesis serving to revivify the concept (despite periodic efforts by courts to entomb it).

Given the transatlantic pedigree of the dilution concept, this chapter explores whether contemporary experience in Europe supports the central arguments of 'Suppressed Origins'. The development of EU law is largely consistent with the idea that dilution law is in part an effort to install a misappropriation regime, at least insofar as the objects of protection are trademarks with a reputation (increasingly, a smaller caveat as the scope of potential trademark subject matter expands and the reputation threshold falls). This has important local consequences: if dilution law is in truth a law against misappropriation, the Court of Justice of the European Union has greater scope to contribute to the creation of a nascent European law of unfair competition. But examining recent European case law also suggests that understanding misappropriation as part of a broader system of unfair competition may moderate the standard US critique of misappropriation claims as formalist, wholly indeterminate and unlimited. Understood in its unfair competition milieu, a misappropriation-based concept of dilution retains some potential for measured delineation of the edges of protection.

Transatlantic comparativism

Why might examination of contemporary European dilution law help understand 'Rational Basis' (or vice versa)? Despite the European origins of dilution, the Court of Justice has sought to illuminate contemporary EU dilution law by reference to US developments. In almost every early case in which the Court tackled dilution, the influence of Schechter and 'Rational Basis' was dutifully acknowledged,[5] as was the derivation from German law and the decision in *Odol*.[6] To be sure, the Court has

[3] *See* Robert G. Bone, 'Schechter's Ideas in Historical Context and Dilution's Rocky Road', 24 *Santa Clara Computer & High Tech L.J.* 469, 471 (2007).

[4] *See* Chapter 3, pp. 63, 72.

[5] *See Intel Corp. v. CPM* (C-252/07) [2009] E.T.M.R. 13 at ¶¶ AG 30–31 (ECJ); *Adidas-Salomon v. Fitnessworld Trading* (C-408/01) [2004] E.T.M.R. 10 at ¶¶ AG 36–39 (ECJ); *Interflora, Inc. & Anor v. Marks & Spencer plc & Anor* (C-323/09) [2012] E.T.M.R. 1 at ¶ 53 n. 39 (CJEU 2011).

[6] *See Intel Corp.* [2009] E.T.M.R. 13 at ¶ AG 10 n. 8; *Interflora* [2012] E.T.M.R. 1 at ¶ AG 53 n. 39.

recognised that its duty is not to interpret 'Rational Basis'.[7] As Advocate-General Sharpston noted in her *Intel* opinion, '[t]he court's task . . . is not to define the doctrine of dilution, as articulated by Schechter or by others, but to interpret the wording of a Community Directive. Only the latter is the law, however much light can be shed on it by the former.'[8] But Schechter's influence is clearly at work providing context.[9]

Recognising the common origin of American and European dilution protection, the Court has thus been eager to look to US law. This has involved not only recognising the influence of 'Rational Basis', but also in some respects reflecting the received version(s) of Schechter and its statutory and judicial implementation, with all its attendant ambiguities and contradictions.[10] The transatlantic repatriation of *Odol* has thus brought with it the incompletely theorised American elaboration and injected that into a European infringement provision that is already riddled with its own uncertainties.

One should not overstate the causal relationship between the citation of American trademark precedent and the influence of Schechter. Resort by the Court to contemporary American concepts in interpreting EU trademark law has not been confined to dilution, and thus cannot be ascribed entirely to the European provenance of American law on this point.[11] However, the extent of ongoing interplay between US and European sources in thinking about dilution suggests that this remains a useful way to consider the arguments advanced in 'Suppressed Origins'.

Dilution provisions in European Union trademark law

'Rational Basis' is conventionally read in ways that arguably are reflected in different components of EU dilution law. However, recent case law from the Court of Justice appears to corroborate, at least in part, Beebe's proposition that dilution protection (barely) conceals an essential prohibition of misappropriation. This raises the possibility that that motivation is endemic to dilution causes of action (and perhaps to many other efforts to extend the outer edge of intellectual property protection), or at least was so hardwired into 'Rational Basis' that one cannot channel Schechter

[7] US courts are also formally responsible in this regard, but they also see the difficulties when dilution is divorced from Schechter's model. *See, e.g., Ringling Bros.-Barnum & Bailey Combined Shows, Inc. v. Utah Division of Travel Development* 170 F.3d 449, 544–46 (4th Cir. 1999).

[8] *See Intel Corp.* [2009] E.T.M.R. 13 at ¶ AG 31.

[9] *See ibid.* at ¶ AG 35.

[10] *See ibid.* at ¶ AG 56 ('It may be helpful to consider also the [blurring] factors set out in the . . . Trademark Dilution Revision Act of 2006').

[11] *See Philips Electronics v. Remington Consumer Products Ltd* (C-299/99) [2002] E.T.M.R. 81 (ECJ 2002); *Lego v. OHIM* (C-48/09 P) [2010] E.T.M.R. 63 (CJEU 2010).

without installing a misappropriation law. If so, the lesson of 'Suppressed Origins' is particularly fundamental.

Readings of Schechter

The conventional characterisation of Schechter's theory of dilution is varied. Three accounts are dominant. First, Schechter argued that the 'preservation of the uniqueness of a trademark constitute[s] the only rational basis for its protection', and a cause of action for dilution would protect the mark's uniqueness.[12] This model most offends purists in common law countries because it raises the spectre of rights in gross in a word (rather than the underlying goodwill). Most marks are not unique, and the same sign can function as a mark for a number of different products. The mark DELTA for water faucets co-exists with the mark DELTA for airline services. But this model has the merit of simplicity, and even some opponents of dilution have been willing to contemplate this form of protection if it were truly restricted (as Schechter's theory appeared to presuppose) to coined or fanciful marks.

Second, an examination of the examples discussed by Schechter in 'Rational Basis' might suggest that dilution protection was a reaction to the narrow scope of protection available at that time under US law, when the mark was used by the defendant on goods that were different from those on which the plaintiff used its mark. The use requirement of US law confined the scope of US trademark rights far more strictly than would be the case in many other systems. For example, in the famous *Borden* case only a decade before Schechter wrote, the Court of Appeals for the Seventh Circuit held that the use of the BORDEN mark on ice-cream did not infringe a registration on the identical mark for milk.[13]

Third, some argued that the dilution cause of action was an attempt to protect a function of marks that was not (according to Schechter) protected at that time, namely, the ability of the mark itself to sell the product, rather than merely identify its source. 'Rational Basis' stresses that the 'selling power' of the mark was its true function, and that required a scope of protection not conferred in 1927, when US trademark law clearly focused on protecting the origin-indication function of marks.[14]

[12] *See* Schechter, *supra* note 2, at 831–32.

[13] *See Borden Ice Cream Co. v. Borden's Condensed Milk Co.* 201 F. 510 (7th Cir. 1912). The case law was beginning to move from the *Borden* approach when Schechter wrote; *see, e.g., Aunt Jemima Mills Co. v. Rigney & Co.* 247 F. 407 (2d Cir. 1917), but this was an ongoing battle in the courts for years to come. *See* Robert G. Bone, 'Taking the Confusion Out of "Likelihood of Confusion": Toward a More Sensible Approach to Trademark Infringement', 106 *Northwestern U. L. Rev.* 1307 (2012).

[14] *See Prestonettes, Inc. v. Coty* 264 U.S. 359, 368 (1924).

'Suppressed Origins' argues that, as an historical matter, these accounts of 'Rational Basis' – while each having an arguable foundation in the text of Schechter's article – are wrong, or at least incomplete. Instead, when viewed in light of his treatment of *Odol*, Schechter advanced dilution law as a weapon against misappropriation.

European dilution provisions

Contemporary European law, which acknowledges an affinity with Schechter and *Odol*, corroborates part of this thesis. It does not appear to map well to readings of 'Rational Basis' as arguing for broad protection for a tiny subset of 'unique' marks, or to dilution as protection against uses on dissimilar goods.[15] However, European experience suggests that dilution is more generally about unfair competition, of which misappropriation is an important part in many countries.[16]

European dilution law is found in two related instruments: the Trademark Directive,[17] which harmonised the national registered trademark laws of the European Union, and the Trademark Regulation, which created a system conferring EU-wide rights on the owner of a Community Trademark (CTM) granted thereunder.[18] Article 5 of the Directive set out the rights conferred on the trademark owner:

> (1) [T]he proprietor shall be entitled to prevent all third parties not having his consent from using in the course of trade:
> (a) any sign which is identical with the trade mark in relation to goods or services which are identical with those for which the trade mark is registered;
> (b) any sign where, because of its identity with, or similarity to the trade mark and the identity or similarity of the goods or services covered by the trade mark and the sign, there exists a likelihood of confusion on the part of the public; . . .

Article 5(2) of the Directive *permitted* Member States of the European Union to extend additional protection against dilution, in these terms:

> Any Member State may also provide that the proprietor shall be entitled to prevent all third parties not having his consent from using in the course of trade any sign which is identical with, or similar to, the trade mark in relation to goods or services which are not similar to those for which the trade mark is

[15] *See supra* p. 84; *infra* pp. 86–87.
[16] European law also has developed by reference to the 'functions' of marks, but that analytical device has by no means been restricted to dilution. *See infra* pp. 93–101.
[17] *See* Directive 2008/95/EC of the European Parliament and of the Council of 22 October 2008, 2008 O.J. (L 299) 25 (consolidating 1988 Directive).
[18] *See* Council Regulation (EC) No. 207/2009 of 26 February 2009 on the Community trademark, O.J. L 78/1 (24 March 2009) (replacing original 1994 Regulation).

registered, where the latter has a reputation in the Member State and where use of that sign without due cause takes unfair advantage of, or is detrimental to, the distinctive character or the repute of the trade mark.

Article 9(1)(c) of the Regulation confers dilution protection on CTMs in terms identical to those found in Article 5(2), except that the threshold requirement for protection is that the mark have a reputation 'in the Community'.[19] And, given the nature of the Regulation (which had to articulate a free-standing EU-wide trademark system), dilution protection was a right conferred on all CTMs that demonstrate the requisite reputation; unlike the Directive, the Regulation does not have optional provisions.

Three substantive points are worth noting on the basis of the text.[20] First, the protection is available to marks that have a 'reputation'. This threshold requirement mirrors conceptually the 'fame' requirement found in Section 43(c) of the US Lanham Act. However, it is much easier to be a mark with a reputation under EU law than a famous mark under US law.[21] As a result, protection against dilution is available to a large subset of marks, rather than the narrow range of unique marks with which Schechter purported to be concerned.

Second, the legislation extended dilution protection *only* against use on dissimilar goods, apparently limiting its focus to the type of third party uses about which Schechter complained in 'Rational Basis'.[22] In *Davidoff v. Gofkid*, however, the Court of Justice held that Article 5(2) extends dilution protection to marks with a reputation where the allegedly infringing use is made with respect to similar goods as well as where that use is made with respect to non-similar goods.[23] The Court reasoned that the Directive could not be interpreted as affording marks with a reputation lesser protection against uses on similar goods than it did against uses on

[19] *See Pago Int'l v. Tirolmilch* (C-301/07) [2010] E.T.M.R. 5 at ¶¶ 27–29 (ECJ).

[20] In addition, the Court has interpreted the provision as requiring that, for any of the dilution claims, the plaintiff must show that the relevant public would make a 'link' between the defendant's sign and the mark of the plaintiff. *See Adidas-Salomon* [2004] E.T.M.R. 10 at ¶ 29. That link is *not* established merely by showing that the mark is unique and has a reputation or that the marks are identical. Instead, a link is established by the fact that 'the later mark calls the earlier mark with a reputation to mind'. *See Intel Corp.* [2009] E.T.M.R. 13 at ¶¶ 60, 64 (ECJ). This broadly matches the 'association' requirement common to the definitions of blurring and tarnishment in the US statute. *See infra* note 27. This interpretation certainly does not put uniqueness at the front and centre of dilution analysis, although 'the more "unique" the earlier mark appears, the greater the likelihood that the use of a later identical or similar mark will be detrimental to its distinctive character'. *Intel Corp.* [2009] E.T.M.R. 13 at ¶ 74.

[21] *Cf. Datacard Corp. v. Eagle Technologies Limited* [2011] EWHC 244 (Pat) at ¶ 291 with *Coach Servs. v. Triumph Learning LLC* 668 F.3d 1356, 1373 (Fed. Cir. 2012).

[22] But see Chapter 3, p. 77 (noting inconsistencies in 'Rational Basis' on this point).

[23] *Davidoff v. Gofkid* (C-292/00) [2003] 1 WLR 1714, [2003] E.T.M.R. 42.

non-similar goods (ignoring the fact that Article 5(1) already addressed uses with respect to similar goods).[24]

Third, the dilution provision in fact contains three different causes of action, each of which affords an independent basis for relief (absent due cause).[25] The first two mirror those explicitly dealt with by the US statute, rendering actionable different (but related)[26] harms: 'detriment' to the distinctive character of the mark ('blurring') and 'detriment' to the repute of the mark ('tarnishment').[27] Indeed, the Court of Justice has explicitly labelled these causes of action using the American vernacular.[28] However, the third cause of action does not exist in US law, and protects against a third party taking unfair advantage of the distinctiveness or repute of the mark.[29] This 'anti-free-riding' cause of action does not depend upon a direct harm to the plaintiff, but rather is aimed at the benefits secured unfairly by the defendant. This third variant of the dilution cause of action most closely approximates the misappropriation rationale that 'Suppressed Origins' sees behind Schechter's work.

To the extent that this was not clear from the text of Article 5(2), the Court of Justice removed any doubts in *L'Oréal SA v. Bellure*.[30] *L'Oréal* involved the sale of smell-alike perfumes in packaging that resembled (in a non-confusing manner) the packaging of plaintiff's high-end perfumes. The plaintiff owned registrations for the word marks and for the appearance of the packaging. The defendant used the plaintiff's word marks in comparison lists that matched the plaintiff's products with the defendant's cheaper imitations. The comparison lists implicated Article 5(1)(a), the double-identity provision, which prohibits use of identical marks on identical goods regardless of confusion. But the plaintiff also argued[31] that the comparison lists and the defendant's packaging took unfair advantage of the plaintiff's mark and thus constituted dilution under Article 5(2).[32]

[24] In the United States there has never been a doctrinal limitation to dissimilar goods. *See, e.g., Starbucks Corp. v. Wolfe's Borough Coffee, Inc.* 588 F.3d 97 (2d Cir. 2009).

[25] *See Intel Corp.* [2009] E.T.M.R. 13 at ¶¶ 27–28.

[26] *See* Stacey L. Dogan & Mark A. Lemley, 'The Merchandising Right: Fragile Theory or Fait Accompli?', 54 *Emory L. J.* 461, 493 (2005) (connecting both forms of liability to search costs); see also Chapter 3, p. 77, n. 102.

[27] *See* 15 U.S.C. § 1125(c)(2)(B) (definition of 'blurring'); 15 U.S.C. § 1125(c)(2)(C) (definition of 'tarnishment').

[28] *See Intel Corp.* [2009] E.T.M.R. 13.

[29] *See Interflora* [2012] E.T.M.R. 1 at ¶ 53 (CJEU 2011).

[30] *L'Oréal SA v. Bellure* (C-487/07) [2009] E.T.M.R. 55 (ECJ 2009).

[31] The Article 5(2) claim had in the first instance only been advanced as regards the packaging; the comparison list was challenged under only Article 5(1)(a). *See L'Oréal SA v. Bellure* [2010] EWCA Civ. 535 at ¶ 50.

[32] Once the Court had held that such nominative use by a third party to refer to the plaintiff's genuine goods fell within the scope of Article 5, the defendant could prevail

The Court of Justice explained the unfair advantage variant of the dilution cause of action in terms that link it, in both substance and metaphor, to the misappropriation impulse and 'reaping/sowing' language of *INS v. Associated Press:*[33]

> Where a third party attempts, through the use of a sign similar to a mark with a reputation, to ride on the coat-tails of that mark in order to benefit from its power of attraction, its reputation and its prestige, and to exploit, without paying any financial compensation and without being required to make efforts of his own in that regard, the marketing effort expended by the proprietor of that mark in order to create and maintain the image of that mark, the advantage resulting from such use must be considered to be an advantage that has been unfairly taken of the distinctive character or the repute of that mark.[34]

The *Odol* court had used similar language to explain the relief it had granted. But the language about 'appropriation [of the] fruits of another's labour' was edited out of the quote used by Schechter in 'Rational Basis'. Beebe suggests that this excision was intended to distance dilution from the misappropriation *language* (or received understanding) of *INS v. Associated Press* given the changes taking place in American legal thought at the time.[35] What Schechter had edited out of *Odol* in 'Rational Basis', the Court of Justice restored in *L'Oréal* (in language that likewise bears the hallmarks of formalistic doctrine). At least the motivation was transparent, even if the full normative contours or limits of the cause of action were not evident (at least from *L'Oréal* itself).

Misappropriation as only part of dilution

When viewed in closer comparison to current US law, however, recent developments in Europe may appear to undermine the argument in 'Suppressed Origins'. The unfair advantage cause of action is one of

only if it was immunised under the Comparative Advertising Directive or if the use did not adversely affect the functions of the mark. The Court held that the defendant's use fell outside the protection of that Directive, which permits lawful comparative advertising, because immunity depended inter alia upon the defendant's goods not being presented as a replica of those of the plaintiff.

[33] *See International News Service v. Associated Press*, 248 U.S. 215, 239–40 (1918) (Pitney J.) ('defendant in appropriating [the plaintiff's labor, skill, and money] and selling it as its own is endeavoring to reap where it has not sown, and by disposing of it to newspapers that are competitors of complainant's members is appropriating to itself the harvest of those who have sown'). Mr Justice Pitney did connect the claim in *INS* to an action for unfair competition. *See ibid.* at 234–35. However, that limit (also seen in the court's order) was obscured by the proximity of broad language of property, a marker of formalism which quickly attracted the fire of Justices Holmes and Brandeis and realist commentators. *See ibid.* at 240 (Pitney J.); *see also ibid.* at 246 (Holmes J. dissenting) ('Property, a creation of law, does not arise from value . . .').

[34] *See L'Oréal* [2009] E.T.M.R. 55 at ¶ 49. [35] *See* Chapter 3, p. 71.

three separate forms of dilution under EU law – and, importantly, one not found in US law. The current US statute exhaustively demarcates the possible causes of action under Section 43(c) as blurring and tarnishment.[36] Thus, for example, the US dilution cause of action no longer provides relief against acts of cybersquatting as such, notwithstanding that cybersquatting is actionable (as a form of unfair competition) under other provisions of the Lanham Act.[37]

European law might therefore suggest that dilution as a whole may encompass something *other* than taking unfair advantage.[38] And dilution under US law is confined to that 'something else', namely, blurring and tarnishment; by formal definition, post-2006 US dilution law is *not* aimed at rendering misappropriation actionable. The US cause of action might, for example, simply be another mechanism for reducing search costs, thus serving the same objectives as the classic infringement cause of action in instances involving different goods.[39]

On reflection, however, this comparison does not rebut Beebe's arguments in 'Suppressed Origins'. First, while US dilution law may lack an *explicit* unfair advantage (or misappropriation) cause of action, this does not mean that misappropriation claims are not effectively pursued in US dilution law.[40] The theoretical void (and doctrinal complexity) in which blurring and tarnishment are situated arguably should enable US courts

[36] *Cf. Ty Inc. v. Perryman*, 306 F.3d 509 (7th Cir. 2002) (rejecting theory of dilution pre-2006 based on free-riding).

[37] Such claims are now brought under a new Section 43(d) which mimics, with small variation, the cause of action available through quasi-arbitral proceedings under the Uniform Domain Name Dispute Resolution Policy (the UDRP) promulgated by the Internet Corporation for Assigned Names and Numbers. *See* UDRP, at ¶ 4(a). The genesis of the UDRP is explicitly found in the unfair competition provision of Article 10*bis* of the Paris Convention, *see* WIPO, Final Report of the WIPO Internet Domain Name Process (30 April 1999), at ¶¶ 173–74, which also captures the essence of the cause of action under Section 43(d).

[38] The broad reading of unfair advantage by the *L'Oréal* Court, when taken with the proof of blurring demanded by the Court in *Intel*; *see Intel* [2009] E.T.M.R. 13 at ¶ 77, might for some time have suggested that dilution in the European Union was for all intents and purposes about misappropriation. But the courts have not read *Intel* as strictly as the US courts read *Moseley*; *cf. Environmental Manufacturing LLP v. OHIM* (C-383/12p)–ECR–(CJEU 2013), and the post-*L'Oréal* unfair advantage case law may further ensure some equipoise between the two dilution claims. *See infra* pp. 97–101.

[39] *Cf.* Dogan & Lemley, *supra* note 26 (explaining blurring and tarnishment in terms of the search costs rationale, but not by reference to nature of goods).

[40] *See* David J. Franklyn, 'Debunking Dilution Doctrine: Toward a Coherent Theory of the Anti-Free-Rider Principle in American Trademark Law', 56 *Hastings L. J.* 117, 119 and 133 n. 96 (2004) (listing cases). Indeed, lacking an explicit misappropriation cause of action, judgments in some confusion-based claims that have pushed back the contours of protection have clearly been fuelled by concerns of unfair advantage. *See Boston Professional Hockey Ass'n, Inc. v. Dallas Cap & Emblem Mfg., Inc.* 510 F.2d 1004 (5th Cir. 1975); *Playboy Enters., Inc. v. Netscape Comms. Corp.* 354 F.3d 1020 (9th Cir. 2004).

with the normative urge to enjoin misappropriation to find a way to do so.[41] Indeed, if this suspicion is warranted, it would vindicate the strategy that Beebe posits was followed by Schechter in 'Rational Basis': in order to provide protection against misappropriation, construct a regime of open-ended, formalistic concepts.

Second, Beebe's exegesis is of *Schechter's* elaboration of dilution in 'Rational Basis', not of that found in current US or EU law. This highlights an important point, which one might not appreciate given the fulsome acknowledgments of Schechter's paternity continually found in US dilution law, namely, that US dilution law is not Schechter's law.[42] To be sure, US courts keep gravitating to some of the formalistic means by which Schechter sought to implement his theory. In particular, courts continue to play with presumptions flowing from the use of identical marks.[43] But this may simply show that judges recognise the enduring practical and political attractions of formalism.

Unfair competition protection in Europe

In Europe, the conceptual dissembling that Beebe detects in 'Rational Basis' (and which may exist in current US law) may mask an important institutional question that determines *who* will shape the outer contours of intellectual property protection in the European Union. The same conscious ambiguities that facilitated the adoption of dilution protection into a US climate suspicious (post-*INS*) of formalist misappropriation claims have enabled the European Court of Justice to expand its prescriptive authority over European intellectual property law. Whereas European trademark law has been substantially harmonised, national

[41] *See* Franklyn, *supra* note 40, at 165. Of course, the lack of any coherent theoretical justification (or doctrinal framework) for dilution also allows courts plenty of room to eviscerate what they often see as an unprincipled extension of trademark rights. *See* Graeme B. Dinwoodie & Mark D. Janis, 'Dilution's (Still) Uncertain Future', 105 *Mich. L. Rev. First Impressions* 98 (2006). In short, there is little constraint on courts effectuating whatever normative first preference they possess. This does cause US dilution law to resemble the critical caricature of a general roving law of unfair competition. *See L'Oréal SA v. Bellure* [2007] EWCA Civ. 968 at ¶¶ 139–40 (Jacob L.J.) ('What one man calls "unfair" another calls "fair" ... There are real difficulties in formulating a clear and rational line between that which is fair and that which is not, once one goes outside the requirement of deception').

[42] *See, e.g., Ringling Bros.-Barnum & Bailey Combined Shows, Inc. v. Utah Division of Travel Development* 170 F.3d 449, 544–46 (4th Cir. 1999).

[43] *See, e.g., Savin Corp. v. The Savin Group* 391 F.3d 439, 452–54 (2d Cir. 2004); *cf. Louis Vuitton Malletier SA v. Haute Diggity Dog* LLC, 507 F.3d 252 (4th Cir. 2007). Formally, courts have rejected an identity *requirement. See Levi Strauss & Co. v. Abercrombie & Fitch Trading Co.* 633 F.3d 1158 (9th Cir. 2011).

legislators were unable to agree on a harmonised European law of unfair competition.[44] In particular, the United Kingdom has long resisted unfair competition claims that went very far beyond the passing-off cause of action, of which *misrepresentation* is the defining element.[45] In continental Europe, on the other hand, protection against misappropriation or parasitic behaviour was a standard component of many laws against unfair competition. By characterising particular behaviour as trademark dilution, rather than unfair competition by misappropriation, the Court of Justice in *L'Oréal* has ensured for itself the power to develop at the European level an important core of unfair competition (involving marks).

There is a certain irony in this. The early drafts of the Directive contained no dilution provision.[46] At that time, the Commission was seeking to promote the use of the CTM system, which would contribute more directly to the free movement objectives of what then was the European Community by providing a single right across the entire territory of the free trade zone. Thus, from an early stage, in contrast to the Directive, the draft Regulation conferred dilution protection, making the Community-wide registration more attractive than national alternatives.[47] Under this model, the Court of Justice would have been able to develop principles of dilution through the Regulation alone, and thus only with respect to marks protected as CTMs.

However, in the final Directive, dilution protection appeared in Article 5(2). This was partly because the philosophy of co-existence

[44] *See* Susanne Augenhofer, 'European Union', in *International Handbook on Unfair Competition* 41, 44 (Henning-Bodewig ed., Verlag C.H. Beck, München, 2013); Directive 2008/95/EC of the European Parliament and of the Council of 22 October 2008, 2008 O.J. (L 299) 25, recital 7. There are EU directives (such as the E-Commerce Directive) that indirectly create unfair competition law by immunising certain conduct from liability under *any* national law. And indeed there are European directives prohibiting defined acts as unfair competition. *See, e.g.*, The Unfair Commercial Practices Directive, Directive 2005/29/EC of 11 May 2005, O.J. L 149/22 (11 June 2005); Directive 2006/114/EC of the European Parliament and of the Council of 12 December 2006 Concerning Misleading and Comparative Advertising, O.J. L 276; (27 Dec. 2006). But these directives can be implemented without creating a private cause of action. *See, e.g.*, The Business Protection from Misleading Marketing Regulations 2008, S.I. 2008/1276 (UK).

[45] *See L'Oréal SA v. Bellure* [2007] EWCA Civ. 968 at ¶¶ 135, 142.

[46] *See* Andreas Sattler, 'Dilution of Well-Known Trademarks – An Analysis of its Foundations in Germany and the European Union', 3 *Zeitschrift für Geistiges Eigentum* 304, 320 (2011).

[47] *See* Proposal for a Council Regulation on the Community trademark, Art. 8(1)(b), COM (80) 635 final, 19 November 1980, Bulletin of the European Communities, Supplement 5/80 at 22. The proposal was clearly aimed at non-competitive products and at a small subset of marks. *See ibid.* at 58.

between national and Community regimes replaced vertical competition as the governing principle of state-federal trademark relations. But it also reflected a concern on the part of the Benelux countries that a directive that did not *permit* such protection would require a reduction in the scope of protection then offered in the Benelux countries. Those countries saw that as undesirable not only on the merits, but also because it was thought that such a pre-emption of national dilution law would signal the intrusion of European law into regulation of unfair competition. This was to be a matter for Member States, because of doubts about the competence to oust national unfair competition law through the Trademark Directive.[48] Article 5(2) thus did not mandate dilution protection in national laws, but it did permit it.

There has been a futility to those efforts to preserve a space for national choice on matters of unfair competition (at least vis-à-vis the use of marks). The reading of Article 5(2) in *L'Oréal* has effectively incorporated a very strong form of misappropriation-based unfair competition protection in European law, now applicable under all national laws of the European Union bar Cyprus.[49] And the scope of EU intrusion into unfair competition via dilution has turned out to be greater than would have been evident on the face of Article 5(2). The decision in *Adidas-Salomon* consolidates this allocation of authority by holding that although Member States were not obliged to offer *any* dilution protection, if they did so they had to extend the full extent of protection encompassed by Article 5(2).[50]

[48] *See* Sattler, *supra* note 46, at 320.

[49] *See* Max Planck Institute for Intellectual Property and Competition Law, *Study on the Overall Functioning of the European Trade Mark System* ¶ 2.148 (February 2011), available at http://ec.europa.eu/internal_market/indprop/docs/tm/20110308_allensbach-study_en.pdf.

[50] Article 5(2) is not the only provision of EU trademark law that presents an opportunity for the Court to opine indirectly on what constitutes unfair competition. For example, each of the defences to trademark infringement under Article 6 of the Directive is conditioned on the defendant's use being 'in accordance with honest practices in industrial or commercial matters'. This proviso, which incorporates verbatim the language of the unfair competition provision of Article 10*bis*(2) of the Paris Convention, has assumed a more dominant role in the Court's reading of defences as it has read the strict elements of Article 6 more liberally in a couple of cases (though the application of that test is nominally left to national courts in cases under the Directive). *See, e.g.*, *Gerolsteiner Brunnen GmbH & Co. v. Putsch GmbH* (C-100/02), [2004] E.T.M.R. 40 (ECJ); *Gillette v. LA Laboratories Oy* (C-228/03), [2005] 2 CMLR 62 (ECJ); *Anheuser-Busch v. Budvar* (C-245/02), [2004] ECR I-10989 (ECJ). Of course, this may only highlight the difficulties in trying to draw too firm a line between trademark and unfair competition law.

'True functions' and misappropriation as formalism

In developing dilution protection under European law, the Court of Justice has relied in part on one concept – the functions of marks – that *is* commonly highlighted in conventional readings of 'Rational Basis'. Use of this device as a means of setting the contours of protection satisfies almost none of the leading scholars assessing Schechter. For Beebe, this was a ruse invented by Schechter to sustain a formalist doctrine in a time of critical or realist thought.[51] For Bone, Schechter's attention to the functions of marks confirmed him as a realist.[52] But, Bone finds little normatively persuasive in Schechter because, in an act of assimilation not uncommon for many (but not all) realists, Schechter assumed too readily that the descriptive functions of marks provided a normative guidepost.[53]

Use of functions has found not much greater favour in contemporary European commentary. The criticism of *L'Oréal* has extended beyond its treatment of unfair advantage. The Court of Justice also offered what was at that time the most comprehensive statement (though not an explanation) of the functions of marks protected by the different types of infringement claim found in Article 5 of the Directive.[54] The use of the 'functions of the mark' to demarcate the outer boundaries of trademark protection was hardly new to the Court, or indeed to other national courts in Europe. The Court had long invoked the functions (most notably, the 'essential function', to indicate origin) of a mark to *limit* trademark rights. In particular, the doctrine had been used to sustain the free movement of goods, an important objective of the European Union that was imperilled by the assertion of national trademark rights. If the mark on goods accurately told the consumer the source or origin of the product, its distribution by a parallel importer could not interfere with the essential function of the mark. In pre-Directive national decisions, this reasoning was the explanation for international exhaustion of rights. Of course, industrial policy (Fortress Europe) modified the international scope of exhaustion.[55] But importantly the function of marks used by the Court (and national courts) was derived from a normative assessment of the social policy behind trademark protection.

Over time, the Court also deployed 'functions' in interpreting the Directive, both the free movement provisions of the Directive and more

[51] *See* Chapter 3, p. 63. [52] *See* Bone, *supra* note 3, at 471.
[53] *See ibid.* at 487, 506. [54] *L'Oréal* [2009] E.T.M.R. 55 at ¶ 58 (ECJ 2009).
[55] *See Silhouette International Schmied GmbH v. Hartlauer Handlesgesellschaft* (C-355/96) [1998] 3 WLR 1218.

generally. For example, starting in *Arsenal v. Reed*,[56] the Court used functions to define the scope of rights. In *Arsenal*, the defendant sold unauthorised merchandise bearing the marks of a prominent English football team. This use nominally fell within the scope of the Directive's double-identity provision. Because liability under that provision does not require confusion, the UK court asked the Court of Justice whether the scope of that provision should be circumscribed by the type of use made by the third party (i.e., use as a badge indicating affiliation rather than as a mark), rendering the defendant's activities non-actionable. In response, the Court emphasised that 'the exercise of [the exclusive] right must ... be reserved to cases in which a third party's use of the sign affects or is liable to affect the functions of the trade mark ... It follows from that case-law that the proprietor of the mark cannot oppose the use of a sign ... if that use is not liable to cause detriment to any of the functions of that mark.'[57]

Arsenal is commonly regarded as a decision in which the Court expanded trademark rights because it refused to limit the scope of rights to trademark uses. But in fact the principle remains facially one of limitation: the outer edges of trademark protection would be set by the effect of unauthorised uses on the functions of a mark. If a third party use did not affect the functions of the mark, it would not be actionable, notwithstanding that it might be a 'use' within Article 5. However, the *Arsenal* judgment also conceived of functions in the plural, acknowledging that the protected functions of the mark might be more than simply the essential function of protecting origin.

Once the possibility of multiple (and multiplying) functions was embraced, the Court then inverted the role of functions. Of course, from the days of Schechter, the notion that marks might serve some function other than source-identification had been recognised in the literature. As noted above, this was what (in the form of the 'selling power' or 'advertising' function of the mark) underlay one understanding of 'Rational Basis' and dilution. But the realist derivation of the normative from the descriptive reached full fruition in *L'Oréal* (and not just in the context of dilution). There, the Court noted that rights were conferred on the mark owner to protect 'the functions of the trade mark ... [including] not only the essential function of the trade mark, ... but also its other functions, in particular that of guaranteeing the quality of the goods or services in question and those of communication, investment

[56] *See Arsenal v. Reed* (C-206/01), [2003] E.T.M.R. 19 (ECJ 2002).

[57] *See Google France v. Louis Vuitton Malletier* (C-236–238/08), [2010] E.T.M.R. 30 at ¶¶ 75–76 (CJEU 2010) (citing *Arsenal*).

or advertising'.[58] Given the conventional accounts of Schechter, it was no surprise that later cases were to acknowledge that the additional functions protected by the double-identity protection of Article 5(1)(a) were also protected by dilution under Article 5(2).[59]

At a doctrinal level, this assimilation of the functions protected under Articles 5(1)(a) and 5(2) was quickly to meet with objection in several quarters.[60] When the *L'Oréal* case returned to the UK courts, the objection was expressed in terms of instrumental trademark policies, concerns about the unlimited (and formalistic) nature of the misappropriation claims, and methodological doubts about relying on functions to set the edges of protection.

The Court of Appeal enjoined the defendant's activities, reading the Court of Justice as endorsing something approaching an absolute right against misappropriation under Article 5(2): 'all free-riding is unfair'.[61] However, the principal focus of the judgment on remand was on Article 5(1)(a), on which the Court of Justice had also provided guidance (vis-à-vis the comparison list).[62] The UK court had referred the question of whether a claim could be made out absent likely confusion, and hence with no effect on the 'essential function' of the plaintiff's mark. The Court replied that the liability under Article 5(1)(a) would turn on whether the defendant's use 'is liable to affect one of the functions of [plaintiff's] marks, such as, in particular, their functions of communication, investment or advertising'.[63]

Lord Justice Jacob felt compelled to conclude that the defendant's use would affect those functions, and thus that there was infringement under Article 5(1)(a). In reaching that conclusion, Lord Justice Jacob was clearly influenced by some of the misappropriation language found in the Court's analysis of Article 5(2).[64] He could hardly be blamed. The Court had effectively declared that the protection conferred by Article 5(1)(a) and Article 5(2) was intended to protect the same extended functions of the mark.[65] (And the Court positively incited the addition of a claim against the comparison lists under Article 5(2), which the plaintiff dutifully took up.[66])

[58] *L'Oréal* [2009] E.T.M.R. 55 at ¶ 58.
[59] *See Interflora* [2012] E.T.M.R. 1 at ¶ AG 64 (CJEU 2011).
[60] *See Interflora* [2012] E.T.M.R. 1 at ¶ 35 (Commission submission); Max Planck Institute, *supra* note 49, at ¶ 2.184.
[61] *See L'Oréal* [2010] EWCA Civ. 535, at ¶ 49.
[62] By the time the answers came back from the Court of Justice, the question of liability for similar packaging had become moot. *See ibid.* at ¶ 4.
[63] *See L'Oréal* [2009] E.T.M.R. 55 at ¶ 63.
[64] *See L'Oréal SA v. Bellure* [2010] EWCA Civ. 535 at ¶¶ 16–18.
[65] *See L'Oréal* [2009] E.T.M.R. 55 at ¶ 58.
[66] *See ibid.* at ¶ 64.

Lord Justice Jacob was not persuaded that defining the scope of protection by reference to the functions of a mark was helpful.

> I am bound to say that I have real difficulty with these functions when divorced from the origin function. There is nothing in the legislation about them. Conceptually they are vague and ill-defined ...
>
> So far as this case is concerned, however, it seems that the Court has indicated the answer as to whether the use is within Art. 5(1)(a) ... I confess I do not know where that line [between permissible descriptive and impermissible use] is, but this case falls the wrong side of it. Why? Because the Court has said so. It regards the use as affecting the communication, advertising and investment functions of the mark.[67]

Thus, Lord Justice Jacob read the decision of the Court of Justice as (a) installing under Article 5(2) an unlimited right against misappropriation that did not take account of questions of fairness, and (b) offering broad protection under Article 5(1)(a) – and, by extension, Article 5(2) – against acts that affected the 'communication, investment or advertising' functions of a mark. The first proposition reflects Beebe's reading of what Schechter had in mind, with misappropriation as the real focus of dilution; the second proposition may cause trademark law to end up in the same place, but through a method that looks more like the conventional understanding of Schechter's justification for dilution.

Some of the concerns expressed by Lord Justice Jacob regarding the outcome in *L'Oréal* are quite instrumentalist: that trademark law should not 'prevent traders from making honest statements about their products where those products are themselves lawful'; and that there was 'a real danger that important areas of trade will not be open to proper competition'. But other aspects of the court's critique are reminiscent of general attacks on the formalism of misappropriation: it is indeterminate and circular. 'The trouble with deprecatory metaphorical expressions such as this ("free-riding" is another), containing as they do clear disapproval of the defendants' trade as such, is that they do not provide clear rules by which a trader can know clearly what he can and cannot do.'[68] And, again, the charge of formalism is common to a number of critics of misappropriation. Both Bone and Beebe are likewise uncomfortable with a claim based upon misappropriation per se.[69]

The parallel between *L'Oréal* and *INS* is worthy of note here. Beebe suggests that Schechter was trying to avoid parallels to *INS* by excising particular formalist language from *Odol*. The assumption is that misappropriation is inevitably a formalist doctrine: a trademark is property, and with

[67] *See L'Oréal SA v. Bellure* [2010] EWCA Civ. 535 at ¶¶ 30–31.
[68] *See L'Oréal SA v. Bellure* [2010] EWCA Civ. 535 at ¶ 17.
[69] *See* Chapter 3, p. 74; Bone, *supra* note 3, at 506.

that inevitably comes a series of rights that give exclusive control over the mark to the mark owner. And, to be sure, language of that type found in Justice Pitney's opinion in *INS* made it an easy target for realists.[70]

But *INS* never was, despite its oft-repeated reaping-and-sowing metaphor, just about rights that flowed from property. *INS* was about misappropriation *as unfair competition*; the scope of the order actually entered by the Supreme Court was narrowly crafted to reflect that fact. This does not undermine Beebe's hypothesis that Schechter wished dilution not to be associated with Justice Pitney's majority judgment in *INS* because clearly that judgment had been held up by realists as an example of what Beebe calls 'classical formalism'.[71] But the cases on unfair advantage post-*L'Oréal* in the European Union suggest that attention to the composite phrase 'unfair competition' (and perhaps the qualifier of 'due cause', though that serves interchangeably with analysis of unfairness) can lead to a more measured doctrine, and a doctrine that is more instrumental in character.[72]

Thus, *L'Oréal v. Bellure* may already represent the high water mark of European dilution law. In *Whirlpool Corp. v. Kenwood*, the plaintiff argued that the defendant's manufacture of a food mixer took unfair advantage of the plaintiff's mark consisting of the shape of its rival mixer. The Court of Appeal rejected the argument that the Court of Justice had read the word 'unfair' out of Article 5(2).[73] Lord Justice Lloyd concluded that the case was a 'very long way away from *L'Oréal v Bellure*'.[74] In particular, he gave weight to the fact that the defendant had its 'own established goodwill in small domestic appliances . . . on which it sought to build and rely . . . It did not need to ride on [plaintiff's] coat-tails, so as to save itself from making promotional efforts in relation to its new product.'[75] The court was paying special attention to the particular conditions of competition that were at play in the kitchen appliance market.[76]

[70] *See International News Service v. Associated Press* 248 U.S. 215, 240 (1918) (Pitney J.).

[71] *See* Chapter 3, p. 70.

[72] I don't mean to put undue weight on the classifications of approaches as 'formalist', 'realist' or 'instrumentalist'. These are contested terms. Rather, I want to suggest that the concept of 'unfair competition' or 'unfair advantage' (when understood as being about competition) can be a measured one, notwithstanding the conventional assumptions about causes of action that start from the premise that there is something wrong with misappropriation.

[73] *See Whirlpool Corp. v. Kenwood* [2009] EWCA Civ. 753 at ¶¶ 114–15 and 136.

[74] *See ibid.* at ¶ 135. [75] *See ibid.* at ¶ 136.

[76] *See ibid.* at ¶ 136 ('[A]s a newcomer in a specialist market of which KitchenAid had a monopoly, and being (necessarily) in the basic C-shape of a stand mixer, the kMix would remind relevant average consumers, who are design-aware, of the KitchenAid Artisan. That, however, is a very different phenomenon, in very different commercial circumstances, from the situation considered in L'Oréal v Bellure').

The Court of Justice has also pulled back from the full force of the misappropriation language in *L'Oréal*. In *Interflora, Inc. v. Marks & Spencer plc*, the Court likewise indicated a heightened regard for free competition, in its most recent ruling regarding purchases of a rival's trademark in keyword advertising.[77] But whereas the *Whirlpool* court had simply insisted on something beyond mere advantage to make out the misappropriation-based claim, the Court of Justice articulated a more measured scope of protection through a mixture of devices: the first detailed development of the protected functions of a mark, a refined definition of blurring, and elaboration on what is taking unfair advantage 'without due cause'.[78] Each reflected instrumental concerns.

Strictly, the Court's analysis of the protected functions of the mark occurred under its discussion of Article 5(1)(a). But because the Court rejected the invitation to curtail the relevant functions protected under that provision, the functional analysis (perhaps only highlighting the Court's erroneous treatment of functions) has relevance also for dilution. Thus, the Court held that the advertising function of the plaintiff's mark would not be affected by a rival purchasing that mark as a keyword (because it did not 'deny[] the proprietor of that trade mark the opportunity of using its mark effectively to inform and win over consumers', through other means).[79] Interestingly, however, the reason for this lack of effect on the mark was couched largely in instrumentalist language about the goals of free competition and consumer choice:

> [A]lthough the trade mark is an essential element in the system of undistorted competition which European law seeks to establish, its purpose is not, however, to protect its proprietor against practices inherent in competition. Internet advertising on the basis of keywords corresponding to trade marks constitutes such a practice in that its aim, as a general rule, is merely to offer internet users alternatives to the goods or services of the proprietors of those trade marks.[80]

[77] *Interflora* [2012] E.T.M.R. 1 (CJEU 2011).

[78] The Court's treatment of 'due cause' maps closely to where the *Whirlpool* court moved by development of the element of unfairness. However, there may be one important difference flowing from where the policy arguments for free competition are doctrinally situated. The due cause proviso conditions all three dilution claims, whereas 'unfairness' is relevant only to the anti-free-riding claim. Given the introduction of third party interests (illogically, perhaps, as regards adverse effect on functions) into the *Interflora* Court's analysis, it makes greater sense to treat these concerns under 'due cause'. But *Interflora* may in time highlight a dynamic that has occurred in US law, namely, that the articulation of legitimate interests of third parties in curtailing the scope of prima facie claims may come to generate more generally applicable defences.

[79] *Interflora* [2012] E.T.M.R. 1 at ¶ 59 (CJEU 2011) (citing *Google France v. Louis Vuitton Malletier* (C-236–238/08), [2010] E.T.M.R. 30 (CJEU 2010), where the Court had stressed the capacity of the proprietor's mark still to appear to consumers in organic results).

[80] *Ibid.* at ¶¶ 57–58.

The same type of concerns informed the Court's (first ever) treatment of the investment function, also protected under Article 5(2) but treated here under Article 5(1)(a). There, the Court emphasised that:

> it cannot be accepted that the proprietor of a trade mark may – *in conditions of fair competition that respect the trade mark's function as an indication of origin* – prevent a competitor from using a sign identical with that trade mark ... if the only consequence of that use is to oblige the proprietor of that trade mark to adapt its efforts to acquire or preserve a reputation capable of attracting consumers and retaining their loyalty.[81]

When the Court turned explicitly to Article 5(2) the same policy considerations appeared to inform the analysis. Thus, the Court held that purchase of a mark with a reputation as a keyword would not cause detriment to the distinctive character of that mark, this 'having merely served to draw the internet user's attention to the existence of an alternative product or service to that of the proprietor of the trade mark'.[82] Likewise, although keyword purchases of a rival's mark have the purpose and effect of taking advantage of the distinctive character and repute of the trademark,[83] they would not be 'without due cause' if the goods offered by the rival are 'alternatives', rather than 'imitations' of the mark owner's goods.[84]

The *Interflora* judgment is not without ambiguities. But the Court has clearly, through a number of devices (some of which, under conventional readings of 'Rational Basis', comport with what Schechter thought central to dilution), indicated that the formalist misappropriation baseline of *L'Oréal* will be modified by more instrumental analysis (even if sometimes dressed up in more formal doctrine, such as 'effect on functions').

This shift has recently been noted by Lord Justice Kitchin, who read this case law as establishing that a dilution claim is not made out simply because the defendant adopted its mark:

[81] *Ibid.* at ¶ 64 (emphasis supplied). This paragraph can arguably be read as a silent acceptance of the argument that *L'Oréal* should have not extended so far the functions protected under Article 5(1)(a). But that is beyond the scope of this chapter. For present purposes, the emphasis on fair competition is key.

[82] *Ibid.* at ¶ 81. Strictly, this conclusion was premised on the condition that the advertisement 'enables the reasonably well-informed and reasonably observant internet user to tell that the goods or services offered originate not from the proprietor of the trade mark but, on the contrary, from a competitor of that proprietor'. *See ibid.* This basically recites the test for adverse effect on the origin function, which is close – but not identical – to the confusion-based claim. *See Datacard Corp. v. Eagle Technologies Limited* [2011] EWHC 244 (Pat) at ¶ 263. It thus raises the same point as noted *supra* note 81 regarding the retreat on protected functions under Article 5(1)(a).

[83] *Interflora* [2012] E.T.M.R. 1 at ¶ 86 (purpose), ¶ 87 (effect).

[84] *Ibid.* at ¶¶ 90–91.

with the intention and for the purpose of taking advantage of its distinctive character and repute, the competitor will derive a real advantage from his use of the mark, and the competitor will not pay any compensation in respect of that use. Consideration must be given to whether the use is without due cause. Specifically, the use of a trademark as a keyword in order to advertise goods which are an alternative to but not mere imitations of the goods of the proprietor and in a way which does not cause dilution or tarnishment and which does not adversely affect the functions of the trademark must be regarded as fair competition and cannot be prohibited.[85]

What the UK and Court of Justice decisions have in common is a concern to situate misappropriation concerns in the unfair competition context, suggesting perhaps that there is a difference between misappropriation as 'unfair competition' and misappropriation of property as a formalist claim. Certainly over time there is some hope that these causes of action might be less formalist and indeterminate.

This will not satisfy all critics of misappropriation-type claims.[86] There may be some who think that a cause of action for misappropriation, or taking advantage of a mark, would (if nothing more) simply be too broad to be useful.[87] But the 'seductive appeal'[88] that critics fear attends misappropriation claims betrays that there is some underlying normative value to which courts instinctually are drawn. To be sure, it may not be an instinct that would satisfy a commentator who saw trademark and unfair competition law in purely economic terms. Thus, Lord Justice Jacob in *L'Oréal* complained that anti-free-riding assertions are 'high in moral content (the thought is clearly that copyists, even of lawful products should be condemned) rather than [in] economic content'.[89] As a matter of formal trademark law, this is an argument with some purchase (though even registered trademark law arguably has always been to some extent concerned with some non-economic values). But most systems augment the economically grounded law of trademark with some ancillary body of unfair competition law.

In *that* context, considerations of fairness are surely relevant; indeed it is hard to see how considerations of fairness could *not* be relevant to *unfair* competition law or causes of action for *unfair* advantage. The challenges that arise from injecting fairness into the calculus are: (1) the supposed indeterminacy of fairness-based standards in an economic context;[90]

85 *Specsavers International Healthcare Ltd v. Asda Stores Ltd (No. 2)* [2012] EWCA Civ. 24 at ¶ 141.

86 *See* Bone, *supra* note 3, at 506.

87 *See* Richard A. Posner, 'Misappropriation: A Dirge', 40 *Hous. L. Rev.* 621, 625 (2003).

88 *See ibid.* at 623.

89 [2010] EWCA Civ. 535, at ¶ 49.

90 Though continental European law suggests that over a period of time, we might develop as certain a vision of permissible conduct defined by the morality of marketplace behaviour as we can get by resort to economics.

(2) the overbreadth of the concept of misappropriation if truly limitless; and (3) if not limitless, the problems of incommensurability that come from weighing fairness with the economic concerns that heavily structure the trademark regime alongside which sits unfair competition. These concerns afflict any misappropriation regime. But they are heightened when the misappropriation claim is simply founded on the act of appropriation of 'property'. Charges (usually intended to be critical) of formalism apply if the right flows simply from the label of property, the circularity of the assimilation of value and right being hard to defend.

If dilution is really about unfair competition, however, then it inevitably wades into these debates. It does not assuage critics to give the misappropriation cause of action the label of dilution.[91] 'Suppressed Origins' suggests that this strategy of conscious ambiguity is, however, effective with legislatures and judges. That may be because it facilitates acting on a genuine normative judicial impulse, namely that fairness is relevant even in the jungle of the marketplace. The European approach draws that instinct into the open, and requires discussion of contested normative policies. US trademark law consciously excludes the misappropriation version of dilution and contains little unfair competition law that is not unregistered trademark infringement; it thus represses that impulse. Instead, the impulse appears deviously in those cases at the edge of US trademark law, but only rarely in the open. (Instead, critics tend to allege that that is what is going on, and those acting on their instinct deny such a calumny.)

Conclusion

Dilution, whether in the United States or the European Union, is really about misappropriation. European law confirms the thesis of 'Suppressed Origins'. But the European experience post-*L'Oréal* suggests that that characterisation of the cause of action need not result in formalist, unlimited protection of property. Instead, if understood as part of unfair competition law, there is hope that it can escape the formalism that (may have) motivated Schechter and provide a measured form of relief reflecting a common normative impulse without imperilling free competition. In this form, courts will have regard to justifications (whether under the rubric of 'due cause' or 'fairness') of third party uses, and weigh in the balance concerns for consumer choice and a robust competitive environment.

[91] *See* Bone, *supra* note 3, at 506.

Of course, if dilution law is simply unfair competition law, the most transparent strategy would simply be to label it as such. This would be the surest tribute to the roots of the doctrine in *Odol*. For political reasons, the European Union has resisted the adoption of a common law of unfair competition. Perhaps the conscious articulation by the Court of Justice of competition-based rationales for setting the boundaries of protection under dilution will persuade legislators that labels should not get in the way of such a project, especially if it is happening already. The decisions of the Court to maintain a low threshold for 'reputation' and to extend protection to uses on similar goods – while departing from conventional accounts of Schechter – corroborate Beebe but also make a transition to an honestly labelled European law of unfair competition appear a less drastic step.

Part III

Geographical indications

5 Spanish Champagne: An unfair competition approach to GI protection

Dev S. Gangjee

Introduction

Should exporters of sparkling wine, produced by the *méthode champenoise* in Spain, be permitted to describe their products as 'Spanish Champagne'? As the 1950s drew to a close, French Champagne producers objected to this labelling practice in the United Kingdom and precisely this question arose before its courts. This dispute is interesting for a number of reasons. First, it has all the ingredients of a good story. Given the profile of Champagne, the dispute attracted considerable press attention during the initial criminal prosecution and subsequent civil litigation. It created diplomatic tensions between France and the UK, generated demands for statutory reform and even gave rise to retaliatory threats against Scotch whisky along the way. The litigation involved high stakes and high pressure, ferment and fizz in liberal measures. Second, the outcome in *Spanish Champagne*[1] is widely recognised as an episode of doctrinal innovation within the common law tort of passing off. The collective interests in the use of Champagne, the nature of the misrepresentation and difficulties associated with proving damage generated evolutionary forces which would enlarge the scope of passing off to better accommodate such disputes in the future. Third, *Spanish Champagne* is additionally remembered for creating lingering uncertainty about how far 'extended' passing off could stretch. There was speculation that these new developments would facilitate the jettisoning of the core requirement of misrepresentation and usher in a pure free riding or misappropriation-based action, sounding in broader notions of unfair competition.[2] This uncertainty was eventually resolved

[1] This encapsulates two related decisions: *J. Bollinger v. Costa Brava Wine Co Ltd* [1960] Ch 262 (for the preliminary points of law to decide whether an action could be maintained in principle); *J. Bollinger v. Costa Brava Wine Co Ltd* [1961] 1 WLR 277; [1961] RPC 116 (at trial).

[2] The cause of the ambiguity is usually traced back to Cross J's *obiter* in a subsequent decision concerning Sherry. *Vine Products v. Mackenzie* [1969] RPC 1, 23 (Ch) ('[*Spanish Champagne*] uncovered a piece of common law or equity which had till then escaped notice – for in such a case there is not, in any ordinary sense, any representation that the

with judicial and academic consensus favouring a broader understanding of misrepresentation, as opposed to pure misappropriation, as its legacy.[3] The contours of 'extended' passing off were established in subsequent decisions concerning the status of geographical designations such as Sherry, Scotch whisky and Swiss chocolate.[4] Its reasoning was also adopted in other common law jurisdictions.[5] Over time, 'extended' passing off came to be perceived as the principal response for the protection of Geographical Indications (GIs) within such legal systems.[6] Its influence is therefore undeniable.

However, for the purposes of this volume, an overlooked fourth aspect deserves our attention. *Spanish Champagne* sets out a distinct methodological approach to protecting GIs, geographical designations such as

goods of the defendant are the goods of the plaintiffs, and evidence that no-one has been confused or deceived in that way is quite beside the mark. In truth the decision went beyond the well-trodden paths of passing off into the unmapped area of "unfair trading" or "unlawful competition".') In the UK, the debates continue unabated. See J. Davis, 'Why the United Kingdom Should Have a Law against Misappropriation' (2010) *Cambridge Law Journal* 561; C. Wadlow 'Passing Off at the Crossroads Again: A Review Article for Hazel Carty, *An Analysis of the Economic Torts*' (2011) *European Intellectual Property Review* 447; H. Carty 'Passing Off: Frameworks of Liability Debated' (2012) *Intellectual Property Quarterly* 106.

3 Unlike conventional passing off, the misrepresentation here relates not to the trade or commercial source of the product, but its membership in a class of products which suggests that it has certain qualities. This was recently confirmed by Arnold J in a dispute concerning the definition of vodka: *Diageo v. Intercontinental Brands* [2010] EWHC 17 (Ch); [2010] E.T.M.R. 17 at [1] (hereafter, *Diageo Ch*). (Describing 'a line of cases stretching back nearly 50 years in which suppliers of products of a particular description have sought to restrain rival traders from using that description, or a confusingly similar term, in relation to goods which do not correspond to that description on the ground of passing-off'.)

4 The authorities are comprehensively reviewed by Arnold J in *Diageo Ch*. See also C. Wadlow, *The Law of Passing Off: Unfair Competition by Misrepresentation* 3rd edn (Sweet & Maxwell, London, 2004) 34, 510–19.

5 See e.g. *Wineworths Group Ltd v. Comite Interprofessionnel Du Vin De Champagne* (1992) 2 NZLR 327 (New Zealand); *Institut National des Appellations d'Origine des Vins et Eaux-de-Vie v. Andres Wines Ltd* 14 CIPR 138, 40 DLR (4th) 239 (1987) (Ontario CA) (Canada); *Shaw Brothers (Hong Kong) Ltd v. Golden Harvest Ltd* [1972] RPC 559 (Hong Kong); *Scotch Whisky Association v. Dyer Meakin Breweries* ILR 1972 Del 124 (India); *William Grant v. Cape Wine Distillers* (1990) 3 SA 897 (although an unfair competition case, also referring to passing off authorities) (South Africa).

6 N. Dawson, 'Locating Geographical Indications: Perspectives from English Law' (2000) 90 *Trademark Reporter* 590, 593 ('Many commentators view the Spanish Champagne case . . . as signaling the origin of the legal protection of geographical indications of origin in English law'); M. Blakeney, 'Geographical Indications and Trade' (2000) 6 *International Trade Law & Regulation* 48, 49 ('The principal development of passing off law in relation to geographical indications occurred with the Spanish Champagne case'); Cf. WIPO 'Document SCT/6/3 Rev. on Geographical Indications: Historical Background, Nature of Rights, Existing Systems for Protection and Obtaining Protection in Other Countries', 2 April 2002 (SCT/8/4), at [16].

Darjeeling, Gorgonzola and Café de Colombia, which signify the link between a product and its region of origin and can also sustain valuable reputations.[7] Instead of its usual parochial classification as the common law approach to GI protection, it may be more helpful to label it as an unfair competition or communicative logic based approach,[8] which is also found in civil law jurisdictions. Doing so allows us to look beyond conventional familial boundaries and enables comparisons with jurisdictions such as Germany, which for several decades also relied on case-by-case judicial recognition for GI products within the framework of its unfair competition statute, the Gesetz gegen den unlauteren Wettbewerb (UWG).[9] This approach is distinct from the registration-based approach favoured in France and influenced by notions of *terroir*, which posits the existence of a unique or distinctive link between a certain class of products and their regions of origin.[10] Both unfair competition and registration-based approaches have to address the same fundamental questions: (1) How is the genuine product identified? (2) How is the region of origin delimited? (3) How do we recognise those legitimately entitled to use the designation and therefore able to claim in such disputes? In responding to these questions, each approach relies on distinct conceptual and institutional resources.

The unfair competition approach deftly manoeuvres around these enquiries by using consumer and trade perception as the points of reference, and there is much to admire in the flexibility as well as frugal elegance of its solutions. The equivalent of a product specification crystallises in the context of the dispute, much like the subject matter of

[7] The international reference point is Art 22.1 of the Agreement on Trade-Related Aspects of Intellectual Property Rights, 15 April 1994, in the Marrakesh Agreement establishing the World Trade Organization, Annex 1C (1994) 33 ILM 1125, 1197 (hereafter, TRIPs). It states that GIs are 'for the purposes of this Agreement, indications which identify a good as originating in the territory of a Member, or a region or locality in that territory, where a given quality, reputation or other characteristic of the good is essentially attributable to its geographical origin'.

[8] In the sense that protection is contingent upon the defendant's (mis)conduct in the form of a communicative act such as the defendant's use of a sign which is misleading. See L. Bently, 'From Communication to Thing: Historical Aspects of the Conceptualisation of Trade Marks as Property' in G. Dinwoodie & M. Janis (eds.), *Trade Mark Law and Theory: A Handbook of Contemporary Research* (Edward Elgar, Cheltenham, 2008) 3, 5.

[9] For a more detailed comparison, see Ch. 3 of D. Gangjee, *Relocating the Law of Geographical Indications* (Cambridge University Press, 2012). For a historical review of the German GI protection regime, see H. Kickler, *Die Geschichte des Schutzes geographischer Herkunftsangaben in Deutschland: Vom zweiten deutschen Kaiserreich bis zum Markengesetz 1995* (PhD dissertation, University of Bayreuth, 2012) (on file with the author).

[10] For an overview of the French appellation system, see Ch. 3 of Gangjee, *Relocating the Law of Geographical Indications*.

copyright law. Yet can we go so far as to agree with Laddie J's assessment that 'in this area the law has advanced in effect to give rise to a civilly enforceable right similar to [the French, registration-based] *appellation controlée*'?[11] This chapter suggests that this simplicity comes at a price, which in turn leads on to a more fundamental insight concerning the objects of protection. For the unfair competition approach, the object of protection is the sign. The scope of protection is designed to recognise and preserve its communicative coherence before a given audience. We therefore protect such geographical designations for the same reasons that we protect all other signs with a commercially valuable reputation, including trademarks. By contrast, the *terroir* approach requires a higher resolution answer to these three questions since an additional object of legal regulation is the underlying product. The product specification, which forms the basis for registration, is designed to capture the distinctive features of the product, its historic link to the region of origin as well as the intergenerational collaborative effort and innovation which has been invested in developing and sustaining the product. The link in turn marks out these products for enhanced protection, where the sign is 'reserved' for producers in the region of origin (regardless of how consumers may perceive it) because the product is believed to be unique or distinctive and its manner of production is valorised. Taking the Lisbon registration system for appellations of origin as an example, once recorded on the register appellations are protected against any form of 'usurpation' across the twenty-seven Members, without the prerequisite that consumers in any Member country are familiar with the appellation or that it has a valuable reputation in that country.[12] Consequently the unfair competition and *terroir* approaches diverge at conceptual, methodological and institutional levels. *Spanish Champagne* therefore highlights this volume's titular 'contested contours', showcasing the divergences at these three levels.

For *Spanish Champagne* to be fully savoured, this chapter is uncorked and decanted in the following measures. The next section sets out the background context, where an unsuccessful prosecution attempt for using trade misdescriptions preceded the civil litigation. Since there is no reported decision from which to reconstruct the reasoning, this section draws on contemporary newspaper reports to retrieve the

[11] *Chocosuisse Union des Fabricants Suisse de Chocolat v. Cadbury Ltd* [1998] RPC 117, 127 (Ch D).

[12] The generous scope of protection is specified in Art 3 of the Lisbon Agreement for the Protection of Appellations of Origin and their International Registration, 31 October 1958, 923 UNTS 205 (1974). For membership details, see: www.wipo.int/treaties/en/registration/lisbon/.

arguments. The failure of the criminal prosecution proved influential in shaping the subsequent passing off claims. It also illustrates the limits of the then dominant international approach to GI protection, developed around the notion of the Indication of Source (IS) within Art 10 of the Paris Convention of 1883[13] and the Madrid Agreement of 1891.[14] *Spanish Champagne* therefore marks the transition between penal and civil approaches to protecting GIs. Finally, the aftermath of this prosecution reveals the broader political economy context that frequently surrounds disputes over GIs, as revealed by declassified Board of Trade correspondence from the UK National Archives. The third section outlines the two key decisions in *Spanish Champagne*. It begins by situating geographical signs within passing off doctrine. The existing authorities appeared to stop short of recognising an interest in *collectively generated goodwill*, whereas such shared use is unavoidable in the case of regional or national specialities. Furthermore, according to the paradigmatic misrepresentation in passing off, the defendants represented their goods to be those of another specific trader, whereas here the defendants claimed that their sparkling wine possessed certain general *characteristics and qualities belonging to a class*. This was misrepresentation as to quality (not commercial origin) and the harm related to the semi-generic usage of the Champagne designation, depleting it of origin-specific significance. Could the tort accommodate these new features? Since this was ultimately answered in the affirmative, the fourth section of this chapter goes on to consider how subsequent case law developed an 'unfair competition style' approach to accommodate the three questions regularly faced by registration-based GI regimes, concerning product definition, region of origin delimitation and the identification of legitimate users. The final section concludes by highlighting some of the institutional and conceptual divergences between registration-based and unfair competition approaches to GI protection.

The penal prosecution: interests and repercussions

The civil litigation in *Spanish Champagne* was preceded by an unsuccessful criminal prosecution, which has not been subjected to scholarly analysis to date. The matter was the subject of a six-day hearing at the Central Criminal Court ('Old Bailey') in London, on charges under the

[13] Paris Convention for the Protection of Industrial Property, 20 March 1883 as revised at Stockholm on 14 July 1967, 828 UNTS 305 (1972).

[14] Madrid Agreement for the Repression of False or Deceptive Indications of Source on Goods, 14 April 1891, 828 UNTS 389 (1972).

Merchandise Marks Acts 1883 to 1957,[15] which resulted in an acquittal by the jury on 24 November 1958. Given the nature of the jury trial, there is no reasoned judgment on record. The decision is treated as something of a black box by the few commentators who refer to it.[16] Nevertheless, it is possible to outline the major thematic arguments as they were reported in *The Times*. An additional and fascinating resource is the 'insider' account of this dispute by the solicitor Robert Keeling.[17] The UK Champagne Association, the French umbrella body for appellation protection known as the *Institut National des Appellations d'Origine* (INAO) and the *Comité Interprofessionnel des Vins de Champagne* (CIVC) initiated the prosecution. They charged the Costa Brava Wine Company with supplying and selling twelve bottles of wine with the descriptions 'Champagne' and 'Spanish Champagne'.[18] Costa Brava was the importer of Perlada Spanish Champagne and had been incorporated only two years previously, in 1956. Those representing Champagne's interests argued that these were false trade descriptions under section 2 of the Merchandise Marks Act of 1887.[19] Written requests to Costa Brava to cease such labelling had met with the response that no

[15] For a synopsis, see C. Grunfeld, 'The Merchandise Marks Act, 1953' (1954) 17 *Modern Law Review* 142. The regime originated as a response to domestic demands for honest product labelling, assisted by the lobbying of imperial and international trade interests seeking a competitive advantage for goods marked with British or colonial origins. The prohibition of false marking on products, including the misuse of trademarks and trade descriptions, was effected via penal sanctions. Trade descriptions included indications of geographical origin. Cf. Ch. 1. in F. G. Underhay, *Kerly's Law of Merchandise Marks*, 3rd edn (Sweet & Maxwell, London, 1909); R. Jacob 'The Protection of Geographical Indications of Origin in the United Kingdom' in H. C. Jehoram, *Protection of Geographic Denominations of Goods and Services* (Sijthoff & Noordhoff, Netherlands, 1980) 135, 136–37.

[16] E.g. F. Honig 'The Law of Unfair Competition' (1961) 51 *Trademark Reporter* 27, 38 (the prosecution at the Central Criminal Court failed, but as the verdict was that of a jury it is difficult to guess the precise reasons which led the jury to acquit).

[17] R. Keeling, 'The "Spanish Champagne" Case' in Alex Bespalof (ed.) *The Fireside Book of Wine* (Simon & Schuster, London, 1984) 160 (with the caveat that Keeling was the solicitor representing the Champagne interests in this dispute).

[18] '"Champagne" Defined in Court – Wine Firm Summoned', *The Times*, 19 July 1958, p. 4.

[19] Section 2: (1) Every person who … (d) applies any false trade description to goods … shall, subject to the provisions of this Act, and unless he proves that he acted without intent to defraud, be guilty of an offence against this Act. (2) Every person who sells, or exposes for, or has in his possession for, sale, or any purpose of trade or manufacture, any goods or things to which any forged trade mark or false trade description is applied, or to which any trade mark or mark so nearly resembling a trade mark as to be calculated to deceive is falsely applied, as the case may be shall, unless he proves either – (a) that… [he had] at the time of the commission of the alleged offence, no reason to suspect the genuineness of the trade mark, mark or trade description, and that, on demand made by or on behalf of the prosecutor, he gave all the information in his power with respect to the persons from whom he obtained such goods or things; or (b) that otherwise he acted innocently; be guilty of an offence against this Act.

purchasers would be likely to be deceived or misled. In contrast, the prosecution asserted that '"Champagne" could only properly be applied to a sparkling white wine produced in the Champagne district of France',[20] since that was the benchmark against which a false trade description was measured. Champagne's defenders argued that it had 'been grown and made in one small area of France for generations. It was made in a particular way and was known by its own characteristics.'[21] Apart from concerns about customers being misled, there was anxiety that such labelling (which the defence alleged was semi-generic) would encourage the slide into genericide for Champagne itself.

The defence's response to this unfolded in two stages. First, a number of prosecution witnesses agreed with the defence 'that it had become the practice in the trade to describe a wine as being of a certain type, for example "South African Sherry" or "Spanish Burgundy"'.[22] Therefore the defence suggested that there was a general practice in the UK wine trade of using place names to describe styles of wines, for which there was ample evidence. They went on to suggest that Champagne was the latest victim of this trend. Reading through the reports, one has the impression that this 'latest victim' suggestion was not supported by much evidence and the generic status of Champagne was insinuated on the strength of the general trend. Keeling recollects that the Queen's Counsel acting for Perlada 'gradually covered the very large table in the well of the court, used to receiving quite a different kind of criminal exhibit, with example after example of wines with mixed-up names ranging from Spanish Sauternes and Australian Burgundy to Palestinian Alicante and Chilean Barsac. If the practice is so widespread for other wines, he said, why can it not apply to Champagne, as it did, for instance, in America?'[23] The prosecution sought to counter this by emphasising that Champagne had never been used in such a geographically qualified manner prior to Perlada's marketing in the UK. Second, building on the generic use argument, the defence contended that such qualified use was not false or misleading. Costa Brava's label suggested that this was a Spanish wine *of the champagne character*, or a Spanish equivalent of Champagne. Both the qualifying use of 'Spanish' and the difference in price were factors

[20] 'Wine Company Sent for Trial – Use of "Champagne" as Trade Description', *The Times*, 26 July 1958, p. 4.

[21] 'Magic of Word "Champagne" – Alleged False Trade Description', *The Times*, 18 November 1958, p. 19.

[22] 'Case of Champagne – Can Spain Produce the Wine?', *The Times*, 19 November 1958, p. 4; 'Wine Company Acquitted – "Spanish Champagne" Verdict', *The Times*, 25 November 1958, p. 7.

[23] Keeling, 'The "Spanish Champagne" Case', 163.

supporting the argument that such use was not misleading.[24] Cumulatively these arguments suggested that the preceding use of 'Spanish' was enough to convert 'Champagne' into a semi-generic term for a style of sparkling wine (which it may not have been if used independently) and such use was not misleading. For good measure, the defence also suggested that since Champagne had 'snob value', it was the preservation of this cachet by preventing the less well-to-do from sampling the more reasonably priced Spanish variety that motivated this prosecution.[25] These strategies would serve the defence well, as the jury eventually deliberated for less than three quarters of an hour before acquitting Costa Brava.[26]

The acquittal provoked a range of responses which reveal the broader constellation of interests affected by the legal determination of this dispute. As expected, producers of sparkling wine by the *méthode champenoise* in Spain were 'greatly encouraged by the favourable verdict' and began to enquire about the possibilities of exporting to the UK.[27] The outcome also reportedly gave great satisfaction to the Australian wine industry, who presumed that now 'Australian champagne' could be used instead of 'Australian sparkling wine'.[28] By contrast, there would have been inevitable disappointment amongst the Spanish Sherry interests who had been closely following the dispute.[29] There was concern that Sherry would also be considered generic for a style of fortified wine, instead of being specifically produced from grapes sourced from the region around the town of Jerez de la Frontera in Andalucía.[30] There was also the threat of retaliation against a prominent UK spirit. Advertisements began appearing in the Spanish press, which advertised Spanish whisky made according to Scottish techniques.[31] Of course, INAO and the CIVC were even more concerned by the outcome, as they envisaged a flood of

[24] '"Neither False nor Misleading" – Evidence on Spanish Wine Label', *The Times*, 21 November 1958, p. 17.

[25] '"Snob Value" of Champagne – Firm Deny False Description', *The Times*, 20 November 1958, p. 17.

[26] 'Wine Company Acquitted – "Spanish Champagne" Verdict', *The Times*, 25 November 1958, p. 7.

[27] 'Spanish Champagne Export Drive – Producers Heartened by Court Ruling', *The Times*, 22 December 1958, p. 7.

[28] 'News in Brief – Satisfaction in Australia', *The Times*, 26 November 1958, p. 8.

[29] 'Madrid Interest in Champagne Ruling – Spanish "Whisky"', *The Times*, 26 November 1958, p. 8.

[30] For the causes leading up to this state of affairs, see J. Simpson, 'Too Little Regulation? The British Market for Sherry, 1840–90' (2005) 47 *Business History* 367; E. Fernández, 'Unsuccessful Responses to Quality Uncertainty: Brands in Spain's Sherry Industry, 1920–1990' (2010) 52 *Business History* 100.

[31] 'Madrid Interest in Champagne Ruling – Spanish "Whisky"', *The Times*, 26 November 1958, p. 8.

similarly labelled sparkling wines from countries including Australia and South Africa.[32] The risk to the livelihoods of the 15,000 families depending upon the Champagne industry is mentioned, alongside a possible retaliation against Scotch whisky. This context helps explain why the options for obtaining civil remedies continued to be explored. Finally, there were reports and editorials criticising the practice of the UK wine trade to make generic use of geographical names to designate styles of wines, such as sherry, burgundy or sauternes. While some called for the enactment of special legislation to protect specific names, others emphasised the complacency, delayed responses and ultimate acquiescence on the part of those claiming protected appellation status.[33]

The various constellations of interests also pursued their agendas through official channels. Archival records indicate that the Industrial Property department of the Board of Trade was drawn into these debates in the period between the criminal prosecution and civil action, when considerable French pressure was brought to bear.[34] The following is a summary of the points and proposals arising out of meetings between the president and other members of the Board of Trade with inter alia a delegation from the UK wine and spirit trade, the Franco-British Parliamentary Relations Committee, the Anglo-French Economic Committee and the Government's Economic Policy Committee.[35] Those in favour of improving the protection of Champagne argued that:

- Unlike other wines, where a decades old practice of generic use had been allowed to develop, semi-generic use of Champagne was very recent and Perlada's product was one of the first to use it in this manner. This was a factual claim which did not threaten the general principle of generic terms being freely available.
- Champagne's cachet for luxury and use during special occasions needed protection. It was closely regulated in France, where specific regulations governed its quality, implying that the reputation was hard earned.

[32] 'Verdict a Danger to Vineyards', *The Times*, 6 December 1958, p. 6.

[33] 'The Truth of Names', *The Times*, 27 November 1958, p. 11; 'Old Name for New Wines', *The Times*, 5 December 1958, p. 13.

[34] The original documents are available at the UK National Archive, in: (BT 209/1167) 'Merchandise Marks Acts: Action Subsequent to the Court's Decision on Spanish Champagne', Board of Trade Files, 1958–1961.

[35] See respectively in (BT 209/1167), (i) Notes of a meeting with a delegation representing various elements of the UK wine and spirit trade on 14 July 1959; (ii) Note of a Meeting with Members of the 'Spanish Champagne' Sub-Committee of the Franco-British Parliamentary Relations Committee on 22nd June 1959; (iii) Draft brief for the Meeting of the Anglo-French Economic Committee of 22 July 1959; (iv) Draft Brief for the President of the Board of Trade for a Meeting with the Economic Policy Committee, 8 June 1959.

Reserving the name for those entitled to use it in France was essential to ensure the continuation of these specific connotations of Champagne.
- No other European country – and this included Spain – sold as Champagne in its home market anything but the genuine French product.
- Without protection, a flood of similarly labelled 'champagnes' from Australia, South Africa and other countries would commence.
- The status of Scotch whisky would be threatened by similar arguments of generic use in important export markets.

In response, the Board of Trade eventually recommended non-intervention and preserving the status quo, for the following reasons:

- There was a difference between the UK approach under the Merchandise Marks regime, where courts decide scope of protection based on whether a use is false or misleading, and the 'French practice of vesting in a trade association the monopoly right to use of a geographical description'[36] after defining the product, region of origin and production method in advance.
- Use that was not considered misleading would not be prohibited and there was no appetite for introducing *appellation* style protection in the UK.
- The option of drafting new legislation specifically reserving the use of Champagne for legitimate French producers was not feasible. This would pose political problems, since Australia, a Commonwealth partner, would object. The precedent of special protected status for Port and Madeira did exist,[37] but valuable consideration has been obtained as a result of the treaty signed with Portugal. Furthermore, protected status by itself was no guarantee of commercial success. Sales figures for both had been declining in recent years.
- Any concession to Champagne would open the floodgates for requests from other producer groups; Spain had already put forward a claim with regard to Sherry. The French government had apparently intervened to halt legal proceedings in a dispute concerning the false labelling of Scotch whisky and this form of 'blackmail' should not be encouraged.

[36] See (BT 209/1167) Note of a Meeting with Members of the 'Spanish Champagne' Sub-Committee of the Franco-British Parliamentary Relations Committee on 22nd June 1959.

[37] See Anglo-Portuguese Commercial Treaty Act 1914; 1914 CHAPTER 1 5 and 6 Geo 5; Anglo-Portuguese Commercial Treaty Act 1916; 1916 CHAPTER 39 6 and 7 Geo 5. Section 1 of the Act of 1914 reflected Art 6 of the Treaty. It stipulated that the use of these terms on wine or any other liquor not originating in the eponymous places would be *deemed a false trade description* under the Merchandise Marks legislation.

- The availability of inexpensive substitutes would lead to an increased taste for and subsequently a larger market for the 'real thing'.

While these arguments helped the government navigate between competing fields of trade pressure and political lobbying, there was greater unease about the French complaint that the UK was arguably in breach of its obligations under Art 10*bis* of the Paris Convention and Art 4 of the Madrid Agreement.[38] The latter was of particular concern, since it states that:

> The courts of each country shall decide what appellations, on account of their generic character, do not fall within the provisions of this Agreement, regional appellations concerning the source of products of the vine being, however, excluded from the reservation specified by this Article.

Thus, if a national court decides that a particular term has become generic (e.g. dijon mustard), its use on products from other than the place bearing that name is not considered misleading under Art 1 of the Madrid Agreement.[39] However, viticultural products are excluded from this judicial scrutiny, with these appellations being *de jure* inoculated against a finding of generic status. While the jury verdict had meant that there was no reasoned judgment available, it might have been construed to suggest that a court had endorsed generic status for a wine appellation, in violation of Art 4.

The UK's response to this alleged treaty violation rested on acquiescence foundations. The Board of Trade noted that the UK had consistently maintained at the international revision conferences that its Merchandise Marks regime fully satisfied all its obligations under the Madrid Agreement. The UK delegate at the revision conference of 1897 made specific reference to customs regulations implementing the Merchandise Marks regime. While prohibiting goods marked with misleading indications, they would permit the use of 'Cape Port' or 'Swiss Champagne'. In such cases the 'indication of origin consists in the precise mention of the locality from which the goods come' and based on such labels, none would be misled as to the locality from which these products originated.[40] Britain repeated this position at the revision conference of 1934 in London, but this was met with strong opposition from the

[38] Letter from the French Ministry of Foreign Affairs, 7 February 1959 (BT 209/1167).

[39] Art 1 essentially requires that any products bearing false or misleading indications of source should be seized on importation or subjected to other such border measures to prevent their circulation.

[40] *Actes de la Conférence de Bruxelles 1897 et 1900* (Bureau de l'Union, Berne, 1901) 303; see also *Report on Unfair Competition, Particularly in Relation to False Marks and Indications* [1922] League of Nations Official Journal 625, 627.

French delegation. Such permissiveness would allow for blameworthy 'usurpations' and did not conform to the fundamental principles of Madrid. The matter had been sufficiently controversial for the Industrial Property department to develop a separate file considering the legality of the UK's position on Art 4.[41] There was doubt expressed as to whether the International Court of Justice[42] would endorse the UK's position in this regard. Therefore at several points in this correspondence, reference is made to the pending civil litigation and its potential as a pressure release valve. The context provided by the archival materials allows us to appreciate the broader web of political economy repercussions emanating from a finding of generic status for a commercially significant product implicated in cross border trade flows. The hopes of several interested parties now rested upon the outcome of the civil action, which could potentially alleviate some of these pressures, or reinforce them.

The *Spanish Champagne* decisions

A fresh round of civil litigation required a new set of legal strategies to be developed, beginning with the basis for the claim and the corresponding identification of injured parties. Instead of the associations which initiated the criminal prosecution, in *Spanish Champagne* the individual claimants were some of the leading Champagne houses.[43] The well-known *maison* of J. Bollinger was joined by eleven other Champagne houses, suing on behalf of themselves and all other persons producing wine in the Champagne district of France which was supplied to England and Wales. To avoid any threshold level disqualification, they were suing in both individual and representative capacities. Two alternative avenues of attack were attempted: (1) a claim that the defendant's application of the trade descriptions 'champagne' or 'Spanish Champagne' to wine made in Spain or from grapes grown in Spain amounted to passing off,

[41] (BT 64/51) 'Industrial Property Conference; Wine Appellations; Note regarding Reservation in Article IV of Madrid Arrangements', Board of Trade Files, 1934–1939.

[42] The notional forum for resolving such disputes over treaty interpretation; notional since it was never approached to interpret any of the WIPO treaties.

[43] While there were four reported decisions, it is the last two which are relevant for our purposes: (i) *J Bollinger v. Costa Brava Wine Co Ltd* [1959] RPC 150 (Ch D) (unsuccessful application by the defendants to strike out part of the statement of claim); (ii) *J Bollinger v. Costa Brava Wine Co Ltd* [1959] RPC 289 (Ch D) (setting out the three points of law to be determined before the trial); (iii) *J Bollinger v. Costa Brava Wine Co Ltd* [1960] Ch 262; [1960] RPC 16 (Ch D) (decision on preliminary points of law) (hereafter, *Spanish Champagne No. 1*); (iv) *J Bollinger v. Costa Brava Wine Co Ltd* [1961] 1 All ER 561; [1961] RPC 116 (Ch D) (trial decision) (hereafter, *Spanish Champagne No. 2*).

or more generally constituted an act of actionable unfair competition; and (2) this conduct also gave rise to a civil remedy for a breach of a statutory duty[44] under the Merchandise Marks Acts. The second option was based on a speculative interpretation of the penal statute and was eventually rejected by the court.[45] However, even the first option rested on untested foundations, because the facts of this dispute did not fit within the conventional passing off mould.

The tort of passing off seeks to prevent those marketplace misrepresentations that are injurious to a trader's goodwill. Lord Oliver's depiction of goodwill, misrepresentation and damage sets out the three interrelated requirements:

> The law of passing off can be summarised in one short general proposition – no man may pass off his goods as those of another ... First, [the claimant] must establish a goodwill or reputation attached to the goods or services which he supplies in the mind of the purchasing public by association with the identifying 'get-up' (whether it consists simply of a brand name or a trade description ...) such that the get-up is recognised by the public as distinctive specifically of the plaintiff's goods or services. Second, he must demonstrate a misrepresentation by the defendant to the public (whether or not intentional) leading or likely to lead the public to believe that goods or services offered by him are the goods or services of the plaintiff... Third, he must demonstrate that he suffers or, in a *quia timet* action, that he is likely to suffer damage by reason of the erroneous belief engendered by the defendant's misrepresentation that the source of the defendant's goods or services is the same as the source of those offered by the plaintiff.[46]

This is a principled elaboration of the archetypal wrongful conduct in passing off:

> A man is not to sell his own goods under the pretence that they are the goods of another man; he cannot be permitted to practice such a deception, nor to use the means which contribute to that end. He cannot therefore be allowed to use names, marks, letters or other indicia, by which he may induce purchasers to believe, that the goods which he is selling are the manufacture of another person.[47]

However, at the time of the dispute, certain limitations were clearly established. To begin with, the tort had not been overtly extended beyond

[44] A duty imposed by a statute on a defendant, which enables a tort-like civil cause of action for a claimant when the duty is breached.

[45] When deciding on the existence of a statutory duty, courts consider the scope and purpose of the statute, the existing remedies it provides and in particular for whose benefit it is intended. The court concluded that the purpose of the statute was consumer protection, as opposed to enabling producers to defend their commercial interests. *Spanish Champagne No. 1*, at 284–85.

[46] *Reckitt & Colman Products Ltd v. Borden Inc.* [1990] RPC 341, 406 (HL).

[47] *Perry v. Truefitt* (1842) 6 Beav 66, 73 (Lord Langdale MR).

misrepresentation to include pure freeriding or misappropriation.[48] The criminal prosecution had collapsed precisely because misleading use could not be established and this remained a concern. Next, the legally protected interest is also clearly identified in passing off. The tort protects the invasion of a property interest by misrepresentation. As opposed to property in the sign or designation itself, it is the 'property in the business or goodwill likely to be injured by the misrepresentation'[49] that is protected. This has traditionally belonged to *an individual commercial entity*, which generates the goodwill through sales or marketplace presence. The trade name or sign is then emblematic of this commercial magnetism. The goodwill is thus preserved by protecting the sign against misuse by unauthorised third parties. A person 'who engages in commercial activities may acquire a valuable reputation in respect of the goods in which he deals ... The law regards such a reputation as an incorporeal piece of property, the integrity of which the owner is entitled to protect.'[50]

In light of these limits, the facts of *Spanish Champagne* raised unsettled issues for each of the three limbs of goodwill, misrepresentation and damage. Let us consider these in turn.

(1) Bollinger and each of the other individual claimants could not claim any exclusivity in the collectively generated goodwill associated with Champagne. Prior to this:

> [T]here was considerable doubt whether any one or more persons could sue, either individually or jointly, alleging passing-off by the use of the word Champagne notwithstanding its great reputation, since it did not represent the wine of any one producer exclusively, and it was not wholly, and in some cases not at all, part of a reputation and goodwill which any particular producer or his predecessors had built up. Any person may set up business as a producer of Champagne provided he does so in the Champagne district of France and complies with the stringent regulations ...[51]

(2) It was also an unconventional misrepresentation, because there was no allegation that the defendants' product was passed off as wine produced by any of the plaintiffs individually. Instead of misrepresentation as to commercial or trade source, there was an alleged misrepresentation about the defendant's membership in a class and consequently about product quality associated with that class.

[48] This continues to be the position and pure misappropriation was emphatically rejected in *L'Oréal SA v. Bellure NV* [2007] EWCA Civ 968 at (Jacob LJ).

[49] *AG Spalding & Brothers v. AW Gamage Ltd* (1915) 32 RPC 273, 284 (HL) (Parker, LJ).

[50] *HP Bulmer Ltd and Showerings Ltd v. J Bollinger SA & Champagne Lanson Père et Fils* [1977] 2 CMLR 625, 629 (Buckley LJ).

[51] *HP Bulmer Ltd and Showerings Ltd v. J Bollinger SA & Champagne Lanson Père et Fils* [1977] 2 CMLR 625, 660 (CA) (Goff LJ) (Champagne Cider and Champagne Perry).

(3) Finally, the familiar category of damage by way of lost sales would be difficult to prove, since none of the individual claimants exclusively owned the goodwill in the first place. Which of the claimants (if any) was losing sales to Costa Brava? These ambiguities explain the dual track nature of the argument that such labelling was either conventional passing off *or* part of a broader species of actionable wrong referred to as unfair competition. Conventional passing off would need to be adapted; refashioned to recognise broader categories of misrepresentation and damage, or possibly even pure misappropriation. Whether such novel claims could be accommodated in the first place required a preliminary decision on points of law.

Before turning to Danckwerts J's reasoning, there is one further element of scene setting, which concerns the status of geographical signs under passing off. At the time of the dispute, the following propositions appeared well settled within the applicable Anglo-American doctrine. First, geographical signs were considered descriptive and not distinctive enough to indicate a single commercial source. The default position was that they would not be protected by passing off.[52] Second, this exclusion could only be overcome if it were established that a sign (which symbolised the protected goodwill) had acquired distinctiveness or secondary meaning, coming to indicate a particular trade source as opposed to describing the geographical provenance of the product.[53] The geographical sign would then start to function as a badge of commercial origin. As one court recently observed:

> In cases of classic passing-off the use of a purely descriptive term to describe the claimant's business will not usually prevent a defendant from using the same name unless the claimant can show that the words in question have acquired a secondary meaning or have become synonymous with its business and that business alone. The more general and descriptive the name is, the more difficult it will be to establish the reputation and goodwill of the claimant in that term and the existence of a misrepresentation by the defendant in its use of the same name.[54]

Third, even in cases where acquired distinctiveness was established, the interests of other traders who wished legitimately to use the geographical

[52] See e.g. *Spalding v. Gamage* (1915) 32 RPC 273, 284 (HL) (Parker LJ) (observing that 'it is extremely difficult to see how a man can be said to have property in descriptive words').

[53] Perhaps the earliest reported case to grapple inconclusively with this issue is *Motley v. Downman* 40 ER 824 (1837). For the subsequent settling of principles, see e.g. *M'Andrew v. Bassett* 46 ER 965 (1864) ('Anatolia liquorice'); *Radde v. Norman* (1872) LR 14 Eq. 348 ('Leopoldshall Kainit' on rock salt); *Wotherspoon v. Currie* (1872) LR 5 HL 518 ('Glenfield Starch'); *Siegert v. Findlater* (1878) 7 Ch D 801 ('Angostura Bitters').

[54] *Diageo v. Intercontinental Brands* [2010] EWCA Civ 920 at [24] (Patten LJ).

sign (for example others who operated in the same region and wished to truthfully use its name) were recognised.[55] Thus the property right was not exclusive, and tailor-made injunctions ensured that these other users could also make use of the sign, provided confusion was controlled for by suitably distinguishing their products. Where there was such a risk of misrepresentation, use would be proscribed even if the defendant was based in the eponymous geographical region.[56] This approach regulated the use of the sign by those within the region. While these three propositions were fairly clear, they did not provide guidance for a situation where a group of otherwise independent commercial entities claimed collectively generated goodwill in a geographical name and sought to prevent those outside the region from using it.

Assessing whether such a novel claim could be recognised was the subject of the decision on points of law in *Spanish Champagne No. 1*. In deciding this, Danckwerts J made the following factual assumptions:

> (1) The plaintiffs carry on business in a geographical area in France known as Champagne; (2) the plaintiffs' wine is produced in Champagne and from grapes grown in Champagne; (3) the plaintiffs' wine has been known in the trade for a long time as 'champagne' with a high reputation; (4) members of the public or in the trade ordering or seeing wine advertised as 'champagne' would expect to get wine produced in Champagne from grapes grown there; and (5) the defendants are producing a wine not produced in that geographical area and are selling it under the name of 'Spanish Champagne'.[57]

With these as the backdrop, the claimants' case was summarised in the following manner:

> The question for determination is whether it is part of English law that where a number of persons produce goods in a defined geographical area which become known by the name of the area and as such acquire a reputation, those persons have a civil remedy against other persons producing goods outside the area who attach its name to their goods.[58]

It was also suggested that the name 'Champagne' was part of each claimant's goodwill which was injured by the defendants' conduct. This aspect was in line with the classic trinity of passing off, where it is the

[55] *Delaware & Hudson Canal Co v. Clark*, 13 Wall. (80 U.S.) 311 (Strong J) ('It must be considered as a sound doctrine that no one can apply the name of a district or country to a well-known article of commerce, and obtain thereby such an exclusive right to the application as to prevent others inhabiting the district, or dealing in similar articles coming from the district, from truthfully using the same designation'); Cf. F. M. Adams, *A Treatise on the Law of Trade Marks*, 2nd edn (Butterworths, London 1876) 73–75.

[56] *Seixo v. Provezende* (1866) LR 1 Ch App 192; *Wotherspoon v. Currie* (1871–72) LR 5 HL 508; *American Waltham Watch Co v. United States Watch Co* (1899) 173 Mass. 85.

[57] *Spanish Champagne No. 1*, at 273. [58] *Ibid.*, at 267.

claimant's own goodwill in the product (as producer/supplier of the product) that is at stake. The Champagne houses claimed that:

> the law was not so limited as to deprive persons so injured of a right of action to protect their property, and that it is not an objection that [they] have no exclusive right to the name 'Champagne' in the sense that they share the right to use it with all other persons who produce wine in the Champagne area.[59]

In other words, there appeared to be two routes to establishing the relevant proprietary interest: establishing exclusive usage of a sign leading to individual goodwill, or demonstrating the existence of collective goodwill associated with a product, which also added value to an individual trader's goodwill, enabling the trader to claim on that basis. Each of these options ought to be acceptable.

The court found these arguments convincing and agreed that passing off could evolve in the direction of preventing new forms of unfair competitive conduct. Danckwerts J first clarified that passing off was grounded in the protection of a proprietary interest in goodwill and then declared that its purpose was to prevent 'unfair competition between traders rather than with the deception of the public . . . for the right of action known as a "passing-off action" is not an action brought by the member of the public who is deceived but by the trader whose trade is likely to suffer from the deception'.[60] On the issue of whether an exclusive right to the goodwill was a prerequisite, he analysed two lines of authorities. One group of cases appeared to involve more than one party with an interest in a geographical sign, but on closer analysis most of these were applications of the secondary meaning or acquired distinctiveness principle and could be accounted for as regular passing off decisions to prevent misrepresentations concerning trade source.[61] However, the second group was more promising and related to personal names. Here there was more than an individual interest because the name might be shared, for example by sons who inherited different facets of the family business.[62]

Two conclusions could be distilled from these personal name authorities: (1) while others may have the right to use the same name and there was no exclusivity in the goodwill, undeserving defendants who were misrepresenting their products could still be subjected to injunctions; (2) all the parties with an interest in the goodwill did not have to be joined to the suit and any one of them could sue on the basis of injury to

[59] *Ibid.*, at 273–74. [60] *Ibid.*, at 274.

[61] *Braham v. Beachim* (1878) 7 Ch D 848 (Radstock Colliery); *The Free Fishers and Dredgers of Whitstable v. Elliott* (1888) 4 T.L.R. 273; *Dunnachie v. Young & Sons* (1883) 10 S.C. (4th) 874.

[62] *Dent v. Turpin* (1861) 2 J. & H. 139; *Southorn v. Reynolds* (1865) 12 L.T. 75.

their individual goodwill. Danckwerts J also relied on US authorities which suggested that a similar approach should be taken to geographical names.[63] Concluding that an action for an expanded notion of passing off should be permissible in these circumstances, he observed:

> There seems to be no reason why such licence should be given to a person, competing in trade, who seeks to attach to his product a name or description with which it has no natural association so as to make use of the reputation and goodwill which has been gained by a product genuinely indicated by the name or description ... In my view, it ought not to matter that the persons truly entitled to describe their goods by the name and description are a class producing goods in a certain locality, and not merely one individual. The description is part of their goodwill and a right of property. I do not believe that the law of passing off, which arose to prevent unfair trading, is so limited in scope.[64]

By suggesting that the collective goodwill nevertheless added a little lustre to each individual claimant, the path was cleared for accommodating this new type of action and the matter proceeded to trial. Here the most controversial issue concerned the nature of the misrepresentation, if any, when 'Spanish Champagne' was used on Costa Brava's labels.

On this issue, Costa Brava reverted to its previously successful defence that the addition of the word 'Spanish' clarified that the geographical origin was not French, so it could not be mistaken for Champagne which is produced in France. It was also accepted that there were large numbers of people in England who knew that authentic Champagne is produced in France. They would know that 'Spanish Champagne' is not the real thing but merely an attempt to capitalise on the prestige value of Champagne.[65] This was buttressed by the argument that the general practice of generic use of former wine appellations would ensure that 'Champagne' was seen here as a style of wine. However, the generic status argument was rejected since the judge found on the evidence that Champagne retained its denotations of French origin for much of the relevant public.[66] As regards the clarificatory effect of 'Spanish', there was evidence to support each side. On the one hand, 'experts and many educated persons, and most persons engaged in the trade, and no doubt wine waiters and the like, know what champagne should be, and will not be deceived'.[67] Yet this had to be balanced against 'a considerable body of evidence that persons whose life or education has not taught them much about the nature and

[63] *Pillsbury-Washburn Flour Mills Co Ltd v. Eagle* (1898) 86 Fed. Rep. 608; *California Fruit Canners' Association v. Myer* (1899) 104 Fed. Rep. 82; *New York and R. Cement Co v. Coplay Cement Co* (1890) 44 Fed. Rep. 277. Danckwerts J preferred the first two of these, finding the contrary opinion in the third decision unpersuasive.

[64] *Spanish Champagne No. 1*, at 283–84. [65] *Spanish Champagne No. 2*, at 563–64.

[66] *Ibid.*, at 564. [67] *Ibid.*, at 566.

production of wine, but who from time to time want to purchase "Champagne", as the wine with the great reputation, are likely to be misled by the description "Spanish Champagne"'.[68] The concern was for those who were not familiar with the wine but wished to celebrate on special occasions by buying 'the real thing'. On this aspect, the decision is very much of its time. From a critical perspective, it seems to be an instantiation of legal institutions reinforcing contemporary class boundaries. However, the court also had to acknowledge that retail arrangements were in the process of being restructured, which emerges from the evidence reviewed at trial. It indicated that self-service (a new development) was gradually being introduced into the alcohol retail model. Consumers would encounter such products directly on the shelves, without interacting with knowledgeable intermediaries as had previously been the case. It also suggested that those without much previous exposure to the sparkling wine were occasionally demanding it.[69] Finally, more compelling evidence for misleading use is found in Keeling's account of the closing arguments at trial. Perlada's use was directed at depleting the special origin and quality related significance of Champagne per se. The defendants themselves had produced a brochure entitled 'Giving a Champagne Party', where they had dropped the 'Spanish' qualifier. According to the plaintiffs' barrister, it was a 'document which patently and blatantly sets out to pass off the defendant's product as and for Champagne ... [not only would it] tempt retailers (as the defendant's own evidence has shown) to sell Perlada as and for Champagne, but it tempts the public to buy it for Champagne occasions'.[70] In attempting to nudge Champagne into generic status in the minds of the British public, the defendant was opening up the space for deceptive conduct. An injunction was consequently granted prohibiting the use of such labelling and there was no further appeal. As a postscript, it is worth mentioning that Spanish sparkling wine producers would go on collectively to develop the Cava designation, which continues to enjoy effervescent sales around the world.[71]

[68] *Ibid.*, at 567.

[69] See *Spanish Champagne No. 2*, at 566–68. For a sense of the growing familiarity with wine amongst UK consumers, linked to the demystification accompanying supermarket sales from the 1970s, see C. Ritchie, 'Beyond Drinking: The Role of Wine in the Life of the UK Consumer' (2007) 31 *International Journal of Consumer Studies* 534. Cf. S. Charters, *Wine and Society: The Social and Cultural Context of a Drink* (Elsevier, Oxford, 2006).

[70] Keeling, 'The "Spanish Champagne" Case', 172–73.

[71] In Spain, Cava is recognised and defined in the *Reglamento de la Denominación «Cava» y de su Consejo Regulador, aprobado por la Orden del Ministerio de Agricultura, Pesca y Alimentación de 14 de noviembre de 1991*. Further details are available at Consejo Regulador del Cava: www.crcava.es/.

Extending 'extended' passing off

Over the half-century of its existence, extended passing off has been developed into a remarkably flexible tort, which can accommodate shared goodwill associated with a regional designation. No prior registration is required for protecting the designation and the action has been widely adopted across common law jurisdictions, with equivalents found within the unfair competition regimes of civil law jurisdictions.[72] However, the protection afforded under passing off also has its limits. The first section of this chapter referred to debates over the extent to which the misrepresentation requirement was attenuated by these cases, being replaced by a misappropriation standard. Despite this, misrepresentation remains central to passing off to date. This constraint on the scope of protection suggests that it does not go as far as the French appellation protection regime or other international or multilateral agreements in preventing not only misappropriation (or pure free riding) but property-like 'absolute' protection as well.[73] Compared to such *sui generis* GI protection systems, other limitations include the vulnerability to generic use[74] and the difficulties faced by collective associations representing GI producers in establishing the requisite goodwill.[75]

These limitations have immediate practical significance for litigants, but a more interesting conceptual difference between unfair competition and registration-based approaches has gone unremarked thus far. If GI protection regimes can be said to have an 'internal' dimension of product

[72] F.-K. Beier & R. Knaak, 'The Protection of Direct and Indirect Geographical Indications of Source in Germany and the European Community' (1994) *IIC* 1; F. Henning-Bodewig & G. Schricker, 'New Initiatives for the Harmonisation of Unfair Competition Law in Europe' (2002) *EIPR* 271, 273.

[73] There are important differences between (i) misrepresentation, (ii) broader unfair competition protection (blurring, tarnishment, freeriding) and (iii) absolute protection. While the first two categories have consumer perception as the starting point, the third reifies the sign, granting protection without first testing for consumer awareness of the meaning of the sign. Art 23.1 of TRIPs is a paradigmatic illustration. See Gangjee, *Relocating the Law of Geographical Indications*, 157–77.

[74] *Vine Products v. Mackenzie & Co Ltd (No. 3)* [1967] FSR 402 (Ch D) (while Sherry by itself retained a specific meaning based on its origin and qualities, the doctrine of laches permitted delocalising additions such as Cyprus or British Sherry due to a century of such usages); *Institut National Des Appellations D'Origine Des Vins Et Eaux-De-Vie et al. v. Andres Wines Ltd et al.*, (1987) 16 CPR (3d) 385 (Ont. HCJ) (finding that the passing off claim failed because Champagne was a generic term in Canada, so there was no misrepresentation).

[75] *Chocosuisse Union des Fabricants Suisses de Chocolat v. Cadbury Ltd* [1999] RPC 826 (CA) (while individual traders can sue in both an individual and representative capacity, trade associations lack any basis for bringing a claim since their interests differ from those of their members).

delineation and regulation, as well as an 'external' dimension of preventing misuse by unauthorised third parties, the extended passing off approach and unfair competition approaches more generally prioritise only the latter.[76] By contrast, *sui generis* registration-based regimes such as the French *appellation controlée* system squarely confront the difficult task of defining the product and identifying the region of origin. This task is challenging because for a given regional product there are inevitable fluctuations in the historic contours of the region of origin, as well as in the methods of production. Pinning down both geographical limits and authentic or official production methods in a product specification is therefore controversial. There are disputes involving those on the periphery of a region, who demand inclusion within the final specification.[77] A consensus also needs to be forged from amongst the prevalent practices that involve different techniques (choices over irrigation practices, methods of harvesting and crushing, etc.) and ingredients (opting for a 100 per cent local grapes requirement or 85 per cent, allowing for flexibility during poor harvests?).[78] Such regimes also have to equitably address imbalances in local power relations and unequal bargaining positions along the supply chain (e.g. where the interests of bottlers diverge from those of grape growers). To take just one example, there has been considerable pressure to adapt the Tequila appellation specification in Mexico to accommodate the interests of multinational spirits producers. The 'rapid expansion of the tequila market has been driven by a shift in ownership of the major tequila companies to transnational liquor conglomerates and accompanied by the concentration, industrialization, and standardization of tequila production ... In order to minimize their exposure to the cycles of surplus and shortage that characterize the industry, the large tequila companies have begun growing their own agave, cutting the independent agave farmers out of the industry altogether.'[79] Additionally, 'traditional agave cultivation techniques are being replaced by a more mechanized, chemically intensive production system, which in turn contributes to groundwater pollution,

[76] *Consorzio del Prosciutto di Parma v. Marks & Spencer plc* [1990] FSR 530 (Ch D).

[77] Many of these difficulties are reviewed in Ch. 3 of Gangjee, *Relocating the Law of Geographical Indications*.

[78] For conflicting interests in the wine industry during the formation of appellation regions, see C. K. Warner, *The Winegrowers of France and the Government since 1875* (Columbia University Press, New York, 1960); K. M. Guy, *When Champagne Became French: Wine and the Making of a National Identity* (Johns Hopkins University Press, Baltimore, 2003). Cf. D. Rangnekar *Geographical Indications and Localisation: A Case Study of Feni* (ESRC Report 2009).

[79] S. Bowen & M. S. Gaytán, 'The Paradox of Protection: National Identity, Global Commodity Chains, and the Tequila Industry' (2012) 59 *Social Problems* 70, 77–78.

soil erosion, and loss of biodiversity'.[80] Finally, even after the initial delineations, the specification needs to be regulated on an ongoing basis, to incorporate change or expansion. This sustained engagement is necessary because these *sui generis* regimes are premised on the historical and geographical embeddedness of the product. Stated bluntly, the product and its link to place have normative significance, helping to define a GI regime as a distinct form of product regulation and sign protection. As the following paragraphs demonstrate, this dimension has limited significance and operates at a much lower level of resolution under an unfair competition approach, which focuses on the meaning of the sign. The unfair competition approach is therefore only a partial substitute for a registration-based *sui generis* GI regime, since the latter additionally regulates the underlying product. In all the passing off decisions mentioned in this chapter, the court proceeds from the assumption that the product specification is drafted, evaluated and monitored by a reliable certification regime of some sort; usually involving a combination of a representative association of producers and a government agency responsible for overseeing the registration process. This ready-made product identity greatly assists courts in defining the genuine or authentic product, as the touchstone for analysing whether the defendant's use constitutes a misrepresentation. One sees this aspect also reproduced in an alternative approach – the common law certification mark decisions – analysed by Daniel Gervais in the response to this chapter.[81]

Let us conclude with an appreciation of how the very flexibility of passing off cuts in both directions, starting with product definition. One of the key features setting 'extended' passing off apart from the more conventional variety is that 'protection is given to a [descriptive] name or word which has come to mean a particular product rather than a product from a particular trader'.[82] Defining the product is important because the goodwill associated with that class of product (e.g. Champagne) is the valuable intangible that is being protected in such actions. Once the product has been defined, we can also assess whether the claimant is entitled to membership in the group of producers that have a shared goodwill associated with the product. This establishes the claimant's standing to bring the action. Finally, a clearly defined product acts as the benchmark when assessing whether the defendant has misrepresented the qualities of their own products. So how is product definition to be approached?

[80] *Ibid.*, at 79. [81] See Chapter 6 in this volume.
[82] *Chocosuisse Union des Fabricants Suisse de Chocolat and Others v. Cadbury Ltd* [1998] RPC 117, 124 (Ch D) (Laddie J).

An issue which arose at an early stage was whether a geographical limitation was required for such collective goodwill situations. Since the product required a 'recognisable and distinctive quality', some of the early judgments suggested that the:

> plaintiff in this sort of action must establish that the district in which goods in question were produced and which gives the goods their name is defined with reasonable precision either by law or custom. The court must obviously be in a position to decide in case of dispute whether or not any given plaintiff is a producer in the district in question.[83]

Here geographical factors such as soil and climate conditions were initially perceived as the basis for giving such products their distinctive qualities and reputation.[84] However both the trial court and the House of Lords concluded in *Advocaat*[85] that a defined region of geographical origin was not an essential requirement in such cases, so long as the product continued to have a defined meaning. As Lord Diplock described it:

> It cannot make any difference in principle whether the recognisable and distinctive qualities by which the reputation of the type of product has been gained are the result of its having been made in, or from ingredients produced in, a particular locality or are the result of its having been made from particular ingredients regardless of their provenance; though a geographical limitation may make it easier (a) to define the type of product; (b) to establish that it has qualities which are recognisable and distinguish it from every other type of product that competes with it in the market and which have gained for it in that market a reputation and goodwill; and (c) to establish that the plaintiff's own business will suffer more than minimal damage to its goodwill by the defendant's misrepresenting his product as being of that type.[86]

It is evident that geographical features and their influence on product quality are not central to the enquiry and 'extended' passing off has been successfully used to prevent the misleading use of non-geographical product descriptions such as whisky[87] and vodka.[88] Thus a fundamental requirement for *terroir* regimes – the link to a defined geographical region

[83] *Vine Products Ltd v. Mackenzie & Co Ltd* [1967] FSR 402, 427 (Ch D) (Cross J).

[84] The authorities were reviewed in *Erven Warnink BV v. J Townend & Sons (Hull) Ltd* [1978] FSR 473, 484–85 (CA).

[85] *Erven Warnink BV v. J Townend & Sons (Hull) Ltd* [1978] FSR 1 (Ch D); *Erven Warnink BV v. J Townend & Sons (Hull) Ltd* [1979] FSR 397 (HL) (Advocaat defined on the basis of its ingredients, as opposed to regional origin).

[86] *Erven Warnink BV v. J Townend & Sons (Hull) Ltd* [1979] FSR 397, 410 (HL).

[87] *Scotch Whisky Association v. Glen Kella Distillers Ltd* [1997] E.T.M.R. 470.

[88] *Diageo Ch*; confirmed on appeal: *Diageo North America Inc. v. Intercontinental Brands* [2010] EWCA Civ 920.

which gives a product its qualities and/or reputation – is reduced to being an optional evidentiary advantage under the unfair competition scheme.

The two types of systems also differ in their approach to defining the ingredients and method of production. *Terroir* regimes adopt a more 'objective' approach which requires specific details (e.g. a minimum alcohol content or number of years for aging) to be indicated as precisely as possible in the application for registration. Since the unfair competition approach to product definition is mediated by consumer perception, fuzzier notions of the 'real thing' are permissible. So long as consumers consider the product to belong to a defined class and there is goodwill associated with that product, consumers need not be aware of the specifics of production. Thus it did not matter in *Advocaat* that consumers mistakenly believed the alcoholic drink in question was made with brandy, or that in *Chocosuisse* some consumers were confused about whether 'Swiss chocolate' signalled origin in Switzerland, or chocolate made according to Swiss recipes, or chocolate produced by reputed Swiss corporations.

> The fact that public have no clear idea of the characteristics of the goods which have the reputation is of little consequence. In the case of Champagne, no doubt many members of the public who know of and rely on the reputation acquired by that designation, know nothing about double fermentation and do not know where the Champagne district of France is. Some may not even know that the wine with the reputation comes from France. This is irrelevant. What is required is to identify the class of goods which has built up and is entitled to exploit the goodwill, not whether the public appreciates the identifying characteristics of the class.[89]

From a litigant's perspective, the strategic advantages of this flexibility are immediately obvious, but the deeper significance is that the unfair competition approach focuses on the sign and its subjective meaning at a fairly abstract or general level, whereas a registration-based system adopts an objective approach to product definition. Prioritising the sign as opposed to the product, or conversely the product as opposed to the sign, lies at the heart of long-standing disagreements between proponents of these two approaches to GI protection.[90]

Conclusion

By laying the foundations for the tort of 'extended' passing off, *Spanish Champagne* is widely regarded as having initiated the common law

[89] *Chocosuisse Union des Fabricants Suisse de Chocolat and Others v. Cadbury Ltd* [1998] RPC 117, 135–36 (Ch D) (Laddie J).

[90] For an overview of these disagreements, see Ch. 1 in Gangjee, *Relocating the Law of Geographical Indications*.

approach to GI protection. The story of this case is interesting for several reasons. It reveals the broader political economy context and range of actors interested in the outcome of a determination on generic status for a valuable commercial product. The across-the-board lobbying, threat of retaliatory sanctions and claims of treaty obligation violations only come to light based on archival materials. Additionally, the judicial outcome stands at the cusp of a penal or Merchandise Marks approach, which had lasted for a century, giving way to a civil or passing off approach. Passing off emerges as a flexible and accommodating tort for protecting collective goodwill, within the limits of a misrepresentation prevention paradigm. It is emblematic of an unfair competition approach, as opposed to registration-based, *terroir* focused protection. The signal feature of this communicative approach is its focus on the meaning of the sign before a given audience. The product and region of origin are incidental. Yet much that is interesting and controversial in the context of registration-based GI systems involves defining the product with clarity, identifying the boundaries of the growing or production region, specifying the method of production and deciding how to recognise collective interests in such regional products, including determining which collective bodies will equitably represent these interests. The 'extended' passing off cases assumed all of this work has been done elsewhere for products such as Scotch whisky, Champagne and Parma Ham. In the process, this body of doctrine does not concern itself with disputes over the raw materials to be used; or determining the appropriate boundaries of the region of origin; or conflicts between the various groups within the GI supply chain. Registration systems are compelled to engage with these questions while this is work that passing off is not designed to do.

This chapter concludes by arguing that the conceptual and institutional divergences between these two approaches map onto contrasting perspectives about the objects of GI protection – the sign and/or the product. In light of this, it is legitimate to ask whether unfair competition approaches and registration-based systems can be meaningfully compared as functionally equivalent alternatives in international GI protection debates. Finally, in focusing on these conceptual aspects, this chapter does not enter into a normative assessment of the unfair competition or *terroir* approaches. This is the challenging task which Professor Gervais picks up on, in the following chapter.

6 A Cognac after Spanish Champagne? Geographical indications as certification marks

Daniel Gervais

Claret is the liquor for boys; port for men; but he who aspires to be a hero must drink brandy. Boswell, *The Life of Samuel Johnson*, April 7, 1779

An introduction (to American champagne)

The *Spanish Champagne* case,[1] adroitly discussed by Dev Gangjee in Chapter 5, is one of the so-called "Drinks" cases. It is very unlikely to happen exactly in the same way in a US court. This is because in the 2006 "Wine Pact"[2] the European Union agreed not to challenge existing uses of so-called semi-generic appellations (including champagne) by producers in the US. Specifically, the Pact allows continued use of semi-generic appellations used in the US before December 13, 2005, provided the term is only used on labels bearing the brand name for which an applicable *certificate of label approval*

[1] *Vine Products Ltd v. Mackenzie & Co Ltd* [1969] RPC 1, referring to *J Bollinger v. Costa Brava Wine Coy. Ltd* [1960] RPC 16, [1961] RPC 116. The cases have a progeny in the UK (*Vine Products Ltd v. MacKenzie & Co Ltd* [1969] RPC 1, HCJ Ch D; *John Walker & Sons Ltd v. Henry Ost & Co Ltd* [1970] RPC 489, Ch D; *HP Bulmer Ltd v. Bollinger SA* [1978] RPC 79, CA; and advocaat: *Erven Warnink Besloten Vennootschap v. J Townend & Sons (Hull) Ltd* [1979] AC 731, HL), but also in Canada (*Institut National des Appellations d'Origine des Vins et Eaux-de-Vie v. Andre Wines Ltd* (1990) 30 CPR (3d) 279 (Ontario CA) aff'g (1987) 16 CPR (3d) 385 (Ontario HCJ), leave to appeal refused [1991] 1 S.C.R. x (note); and *Dairy Bureau of Canada v. Annable Foods Ltd* (1993) 46 CPR (3d) 289 (British Columbia SC) 309); and New Zealand (*Comité Interprofessionel du Vin de Champagne v. Wineworths Group, Ltd* [1991] 2 N.Z.L.R. 432 (H.C.)).

[2] European Community and the USA, *Agreement between the European Community and the United States of America on trade in wine* ("Wine Pact"), OJ L 87, 2 (March 24, 2006). *See also Agreement In The Form Of An Exchange Of Letters Between The United States Of America And The European Community On Matters Related To Trade In Wine*, Document EL/USA/CE/en 1 and en 2 (Nov 23, 2005), online at http://1.usa.gov/1cEDncF (visited November 20, 2012). Under 27 CFR § 4.24(c) and 27 CFR § 12.31, "geographic significance" that has not been found by the Administrator of the Alcohol and Tobacco Tax and Trade Bureau (Department of the Treasury) to be generic or semi-generic is protected. For a discussion on the Wine Pact, *see* Daniel Gervais, "Reinventing Lisbon: The Case for a Protocol to the Lisbon Agreement," 11:1 *Chi. J. Int'l L.* 67, 115–16 (2010).

(COLA) has been issued.[3] This means that American champagne is here to stay for the predictable future.

However, this is not the end of the story of Geographical indications (GIs) in the US, far from it, for at least two reasons. First, internationally, the Wine Pact did not "affect the rights and obligations of the Parties under the WTO Agreements,"[4] which includes the Agreement on Trade-Related Aspects of Intellectual Property (TRIPS Agreement)[5]. Ongoing discussions at the WTO might thus lead to changes in US law. Second, the Pact only applies to wine, which leaves spirits and a host of other products to which GIs might apply, including the recent example of Darjeeling tea.[6] Let us see how the story might unfold in the US.

Telling the US side of the GI story takes us a few hundred miles southwest of Champagne, to the Cognac region of France. "Cognac" is a well-known term in the US. Indeed, there have been a number of cases dealing with that particular type of brandy. Before pouring into that discussion, however, I should note that the spirit of *Spanish Champagne* informed the Cognac-related discussion in the US. The link is found in the emergence of a notion of collective goodwill in *Spanish Champagne* and other Drinks cases. This conceptual construction, namely the recognition of a notion of goodwill not linked to a single producing entity but rather to a "collectivity" of producers (here operating in a given geographical area), proved key in protecting French Champagne makers under unfair competition law in the UK. As we will see, it undergirds US law as well.

The recognition of collectively owned goodwill suggests two additional liminary normative observations. First, there is nothing inherently shocking about the notion of goodwill as "collective" if one accepts that a trademark is protected as an indicator of a perceived origin (usually defined as the producer) because that origin may well be a *group of producers*. Second, both single-producer and "group of producers" marks can be solidly grounded in the central tenet of trademark law, namely

[3] COLAs are issued by the Alcohol and Tobacco Tax and Trade Bureau, under 27 CFR § 4.30. *See* Alcohol, Tobacco Tax and Trade Bureau, Department of the Treasury, Labeling Requirements for Wine, 27 CFR § 4.30. Provisions implementing Article 6 were introduced in December 2006 by § 422 of the appropriately named Tax Relief and Health Care Act of 2006. The label must identify the wine as produced in the US. 27 CFR. § 4.24(b)(1).

[4] Wine Pact, *supra* note 2, Art. 12(1).

[5] Agreement on Trade-Related Aspects of Intellectual Property Rights ("TRIPS Agreement"), Marrakesh Agreement establishing the World Trade Organization, Annex 1C (April 15, 1994).

[6] *See* Jim Yardley, "Darjeeling Journal: Good Name Is Restored in Terrain Known for Tea," *The New York Times*, December 16, 2012, available at http://nyti.ms/134NKj7.

that it aims to provide potential purchasers with useful source or product information in making a purchasing or similar decision.[7]

While there are key parallels to be drawn with *Spanish Champagne* and US law, there are also important differences between the legal environment in which that case bubbled up and the current US regime, particularly the development of *certification marks*. Those marks will be a central feature of the discussion below. They are defined in the US statute as:

> [Marks] used upon or in connection with the products or services of one or more persons other than the owner of the mark to certify national or other origin, material, mode of manufacture, quality, accuracy, or other characteristics of such goods or services or that the work or labor on the goods or services was performed by members of a union or other organization.[8]

In adding marks that certify not a producer but rather "national or other origin, material, mode of manufacture, *quality*, accuracy, or *other characteristics* of such goods or services" to the statute, Congress arguably codified a notion of collective goodwill in a way that is compatible with the international notion of GI. Indeed, the TRIPS Agreement (incidentally, TRIPS was the first multilateral instrument to use the term "Geographical Indications") defined GIs as "indications which identify a good as originating in the territory of a Member, or a region or locality in that territory, where a given *quality*, reputation *or other characteristic* of the good is essentially attributable to its geographical origin."[9] There is thus a fair degree of parallelism between the international notion of GI and that of geographic certification marks in US law.[10] That said, after this quick sip of Champagne as our backdrop, it is now time to move on to Cognac.

The *Cognac* cases

The story of Cognac in US trademark law points to three main cases. The first dates back to 1944. The date matters because, although the case is silent on that point, sympathy for France may have been a factor at that particular juncture in US history. The case was in fact a consolidation of twelve cases involving applications for the trademarks COLOGNAC and CALOGNAC for brandy and oppositions to those applications by Otard, a genuine Cognac maker.[11] The oppositions were not made on the basis

[7] Which, when seen from the flip side, translates into the more common "negative view" of trademark rights as a prohibition of using misleading or confusing information on a product or its packaging.

[8] Lanham Act § 45, 15 U.S.C.A. § 1127.

[9] TRIPS Agreement, Art. 22.1.

[10] By which I mean the use of a certification mark to certify geographic origin.

[11] *Otard, Inc., v. Italian Swiss Colony* 141 F.2d 706 (Cust & Pat. App. 1944).

of pre-existing registrations for other marks (such as COGNAC). Instead they were made under the terms of the statute in force at the time, which allowed certain parties (this would emerge in the case, as we shall see) to oppose the use of descriptors as marks if those would confuse or mislead the consumer.[12]

The oppositions were considered, first, by the Examiner of Trade-Mark Interferences, who basically did not recognize the opposers' right to oppose the applications and thus rejected the oppositions without stating much in terms of reasons.[13] The opposers appealed the matter to the Commissioner of Trademarks, who was more sympathetic to their arguments, at least to the extent that he accepted both the opposers' standing and the fact that a symbol could be both a geographic descriptor and a mark. This "dual purpose" is now well accepted in US trademark law[14] and was "codified" in the Wine Pact and US legislation's recognition of "semi-generic" appellations. Having overruled the Examiner on those points, the Commissioner then decided to treat the matter as any other trademark application:

> It seems to me the only question requiring determination is whether it appears reasonably likely that people seeing the name "Calognac" on brandy will believe the brandy to be cognac; in other words whether "Calognac" will be reasonably likely to impress purchasers and the public as merely a corruption or a mere misspelling of the word "cognac" and to mean nothing else but cognac either descriptively or geographically or both.[15]

On the basis of evidence before him, the Commissioner affirmed the rejection of the opposition. He basically found that the addition of a syllable (in COLOGNAC and CALOGNAC) in particular "differs from the word 'Cognac'."[16] At least he had heard the case on the merits.

The matter was then submitted to what was to be its final level, the Court of Customs and Patent Appeals. This is where it becomes particularly important for our purposes, because the Court made a number of key findings that have informed certification mark cases up to the present day.

[12] Under Section 5 of the Trade-Mark Act of 1905, 15 U.S.C.A. § 85. The relevant portion read as follows: "Trade-marks which are identical with a registered or known trade-mark owned and in use by another and appropriated to merchandise of the same descriptive properties, or which so nearly resemble a registered or known trade-mark owned and in use by another and appropriated to merchandise of *the same descriptive properties as to be likely to cause confusion or mistake in the mind of the public or to deceive purchasers* shall not be registered." (Emphasis added.)

[13] 141 F.2d 706, at 707.

[14] The test is whether the "primary significance of the term in the minds of the consuming public is not the product but the producer." *Kellogg Co. v. National Biscuit Co.* 305 U.S. 111, 118 (1938).

[15] 141 F.2d 706, at 707.

[16] Cited in *ibid.* at 710.

First, in agreement with the Commissioner, the Court accepted the opposers' standing, noting that a "party, upon a showing of probable injury, might maintain an action for cancellation of a registered mark found to be descriptive."[17] Second, and more importantly, the Court accepted the opposers' evidence to justify their claim in a way that seemed to provide a solid normative grounding for their case:

"Cognac" is a name applied to a type of brandy distilled from wines made from grapes grown in a limited territorial region of France, often referred to as the Cognac district, the boundaries of which are defined by French law. . . . There is a certain quality in the soil of the region which gives to the grapes there grown a particular character or flavor, which enters into the brandy made from them, and that that quality of soil is not found elsewhere in France, nor, it is claimed, in any other part of the world. It is recognized as a superior brandy.[18]

Third, unlike the Commissioner, the Court considered the fact that specific US regulation of *labels* could be relevant in informing the trademark analysis, noting that Regulation No. 5 of the Federal Alcohol Administration of the Treasury Department[19] defined "Cognac" or "Cognac brandy" as "grape brandy distilled in the Cognac Region of France."[20]

Having thus situated the matter, the Court noted the "sui generis" nature of the case:

The peculiarity of the case grows out of the fact that "Cognac" is not claimed to be a technical trade-mark used as such, *or subject to exclusive ownership*. Appellee would have the right to use it in the same manner that appellant uses it – that is upon brandy imported from the Cognac region of France, but there is no claim on the part of appellee that it would be entitled to use it on domestically produced brandies or on any brandies other than that coming from the described region. *It is, in fact, a substantive name which for hundreds of years has meant brandy of a particular type.*[21]

Indeed, as I explain in greater detail below, it is in the nature of a certification mark that anyone who complies with the standard certified by the mark can use it. It is equally true that there is a "substantive" quality to a certification mark, a reputation built over a long period of time.[22]

It should come as no surprise that the Court disagreed with the Commissioner's factual conclusions. While the last words of the opinion

[17] 141 F.2d. 706, at 710. [18] 141 F.2d 706, at 708.
[19] Federal Alcohol Administration Act of August 29, 1935, 27 U.S.C. § 201 et seq., 27 U.S.C.A. § 201 et seq.
[20] *Ibid.* [21] 141 F.2d 709 (emphasis added).
[22] This is recognized in TRIPS, which does refer to the reputation associated with a GI. *See supra.*

seem to be borrowed from the same "syllable by syllable" analysis book as the Commissioner's, its outcome strikes me, as the excerpt below should show, as informed by the importance and value it attached earlier in the opinion to Cognac as a GI, and the applicants' apparent desire to free-ride on a well-known name:

> The application for its registration does not divide the term into syllables. The first letter of it, and the last four letters are identical with similar letters of Cognac. If the next two letters (A and L) were eliminated there would remain only the word Cognac. Certainly, the two terms are quite similar in appearance. *We are unable to escape the conclusion that appellee, whatever its motive, in trying to establish a trade-mark sought one as nearly like Cognac as it could find or coin*, and in adopting "Calognac" it certainly made a close approach.[23]

This takes us to our second case, four decades later. A highly inventive entrepreneur, perhaps having seen that applications for COLOGNAC and CALOGNAC had not been successful in the 1940s, applied for COLAGNAC, again for brandy.[24] The case evidently has strong similarities to the previous one but it was also different in part because the opposer was not a producer of Cognac but rather an entity responsible under French law for defending the word Cognac, that is, what, in *Spanish Champagne* parlance, could be described as the trustee or agent of the owners of the "collective goodwill" in the Cognac "brand."[25]

The 1946 Trademark (Lanham) Act with its specific provision for certification marks, had been adopted before the application at issue (but after the previous case). Indeed, one of the first steps taken by the Board was to note that certification marks were now defined in the statute and included marks used to denote a regional origin.[26] Additionally, the statute also contained a prohibition of the registration of a mark

[23] 141 F.2d 709 (emphasis added).

[24] *Bureau National Interprofessionnel du Cognac and Schieffelin & Co. v. International Better Drinks Corporation* 6 U.S.P.Q. 2d 1610 (Trademark Tr. & App. Bd. 1988). The application was filed in 1984.

[25] As described by the Board in its opinion, at *1: "[A]n interprofessional association having the status of a corporate body, created by decree in 1941 under the authority of the French Ministry of Agriculture and Ministry of Economy and Finance to oversee the protection of the term 'COGNAC' (as a designation for a type of brandy) and the interests of the 'COGNAC' trade, namely, the vintners, trading firms and various auxiliary professions."

[26] The terminology was new, but not the notion of a collectively owned mark. Section 62 of the Trade-mark Act of 1905 referred to standardization marks. The statute was amended in 1936 and again in 1938 to provide for registration of collective marks owned by foreign associations. *See* Registration of Collective Marks, 75th Congress, 3d session, Senate Report No. 1770 (1938). Some of these marks were used to denote a form of certification by the association.

which "when applied to the goods of the applicant, is primarily geographically descriptive or deceptively misdescriptive of them."[27]

As in *Spanish Champagne*, one can see GI building blocks being added to the previous (*Otard*) case by the Trademark Appeal Board. First, here again the Board quickly accepted the opposer's standing as defining a *common law certification mark*, a much clearer basis than in *Otard*:

> We believe it is clear that the designation "COGNAC" serves as a certification of regional origin, as well as of the quality of the brandy products entitled to bear the designation under French laws and regulations, which quality results from the use of the required type of grape, methods of distillation, aging conditions, etc. Moreover, under French law, opposer Bureau is responsible for certifying the genuineness of brandy bearing the designation "COGNAC" and for protecting the designation "COGNAC" as an appellation of origin. Under the circumstances, we are of the opinion that (as contended by opposer Bureau in its brief on the case) the term "COGNAC" is a common law regional certification mark controlled (but not used) by opposer Bureau (and that opposer Bureau is therefore entitled to rely upon it herein for purposes of its allegation of likelihood of confusion under Section 2(d) of the Act).[28]

The Board then turned to the substance of the opposition. The test was presented as follows, putting the focus squarely on the consumer:

> If a mark is the name of a place known generally to the public, purchasers who encounter goods bearing the mark would think that the goods originate in that place [i.e., purchasers would make a "goods-place association"] . . . the goods do not come from the named place, and the deception is material to the purchasing decision, the mark is deceptive under Section 2(a); if the deception is not material to the purchasing decision, the mark is primarily geographically deceptively misdescriptive under Section 2(e)(2) of the Act.[29]

The last step for the Board was simple enough. It referred to *Otard* and decided that the outcome should be the same here.

This leaves the third case, decided a decade later, which, factually, is closer to *Spanish Champagne* because the mark at issue was CANADIAN MIST AND COGNAC, that is, a direct use of the relevant GI (Cognac) by the trademark applicant.[30] The opposer, the *Institut National des Appellations d'Origine*, was also a "GI defending entity" as in the previous case. However, it was not just responsible to defend Cognac but indeed a vast number of protected wine and spirit appellations (GIs) in France.

[27] 15 U.S.C.A. § 1052(e)(2) (1946). [28] 6 U.S.P.Q. 2d 1614.

[29] 6 U.S.P.Q. 2d 1615.

[30] *Institut National des Appellations d'Origine v. Brown-Forman Corp.* 47 U.S.P.Q. 2d 1875 (Trademark Tr. & App. Bd. 1998). Apparently, the applicant's concoction actually contained some French brandy.

The opinion parallels the previous 1988 case. First, the Board was quick to accept COGNAC as a common law certification mark. Second, it also noted the protection of COGNAC under labeling regulations.[31] However, it added a significant stone to the construction of our 'GIs-as-certification-marks-edifice' in its clear finding that:

[I]f the use of a geographic designation is controlled and limited in such a manner that it reliably indicates to purchasers that the goods bearing the designation come exclusively from a particular region, then that term functions as a regional certification mark, just as a term which reliably indicates to purchasers that the goods come from a particular producer functions as a trademark ... [T]he issue is not whether the public is expressly aware of the certification function of the mark or the certification process underlying use of the mark, but rather is whether the public understands that goods bearing the mark come only from the region named in the mark. ... Neither the statute nor the case law requires that purchasers also be expressly aware of the term's certification function.[32]

The Board drew on well-accepted principles of trademark law. A consumer may not know exactly where or who the "source" of a product is, but when she has come to expect a certain quality or other feature, then that expectation creates goodwill which trademark law will protect. In economic terms, there would be a loss, and little obvious surplus created, by letting anyone make a product called "cognac" if the consumer used to "the real thing" was no longer able to find or identify it. This left the Board with a decision on the proper statutory ground for the opposition.[33] It rejected the part of the opposition claiming that the applicant for CANADIAN MIST AND COGNAC was trying falsely to suggest a connection with opposers under Section 2(a) of the Act.[34] The conclusion drawn here is rather technical: the opposer was not an *actual user* of the common law mark COGNAC. To win under Section 2(a), the opposers would have to show that there was an attempt to suggest a connection with *individual Cognac producers*, which the evidence did not demonstrate:

Opposers have not explained how applicant's mark CANADIAN MIST AND COGNAC, or even COGNAC alone, can point uniquely and unmistakably to each of these discrete entities, or to all of them, or to any of them.[35]

The Board then moved to the more common Section 2(d), which deals with likelihood of confusion with a pre-existing mark. More common

[31] Namely 27 CFR § 5.22(d)(2). [32] 47 U.S.P.Q. 2d 1875, at 1884.
[33] The appeal was heard on summary judgment and, therefore, without adducing additional evidence.
[34] 15 U.S.C.A. § 1052(a). [35] 47 U.S.P.Q. 2d 1875, at 1887.

perhaps, though not necessarily for certification marks. Still, the Board decided that the test was the same for all marks:

> There is nothing in the language of Section 2(d) which mandates or warrants application of one level of likelihood of confusion analysis . . . in cases where the plaintiff's mark is a trademark or service mark, but a different and more limited likelihood of confusion analysis in cases where the plaintiff's mark is a certification mark.[36]

In other words, deception (or a higher level of evidence) was unnecessary. Certification marks should be treated, for purposes of an infringement analysis, in the same way as ordinary trademarks.

The Board's conclusions are clear, and they were not arrived at by happenstance. In fact, the applicant had submitted rather forceful arguments why certification marks were different. His main argument was that, consistent with the nature of certification marks, the Board should apply a deceptiveness or misdescriptiveness analysis under Section 2(d) virtually identical to that used under Section 2(a) or Section 2(e)(1), rather than a traditional analysis of likelihood of confusion as to source or sponsorship, because the issue in Section 2(d) cases involving certification marks is the purchaser's confusion as to the nature of the goods, i.e., *whether they are certified or not*. Here, said the applicant, there was no confusion because the product did contain some real Cognac (i.e., the certified product). Put differently, he argued that there had to be an element of deception for the opposer to prevail, and failed.

My sense is that we are left, after the three *Cognac* cases, with the following "takeaway":

- US courts are prepared to recognize the quality or characteristics attributable to geographic origin as a form of collective goodwill.
- The previous point is reinforced by the protection of GIs on wines and spirits in specific labeling regulations.
- They are prepared to recognize agents of this collective goodwill as having a sufficient interest to defend their rights under the Lanham Act.
- The notion of certification mark is the proper vehicle to protect this form of collective goodwill.
- Certification marks exist also at common law.
- The test for infringement of (and, it seems, generally speaking as well) certification marks should otherwise be treated like all other marks.

[36] *Ibid.*, at 1891.

This also means that the normative claims of certification mark owners in GIs are rooted, like their trademark siblings, in confusion. Whether a particular symbol or word conveys primarily a geographic origin significance or not is, therefore, directly relevant. Logically, therefore, as consumers of wine, food and other "geographically determined" products understand information conveyed by food and wine labels better, they will also expect those labels to be accurate *when the information conveyed is perceived as denoting a geographical origin*. Geographic certification mark infringement should be subject to a dynamic legal test, for which a threshold might be crossed when the consumer search costs increase because the consumer is better informed about what a wine label conveys and finds information now perceived as geographical in nature confusing or inaccurate.[37] To quote Judge Rich, "Rights in this field do not stay put. They are like ocean beaches; they shift around. Public behavior may affect them."[38]

It is conceivable that what was primarily a generic identifier of a type of product would, in time, become a GI protected as a certification mark.[39] GIs could lead US consumers to become more discerning when buying wines based on their origin and may reduce the confusion (if any) in buying "champagne" not made in the Champagne region of France.[40]

Certification marks

The notion of collectively owned goodwill is not new. In his detailed study of certification marks,[41] Jeffrey Belson shows many marks owned by Guilds (but to be used by Guild members) dating back to 1420, such as those shown in Figure 6.1.

[37] *See* Margaret Ritzert, "Champagne is from Champagne: An Economic Justification for Extending Trademark-Level Protection to Wine-Related Geographical Indicators," 37 *AIPLA Q. J.* 191, 204–05 (2009).

[38] Rich J., "Trademark Problems as I See Them—Judiciary," 52 *Trademark Rep.* 1183, 1185 (1962).

[39] McCarthy noted this possibility of "resuscitation" of a once-generic symbol: "I believe that the door should remain open (even if only open slightly) to an assertion of trademark status in formerly generic names. The only purpose is to accommodate the rare and extraordinary event that a generic name over a period of years loses its generic significance and achieves trademark significance." 1 J. McCarthy, *McCarthy on Trademarks and Unfair Competition* (4th edn., Deerfield, IL: Clark Boardman Callaghan, 2012) § 12:47.

[40] For a similar point made with respect to French cheeses, *see* Ivy Doster, "A Cheese by Any Other Name: A Palatable Compromise to the Conflict over Geographical Indications," 59 *Vand. L. Rev.* 873, 898 (2006). *See also* Justin M. Waggoner, "Note, Acquiring a European Taste for Geographical Indications," 33 *Brook. J. Int'l L.* 569, 570 (2008).

[41] Jeffrey Belson, *Special Report: Certification Marks* (London: Sweet & Maxwell, 2002).

Figure 6.1: Traditional Coopers (Guild) Marks

The marks shown in Figure 6.1, belonging to the London Coopers, were registered at the London Guildhall in 1420. They were made of iron.[42] However, after the sixteenth century, when the monarchy and, later, Parliament increased their intervention in Guild affairs, the protection of marks was gradually taken over by wards and boroughs and later by uniform regulations throughout the realm.[43] The matter was, however, seen as trade regulation, not trademark law. Statutory changes in the UK would take long to recognize trademarks as including certification.[44]

The US picture is a little different. The *Cognac* cases discussed above show the willingness to recognize collective goodwill in the form of common law certification marks, starting with *Pillsbury-Washburn Flour Mills Co v. Eagle* in 1898.[45] In that case, the Court enjoined a Chicago company from using Minnesota on flour produced in Milwaukee, Wisconsin but advertised as made in Minneapolis. The Court accepted that there was deception because Minnesota producers had high standards and frequent inspections, which apparently was not the case in Wisconsin.[46]

[42] *See ibid.*, at 130. [43] *See ibid.*, at 8–9.

[44] *See ibid.*, at 11–12 and 20–21. *See also* Trade Marks Act 1994, s. 50 and Sched. 2, para. 3(2) (UK).

[45] [1898] Fed. Rep. 608. [46] [1898] Fed. Rep., at 611.

There are two key features of the modern notion of (registered) certification mark in Anglo-American systems. First, as with the Guild marks – which applied to goods and services offered by members of a Guild but not the Guilds themselves – the law precludes the owner from using the mark on the certified goods, in order to maintain the owner's independence as a certifier.[47] Second, and this would have likely been different with the Guilds, certification cannot be refused to anyone who complies with the standard.[48]

GIs as certification marks

GIs, like (all) marks, depend on reputation and associated goodwill. In the case of a geographic certification mark, that collective goodwill is linked to a region or locality. One of the central findings of *Spanish Champagne* was that the collective nature of the mark did not preclude relief for passing off. The progeny of the *Drinks* cases[49] was a shift from the need to have central quality control justifying the protection, to the current situation where *any affected producer* may file a claim in civil courts without having to show this level of control or agreement of the collective.[50] New Zealand courts have also been willing to protect French "Champagne" makers.[51] In the US, courts have generally taken a less liberal approach on the right of action by individual users, and thus given the holder of the certification mark more control.[52] The owner "acts as the representative of the mark users."[53]

Spanish Champagne and related cases also marked an extension of the scope of passing off. That extension was one of recognizing collective

[47] *See* Belson, *supra* note 41, at 32.

[48] *See ibid.* WIPO makes a similar point: "[C]ertification marks are given for compliance with defined standards, but are not confined to any membership. They may be granted to anyone who can certify that the products involved meet certain established standards. The internationally accepted 'ISO 9000' quality standards are an example of such widely-recognized certifications." WIPO, *About Trademarks*, available at http://bit.ly/1fpO5Vp (last visited January 14, 2013).

[49] *See supra* note 1.

[50] This shift is apparent in *John Walker & Sons Ltd v. Henry Ost & Co. Ltd* [1970] R.P.C. 489 (Eng. Ch. Div.); and *Erven Warnink Besloten Vennootschap v. J Townend & Sons (Hull) Ltd* (1979), [1979] AC 731, [1979] 5 F.S.R. 397, [1980] R.P.C. 31, [1979] 2 All ER 927, [1980] R.P.R. 31 (UK HL).

[51] For Canada and New Zealand, *see supra* note 1.

[52] For example, in *State of Idaho Potato Com'n. v. G & T Terminal Packaging, Inc.* 425 F.3d 708, 721–22, 76 U.S.P.Q. 2d 1835 (9th Cir. 2005), the Ninth Circuit found that selling genuine Idaho potatoes using the name IDAHO constituted counterfeiting of the certification mark IDAHO for potatoes because the mark owner did not have the opportunity to exercise quality control.

[53] *See* McCarthy, *supra* note 39, at § 19:92.50.

goodwill typically evidenced by the existence of a reputation. This reputational element is what is used to justify or at least explain the higher price sought by producers of GI goods in systems where GIs are protected by a *sui generis* regime. While cultural, historical and other differences between marks and *sui generis* GIs may remain, there are very few if any differences between geographic certification marks as used in the US that would require the existence of a *sui generis* regime to protect effectively what the TRIPS Agreement defines as a geographical indication.

There are a few issues that must be examined, however, before concluding that certification marks can be a valid bridge between the *sui generis* GI world and Anglo-American trademark systems. As a matter of trademark law, the owner of a certification mark – not the state – controls the certification standards.[54] Certification marks can be applied to wine produced in the Champagne region of France or to Cognac in accordance with methods approved for use there.[55] US examples of geographic certification marks include IDAHO POTATOES, PARMIGIANO-REGGIANO, ROQUEFORT, STILTON, REAL CALIFORNIA for cheese, PARMA for ham, DARJEELING for tea, WASHINGTON for apples, and the FLORIDA SUNSHINE TREE for citrus.[56]

So why would certification marks not be adequate to protect GIs? The possible reasons I found in the literature are: (a) the role of the state (or absence thereof) in enforcing certification marks; (b) transferability (e.g., by sale) of the certification mark; (c) the alleged greater value of GIs compared to marks; and (d) the better fit for traditional knowledge with GIs than certification marks. Let us consider each one briefly.

The role of the state in protecting GIs

GIs are commercial symbols. That is not to say that those who say GIs are not, or are "more than just" marks, do not have a point. At their most basic level, trademarks indicate the source or origin of a product or

[54] 15 U.S.C.A. § 1064(5)(A) (2006).

[55] *See* www.champagne.fr/en/alcoholic_fermentation.aspx (last visited November 20, 2012). *See also* Molly Torsen, "Apples and Oranges (and Wine): Why the International Conversation Regarding Geographic Indications is at a Standstill," 87 *J. Pat. & Trademark Off. Soc'y* 31, 48, 49 (2005).

[56] *See* Justin Hughes "Champagne, Feta, and Bourbon: The Spirited Debate About Geographical Indications," 58 *Hastings L. J.* 299, 310 (2006). A vast majority of certification marks in the US are not for geographic origin, however. They include marks registered by unions and various standardization bodies, such as Underwriters' Laboratories. *See* Belson, *supra* note 41, at 26–28.

service.[57] In the famous words of Learned Hand: "[A] trademark is not property in the ordinary sense, but only a word or symbol indicating the origin of a commercial product."[58] Do GIs actually do *more* or *something different*?

Perhaps the GI world can be mapped according to a division of labor. In the "common law world," protection against *false information* that a geographically incorrect indication might convey is a matter dealt with by individual trademark owners under trademark law, and occasionally by consumer protection agencies.[59] However, the Lanham Act also provides relief for false designation of origin quite apart from the rights of the owner of the certification mark.[60] In countries where Geographical Indications are protected by *sui generis* regimes, which consider GIs as better or as having higher status than ordinary trademarks, governmental authorities, sometimes in partnership with producer associations, monitor and enforce the proper use of the indication. It is this *conflation of roles* that seems to give GIs a special status in the realm of commercial symbols.[61] Collective goodwill may lead to issues of fiduciary, agency or

[57] At least, that is the traditional explanation. *See* McCarthy, *supra* note 39, at § 3:3: "[T]he proponent of trademark rights must show that this designation in and of itself serves the function of indicating the origin of the product – that is, that it functions as a 'trademark.' The prime question is whether the designation in question, as actually used, will be recognized in and of itself as an indication of origin for this particular product or service." (Notes omitted.)

[58] *Industrial Rayon Corp. v. Dutchess Underwear Corp.* 92 F.2d 33 (2d Cir. 1937), cert. denied, 303 U.S. 640, 82 L. Ed. 1100, 58 S. Ct. 610 (1938).

[59] Under section 5 of the Federal Trade Commission (FTC) Act in the US, the FTC is empowered to protect the public from "unfair methods of competition" and "unfair or deceptive acts or practices in or affecting commerce." 15 U.S.C.A. § 45(a)(2). As far as trademark law is concerned, one should say "perceived as incorrect" because the test is not objective correctness but rather consumer perception and the possible confusion/deception that might be present. However, trademark law is also relevant for two main reasons: first ¶ 43(a)(1)(B) of the Lanham Act (15 U.S.C.A. § 1115(a)(1)(B)) is not limited to trademark holders, second, ¶ 2(a) of the Act bars registration of geographically deceptive terms.

[60] As McCarthy notes: "The Eighth Circuit has held that § 43(a) embodies and carries forward the common law cases which permitted a group of manufacturers in a locality to assert the right to truthfully use a geographic designation as against a manufacturer who does not make the product in the named locality. This claim exists apart from any trademark or certification mark rights in plaintiff, for it is founded on the false advertising prong of § 43(a)." He is referring here to *Black Hills Jewelry Mfg. Co. v. Gold Rush, Inc.* 633 F.2d 746, 208 U.S.P.Q. 631 (8th Cir. 1980). McCarthy, *supra* note 39, at § 27:49.

[61] For example in Panama, under Panama Law No. 20 on the Special Intellectual Property Regime Upon the Collective Rights of Indigenous Communities for the Protection of their Cultural Identity and their Traditional Knowledge, Ley No. 20, of June 26, 2000, the state has a duty to protect certain GIs associated with traditional knowledge. This raises issues of guardianship and even expropriation. *See* Commonwealth of Aust. Dep't of Communications, Information Technology & the Arts, Report of the Contemporary

other rules to represent the collective owner of the mark/GI. Should the state own the right or exercise it? When it does, the difference between a GI and a mark is real, but it seems exaggerated to consider it as defining GIs qua GIs, for a number of reasons.

First, governmental authorities generally play a different role in trademark origination in civil and common law countries, yet both are indisputably protecting trademarks qua trademarks. "Under common law, trademarks come into existence through use. The United States' regime, thus, represents a so-called use-based system; whereas, the German system, adopting the civilian law, confers trademark rights upon registration."[62] In other words, the *ex ante* component found in civil law trademark regimes, and absent in the common law world where trademark protection evolved from the tort of passing off, already establishes a different role for government. Indeed, that difference in the role of the state in trademark issuance has not prevented the adoption of uniform rules such as those contained in the TRIPS Agreement.[63]

Second, the role of the state does not necessarily mean that GIs are more valuable because they are somehow better at quality control or assurance than trademarks. Trademarks can do that as well. As Justice Frankfurter noted in *Mishawaka Rubber & Woolen Mfg. Co. v. S.S. Kresge Co.*, a trademark "promotes honesty and comports with experience to assume that the wrongdoer who makes profits from the sales of goods bearing a mark belonging to another was enabled to do so because he was drawing upon the good will generated by that mark."[64] The goodwill that results from use of the mark may be described as the mental link that will be formed between a buyer's mind and the product or service (and, notionally at least, its "origin"). In common law jurisdictions, uses that infringe on the value of another's goodwill in commerce may be enjoined, independently of registration. As the two more recent *Cognac* cases show, an *unregistered* certification mark can be protected in the presence of consumer confusion. It can also be used to claim injunctive relief.[65]

Visual Arts and Crafts Inquiry 152 (2002), www.arts.gov.au/public_consultation/earlier-consultations/cvac_inquiry/report. The link between GIs and traditional knowledge is discussed more specifically at pp. 148–49 below.

[62] Rudi Rayle, "The Trend Towards Enhancing Trademark Owners' Rights – A Comparative Study of U.S. and German Trademark Law," 7 *J. Intell. Prop. L.* 227, 240 (2000)

[63] See Daniel Gervais, *The TRIPS Agreement: Drafting History and Analysis* (3rd edn., London, Sweet and Maxwell, 2008) 263–90.

[64] 316 U.S. 203, 207 (1942).

[65] *Florida v. Real Juices, Inc.* 330 F. Supp. 428 (M.D. Fla. 1971) (unregistered certification mark SUNSHINE TREE used to certify Florida citrus products).

Courts are a governmental authority. They form part of a quality control loop because they will punish a trademark holder who fails to maintain *any* quality control of its product (such as in cases of naked licensing) by deeming the mark abandoned.[66] As the Seventh Circuit noted in a recent opinion:

> There is no rule that trademark proprietors must ensure "high quality" goods – or that "high quality" permits unsupervised licensing. [. . .] The sort of supervision required for a trademark license is the sort that produces consistent quality. [. . .] How much control is enough? The licensor's self-interest largely determines the answer. Courts are apt to ask whether "the control retained by the licensor [is] sufficient under the circumstances to insure that the licensee's goods or services would meet the expectations created by the presence of the trademark."[67]

It is true, however, that, in the common law world, policing (including bringing a lawsuit against infringers) of geographic certification marks remains largely in private hands. In those jurisdictions, the role of the state (here, courts) in GI enforcement is *ex post*. The *ex ante* substantive determination by a governmental authority that a GI is justified by a special characteristic is thus a notable administrative difference – and one which may prompt GI holders to codify their practices to convince such authority. However, presumably the holder of *any* trademark (and in particular a certification mark) wants to develop the same degree of credibility in the marketplace as the GI user.[68] In addition, the Lanham Act does link registration of a certification mark with the applicant's ability to control quality.

Section 4 of the Act provides that such marks are registrable by persons "*exercising legitimate control over the use* of the marks sought to be registered."[69] Applicants "are also required to furnish a copy of the standards to demonstrate how they exercise control over the use of the mark and to establish that they are, in fact, engaged in a certification program."[70] Then, those marks shall be entitled to protection "when used so as to represent falsely that the owner or a user thereof makes or sells the goods

[66] *General Motors Corp. v. Gibson Chemical & Oil Corp.* 786 F.2d 105 (2d Cir. 1986) also comes to mind: "The critical question in determining whether a licensing program is controlled sufficiently by the licensor to protect his mark is whether the licensees' operations are policed adequately to guarantee the quality of the products sold under the mark." A progressive lowering of standards is much less likely to result in a finding of abandonment, however.

[67] *Eva's Bridal Ltd v. Halanick Enterprises, Inc.* 639 F.3d 788, 790 (7th Cir. 2011).

[68] Indeed, a "certification mark is symbolic of a guarantee or the meeting of certain standards." 1 McCarthy, *supra* note 39, at § 4:16.

[69] 15 U.S.C.A. §1054 (emphasis added).

[70] Terry E. Holtzman, "Certification Marks: An Overview," 81 *Trademark Rep.* 180, 192 (1991).

or performs the services on or in connection with which such mark is used."[71] Finally, the US statute also provides that a petition to cancel a registration may be filed "in the case of a certification mark on the ground that the registrant *does not control, or is not able legitimately to exercise control* over, the use of such mark."[72]

In sum, it seems to me that, while the process is different, the outcomes are comparable. The difference in the role played by the state does not strike me as somehow proving the fundamentally or ontologically different nature of GIs.[73] In both cases (whether marks or GIs as *sui generis* symbols), what matters in the end is the quality of the "certifier" (the perceived origin of the good or service in the case of a mark or the organization ensuring the integrity of the certification mark or GI) and its ability to convince the public that the GI or certification mark does certify an origin perceived to add value to the product.

Transferability

Rules that favor transferability of trademarks without the transfer of the entity identified as the "origin" of the product are recent.[74] Traditionally, the goodwill generated by and attached to a mark was seen as existing symbiotically with the mark and thus could not be separated.[75] Rules prescribing transferability now abound, and in certain cases (for example if all the necessary know-how is transferred and quality remains the same) transferability is contingent on maintaining the semiotic function of the mark in the consumer's mind.[76] For that reason, transferability of

[71] 15 U.S.C.A. § 1054. [72] 15 U.S.C.A. § 1064(5) (emphasis added).

[73] This has been described as being in "stark contrast" to the US system. *See* Emily Nation, "Geographical Indications: The International Debate over Intellectual Property Rights for Local Producers," 82 *U. Colo. L. Rev*. 959, 990 (2011). However, the government is involved in seizure of counterfeit goods at the border and criminal prosecution of trademark counterfeiters. The real issue is the *ex ante* determination and "seal of quality" that it provides. Ironically, when the US government does certify the quality or other characteristic of a product, it uses a mark to do so (e.g., USDA Organic). *See* Michelle Traher, "USDA Organic Certification for the Innovative Farmer," 19 *J. Contemp. Legal Issues* 254, 255 (2010).

[74] Mark A. Greenfield, "Goodwill as a Factor in Trademark Assignments – A Comparative Study," 60 *Trademark Rep*. 173, 173–74 (1970).

[75] *Comm'rs of Inland Revenue v. Muller & Co.'s Margarine Ltd* [1901] AC 217, 22: "For goodwill has no independent existence. It cannot subsist by itself. It must be attached to a business. Destroy the business and the goodwill perishes with it."

[76] As Calboli explains: Article 6*quater* ... rather than plainly stating that misleading assignments are invalid, ... stated that these agreements may be considered invalid. Despite this awkward language, the question was solved by Article 10*bis* of the Paris Convention, which forbids any act that could mislead consumers, including deceptive or confusing trademark assignments, as acts of unfair competition." (Notes omitted.) Irene

a GI (linked to a specific geographic origin) may not be possible. A contract could not validly state that "Champagne" (as protected and defined under the French Appellation of Origin system, essentially a subset of GIs) may be made in Morocco or New Zealand.[77] Yet, *any* trademark transfer or license is tricky. Indeed, the transfer of many certification marks[78] would be as nonsensical as Champagne made in Bordeaux ("Wisconsin" cheese made in Louisiana?[79]). Again, this strikes me as a distinction between trademark law and *sui generis* GI regimes without a substantive difference.

The (greater) value of GIs

Both trademarks and GIs (if perceived as *sui generis* symbols) can influence behavior and consumption patterns. This is especially true when demand is elastic, as is typical with more expensive and luxury goods.[80] A GI allows the producer relying on that elastic nature to incorporate the value perceived by the consumer in buying a good made in *x* into the product.[81] While I fully accept this, is this fundamentally different from paying *y* more for a bag because it bears the Louis Vuitton mark? *All marks* may contain information designed to appeal visually or otherwise to modify a purchasing decision, two functions that Catherine Ng has called informational and magnetic value, respectively.[82] "Champagne" might be seen as an information-conveying sign ("this wine is from the Champagne region of France") *and* as a sign with magnetic value ("I am getting the real thing and am willing to pay more for it"). Naturally, a GI *must* have informational value (because it identifies a specific region), but arguably a trademark must as well because to exist as a trademark it must link a product or service (mentally) to its perceived "origin."

Calboli, "Trademark Assignment 'With Goodwill': A Concept Whose Time Has Gone," 57 *Fla. L. Rev.* 771, 818 (2005).

[77] *See* www.inao.gouv.fr; and James E. Wilson, *Terroir: The Role of Geology, Climate and Culture in the Making of French Wines* (Berkeley, University of California Press, 1998).

[78] The term "certification mark" in the Lanham Act means any word, name, symbol, or device, or any combination thereof: "(1) used by a person other than its owner, or (2) which its owner has a bona fide intention to permit a person other than the owner to use in commerce and files an application to register on the principal register [...] to certify regional or other origin, [...] or other characteristics of such person's goods or services or that the work or labor on the goods or services was performed by members of a union or other organization." Lanham Act § 45, 15 U.S.C.A. § 1127.

[79] *See* US certification marks 1548738; 1548739; 2964548 and 77205580.

[80] *See* Ritzert, *supra* note 37, at 209–10. [81] *See ibid.*, at 217–19.

[82] *See* Catherine Ng, "A Common Law of Identity Signs," 20 *Int. Prop. J.* 177, 221–22 (2007).

Recent research also suggests that GI protection may impact global food consumption patterns and lead to shifts in agricultural models.[83] However, surely all trademarks have the ability to guide consumers. I am not only referring here to product marks (e.g. COCA-COLA®) but also to certification and collective marks that indicate that a product is organic or kosher, for example.

GIs, like (all) marks, undeniably can increase the value of a product in the market and exponentially increase the profits, in particular if there is not a huge difference in production costs.[84] This, in turn, translates into much higher land value where production under a protected GI or a geographic certification mark is allowed.[85] Indeed the same has happened to US regions producing products associated with a geographic certification mark in high demand, such as NAPA for wines, FLORIDA for orange juice, and VIDALIA for onions produced in Eastern Georgia.[86]

Cultural resources and traditional knowledge

The supposed greater linkages between GIs and culture than is the case with other marks are not an altogether convincing narrative. Andy Warhol's use of soup cans[87] and the many artists who have used iconic

[83] *See* Elizabeth Barham, "Translating *Terroir*: The Global Challenge of French AOC Labelling," 19 *J. of Rural Stud.* 127, 128 (2003) ("Most authors identify origin labeled products as important manifestations of 'local,' 'quality,' or 'endogenous' food systems. They are seen as contributing to the 'consumer turn' which may portend major shifts in the conventional agricultural model. Gilg, in fact, estimates that as global agricultural production differentiates into a bipolar system of high volume 'day-to-day' foods produced and distributed by multinational corporation and lower volume niche or specialty products such as those produced under labels of origin, the latter category could come to account for as much as 30 percent of overall food sales due to their higher value" (notes omitted). The reference to Gilg is to Andrew Gilg, *Countryside Planning: The First Half Century* (2nd edn., New York, Routledge, 1996) 71.

[84] This is not binary. A producer of GI-related products may have to follow additional quality control etc. steps that may increase production cost. But if the cost of production of bubbly wine goes from $5 to, say, $7 to benefit from the CHAMPAGNE GI, but the sale price goes from $15 to $45, then profit is increased by 380% ($10 to $38).

[85] *See* Thiébault Dromard, "Le champagne en quête de nouvelles terres," *Le Figaro*, December 17, 2007, available at www.lefigaro.fr/vins/2007/10/26/05008-20071026ARTFIG00048-le-champagne-en-quete-de-nouvelles-terres.php. According to this article, the price of a hectare of land (approximately 2.5 acres) moving from outside to inside the appellation zone would jump by 35,000% to almost $1,500,000.

[86] Napa is an interesting case study. The property lies within the larger Napa Valley AVA, American Viticultural Area, or appellation. The Napa Valley AVA encompasses the entire 300,000 acres of Napa County. Approximately ten percent of this land is utilized as vineyards. Within the Napa Valley AVA and its 240 wineries, the microclimates are distinctive. Due to these differences, the Napa Valley AVA has been further subdivided into fourteen sub-appellations.

[87] CAMPBELL'S of course.

marks in their work, and those that people proudly wear on T-shirts, bags, etc. make a strong case that trademarks are powerful cultural memes in the same way, perhaps even more so, than CHAMPAGNE, GRUYÈRE or CHIANTI.

One might counter that GIs tend to be older and rooted in the *land*. That point is valid, but again it should not be overemphasized. While GIs can symbolize the link between a product and its geographical origin, they often depend (to be worth protecting) on the existence of a reputation, and decades or centuries may be necessary to establish one in the relevant public's eye, just as trademarks also grow with use. In fact, many countries and international instruments recognize well-known/famous marks and protect them more than ordinary marks.[88]

Historically, a number of GIs, especially those linked with land seen as "*terroir*" or traditional knowledge, may have deeper roots than most ordinary trademarks. The *terroir* implicates a certain emotional resonance in Europe and runs deep. Indeed, it is not an exaggeration to say that it is sometimes linked to national identity.[89] This may explain why traditional knowledge holders increasingly argue that GIs might protect part of their special relationship to their land.[90] Politically, it is also relevant that GIs on many food products are based in the developing world and often owned by women.[91] However, the exploitation and protection of GIs is unlikely to be a capacious vehicle for this deep history, unless it can be communicated to and understood by consumers of different cultural backgrounds, especially internationally.

This normative undergirding of GI is subject to other theoretical challenges. As illustrated in *Otard* above, people can move (outside the region), taking their know-how with them, though not the physical link

[88] Paris Convention for the Protection of Industrial Property, Art. 6*bis*.

[89] Some readers may be familiar with José Bové and his popular campaign against American fastfood chains, globalization, genetically modified food and a few other worthy causes. *See* David Downie, "Let Them Eat Big Macs," Salon.com, July 6, 2000, available at www.salon.com/business/feature/2000/07/06/frenchfood/index.html.

[90] *See* Teshager Worku Dagne, "Law and Policy on Intellectual Property, Traditional Knowledge and Development: Protecting Creativity and Collective Rights in Traditional Knowledge Based Agricultural Products Through Geographical Indications," 11 *Estey J. of Int'l L. & Trade Pol.* 78–127 (2010).

[91] On the developing countries' interest, *see* Justin Hughes, "Coffee and Chocolate – Can We Help Developing Country Farmers Through Geographical Indications?" (2010), available at http://papers.ssrn.com/sol3/papers.cfm?abstract_id=1684370. On the gender-related issues of GIs in the developing world, *see* Terra L. Gearhart-Serna, "Women's Work, Women's Knowing: Intellectual Property and the Recognition of Women's Traditional Knowledge," 21 *Yale J. L. & Feminism* 372, 401–02 (2010).

between place and product.[92] Indeed, allowing producers in other regions to produce and use the GI on their product may, under various doctrines such as acquiescence or laches, lead to a loss of right and possibly genericide.[93] That very case has been made against protecting "Champagne."[94] Overall, however, while there may be a higher degree of connection between GIs and the land and certain forms of traditional knowledge, the similarity in *acquiring value through time and use* is very strong. In my view, it does not justify in and by itself a *sui generis* regime, especially for products like wine whose commercial value (as any other product) may be greater than the traditional and/or cultural value. Finally, I would go back to Andy Warhol and underscore the deep cultural resonance of at least certain famous marks.

Looking ahead

The historical and cultural roots of GIs have led a number of countries to want to play a greater role in their recognition. They tend to emphasize their higher normative profile compared to other commercial symbols. At bottom, the argument is that the collective goodwill of a region (however its producers are represented and manage the use of the GI) has intrinsically a higher value than the goodwill associated with a normal commercial trademark. This is not because trademarks cannot recognize collective goodwill; they do.[95] Just not *that kind* of goodwill.

Indeed, other than well-known marks, GIs in Europe trump normal trademarks. For example, Torres is a well-known Spanish producer of wine. Some of its trademark registrations for TORRES date back almost one hundred years.[96] In the early 1990s, Portugal registered TORRES as

[92] Arguably, the more human factors are involved, the weaker is the rationale for protecting a GI only in a specified region. *See* Kal Raustiala and Stephen R. Munzer, "The Global Struggle over Geographic Indications," 18 *Eur. J. Int'l L.* 337, 353 (2007).

[93] A major point of contention in international negotiations is precisely genericide. Under the Lisbon Agreement for the Protection of Appellations of Origin and their International Registration ("Lisbon Agreement"), 923 UNTS 205 (October 31, 1958), genericide is only possible if the GI has become generic *in the country of origin*. *See* Gervais, "Reinventing Lisbon", *supra* note 2, at 99–100.

[94] "One can compare the results for aspirin to the results for champagne. As a result of genericide, when competing producers of the same type of painkiller called their product "aspirin," Bayer lost the exclusive right to the name. Champagne is already a generic or descriptive term." Deborah J. Kemp and Lynn M. Forsythe, "Trademarks and Geographical Indications: A Case of California Champagne," 10 *Chap. L. Rev.* 257, 267–68 (2006). As between the EU and the US, the matter was resolved under the Wine Pact. *See infra* note 104.

[95] As with certification marks.

[96] *See* Nina Resinek, "Geographical Indications and Trade Marks: Coexistence or 'First in Time, First in Right' Principle," 29 *Eur. Int. Prop. Rev.* 446, 449 (2007).

a protected GI under Articles 40(2) and (3) of EC Regulation 2392/89.[97] Under the absolute priority principle (that is, GIs trump pre-existing marks), the Spanish producer would have had to abandon a reputable trademark, causing untold damage to its goodwill and revenue. The Regulation at issue was later amended to allow for co-existence, for well-known "brands" that predate the official recognition of the appellation by at least twenty-five years.[98]

However, this is not unique to GIs. For example, the Olympic marks trump other marks under a special US statute.[99] In a famous example of how those statutes are applied, "[t]wo teachers took students, who had Coca-Cola in their lunches, to a cricket match – Pepsi was the event's official sponsor. Event officials would not permit the students' 'entry until they peeled off the Coca-Cola labels and scraped off the logos from all the bottle tops and lids.'"[100]

The EU has argued that higher *sui generis* protection for GIs is not harmful. EU negotiators have used the Cava example to argue that having to stay away from a GI like Champagne has not caused harm to Spanish producers of (now) Cava wines.[101] They note that Cava wine consumption has increased in France after Cava producers were no

[97] Council Regulation (EEC) No. 2392/89 of 24 July 1989 laying down general rules for the description and presentation of wines and grape musts (OJ L 232, 09/08/1989 pp. 0013–0039).

[98] *See* Art. 1(7) of Council Regulation (EEC) No. 3897/91 of 16 December 1991 amending for the third time Regulation (EEC) No 2392/89 laying down general rules for the description and presentation of wines and grape musts (OJ L 368, 31.12.1991, pp. 5–6).

[99] The Ted Stevens Amateur Sports Act (ASA) "grants the US Olympic Committee (USOC) an almost absolute right to control the use of any Olympic-related words, marks, mottos or insignia by others." Edward Vassallo, et al., "An International Look at Ambush Marketing," 95 *Trademark Rep.* 1338, 1350 (2005). Like many *sui generis* GI regimes, the ASA does not require the USOC to show any likelihood of confusion. Canada, China, Greece, Italy and Australia, to name just a few have similar legislation. *See* Ari J. Sliffman, "Unconstitutional Hosting of the Super Bowl: Anti-Ambush Marketing Clean Zones' Violation of the First Amendment," 22 *Marq. Sports L. Rev.* 257, 267 (2011).

[100] *Ibid.* at 268. Those special Olympic mark statutes do not protect the trademark holders (such as Coca-Cola or Pepsi in this example) directly, but rather as official Olympic sponsors.

[101] General Council Trade Negotiations Committee, Note by the Secretariat: Issues Related to the Extension of the Protection of Geographical Indications Provided for in Article 23 of the TRIPS Agreement to Products other than Wines and Spirits P 9, WT/GC/W/546 (May 18, 2005), at 47–48 and 63 [hereinafter "Extension Note"]. *See also* Hughes, "Champagne, Feta, and Bourbon," *supra* note 56, at 369 ("Have Champagne district sparkling wine sales displaced Spanish sparkling wine sales in Spain? Have Cava sales dropped in the rest of Europe? The answer to each question looks to be no."); and Leigh Ann Lindquist, "Champagne or Champagne? An Examination of U.S. Failure to Comply with the Geographical Provisions of the TRIPS Agreement," 27 *Ga. J. Int'l & Comp. L.* 309, 312–13 (1999).

longer to indicate it was made like champagne.[102] This is a possible reply to the US negotiators who fear that banning a list of terms such as parmesan, asiago, camembert, edam, feta, gouda, balsamic vinegar, kalamata olives, and pilsner might threaten US producers of goods using those terms.[103] Clearly, beyond the normative and theoretical issues at play, there are billions of real dollars at stake.[104]

How can we move the international ball forward? The US prefers a trademark approach, and the "first in time, first in right" approach.[105] The TRIPS Agreement allows countries to pick this system and the analysis above supports the use of geographic certification marks to protect what Article 22.1 of the TRIPS Agreement defines as "Geographical Indications."[106] Under such a system, the *Torres* case could not happen because the mark owner was there before the GI emerged.[107] Under a trademark regime, the first user (almost always) wins.[108]

[102] *See* "L'Espagne effervescente en France," *Vins Magazine*, no. 45 (Winter 2002), at 16.

[103] Extension Note, *supra* note 101, at 47. PILSNER was the first GI registered under the Lisbon Agreement.

[104] *See* Frances G. Zacher, "Comment, Pass the Parmesan: Geographic Indications in the US and the European Union – Can There Be Compromise?," 19 *Emory Int'l L. Rev.* 427, 434 (2005). In various doomsday scenarios that seem to inform US negotiators' positions, "American producers like Kraft and Anheuser-Busch predict enormous losses resulting, in part, from disruptive relabeling and remarketing campaigns if existing products become subject to stricter regulations." Nation, *supra* note 73, at 992. The US position is indeed that GI protection (beyond wines and spirits, a matter mostly dealt with under the EU–US Wine Pact, is that GIs would "create chaos and simply prove unmanageable." "That's a Fine Chablis You're Not Drinking: The Proper Place for Geographical Indications in Trademark Law," 17 *Fordham Intell. Prop. Media & Ent. L. J.* 933, 944 (2007). On the Wine Pact, *see supra* note 2. While one could dispute the major losses, the immediate gains for those companies are harder to see. The interest of US GI-based production and other trade interests would have to be factored into any negotiation.

[105] "The first user, then, to appropriate and use a particular mark – the 'senior' user – generally has priority to use the mark to the exclusion of any subsequent – or junior – users." *Emergency One, Inc. v. American Fire Eagle Engine Co., Inc.* 332 F.3d 264, 268 (4th Cir. 2003). *See also Ford Motor Co. v. Summit Motor Products, Inc.* 930 F.2d 277, 292 (3d Cir. 1991).

[106] *See* Gervais, "Reinventing Lisbon", *supra* note 2, at 105–06. Concerning first in time under the Lisbon Agreement, *see ibid.*, at 97.

[107] *See* Andrew Simpson, Christine James and Michael Grow, Report – Question – Q191: The Relationship between Trademarks and Geographical Indications: Report of the US Group, AIPPI Report 11 (2006), available at www.aippi-us.org/images/AIPPI-Q191 (2006)(2).DOC.

[108] Under US law, there is a limited exception for a junior registered user vis-à-vis a senior unregistered user. Essentially, the senior user/nonregistrant may retain exclusive rights only in the area of its actual use and its zone of natural expansion. *See Wrist-Rocket Mfg. Co. v. Saunders Archery Co.* 578 F.2d 727 (8th Cir. 1978).

This leaves legacy issues with use of European and other GIs in the US. As I mentioned above, there may well be cases where what was a generic descriptor may acquire dual meaning (that is, be also seen as a GI by consumers). If that second GI use becomes predominant, a GI symbol might emerge from the ashes of a generic commercial term, and the protection might even be tailored to recognize the dual use. It is extremely rare for a genericized trademark to be restored to trademark status, though it does happen: "In the entire history of American trademark law, the courts have held that only two terms that had been generic names were reclaimed from the public domain by a change in public usage to become protectable trademarks: SINGER for sewing machines and (arguably) GOODYEAR for rubber products."[109] However, that may be more likely to happen for geographic certification marks. Indeed, it seems fair to suggest that foreign GIs known in the US for a variety of reasons (international travel, advertising, etc.), which are currently "generic" might acquire goodwill which could then entitle them to certification mark status, assuming of course that the public correctly learns the lesson that the mark owner is endeavoring to impart.

A second issue is the need (to comply with the TRIPS Agreement) to protect certain GIs, namely those used in connection with wines and spirits.[110] Even in the absence of consumer confusion, that is beyond the traditional confines of trademark law. In the US, a non-trademark solution has been found, as mentioned already, by using US Bureau of Alcohol, Tobacco, Firearms and Explosives (ATF) regulations (labels).[111]

As a normative matter, however, and beyond such considerations, a common law jurisdiction should find it easier to transition to a GI-friendly legal environment by staying within the more capacious bounds of trademark law.[112] It brings with it the dynamic nature of consumer perceptions and thus avoids putting the protection cart before the

[109] McCarthy, note 39 *supra*, at § 12:30. McCarthy also noted that the Federal Circuit had adopted the view that a generic name can change its meaning, "holding that the proponent of trademark rights in 'opry' as a mark for country western shows could prove that the term had been reclaimed from public domain status since the Eighth Circuit had held eight years previous that 'opry' was a generic name for such shows." *Ibid.*

[110] Art. 23.1 of the TRIPS Agreement.

[111] *See* note 3 *supra*. *See also* Jacques Audier, "International Institutions and Accords," in Richard Mendelson, *Wine in America: Law and Policy* (New York, Aspen Publishers, 2011), 438.

[112] I am relying here not only on Dr. Gangjee's chapter in this book (Chapter 5) but also his previous work. *See* Dev Gangjee, "Quibbling Siblings: Conflicts Between Trademarks and Geographical Indications," 82 *Chi.-Kent L. Rev.* 1253, 1254–57 (2007). *See also* Kemp and Forsythe, *supra* note 94.

perception horse. At any given point in time, some consumers will have transitioned in their perception of a generic term to its GI meaning, and others will not.[113]

Let us separate prospective buyers into two groups. Let us call them *cognoscenti* and *ignorami*. The societal costs to be borne here and the related externalities that should matter are those imposed on the *cognoscenti* by allowing the *ignorami* to expect to find the terms they perceive as generic versus the costs imposed on *ignorami* for letting the *cognoscenti* purchase products on which they can trust the information they perceive to be geographical in nature.

There is not necessarily a single, simple solution to this problem. One could do math and wait for a 50 percent (or other more or less arbitrary) threshold to be crossed by the army of *cognoscenti* and tip the scales in their favor, as in the predominant use cases. Alternatively, one could posit that the *cognoscenti* know more – including the fact that the information on labels is transitioning from product to origin description– so that disclaimers or other methods could be employed to allow dual use (that is, both as indicating type and source) to continue. This may leave courts in a bind because there will be a likelihood of confusion at both ends. It may be easier to solve confusion at the *cognoscenti* end by using devices such as disclaimers, as already noted. Perhaps that is a viable solution, until the army of *ignorami* is so decimated that the issue with respect to a given product disappears.[114]

My point is not to pick one of these (or indeed other possible) solutions. Rather, my point is that by staying within a uniform system (trademark law), we leave it to courts to decide when the adequate threshold has been crossed with respect to a specific product. In other words, it may be easier if the battle is fought within the trademark system in "countries in transition" towards better GI protection rather than between two separate systems, that is, by introducing a new, *sui generis* GI regime.

What the *Spanish Champagne* and *Cognac* cases have shown is that trademark law can accommodate the form of collective goodwill (in the US, as registered or unregistered certification marks) that GIs aim to protect. A *sui generis* system is simply not required.[115] Hard questions

[113] Which seems to justify (*ex post* perhaps) the use of a term such as semi-generic, which otherwise seems ontologically warped.

[114] The Wine Pact's approach to grandfather users (that is, not to allow new users) is arguably a step towards that result, but education of the consuming public may work best.

[115] Indeed, in proposing a protocol to the Lisbon Agreement – an option that WIPO is now pursuing – I had indicated that the Lisbon Agreement did not require a *sui generis* system. *See* Gervais, "Reinventing Lisbon", *supra* note 2, at 87–89.

remain on the management of collective goodwill in traditional knowledge and innovation. Those may take longer to solve because the matter is not just one of registration and allowing commercial producers to defend their rights, individually or collectively. The debate is also infused with broader questions of sovereignty and recognition of "past sins" in a postcolonial context. The fact that this comment is about Champagne and Cognac, elite products from a Western nation, should not escape us. It informs how law may protect forms of collective goodwill, but it does not provide a complete answer.

Part IV

Design protection

7 The Fashion Originators' Guild of America: Self-help at the edge of IP and antitrust

*C. Scott Hemphill and Jeannie Suk**

Women do not buy hats. They buy fashion. ... Virtually their sole purpose is to make the wearer happy in the thought that she has a beautiful thing which is in fashion. ... Men may joke, but it is this curious quality of "fashion" which sells hats, and is, therefore, of great economic value.[1]

The question of intellectual property for fashion design has attracted enormous public attention in recent years. One reason is fashion's economic importance as a global business. Another is that fashion design presents an "edge" case for United States' intellectual property, as fashion design lacks the robust copyright protection accorded to other types of creative activity.[2] A third is the outlier status of the United States among countries with fully developed intellectual property regimes in withholding protection for fashion design. These features have given rise to renewed calls for protection, and active consideration of various legislative schemes to achieve that goal.[3]

The question whether to protect fashion design from copying has a storied past. Since 1914 there have been more than eighty proposals in Congress to provide protection for design. In the 1930s, as American fashion was coming into its own as a cultural force, designers worried

* We are grateful to Sara Marcketti for helpful insights, and to Terry Fisher and participants in the Intellectual Property at the Edge conference for valuable comments. We received excellent research assistance from Sam Birnbaum, Chrissy Calogero, Alex Chen, Ashley Chung, Sean Driscoll, Derek Fischer, Adam Goodman, Shane Hunt, Annie Liang, Christina Ma, Sonia McNeil, Ashley Nyquist, Sean O'Neill, Justin Patrick, Graham Philips, Krysten Rosen, Shivan Sarin, Eden Schiffmann, Lauren Schloss, Matthew Schmitten, Elizabeth Stork, Marissa Weinrauch, Crystal Yang, and Sunshine Yin. Many thanks to Janet Katz in the Harvard Law School Library, and librarians at the Fashion Institute of Technology and National Archives, for help in navigating archival materials.

1 *Millinery Creators' Guild, Inc. v. FTC*, 312 U.S. 469 (1941) (No. 251), 1940 WL 46567, Brief for Petitioners, at 3.

2 For a critique of this discrepancy see C. Scott Hemphill & Jeannie Suk, "The Law, Culture, and Economics of Fashion," 61 *Stan. L. Rev.* 1147 (2009).

3 Innovative Design Protection and Piracy Prevention Act of 2011: Hearing before the Subcomm. on Intellectual Property, Competition, and the Internet of the H. Comm. on the Judiciary, 112th Cong. (2011) (statement of Jeannie Suk).

about knockoffs. Then, as now, they lacked intellectual property protection for original fashion designs. In 1930, the Vestal Design Copyright Bill proposed copyright protection for industrial patterns, shapes, and forms, which would have covered designers of fashion and other useful articles. The Bill was never enacted, mainly due to concerns that it was too difficult to determine whether one design infringed another.[4]

Fashion designers were discouraged by the rampant practice of design copying. Copies were often sold at a fraction of the price, even in the same stores as the originals. Although today the near-singular focus of fashion law reform is legislative reform, designers in the 1930s pursued a range of possible solutions in their attempt to stop those who reproduced their designs and undermined their profitability by selling cheaper copies. Then, as now, designers sought legislative protection. But they also pursued a regulatory solution, as part of New Deal responses to the Great Depression. They ultimately settled on a seemingly effective but controversial solution: a set of self-help measures targeting both copyists and retailers willing to merchandise knockoffs.

The resulting boycott, devised by the Fashion Originators' Guild of America (hereinafter the "Guild"), was arguably the "largest scale private intellectual property scheme ever implemented."[5] At its height, a staggering 4,000 new designs were protected each month.[6] The designers' organized efforts at self-help to create design protection eventually gave rise to antitrust lawsuits in federal and state courts, culminating in a pair of 1941 Supreme Court cases involving dresses and hats.[7]

This chapter tells the story of the Depression-era fashion designers, and the solutions they pursued to remedy the lack of intellectual property protection for their work. It describes the Guild's formation and activities within the social, economic, and legal context of the Depression, and the fatal government scrutiny that eventually led to the Guild's demise. Finally, it suggests some lessons as to both means and ends drawn from this story of fashion: about self-help as a private solution to a public lack on the one hand, and about intellectual property protection for design on the other.

***

[4] Steven Wilf, "The Making of the Post-War Paradigm in American Intellectual Property Law," 31 *Colum. J. L. & Arts* 139, 186–87 (2008).

[5] Jonathan Barnett et al., "The Fashion Lottery: Cooperative Innovation in Stochastic Markets," 39 *J. Legal Stud.* 159 (2010).

[6] Thomas F. Conroy, "Guild's Work Good in Upper Brackets," *N. Y. Times*, Feb. 23, 1936, at N17.

[7] *Fashion Originators' Guild of Am., Inc. v. FTC*, 312 U.S. 457 (1941) [hereinafter *FOGA*]; *Millinery Creators' Guild, Inc. v. FTC*, 312 U.S. 469 (1941).

"The King of Fashion" was the title Maurice Rentner gave himself.[8] Seventh Avenue also called him "The Dean," perhaps because most of the garment industry's top executives had at some point worked for him. "Napoleon" was another moniker, which apparently referred to his slight but elegant stature at five feet four inches.[9]

Rentner's Polish Jewish family had arrived in New York in 1902 when he was thirteen.[10] New York was already the center of a garment industry peopled largely by the influx of immigration.[11] As industrialization saw the move from homemade to factory-made clothing, Rentner began work as an errand boy delivering thread for shirtwaists, and then as a traveling salesman of children's clothing. In his twenties, Rentner bought a glove business that grew to become Maurice Rentner, Inc., a high-end producer of ladies' apparel, with six factories to its name. By World War I, Rentner had grown the company into a significant fashion house whose elegant gowns were sold only in exclusive stores like Bonwit Teller, I. Magnin, and Lord & Taylor. Rentner wanted his dresses to be "quietly expensive." French *haute couture* was the model.[12]

After World War I, the apparel industry expanded rapidly. In the 1920s fashion's visibility rose as increasing ease of communication and transportation diffused "big-city" fashion. Rentner began to turn away from Seventh Avenue's reliance on Paris as the Mecca for fashion design. He became a pioneer in American ready-to-wear, daring to produce designs rather than simply continue to copy from Paris models. As American ready-to-wear shifted, Rentner was among the first American manufacturers to develop in-house designers. He was known for well-crafted but uncomplicated silhouettes with unexpected detailing in sumptuous fabrics, in a casual but graceful mode that combined style and comfort. Rentner disseminated his design concepts in his own fashion magazine, *Quality Street*.[13]

[8] Madelyn Shaw, "Maurice Rentner: American Designer and Manufacturer," in *Contemporary Fashion* 564, 565 (2nd edn., Taryn Benbow-Pfalzgraf (ed.), St. James Press, Detroit, MI, 2002).

[9] "Maurice Rentner is Dead at 69; Noted as Dress Manufacturer," *N. Y. Times*, Jul. 8, 1958, at 27 [hereinafter "Obituary"]; "Dress War," *Time*, Mar. 23, 1936, at 88.

[10] "Obituary," *supra* note 9, at 27.

[11] Roger D. Waldinger, *Through the Eye of the Needle: Immigrants and Enterprise in New York's Garment Trades* 49–50 (New York University Press, 1986); Nancy L. Green, *Ready-To-Wear and Ready-To-Work: A Century of Industry and Immigrants in Paris and New York* (Duke University Press, Durham, NC, 1997); Daniel Soyer (ed.), *A Coat of Many Colors: Immigration, Globalism, and Reform in the New York City Garment Industry* 6 (Fordham University Press, New York, NY, 2005).

[12] "Obituary," *supra* note 9; Shaw, *supra* note 8; "Dress War," *supra* note 9.

[13] "Dress War," *supra* note 9; Waldinger, *supra* note 11; Shaw, *supra* note 8.

The dress industry of course felt the impact of the Depression, and myriad apparel businesses went bankrupt in the 1930s. Demand for cheap dresses increased, and prices and quality decreased dramatically. Rentner was troubled by the impact of copies on the profitability of New York fashion houses attempting to sell original designs. Copies of his company's dresses were immediately being sold at lower prices, practically adjacent to the originals. Sketch artists in New York would go to such lengths as to intercept brand new dresses from delivery boys on the way to the stores, resulting in knockoffs for sale that very day at less than half the price of the originals. Rentner had begun his dress industry career copying French designs, and he knew all too well the phenomenon of extracting value from others' design investments.[14] His self-conception had effectively evolved from copyist to creator, which accompanied a similar American stirring in the industry, at least among the fashion houses.

Design copying was generally not illegal, since copyright protection did not extend to apparel.[15] Designers thus had no resort to lawsuits and courts to stop copyists from using the designs and devaluing the original products.

But Rentner had an idea. He set out to recruit other fashion houses to join in the creation of a new organization called the Fashion Originators' Guild of America. The Guild began in 1932 with twelve members, the most important fashion houses in New York. Its stated *raison d'être* was to protect "originators of fashions and styles against copying and piracy,"[16] which the members considered a plague on a still-emerging American dress business. The members entered an agreement that they would all refuse to sell their products to stores that also sold copies of their designs. If stores responded to this pressure and stopped selling copies, it would drive copyists out of those stores, and potentially out of the market entirely. This plan was Rentner's vision of how dressmakers would fight copying in the absence of legal protection for fashion design.

First, the distinction between fashion originals and copies had to be recognized and implemented. The Guild resolved that its members

[14] Sara B. Marcketti, "Codes of Fair Competition: The National Recovery Act, 1933–1935, and the Women's Dress Manufacturing Industry," 28 *Clothing & Textiles Res. J.* 189, 193–94 (2010) [hereinafter Marcketti, "Codes"]; "Dress War," *supra* note 9. Marcketti's work is indispensable for anyone interested in design piracy in the 1930s.

[15] Registration of Claims to Copyright, 37 C.F.R. § 201.4(7) (1938); *Cheney Bros. v. Doris Silk*, 35 F.2d 279, 281 (2d Cir. 1929).

[16] Sara Marcketti & Jean L. Parsons, "Design Piracy and Self-Regulation: The Fashion Originators' Guild of America, 1932–1941," 24 *Clothing & Textiles Research J.* 214, 217 (2006) (quoting FOGA's incorporation papers).

would not copy from European design models, as that was not "conducive to stimulating original designing and to providing an incentive for domestic creators to stress their individual conceptions of the current modes."[17] To promote original designing, in 1933 the Guild began putting on seasonal shows of original dress and coat designs – the predecessor to modern-day New York Fashion Week.[18]

The Guild created a registry for members to register their original designs. A member simply had to submit a sketch and a description of the design along with a signed affidavit of originality. The Guild would reject designs it deemed generic. Rather than committing the Guild to the design's originality, the registration process simply created a repository of designs that members averred were original. Registered products were embossed with a label that indicated "An Original Design Registered by a Member of Fashion Originators' Guild," or "Registered Original With FOGA." The member had exclusive rights to sell the registered design for six months.[19]

The Guild's membership consisted of designers and manufacturers of higher-price dresses and eventually rose from twelve to 176 members.[20] At its height, the Guild's registry took in over 40,000 designs in a year.[21]

Second, the scheme depended on the cooperation of retail shops and department stores not to sell the products of copyists. As a condition of selling Guild members' products, retailers were obliged to sign a "Declaration of Cooperation" that they would not deal in copies. The Guild had a system to distinguish and punish non-cooperative retailers. On white cards, the Guild listed the names of cooperating retailers. On red cards, it listed the names of retailers who refused to sign the pledge or otherwise failed to cooperate. The cards were regularly updated. Guild members refused to sell to red-carded businesses. Furthermore, certain Guild affiliates, who were textile manufacturers, were not supposed to sell textiles to clothing manufacturers who did business with red-carded retailers.[22]

The Guild also facilitated retailers' compliance with the system by instituting a legally ingenious warranty system. Cooperating retailers

[17] "Guild Not to Copy Models of Retailers," *Women's Wear Daily*, Apr. 11, 1935, at 26.

[18] Véronique Pouillard, "Design Piracy in the Fashion Industries of Paris and New York in the Interwar Years," 85 *Bus. Hist. Rev.* 319, 338–39 (2011).

[19] Marcketti & Parsons, *supra* note 16, at 218; "Dresses Ready-To-Wear," 38 *Printers' Ink Monthly* 5, 6–7 (Jan. 1939); Sara Beth Marcketti, *Design Piracy in the United States Women's Ready-to-Wear Apparel Industry: 1910–1941*, at 133 (2005) (unpublished Ph.D. dissertation, Iowa State University) [hereinafter Marcketti, *Design Piracy*]. Marcketti adds that "in practice," designs were protected for only three months.

[20] *FOGA*, *supra* note 7, at 462.

[21] Albert Post, Letter to the Editor, "Style Piracy," *Life*, Sept. 6, 1937, at 6.

[22] *FOGA*, at 461–62.

added a provision to their order forms, insisting that the manufacturer warrant that the dress was not a copy. The retailer reserved the right to return to the manufacturer any merchandise that violated the warranty. The Guild helpfully provided an ink stamp to be used to add the warranty provision to an order form.[23]

In 1936, the majority of moderate- to high-priced dresses in the market (those that wholesaled for $10.75 and above) were made by Guild members, so it was not easy for department stores to refuse to cooperate if they wanted to meet consumer demand for those categories of dresses. The number of retailers who signed on to cooperate eventually rose to 12,000 nationally.[24]

Third, the enforcement of the system of cooperation was crucial to this fight against design copying. The Guild undertook regularly to audit the books of its members and to fine those found in violation of the agreement not to sell to red-carded retailers. The Guild also employed a team – at one point, a staff of twenty-nine investigators – that visited stores to peruse the merchandise and ascertain whether the stores were selling copies of registered original designs.[25]

To decide the fate of retailers accused of selling copies, the Guild set up an internal tribunal and an appeal system to determine whether the merchandise alleged to be a copy was in fact a copy. Once the tribunal concluded that a retailer was selling copies, the retailer would be red-carded and members had to cease doing business with that retailer. The Guild also made it difficult for its members to defect; a member who chose to leave would be banned from the Guild for six months and fined $5,000.[26] In sum, the Guild ran a quasi-legal enforcement system consisting of rules born of agreement, enforcement measures, and officials to police the rules; tribunals to adjudicate claims of rule violation; and effective punishment.

Finally, the Guild engaged in an extensive advertising campaign in newspapers and magazines to explain the Guild's cause. For example, an advertisement in *Women's Wear Daily* explained that a cooperating retailer was "giving necessary encouragement to the trade as a whole to accord greater consideration to the element of quality in fabrics and in

[23] Commission Exhibit 537, Fashion Originators' Guild of America, No. 2769, 28 F.T.C. 430 (1939) (card from Guild instructing cooperating retailer to expect rubber stamp "to be affixed by you on all apparel orders"). The card is contained in Box 1902, Fashion Originators' Guild, Docketed Case Files, Records of the Federal Trade Commission, RG-122, National Archives in College Park, Maryland [hereinafter *FOGA Docket*].

[24] *FOGA*, at 461–62.

[25] *Ibid.* at 463; "Guild Expands Shopping Staff," *N. Y. Times*, Sept. 1, 1936, at 38; *FOGA*, at 462–63.

[26] *FOGA*, at 462–63.

workmanship. This conforms directly to the government's endeavors, through the National Industrial Recovery Act, to elevate standards as a means of augmenting the earning power of labor." Such messages dovetailed with the Guild's assertion, discussed further below, that copyists employed sweatshop labor to be able to produce goods so cheaply. The Guild also used the advertisements to promote a benefit of design protection that resonates with the debates today, that protection would "broaden the diversity of fashions."[27]

While the Guild was launching, in the midst of the Depression, early New Deal interventions were in the works to spur economic recovery by correcting an unregulated market. They included Congress's passage in 1933 of the National Industrial Recovery Act (hereinafter the "Act"). The Act established the National Recovery Administration (hereinafter "NRA"), to oversee cooperation among government, industry associations, corporations, and labor unions, for the purpose of stabilizing the industries. Reflecting New Deal ambivalence toward economic competition, the Act in effect suspended antitrust laws for this purpose. It provided that a particular industry's trade association could create codes of fair practices and competition for that industry. Such industry-specific codes would have the force of law, once submitted to and approved by President Roosevelt. Formulated by industry consensus, the codes would be enforced by each industry, with help from the Federal Trade Commission (hereinafter "FTC") and the federal courts.[28]

Even before the Act, the FTC Trade Practice Conferences had enabled industries to form their own standards of practice to regulate unfair competition. Some industries that had a strong design component, such as upholstery textile and embroidery, secured design protections through these trade practice conferences, but, unlike other rules regulating unfair competition, the design protection rules were deemed "recommended industry practices," not law.[29] The dress industry never did receive design protection through the trade practice conferences, but when the Act was passed, dress industry players argued that legally binding design protection provisions should be part of the industry-specific codes of fair practices that the Act contemplated.

[27] Advertisement, "A Message from the Dress Creators' League of America," *Women's Wear Daily*, July 11, 1933, at 11.

[28] Dalia Tsuk Mitchell, *Architect of Justice: Felix S. Cohen and the Founding of American Legal Pluralism* 76 (Cornell University Press, Ithaca, NY, 2007); Wilf, *supra* note 4, at 151; National Industrial Recovery Act, Pub. L. No. 73-90, 48 Stat. 195 (1933).

[29] Upholstery Textile Industry, 2 CCH Trade Reg. Serv. ¶ 12,250 (8th edn. 1937); Embroidery Industry, 2 CCH Trade Reg. Serv. ¶ 12,608 (8th edn. 1937); FTC, Annual Report 113 (1938) characterizing Group II rules.

The industry codes were presented by forty-three different industries – including the lumber, automobile, and motion picture industries – at public hearings held by the NRA. The dress industry's initial Hearing on the Codes of the Dress Industry, known as the "dress code" hearings, focused on fair labor and trade practices – workers' wages and hours, and the relationship between manufacturers and contractors. The goal was to limit labor exploitation that resulted from fierce, potentially ruinous competition among manufacturers seeking to cut costs and undersell each other.[30]

Industry representatives from apparel firms and trade associations nationwide testified at the dress code hearings held between 1933 and 1935. Rentner represented the Guild as its chairman. His testimony depicted design piracy as a prevalent means for manufacturers to achieve cheaper production and undersell the competition. Copyists could skimp on wages by skipping the costly design process. Rentner believed that competition in the industry should take place not on the ground of price, but rather on the terrain of quality. Samuel Zahn, chairman of the Dress Creators' League of America, testified as well, arguing that unregulated copying encouraged the rushed shortness of the fashion cycle, which in turn led to lower quality goods and poorer working conditions for laborers. Protection against design copying would make the period of salability of fashion merchandise last longer and push manufacturers' investments towards designing rather than copying. Rentner and Zahn tarred design copying with the brush of sweatshop labor, reasoning that firms that focused on making goods so cheaply were wont to exploit workers in the process. In short, the Guild sought to recruit labor in the effort to include design protection in the NRA dress code.[31]

But to know what design copying was, one had to posit a distinction between an original design and a copy. That elicited questions about the role that imitation played in the fashion trends that fueled consumers' demand for new clothes. The dress code hearings thus became the occasion for public debate of these very questions of innovation and intellectual property in fashion, as they related to the NRA's general goal to limit harmful competition in the industry.

Was there such a thing as originality in fashion? Wasn't imitation important, even essential, to the fashion trend cycle? Rentner claimed that originality in fashion was perfectly consistent with some amount of imitation, and "no fashion creator will assert that everything about every

[30] Marcketti, "Codes," *supra* note 14, at 194, 196.

[31] *Ibid.* at 195; National Recovery Administration, Hearing on the Code of Fair Competition for the Dress Manufacturing Industry 31, 114–16 (1934) [hereinafter NRA Hearing]; Marcketti & Parsons, *supra* note 16, at 223–24.

dress he offers is new."[32] But he argued that originality inhered in "combining" elements of existing sources from which the designer creates a design. Rentner's position distinguished between imitation in fashion trends and copying particular designs. Style trends were of course based on imitation and inspiration. But the fact that all designers engaged in this process of "adaptation" did not mean that their designs could not be deemed original works.

Medium and low-priced dress manufacturers testified against protection. They argued that design protection would introduce legal uncertainty about whether manufacturers were infringing a protected design, especially since it would be very difficult to determine originality in fashion. They also emphasized the unfairness to lower-income women who would be deprived of lower-priced versions of fashionable styles. Poor women would have to wear their lack of wealth on their sleeve, so to speak, if denied access to low-priced dresses that looked like the originals.[33]

Indeed, the stratification of higher- and lower-priced dress markets and consumers centrally animated the debate about design copying, and would eventually lead to an identity crisis for the Guild. The Guild's members were creators of high-end dresses, and its anti-copying activities were perceived as protecting high-end designers against copyists. The copies, always sold at lower-price points, reflected the cost-saving advantages of circumventing the design process as well as the lower-quality materials and workmanship used to bring prices down. When these design copies rapidly appeared in stores and on women in the streets, purchasers of the originals became dismayed at the availability of the cheaper and lower-quality versions, and some returned their purchases to the retailer, who would then cancel orders or not reorder the items. The entry of the copies into the market effectively meant that the time window for the original dress as desirable and salable merchandise was closing, almost as quickly as it had opened.[34]

Other industries such as the silk textile industry succeeded in adopting design protection provisions in their codes through the NRA process. But, despite extensive debates at the dress code hearings about design copying, the dress industry did not reach consensus on design protection. The dress code ultimately regulated labor and trade standards including working hours, conditions, and wages, but not copying.

[32] *Ibid.* at 221 (quoting Mildred Finger, *Memoirs of Maurice Rentner from Varying Perspectives* 105 (Fashion Institute of Technology, New York, NY, 1982)).

[33] A.C. Johnston & Florence A. Fitch, *Design Piracy: The Problem and its Treatment under NRA Codes* 47–50 (National Recovery Administration, Washington DC, 1936).

[34] NRA Hearing, *supra* note 31, at 56; Marcketti & Parsons, *supra* note 16, at 223.

A proposed amendment to add design protection was dropped because the industry was too divided, with strong opposition from "popular" (i.e., lower-priced) manufacturers and retailers. The NRA was reluctant to proceed in the absence of complete industry acceptance, especially with the perceived difficulties of determining originality and the administrative burdens of running a fashion design registration system. Overall, though, Rentner perceived the dress code's limitations on labor cost-cutting measures as tending to lessen the unfair advantages that low-priced copyists enjoyed.[35]

The NRA dress code itself was short-lived, however. Within months, the Supreme Court declared unconstitutional Congress's delegation to the president of the power to approve the industry-created codes.[36] The New Deal principles that animated the Act, however, remained in the Guild's project to promote cooperation among fashion industry players, stabilize "the customs and commercial usages of trade," and restrain untrammeled competition.[37] The Guild's system was of a piece with the New Deal promotion of industry-wide cartels for these purposes.

Around this time, the Millinery Creators' Guild, modeled on the Fashion Originators' Guild, was formed with the same goal, to provide protection for fashion designers of hats. The milliners' group implemented a similar system, and over 1,600 cooperating retailers agreed not to sell hats that were copies.[38]

As the Depression continued, the demand for cheap dresses soared. The Guild continued its fight by registering members' designs and red-carding retailers who violated its rules. But the demand for cheaper dresses deepened a dangerous fault line that had surfaced at the dress code hearings. Initially the Guild had registered only high-end dress designs, priced at $16.75 wholesale or higher. The success of the Guild's anti-copying system made it increasingly difficult for mid-price dress-makers to make do with simply copying higher-price dress designs. The mid-price manufacturers were thus spurred to engage in original design themselves and sought to register their designs with the Guild as well. Rentner felt it was important to offer the Guild's protections to those who were creating designs, even if they were in lower price brackets.

[35] Karl Fenning, "N.R.A. Codes," 16 *J. Pat. Off. Soc'y* 189, 199 (1934); National Recovery Administration, Code of Fair Competition for the Dress Manufacturing Industry 2–6 (Oct. 31, 1933) (Reg. No. 228-01); Pouillard, *supra* note 18, at 341–43; Johnston & Fitch, *supra* note 33, at 136.

[36] *A.L.A. Schecter Poultry Corp. v. United States*, 295 U.S. 495 (1935).

[37] Marcketti, *Design Piracy*, *supra* note 19, at 126 (citing FOGA's incorporation papers).

[38] "Business World: Millinery Guild Adopts Label," *N. Y. Times*, Oct. 16, 1935, at 42; *Millinery Creators' Guild v. FTC*, 109 F.2d 175, 176 (2d Cir. 1940).

After all, that was the Guild's defining principle and purpose – to protect and encourage originators.[39]

The Guild accepted the mid-price designs for registration. The price floor for registrable dresses was dropped from $16.75 to $10.75 in early 1935. At this point, though, retailers grew uncomfortable with the expansion of the Guild's cadre of designers. The Guild obligated retailers to return to the manufacturer any dresses the Guild deemed to be copies. Retailers were not eager to take on the burden of including the lower-price ranges in the merchandise subject to Guild surveillance. Lower-price dresses were bought in greater bulk, and cooperating department stores worried about competing in the lower-price ranges with non-cooperating chain stores that sold dresses free of Guild restrictions.[40]

Despite growing retailer disgruntlement, by late 1935 the Guild further extended its reach to original dresses priced below $10, even $6.75. The Guild soon issued a new "declaration of cooperation" stating that retailers who had previously agreed not to sell copies of high-end dresses must henceforth not sell copies of virtually any dresses. More than one hundred styles per month were declared copies. One retailer claimed that covering the lower-price ranges created the "impossible condition" of essentially subjecting all manufacturers and retailers to the Guild's dominion. Retailers resented the expansion beyond the original cooperation agreement, which had contemplated a manageably limited system protecting only original designs priced above $16.75.[41]

By early 1936, the reduction of copying credited to the Guild was significant: 75 percent reduction at the $16.75 range, and 40 percent reduction in the $10.75 range. But retailers' unease with the Guild's perceived heavy-handed overreaching had turned into outright frustration and anger, bordering on revolt. Beginning with the high-end Strawbridge & Clothier, department stores witnessed incidents in which store managers openly disobeyed Guild investigators who came in and demanded that certain dresses be removed as copies. The stores included heavy hitters Bloomingdale's and R.H. White, owned by Filene's. Other members of a major department store group, Associated Merchandising Corp., followed in rebellion, and one by one got red-carded. By February

[39] "Dress War," *supra* note 9; Thomas F. Conroy, "Guild Pushes Fight to Protect Styles," *N. Y. Times*, Feb. 16, 1936, at F9.

[40] "Business World: Expand Dress Style Registration," *N. Y. Times*, Mar. 22, 1935, at 41; "Dress War," *supra* note 9; Conroy, "Guild Pushes Fight to Protect Styles," *supra* note 39.

[41] "Business World: Buyers to Use Dress Stamp," *N. Y. Times*, Oct. 15, 1935, at 41; "Fashion Originators Will Not Set Prices," *N. Y. Times*, Dec. 5, 1935, at 47; "Dress War," *supra* note 9; "Dress Group Decides Against Ban on Copies," *N.Y. Times*, Oct. 11, 1935, at 38; Conroy, "Guild Pushes Fight to Protect Styles," *supra* note 39.

1936, two dozen such stores were red-carded. R.H. White asked individual manufacturers to continue doing business together despite the red-carding, but was rebuffed. The retailer community was outraged.[42]

Sylvan Gotshal was counsel for the Guild's fabric division. His recent distinctions included founding the New York law firm, Weil, Gotshal, and Manges, in 1931, and serving on the drafting committee for the failed Vestal Design Copyright Bill in 1930. In disagreement with the Guild's tactics, Gotshal resigned from his position at the Guild. He presciently stated: "Attempts at coercion of this type against one group of retailers is only going to serve to consolidate the efforts of all those opposed to any protection whatsoever, and in the long run the guild will collapse."[43] He advocated withdrawing the red cards the Guild had issued to the retailers, and entering into arbitration to resolve the situation. The Guild was eventually able to compromise with some retailers, and agreed to withdraw dresses in the range of $6.75 to $7.75 from the Guild's protection.[44]

But it was too late. An all-out "dress war" became unstoppable when Filene's decided to sue the Guild in federal court in March 1936, four years after the Guild's incorporation. Filene's sought a preliminary injunction in a federal district court in Boston, claiming that the Guild violated federal antitrust law. Filene's claimed that the Guild's entire system – red-carding, boycotting non-cooperating retailers, and requiring retailers to accept the Guild's judgment that a dress was a copy – constituted a violation of the Sherman Act.[45]

The court thought it was apparent that the Guild's scheme was "calculated to benefit rather than prejudice public interest," and that its methods were not designed to "enhance prices or to curtail or cheapen production." The question was "whether the coercive influences exerted upon the members directly, and indirectly upon conforming retailers, unduly restrain the free flow of trade to the extent that it can be said that the interest of the public are prejudiced in any way." The court concluded that the fact that members "voluntarily submit to restrictions upon their right to sell to nonconforming retailers" and could resign Guild membership at will meant there was no "unlawful suppression of competition." As for the retailers, again the availability of the choice

[42] Conroy, "Guild Pushes Fight to Protect Styles," *supra* note 39; "Dress War," *supra* note 9; "Fashion Guild Stand Backed by Producers," *N. Y. Times*, Feb 19, 1936, at 35; *Wm. Filene's Sons Co. v. FOGA*, 14 F. Supp. 353, 356 (D. Mass. 1936) [hereinafter *Filene's*].

[43] "Guild Stands Firm on Dress Program," *N. Y. Times*, Feb. 21, 1936, at 31.

[44] *Ibid.*; "Fashion Guild Ban on Store Here Ends," *N. Y. Times*, Feb. 28, 1936, at 30; "Designs Filed at Peak," *N. Y. Times*, Sept. 13, 1936, at F8.

[45] "Dress War," *supra* note 9; *Filene's*, *supra* note 42, at 357.

made the court unwilling to find a "denial or abridgement of the right of fair competition. The right to compete by unfair means I assume is not a right which the anti-trust laws were designed to protect." The retailer who chose not to cooperate with the Guild could work with non-members, who were still a majority of dressmakers in New York. The retailer could "retain his full freedom to sell pirated articles, or he may take the other course and consent to rules adopted by the trade for the purpose of abating the evil of piracy." The judge denied Filene's request for a preliminary injunction.[46]

The case was referred to a special master, who found that the Guild had not tried to fix prices, limit production, or cause quality deterioration. He concluded that the Guild was "beneficial, rather than prejudicial, not only to the interests of the dress industry but as well to the interests of the public." The Guild's members and affiliates "carried with them no monopolistic menace" and did not unduly restrain competition.[47]

Filene's fared no better on appeal in the First Circuit, which concluded that the Sherman Act "does not preclude the members of an industry in which evils exist ... from action collectively in the elimination of such evils and establishing fair competitive practices." Crediting the special master's finding that a retailer who chose by non-cooperation with the Guild to "cut itself off from certain sources of supply" still had "substantial and reasonably adequate markets to which it could resort for the purchase of ready-to-wear dresses," the First Circuit found no unreasonable restraint of trade or monopoly.[48]

Though the Guild thus succeeded in fending off the Filene's lawsuit, legal troubles were far from over. Discord in the dress industry around the Guild's activities had caught the attention of the FTC, which earlier had conducted an inconclusive investigation into the Guild's activities. While the *Filene's* case was still making its way through the First Circuit, the FTC issued a complaint charging the Guild with unlawful restraint of trade in April 1936. The next month, the FTC similarly charged the milliners' group. This set off a process that would eventually hasten the demise of the Fashion Originators' Guild of America.[49]

[46] *Filene's*, *supra* note 42, at 359, 361.

[47] *Wm. Filene's Sons Co. v. Fashion Originators' Guild of Am.*, 90 F.2d 556, 560 (1st Cir. 1937).

[48] *Ibid.* at 559, 560–61.

[49] "Commission Holds Guild a Monopoly: Issues Complaint Against Body and Four Other Groups for Conspiracy," *N. Y. Times*, Apr. 21, 1936, at 42; "Milliners Cited as Curbing Trade: Federal Board Lays Unfair Practices to Two Groups in New York City," *N. Y. Times*, May 27, 1936, at 34.

The FTC held hearings on the matter, in New York and Boston, between July 1936 and January 1938.[50] The Guild's message in those hearings had some internal tension. On the one hand, despite the Guild's apparent success in fighting copyists, it argued that copyists were still quite free, as they could sell goods to any non-cooperating retailer – and many retailers were not cooperating, in fact. That is, especially the smaller retailers who focused on selling copies could still thrive, even in a market regulated by the Guild, since they had no need to do business with Guild members.[51] It was mainly large retailers selling a broader range of goods who would feel the pressure to cooperate in order not to lose access to high-price originals.

On the other hand, the Guild's somewhat contrary message had been that the success of its elaborate system would aim at eliminating the market for copies: "[W]here there are no buyers for the copies, there will be no copy makers . . ."[52] As for the difficulty of distinguishing copying from the imitation that led fashionable women to converge on fashion trends, the Guild emphasized that there was an important difference between "styles" and "designs." Styles were what comprised trends, and could be freely imitated in the modes of fashion. They were too general to be protectable. But designs were particular instantiations of a style, whereby a creator combined design elements into a distinctive original work that should not be copied at will.[53]

An FTC attorney likened the Guild's methods to those of Hitler. The Guild sought to justify its scheme by submitting proof of the untenable industry conditions that drove the Guild to devise its system, and of the economic benefits secured by its activities. However, the FTC examiner conducting the hearings refused to accept this evidence. From the Commission's standpoint, the boycott was illegal "per se," without regard to any purported justification.[54]

[50] For a listing of witnesses and testimony, see Transcript of Record at 165–4451, *Fashion Originators' Guild of Am. v. FTC*, 312 U.S. 457 (1941) (No. 537) [hereinafter Transcript of Record].

[51] See, for example, an article titled "Shops Cut In on Low-End Field," part of the press clippings file contained in Box 1856, Fashion Originators' Guild, Auxiliary Case Files, RG-122, National Archives in College Park, Maryland.

[52] Commission Exhibit 99-a, Fashion Originators' Guild of America, No. 2769, 28 F.T.C. 430 (1939) (letter from FOGA to retailers (June 16, 1933)) (contained in Box 1904, *FOGA Docket*).

[53] Transcript of Record, *supra* note 50, at 4312–15.

[54] "Fashion Guild Called 'Hitler' of Dress Field; Defended as Preventer of Style Piracy," *N. Y. Times*, Sept. 22, 1938, at 32; Transcript of Record, *supra* note 50, at 4307–08; *ibid.* at 4a (Guild petition in Second Circuit).

At this time, Claire McCardell was a fashion designer working for the dress manufacturer Townley Frocks. History would remember her as the inventor of the "American Look." Departing from the fashions of Paris, where she was trained, McCardell designed for the American everywoman in a style that was "easy, confident, athletic ... free and optimistic." The clothes were mass-produced, affordable, clean, casual, and comfortable. McCardell was so committed to design originality that she even refused to visit collections while vacationing in Paris, to avoid the influence of other designers.[55]

In 1938 McCardell designed a dress called the "Monastic" that instantly brought her fame. The design exemplified the new spirit of fashion as it took a break from Europe. Named after the shapeless robes of clerics, the dress was unwaisted and had the same front and back. It hung from the shoulders, meant to fit any woman, and had no constraints in the form of bust darts or corseting. Worn with a belt, it "did great things for the female figure," and "ma[d]e your waist look tiny."[56]

Marketed as the "Nada Frock" for $29.95 only at Best & Company, the dress was hugely popular, and very widely and quickly copied. An advertisement entitled "Fair Warning" placed by Best & Company sternly declared the design to be a registered original that the Guild would act to protect against infringing copies.[57] But it had little effect. Knockoffs of the dress flooded into the market faster than the originals could be produced. Because of the large number of copies for sale, Henry Geiss, the owner of Townley Frocks, tried to convince McCardell to let the Monastic go and move on to other designs for the next season's collection, but she wanted to keep the design in the collection. Geiss went repeatedly to the Guild for help fending off copyists. But knockoffs were so uncontrollable that the Guild finally declared the Monastic an "open item" that could freely be copied with impunity, eventually selling "for the devastating price of thirty dollars a dozen." As a result of the

[55] "The American Look," *Time*, May 2, 1955, at 87; Constance C.R. White, "Celebrating Claire McCardell," *N. Y. Times*, Nov. 17, 1998, at B15.

[56] Rebecca J. Robinson, *American Sportswear: A Study of the Origins and Women Designers from the 1930's to the 1960's* (2003) (unpublished M. Design dissertation, University of Cincinnati) (manuscript at 116); Bill Cunningham, "Claire McCardell," *Chicago Tribune*, July 31, 1972, at B2; Bernadine Morris, "Looking Back at McCardell: It's a Lot Like Looking at Today," *N. Y. Times*, May 24, 1972, at 58; Kohle Yohannan & Nancy Nolf, *Claire McCardell: Redefining Modernism* 41 (Harry N. Adams, New York, NY, 1998).

[57] The advertisement, apparently from 1938, can be found in Box X38.2.2.6, in the Claire McCardell materials kept by the Special Collections Library of the Fashion Institute of Technology in New York City.

losses and the legal fees associated with desperate attempts to protect the design, Townley Frocks went under that year.[58]

Though the Monastic was in the high-end category that the Guild was originally created to protect, its fate exemplified how the dissatisfaction over the Guild's inclusion of low-price dresses eroded the industry's overall respect for the Guild's rules. The protective efforts regarding the Monastic failed in the period of government investigation into the Guild's activities, a period in which increasing criticism accompanied a marked decrease in the Guild's authority in the industry.[59]

The FTC completed its investigation in February 1939 and issued a cease and desist order against the Guild. The order prohibited the Guild from engaging in activities in combination to limit competition by preventing retailers from buying dresses from manufacturers. It also forbade the Guild from refusing to deal with businesses that did not accept its rules.[60] The Guild filed an appeal in the Second Circuit.

By that point, the FTC had already issued a similar cease and desist order against the milliners' group, prohibiting the same practices.[61] The milliners' Second Circuit appeal was decided first, in January 1940. The court thought the question was about "the alleged evil of style piracy, and whether its abolition will eliminate a socially useful type of competition." The court acknowledged that the creator "suffers a real loss when the design is copied as soon as it appears" and that "the imitator in turn reaps a substantial gain by appropriating for himself the style innovations produced by the creator's investment."[62]

But the court explained that to outlaw piracy "would afford a virtual monopoly to the creator of an unpatented and uncopyrighted design." Congress had "not yet . . . seen fit to extend the privileges of a monopolist to the inventor of an unpatentable idea," and "the courts have refrained from enjoining the pirate because they will not support a monopoly in an unpatentable idea. It would be strange to say that the [milliners] may establish this same monopoly by extrajudicial methods."[63]

The court observed that "piracy has been lethal in its effect on hat prices, and one of its results has been to make the latest fashions readily available to the lowest purchasing classes." That is, consumer access to inexpensive hats came at the expense of high-end hat makers. The court

[58] Yohannan & Nolf, *supra* note 56, at 42; "The American Look," *supra* note 55; Robert Riley et al., *American Fashion: The Life and Lines of Adrian, Mainbocher, McCardell, Norell, and Trigere* 232 (1st edn., Sarah Tomerlin Lee (ed.) Quadrangle/New York Times Book Co., New York, NY, 1975); Robinson, *supra* note 56, at 117.

[59] Marcketti, *Design Piracy*, *supra* note 19, at 137–42, 159.

[60] FTC, Annual Report 73, 101–02 (1939).

[61] *Ibid.* at 105.

[62] *Millinery Creators' Guild v. FTC*, 109 F.2d 175, 177 (2d Cir. 1940).

[63] *Ibid.*

thought it was "safe to say that the members ... instituted their anti-piracy campaign to protect their markets and price levels."[64] The smoking gun was the testimony of a hat company representative that the defendants:

> had gotten together all of the leading milliners, so-called, to try to create a greater interest in women wearing hats and raising the prices for a better grade milliner because, for instance, the average milliner 15 years ago easily got $30 for every hat they sold, today the God damn thing sells for $1.95, I mean they sell for $1.95 around town, as a result of which they practically ruin every milliner.[65]

The court found the purpose of the milliners' combination was to "maintain their price structure, and to eliminate a distasteful 'evil' which the law nevertheless recognizes to be a socially desirable form of competition." That is, "what is desirable competition to the consumer may be outlaw traffic to the established manufacturer." The Second Circuit thus held that the milliners' boycott violated antitrust law.[66]

This decision set the stage for the Fashion Originators' Guild's Second Circuit appeal, which resulted in an opinion by Judge Learned Hand. This was not Judge Hand's first engagement with fashion. In a famous earlier case, *Cheney Bros. v. Doris Silk Corporation*, he had examined a copying claim involving fabric patterns.[67] There, the plaintiff had asserted a misappropriation claim using an analogy to protection for "hot news" previously recognized by the Supreme Court.[68] Judge Hand had rejected the extension of that principle to fabric patterns. Noting the absence of federal copyright protection for fabric patterns, Judge Hand had emphasized that his hands were tied, "even though there be a hiatus in completed justice" in allowing such design copying to go unregulated.[69]

For Judge Hand, the milliners' case, combined with earlier cases about boycotts and his own opinion in *Cheney Bros.*, controlled the Fashion Originators' case. Once the dress or fabric was offered for general sale, there was no residual property protection. Echoing his *Cheney Bros.* opinion, Hand explained: "It may be unfortunate – it may indeed be unjust – that the law should not thereafter distinguish between 'originals' and copies; but until the Copyright Office can be induced to register such designs as copyrightable under the existing statute, they both fall into the public demesne without reserve."[70] A boycott aiming to create protection for something that existing intellectual property law did not protect had to be rejected.[71]

[64] *Ibid.* [65] *Ibid.* at 178. [66] *Ibid.* at 176, 178. [67] 325 F.2d 279 (2d Cir. 1929).
[68] *International News Service v. Associated Press*, 248 U.S. 215 (1918).
[69] *Cheney Bros. v. Doris Silk Corp.*, 35 F.2d 279, 280–81 (2d Cir. 1929).
[70] *Fashion Originators Guild of Am. v. FTC*, 114 F.2d 80, 84 (2d Cir. 1940).
[71] *Ibid.* at 84–85.

The sharp inconsistency between the First and Second Circuit's conclusions about the Guild – that the boycott was permissible according to one court, but prohibited according to the other – was resolved by the Supreme Court. A unanimous opinion authored by Justice Hugo Black in *Fashion Originators' Guild of America v. FTC*[72] (hereinafter "*FOGA*") embraced in sweeping terms the FTC's view that the Guild violated federal antitrust law. The hat designers' case, *Millinery Creators' Guild v. FTC*,[73] was decided the same day, on the authority of *FOGA*.

The Supreme Court unreservedly accepted the FTC's argument that the Guild's justification for, and any salutary effects of, the boycott were irrelevant as a matter of antitrust doctrine. The Court seemed particularly perturbed that the Guild had set up "an extra-governmental agency," with elaborate institutions of enforcement and self-governance. In other words, the Guild's quasi-judicial tribunals and trappings of process granted to alleged copyists to adjudicate their guilt only deepened rather than ameliorated the offense, by "trench[ing] upon the power of the national legislature."[74]

The Court's ruling went beyond Judge Hand's Second Circuit opinion in a crucial respect. Hand had accepted that the Guild's boycott was permissible to the extent it attacked *illegal* copying, for example, of unpublished designs (which enjoyed common law protection), or designs acquired by fraud.[75] At the Supreme Court, the Guild relied heavily on this concession, arguing that design copying generally was illegal, as a form of unfair competition or an infringement of the "hot news" right the Court had previously recognized. In an early unpublished draft of the opinion, Justice Black gave careful substantive attention to the proposition, offering that "there is much force in petitioners' arguments" that a hot news right could be applied to these facts.[76] The draft reluctantly concluded that the extension must be denied, for fear that the principle might then be extended to "every type of design." In the final opinion, this analysis was omitted, in favor of the sweeping conclusion that a boycott to enforce extant state law protection would be no less illegal.[77]

After the Supreme Court case, the Guild was reduced to a shadow of its former self. The possibility that designers might recreate the protections they had enjoyed by proceeding on an individual and non-compulsory basis with retailers appears to have gone nowhere. Designers

[72] 312 U.S. 457 (1941). [73] 312 U.S. 469 (1941).
[74] *FOGA*, *supra* note 7, at 465 (internal quotation marks omitted).
[75] *Fashion Originators Guild of Am. v. FTC*, 114 F.2d 80, 84 (2d Cir. 1940).
[76] Box 262, Fashion Originators' Guild of America Case File, Hugo LaFayette Black Papers, Manuscript Division, Library of Congress, Washington DC.
[77] *FOGA*, *supra* note 7, at 456, 468.

increased their pursuit of design patents as an alternative. The Guild hoped for a reduction in the time required to issue a design patent, to make approval possible six or seven weeks from the date of filing. The old retailer warranty was replaced by a new Guild-provided stamp, requiring the seller to warranty that the design was not protected by a design patent. Ultimately, however, the design patent route fizzled.[78]

After a pause for World War II, the Guild's activities were limited to advocacy for design legislation and promotion of industry and American design. After the War, the fashion industry saw an influx of European couturiers that eventually came to dominate the high-end fashion market in the United States in the latter half of the twentieth century.[79]

Rentner continued to work on fashion industry interests, for example as a board member of the Fashion Institute of Technology. He died in 1958, but Maurice Rentner, Inc. survived after a merger with Anna Miller & Co., a company owned by his sister. The head designer then was Bill Blass, who would eventually buy the business and operate it under his own name. Rentner's beloved Guild, however, did not long survive him, and it ceased operating entirely in the 1960s. Bill Blass, in 1962, became a founding member of the now-existing modern counterpart to the Guild, the Council of Fashion Designers of America (hereinafter "CFDA"), which began as an organization focused on boosting the fashion industry through public relations and promotion of fashion as high art. Only after four decades did the CFDA seriously take up its well-known contemporary cause of legal protection for fashion design.[80]

After *FOGA*, the quest for new fashion legislation continued. In these debates, the same issues tended to recur. For example, in 1936, during the heyday of the Guild, opponents of legislation "cited the impracticability of protecting certain basic designs, such as polka dots."[81] Such worries required the counter-reassurance, repeated in ensuing

[78] "Fashion Designers Seek Protection," *N. Y. Times*, June 8, 1941, at F6; Elizabeth R. Valentine, "Supreme Court Upsets Fashions," *N. Y. Times*, Mar. 9, 1941, at E10; "Revises Program to Protect Design," *N. Y. Times*, Oct. 25, 1941, at 23; "Patents on Styles Deemed Effective," *N. Y. Times*, Sep. 15, 1949, at 40; Thomas F. Conroy, "Fight to Continue on Style Piracy," *N. Y. Times*, Mar. 9, 1941, at F7.

[79] Shaw, *supra* note 8.

[80] *Ibid.*; Isadore Barmash, "2 Apparel Groups to Weigh Merger at Meeting Today," *N. Y. Times*, Dec. 23, 1965, at 39, 46; Council of Fashion Designers of America, History, http://cfda.com/about/history (last visited Nov. 4, 2012); Amy Fine Collins, "The Lady, the List, the Legacy," *Vanity Fair*, April 2004, at 260; Eric Wilson, "O.K., Knockoffs, This Is War," *N. Y. Times*, Mar. 30, 2006, at 1.

[81] "Replies on Design Bill," *N. Y. Times*, Apr. 15, 1936, at 31.

decades, that "[t]here is no intention whatsoever of registering basic designs of this character, which are definitely in the public domain of apparel designs."[82]

Today, not all fashion designs are treated alike. When *FOGA* was decided, the law treated dress (and hat) designs and fabric designs identically – neither was protected. In 1959, a district court case accorded protection to fabric designs, relying on dicta in an earlier Supreme Court case that pointed out that utility does not eliminate copyrightability. The Copyright Office changed its rules to accord copyright to fabric designs, but remained hostile to dress designs. This discrepancy persists today.[83]

★★★

The rise and fall of the Fashion Originators' Guild carries several lessons.[84]

First, designers have cared deeply about protection, and have been willing to go to great lengths to stop design copying. Today's proposals to add fashion design to federal copyright law continue to spawn debates about whether and to what extent designers do or should want protection from copying. The fashion design community's will to protect its designs even where law did not protect them is undeniable in the historical example of the Guild.

Second, the struggle in contemporary debates about whether fashion is really capable of protectable originality, given that its distinctively short cycles of trends necessarily entail imitation, is not new. From the start, American fashion designers posited the distinction between general "styles" versus specific "designs" – overall trends versus distinctive variations – that suggested that the relational dynamic of originality and copying had both conceptual purchase and economic significance for fashion designers.

Third, the Court's opinion in *FOGA* casts a pall over private self-help measures that might attempt to mimic the effect of intellectual property protection that has not yet been granted by the legislature.[85] An

[82] *Ibid.*

[83] *Peter Pan Fabrics, Inc. v. Brenda Fabrics, Inc.*, 169 F. Supp. 142 (S.D.N.Y. 1959); *Mazer v. Stein*, 347 U.S. 201, 213 (1954); Works of Art (Class G), 37 C.F.R. § 202.10(b) (1956); Kal Raustiala & Christopher Sprigman, "The Piracy Paradox: Innovation and Intellectual Property in Fashion Design," 92 *Va. L. Rev.* 1687, 1747 n. 113 (2006) (noting the discrepancy).

[84] For an earlier suggestion of the Guild's modern relevance, see Randal C. Picker, "Of Pirates and Puffy Shirts," *Va. L. Rev. in Brief 1* (2007).

[85] For a suggestion that self-help might have been more efficient than statutory protection, see Robert P. Merges, "Contracting into Liability Rules: Intellectual Property Rights and Collective Rights Organizations," 84 *Cal. L. Rev.* 1293, 1365–66 (1996).

exception might have existed, as Judge Hand suggested, for self-help designed to enforce an existing legal right, as opposed to creating a right the law does not already recognize.[86] However, the Supreme Court's sweeping rejection of the Guild's argument stymies this suggestion. Either way, schemes like the Title Registration Bureau, set up by the Motion Picture Association of America to govern the allocation of titles for unreleased films, may be subject to serious doubt, because they, like the Guild's system, serve as privately organized substitutes for copyright or trademark protection.[87]

Fourth, if design protection were to succeed in turning more fashion producers away from copying and toward designing, the desired increase in lower-price producers' design originality could breed a delicate risk to the protection system itself. The Guild eventually came to recognize that high price and protection-worthy design were not necessarily linked, but the extension of coverage to lower-price designers fatally frayed industry support for the protection scheme. Today, expensive luxury fashion still provides the goods most popularly considered protection-worthy, and many such goods already receive a certain amount of protection under trademark law. Meanwhile, designers at lower-price levels of lesser fame, who lack those already existing protections, are perhaps *more* vulnerable to copyists' impact on their businesses, as their intellectual property lies in creativity rather than branding. The problem of extending design protection down market to lower-price originators on the one hand, and keeping a perceived adequate unregulated space of free copying on the other hand, poses questions of industry equilibrium that any fashion design protection scheme must confront.

Finally, perhaps originality is overrated as a basis for design protection. Jettisoning originality and focusing instead on the designer's role in providing consumers with desired, distinctive, of-the-moment articles – even articles that are not newly created but rather curated or compiled from creations of the past – is a potential alternative basis for according protection for fashion design even in the absence of copyright protection. Insofar as originality currently provides a restriction on protectability, however, forgoing the constraint of the originality requirement in this way would potentially expand the scope of protection for fashion design beyond that which exists for other creative works in an already expansive copyright regime.

[86] *Fashion Originators' Guild of Am. v. FTC*, 114 F.2d 80, 84 (1940).
[87] Cf. 1 Melville B. Nimmer & David Nimmer, *Nimmer on Copyright* § 2.16 n. 13 (rev. edn., Matthew Bender, Newark, NJ, 2011) (suggesting obliquely that "such private legislation" might be invalid).

8 Protection for fashion: The European experience

Annette Kur

Introduction

Designing fashion requires a high degree of creative skills and imagination, paired with a keen sense for trends and solid knowledge about the technical aspects of tailoring and treating fabrics. In all those aspects fashion design is in no way inferior to designing household appliances, furniture, or new cars. Whereas those activities are usually distinguished from creation of artworks or literature that falls under copyright, at least in Europe it is in principle readily accepted that design efforts in all fields are worthy of protection, primarily under the regime of industrial design protection that was specifically crafted for them. Nevertheless, even in Europe, fashion did have a special role at the edges of IP. Although even before European design legislation was harmonized around the turn of the millennium, most countries did provide for protection relating to all fields of design, including fashion, the situation was not considered as optimal by the fashion industry. Especially in countries where design registration depended on substantive examination, the procedure was considered as too lengthy and burdensome for an industry characterized by constant change and brief life-cycles of the individual creations. Fashion designers are therefore likely to prefer protection without formalities, be it on the basis of copyright or other legal titles.

In Germany, which is the focus of this chapter, such protection was granted fairly generously from the 1970s, based on specific case law developed under the general clause of the Act Against Unfair Competition (UWG). That line of jurisprudence provided inspiration for the special type of unregistered design protection that was introduced by the Community Design Regulation, offering short-time, informal protection for any novel and individual design, including fashion.[1]

[1] Council Regulation (EC) No 6/2002 of December 12, 2001 on Community designs [2002] OJ L 3/1.

In comparison with the situation in the US, this appears to be a happily ended story, at least in the eyes of fashion designers. However, whether and in what way the fashion industry has actually benefited from the introduction of the Unregistered Community Design (UCD) is hard to ascertain. Reported litigation is scarce, and other actual data, in particular concerning the economic impact of protection, are not available. What seems to be clear, though, is that demand for longer protection has not fully subsided. In such cases, recourse is taken, with varying success, to trademark law or unfair competition rules that have not been harmonized in this particular aspect.[2]

Instead of matching the account given by Scott Hemphill and Jeannie Suk of fashion designers' unorthodox means in the fight against knockoffs,[3] this chapter will try to paint the larger picture of how fashion protection developed over time in Europe. Starting with the German experience, it briefly sketches the genesis of the UCD protection, ending with references to case law addressing the availability of trademark and (subsequent) unfair competition protection for fashion articles. No attempt is made, though, to judge the failure or success of EU design legislation and its suitability as a model for future US legislation.

Germany: pre-harmonization protection for fashion

Until recently, when Berlin developed a certain reputation as one of the most innovative European fashion design capitals, Germany was not much associated with fashion. It is little wonder therefore that, unlike in France, the issue of how to protect creative achievements of the fashion industry did not figure prominently in the German legal debate during the first half of the last century. True, there was a rich

[2] Legislation in the EU Member States has been harmonized in regards of misleading and comparative advertising (Directive 2006/114/EC of the European Parliament and the Council of December 12, 2006 concerning misleading and comparative advertising (codified version), [2007] OJ EC L 149/22) as well as in regards of unfair commercial practices (Directive 2005/29/EC of the European Parliament and the Council of May 11, 2005 concerning unfair business-to-consumer commercial practices in the internal market and amending Council Directive 84/450/EEC, Directives 97/7/EC, 98/27/EC and 2002/65/EC of the European Parliament and of the Council and Regulation (EC) No 2006/2004 of the European Parliament and of the Council ("UCD Directive"), [2005] OJ L 149/22). As is apparent from its title, the latter Directive only covers unfair marketing practices in the business-to-consumer relationship and does not regulate matters of fair conduct between entrepreneurs, such as, in particular, imitation of products.

[3] See Chapter 7 in this volume.

body of case law dealing with so-called slavish imitation under the aspect of unfair competition. Based on Section 1, the so-called general clause, of the UWG, competitive actions were held to be illicit in presence of "aggravating circumstances," such as consumer confusion resulting from close imitation of products originating from another party. Some of those decisions concerned "fashion(able) items" in a larger sense, meaning that the imitated products were supposed to please the eye, but without addressing imitation of fashion as a proper category of its own.[4]

Apart from protection under the aspect of unfair competition, items such as embroidery,[5] artificial flowers,[6] and patterns of cloth or lace[7] had been declared eligible in principle for copyright protection, although the individual items actually at stake regularly lacked creative character and therefore did not qualify for protection. Furthermore, regarding apparel and similar items such as shoes, the majority opinion in Germany held that they were not protectable at all under copyright, because, in view of their functional character and the limited space left for individual expression, they could never rise beyond the threshold of mere (skillful) craftsmanship. Distancing itself from that position, the Federal Supreme Court (BGH) declared in a landmark decision of December 14, 1954 ("*Mantelmodell*") that not only could the drawings and sketches made in the process of creating new fashion be protected under copyright as works of applied art, but that the same applies to apparel resulting from such creative activities.[8]

The decision met with mixed reactions in the literature. While it was welcomed by some as overdue,[9] others remained skeptical, contending that while copyright may indeed apply to haute couture, it should not cover

[4] For an overview see F.-K. Beier, "Der Schutz von Modeschöpfungen in Deutschland und Frankreich," *GRUR* Ausland 1955, 337.

[5] Reichsgericht (Supreme Court of the German Reich, "RG") April 9, 1937, *GRUR* 1938, 68.

[6] RG, March 19, 1932, RGZ 135, 385.

[7] RG, June 12, 1937, RGZ 155; Landgericht (District Court, "LG") Dresden, May 16, 1930, *GRUR* 1930, 1209; LG Berlin, March 14, 1935, *GRUR* 1936, 204; Oberlandesgericht (Higher Regional Court, "OLG") Dresden, October 11, 1932, MuW 1933, 207.

[8] BGH *NJW* 1955, 460 – *Mantelmodell* (coat model). The decision concerned the unauthorized copying of a winter-coat manufactured by the defendants on the basis of sketches provided by the plaintiff. The appeal court and the court of first instance had dismissed the claim; the BGH advised the appeal court to extend the examination to other grounds of protection, in particular copyright. The final outcome of the case is unknown.

[9] F.-K. Beier, *supra* note 4, at 339.

ready-to-wear apparel.[10] However, pursuant to the BGH, that distinction is irrelevant: As pointed out in "*Mantelmodell*," the mode of manufacture does not influence or change the artistic character of an item, the only decisive test being whether "observers that are reasonably familiar with evaluating art" would find a sufficient degree of individual creative character.

In spite of that ruling, copyright never became a stronghold for fashion protection in Germany. Due to the so-called theory of the tiers ("*Stufentheory*"),[11] established German doctrine holds that the threshold for copyright protection of works of applied art is rather high and cannot be met by items which only display a minimum degree of creativity. The purpose of that approach is to reserve a meaningful scope of application for design legislation, so as to avoid a total overlap of protection.[12]

While copyright protection for fashion therefore remained a purely theoretical option, more realistic chances were provided by registration under the (previous) Industrial Design Act. However, not much use was made of that alternative either. Although offering a relatively simple registration procedure without substantive examination, the system, with its formal requirements, was considered as too costly and time-consuming. Further complaints concerned the fact that the novelty requirement was difficult to comply with by an industry characterized by slightly varied reprises of former trends and styles rather than by linearly progressing innovation.[13]

Another line of cases, which started with a decision of the BGH in 1973 ("*Modeneuheit*"), proved to be more efficient than design protection and more readily available than copyright.[14] The plaintiff, a French

[10] For instance K. Nicolini in her comment on the *Mantelmodell*-decision, *NJW* 1955, 461.

[11] The theory was first conceived by the German scholar Eugen Ulmer. See E. Ulmer, *Urheber- und Verlagsrecht* (3rd edn., Springer, Berlin, 1980) § 25 III. It was finally declared obsolete in a recent decision by the BGH, 13 November 2013, 1 ZR 143/2013 – *Geburtstagszug* (birthday train), Beck RS 2013, 22507.

[12] The approach is explained in a BGH decision concerning jewelry (brooch and ear-clips) in the shape of a thistle: "[While] case law in the field of musical and literary creations acknowledges the so-called 'small change' that covers simple creations that are only barely susceptible to protection ... the case law on applied art, to the extent that it is entitled to design protection, has always applied stricter criteria. ... Since even a design that is susceptible to design protection must stand out from unprotected average designs, ... an even greater difference must apply for copyright protection, i.e., the work must clearly surpass works of average design." BGH June 22, 1995 – Case No. I ZR 119/93, 38 *IIC* 140 (1997) – *Silberdistel* (silver thistle).

[13] The risks concerning novelty were somewhat limited by the fact that the relevant prior art was restricted to designs that were known, or could have been known, to designers in Germany; BGH, May 8, 1968 – Case No. I ZR 67/65, *NJW* 1968, 2193 – *Rüschenhaube* (lady's bonnet with ruchets).

[14] BGH, January 19, 1973 – Case No. 1 ZR 39/71 – *Modeneuheit* (fashion novelty); *GRUR* 1973, 478.

company, was a widely known manufacturer of fabric, with customers inter alia in the famous haute couture firms. The defendant produced ready-made apparel. In the spring/summer season of 1968, the plaintiff had offered for sale a combination of matching fabrics (silk and wool) characterized by subtle changes in the coloring achieved by specific weaving and dyeing techniques. Having ordered some fabric samples from the plaintiff, the defendant had allegedly commissioned another manufacturer to produce the same kind of matching silk and wool, and had tailored these fabrics into dresses that were sold in a chain of low-budget department stores in Germany. The plaintiff filed suit for copyright infringement and unfair competition. Concerning copyright the courts of lower instance had found that the fabric did not reveal a sufficient degree of individual creative character; however, the claim was granted under the general clause of the UWG. The decision was confirmed by the BGH: While in principle, imitation of products that are not protected by any intellectual property law must remain permissible, this is different in case of "fashion novelties" where (a) the imitated product has a certain "competitive individuality" (*wettbewerbliche Eigenart*) distinguishing it from merely commonplace (or, in the fashion sector: "trendy") articles, and (b) the imitated product is the result of efforts and financial investment which could not be recouped if others were free simply to imitate the achievement.[15] In view of the short-lived character of fashion items, the BGH added that protection should in general be granted for only one season, leaving it open whether an extension could be accorded under certain circumstances.

Further decisions followed.[16] While the basic tenets announced in the first case were not questioned, the duration of protection was subsequently extended to two consecutive seasons, in particular where the garment at stake was to be worn in the intermediate season – days of neither much heat nor cold – which in wet, temperate climate zones like in Germany extends over a good part of the year. More than that was not readily conceded. In "*Trachtenjanker*",[17] concerning a close imitation of a

[15] In that regard, the approach adopted in the BGH's reasoning is similar to that of the US Supreme Court in *International News Service v. Associated Press*, 248 U.S. 215 (1918) regarding "hot news," while the same approach was rejected by the Second Circuit as inapplicable to fabric patterns, *Cheney Bros. v. Doris Silk Corp.*, 35 F.2d 279, 280–81 (2d Cir. 1929). See Hemphill and Suk, Chapter 7 in this volume, note 67 and accompanying text.

[16] See, for instance, BGH November 10, 1983 Case No. I ZR 158/81, 15 *IIC* 777 (1984) – *Hemdblusenkleid* (shirt dress); decision of May 23, 1991 Case No. I ZR 286/89 – *Kastanienmuster* (chestnut pattern); decision of January 30, 1992 Case No. I ZR 113/90 – *Pullovermuster* (patterned sweater).

[17] BGH November 6, 1997 Case No. I ZR 102/95, *GRUR* 1997, 477 – *Trachtenjanker* (Bavarian jacket).

jacket in traditional Bavarian style with the pockets being shaped like small Bavarian leather backpacks, it was pointed out that protection under the fashion novelties jurisprudence was definitely no longer available after two years from market launch. However, it was also indicated that more extended protection might be granted under unfair competition aspects if the article had an inherent capacity to indicate commercial origin,[18] but that this would only be found in exceptional cases.

The path to European harmonization

Although the fashion industry was not left without protection in Germany, the legal situation was largely considered as unsatisfactory. The case law based on the UWG did not provide a clear and stable legal basis for protection. Without questioning the basic need for protection in the relevant cases, doubts were raised against the legitimacy of courts granting a quasi-IP right *praeter legem*, without ever having received a clear mandate to do so.[19]

On the European level, the uncertainties were even more hazardous. No harmonization was (or is) achieved with regard to unfair conduct between competitors.[20] Also, industrial design protection was regulated quite differently, with some countries following a patent-like approach with a strict novelty requirement and monopoly-type protection, and others favoring a system similar to copyright with a (low) originality threshold and protection against copying only. No attempt was made until the late 1980s to overcome the differences by proposing harmonized legislation.

With the European legislature remaining inactive, academic initiatives rose to the challenge.[21] In particular, a proposal was elaborated within

[18] This does not mean that the requirements for protection of unregistered trademarks would have to fulfilled; see the comments at pp. 187–88 regarding BGH *GRUR* 2006, 79 – *Jeans*; English translation in 38 *IIC* 128 (2007) with brief explanations on the regulatory background in notes 29 and 32 *infra*.

[19] The issue as to what extent courts can and should grant protection against imitation beyond the area covered by intellectual property rights has provoked much scholarly debate (not only) in Germany. For an overview see A. Ohly, "The Freedom of Imitation and its Limits – A European Perspective," 41 *IIC* 206 (2010); for an early account of the legal situation in Austria, Germany and Switzerland see F. Schönherr, "Slavish Imitation in German, Austrian and Swiss Case Law," 6 *IIC* 60 (1975).

[20] The European harmonization directive on unfair commercial practices (*supra* note 2) only applies to B2C measures, whereas it "neither covers nor affects the national laws on unfair commercial practices which harm only competitors' economic interests or which relate to a transaction between traders" (Recital 6 of the UCP Directive).

[21] In addition to the Max Planck group, whose proposal is presented below, this concerned a loose grouping of eminent European scholars who held meetings in the North of Italy

the Max Planck Institute in Munich, under the chairmanship of the Institute's late director Friedrich-Karl Beier.[22] The work took its cue from a comparative analysis of the current design laws, and from a survey undertaken among European designers. Its chief purpose was to make design protection more easily available in practice: The threshold for protection should be relatively low ("individual character" instead of "originality"/"creativeness"), there should be a twelve-month grace period during which the designer could use the design openly on the market without thereby destroying its novelty at the time of application, and the governing perspective – both with regard to the threshold for protection and for assessing infringement – should be that of the relevant users instead of design experts. Furthermore, the Max Planck draft proposed to combine regular design protection obtained through registration with short-term protection of unregistered designs. In that regard, the proposal was clearly inspired by the German case law concerning fashion novelties, thereby aiming at harmonization "through the back-door" of one specific type of unfair competition protection that would otherwise have been impossible to achieve.

When the proposal was made public in 1990,[23] the deadline for completion of the Internal Market, to be achieved by the end of 1992,[24] was drawing near. Feeling the time pressure, the Commission readily accepted the proposal as a basis for its own harmonization efforts. A Green Paper on the Legal Protection of Industrial Designs was published in 1991,[25] and subsequently led to the enactment of the European Design Directive (71/98/EC; "DD") and the Community Design Regulation (6/2002; "CDR"). Both instruments reflect a number of features contained in the Max Planck proposal. This applies in

(the "Treviso group"); see Disegno Industriale e Protezione Europa, Records of an international congress held in Treviso, October 12–13, 1989, edited by Camera di comercio industria artigianato agricoltura Treviso (Giuffrè, Milan 1989). The group favored a copyright-type of regulation, as endorsed inter alia by H. Cohen Jehoram, "Cumulative Design Protection, a System for the EC?" (1993) *EIPR* 83, 87.

[22] The group further consisted of Kurt Haertel, former president of the German Patent Office and one of the fathers of the European Patent Convention, Prof. Marianne Levin (Stockholm) and this author, at that time a complete novice to the field.

[23] F.-K. Beier, K. Haertel, M. Levin and Annette Kur, "On the Way to a European Design," 22 *IIC* 523 (1991).

[24] Due to the "Single European Act" (first substantive revision of the Rome Treaty (1958)), signed in Brussels and Luxemburg in 1986.

[25] Commission Document III/F/513/91 (June 1991). The Commission's Green Paper and the inspiration it took from the Max Planck proposal are sharply criticized by H. Cohen Jehoram, "The EC Green Paper on the Legal Protection for Industrial Design – Half Way Down the Right Track," (1992) *EIPR* 75; in reaction to that A. Kur, "The Green Paper's Design Approach – What's Wrong With It?," (1993) *EIPR* 374.

particular to short-term informal protection, which is anchored in Article 11 CDR;[26] it also concerns the twelve-month grace period and the low protection threshold. Furthermore, as recommended in the Max Planck proposal, registration on the Community level as well as in most Member States is without substantive examination, thus leading to fast and relatively cheap (though insecure[27]) protection.

Claims for subsequent protection: The Benetton cases

It is difficult to judge whether the harmonization of design protection in Europe has actually achieved its goals in general, and regarding the fashion industry in particular. At least in its registered form, design protection to date is not frequently used by fashion firms or designers, for reasons that remain unclear. Concerning the UCD, no data or empirical studies seem to exist about the actual frequency and impact of claims based on that right.

In any case, the availability of protection under the UCD does not seem to have preempted further claims based on unfair competition or IP law for protection of product design; protection after the lapse of the UCD is still in demand.[28]

One exemplary case is presented by the dispute between the firms G-Star and Benetton over alleged imitation by Benetton of the "Elwood" jeans. In Germany, the case was brought on the basis of the UWG.[29] Several years after first marketing of the jeans by G-Star, Benetton started selling very similar pants, showing the same pattern of stitches at the crotch, the knees, and the back of the jeans. In defence against G-Star's claim, Benetton argued that European design legislation imposes a three-year limit for protection of unregistered designs, meaning that even close reproductions should be admissible after that period. The BGH agreed that, in principle, a finding of unfairness of the

[26] Informal protection lasts for three years (whereas only two years were proposed in the Max Planck draft).

[27] Whether a Community design is actually valid will only be tested upon request of invalidation (Art. 52 CDR) or by way of counterclaim in infringement proceedings (Art. 84 CDR).

[28] As is pointed out below, the opinion is endorsed in this brief chapter that even if certain protection gaps persist in spite of the rather generous coverage of fashion articles by European design legislation, additional protection should not be granted where it disrupts the systemic boundaries limiting protection under design legislation as well as under trademark law.

[29] BGH *GRUR* 2006, 79 – *Jeans*; English translation in 38 *IIC* 128 (2007). Protection under Section 4 no 9 lit b UWG is to be distinguished from protection under the German Trademark Act for unregistered marks; see *infra*, note 32.

imitation could not be grounded on objectives running parallel to those on which protection for unregistered designs is based, in particular the "competitive individuality" of the item. However, that did not rule out the possibility to grant protection based on the inherent distinctive character of the design, the imitation of which might result in an "avoidable deception as to origin" among the target group, which is prohibited pursuant to Section 4 no 9 lit b UWG.[30]

As a matter of principle, the BGH's ruling in the "*Jeans*" case is in sync with previous decisions holding that whereas special protection for "fashion novelties" is short-lived, it is not excluded that longer protection is granted on the basis of an inherent capability to distinguish.[31] On the other hand, that approach is problematic for a number of reasons. First, the distinction between the "capability to distinguish" and the "competitive individuality" of a shape is rather unclear; for practical matters, both are frequently vested in exactly the same features of the protected item. Second, if it is assumed (as seems to be suggested by the BGH) that "capability to distinguish" is found where the shape has acquired a certain degree of secondary meaning (or "acquired distinctiveness" in European parlance), protection remains questionable where the level of public awareness is inferior to the threshold regularly required for protection of unregistered marks under trademark law.[32] Third, the Court did not consider whether the post-three-year protection granted in the actual case might clash with fundamental legal principles concerning the aesthetic functionality of product shapes.

The latter aspect was addressed in the second notable decision concerning the "Elwood" jeans, litigated in the Netherlands. Following extensive marketing campaigns, the jeans had been registered as a Benelux trademark. In an infringement suit filed against it, Benetton contested the protectability of the mark based on Article 3(1)(e)(iii) Trademark Directive (95/2008/EC; "TMD"), which excludes signs from protection that consist exclusively of shapes giving essential value to the goods. According to the Dutch Supreme Court, the appearance of the jeans had indeed conferred essential value to the garment when it was

[30] It is important to note here that it was not even argued by G-Star that the consumers were actually deceived by the similarity, due to the fact that the jeans were clearly marked with Benetton's trademark.

[31] As pointed out in *Trachtenjanker*, *supra* note 17.

[32] The conditions for, and extent of, protection for unregistered marks are not harmonized in Europe. In Germany, the general threshold for trademark protection of shapes such as in the case at bar would be rather high (not less than 50 percent of the target public), whereas the threshold for granting protection under Section 4 no 9 lit b is considerably lower.

first marketed, whereas at the time of registration, its commercial value was rather due to the fact that the interested circles recognized the arrangement of stitches as indicating commercial origin. The question was therefore referred to the Court of Justice of the European Union (CJEU) whether the jeans must nevertheless remain excluded from protection. The CJEU confirmed, referring to the wording of Article 3(1)(e) and Article 3(3) TMD, that whenever a shape is found to be caught by the exclusion clause, it can never be registered as a trademark, irrespective of the distinctive character it may later-on acquire.[33]

Concluding remarks

This is not the place to question the wisdom of the CJEU's reasoning in *Benetton.*[34] It must be noted, though, that the judgment practically results in a categorical exclusion from trademark registration of any kind of apparel, no matter how much its appearance may become associated in the public's mind with specific firms or designers.

Does that pose a major problem for the fashion industry? The answer is most likely negative. Though *trademark* protection may be out of reach, the fact remains that *design* protection is easy to obtain through registration, and even without that, informal protection is granted for a time period which will in many cases be sufficient to cover the full marketing period.[35] Furthermore, trademark protection remains available for the labels and logos of fashion design, and also for specific features usually referred to as "position marks," like the red flag at the rear pocket of Levi's jeans or the red and white rectangle stitched on Hilfiger clothes.[36]

True, there may be protection gaps that courts could be tempted to fill by unfair competition law or similar rules regulating marketing conduct. However, decisions such as that of the German BGH risk disrupting the systemic boundaries limiting protection under design legislation as well

[33] CJEU Case C-371/06, *Benetton v. G-Star*, [2007] ECR I-7709.

[34] For a more extensive analysis and critique see A. Kur, "Too pretty to protect?", Max Planck Institute for Intellectual Property & Competition Law Research Paper No. 11–16, at http://papers.ssrn.com/sol3/papers.cfm?abstract_id=1935289.

[35] It must be noted that designers can only benefit from informal protection if the design has been made available "in the territory of the EU" (Art. 111a(5) CDR). American fashion which is not launched simultaneously in the EU will remain unprotected unless it is registered.

[36] Harder cases are presented when such features become an integral part of the product's attractiveness, such as contrast-coloured stripes running along the sides of tracksuits. It is remarkable that the CJEU completely disregarded the aesthetic functionality of such features and the resulting constraints for competition in Case C-408/01, *Adidas v. Fitnessworld*, [2003] ECR I-12537.

as in trademark law. Instead of expanding the protection granted under the pertinent IP laws in a clandestine way, it should be accepted that, without design registration and after the lapse of the three-year period of informal protection, even plain imitation of fashion design is admissible, as long as the different commercial sources are clearly indicated, and provided that no actual consumer confusion is likely to occur.

Part V

Traditional knowledge

9 "Ka Mate Ka Mate" and the protection of traditional knowledge

Susy Frankel

Introduction

[The] traditional knowledge debate can also lead the intellectual property policy community to reflect deeply about the central tenets of the IP system, its core principles and cultural assumptions, indeed its very legitimacy and fundamental policy rationale. For the policy domain of IP the traditional knowledge debate has been a tonic, helping to open up a more informed, more inclusive, more broadly based discourse on the role, the principles and the legitimacy of the IP system.[1]

When the debate about the relationship between intellectual property and traditional knowledge began, the stance taken by both those in favour of some protection and those against protection was that traditional knowledge and intellectual property are incompatible. Indeed, the intellectual property system was not designed to protect traditional knowledge, even if in some instances it has protected an aspect of a work of traditional knowledge, such as a song receiving copyright protection.[2] As dialogue about the relationship between the two areas has grown, however, there is a new focus to the debate. That focus has shown ways in which those seeking to protect traditional knowledge might both obtain protection that is distinct from intellectual property and also how they might utilise the intellectual property system.[3] There is also discussion, which as yet falls short of agreement,

[1] Antony Taubman, 'Trading Places: New Dialogues, New Pathways – A Preface to Indigenous Peoples' Innovative Knowledge: IP Pathways to Development' in Peter Drahos and Susy Frankel (eds), *Indigenous Peoples' Innovative Knowledge: IP Pathways to Development* (Australian National University e-press, 2012), ('Drahos and Frankel').

[2] For a detailed discussion of the ways in which the intellectual property system does not fit and consequently cannot protect traditional knowledge see Susy Frankel, *Intellectual Property in New Zealand* (2nd edn, LexisNexis, Wellington, 2011) ch 2.

[3] One suggestion has been the use of geographical indications. See, for example, Daniel Gervais, 'Traditional Innovation and the Ongoing Debate on the Protection of Geographical Indications' in Drahos and Frankel, above n 1. I have disputed geographical indications' overall utility for protecting innovative indigenous traditional knowledge; see Susy Frankel, 'The Mismatch of Geographical Indications and Traditional Knowledge' (2011) 29 (3) *Prometheus* 253

about how the intellectual property system might be adjusted to take account of traditional knowledge in appropriate circumstances.[4] In some jurisdictions aspects of intellectual property law have been amended to interface with traditional knowledge related claims.[5] Such initiatives have primarily arisen from local interests, but the international discussion of the protection of traditional knowledge has been dynamic. The TRIPS Agreement[6] has placed intellectual property in a trade setting and, accordingly, the rationales for intellectual property have been exposed to new analyses and new ideas. This is so even if politics, and the effective cessation of the Doha Round of negotiations at the World Trade Organization (WTO), has prevented progress on the specific issues relating to traditional knowledge.[7] An increase in trade has also resulted in an increase in opportunities for trade in products of traditional knowledge and cultural heritage.

Trade has contributed to a 'more broadly based discourse' than the dead-end focus of how traditional knowledge does not fit intellectual property.[8] The link between trade and intellectual property has at international level created a focus on how they can work together. That focus has resulted in the tradability of traditional knowledge as the parallel discourse, even if traditional knowledge is not recognised as having the equivalent legal status of traditional intellectual property. Although the dialogue on the nexus between trade and traditional knowledge is undeveloped and stagnant at the WTO, the same is not true at the World Intellectual Property Organization (WIPO). The WIPO discussion has, since its inception, made significant progress and the Intergovernmental Committee (IGC) is now charged with

[4] The proposal for a requirement, in the TRIPS Agreement, of disclosure of the origin of genetic resources and associated traditional knowledge as a requirement of a patent application is such an example.

[5] See for example, the Trade Marks Act 2002 (NZ), s. 17(1)(b), which allows Māori to object to the registration of offensive trade marks. See also Susy Frankel, 'Third-Party Trade Marks as a Violation of Indigenous Cultural Property – A New Statutory Safeguard' (2005) 8 *Journal of World Intellectual Property Law* 83.

[6] Agreement on Trade-Related Aspects of Intellectual Property Rights, 15 April 1994, Marrakesh Agreement Establishing the World Trade Organization (WTO Agreement), 1869 U.N.T.S. 299, 33 I.L.M. 1197 (1994).

[7] See generally Michael Blakeney, 'The Pacific Solution: The European Union's Intellectual Property Rights IPR Activism in Australia and New Zealand's Sphere of Influence' in Drahos and Frankel, above n 1.

[8] I describe this as a 'dead-end focus' because spotting the differences does not resolve the issues about when and why traditional knowledge should be protected. As is discussed below, because of the misfit between traditional knowledge and existing intellectual property laws *sui generis* protection of traditional knowledge is most appropriate, but that *sui generis* protection must have a substantive interface with the intellectual property system.

negotiating a treaty.[9] Drafts exist, but there is significant opposition, most notably from the United States. This chapter addresses some specifics of that opposition.

One interesting feature of the WIPO process is that it is developing an international agreement ahead of many of its members having relevant domestic laws. This perhaps contrasts to other international intellectual property treaty-making processes where domestic norms are well embedded and the international process is a negotiation about bringing those domestic norms into greater international harmony. It is wrong, however, to conceptualise the WIPO–IGC process as a complete contrast to other treaty processes. After all, the negotiation of international agreements usually requires the parties to change their domestic laws. In the WIPO–IGC process one difficulty is the relative lack of norms at domestic law for the WIPO process to draw on. The reason, however, for an international process is precisely because it is the considerable increase in international trade in intellectual property and cultural goods that has given rise to the call for the protection of traditional knowledge. Uses of Māori culture, for example, include uses by multi-national businesses, including Ford, Lego, Sony and Fiat. In all of those instances the companies have extracted value from Māori culture in order to sell products and in some instances to create new works of intellectual property. The issues over the protection of traditional knowledge are not, therefore, isolated to some parts of the world and they go to the heart of intellectual property law and the values that it has in encouraging anyone to make use of anything that is in the so-called public domain to create and innovate.[10] It is for these reasons that the protection of traditional knowledge needs to be addressed both within the intellectual property system and outside of it, where traditional knowledge protection does not fit the intellectual property system. In other words, although traditional knowledge is treated as on, or beyond, the edge of intellectual property its protection has a role both at the edge of intellectual property law and in the heart of the law.

In the early days of the debate about traditional knowledge WIPO conducted an investigation into traditional knowledge[11] and subsequently created the IGC to discuss whether and how traditional

[9] See WIPO Intergovernmental Committee at www.wipo.int/tk/en/igc/. See also Silke von Lewinski, Chapter 10 in this volume.

[10] Different cultures have different views of what is or ought to be in the public domain; see discussion below.

[11] For a discussion of that investigation see WIPO, Report on Fact-Finding Missions on Intellectual Property and Traditional Knowledge (1998–1999) at www.wipo.int/tk/en/resources/publications.html.

knowledge should be protected. The WIPO process is divided into considering traditional knowledge and the related categories of traditional cultural expressions (TCEs) and genetic resources. Defining traditional knowledge poses some difficulties because of its wide scope,[12] but it can be defined for those who find definition necessary. One definition is that traditional knowledge is:

> [I]ntellectual activity in a traditional context, and includes the know-how, skills, innovations, practices and learning that form part of traditional knowledge systems, and knowledge embodying traditional lifestyles of indigenous and local communities, or contained in codified knowledge systems passed between generations and continuously developed following any changes in the environment, geographical conditions and other factors. It is not limited to any specific technical field, and may include agricultural, environmental and medicinal knowledge, and any traditional knowledge associated with cultural expressions and genetic resources.[13]

In this chapter I refer to traditional knowledge, rather than distinguishing between traditional knowledge and TCEs. I also refer to mātauranga Māori, which might best translate as the knowledge and the process of acquiring that knowledge.

> 'Mātauranga' derives from 'mātau', the verb 'to know'. 'Mātauranga' can be literally translated as 'knowing' or 'knowledge'. But 'mātauranga' encompasses not only what is known but also how it is known – that is, the way of perceiving and understanding the world, and the values or systems of thought that underpin those perceptions. 'Mātauranga Māori' therefore refers not only to Māori knowledge, but also to the Māori way of knowing ... Mātauranga Māori incorporates language, whakapapa, technology, systems of law and social control, systems of property and value exchange, forms of expression, and much more. It includes, for example, traditional technology relating to food cultivation, storage, hunting and ... it includes arts such as carving, weaving, tā moko (facial and body tattooing), the many performance arts such as haka (ceremonial dance), waiata (song), whaikōrero (formal speechmaking), karanga (ceremonial calling or chanting), and various rituals and ceremonies.[14]

[12] The problem with definition can be its failure to recognise the rational boundaries and dynamics of possessing knowledge, rather than the analytical facets of the knowledge. See the 'Quicksands of Definition:' in Peter Drahos and Susy Frankel 'Indigenous Peoples' Innovation and Intellectual Property: The Issues' in Drahos and Frankel, above n 1 at 9–10.

[13] 'The Protection of Traditional Knowledge: Revised Objectives and Principles', WIPO Document WIPO/GRTKF/IC/18/5 (10 January 2011), see Annex at 18. For an explanation of what is meant by traditional cultural expressions see 'The Protection of Traditional Cultural Expressions: Draft Articles', WIPO Document prepared by the Secretariat, WIPO/GRTKF/IC/18/4 REV (14 April 2011).

[14] Waitangi Tribunal, Ko Aotearoa Tēnei: A Report into Claims Concerning New Zealand Law and Policy Affecting Māori Culture and Identity (2011), ('*Ko Aotearoa Tēnei*').

Those who seek to protect traditional knowledge face many objections. The most often heard objection, particularly on the international stage, is that it lacks the characteristics of intellectual property. In this chapter I use the story of Ka Mate Ka Mate to explain why protection is called for. As part of that explanation I use aspects of a United States' submission to the WIPO–IGC negotiations, which questions how traditional knowledge can or should be protected. This chapter shows how each of the questions in the United States' submission is answerable and that such abstract questions are a distraction from the real issue of how people, who are often in considerable need of economic development, can best utilise the resources they have to achieve that development. If an underlying rationale is needed for the protection of traditional knowledge then the need for economic and related cultural development is a key feature of such a rationale.

In some instances holders of traditional knowledge derive economic benefit from applied uses of their knowledge. Many holders of traditional knowledge need economic development opportunities. The protection of their traditional knowledge may very well provide the legal tool to support such opportunities, although legal tools alone are not enough to stimulate economic development. The need for such economic development is well recognised, yet third parties rather than traditional knowledge holders often derive considerable economic benefit from uses of traditional knowledge. Another reason for the protection of traditional knowledge is to enable its continuous development and to support, particularly, indigenous peoples' cultural development. Consequently, protecting traditional knowledge is a means of encouraging creativity and innovation. In this chapter I use the story of Ka Mate Ka Mate to illustrate these points and to show how it, and other examples of the creative outputs of traditional knowledge, should be protected.

Ka Mate Ka Mate has been the subject of two Waitangi Tribunal disputes and several trade mark related cases. This chapter describes the Waitangi Tribunal process as well as the trade mark cases. The chapter then turns to show how Ka Mate has become valued both within New Zealand and around the world. It has been used (Māori say misused) in a number of countries other than New Zealand, including Italy where it featured as part of a Fiat commercial. There the claimed offence was not only that it was commercialised without permission, but also because women performed this haka. Haka can be written for women, but that one was not. That was not, however, the only objection to how it was used. It was incorrectly performed in a variety of ways and was used to sell motor vehicles, with no acknowledgement of the culture from which it came or recompense to members of that culture in any way.

Te Rauparaha and Ka Mate Ka Mate

Te Rauparaha was a chieftain and warrior of considerable mana (prestige and standing). He not only won several wars between his people, Ngāti Toa, and other Māori iwi (tribes), but he also fought the British and, although the British eventually came to control New Zealand, many battles with Māori were not easily won. Te Rauparaha died in 1849 and his image is legend.[15]

In one battle between his and another iwi Te Rauparaha was fleeing from the East Cape of the North Island and he hid from his pursuers. The place he chose to hide was in a kumara (a type of sweet potato) pit. The Waitangi Tribunal described this story as follows:[16]

> As Ngāti Te Aho chased [Te Rauparaha] and his people through the central North Island, Te Rauparaha sought the protection of his distant relative Te Heuheu of Ngāti Tūwharetoa. Te Heuheu sent him to lake Rotoaira, the home of a chief named Wharerangi. With Ngāti Te Aho nearly upon him, Wharerangi hid Te Rauparaha in a kūmara pit, then Wharerangi had his wife, Te Rangikoaea, straddle the pit to conceal him. Te Rauparaha lay quietly in the pit beneath the kuia while Ngāti Te Aho searched the village. It must be understood that to place a woman's genitals above the head of a chief was unthinkable, but this action saved his life. When Ngāti Te Aho passed through Rotoaira without finding him, Te Rauparaha burst from the pit and performed his now famous ngeri ...

According to Collins[17] it was the last stanza of Te Rauparaha's chant that was combined with actions and was performed as a haka. The haka has become known 'Ka Mate Ka Mate'. Its words and translation are shown in Table 9.1.

After Te Rauparaha died, the haka Ka Mate continued in importance to his people, Ngāti Toa. Today his descendants describe themselves as the kaitiaki (guardians) of Ka Mate. It is their heritage and their taonga (treasure). They have sought attribution and ownership of the haka and consequent control of its uses. Ka Mate has also been described as the 'most maligned, the most abused of all haka'.[18] This is in part because of the role it, and other haka, have played in New Zealand.

[15] One image can be found at Ministry of Education, Arts Online http://artsonline2.tki.org.nz/resources/units/visual_culture/wearable_art/te_rauparaha.php. That image is a watercolour of the Ngāti Toa (tribe) chief Te Rauparaha wearing a European naval uniform. He has a moko (facial tattoo) and he is posing alongside a flowering flax bush, and there is a bay in the background.

[16] *Ko Aotearoa Tēnei*, above n 14 at 40–41.The Tribunal cites Heni Collins, *Ka Mate Ka Ora: The Spirit of Te Rauparaha* (Steele Roberts, Wellington, 2010). That source also records variations on this story.

[17] Collins, above n 16.

[18] Tīmoti Kāretu, *The Dance of a Noble People* (National Library New Zealand, 1993) at 68.

Table 9.1 *Ka Mate Ka Mate and translation*

Ka Mate ! Ka Mate !	It is death! It is death!
Ka ora ! Ka ora !	It is life! It is life!
Ka Mate ! Ka Mate !	It is death! It is death!
Ka ora ! Ka ora !	It is life! It is life!
Tēnei te tangata pūhuruhuru	Here is this hairy person
Nāna i tiki mai whakawhiti te rā	Who has made the sun shine upon me!
A, hūpane, kaupane	One step up, another step up
Hūpane, kaupane, whiti te rā!	One step up, another step up, the sun shines!

Haka in New Zealand

Haka has become a significant part of New Zealand society. School children are taught haka and around the country there are competitions known as kapahaka. Māori have shared haka with Europeans, particularly on ceremonial occasions. Elsdon Best, an anthropologist who was in New Zealand in the nineteenth century, said 'accompanied by songs, [haka] were performed at a reception to visitors, to entertain them after a reception, to avenge insults, at peace-making ceremonies, during mourning rites, as a means of divination, where a good haul of fish was made, and many other occasions'.[19] From this time haka progressively became something for tourists[20] as well as locals. The status of haka was perhaps shown by its inclusion in the national holiday, Waitangi Day, which is the day Māori and the British signed a treaty (discussed below).[21]

In the 1970s, Māori and Ngāti Toa in particular, objected to uses of the haka which were inappropriate, racist or in some way debasing.[22]

[19] *Games and Pastimes of the Māori* (Dominion Museum Bulletin, Wellington, 1925 – reprinted without textual alterations, Te Papa Press, 2005). See also Alan Armstrong, *Maori Games and Haka* (Reed, Wellington, 1964) stating: 'The haka is a composition played by many instruments. Hands, feet, legs, body, voice, tongue, and eyes all play their part in blending together to convey in their fullness the challenge, welcome, exultation, defiance or contempt of the words ... It is disciplined, yet emotional. More than any other aspect of Māori culture, this complex dance is an expression of the passion, vigour and identity of the race. It is at its best, truly, a message of the soul expressed by words and posture.'

[20] See Susy Frankel and Megan Richardson, 'Cultural Property and "the Public Domain" Case Studies from New Zealand and Australia' in Christoph Antons (ed), *Traditional Knowledge, Traditional Cultural Expressions and Intellectual Property Law in the Asia-Pacific Region* (Kluwer Law International, The Netherlands, 2009).

[21] See Tīmoti Kāretu, above n 18 at 11, 68; Wira Gardiner, *Haka: A Living Tradition* (Hodder Moa Beckett, Auckland, 2001) at 101; and Vernon Reed, *The Gift of Waitangi* (AH and AW Reed, Wellington, 1957).

[22] One such event involved a university student rendition of Ka Mate which resulted in a human rights inquiry, see Human Rights Commission in *Racial Harmony in New Zealand: A Statement of Issues* (Human Rights Commission, 1979). See also, Kayleen

But, as Megan Richardson and I note elsewhere, there has not only been a culture of objection, there has also been active encouragement of Māori and non-Māori to use the haka appropriately for non-commercial exploitation.[23] Also, haka is not just a historic art form, it is developing. New hakas are created and written by both Māori and non-Māori in the twenty-first century.

Ka Mate in New Zealand

Without a doubt, Ka Mate, has earned the title of 'The Haka' because of the role it has played in New Zealand sport and, in particular, as the signature haka of the national rugby team, the All Blacks. The All Blacks started to use Ka Mate in 1905 and originally used it only when the team played overseas. In the 1987 World Cup they started to use it in every game they played. Ngāti Toa have stated that they are proud that the All Blacks use this haka. An anthropological study of attitudes to Ka Mate in New Zealand concluded 'for many New Zealanders as well as for many non-New Zealanders, it would appear that the haka is not primarily associated with [its origins] ...; rather, it is associated with a national rugby team known as the "All Blacks"'.[24] Although since that study Ngāti Toa's claim to the haka has been so well publicised they may be equally, if not more so, associated with its origins today.

Ngāti Toa's claim over Ka Mate sought control, particularly of commercial uses, over the haka, although Ngāti Toa have stated publicly that they do not mind respectful non-commercial uses of the haka. In 2012 the government of New Zealand agreed, in a deed of settlement with Ngāti Toa, to recognise Ngāti Toa's connection with the haka.[25] This recognition will involve a law, yet to be enacted, which will require attribution of the haka to both Te Rauparaha and Ngāti Toa, in certain circumstances. The settlement is for attribution and falls short of control, which is discussed further below. The haka has also been used to parody the All Blacks. One example is the so-called handbag incident. There the Australia Rugby team advertised a forthcoming test match against the All Blacks with a video showing the All Blacks holding handbags while performing the haka. The reason for this parody was that one of the All

Hazelhurst, *Racial Conflict and Resolution in New Zealand: The Haka Party Incident and its Aftermath, 1979–1980* (Australian National University, 1988).

[23] See discussion in Frankel and Richardson, above note 20, citing discussion in Wira Gardiner, *Haka: A Living Tradition* at 15–16.

[24] David Murray, 'Haka Fracas? The Dialectics of Identity in Discussions of a Contemporary Māori Dance' (2000) 11 *Aust. J of Anthropology* 345, 346.

[25] See Ngāti Toa Deed of Settlement, signed 7 December 2012, at http://nz01.terabyte.co.nz/ots/fb.asp?url=livearticle.asp?ArtID=1384035515.

Blacks had been injured by a handbag in a pub. One issue arising from the advertisement is who or what was being parodied: the All Blacks, the haka, or both?[26] The free speech issues this raises are discussed further below.

The All Blacks, New Zealand's national rugby team, although they use Ka Mate have also had another haka written by a Māori author especially for them. That haka is increasingly used in preference to Ka Mate. Perhaps most notably it was used in 2011 at the final of the Rugby World Cup. The culture of haka is alive and thriving. Māori do, however, exercise customary control over some uses of both old and where appropriate new haka. In order to reclaim greater control over Ka Mate Ka Mate, Ngāti Toa have tried to register the words as a trade mark and have brought two claims to the Waitangi Tribunal.

Registered trade marks

Because they could not claim in any court any protection to prevent others from misusing Ka Mate, Ngāti Toa filed an application to register as a trade mark 'Ka Mate'.[27] To date, the Intellectual Property Office of New Zealand (IPONZ) has not granted that application, although IPONZ has now registered as a trade mark a series of images of 'KA MATE KA ORA'.[28] Those registrations achieve the effect of protecting aspects of the haka, but they do not protect the whole haka from derogatory treatment or all commercial uses, as Ngāti Toa would wish. Thus, although making the best uses of the resource available, i.e. using trade marks because no other protection exists, Ngāti Toa have not been able to protect all that they seek to protect.[29] For this and other reasons Ngāti Toa brought claims to the Waitangi Tribunal.

The Waitangi Tribunal

The Waitangi Tribunal is a tribunal of inquiry established by statute.[30] The Tribunal investigates claims made under the Treaty of Waitangi

[26] See Frankel and Richardson, above n 20.

[27] The Trade Mark Register shows that the application is 'under an opposition proceeding'; see Trade mark 814421.

[28] Trade mark 827077, registered in relation to a variety of goods, including clothing and headgear, in classes 18, 25, 28, 35 and 41. Owned by a Māori organisation called Te Runanga o Toa Rangatira Incorporated, which is the iwi (tribal) authority for Ngāti Toa. The Trade Marks Register also shows three cancelled applications for all of the words of the haka; Trade marks 305166, 305167 and 305168.

[29] *Ko Aotearoa Tēnei*, above n 14, discusses other uses of trade marks to protect mātauranga Māori at 38–39 and 59.

[30] Treaty of Waitangi Act 1975, s. 5.

Table 9.2 *Article 2 of the Treaty of Waitangi*

Ko te tuarua	Article the second
Ko te Kuini o Ingarani ka wakarite ka wakaae ki nga RaNgātira ki nga hapu – ki nga tangata katoa o Nu Tirani te tino raNgātiratanga o ratou wenua o ratou kainga me o ratou taonga katoa	Her Majesty the Queen of England confirms and guarantees to the Chiefs and Tribes of New Zealand and to the respective families and individuals thereof the full exclusive and undisturbed possession of their Lands and Estates Forests Fisheries and other Preemption over such lands

(Te Tiriti O Waitangi). The Treaty is a founding document of New Zealand.[31] In essence it sets out the agreement between Māori and the Crown over the governance of New Zealand and is consequently of constitutional significance. The Treaty of Waitangi is in both Māori and English and both versions are official versions. They are not direct translations of each other.[32] The Second Article, Ko te tuarua, and, in particular, its reference to taonga is of direct relevance to mātauranga Māori and its relationship with intellectual property. The relevant Article in both Māori and English, which have equal status, is set out in Table 9.2.[33]

As it has inquiry powers, the Tribunal does not make rulings that have the force of law, but rather it makes recommendations to government.[34] As such, it recommends policy and does not draft law. Another limitation on the role of the Tribunal is that its jurisdiction is confined to making recommendations where there is a connection to the Treaty.

The descendants of Te Rauparaha, Ngāti Toa, have complained to the Waitangi Tribunal on two occasions about te tino rangitiratanga (literally, chieftainship, but perhaps more accurately self-determination and control)[35] over Ka Mate and the treatment of it as part of the body of

[31] For the Treaty's history see Claudia Orange, *The Treaty of Waitangi* (Bridget Williams Books, Wellington, 1992). For many years New Zealand courts doubted the legal importance of the Treaty of Waitangi, see *Wi Parata v. Bishop of Wellington* (1877) 3 NZ Jur (NS) SC 72.

[32] Treaty of Waitangi Act 1975, s. 2, which defines 'the Treaty' as including both the English and Māori versions set out in sch. 1 of the Act.

[33] This table is reproduced from Frankel, above n 2. See ch 3 of that text for further discussion of the Treaty of Waitangi.

[34] The government then decides how to respond to the recommendations. There are other institutions involved in the Treaty of Waitangi process. A key one is the Office of Treaty Settlements, which negotiates settlement with Māori where a settlement, such as in land claims, is the appropriate remedy.

[35] Te tino rangitiratanga is guaranteed to Māori under Article 2 of the Treaty of Waitangi; see Māori version of the Treaty.

knowledge and understanding; that is mātauranga Māori (Māori culture). In both inquiries the Tribunal recommended to the government that Ngāti Toa have a greater degree of control over Ka Mate. One of these inquiries related to Ngāti Toa's rights generally, including land rights. In that inquiry, based on the Tribunal's recommendation, the Crown, in the settlement letter following the recommendation, said it would 'record the authorship and significance of the haka' to Ngāti Toa.[36] Whatever that meant it falls short of a promise of giving rights or full protection of Ngāti Toa's interest in 'Ka Mate' and, as discussed above, has now resulted in a deed of settlement providing that there will be legislation requiring attribution of the haka to Ngāti Toa and Te Rauparaha. The other inquiry arose from a claim brought by Ngāti Toa and six other iwi[37] relating to intellectual property. That claim addressed, among other issues, the effect of intellectual property law on Ngāti Toa's interest in relation to Ka Mate Ka Mate and other taonga of Māori. The analysis in the Tribunal's report in this inquiry recommended greater measures be put in place to protect traditional knowledge.

The claim as an aspect of Ngāti Toa's culture and intellectual property

The claim to te tino rangitiratanga over Ka Mate was part of the claim that the Crown had not protected taonga as it is obligated to do under Article 2 of the Treaty of Waitangi. One strand of the claim was that the existing intellectual property system did not recognise Māori rights and that the Crown had allowed a system of intellectual property that had, in some instances, abrogated the treaty rights. In this chapter, I refer to this claim by its shortened report name *Ko Aotearoa Tēnei*.[38]

[36] New Zealand Press Association and Yvonne Tahana, 'Ka Mate Haka Rights Part of $300m Treaty Deal', *The New Zealand Herald*, 11 February 2009.

[37] The claimants were Haana Murray of Ngāti Kurī, Hema Nui a Tawhaki Witana of Te Rarawa, Te Witi McMath of Ngāti Wai, Tama Poata of Ngāti Porou, Kataraina Rimene of Ngāti Kahungunu and John Hippolite of Ngāti Koata.

[38] *Ko Aotearoa Tēnei*, above n 14. Translated *Ko Aotearoa Tēnei* means: 'This is Aotearoa/ New Zealand.' Aotearoa is the name for New Zealand. The claim resulted in a Report from the Waitangi Tribunal in 2011. In essence the report on the claim is about Māori culture and identity; New Zealand's laws, government policies and practices affect that culture; and whether Māori are able to live and develop (both culturally and economically) as Māori. There are two chapters of *Ko Aotearoa Tēnei* which directly discuss intellectual property law and the protection of Māori culture. The first is focused on cultural expressions and related traditional knowledge and the second discusses biological and genetic resources. The first chapter, 'Taonga Works and Intellectual Property' is most relevant here.

Ngāti Toa, in *Ko Aotearoa Tēnei*, sought the right to control the commercial exploitation of the haka[39] and to ensure that where it is performed it is done in a culturally appropriate way.[40] This claim was based on the Treaty of Waitangi guarantee of te tino rangitiratanga over their taonga works and related mātauranga Māori that is expressed in those works. The control Ngāti Toa sought for the haka and more broadly included that Māori maintain and develop their relationship with their taonga works. The relationship is one of guardianship over the taonga. Kaitiaki can be both a collective and an individual role. Māori iwi are kaitiaki of their taonga, such as Ngāti Toa are kaitiaki of the haka. Also individual Māori may be kaitiaki of some taonga. The author of a modern haka may, for example, be the kaitiaki of that haka. The kaitiaki relationship is one that relates to the past, present and future. As kaitiaki of taonga there is an ancestral relationship (whakapapa) and consequently kaitiaki are both guardians of that heritage and of the taonga and mātauranga Māori for future generations. As well as being able to be kaitiaki of their taonga, the claimants wished to be free to develop that relationship and, where they as kaitiaki consider it appropriate, to economically exploit and benefit from that relationship.

The Waitangi Tribunal in its report was careful to recognise that there are competing interests, such as the rights of the general public to use Māori culture and of existing intellectual property owners, which should be considered alongside the Māori interests in taonga works. Some people with competing interests, including New Zealand artists and designers as well as other holders of intellectual property rights, gave third party evidence at the hearings of the claim.[41] The current position is that those competing interests usually trump the Māori interest. *Ko Aotearoa Tēnei* recommends shifting that balance so that the Māori interests can, in appropriate circumstances, be the key interest that the law protects. The Tribunal also, in its recommendations, wanted to make sure that the recognition of other interests was balanced and did not result in marginalising the Māori interest or making it impossible for Māori to develop their culture. Therefore, the approach of the Tribunal was to recommend a regime that will shift the balance, but will not make it impossible for all New Zealanders to use Māori culture.

[39] *Ko Aotearoa Tēnei*, above n 14 at 41.

[40] See also Ngati Toa Rangatira, Letter of Agreement from the Crown, available at http://nz01.terabyte.co.nz/ots/DocumentLibrary/NgatiToaofferletter.pdf, where it is stated, at paragraph 42, that 'the expectation of Ngāti Toa that the primary objective of this redress is to prevent the misappropriation and culturally inappropriate use or performance of the haka "Ka Mate"'.

[41] *Ko Aotearoa Tēnei*, above n 14 at 74–77.

The Tribunal in its deliberations also noted that protecting Māori culture is about protecting New Zealand. It said that 'Taonga works are not just about Māori identity – they are about New Zealand identity, and a regime that delivers kaitiaki control of taonga works will also deliver New Zealand control of its unique identity.'[42] In relation to Ka Mate this might arguably be particularly so. At the time of writing the government has not yet responded to the recommendations of *Ko Aotearoa Tēnei*.

Why protect or not protect traditional knowledge and Ka Mate?

The key rationale in favour of protecting traditional knowledge is the kaitiaki relationship with it and the consequential benefits that flow from protecting that relationship, which include the protection of culture and the further encouragement of creativity and innovation. Once a relationship is established with a taonga, such as the Ka Mate, the choice to exploit the economic value of Ka Mate, it is said, ought to be the choice of the Ngāti Toa people. Yet, there is objection to protecting taonga works, and traditional knowledge more generally, both in New Zealand and worldwide.

In the WIPO–IGC process, the United States is one of the main opponents of forming a treaty to protect traditional knowledge. Some key aspects of the United States' objections are set out here.[43]

> ... what objective was sought to be achieved through according intellectual property protection (economic rights, moral rights) [to traditional knowledge (TK)]? Historically, information had been freely shared, except in limited circumstances, and for periods of limited duration. Furthermore, even with the limited circumstances of Intellectual Property rights such as Copyright and Patent, such legal systems had within them a concept of fair use or research use. How should these norms be balanced with any new exclusive rights granted on TK? ...
>
> Who should benefit from any protection of TK? Who should hold the rights to protectable TK? Should holders of TK that reside within the traditional origin of the TK and those who no longer reside within the same area be treated in the same way? How would a new system to protect TK change the right of TK holders to continue to use their TK? ...[44] If TK was protectable by patent,

[42] *Ko Aotearoa Tēnei*, above n 14.

[43] Intergovernmental Committee on Intellectual Property and Genetic Resources, Traditional Knowledge and Folklore, Eighteenth Session, Geneva, 9 to 13 May 2011, 'The Protection of Traditional Knowledge: Revised Objectives and Principles', Annex at p 8.

[44] The question omitted from here is 'How would the international concept of non-discrimination apply?' For discussion of that question see Susy Frankel, 'Attempts to Protect Indigenous Culture through Free Trade Agreements' in Christoph Graber, Karolina Kuprecht and Jessica Lai (eds), *International Trade in Indigenous Cultural Heritage* (Edward Elgar, Cheltenham, 2012).

copyright or other traditional intellectual property rights, should TK also be protectable by other means, i.e., new national laws?

The following sections address these questions, although in a slightly different order, through the specific example of Ka Mate Ka Mate and its story.

What objective was sought to be achieved through according intellectual property protection (economic rights, moral rights)?

The objectives in the WIPO process are clearly set out in its working documents and include that the protection of traditional knowledge should aim to:[45]

- recognise value;
- promote respect;
- meet the rights and needs of holders of traditional knowledge;
- promote conservation and preservation of traditional knowledge;
- empower holders of traditional knowledge and acknowledge the distinctive nature of traditional knowledge systems;
- support traditional knowledge systems;
- contribute to safeguarding traditional knowledge;
- repress unfair and inequitable uses or misappropriation and misuse;
- respect for and cooperation with relevant international agreements and processes;
- promote innovation and creativity; and
- promote community development and legitimate trading activities.

These objectives are broader than those usually framed in intellectual property law,[46] and the list of objectives is not exhaustive of what traditional knowledge owners may seek to achieve. Where intellectual property protection is involved, however, the short answer to the question of 'what objective' is sought, is both economic and moral rights. One motivation for seeking economic rights is that those seeking them need an economic return to develop as people and cultures in the twenty-first century. That, however, does not tell the whole story. This categorisation is an intellectual property perspective, where the labels 'economic' and 'moral' have existing meanings that reflect different aims from those sought for the protection of traditional knowledge. That difference is precisely why existing intellectual property rights cannot protect

[45] See above n 43, Annex at 6–7.
[46] See Silke von Lewinski, Chapter 10 in this volume.

traditional knowledge. This division into intellectual property categories, Ngāti Toa explained to the Waitangi Tribunal, causes a fundamental misunderstanding about what they seek in claiming te tino rangitiratanga over Ka Mate and other taonga. This is, in part, why a *sui generis* regime that interfaces with intellectual property, but is different from intellectual property, is what the Tribunal recommends. Additionally, the focus on whether the purpose of protection is economic or moral may not fully address that a key goal of protecting traditional knowledge is to maintain and develop a culture and consequently promote and support creativity and innovation of that culture.

Who should benefit from any protection of TK? Who should hold the rights to protectable TK?

Simply, the kaitiaki of a taonga work should benefit. Ngāti Toa as the kaitiaki of Ka Mate would benefit from its protection. The kaitiaki of the haka is well known. Who is a kaitiaki can be disputed and this is one of the reasons that the Waitangi Tribunal recommends that kaitiaki need to demonstrate their kaitiaki status in order to benefit from the protection.[47] Ngāti Toa and other kaitiaki importantly view themselves as guardians for future generations and so the benefit extends beyond the existing beneficiaries. Undoubtedly, the beneficiaries of traditional knowledge protection will not always be so readily identifiable, but frequently they are, in ways that the culture concerned recognises. In any event, it does not follow that because there is doubt, in some situations, over who is entitled to benefit from protection, that doubt should mean there is no protection overall. After all, orphan works are still copyright works.[48]

In the area of who should benefit there is likely to be an overlap with customary law.[49] The claimants of the traditional knowledge are those whose tradition is being protected. The beneficiaries are, therefore, the kaitiaki of traditional knowledge (or related mātauranga Māori). Such an approach is, in essence, a pluralistic approach to recognising who benefits from any rights. Also, a pluralistic approach can function to recognise that customary law is frequently not static and should not be treated as

[47] As discussed below, the Waitangi Tribunal recommends a new commission with an adjudicative role, which would include adjudicating, if necessary, between competing claims of kaitiaki status.

[48] An orphan work is a work where the author and/or owner of the copyright work cannot be identified.

[49] For a discussion of pluralism in the protection of traditional knowledge in the Pacific region, see Miranda Forsyth, 'Do You Want It Gift-Wrapped?: Protecting Traditional Knowledge in the Pacific Island Countries', in Drahos and Frankel, above n 1.

such. The recommendations of the Waitangi Tribunal effectively require those seeking protection of taonga works and associated mātauranga Māori to establish their role as kaitiaki. They can only really do so by reference to their custom.

What makes something a taonga work and who are the kaitiaki?

The Tribunal explained that what makes a work a taonga work is the relationship between Māori and the work. The relevant Māori could be an individual, a family (whānau); an extended family group (hapū) or a tribal group (iwi). In all cases, the relevant people are the kaitiaki of the taonga work and it is that relationship between the kaitiaki and the taonga work, for which the Tribunal found Article 2 of the Treaty of Waitangi guarantees an appropriate degree of protection. In the case of Ka Mate the kaitiaki are an iwi, Ngāti Toa.

The consequence of the focus on the relationship is that there are works that involve Māori elements which may not be taonga works. The Tribunal described these works as taonga-derived works and concluded that such works have no kaitiaki and, therefore, protection of them is necessarily less.[50] Ka Mate Ka Mate has a known and identifiable kaitiaki and is, therefore, a taonga work, not a taonga-derived work.

The distinction between taonga-derived works and taonga works might also be seen as reflecting the reality that allowing non-Māori to use Māori culture is also a benefit for Māori, as such use contributes to the culture's survival. It is for that reason that the Tribunal also said it did not recommend mātauranga Māori be treated as owned by Māori. The Tribunal said that 'building a legal wall around mātauranga Māori would . . . choke it'.[51]

One consequence of determining who benefits on the basis of a kaitiaki relationship is that the question, '[s]hould holders of TK that reside within the traditional origin of the TK and those who no longer reside

[50] 'There is another, more amorphous category of works. These are works that have a Māori element to them, but that element is generalised or adapted, and is combined with other non-Māori influences. Works like these are inspired either by taonga works or by the mātauranga Māori underlying those works, but the connection to mātauranga Māori is far more tenuous than is the case for taonga works themselves. We call these taonga-derived works. We put them into a different category because they are so generic or derivative they have no whakapapa and no kōrero except at a generalised level. Most importantly, taonga-derived works have no kaitiaki. By this we mean there is nothing about the Māori element of the work that would lead one to conclude that the responsibilities of kaitiakitanga in respect of it belong to a particular community or kin group. In short there is no natural connection with a kaitiaki community.' *Ko Aotearoa Tēnei*, above n 14 at 84–85.

[51] *Ko Aotearoa Tēnei*, above n 14 at 92.

within the same area be treated in the same way?' is answered 'yes'. The test is not residence but a kaitiaki relationship.

Another consequence is that the question '[h]ow would a new system to protect TK change the right of TK holders to continue to use their TK?' is also answered with reference to the kaitiaki relationship. The role of being a guardian of a taonga work includes developing it for uses for current and future generations.

If TK was protectable by patent, copyright or other traditional intellectual property rights, should TK also be protectable by other means, i.e., new national laws?

For the most part traditional knowledge is not protectable by traditional intellectual property rights and it is because of this that other means of protection for traditional knowledge are necessary.

The broad recommendations that the Waitangi Tribunal made in order to achieve the protection of taonga works and mātauranga Māori are:

1. New standards of legal protection governing the use of taonga works, taonga-derived works, and mātauranga Māori.
   (a) A general objection mechanism to prohibit the derogatory or offensive public use of taonga works, taonga-derived works, or mātauranga Māori.[52]
   (b) A mechanism by which kaitiaki can prevent any commercial exploitation of taonga works or mātauranga Māori (but not taonga-derived works) unless and until there has been consultation and, where found appropriate, kaitiaki consent.[53]
2. An expert commission to have wider functions in relation to taonga works, taonga-derived works, and mātauranga Māori.[54]

Ko Aotearoa Tēnei sets out how the proposed expert commission should have adjudicative, facilitative[55] and administrative functions.[56]

[52] The Tribunal recommended that anybody should be entitled to object to the derogatory or offensive public use of taonga works, taonga-derived works, or mātauranga Māori.

[53] The Tribunal recommended that only kaitiaki should be entitled to object to any non-derogatory or non-offensive commercial use of taonga works or mātauranga Māori.

[54] The Tribunal recommended that the government establish a commission. The commission should have multi-disciplinary expertise (encompassing mātauranga Māori, IP law, commerce, science, and stewardship of taonga works and documents at both commissioner and secretariat levels).

[55] The facilitative function of the commission includes producing guidelines and best-practice information for both kaitiaki and other users of Māori culture.

[56] The recommended administrative function relates to maintaining a register of kaitiaki in respect of particular taonga works. The register is voluntary because kaitiaki must be free to keep their taonga and mātauranga Māori secret if they wish.

The adjudicative functions would involve hearing complaints about 1 (a) and (b) above and deciding what steps must be taken to remedy the situation.[57] This adjunctive function is not only for fully fledged disputes, but the Tribunal also recommended that the commission has the power to give rulings where parties are uncertain if they should proceed or otherwise. The Tribunal suggested such a mechanism, with the aim that it should ameliorate any chilling effect from uses of Māori culture.

If the commission finds that a work is a taonga work,[58] the Tribunal recommendations are that kaitiaki must be involved in any decision about the taonga work's future, if any, commercial use. *Ko Aotearoa Tēnei* does not predetermine the exact scope of any kaitiaki rights. It says that should depend on the degree of the kaitiaki relationship. Thus, the nature of the relationship that kaitiaki has with the taonga work or mātauranga Māori, and the balancing of competing interests, will lead to a determination of an appropriate level of kaitiaki control.

The Tribunal recommends laws other than intellectual property laws as well as changes to intellectual property laws. It said:[59]

> This approach is not intended to create a new category of proprietary right, but is rather a way of recognising the relationship of kaitiaki with taonga works and some aspects of mātauranga Māori where it is proposed to exploit those things commercially. It is important to understand that our recommendations do not represent a wholesale change to the current system of IP protection, particularly copyright and trade mark protection. Nor would they grant perpetual copyright to kaitiaki. These recommendations are sui generis in that they would operate outside the Copyright Act 1994, the Trade Marks Act 2002, the Designs Act 1953, the internet registration system, and any other relevant Acts which protect IP or related rights. They would have independent legal enforceability in their own right. However, as we noted above, this sui generis system must effectively interface with the IP system so that no irresolvable conflict arises between them. The commission should provide that point of interface.

The last part of this passage emphasises the needs of any *sui generis* system and the intellectual property system to work together so that when there is conflict there is a mechanism for that conflict to be resolved.[60] This is

[57] This will also involve determining whether any particular work is a taonga work, or a taonga-derived work or otherwise, and who is kaitiaki of any taonga work. *Ko Aotearoa Tēnei*, above n 14 at 92.

[58] Such a finding is dependent on there being a proven kaitiaki.

[59] *Ko Aotearoa Tēnei*, above n 14 at 92.

[60] In New Zealand some of this interface already exists. New Zealand trade mark law includes a system where Māori can object to the registration of trade marks on the grounds that the trade mark applied for is culturally offensive or is likely to cause offence; Trade Marks Act 2002, s. 17(1). See also Frankel, above n 5 at 83; Susy Frankel, 'Trade Marks, Traditional Knowledge and Cultural Intellectual Property' in Graeme B.

important because for a *sui generis* system to be effective it needs to be made to work simultaneously with existing law. There are two alternatives. First, intellectual property law will dominate and defeat the purpose of the *sui generis* law. The second is that the *sui generis* system, as the later in time, might in some jurisdictions be deemed to overrule any prior conflicting laws.[61] Neither of these alternatives is the intention either of the Waitangi Tribunal or, I suggest, of those engaged in the WIPO–IGC process. Thus, it is important that protection of traditional knowledge not only be *sui generis*, or, as might be described in this volume, 'at the edge of intellectual property', but also be recognised by the regimes in the core of intellectual property law.[62]

Intellectual Property rights ... had within them a concept of fair use or research use. How should these norms be balanced with any new exclusive rights granted on TK?

The name 'traditional knowledge' is in some ways regrettable because it is apt to misinterpretation. The ability to extract and use knowledge is the cornerstone of much intellectual property and the protection of traditional knowledge suggests, to some, an incursion on that claim. However, that is not what was really claimed. The Waitangi Tribunal did not recommend absolute rights over Ka Mate or other taonga works. Its recommendations are tailored to that which Māori can, in the Tribunal's words, reasonably expect. The Tribunal's recommendation for protection of Ka Mate, and other taonga works, is to give kaitiaki control over the commercial exploitation, without which such protection gives the kaitiaki no return. The second element of protection is a right to object to offensive treatment of taonga. Neither recommendation, if brought into law, should stop others learning about the haka or using the knowledge it conveys. Nor indeed do they limit all fair use of the haka. The rights recommended are not absolute. However, the types of fair use are differently circumscribed than those found under copyright.

Parodying Ka Mate raises complex issues, which are worthy of a separate paper.[63] As a cultural icon the haka is almost certainly likely to

Dinwoodie and Mark D. Janis (eds), *Trade Mark Law and Theory: A Handbook of Contemporary Research* (Edward Elgar Press, USA, 2007).

[61] This could also create problems with existing international intellectual property treaty compliance.

[62] For a further discussion of the importance that traditional knowledge interfaces with existing intellectual property law see Susy Frankel, 'A New Zealand Perspective on the Protection of Mātauranga Māori' in Graber, Kuprecht and Lai, above n 44, 439 at 450–54.

[63] In New Zealand there is no statutory permitted act or fair use of copyright for parody.

be the subject of parody or social comment.[64] However, under New Zealand copyright law there is no fair use or permitted act for parody. Also, one might say that parody is a cultural construct. One person's parody is another's offence. There is no international view of what amounts to parody and legitimate free speech, and all rights are subject to reasonable limitations.[65] Whether protection of traditional knowledge from offensive or derogatory treatment is a reasonable limitation is debatable on any given facts. Several uses of Ka Mate remain in the public domain and have not been complained about.

One that caused complaint was Fiat's use of Ka Mate, or an imitation of it, in a commercial for a car.[66] In New Zealand, the advertisements were widely thought to be culturally offensive.[67] The government intervened to ask the producers to change the advertisement to be 'either performed by a Māori group or to have a haka composed for women to perform'.[68] Fiat declined both options and continued to air its advertisement. No further action was taken.

The association between the All Blacks and Ka Mate places the haka as something aggressively masculine. So much so, that even in the United States one sports team uses the haka to build some macho feeling.[69]

As to this use, Ngāti Toa said '[we have] no problem with the team using the haka – but they could do with a bit of discipline and technique'. 'You can't fault their enthusiasm' said Teariki Wi Neera, who is on Ngāti

[64] See Susy Frankel, 'From Barbie to Renoir: Intellectual Property and Culture' (2010) 41 *Victoria University of Wellington Law Review* 1 at 4. See also Robert Jahnke and Huia T. Jahnke, 'The Politics of Māori Image and Design' (2003) *He Pukenga Kōrero* 7 (1), 5–31 at 14 where the authors state 'the artifice of humour and wit can also conceal deceit. Beneath the charade of caricature is a colonial world view that sanitises the other with historical stereotypes of homogeneity and nationalism.' And for a similar discussion outside of the New Zealand context see Susan Scafidi, 'Intellectual Property and Cultural Products' (2001) *Boston University Law Review* 81 at 842.

[65] Lisa Ramsey advocates, therefore, that domestic law should define its 'speech-friendly' parameters before agreeing to international law limitations, see Lisa Ramsey, 'Free Speech and International Obligations to Protect Trademarks' (2010) 35 *Yale Journal of International Law* 405.

[66] A video of the advertisement can be found at http://stuffucanuse.com/italian_haka/fiat_haka.htm.

[67] For a discussion in the media, see Peter Lewis, 'Australia and New Zealand Take Rivalry to the Rugby Pitch' at www.abc.net.au/am/content/2006/s1681115.htm.

[68] See Steven Jackson and Brendan Hokowhitu, 'Sports, Tribes and Technology: The New Zealand All Blacks Haka and the Politics of Identity' in M. Silk, D.L. Andrews and C. Cole (eds), *Sport and Corporate Nationalisms* (Berg, New York, 2005).

[69] The San Mateo Bulldogs American Football team has posted footage of its pre-match haka on its Facebook page and it is clearly based on Ka Mate; see Ian Steward, 'Stamp of Approval to go to American haka' at www.stuff.co.nz/national/5717467/Stamp-of-approval-to-go-on-American-haka. The team claims using the haka has propelled it into winning the Northern California championship.

Toa's Ka Mate sub-committee. But he said their rendition was a bit like 'a bad Coke ad'. 'We're incredibly proud of Ka Mate and we prefer to see it done properly.' Wi Neera said Ngāti Toa would be happy to provide some instruction, an offer Bulldogs' assistant coach, Tim Tulloch, said his players would be 'ecstatic' to receive.[70]

The balance of norms that Ngāti Toa seems to advocate in the above scenario is exactly that which the Waitangi Tribunal recommended; an ability to object to offensive and derogatory use, but to allow other uses where they are not directly commercial. The Tribunal does not answer what amounts to offensive or derogatory treatment. It makes clear that it leaves this for future determination. That is hardly surprising; after all fair use is not always narrowly prescribed, rather it depends on the facts.[71] The Tribunal makes it clear, however, that use of Māori imagery is not per se offensive. Kaitiaki have rights that flow from the kaitiaki relationship. That relationship must be shown and the rights that flow are proportionate to that relationship.

Concluding thoughts – beyond Ka Mate Ka Mate and beyond New Zealand

All over the world, indigenous people seek greater control of their culture. In part this has occurred because many indigenous peoples are in need of economic development in a world where there has been increasing trade in indigenous culture and trade that utilises indigenous culture, without always a corresponding benefit for the peoples from whom that culture originates. The uniqueness of New Zealand is perhaps that the indigenous peoples are in a position to bring such a claim, as that brought to the Waitangi Tribunal, both because they have rights to their land[72] and because the Waitangi Tribunal procedure provides a forum for such a claim. That is a political uniqueness. The normative basis for protecting traditional knowledge is strong and

[70] *Ibid.* at page 387, lines 5–9.

[71] See Rebecca Tushnet, Chapter 19 in this volume.

[72] In Peter Drahos and Susy Frankel, 'Indigenous Peoples' Innovation and Intellectual Property: The Issues' in Drahos and Frankel, above n 1, we state: 'In the case of Aboriginal people in Australia the place–time nature of their system means that land rights justice is the primary necessary first step. Land rights justice, although not completely resolved, is considerably closer to having been achieved in New Zealand through the Waitangi Tribunal and Treaty Settlement Process. That is perhaps why Māori were able to bring the WAI 262 claim about the protection of their knowledge, culture and identity to the Waitangi Tribunal. This claim shows how progress on land rights justice opens the way to progress on the protection of indigenous knowledge and culture more broadly.'

is well-defined.[73] It includes the WIPO objectives and principles, domestic obligations such as those in New Zealand and what might be described as recognition of fair play in the international trade of knowledge assets.

Those normative underpinnings for the protection of traditional knowledge flow well beyond the shores of New Zealand. The WIPO–IGC process may not yet be complete, but its existence is implicit recognition that calls for protection of traditional knowledge will not evaporate. As the quote at the beginning of this chapter says, the traditional knowledge debate provides a means to a more informed and inclusive discourse about why we have an intellectual property system.

[73] If compared to publicity rights, for example, the normative basis of traditional knowledge protection is comparatively much more solid; see Stacey L. Dogan, Chapter 1 in this volume.

10 Comments on Susy Frankel: "'Ka Mate Ka Mate' and the protection of traditional knowledge" – an international perspective

Silke von Lewinski

Introduction

In respect of the protection of traditional knowledge, it is difficult to add a comment to Chapter 9 based on comparative law – in particular based on German or other European laws – given the lack of domestic *sui generis* protection in European countries. It is also known that intellectual property generally may cover only quite limited aspects of traditional knowledge, as is the case for trademark protection.[1] Although in Europe traditional knowledge exists and is in part practiced – for example, many people use grandmothers' recipes to fight a flu, etc., and Bavarians, at least in the countryside, still practice their folk dances, such as *Schuhplattler* – there is often either no identifiable source of traditional knowledge, or those people who are identifiable as the source of a particular traditional knowledge, such as Bavarians, have not called for any protection. It seems that in comparison with Maori and other indigenous peoples who have suffered colonization or marginalization, their traditional knowledge, including cultural expressions, is less essential for their survival as a separate group, or they may not have felt threatened to the same extent in practicing their ways of life and thus have not felt the same need to call for the kind of protection that Maori and many others have claimed. Indeed, any discourse in Germany or most other European countries on the protection of traditional knowledge seems to be marginal and only imported in particular through the World Intellectual Property Organization (WIPO) process mentioned in Chapter 9. This chapter therefore will focus on some of the texts developed and discussed

[1] Similarly as in New Zealand, see Susy Frankel, Chapter 9 in this volume, pp. 193–214. See also there, p. 209. On geographical indications, see Daniel Gervais, Chapter 6 in this volume, at pp. 105 ff. On the fact that different intellectual property rights can only partially, if at all, meet the needs of indigenous peoples in protecting their folklore, see Lucas-Schlötter, "Folklore", in von Lewinski (ed.), *Indigenous Heritage and Intellectual Property* (Kluwer Law International, Alphen aan den Rijn, 2008), 383–413; von Lewinski, "Final Considerations", in *ibid.*, 509 ff, in particular 510.

with a view to a possible international instrument on the protection of traditional knowledge, under the aegis of WIPO.

While trade, as Professor Frankel has correctly pointed out (Chapter 9, page 194), has certainly been an element triggering claims for traditional knowledge protection, it has also been the mere use, whether commercial or not, of traditional knowledge without the consent of indigenous peoples which has contributed to the emergence of this discussion. At the same time, one has to consider the fact that traditional knowledge regularly is seen as covered by land rights and has to be placed in the broader context of the right of self-determination of indigenous peoples, and, thus, different aspects of traditional knowledge have been discussed in different international organizations. It seems quite natural that those aspects that are most comparable to traditional intellectual property have been discussed in the framework of WIPO. In fact, the competence of WIPO stretches to "intellectual property" as defined in broad terms in Article 2(viii) of the Treaty on the WIPO ("... and all other rights resulting from intellectual activity in the industrial, scientific, literary or artistic fields"). As a consequence, the discourse within WIPO on traditional knowledge has largely followed the concepts of classical intellectual property rights.

This pragmatic approach, i.e., of using an existing international organization that traditionally has been dealing with matters similar to, but certainly not fully matching, traditional knowledge and its background, has, from the outset of discussions within WIPO, reflected the clash of concepts of traditional intellectual property on the one hand and the claimed protection for traditional knowledge on the other hand. In particular, governmental experts of countries for which this topic has little salience, such as many European countries, learned about the specifics of traditional knowledge only within the WIPO process; otherwise, they had dealt only with traditional intellectual property rights, such as patents, trademarks and copyright. It is obvious that discussions among such governmental experts initially have focused on the concepts of classical intellectual property rights and often today still reflect such concepts. For example, Italy stated several times that, if the conditions for a work of an author to be protected by authors' rights are not fulfilled, there is no justification to apply authors' rights or a similar intellectual property right to an object (in this case, traditional cultural expressions).[2]

[2] See WIPO, Intergovernmental Committee on Intellectual Property and Genetic Resources, Traditional Knowledge and Folklore, Eleventh Session – Adopted Report, WIPO Doc. GRTKF/IC/11/15, para. 85, available at: www.wipo.int/edocs/mdocs/tk/en/wipo_grtkf_ic_11/wipo_grtkf_ic_11_15.pdf.

While the WIPO Secretariat already in 2006 submitted to the Intergovernmental Committee text proposals that took into account a number of specifics of traditional knowledge,[3] the latest documents,[4] based on discussions by Member States and, in part, prepared and presented by a facilitator from New Zealand (Kim Connolly-Stone), in certain aspects again or still reflect copyright terms and concepts.

Authors' rights and traditional knowledge: Commonalities and differences

Given the focus of this book on "intellectual property at the edge," this chapter follows up on the very sound and wise recommendations of the Waitangi Tribunal set out in the chapter by Susy Frankel as a basis to shed light on that very edge or border between classical intellectual property and traditional knowledge. Therefore, these comments highlight key commonalities and differences of, in particular, authors' works and their protection versus traditional cultural expressions and the related claims for protection, or even of customary laws protecting them.

Objective of protection

Before looking at individual elements of protection, a general look at the objective of protection seems useful. Broadly speaking, the objective of "copyright" protection according to common law countries' copyright systems is mainly to promote the well-being of society through the promotion of innovation and creativity. In contrast to this utilitarian approach, "authors' rights" (*droit d'auteur*, *Urheberrecht* . . .) systems have the main purpose of recognizing the achievement of an author, by rewarding the mere fact of creating works that enhance cultural diversity; such recognition of the value added by an author to a society's culture by means of protecting the (economic and personal) relationship of the author to his work is by itself a justification for protection, irrespective of whether the protection indeed promotes creativity.[5]

[3] See, in particular, The Protection of Traditional Cultural Expressions/Expressions of Folklore: Revised Objectives and Principles, WIPO Doc. GRTKF/IC/9/4, available at: www.wipo.int/edocs/mdocs/tk/en/wipo_grtkf_ic_9/wipo_grtkf_ic_9_4.pdf; this document was based on an earlier one (WIPO Doc. GRTKF/IC/8/4) of 2005.

[4] The Protection of Traditional Cultural Expressions: Draft Articles, WIPO Doc. WIPO/GRTKF/IC/22/4, of April 27, 2012, available at: www.wipo.int/edocs/mdocs/tk/en/wipo_grtkf_ic_22/wipo_grtkf_ic_22_4.pdf; for the outcome of that session, see www.wipo.int/edocs/mdocs/tk/en/wipo_grtkf_ic_22/wipo_grtkf_ic_22_ref_facilitators_text.pdf.

[5] See von Lewinski, *International Copyright Law and Policy* (Oxford University Press, 2008), 3.11–3.15.

In respect of traditional knowledge, the WIPO discussions have set out a number of objectives,[6] including both the recognition of the value of and promotion of respect for traditional knowledge as well as the promotion of innovation and creativity. In addition, other objectives go beyond those of intellectual property rights, such as the promotion of community development and the promotion of conservation and preservation of traditional knowledge. As furthermore the Waitangi Tribunal has pointed out, the recommended protection is to recognize the "relationship of kaitiaki with taonga works . . ."[7] (which reminds us of authors' rights, which protect the (personal and economic) relationship between the author and his work; see, e.g., Article 11 of the German Copyright Act). Still, for all those objectives, one should be careful not to take them simply over from copyright, or to impose additional objectives that are rooted mainly in Western thinking, without focusing on the actual reasons why indigenous peoples have claimed protection. As stated above, the Waitangi Tribunal pointed to the essence of what should be protected (the relationship with taonga works), and the Maori had made clear what their needs are, namely, to control the use of their traditional cultural expressions (TCEs) in order to fulfill their responsibilities as caretakers thereof; other purposes like promotion of creativity do not seem to be among them, and even if protection of TCEs may lead to the economic development of indigenous peoples and therefore may be helpful to them, this may not necessarily be for them the main reason to claim protection of TCEs – all the more so since some of them object to commodification and commercialization of their TCEs.[8]

Subject matter of protection

Regarding the subject matter of protection, the common feature of works/original works of authorship and TCEs is the domain called "literary and artistic domain" in the Berne Convention, which also covers music, dance and similar fields of "art" in the broad sense. Furthermore, what is (to be) protected are only "expressions" (in contrast to mere ideas, concepts, etc.) by humans (whether they can still be identified or not, as usually in the case of TCEs, and irrespective of who is finally recognized as the rightholder).[9]

[6] See Frankel, Chapter 9 above, p. 206. [7] *Ibid.*, p. 210, note 59.
[8] Similarly, for terms such as "economic and moral rights", *ibid.*, p. 206.
[9] Even if under the copyright system, a corporation may be recognized as the first rightholder, a work is always initially created by a human being.

Some differences regarding the subject matter of protection are reflected in the claims of indigenous peoples and, e.g., Article 1 of the initial WIPO proposal,[10] which also covers individual words, signs, names, and symbols as well as musical instruments, ceremonies, rituals and other performances;[11] under authors' rights and copyright, the first-mentioned items would regularly not be protected, due to a lack of originality or sufficient creativity, respectively, and the latter ones would regularly be protected as performances under performers' rights (and musical instruments would regularly not be protected). Furthermore, the above Article 1 shows that the function of a work protected by authors' rights on the one hand and of TCEs on the other hand is fundamentally different: An author usually creates a work out of the need personally to express himself in an artistic way, even if ulterior aims (such as entertainment, spreading of certain thoughts and ideas, earning money by commercialization) may also play a role.

In contrast, TCEs have a specific function within indigenous and other cultural communities, to be explained against the background of the prevailing holistic world view, according to which every element is interrelated and has to be respected equally, such as the land, animals, plants, humans, their ancestors and spirits. TCEs in this context usually represent the link of an individual member of a community with the other members, the land, the ancestors and the entire surrounding world. Making a design, dancing a ceremonial dance or singing a folklore song often serve to reaffirm these links, to reconnect and bring into harmony the individuals and their surrounding world. Such activities assert self-identification and thereby strengthen the identity of an entire community and the position of its individual members within that community, and they may even be essential for survival as a distinct community. Also, the context of self-determination becomes evident here. TCEs may even contain concrete information that may be useful for the life or even survival of an indigenous community, such as information on the topography of the surrounding land, on the places of waterholes in a desert, etc. Accordingly, the function of TCEs is usually much more profound and essential to indigenous peoples as compared to that of authors' works in Western societies.[12]

The special function of TCEs, as just described, may explain, among others, the particular conditions of protection as set out in Article 1 of the

[10] WIPO Doc. GRTKF/IC/9/4, above n. 3, Annex, p. 11.

[11] Similarly, WIPO Doc. WIPO/GRTKF/IC/22/4, above n. 4, Art. 1, which even includes sacred places (Option 2, 1(d)).

[12] Cf. also the broad Maori-definition of matauranga, Frankel, Chapter 9 above, p. 196.

WIPO proposal,[13] as in particular the need for a TCE to be characteristic of a community's cultural and social identity and cultural heritage and to be maintained, used, or developed by such community or by individuals having the right or responsibility to do so in accordance with the customary law and practices of that community. These conditions in fact reflect the function of TCEs, i.e. to constantly reestablish the links of community members with their surrounding world and thus reaffirm the identity of the community; equally, TCEs retain that function only as long as they are maintained, used or developed as described in the WIPO text or, in short, as long as they are being practiced or "lived." Where folklore is no longer living and no longer serves the self-identification and linkage of the community, its members and the surrounding elements, it is no longer important for the community and therefore not in need of protection. Correspondingly, for the Waitangi Tribunal, it is also this special function in respect of the relationship between Maori and their taonga works, which is essential for the Tribunal.[14] At the same time, one should critically note that the Tribunal uses the term "work" (though in connection with "taonga"), which is a longstanding term with a specific meaning in the field of copyright/authors' rights and that thus might lead to misunderstandings.

Rightholders and beneficiaries of protection

In respect of the rightholders and the beneficiaries of protection, under the authors' rights system, it is always the creator of a work who is the first rightholder and, at least in part, also its beneficiary (depending on the contracts for exploitation that he concludes subsequently); according to the aim of the continental law system, the author himself should also be at least one of the beneficiaries of protection. Under the copyright system, in contrast, a juridical person may be the first rightowner, and contractual partners may often benefit even more strongly from copyright than contractual partners of authors under the authors' rights system.[15]

In contrast to protection of authors' rights, protection of TCEs is generally claimed to benefit not the individual or group of individuals who created a TCE at the outset (apart from the fact that most often these individuals can no longer be identified, all the more since TCEs regularly evolve through practice) but, as pointed out by the Waitangi

[13] WIPO Doc. GRTKF/IC/9/4, above n. 3, Annex, p. 11.
[14] See Frankel, Chapter 9 above, pp. 208 and 210 (note 59).
[15] See for a comparison of both systems in this respect von Lewinski, above n. 5, 3.37–3.43.

Tribunal, those who are the guardians or kaitiaki of the TCEs.[16] Similarly, WIPO proposed that the beneficiaries be those indigenous peoples and traditional and other cultural communities in whom the custody, care and safeguarding of the TCEs are entrusted in accordance with their customary law and practices and, in addition, who maintain, use or develop the TCEs, which must be characteristic of their cultural and social identity and cultural heritage.[17] Such rules again show that the purpose of claimed protection of TCEs is not at all the promotion of creativity as such but is rooted in the function of TCEs within a community as described above. In this respect, among others, the fundamental difference as compared to authors' rights or copyright protection necessitates a *sui generis* approach, as confirmed by the Waitangi Tribunal.[18]

Form and contents of legal protection

Both under authors' rights/copyright and claims for TCE-protection, the control of uses (be it for economic or personal/moral reasons)[19] is the aim to be achieved.

Under the authors' rights and copyright systems, the author's right to control uses of his work is shaped as a property right, i.e. a right of the author to authorize or prohibit any third person to use the work in the described, restricted ways or without such restrictions; such rights are regularly covered by the fundamental right of property, whether or not explicitly mentioned in the different constitutions, in particular in Europe. Moreover, such a property right regularly covers both commercial and non-commercial uses; for the latter, specific exceptions and limitations may apply in individual cases. Also, a property right allows the granting of licenses to third persons or otherwise to commercialize the right.

However, this concept of private property as developed in Western legal systems does not exist in a comparable way in indigenous or other local communities and would not seem appropriate either. As clearly pointed out by the Waitangi Tribunal, it does not recommend creation of a new category of proprietary right.[20] This approach is consistent with the function of TCEs within such a community, and the fact that under customary law TCEs usually do not "belong" in the meaning of Western property rights to a person or persons, but are placed under the

[16] Frankel, Chapter 9 above, pp. 207–209; also p. 198 for the presentation of the Maori.

[17] WIPO Doc. GRTKF/IC/9/4, above n. 3, Art. 2, (Annex, at 16). Similarly, WIPO Doc. WIPO/GRTKF/IC/22/4, above n. 4, Art. 2, which refers to the conditions of protection under Art. 1.

[18] Frankel, Chapter 9 above, p. 210 , note 59.

[19] For Maori claims, see *ibid.*, pp. 199 f, 203 f.

[20] *Ibid.*, p. 210, note 59.

guardianship of those who are the beneficiaries, namely the caretakers or guardians (kaitiaki), who may be persons, clans, families, communities or other groups, and who have a responsibility or burden under customary law to ensure that the individual TCE is used in accordance with customary law – and this even for the past, present and future.[21] Accordingly, the Waitangi Tribunal has consistently recommended mechanisms allowing the beneficiaries to control certain uses by prohibiting derogatory or offensive public use and preventing any commercial exploitation.[22]

The initial WIPO proposal provided for a quite complex, threefold system of protection.[23] This system has been criticized in particular for its complexity[24] and has not been retained in the recent proposals. Nevertheless, it included (for certain TCEs that would have to be registered by indigenous peoples in a registry to be created at national level) the useful concept of "prior informed consent," which arguably is not comparable to an exclusive or property right, since it does not allow for licenses and thus could avoid unwanted commodification and potential right ownership by third persons. Instead of such specified provisions as under this initial proposal, the new proposals largely leave discretion to national legislators by broad formulations, such as "adequate and effective legal, administrative or policy measures" to be introduced.[25] Interestingly, protection of economic interests, at least under Option 2 of these new proposals, seems to be limited to commercial exploitation. However, though the header of lit. (e) regarding economic interests states that lit. (e) "deals with commercial exploitation," this is not explicitly repeated in all three alternatives of Option 2. "Moral" interests are not explicitly limited to commercial exploitation. This approach would seem to correspond to the one taken by the Waitangi Tribunal.[26] Still, in two alternative formulations, terms borrowed from copyright/authors' rights are being used to describe the individual acts to be covered by protection; namely, "fixation, reproduction, public performance, translation or adaptation,

[21] *Ibid.*, pp. 203 f; see also *ibid.*, p. 198.

[22] *Ibid.*, p. 209, notes 52, 53.

[23] WIPO Doc. GRTKF/IC/9/4, above n. 3, Art. 3; it included the requirement of "prior informed consent" for certain, registered TCEs, a remuneration right for others, and yet different protection for secret TCEs.

[24] See, for example, Intergovernmental Committee on Intellectual Property and Genetic Resources, Traditional Knowledge and Folklore, Eighth Session – Second Draft Report, WIPO Doc. GRTKF/IC/8/15 Prov. 2, para. 122, available at: www.wipo.int/edocs/mdocs/tk/en/wipo_grtkf_ic_8/wipo_grtkf_ic_8_15_prov_2.doc and, regarding the requirement for registration, *ibid.*, para. 100; von Lewinski, "Adequate Protection of Folklore – A Work in Progress," in: P. Torremans (ed.), *Copyright Law: A Handbook of Contemporary Research*, Camberley (Edward Elgar, Cheltenham, UK, 2007), 207, 222–23.

[25] WIPO Doc. WIPO/GRTKF/IC/22/4, above n. 4, Art. 3, Option 2.

[26] See text at n. 22 above.

making available or communicating to the public; and distribution."[27] Such language does not seem to be appropriate for the protection of TCEs, since it repeats categories of uses understood in a certain way in the field of copyright, but does not correspond to the tradition of indigenous peoples not to use categories for what could simply be called "uses."

Limitations of protection

In connection with the kind of rights granted, the question as to the limitations of such rights arises. Under authors' rights and copyright, the exclusive rights of authors have traditionally been limited by law in favor of certain privileged purposes, such as education, research and information on current events. Given the particular purpose of TCEs and of their (claimed) protection, the Waitangi Tribunal carefully tries to draw a line between uses that Maori should be able to prevent – namely, offensive and derogatory uses on the one hand and commercial exploitation on the other hand – and those uses which Maori usually do not have an interest in controlling.[28] In fact, indigenous peoples traditionally have shared their TCEs with outsiders, where they could expect a respectful and proper use of their TCEs. This approach, which largely follows Maori customs, indeed seems more appropriate than the description of classical exceptions or limitations following authors' rights/copyright legislation.

While all WIPO proposals exempt customary uses from protection and thereby take into account the specifics of TCEs and their use, the initial WIPO proposal also provided for classical exceptions or limitations known from authors' rights/copyright legislation, such as teaching, criticism and review, or news reporting.[29] One could doubt whether this was an appropriate approach, given the specificities of TCEs and their use. For example, if a particular way of using a TCE for the purpose of teaching were offensive, for example, because it is taken out of context, indigenous peoples would not consider as appropriate such a full-fledged exception or limitation as proposed by WIPO.[30] Also, some TCEs under customary law may be under the exclusive guardianship of a particular group or person (e.g., a shaman often must not give away his knowledge unless to specific, selected people under particular circumstances),

[27] WIPO Doc. WIPO/GRTKF/IC/22/4, above n. 4, Art. 3, Option 2, alternatives 2 and 3 (the quoted passage is from alternative 2).

[28] See also Frankel, Chapter 9 above, pp. 211–213.

[29] WIPO Doc. GRTKF/IC/9/4, above n. 3, Art. 5(a)(iii).

[30] For the similar exception in Art. 3(4) in favour of cultural institutions, see the concerns expressed by representatives of indigenous peoples regarding offensive uses, WIPO Doc. WIPO/GRTKF/IC/22/4, above n. 4, Annex, p. 15 (comment by facilitator).

so that a general teaching exception would conflict with such customary law rules and traditions; an overarching concept of free speech so fundamental in the United States is not part of indigenous culture. The more recent proposals again leave more discretion to national legislation and refrain from specifying too much detail in this respect ("appropriate limitations or exceptions"), but some alternative formulations still take over elements from international copyright law; namely, the second and third steps of the three-step test.[31] Moreover, they stipulate a few concrete uses of TCEs that should be permitted by law; namely, uses in archives, libraries, museums or cultural institutions for non-commercial cultural heritage purposes, including for preservation, display, research, presentation and education, and, in one alternative, even use for the creation of an author's work inspired by or borrowed from TCEs.[32]

Conclusions

Overall, the international and global debate on how to protect TCEs has matured, especially after more than ten years of discussions in WIPO's Intergovernmental Committee, to acknowledge that, although certain needs may be met by individual aspects of intellectual property rights, the only solution that can be congenial to the specifics of TCEs is a *sui generis* approach, as also confirmed by the Waitangi Tribunal. One should avoid using terms that have acquired, through history, a proper meaning in the field of intellectual property. One should also refrain from imposing Western thinking (and thus recalling early paternalistic behavior) on any concept of protection, in particular as regards the objectives of protection: For example, where (mostly non-indigenous) politicians or others consider TCE-protection as a tool to promote trade and development, creativity, or the economic development of the entire country, one should carefully analyze whether the protection of TCEs in such cases would in fact serve indigenous peoples or whether such protection is rather (mis-)used for ulterior motives. In the end, indigenous peoples know best for what purposes they desire protection, and how they aim to achieve or improve their development.

[31] WIPO Doc. WIPO/GRTKF/IC/22/4, above n. 4, Art. 3, Options 1 and 2, para. 4. These two steps, as also contained, for example, in Art. 9(2) of the Berne Convention, Art. 13 of the TRIPS Agreement and Articles 10 of the WIPO Copyright Treaty and 16 of the WIPO Performances and Phonograms Treaty, read (example from TRIPS): "which do not conflict with a normal exploitation of the work and do not unreasonably prejudice the legitimate interests of the right holder."

[32] WIPO Doc. WIPO/GRTKF/IC/22/4, above n. 4, Art. 3, Options 1 and 2, para. 4, though put into brackets again in the latest version; see n. 4 above, at the end.

Part VI

“Paracopyright”: Technological protection measures

11 Paracopyright – a peculiar right to control access

*Joseph P. Liu**

Introduction

During the mid-1990s, the advent of digital and networked computer technology began to place increasing pressure on the markets for copyrighted works. Even before this development, unauthorized copying had always been a problem for the copyright industries. However, the ease and perfection of digital copying, combined with the low cost of distributing copies around the world, began to place increased stress on copyright markets and the copyright industries. These industries were concerned that the ease and ubiquity of unauthorized digital copying would undercut the demand for authorized copies of their works, thereby threatening their existing revenues. Some observers were concerned that this would, in the long run, undermine the incentives to create copyrighted works in the first place.

More specifically, copyright owners expressed concern that the then-existing rights under copyright law were insufficient to keep unauthorized copying below a manageable level. Although copyright owners in the digital world still had a full set of rights that could be enforced against unauthorized copiers, they were concerned that it would become increasingly more difficult to enforce these rights effectively. This was because large scale copying and distribution of unauthorized copies no longer required any sophisticated technology or scale, but could be effectuated in a distributed fashion by consumers themselves.

It was in this context that copyright owners advanced proposals to amend the copyright laws to deal with this enforcement problem. In their view, simply adding new formal rights would be unlikely to solve this problem, since the main issue was not the lack of rights, but the inability to enforce them effectively. So instead the focus turned not to law, but to technology. The hope was that copy-protection technologies, such as

* Research for this book chapter was funded through a generous grant from the R. Robert Popeo J.D.' 61 Law Fund for Faculty Research.

those already in place in the software industry, might be able to reduce the extent of unauthorized copying, such that copyright owners could earn an adequate return on their investments.

One problem with this view was the hard fact that such technologies were always subject to circumvention. In other words, no technology could assure perfect protection of the work from unauthorized copying. The history of attempts to create a perfect copyright protection technology is littered with failure. Although the software industry had long tried to protect its products using such technologies, resourceful individuals were always able to find ways around these technologies. Similarly, early attempts by the music industry technologically to secure recorded music were quickly defeated, sometimes within hours of a new technology's distribution.

Thus, the impetus arose to provide legal support for these technologies. If such technologies could be supported by law, perhaps the combination of law and technology could do together what neither could do alone. The law could do this by imposing liability on the circumvention of technologies that protected copyrighted works. This, by itself, would do little to improve the situation, since it still presented the same enforcement problem. However, the law could go further to ban technologies that enabled circumvention. As long as such technologies could be kept from the market, casual consumers would not be able to engage in circumvention. And, although sophisticated individuals could still engage in circumvention, the lack of easy circumvention by consumers would cause them to seek out authorized versions of the works.

This was the basic idea behind the Digital Millennium Copyright Act of 1998 (DMCA),[1] the US Congress's major response to the digital challenges described above. By passing the DMCA, Congress sought to provide legal support for the use of technology by copyright owners to protect their copyrighted works. It did this by creating a new cause of action against the circumvention of technologies that controlled access to copyrighted works. It also banned the sale of technologies that had few purposes other than to circumvent technologies that control access to, or prevent copying of, copyrighted works – the so-called "anti-trafficking" provisions.[2]

Together, these two provisions facilitated enforcement of copyrights in digital works. Before passage of the DMCA, a consumer using a computer could easily copy an unprotected copy of, say, a sound recording in

[1] 17 U.S.C. §§ 1201 *et seq.*
[2] David Nimmer, "A Riff on Fair Use in the Digital Millennium Copyright Act," 148 *U. Pa. L. Rev.* 673 (2000)

the form of a CD. After passage of the DMCA, access to, and copying of, a sound recording could be restricted through use of a technology, such as encryption. Moreover, consumers would no longer have easy access to technologies that could circumvent such technologies to enable access or copying. While not perfect, the combination of law and technology would serve to keep unauthorized copying to a manageable level.[3] This "enforcement facilitation" function was what the DMCA was intended to accomplish.

Interestingly, however, the DMCA did more than just facilitate enforcement. Enforcement could have been facilitated by simply enacting the provisions that dealt with trafficking. For example, section 1201(b) of the DMCA bans the sale and distribution of technologies that facilitate the circumvention of technologies that protect copyright rights. Simply enacting this provision would have done much to address the problem of enforcement by preventing easy access to such technologies.

The DMCA also, however, created a new cause of action against circumvention of technologies that controlled *access* to copyrighted works. This represented an extension of the scope of potential copyright liability. Traditionally, merely accessing a copyrighted work did not, without more, lead to copyright liability. For example, merely reading a book or listening to a CD does not infringe a copyright right. If a technology prevented me from reading a literary work, under traditional copyright law, circumventing that technology would lead to no liability. Under the DMCA, however, obtaining such access to a work would lead to liability even if no underlying copyright right were infringed. Thus, for example, circumventing the encryption that protects a DVD in order merely to view the movie would lead to liability, even though no underlying copyright interest was violated. The DMCA's anti-circumvention provisions thus represented an extension of the practical scope of copyright rights, creating a new form of what some scholars called "paracopyright."[4]

This was not accidental. Congress was fully aware that it was extending the effective scope of copyright in this fashion. The legislative history, in fact, indicates that Congress intended this to be a feature of the new

[3] But *see* Fred von Lohmann, "Measuring the Digital Millennium Copyright Act Against the Darknet: Implications for the Regulation of Technological Protection Measures," 24 *Loy. L.A. Ent. L. Rev.* (2004).

[4] *See* Jane C. Ginsburg, "Copyright Legislation for the 'Digital Millennium,'" 23 *Colum.-VLA J. L. & the Arts* 137, 140–43, 147–48 (1999); Michael Landau, "Has the Digital Millennium Copyright Act Really Created a New Exclusive Right of Access?: Attempting to Reach a Balance between Users' and Content Providers' Rights," 49 *J. Copyr. Soc'y U.S.A.* 277 (2001).

legislation. By supporting the efforts of copyright owners to use technology to control *access* to copyrighted works, Congress believed it was paving the way for more efficient markets in access to copyrighted works. Copyright owners could now use technology to sell more limited access to copyrighted works – for example the ability to read an article once, or watch a video only during a twenty-four-hour window – for a lower price, thereby facilitating price discrimination. Consumers would, the theory went, also be better off because they would now be able to gain access to works at lower cost if they merely wanted to access a work briefly, or at higher cost if they wanted unlimited access.[5]

Thus the DMCA was enacted not only to facilitate enforcement of existing copyrights but also to facilitate more fine-grained copyright owner control of access to copyrighted works.[6] This separate and distinct rationale can be seen in other provisions of the DMCA. For example, section 1202 deals extensively with so-called copyright management information (CMI). CMI is defined as information attached to a copy of a copyrighted work that sets forth the owner of the copyright, contact information, terms of use, etc. The DMCA imposes liability on the removal or alteration of CMI with an intent to facilitate infringement. Congress envisioned future markets where digital copies of copyrighted works would contain embedded information regarding licensing terms, etc., and these provisions were designed to support this vision of a more efficient market.

The creation of a new right to control access through technology – the extension of copyright beyond its pre-existing boundary or "edge" – was not without controversy. Indeed, it was heavily contested. Many commentators argued that such an extension of copyright was unwarranted, as then-existing laws were sufficient to provide incentives for the creation and dissemination of copyrighted works.[7] Other commentators expressed concern that giving copyright owners such extensive rights

[5] David Nimmer, "Appreciating Legislative History: The Sweet and Sour Spots of the DMCA's Commentary," 23 *Cardozo L. Rev.* 909 (2002). Note that the equivalent DMCA-like provisions enacted by some European countries tie anti-circumvention liability more closely to acts of infringement. *See* Severine Dusollier, Chapter 12 in this volume.

[6] Jane C. Ginsburg, "From Having Copies to Experiencing Works: The Development of an Access Right in U.S. Copyright Law," 50 *J. Copyr. Soc'y U.S.A.* 113, 125–31 (2003).

[7] *See, e.g.*, Pamela Samuelson, "Intellectual Property and the Digital Economy: Why the Anti-Circumvention Regulations Need to Be Revised," 14 *Berkeley Tech. L. J.* 519, 534–37 (1999); Landau, "Has the Digital Millennium Copyright Act Really Created a New Exclusive Right of Access?," at 311; Dan Burk & Julie Cohen, "Fair Use Infrastructure for Rights Management Systems," 15 *Harv. J. L. & Tech.* 41, 42 (2001); Glynn S. Lunney, Jr., "The Death of Copyright: Digital Technology, Private Copying, and the Digital Millennium Copyright Act," 87 *Va. L. Rev.* 813 (2001).

would wind up limiting, rather than increasing, public access to works. Still other commentators suggested that the underlying model of perfect price discrimination represented not an ideal vision of an efficient market, but a dystopian vision of centralized and excessive control over how consumers interacted with copyrighted works. Supporters of these provisions, however, argued that they would pave the way for more widespread and inexpensive access to and distribution of copyrighted works, ultimately benefiting both copyright owners and consumers.

In this chapter, I propose to take a comprehensive look at the many cases that have been decided since enactment of the DMCA, grappling with the scope of this new right to control access. A close look at the case law reveals that the new access right is more peculiar and more complicated than either of the competing views above suggests. While the new access right has, to a certain extent, played a role in supporting copyright owner interests and facilitating enforcement of these rights, and while it has played a role in metering and limiting access to copyrighted works, it has also been invoked in a large number of cases seeking to extend copyright owner control into areas that were never intended or envisioned by Congress.

Indeed, a significant portion of the actual case law has ventured rather far from the underlying copyright interests that motivated the passage of the legislation in the first place. To be sure, many cases appear to further the primary goals of the DMCA, by, for example, banning technologies clearly designed to circumvent access to copyrighted works, such as those fixed on DVDs or made available through cable or television signals. A surprisingly large number of cases, however, involve attempts to use the DMCA to control the behavior of consumers in ways unrelated to copyright, for example to prevent cheating in online games, or to bar automated access to a website, or even to prevent the use of hardware with a competing service. Moreover, courts have not always carefully limited the new right to cases that involve legitimate copyright interests.

The reason for this, I suggest, is the failure of Congress to anticipate how complicated the issue of "access" would be in a world in which digital copies of works are ubiquitous. The term "access," itself, can have many different meanings, depending on the kind of underlying copyrighted work. For example, accessing a literary work may mean something very different from accessing a digitized sound recording or a piece of computer software.[8] Moreover, the reasons for controlling access to a copyrighted work, and the reasons for trying to obtain access

[8] Dennis S. Karjala, "Access to Computer Programs Under the DMCA," 25 *J. Marshall J. Computer & Info. L.* 641 (2009).

to that work, can be quite varied and do not always map cleanly onto an underlying copyright interest. Finally, the ubiquity of "work[s] protected under this title" in the online environment means that a broad-ranging and unqualified right to control all forms of access to such works can lead to a very broad right to control all kinds of online behavior.[9]

In the end, this suggests that courts must develop, as they have begun to, a more nuanced understanding of what it means to control "access" to a copyrighted work, one that ties the access right more firmly to the copyright interests that prompted its creation. Many courts have begun developing precisely such an understanding, although not without some effort and twisting of the language of the statute. Thus, in some cases, the worst potential abuses have been avoided. In other cases, however, the courts have allowed more literal interpretations of access to extend these rights too broadly. More work therefore needs to be done to develop a better understanding of this new right to control access and to tie it more firmly to the copyright interests that gave rise to its creation. In short, more work needs to be done to tie "paracopyright" more closely to "copyright."

The statute

Unlike most other chapters in this volume, this particular chapter deals with a new intellectual property right that is a creature of statute, and a quite recent statute at that. Thus, the origins of this new right are relatively recent and easily recalled by most in the field. As a result, this chapter does not attempt to unearth an untold story behind this new right, or seek to develop in more detail the origins of the right. Instead, it will focus on both the text of the originating statute and the subsequent and still-recent history of this right in the decade since passage. The early history of this right is currently being written, and we have here an opportunity to see, in real time, how this right has developed and is still developing. Accordingly, after starting with the text of the statute, this chapter moves on to consider the body of early case law that it has generated. As we will see, while the DMCA has arguably succeeded, at least by its own terms, in facilitating the enforcement of copyrights, its attempt to create a new right of access has met with more mixed results.[10]

[9] Note interestingly that the European equivalent to the DMCA focuses, not on "access" as the operative new right, but rather on "acts, in respect of works or other subject matter, which are not authorized by the rightholder," which is potentially even broader in its scope, as discussed in Chapter 12.

[10] *See generally*, June M. Besek, "Anti-Circumvention Laws and Copyright: A Report from the Kernochan Center for Law, Media and the Arts," 27 *Colum. J. L. & Arts* 385 (2004).

The text of the DMCA reflects the same division of purposes described in the preceding section. The first section creates a new right to control access to copyrighted works that are protected by technology. Section 1201(a)(1)(A) states: "No person shall circumvent a technological measure that effectively controls access to a work protected under this title." The following subsection bolsters this right by banning the sale and distribution of technologies that undermine this right. Section 1201(a)(2) (emphasis added) states:

No person shall manufacture, import, offer to the public, provide, or otherwise traffic in any technology, product, service, device, component, or part thereof, that—

(A) is primarily designed or produced for the purpose of circumventing a technological measure that effectively *controls access* to a work protected under this title;
(B) has only limited commercially significant purpose or use other than to circumvent a technological measure that effectively *controls access* to a work protected under this title; or
(C) is marketed by that person or another acting in concert with that person with that person's knowledge for use in circumventing a technological measure that effectively *controls access* to a work protected under this title.

Thus, 1201(a) is primarily concerned with protecting the right to control access to copyrighted works.

A separate subsection, 1201(b), covers technologies that prevent not unauthorized access to copyrighted works, but unauthorized copying. Its structure is identical to the structure of 1201(a)(2), but substitutes for control of "access" the protection of a "right of a copyright owner" (emphasis added):

No person shall manufacture, import, offer to the public, provide, or otherwise traffic in any technology, product, service, device, component, or part thereof, that—

(A) is primarily designed or produced for the purpose of circumventing protection afforded by a technological measure that effectively *protects a right of a copyright owner* under this title in a work or a portion thereof;
(B) has only limited commercially significant purpose or use other than to circumvent protection afforded by a technological measure that effectively *protects a right of a copyright owner* under this title in a work or a portion thereof; or
(C) is marketed by that person or another acting in concert with that person with that person's knowledge for use in circumventing protection afforded by a technological measure that effectively *protects a right of a copyright owner* under this title in a work or a portion thereof.

Section 1201(b) contains only an anti-trafficking provision and does not contain a section that parallels 1201(a)(1)'s anti-circumvention provision. The legislative history makes it clear that this is because Congress felt such a parallel provision unnecessary, since the underlying infringement of a "right of a copyright owner" was already proscribed by other provisions of the Copyright Act.

The parallel structure of the DMCA's two sections clearly indicates that Congress was aware that it was furthering two separate and distinct purposes: (1) facilitating the enforcement of existing copyright rights (in 1201(b)); and (2) creating a new right to control access to copyrighted works (in 1201(a)(1)). In practice, the line between a technology that "controls access" and one that "protects a right" may be fuzzy, as some technologies may arguably do both. Indeed, a number of early cases appeared to elide the differences between these two definitions. Nevertheless, the structure of the DMCA indicates a clear distinction and a desire to further two separate purposes.[11]

Finally, the DMCA contains a separate provision, 1202, that provides additional support to the vision of a more efficient market for digital copyright works. It states:

(a) **False Copyright Management Information**.— No person shall knowingly and with the intent to induce, enable, facilitate, or conceal infringement—

(1) provide copyright management information that is false, or
(2) distribute or import for distribution copyright management information that is false.

(b) **Removal or Alteration of Copyright Management Information**.— No person shall, without the authority of the copyright owner or the law—

(1) intentionally remove or alter any copyright management information,
(2) distribute or import for distribution copyright management information knowing that the copyright management information has been removed or altered without authority of the copyright owner or the law, or
(3) distribute, import for distribution, or publicly perform works, copies of works, or phonorecords, knowing that copyright management information has been removed or altered without authority of the copyright owner or the law,

knowing, or, with respect to civil remedies under section 1203, having reasonable grounds to know, that it will induce, enable, facilitate, or conceal an infringement of any right under this title.

[11] R. Anthony Reese, "Will Merging Access Controls and Rights Controls Undermine the Structure of the Anticircumvention Law?," 18 *Berkeley Tech. L. J.* 619, 655 (2003).

The law of access

Whenever Congress enacts a new statute, it takes some time for the courts to work out how it applies in specific cases. Even the most competent Congress will not be able to foresee all the varied circumstances in which the law will be applied. Ambiguities in the text of the statute will always exist, and the legislative history may not always be able easily to settle such ambiguities. This is particularly the case when the statute governs an area of rapid technological change. New copyright statutes that target a specific area of technology do not have a good track record.[12]

For these reasons, it is particularly interesting to take a look at the case law that has developed in the decade since enactment of the DMCA, as it gives us a snapshot of the issues and ambiguities that the courts have had to address in interpreting this new statute. How has the DMCA fared? In particular, how has this new right to control access developed over time? The survey that follows attempts to organize the case law more formally by taking an analytical look at the various reasons why copyright owners might assert a right to control access to a copyrighted work.

As the following survey suggests, the idea of "access" plays a more complicated role in copyright markets than Congress ever originally anticipated. The case law highlights how a broad right to control access can be leveraged, not only to prevent infringement or meter access to copyrighted works, but to control activities that are unrelated to any legitimate copyright interest. Confronted with a significant number of such cases, and sensing the disconnect between the language of the DMCA and the copyright interests it was intended to protect, courts have been forced to begin developing, in almost a common law fashion, a new law of access under the DMCA.

Controlling access to facilitate copyright enforcement

Why might a copyright owner want to control access to a copyrighted work? One reason might be to prevent infringement. In other words, a right to control access might be valuable, not in and of itself, but as an indirect way to prevent unauthorized copying. For example, take the technology of encryption. In some ways, encryption is a classic way to control access to a work. If a copyright owner encrypts a movie, that movie cannot be accessed without authorization. The technological measure thus controls access to the work. At the same time, the

[12] *See, e.g.*, Audio Home Recording Act of 1992, *codified at* 17 U.S.C. §§ 1001 *et seq.*

technology may also effectively prevent unauthorized copying of the work, since one cannot copy the unencrypted material and then subsequently distribute it to others. Thus, the technology may also play an important role in facilitating enforcement of other, traditional copyright rights.

A key example of this is perhaps the most famous DMCA case, *Universal* v. *Corley*.[13] In that case, a number of major motion picture studios brought a DMCA lawsuit against the owners and operators of a website. The website initially distributed, and then later posted links to, a software program called DeCSS. This program enabled users to defeat the encryption (called Content Scramble System or CSS) that movie studios used to control access to motion pictures distributed on DVDs. As a result, users of DeCSS could make and distribute unauthorized, unencrypted copies of the motion pictures. The motion picture companies argued that DeCSS was a technology designed to circumvent technological measures that controlled access to copyrighted works. Thus, the operators of the website were liable for distributing this technology.

The US District Court in the Southern District of New York decided the case in favor of the major motion picture studios and, in doing so, provided some of the first judicial interpretations of key provisions of the DMCA. In particular, the District Court held that CSS was a technological measure that "effectively controlled access" to a copyrighted work, and thus was the type of technology Congress had intended to protect. The Court also interpreted a number of statutory exceptions to DMCA liability, finding them inapplicable to the particular facts. Specifically, the Court rejected arguments that DeCSS was authorized by statutory exceptions for reverse engineering, encryption research, or security testing. Finally, the Court rejected the argument that DMCA liability was subject to copyright law's general fair use defense, concluding instead that Congress had expressly given the authority to craft exceptions not to the courts, but to the Library of Congress.

The US Court of Appeals for the Second Circuit affirmed the lower court's decision. The Second Circuit's opinion focused less on interpreting specific provisions of the DMCA and more on the defendants' First Amendment arguments. The defendants had raised, and the District

[13] 273 F.3d 429 (2nd Cir. 2001). *Corley* was the first appellate court decision on the anti-circumvention provisions of the DMCA. The District Court opinion, *Universal* v. *Reimerdes*, was issued in 2000. *Universal City Studios, Inc.* v. *Reimerdes*, 111 F.Supp.2d 294 (S.D.N.Y. 2000). Prior to that decision, there were two district court opinions, although neither resulted in an appellate decision. *Sony Computer Entertainment America, Inc.* v. *Gamemasters*, 87 F.Supp.2d 976 (N.D. Cal. 1999); *RealNetworks, Inc.* v. *Streambox, Inc.*, 2000 WL 127311 (W.D. Wash. 2000).

Court had rejected, a number of arguments that imposing DMCA liability on the website operators for linking to the DeCSS program violated their First Amendment rights. The Court of Appeals largely affirmed the District Court's holding and had relatively little to say about the specific interpretations of the DMCA provisions. Thus, to some extent, for purposes of the argument in this chapter, the appellate Court opinion is important more for its affirmance than for anything specifically in the opinion itself.

The *Corley* decision firmly advanced the enforcement-facilitating goals of the DMCA. Although, strictly speaking, the decision in *Corley* viewed CSS as an access-control technology, the underlying interest at issue was clearly preventing unauthorized copying.[14] The plaintiffs were not concerned that consumers would be able to play their lawfully purchased DVDs on unauthorized DVD players. Rather, they were concerned that decrypting the movies would allow the movies to be copied, shared, and played by others who had not purchased the DVD. In this sense, CSS was aimed at both controlling access and preventing unauthorized copying (and the plaintiffs in the case asserted claims under both 1201(a)(2) and 1201(b), although the courts never separately addressed the 1201(b) claim).

Many subsequent cases followed in *Corley*'s footsteps. A number of cases involved the exact same technology at issue in *Corley*, i.e. CSS. For example, in *321 Studios* v. *Metro Goldwyn Mayer Studios*,[15] the District Court found liable a company that distributed software that allowed individuals to make backup copies of movies on DVDs. Consistent with the *Corley* opinion, the Court in *321 Studios* held that CSS was a technological measure that controlled access to copyrighted works, and that the defendant's software was created to circumvent the technology. And just as in *Corley*, the Court rejected both fair use and First Amendment arguments. Similarly, in *RealNetworks* v. *DVD Copy Control Assoc.*,[16] the District Court held liable a company that distributed DVD backup software, reaching many of the same conclusions. These cases reinforced and followed directly from the specific result in *Corley*.

These cases represent a fairly standard use of access control to further a core copyright interest. The particular right may be new, in the form of

[14] Robert C. Denicola, "Access Controls, Rights Protection, and Circumvention: Interpreting the Digital Millennium Copyright Act to Preserve Noninfringing Use," 31 *Colum. J. L. & Arts* 209 (2008).

[15] 307 F.Supp.2d 1085 (N.D. Cal. 2004). *See also Macrovision* v. *Sima Products Corp.*, 2006 WL 1063284 (S.D.N.Y. 2006) (sale of chips that allow consumers to eliminate copy-protection measures embedded in DVD movies by Macrovision).

[16] 641 F.Supp.2d 913 (N.D. Cal. 2009).

a right to control access. And the right to ban trafficking may be more extensive than the rights that copyright owners would ordinarily enjoy under standard doctrines of third-party liability. Thus, there may well be disagreement over whether these additional anti-trafficking rights are warranted or optimal. Nevertheless, these new and broader rights serve a traditional copyright interest, insofar as they address the main concern: preventing unauthorized copying of a copyrighted work.

Controlling access to prevent initial access

Another reason to employ an access-control technology is to exclude those who have not paid for initial access to the work. Here, the concern is not so much the prevention of unauthorized copying. Instead, the concern is truly and solely about access. In fact, there may be no unauthorized copying involved at all. The copyrighted work may be streamed or broadcast to the recipient in encrypted form, and thus result in the making of no additional permanent or storage copies. Nevertheless, the copyright owner may have an interest in preventing access to the broadcast or stream by those who have not paid for such access.

A classic example of this kind of access control can be found in the cases involving the decryption of encrypted cable or satellite television signals. Subscribers to cable or satellite television are required by the cable or satellite companies to have an authorized set-top device that enables decryption of the signals so that they can be displayed on the subscriber's television. Many individuals and companies have used or sold devices that contain technologies that enable individuals to decrypt these signals, and thereby obtain access to the television broadcasts, without paying subscription fees.

The federal courts have decided dozens of such cases in the wake of the DMCA. Copyright owners have brought suit against companies offering devices that allow consumers to access satellite television signals without authorization.[17] Copyright owners have also brought suit against companies providing technologies that allow consumers to authorize pay-per-view cable broadcasts without payment.[18] In almost all of these

[17] *See U.S.* v. *Whitehead*, 532 F.3d 991 (9th Cir. 2008) (criminal prosecution brought against individual who sold counterfeit "access cards," which allowed individuals to access DirectTV broadcasts without authorization); *Echostar Satellite, L.L.C.* v. *Viewtech, Inc.*, 543 F.Supp.2d 1201 (S.D. Cal. 2008) (case against vendor of technology that allowed decryption of satellite television signals).

[18] *See CoxCom, Inc.* v. *Chaffee*, 536 F.3d 101 (1st Cir. 2008) (digital filter allowing customers to order pay-per-view shows without paying).

cases, the courts have rather easily found violations of the DMCA's anti-circumvention and anti-trafficking provisions.

Here, the interest being furthered is not a traditional interest in vindicating a pre-existing copyright right. Instead, these are cases where the DMCA has in fact created a new right of access. Without the DMCA, the act of decrypting a scrambled satellite TV signal likely would not, by itself, lead to copyright liability. The signal is being streamed directly to the consumer, either over the airwaves or via a physical cable. So long as no copies are being made of the signal, no pre-existing copyright right is being violated.[19]

While these cases arguably extend the scope of copyright law, these cases seem less problematic insofar as they still implicate a right related to the copyright owner's core interest, i.e. getting a return on their investment in creating and disseminating the underlying work. Moreover, such acts of circumvention likely violate other telecommunications laws that existed prior to enactment of the DMCA. In this sense, while the access right certainly facilitates enforcement, it does not materially change the status quo ante, at least in these particular markets.

Controlling access to meter access and enforce licensing provisions

Perhaps more interesting are cases where an individual legitimately possesses a copy of a copyrighted work, and may already have obtained some initial access to the work, but a technology seeks to control the degree or amount of access to the work. One example can be found in the area of computer software. Many computer software programs are protected by technological measures. Some of these measures are meant to prevent unauthorized copying and use of the software by third parties, and thus serve the traditional interest in facilitating enforcement of existing copyright rights. For example, for certain expensive software programs, purchasers are required to have a physical device, called a dongle, attached to the computers before the software programs can be run. This ensures that unauthorized copies of the software cannot be run without an additional physical device.[20]

[19] Note that it is possible that some courts might find that infringing copies were made if the set-top box temporarily stores or "caches" the content in its hard drive. *See, e.g., MAI Systems Corp.* v. *Peak Computer*, 991 F.2d 511 (9th Cir. 1993).

[20] *See MGE UPS Systems, Inc.* v. *GE Consumer and Indus., Inc.*, 622 F.3d 361 (5th Cir. 2010) (suit against computer servicing company that uses hacked version of software that permitted operation without dongle); *MGE UPS Systems, Inc.* v. *Fakouri Elec. Engineering, Inc.*, 422 F.Supp.2d 724 (N.D. Tex. 2006) (using hacked copy of software that permitted operation without dongle); *Microsoft Corp.* v. *EEE Business Inc.*, 555 F.Supp.2d 1051 (N.D. Cal. 2008) (defendant imported student-marketed versions of

Other measures are meant to enforce restrictions found in licensing terms, for example on the length of time that the software can be used, the number of people who can use it, the identity of the individuals who can use it, etc. Thus, for example, a company may have a license to use a piece of software for a year, and a technological measure may disable access to the software after that year. Circumventing the technological measure would give rise to liability under the DMCA.[21]

These restrictions can also be applied to other kinds of copyrighted works. Thus, for example, encrypted DVDs and computer games often have so-called "region codes," which allow the movies and games only to be played by authorized players sold in a certain geographic area. Disabling the region codes allows the DVDs and games to be played in other geographic areas. When a DVD or game is played in this fashion, there may be no violation of the underlying copyright, since no additional copies are being made. However, this undercuts the copyright owner's attempt to enforce certain restrictions on access to the work. [22]

A similar restriction can be found in technologies that place time limits on how long a particular work can be access or viewed. For example, some movie studios permit consumers to download digital copies of motion pictures onto their computers or other devices as "rentals." The movies can then be viewed a certain number of times, or within a certain fixed time period. After that period is over, the digital file is deleted. Circumventing such a technological restriction would enable consumers to keep and view the movie repeatedly, beyond the scope of use intended by the copyright owner. Similar restrictions can and have been imposed on other kinds of works, for example literary works in eBook formats.[23]

Microsoft software, along with labels that contained 15-digit code to enable software); *Apple, Inc.* v. *Psystar Corp.*, 673 F.Supp.2d 931 (N.D. Cal. 2009) (liability for sale of decrypted versions of MacOS software). *See also Sony Computer Entertainment America, Inc.* v. *Filipiak*, 406 F.Supp.2d 1068 (N.D. Cal. 2005) (case discussing statutory damages in context of sale of "mod chips" for Sony Playstation consoles); *Sony Computer Entertainment America, Inc.* v. *Divineo, Inc.*, 457 F.Supp.2d 957 (N.D. Cal. 2006) (Sony Playstation mod chips).

[21] *See MedioStream, Inc.* v. *Microsoft Corp.*, 749 F.Supp.2d 507 (E.D. Tex. 2010) (company shares software API, protected by technological protection measure, for evaluation and receiving company uses after expiration).

[22] *See Sony Computer Entertainment America, Inc.* v. *Gamemasters*, 87 F.Supp.2d 976 (N.D. Cal. 1999) (device allowing consumers to play computer game while disregarding the region coding).

[23] *See U.S.* v. *Elcom Ltd*, 203 F.Supp.2d 1111 (N.D. Cal. 2002) (criminal prosecution against individual who created a program that allowed individuals to read eBooks without restrictions). *See also Agfa Monotype Corp.* v. *Adobe Systems, Inc.*, 404 F.Supp.2d 1030 (N.D. Ill. 2005) (rejecting DMCA claim based on attempt to use "embedded bits" to control use of embedded fonts, holding that this measure did not

In these cases, we see a significant extension of copyright law beyond the pre-existing scope of copyright rights, though arguably not beyond prior licensing practices. Prior to the DMCA, copyright owners had very little ability to control and meter how individuals used their works once they had obtained access to a copy of the work. An individual could read a book once, twice, or a dozen times. In some cases, for example with computer software, copyright owners attempted to exert control over the extent of use via contract law, using licensing terms. But these were often difficult to enforce.

The DMCA provides additional support to these efforts by creating a separate cause of action against circumvention of technologies that control or meter access to copyrighted works in this way. Thus, once a copyright owner limits access to a work using technology, consumers no longer have the ability to access those works on demand. Any attempt to circumvent the technology leads to liability. Moreover, the technology to engage in circumvention is kept off the market by the DMCA's anti-trafficking provisions. The DMCA thus allows copyright owners effectively to exert far greater control over how their works are accessed, through the use of technology rather than via difficult-to-enforce licensing terms.

This use of access control, while an extension beyond the pre-existing scope and boundary of copyright law, is very likely within the ambit of what Congress intended.[24] The legislative history of the DMCA contained statements supporting the idea of a new digital marketplace, where copyright owners would exert greater control over access to their works. Congress expected that this greater control would in fact broaden access to copyrighted works and make the markets more efficient, by allowing copyright owners to sell various levels of access at different price points. Essentially, the DMCA would facilitate efforts to engage in price discrimination. Although there has been robust debate about whether this is a desired result as a matter of copyright policy more generally, it is relatively clear that it is within what Congress contemplated when passing the DMCA.

And to a large extent, the subsequent case law on access has supported this goal. In many of the above cases, copyright owners have in fact deployed technologies to limit and meter use of their works.

"effectively control access" to the fonts); *Monotype Imaging, Inc.* v. *Bitstream, Inc.*, 376 F.Supp.2d 877 (N.D. Ill. 2005).

[24] *See* Jane C. Ginsburg, "The Pros and Cons of Strengthening Intellectual Property Protection: Technological Protection Measures and Section 1201 of the US Copyright Act," 16 *Information & Communications Technology Law* 191 (2007).

Technologies that would enable circumvention of these measures are not widely available, and in cases where they have been available, copyright owners have successfully brought suit under the DMCA. Thus, this reason for controlling access to copyrighted works has found support in the courts.

Controlling access to prevent "misuse"

Although many of the cases discussed above have protected access as a means of vindicating either a core copyright interest or a more expansive vision of metered use of copyrighted works, some cases have used access to get at interests that are arguably further afield. One example involves the use of the DMCA's access-control provisions to prevent "cheating" in online games. For example, *MDY Industries* v. *Blizzard Entertainment*[25] involved a claim by Blizzard Entertainment, the creator of the popular online game *World of Warcraft*. The defendant in that case, MDY, had created a software program that allowed game players to play the game automatically, i.e. without their active involvement or presence. This allowed a player's online character to acquire experience and additional powers. Blizzard viewed this as a form of cheating in the game and deployed technical measures to prevent this kind of software from being used. Defendant MDY circumvented a number of these measures. Blizzard successfully brought a claim under the DMCA, asserting that MDY circumvented a technological measure that controlled access to an underlying copyrighted work, namely the game software residing on plaintiff's servers.

In one sense, *MDY* can be seen as analytically similar to the cases in the prior section. Blizzard placed conditions on the use of its software. It uses a technological measure to enforce those conditions. A third party circumvented the technology to violate those conditions, thereby obtaining access to the copyrighted software. Thus, these cases could be viewed as little different from the cases that meter use or enforce a licensing provision.

Yet *MDY* is also different in a material fashion. Blizzard is not concerned about mere access to the software. It is not concerned that individuals may be using the Blizzard software after their subscriptions have expired. Indeed, all of the individuals who used the software were existing subscribers and had full access to play the game whenever they wanted. Blizzard was concerned, not about unauthorized access, but about cheating. Or to put it more generally, Blizzard was concerned

[25] 629 F.3d 928 (9th Cir. 2010).

about a use of its software that might harm its business model by making the gameplay less enjoyable for other consumers.[26]

This may well be a legitimate concern and interest on the part of Blizzard. And indeed, Blizzard might be able to further this interest via contract law, by enforcing its terms of service. But it is important to note that this is, at bottom, not a copyright interest, even under the broader definition implicitly set forth by the DMCA. It has nothing to do with preventing infringement of the underlying software. It has nothing to do even with preventing unauthorized access, qua access, to the underlying software, since Blizzard is perfectly happy for the individuals to play the game directly. Nevertheless, because the technology deployed by Blizzard to prevent cheating also happened to affect access to the underlying software, Blizzard was able to leverage the DMCA's use of "access" to bring a claim against consumers who were using the software in a fashion Blizzard objected to.

At least one District Court, however, rejected a DMCA claim on similar facts. In *Jagex Ltd* v. *Impulse Software*,[27] the court addressed a DMCA claim brought by the creators of the massively multiplayer online game *Runescape*. Just as in *MDY*, the defendant in *Jagex* distributed software that allowed players to play the game automatically, without their active involvement. The court ultimately dismissed the case, both because of doubts about the ownership of the underlying copyrights, but also because of a technical distinction between *Jagex* and *MDY*, where access to the software at issue in *Jagex* was not in fact restricted by the particular technological measure deployed in that case.[28]

Another analytically similar case can be found in *Coupons, Inc.* v. *Stottlemire*.[29] Although not a computer game case, *Coupons, Inc.* similarly involved an act of "cheating." In that case, the plaintiff was an online coupon company, which distributed coupons to consumers electronically via the internet. To prevent consumers from printing and using their coupons more than once, the plaintiff placed a small piece of software code on the consumer's computer. The defendant distributed software that allowed consumers to remove the code and print multiple coupons. The plaintiff brought a DMCA claim, asserting that the defendant's software circumvented a measure designed to protect a copyrighted

[26] *Cf.* Justin Van Etten, Case Comment, "Copyright Enforcement of Non-Copyright Terms: *MDY* v. *Blizzard* and *Krause* v. *Titleserv*," 2011 *Duke L. & Tech. Rev.* 7 (2011).

[27] 750 F.Supp.2d 228 (D. Mass. 2010).

[28] *Compare Evony, LLC* v. *Holland*, Slip Copy, 2011 WL 1230405 (W.D. Pa. 2011) (similar case, but court enforces default judgment against defendant, finding that allegations sufficient to make out a case for trafficking).

[29] 588 F.Supp.2d 1069 (N.D. Cal. 2008).

work, namely the coupons. This last case highlights even more expressly how some of the new rights in the DMCA can be leveraged to vindicate interests that have little to do with the copyrights themselves.

More generally, as more and more activity moves online, individuals and companies will seek to control how individuals behave, in ways that maximize their profits, but have nothing directly to do with copyright law. Individuals and companies may deploy technological measures to control individual behaviors. And when such measures are undercut or circumvented, the ubiquity of protected copyrighted material online means that there will often be some copyrighted work to which an individual will have obtained access, thanks to the act of circumvention. Without a clearer idea of the copyright interests underlying the DMCA, and without some limitations on our conception of "access," this may lead to troublesome results.

Controlling access to websites and computers

Yet another set of troubling cases involve uses of the DMCA to restrict access, not to particular copyrighted works, but to websites and computers in general. In these cases, the plaintiffs attempt to use the DMCA to prevent someone from accessing a website or computer without authorization. In these cases, the plaintiff deploys a technological measure to restrict access, and the defendant circumvents the measure. Because accessing a website or computer often leads to access to a copyrighted work (whether computer software running on the server or copyrighted material residing on the website), plaintiffs can claim that the very act of access to the computer gives rise to liability under the DMCA, whether or not any underlying copyrighted work has actually been infringed.

A number of these cases involve unauthorized use of a password to gain access to a computer or website. For example, in *I.M.S. Inquiry Mgmt. Sys.* v. *Berkshire Info. Sys.*,[30] the defendant was an internet advertising firm that used a password to access a competitor's website without authorization, in order to gain access to information. The password had been acquired from someone who was authorized to use it. Nevertheless, the plaintiff brought a DMCA claim, arguing that the defendant, by using the password without authorization, circumvented a technological measure designed to prevent access to a copyrighted work (namely materials on the website). The District Court ultimately dismissed the

[30] 307 F.Supp.2d 521 (S.D.N.Y. 2004).

case, holding that, although the password system was a "technological measure" within the meaning of the DMCA, the use of a password was not an act of circumvention. Similarly, in both *Egilman* v. *Keller & Heckman*[31] and *R.C. Olmstead, Inc.* v. *CU Interface*,[32] US District Courts rejected DMCA claims based on the unauthorized use of a username and password to gain unauthorized access to a website or computer, largely following the reasoning in *I.M.S.*[33]

Although plaintiffs have not been successful on this front when dealing with passwords, they have had more success with other measures designed to control access to websites. In *Ticketmaster LLC* v. *RMG Technologies*,[34] the plaintiff Ticketmaster sold event tickets online. In order to prevent automated programs from buying tickets or otherwise accessing its Web pages automatically, Ticketmaster used a "captcha" system, which required an individual to type in a code displayed in a fashion (i.e. as a distorted image) so as to defeat an automated system. Defendant sold software that allowed a computer program to successfully negotiate the captcha system, thereby accessing the underlying Web pages. Ticketmaster sued under the DMCA, arguing that the captcha system was a technological measure that effectively controlled access to the copyrighted material on its website. The District Court in *Ticketmaster* accepted this argument, holding that the captcha system did in fact constitute a technological protection measure.

The *Ticketmaster* case is not an isolated case. In *Craigslist* v. *Naturemarket*,[35] another US District Court reached a very similar result. In that case, the online classified advertising company Craigslist used captcha technology to prevent other companies from automatically posting classified advertisements on its website. The defendant sold software and services that enabled third parties to automatically negotiate the captcha process, thereby automatically posting classified advertisements. Just as in *Ticketmaster*, Craigslist sued under the DMCA, and the District Court found a cause of action.

These cases are troubling because they suggest that the DMCA's right to control access can be extended well beyond what is necessary to protect copyrighted works, to create a right to control access to websites and computers more generally. One can imagine circumstances where it might be quite appropriate to enforce a technological measure designed to control access to a particular computer that contains copyrighted

[31] 401 F.Supp.2d 105 (D.D.C. 2005). [32] 657 F.Supp.2d 878 (N.D. Ohio 2009).

[33] *See also Ground Zero Museum Workshop* v. *Wilson*, 813 F.Supp.2d 678 (D. Md. 2011) (reaching a broadly similar result).

[34] 507 F.Supp.2d 1096 (C.D. Cal. 2007). [35] 694 F.Supp.2d 1039 (N.D. Cal. 2010).

material. For example, imagine a computer that contains a host of copyrighted music files, protected by an access-control measure. If that measure were defeated in order to access the copyrighted music, this would seem to be a relatively straightfoward DMCA case.

The problem is that the DMCA, by its terms, applies equally to a case where the computer contains no copyrighted material that the owner of the computer is interested in protecting. For example, imagine a situation where the computer contains mostly data, and only minimal copyrighted material.[36] Circumventing an access-control technology to access the data would lead to liability under the DMCA, even if there is no underlying copyright interest, since it would lead to access to both the minimal copyrighted material and the software running on the server. Or take the *Ticketmaster* and *Craigslist* cases above. Neither Ticketmaster nor Craigslist were concerned about protecting the copyrights in its Web pages. Neither was concerned that others would copy the copyrighted material and sell it or use it in competition. Instead, these companies wanted to prevent competitors and other companies from accessing their websites.

Whether owners of websites should have the right to prevent such access as a general matter, and whether they might have claims under other statutes, such a broad right is not a *copyright* interest.[37] When Congress enacted the DMCA, it did not intend to create a wide-ranging right to control access to websites or computers via passwords or other technical measures. (Such a right, if it exists at all, should be the subject of a separate statute designed for just this purpose, such as the federal Computer Fraud and Abuse Act.[38]) Instead, when Congress enacted the DMCA, it intended to prevent individuals from breaking encryption systems to access and copy copyrighted works. In none of the above cases is there any real interest in protecting an underlying copyrighted work or preventing copyright infringement. Instead, the plaintiffs in these cases take advantage of the fact that accessing a website or computer invariably leads to "access" to copyrighted material.

Courts therefore need to find a way to sort through these cases to ensure that a DMCA claim based on unauthorized access to a computer or website truly furthers an underlying copyright interest. One way would be to interpret "access" more narrowly, to apply to cases where the technological measure controls access to a particular copyrighted work,

[36] *See* Ginsburg, "From Having Copies," (describing this hypothetical).
[37] *See* Computer Fraud and Abuse Act, 18 U.S.C. § 1030.
[38] Note that a very interesting parallel discussion is currently taking place regarding the breadth of the term "access" in the Computer Fraud and Abuse Act, 18 U.S.C. § 1030.

and not a computer more generally. Another possibility would be to import into the DMCA a requirement that the act of circumvention be related to a copyright interest, i.e. that it have a nexus to infringement. Some of the cases in the following section adopt this approach. Yet another approach might be to interpret "work[s] protected under this title" more narrowly to prevent or limit attempts to expand control over unprotected material.[39] More generally, this suggests a need to tie the access-control right more firmly to an underlying copyright interest.

Hardware and software tying

A final example of the potential mischief caused by an expansive understanding of "access" can be found in the cases that attempt to use the DMCA to facilitate a strategy of tying hardware, software, or services. Fortunately, several appellate courts have interpreted the DMCA more narrowly to limit the ability of plaintiffs to extend the DMCA in this fashion. At the same time, however, other courts have been more willing to permit plaintiffs to use the DMCA's access-control provisions in this fashion. Accordingly, this is an area that warrants further development.

The Court of Appeals' decisions in *Chamberlain Group* v. *Skylink Technologies*[40] and *Lexmark Intern.* v. *Static Control Components*[41] are the two most prominent examples of attempts to use the DMCA to facilitate hardware tying. In *Chamberlain*, the plaintiff asserted a DMCA claim to prevent the defendant from making a compatible remote control for its garage door opener. The plaintiff claimed that the remote control circumvented a technological measure that controlled access to the software that ran on the garage door opener, when it caused the garage door opener to function (and thus run the software). In *Lexmark*, the plaintiff asserted a DMCA claim to prevent the defendant from making and selling toner cartridges that were compatible with plaintiff's laser printers. The plaintiff claimed that the toner cartridges circumvented a technological measure that attempted to restrict compatible toner cartridges to ones authorized by the plaintiff. The DMCA claim was based on the claim that the defendant's toner cartridges caused the laser printer to run, thereby accessing the laser printer software without authorization.

Both of these cases presented situations that were clearly outside what Congress intended when it passed the DMCA. Congress did not intend to facilitate hardware tying when it enacted the DMCA. Instead, its main concern was preventing copyright infringement. Neither *Chamberlain* nor

[39] *See* Ginsburg, "The Pros and Cons."

[40] 381 F.3d 1178 (Fed. Cir. 2004).

[41] 387 F.3d 522 (6th Cir. 2004).

Lexmark involved a good faith concern about protecting copyrighted works. In *Chamberlain*, the plaintiff was not afraid of unauthorized copying of its garage door opener software. In *Lexmark*, the plaintiff was not concerned about protecting its laser printer software. Rather, in both cases, the plaintiffs used the DMCA opportunistically, in an attempt to prevent others from making and selling compatible products. These claims were made possible by the fact that computer software happened to be a component of these products.

Fortunately, in both cases, the Courts of Appeals found ways to interpret the DMCA in a limited fashion, to avoid these results. Although these cases were clearly outside the intended scope of the DMCA, unfortunately they were not so clearly outside the plain language of the DMCA. Moreover, the lack of any fair use defense, per *Corley*, made it more difficult for the appellate courts to find a way to insulate these activities from DMCA liability. In the end, however, the two courts adopted different strategies for reaching their results. In *Chamberlain*, the Federal Circuit held that DMCA liability required some nexus to an underlying copyright infringement concern. In *Lexmark*, the Sixth Circuit held that the particular technology did not effectively control "access" to the software, since the software itself remained unprotected. Thus, in each case, the court found a way to interpret the DMCA in a fashion that was true to Congressional intent.[42]

A number of cases have involved attempts to tie services rather than products. For example, *Storage Technology Corp.* v. *Custom Hardware Engineering & Consulting*[43] involved a DMCA claim brought against a computer hardware service company. In order to service the plaintiff's computers, the defendant ran certain diagnostic and maintenance software residing on those computers and owned by the plaintiff. The plaintiff claimed that, by circumventing certain technical measures to run that software, defendant violated the DMCA. Here, the plaintiff attempted to invoke the DMCA to prevent third parties from servicing its computers. Again, this result was not what Congress intended when passing the DMCA. And again, the Federal Circuit, following its opinion in *Chamberlain*, denied liability, finding no nexus to copyright infringement.

Although several appellate courts have interpreted the DMCA's access provisions to avoid this misuse of the DMCA, other courts have not been

[42] *See* Timothy K. Armstrong, "Fair Circumvention," 74 *Brook. L. Rev.* 1 (2008); Dan L. Burk, "Legal and Technical Standards in Digital Rights Management Technology," 74 *Fordham L. Rev.* 537 (2005); Steve P. Calandrillo, "The Dangers of the Digital Millennium Copyright Act: Much Ado About Nothing?," 50 *Wm. & Mary L. Rev.* 349 (2008); Robert C. Denicola, "Access Controls."

[43] 421 F.3d 1307 (Fed. Cir. 2005).

so careful. A very large number of such cases have involved attempts to tie cellphone hardware to cellphone services. For example, both *TracFone Wireless* v. *Dixon*[44] and *TracFone Wireless* v. *GSM Group*[45] involved cases brought by cellphone manufacturers against companies that had purchased plaintiff's phones and removed technologies that restricted operation of the cellphones to the plaintiff's network, thereby allowing the phones to be used on different networks.[46] Again, in none of these cases was the primary concern protecting the software that resided on the cellphones. Instead, the claims were brought in an effort to tie the cellphones to a particular cellphone carrier. Once again, this was clearly outside what Congress intended when it enacted the DMCA.[47]

With respect to the cellphone cases, the courts have yet to reach a result akin to the results in *Chamberlain* and *Lexmark*. Instead, partial relief from liability had in the past come in the form of a regulatory exemption, promulgated by the Library of Congress as part of its triennial rulemaking. Recognizing the disjunction between the intended scope of the DMCA and these cases, the Library of Congress in the past created an exemption for circumventing software on cellphones solely for the purpose of making the cellphones compatible with other networks.[48] However, in its most recent rulemaking, the Library of Congress refused to renew this exemption for cellphones purchased in the future, on the grounds that there were sufficient numbers of unlocked phones on the market such that the DMCA did not prevent consumers from obtaining easy access to such phones.

[44] 475 F.Supp.2d 1236 (M.D. Fla. 2007). [45] 555 F.Supp.2d 1331 (S.D. Fla. 2008).

[46] *See also TracFone Wireless, Inc.* v. *Zip Wireless Products, Inc.*, 716 F.Supp.2d 1275 (N.D. Ga. 2010); *TracFone Wireless, Inc.* v. *SND Cellular, Inc.*, 715 F.Supp.2d 1246 (S.D. Fla. 2010) (awarding damages for default judgment); *TracFone Wireless, Inc.* v. *Anadisk LLC*, 685 F.Supp.2d 1304 (S.D. Fla. 2010) (same kind of case, no discussion of regulatory exemption).

[47] *Davidson & Associates* v. *Jung*, 422 F.3d 630 (8th Cir. 2005) arguably falls within this category as well. In *Davidson*, the plaintiff owned the copyright to a computer game, which consumers could play on their own computers. Consumers could also log onto plaintiff's online service, which would enable consumers to play against other consumers. The defendant in the case created a competing service, which enabled consumers to play each other without using plaintiff's online service. In so doing, the defendant circumvented a measure that plaintiff used to verify that the consumers were playing legitimate copies of the software. Arguably, this was a form of tying, insofar as the plaintiff wanted to tie the computer software to a particular online service. However, there was evidence in the case that defendant's service permitted unauthorized copies of the software to be run. Thus there is at least some nexus with copyright infringement.

[48] 37 C.F.R. 201. At the same time, real questions existed as to the breadth of this exemption, as a number of courts nevertheless found potential liability where the circumvention was arguably not "solely" for the purpose of compatibility. *E.g. TracFone Wireless, Inc.* v. *Zip Wireless Products, Inc.*, 716 F.Supp.2d 1275 (N.D. Ga. 2010) (holding that case may fall outside regulatory exemption).

The cellphone cases thus represent a clear example of the continuing mischief potentially caused by an expansive and overly literal interpretation of the term "access." Such cases should, in an ideal world, fall outside the scope of DMCA liability in the first instance, and therefore not be subject to the vagaries of the DMCA's rulemaking process. Indeed, as the most recent rulemaking indicates, the nature of the rulemaking inquiry is not easily amenable to such considerations, since it by definition focuses on whether consumers can obtain access to copyrighted works, and not on whether DMCA liability is even appropriate or intended by Congress. Thus a real risk continues to exist that hardware manufacturers will be able to leverage a broad "access" right to tie their hardware to specific services or other products.

The troublesome nature of access

The pattern of cases above highlights the fact that the DMCA's understanding of a right to control "access" to copyrighted works must, necessarily, be more nuanced than originally suggested in the text and legislative history of the DMCA. The DMCA itself mentions "access" in a rather straightforward fashion, never defining it, and the legislative history behind this provision suggests that Congress had a rather simple understanding of access. Congress likely had in mind the simple case of a technological measure that restricted access to a movie or piece of music, and wanted to target actions and technologies that circumvented such measures.

Reinforcing the idea that Congress thought of "access" in simplistic terms is the absolute nature of the right. Unlike, say, copyright's reproduction right, the right to control access via technology is subject to no general fair use defense.[49] Thus, courts are not empowered to adjust the scope of this right to adapt it to new circumstances or to adjust to permit potentially legitimate interests in obtaining access. Instead, exceptions are either written into the statute or subject to exemption via a rulemaking process. This suggests that Congress believed the access right would raise fewer concerns, in some ways, than the other copyright rights.

Congress failed to anticipate, however, a number of factors that have given the access right a far broader scope than ever originally intended. One factor is the inherent ambiguity in the term "access." What does it mean to access a copyrighted work? Must one be able to copy the work? With respect to software, does any act that causes the software to run

[49] *See* Ginsburg, "From Having Copies," (suggesting that anti-circumvention liability should be subject to a fair use or fair access defense).

constitute an act of access? This issue was presented expressly in the *Lexmark* case, in which the court decided that merely running a piece of software does not mean one has "accessed" the software within the meaning of the statute. Courts have thus had to define "access" more carefully.[50]

Another factor is the wide range of reasons copyright owners might have for seeking to control access. One reason might be to prevent copyright infringement. Another reason might be to charge for access as a means of price discrimination. Both of these are reasons that fall within the DMCA's intended ambit. However, as the subsequent case law reveals, copyright owners in fact have many other reasons for seeking to control access. One reason might be to control consumer behavior or further a particular business model that is unrelated to a traditional copyright interest. Another reason might be to prevent unauthorized access to a website for reasons entirely unrelated to a concern about protecting copyrighted material. Yet another reason might be to try to restrict competition in a particular non-copyright market.

These latter reasons have little or nothing to do with an underlying copyright interest, but instead opportunistically take advantage of the broad access right to accomplish another goal. An absolute access right, unconnected to any copyright interest, would lead to absurd results. Indeed, the reasons for controlling access, and for seeking to obtain access, are, if anything, even more wide ranging and nuanced than the reasons one might have for reproducing a copyrighted work.[51] Accordingly, we see attempts to leverage the absolutist nature of the right to accomplish these unrelated goals. We have also seen courts, in response, importing into the access right a necessary nexus to an underlying copyright interest. The analysis in this chapter highlights some of the reasons why such a move, i.e. importing a nexus to a copyright interest broadly understood, may be both desirable and necessary to take into account the wide range of reasons for controlling and obtaining access to copyrighted works.

A final unaccounted for factor is the ubiquity of "work[s] protected under this title" in the online environment. Many activities online lead to access to copyrighted works. Merely visiting a website results in access to a host of copyrighted materials. Technologies that control activities online have the de facto effect of controlling access to copyrighted works. An overly broad understanding of access can lead to excessive control,

[50] Reuven Ashtar, "Licensing as Digital Rights Management, From the Advent of the Web to the iPad," 13 *Yale J. L. & Tech.* 141 (2011).

[51] Ginsburg, "From Having Copies," (proposing that a right to control access be accompanied by many of the same defenses and limitations that apply to other copyright rights). For further development of defenses arguments, *see also* Ginsburg, "The Pros and Cons."

not only of the use of copyrighted materials, but general behavior online. Thus we see the cases that have leveraged the access right into a right to control access to Web pages or to servers, or leveraged it into a right to control the behavior of individuals online. Although the plaintiffs in these cases may have legitimate business reasons for seeking to control individual behavior in these ways, it is hard to see why copyright law should facilitate these attempts to exert control.

Finally, the ubiquity of access applies offline as well, as can be seen from the tying cases. Computer software now sits at the juncture of so many of our everyday products. And software is often used to control how real-world devices and products operate and interoperate. Taken literally, an overly broad understanding of the term "access" leads to absurd results. This does suggest, ultimately, that the courts have properly begun to recognize limits on how far the access right should extend.

This chapter has focused largely on looking at actual DMCA case law to highlight some of the complexities associated with the DMCA's new right to access, but has spent relatively less time on the various proposed solutions. Several appellate courts have, as noted above, interpreted "access" in a more nuanced fashion, to preclude overly expansive applications of the DMCA. Still other courts have imported into the DMCA a general requirement that circumvention of access be tied to an underlying copyright interest. Yet another potential response might be to interpret "work[s] protected under this title" in a more nuanced fashion, to exclude some of the potential for abuse.[52] Whether one or many of these solutions ultimately find favor with the courts, it is clear that the courts need to find doctrinal avenues to ensure that some of the complexities associated with this new right of access are carefully considered, and that this new right be tailored to fulfill identified copyright interests.

Conclusion

In the end, the subsequent case law interpreting the DMCA's access right highlights the inherently more complicated nature of a right to control access in the digital environment. Courts have begun to implicitly recognize these complications and have started to adopt doctrines that will give them some room to interpret the access right in a way that ties it to the underlying copyright interests. In the end, this reflects some of the complexities inherent in creating a new right, in a complex and fast-changing technological environment, extending the boundaries at the very edge of our existing intellectual property rights.

[52] Ginsburg, "The Pros and Cons," (exploring this possible approach).

12 The protection of technological measures: Much ado about nothing or silent remodeling of copyright?

Séverine Dusollier

The enactment of anti-circumvention provisions in the European Union (EU) has witnessed the same fierce opposition as in the United States (US), generally based on the fear that such an extensive protection, instead of aligning itself on the contours of copyright, would enlarge the control of copyright holders on access to and use of works, and create what some have called "paracopyright."[1] The designated culprit of such an extension has been found in the criteria used to define the technological protection measures (hereafter TPM) protected by the European Copyright Directive,[2] i.e. the lack of authorization by the right holders. Article 6(3) of the 2001 Directive indeed defines technological measures as "any technology designed to prevent acts not authorized by the right holder." In comparison to the US Digital Millennium Copyright Act of 1998 (DMCA), where two categories of TPM are protected, on one hand measures preventing copyright infringement, on the other hand, measures controlling access to a copyrighted work, the EU protection of TPM, through this vague wording, seems to extend to any use unauthorized by the copyright owners irrespective of its link with the exclusive rights.

Critique has therefore been intense against the anti-circumvention provisions contained in the so-called Infosoc Directive of 2001. Yet, surprisingly, all has been rather quiet on the judicial front as far as Digital Rights Management (DRM) is concerned. No ink cartridge, garage

[1] M. Nimmer, *Nimmer on Copyright* (Matthew Bender & Co., Lexis/Nexis, 2001), 12A-72; this terminology also appears in the preparatory work of the Digital Millennium Copyright Act of 1998, see Report of the Committee of Commerce to accompany H.R. 2281, House of Representatives, 105th Congress, 2d Session, Rept. 105-551 Part 2, 24.

[2] S. Dusollier, "Tipping the Scale in Favor of the Right Holders: The Anti-Circumvention Provisions of the European Directive," in *Digital Rights Management – Technological, Economic, Legal and Political Aspects in the European Union* (E. Becker, W. Buhse, D. Gunnewig & N. Rump (eds.), Berlin, Springer-Verlag, 2003), 462–78; Institute for Information Law (IVIR*), Study on the Implementation and Effect in Member States' Laws of Directive 2001/29/EC on the Harmonisation of Certain Aspects of Copyright and Related Rights in the Information Society*, 2007, at 73–75.

door opener, or online game cheating, to mention some case law described by Joseph Liu in Chapter 11 in this volume, has crossed the European sky.

Another ground for discontent has been the risk that TPM would be applied to curtail copyright exceptions.[3] The EU lawmaker has devised a particular solution to this issue, requiring the safeguarding of some exceptions to some users, and in some limited cases, in Article 6(4) of the 2001 Directive. But the provision safeguarding the exceptions has so far not been put into practice before courts or administrative bodies in charge of such conciliation between exceptions and TPM. Would that indicate, as for the range of technological devices to be protected, that the critique was not justified and that the copyright exceptions had (and still have) nothing to fear?

This chapter investigates both questions and considers whether paracopyright, in the form of an extended protection towards the control of access to and use of the work, has finally settled in the copyright regime through the guise of anti-circumvention provisions. Part I of this chapter discusses the definition of technological measures aimed at by the EU lawmaker and whether it has led to excessive protection in national case law, lacking any nexus to copyright, following the methodology of Joseph Liu's chapter. Part II will come back to the issue of exceptions and analyze whether, albeit the lack of any formal complaints by users, copyright exceptions have not been transformed by anti-circumvention laws.

PART I: THE PROTECTED TECHNOLOGICAL MEASURES IN RELATIONSHIP WITH COPYRIGHT SCOPE

European anti-circumvention provisions

The European equivalent of the DMCA is the Directive 2001/29 of May 22, 2001 on the harmonization of certain aspects of copyright and related rights in the information society.[4] At the time of the Directive, comparison was often made with its US counterpart, particularly concerning the

[3] S. Dusollier, "Exceptions and Technological Measures in the European Copyright Directive of 2001," *International Review of Industrial Property and Copyright Law* (2003), 62–83; IVIR Study, *supra* note 2, at 101. S. Bechtold, "Comment on Article 6 of the Directive," in T. Dreier & B. Hugenholtz (eds.), *Concise European Copyright Law* (Kluwer Law International, Alphenaan den Rijn, 2006), 393.

[4] It should be noted that, contrary to the DMCA, the European Directive is not of direct application as it is a harmonization measure that provides rules and principles that the Member States need to implement in their national laws while keeping some maneuver in doing so.

anti-circumvention provisions.[5] It was generally concluded that such provisions, whatever their side of the Atlantic, shared an extension of copyright towards access and use of works.[6]

The European text has a rather indirect and blurry way to include access to and use of works within its ambit. Its Article 6 deals with technological measures of protection that are defined as: "any technology, device or component that, in the normal course of its operation, is designed to prevent or restrict acts, in respect of works or other subject matter, which are not authorized by the right holder of any copyright or any right related to copyright as provided for by law or the sui generis right." Additionally the definition of the effectiveness of the TPM, a further prerequisite to the protection, refers to access controls.

Such a definition has been understood as opening a broad scope of protection to technological locks. The triggering factor of the protection against circumvention lies in the absence of authorization of the copyright owner. As soon as the technological protection embeds this prohibition or control of use in the digital format or enabling device, it would be legally secured against tampering, for the terminology of the provision appears extremely broad, as it focuses on the absence of authorization by the rights owners, not by the law. Despite the fact that the provision indicates that the rights protected are those "provided by the law," scholars have generally construed the protection as going beyond the control of activities recognized as an exclusive right by copyright law, arguably reaching mere acts of access or use.[7]

Indeed, the emphasis put on the "act not authorized by the right holder," rather than on the legally defined scope of exclusive rights is puzzling. Obviously, since the right holder has decided to protect technically some defined uses related to her work, it means that she was not willing to authorize such activities. Through the definition contained in Article 6(3) of the Directive, referring to what the copyright owner is willing and able to protect through technology, any TPM is then addressed by the EU anti-circumvention protection.

[5] J. de Werra, "The Legal System of Technological Protection Measures under the WIPO Treaties, the Digital Millennium Copyright Act, the European Union Directives and other National Legislations (Australia, Japan)," 189 *Revue Internationale du Droit d'Auteur* (July 2001), 66–213; S. Dusollier & A. Strowel, "La protection légale des systèmes techniques: Analyse de la directive 2001/29 sur le droit d'auteur dans une perspective comparatiste," *Propriétés Intellectuelles* (2001), 10–27; See also the proceedings of the ALAI Conference held in New York in 2001, *Adjuncts and Alternatives to Copyright*, ALAI-USA, Inc., 2002.

[6] See *supra* note 2. [7] IVIR Study, *supra* note 2, 95–97.

Should this broad interpretation prevail, the technological capacity would dictate the legal scope of protection. The scope of copyright would not be decided according to what its proper scope should be, but according to what the technology can do. Any use of a work would enter, through the legal prohibition of the circumvention of a TPM, in the arena of control granted to copyright holders.

However, not all scholars have interpreted the scope of the Directive so extensively[8] and some elements in the legislative history of this provision may incline to establish more firmly a connection between the technically protected uses and the legally protected ones. The proposal for a directive of 1997, as well as further versions until the common position of 2000, only required the Member States of the EU to prohibit the circumvention of "technological measures designed to prevent or inhibit the infringement of any copyright or any rights related to copyright as provided by law."[9]

In the Explanatory Memorandum to the Proposal, the Commission had insisted that:

> Finally, the provision prohibits activities aimed at an infringement of a copyright, a related right or a sui generis right in databases granted by Community and national law: this would imply that not any circumvention of technical means of protection should be covered, but only those which constitute an infringement of a right, i.e. which are not authorized by law or by the author.[10]

This could indicate that the substitution of the expression "acts not authorized by the rights holders" at the stage of the Common position in 2000, aimed indeed at encompassing a broader scope than the exclusive rights.[11] Having said that, the same statement could also be said to

[8] T. Hoeren, "Access Right as a Postmodern Symbol of Copyright Deconstruction?," in *Adjuncts and Alternatives to Copyright*, *supra* note 5; Bechtold, *supra* note 3, at 387.

[9] Proposal for a European Parliament and Council Directive on the harmonization of certain aspects of copyright and related rights in the Information Society, COM/97/0628 final, Official Journal, C-108, 07/04/1998, at 6. See also the Explanation of the Common Position, 28 September 2000, no. 45 ("access to works or other subject-matter is not part of copyright").

[10] Explanatory Memorandum to the Proposal for a Directive on Copyright in the Information Society, available at http://eur-lex.europa.eu/LexUriServ/LexUriServ.do?uri=CELEX:51999PC0250:EN:NOT, at 41.

[11] IVIR Study, *supra* note 2, 79. That would be confirmed by the Statement issued by the European Council, that explains that the new definition of the protectable technological measures "is broader than the one provided for in the Commission's amended proposal or the one set out in Parliament's amendment" (see Statement of the Council's reasons, Directive of the European Parliament and of the Council on the harmonisation of certain aspects of copyright and related rights in the information society, Common Position (EC) No 48/2000 of 28 September 2000 adopted by the Council, Official Journal, C 344, 01/12/2000, pp. 1–22, § 43).

indicate only that TPM are protected, even though the person performing the circumvention does so to benefit from one exception.

Yet, this interpretation has been denied by the European Commission in its 2007 evaluation report on the Directive.[12] This report clearly affirms the required connection between copyright and the TPM, as follows:

> The wording "acts not authorised by the rightholder" in Article 6(3) aims to link TPM to the exercise of the exclusive rights mentioned in this paragraph. Therefore, the Directive aims to establish a connection between the technological measure and the exercise of copyright. This implies that Article 6(3) only protects technological measures that restrict acts which come within the scope of the exclusive rights. (. . .) Moreover, it is clear that the mention of "access control" is no more than an example to define an effective TPM. It cannot be relied upon to widen the scope of the legal definition of TPM under Article 6(3) beyond what is in the rightholders' normative power to prohibit.[13]

Some Member States have similarly emphasized the link that should exist between what a technological measure could encapsulate and what a copyright owner is legally entitled to control.[14] This is the case of the UK whose protection against circumvention only applies where TPM protects a copyright work, which is limited to "the prevention or restriction of acts that are not authorised by the copyright owner of that work and are restricted by copyright."[15] Similar definitions, firmly attaching TPM ambition to copyright scope, can be found in Austria, Denmark and Germany.[16]

In addition, one UK court decision convincingly affirmed that:

> When speaking of "acts which are not authorised" it is implicit that one is considering only acts which need authorisation, i.e. acts which are otherwise restricted. To "authorise" a man to do something he is free to do anyway – something which needs no authority – is a meaningless concept. So we think the UK draftsman was merely making explicit that which was implicit in the Directive – and indeed in the original 1996 Treaty obligations.[17]

[12] Commission Staff Working Document, Report to the Council, the European Parliament and the Economic and Social Committee on the application of Directive 2001/29/EC on the harmonisation of certain aspects of copyright and related rights in the information society, November 30, 2007, SEC(2007) 1556.

[13] *Ibid.* at 7.

[14] U. Gasser & M. Girsberger, "Transposing the Copyright Directive: Legal Protection of Technological Measures in EU-Member States – A Genie Stuck in the Bottle?," November 2004, Berkman Working Paper No. 2004-10, available at http://ssrn.com/abstract=628007.

[15] Section 296ZF (3) of the Copyright, Designs and Patent Act of 1988. See also part (b) of this section that reads that "use of a work does not extend to any use of the work that is outside the scope of the acts restricted by copyright."

[16] IVIR Study, *supra* note 2, Part II, at 52.

[17] *Higgs* v. *The Queen*, [2008] EWCA Crim 1324, at 32.

Case law

Surprisingly enough, anti-circumvention provisions yielded less case law than theoretical criticism. To follow Liu's analysis, in Chapter 11, of the post-DMCA court decisions and its division between canonical and intended cases and those whose purpose has nothing to do with preventing copyright infringement, this section will first draw a similar line between the expected and unexpected cases, i.e. between the "core" cases where limiting copyright infringement is aimed at, and some other court decisions apparently lacking some nexus to copyright protection. The latter proved to be rather scarce in the countries reviewed.[18] Many decisions concern the use and sale of modchips for videogames that have generated a mixed judicial response. I will focus my attention on that particular application of anti-circumvention provisions.

Expected and unexpected cases

As in the US, DVD hacking has provided some of the first decisions in Europe. However, provision or trafficking in DeCSS code has not made the headlines of many court cases, except perhaps for one Finnish decision that has unexpectedly declined to enforce the protection against circumvention of the DVD, considering that the huge circulation of the hacking tool had rendered ineffective the CSS protection, therefore making the DVDs ineligible for protection against circumvention.[19] In other cases, the technological measure that was tampered with either prevented musical CDs from being burned,[20] or software from being used without authorization,[21] or controlled the individual access to a videogame[22] or to copyrighted maps,[23] all cases that demonstrate some link with copyrighted works and copyright protection.

[18] Not all 27 Member States' case law has been analyzed, as court decisions of all countries are difficult to find in another language than their original one. Our informal survey has been limited to the UK, Belgium, France, Germany, Italy and the Netherlands. Even for those countries, we might have missed some court decision dealing with circumvention of technological measures.

[19] Helsinki District Court, Case R 07/1004, May 25, 2007, unofficial English translation available at www.valimaki.com/org/docs/css/css_helsinki_district_court.pdf.

[20] BGH, July 17, 2008, GRUR, 2008, at 996; LG Köln, Urteil v. November 23, 2005 – Az: 28 S 6/05 (2006) Jur-PC Web-Dok. 49/2006, Nos. 1–63, available at www.jurpc.de/rechtspr/20060049.htm.

[21] Anvers (9th ch.), 28 February 2002, *Auteurs & Media*, 2002, at 340; Corr. Charleroi, October 23, 2003, no. 2626; Corr. Gand, April 23, 2008, no. 2008/1322; Mons, May 4, 2007, no. 135 H 04. Note that in those cases another legal provision than the national implementation of the 2001 Directive applies. Such a legal provision has an explicit link with the exclusive rights in the software.

[22] BGH, February 11, 2010 – I ZR 178/08 (OLG Hamburg) Half-Life 2.

[23] BGH, April 29, 2010 – I ZR 39/08 (OLG Hamburg) Session-ID.

In Germany, freedom of expression and freedom of the press were applied to deny the application of an anti-circumvention provision to an online news site that had reported about an allegedly illegal circumvention device (and linked thereto).[24]

Odd cases, which would confirm the potential excess of anti-circumvention provisions are difficult to find in Europe. In Belgium, a person having tampered with the SIM card of cell phones[25] to make them operate on other telecommunications networks had been convicted of infringement of copyright anti-circumvention provisions, though this ground was in the end not even discussed by the criminal judge.[26]

Modchips and videogames: the uneasy case

Videogames are generally protected by built-in authentication measures and copy-protection that ensure many functions: they guarantee the authenticity of a game inserted in a console, verify the authorized region where the game was marketed and prevent the playing of unauthentic or pirated games. Modchips (that stand for modification chips) disable these mechanisms so as to allow the running of games bought in other markets, unlicensed games created by the user herself or a third party, or even copied games. More recently, modchips have also been used to transform the console in a genuine computer capable of performing other functions than those assigned by the console maker.

Litigation related to modchips has been considered in Liu's chapter (Chapter 11) as belonging to the normal remit of the anti-circumvention provisions. This does not seem so straightforward however, particularly if one looks to the diverging case law on that issue, namely in Europe. Whereas selling or making available modchips in any way has been condemned on the basis of anti-circumvention provisions namely in Belgium,[27] France,[28] the UK[29] and Germany,[30] some doubts have been

[24] BVerfG, December 15, 2011, 1 BvR 1248/11, Absatz-Nr. (1 – 38), available at www.bverfg.de/entscheidungen/rk20111215_1bvr124811.html.

[25] Mobile communications in Europe operate with chip cards inserted in phones and related to the provider with which the user has a subscription. Some so-called SIM cards are locked to prevent users from moving to another operator (to preserve the duration or other conditions imposed on the subscription).

[26] Civ. Namur, January 7, 2004, *R.D.T.I.*, October 2005, 113, note Dusollier & Potelle.

[27] Corr. Charleroi, October 23, 2003, no. 68.L7.343/02; Corr. Gand, April 23, 2008, no. 68.98.1806/07/FS1; Mons, May 4, 2007, no. 135 H 04.

[28] CA Paris, September 26, 2011, *Nintendo c. Absolute Games & Divineo*, available at www.legalis.net/spip.php?page=jurisprudence-decision&id_article=3238.

[29] *Kabushiki Kaisha Sony Computer Entertainment Inc. (t/a Sony Computer Entertainment Inc.)* v. *Ball & Ors* [2004] EWHC 1192 (Ch) (May 17, 2004), available at www.bailii.org/ew/cases/EWHC/Ch/2004/1192.html.

[30] LG München, March 13, 2008, 7 O 16829/07, *MMR*, 2008, 839.

raised in Spain[31] and in first degree decisions in France[32] and Italy[33] as to the lacking connection between copyright protection and the use secured and restrained by videogame consoles.

Trafficking in modchips is indeed a difficult application of anti-circumvention provisions. True, modchips tamper with a set of protection measures set around videogames being without any doubt copyrighted works. They disable the protection that indirectly secures the regional distribution market of authentic videogames. Yet, as such, modchips do not copy protected works and their use to play imported or unlicensed games is, in some senses, external to the key purpose of copyright protection to the extent it circumvents the prohibition of parallel imports or alternative manufacturing of games. Playing games acquired in a different region than that of the device does not arguably infringe any exclusive rights of the copyright owner, as no distribution or resale act occurs.[34] A further difficulty is that the mere use of pirated games, enabled by modchips, does not clearly constitute an infringement of copyright save for a strict application of the temporary reproduction right. Under European law, a RAM-copy, such as that occurring when playing a game, contravenes the copyright if it is not a technical and essential part of a lawful use and has an independent economic significance.

The broad interpretation that the Court of Justice of the European Union (CJEU) has given to the temporary reproduction right might confirm the analysis of the mere use of a counterfeited work being a copyright infringement, thereby triggering the protection of the TPM controlling such use.[35] Only transient copying, occurring during a lawful use of a work, upon the condition that it is an integral and essential part of such use and does not have any other significant economic independence would be exempted under a rule of exception. The lawfulness of the use of pirated games is undoubtedly lacking, but the question is less certain for unlicensed games or games created by the user herself, the owner of the right in the console

[31] Audiencia Provincial de Las Palmas, March 5, 2010, Modchips y Swap Magic; Juzgado de instrucción no. 004 Salamanca, November 20, 2009, *Nintendo* v. *Movilquick*.

[32] TGI Paris, December 3, 2009, *Nintendo* v. *Divineo*, available at http://juriscom.net/2009/12/tgi-paris-3-decembre-2009-nintendo-c-sarl-divineo-et-autres/.

[33] Tribunale del riesame di Bolzano, December 31, 2003, available (in Italian) at www.diritto.it/sentenze/magistratord/ord_bo_31_12_03.html.

[34] As agreed by the European Commission's evaluation of the Directive, see *supra* note 12, at 8.

[35] CJEU, July 16, 2009, *Infopaq International*, C-5/08; CJEU, January 17, 2012, *Infopaq International*, C-302/10; CJEU, October 4, 2011, *Football Association Premier League*, C-403/08, & *Karen Murphy*, C-429/08. For a comment on its effect on anti-circumvention protection, see G Westkamp, "Code, Copying, Competition: The Subversive Force of Para-Copyright and the Need for an Unfair Competition Based Reassessment of DRM Laws after Infopaq," 58 *J. Copyright Soc'y* (2011), 665.

having no copyright in such games. As to regional coding, if the use of games imported from another region than that of the console is not illegal, this also renders the RAM-copy thereof an integral part of a lawful use.

In modchips cases, only the UK decisions have directly addressed the issue by considering that running counterfeited games constitutes an infringement of copyright due to the illicit temporary copying.[36]

An added difficulty results from the diverging protection of TPM applying to software or to other types of works. Indeed the 2001 Directive left intact the former protection of technological measures applied to computer programs, which was more limited: Only acts of trafficking in circumventing devices were aimed at (whereas the act of circumventing is also covered by the 2001 Directive) and they should have the *sole purpose* of circumventing to be considered as illegitimate (compared to the less restrictive standard of "limited commercially significant purpose or use other than to circumvent" found in the 2001 Directive). In some court decisions, when videogames were qualified as being software, it might have led to some doubts as to whether modchips have the sole purpose of circumventing the protection of games, as they could generally serve other legitimate purposes (even though minimal). This has informed an Australian decision[37] as well as the decision of the Italian district court. In other countries, this challenge has been avoided either by considering videogames as multimedia works to which the protection of the 2001 Directive applies, or as embracing a rather broad construction of the criteria of the sole purpose.[38]

A French district court rejected the request of Nintendo to condemn the sale of modchip-like tools.[39] The court considered that the modchip aimed at achieving interoperability of the Nintendo console with other games, which was not prohibited by the law, making a rather surprising application of the French law that provides that the TPM should not hamper interoperability.[40] On appeal,[41] the exception for interoperability was properly limited to the requirement to claim such benefit in the way

[36] *Gilham* v. *R* [2009] EWCA Crim 2293; *Nintendo Company Ltd & ANR* v. *Console PC Com Ltd* [2010] EWHC 1932 (Ch).

[37] High Court of Australia, *Stevens* v. *Kabushiki Kaisha Sony Computer Entertainment* [2005] HCA 58 (October 6, 2005).

[38] In the Netherlands, Rb. Alkmaar November 30, 2000, Computerrecht, 2001–3, note K. Koelman.

[39] TGI Paris, December 3, 2009, *Nintendo* v. *Divineo*, available at http://juriscom.net/2009/12/tgi-paris-3-decembre-2009-nintendo-c-sarl-divineo-et-autres/.

[40] Actually this provision, albeit somewhat vague, aims at directing makers of devices that need to interoperate to DRM to address a request to an ad hoc administrative body to get the necessary information. It was not thought as providing a limitation of the protection against circumvention to achieve interoperability.

[41] Court of Appeal, Paris, September 26, 2011, no. 10/01053.

organized by law. The decision has been reversed and the modchips were considered as having been designed solely to circumvent the TPM affixed to the videogames and consoles.

In Italy, two district courts[42] had also refused to condemn the modification of PlayStations that aimed at enabling playing games imported from other regions. The decision of the *Bolzano* court considered that the main objective of the modchips was "to overcome monopolistic obstacles and to have a better use of the PlayStation." Namely, the chip was deemed to serve legitimate purposes such as playing imported games, backup copies, games of other brands, or even transforming the console into a genuine and unfettered computer. The judge did not find any relationship of the TPM with copyright but considered that the modchip rather reinstalls all functionalities that a legitimate owner should benefit from. This opinion was reversed on appeal,[43] followed by the Italian Supreme Court in 2007, which held that modchips are unauthorized circumventing devices.[44]

From Italy again a decisive interpretation could come, as a Milan Court has recently referred some questions to the CJEU for preliminary ruling as to the scope of the protection of TPM under the 2001 Directive and its application to modchips.[45] The referred questions enquire whether anti-circumvention provisions apply to a recognition code that prevents interoperability between the console and complementary products or equipment, not marketed by the same undertaking as the seller of the console. The CJEU should then soon shed some light on this unclear issue or, as has regularly been the case in the last years, it might add further complexity and uncertainty.[46]

PART II: THE INTERFACE BETWEEN TPM AND EXCEPTIONS

Article 6(4) of the Directive: a European oddity

As to the exceptions to copyright, the solution put forward by the European Directive in its Article 6(4) is a bold one as it induces

[42] Tribunale del riesame di Bolzano, December 31, 2003, available (in Italian) at www.diritto.it/sentenze/magistratord/ord_bo_31_12_03.html; Trib. Vincenza, June 27, 2003, nr. 53/03.

[43] Corte di Appello di Trento, May 18, 2006.

[44] Corte Suprema di Cassazione, September 3, 2007, no. 33768.

[45] Reference for a preliminary ruling from the Tribunale di Milano (Italy) lodged on July 26, 2012 – *Nintendo Co., Ltd and Others* v. *PC Box Srl and 9Net Srl*, Case C-355/12.

[46] The conclusions of the Advocate General were released on September 19, 2013; see the case C-355/12 on curia.europa.eu.

implementation of copyright exceptions in the very design of the technical, business and contractual models for distributing copyrighted works. Indeed, while the US have only considered the solution to that "fair use" issue at the level of the sanction for circumvention,[47] the EU has chosen to rule on the matter even before the enforcement stage.

Its first principle is to entrust the right holders with the task of reconciling the technological measures with the safeguarding of the exceptions. The first subsection of Article 6(4) states:

> [I]n the absence of voluntary measures taken by rightholders, including agreements between rightholders and other parties concerned, Member States shall take appropriate measures to ensure that rightholders make available to the beneficiary of an exception or limitation (. . .), the means of benefiting from that exception or limitation, to the extent necessary to benefit from that exception or limitation and where that beneficiary has legal access to the protected work or subject-matter concerned.

The intervention of the lawmaker is therefore subsidiary to that of the authors and other rights owners. Adoption of any voluntary measures by right holders should be the preferred solution. The state should intervene only in default of such measures. The second subsection of Article 6(4) provides for a similar solution (appropriate measures of the states if right holders fail to do so) as to private copying. In that case, the intervention of the legislator is not mandatory, but optional. Here also, the initiative lies on the right holders. In a way, this solution implies that the exceptions are given a positive meaning and not only a defensive nature. It was certainly the first time that authors were asked to facilitate the exercise of exceptions to their rights.

However, the accommodation of the exceptions is limited in different ways. First, the intervention of the Member States is only subsidiary to the primary intervention of the copyright owners themselves. Second, it applies only to some exceptions, such as library privileges, use for education, use by disabled persons, etc. And, finally, this approach does not apply if the work is made available on demand on agreed contractual terms, which could potentially cover many online services.

Fragmented solution within the Member States

Member States have implemented the accommodation of the exceptions within anti-circumvention measures rather differently. Some have done

[47] The DMCA sets up a rulemaking procedure where defined acts of circumvention are declared as being outside of the prohibition.

nothing, others have set up specific mechanisms, whether administrative or judicial, to complain of a technical limitation of an exception, or have simply referred the issue to the courts or to a mediation procedure.[48] This rather kaleidoscopic regime was largely criticized as it could not give security to European beneficiaries of exceptions. The recourse offered to the users in some countries may also have been perceived as too burdensome compared to the benefit of some exceptions. No user will start a lawsuit for the sole benefit of making a private copy of a CD or DVD she bought for a few euros.[49]

The absence of complaints: A solution in quest of an issue?

In any event, in the decade following the adoption of the 2001 Directive, almost no beneficiary of exceptions safeguarded by Article 6(4) of the Directive has, to my knowledge, complained before the dedicated administrative body or to any court about the operation of technological measures and reclaimed the due benefit of the privileged use. For instance, the 2008 report of the French Authority for the Regulation of Technological Measures (ARMT), whose primary mission was to hear the requests of users who could not benefit from an exception, was never seized.[50] In Belgium, where the conflict was referred to courts competent to issue injunctions in case of a technological measure unduly impeding a privileged exception, no case was ever brought to justice.

Would that be an indication that the concerns were overstated and that technological measures do not curb the benefit of exceptions as they were deemed to do? Yet, a 2009 empirical study,[51] carried out by Patricia Akester and based on many interviews with right holders and users alike, has shown that the latter declare that they are being adversely affected by the use of DRM.

Many factors can explain the lack of cases on the interface of exceptions and technological measures. First, most restraining TPM have been gradually abandoned. The music industry, for instance, has renounced protecting CDs against copying due to the hostility of consumers. Second, the room left to the initiative of right holders has yielded some

[48] IVIR Study, *supra* note 2, Part II, *The Implementation of Directive 2001/29/EC in the Member States*, 65–74 and the table at 95; Gasser & Girsberger, *supra* note 14.

[49] Systems of collective redress upon a complaint by consumers' associations could prove more effective in that regard.

[50] Annual Report, ARMT, 2008.

[51] P. Akester, "The Impact of Digital Rights Management on Freedom of Expression – The First Empirical Assessment," 1 *International Review of Intellectual Property and Competition Law* (2010), 31.

private arrangements, namely through contracts, to accommodate the needs of the beneficiaries of exceptions. In Germany for instance, scientific publishers have agreed with libraries to enable them to carry on some privileged uses for archiving purposes, despite the presence of a technological measure. Then the procedures set up to the benefit of users might be too costly and complex to engage, particularly for individuals or small institutions. But that might not be a decisive factor, as no cases were initiated in the countries where a collective action has been conferred to the representatives of the beneficiaries of exceptions (e.g. an association of libraries) either.

Finally, technological measures have evolved from genuine locks, blocking access to works or preventing their copy, to more refined systems controlling the use while allowing many activities. Users might then be sufficiently happy with the breathing space offered to them and not feel the need to rely on copyright exceptions. Downloading films or music on iTunes, for instance, entitles the buyer to make some copies and to transfer the file to a limited set of personal devices, which creates a sphere of personal use that might not be exactly identical to what is allowed under the private copy exceptions or limitations but could be flexible enough to meet the needs of users.[52]

Conclusion

Actual application of anti-circumvention in Europe has all the appearance of a quiet sea. This significantly contrasts with the accusation of creating paracopyright with no other legitimacy than the desire for more control of copyright owners over use of their works.

The scope of anti-circumvention provisions has rarely reached contested territory, where any trace of copyright infringement would be lacking and even copyright exceptions, which were considered as being the sacrificed victims of the protection of TPM, seem to have been largely preserved from an excessive technological restraint, at least if one considers the lack of recourse to the solution imposed by Article 6(4) of the 2001 Directive.

In my view, that does not mean that problems have been exaggerated or are nonexistent. I would rather suggest that a more insidious shift of copyright control lurks behind this apparent quietness. TPM have succeeded in embarking new business models in entertainment and cultural artefacts to the extent that the technical choices have already won over

[52] Some users also confess that they download works from file-sharing networks if the copy they legally bought is restricted in some way.

legal balances and design. They do not prohibit or block any use anymore, which might explain the shortage of complaints about their possible excess. Instead, current technological protection measures control and modulate use of works. The French philosopher Deleuze said about the electronic card imagined by Guattari for the future of urban cities: "[W]hat matters is not the gate, but the computer that identifies the position of each, whether legal or illegal, and operates a universal modulation."[53] He considered that the disciplinary society described by Foucault, including locking up and prohibition, was now transforming into a society of control and of freedom under probation.

Technologies of discipline constrain, lock up and prevent while the technologies of control authorize but in a regime of probation. Deleuze said that the regulation enforced by the first ones is a sort of mold, while that enforced by the second ones operates as a modulation. DRM are closer to a modulation mechanism of regulation, since they determine and adjust the extent of the use of the work allowed, depending on the user, on the license she entered into or on the remuneration she paid. They do not block the access to works but make it subject to the disciplinary conditions as decided by the right holder. Where the right owners decide to provide digital content with some defined usage rules, e.g. including a number of copies, a number of allowed viewings, etc., this usage becomes the norm for the recipients and users of such content, even though the usage they are entitled to enjoy from such works under the law might be broader and less restricted.

Today, DRM do not prevent copying, but regulate it as to the number of copies allowed, the media or device where they are installed and the authorized sphere in which they occur. Usages authorized by iTunes, Amazon or others might be an imperfect substitute to the legal private copy, depending on its scope in some countries. Modchips cases prove that parallel imports sustained by the distribution right limited by the first sale doctrine are replaced by a regional fragmentation of the markets and game/console tying through technological tricks. Finally, the example of the contractual arrangements agreed upon between some European libraries and publishers proves that the legally defined exception for archival purposes has left the floor to bilateral agreements and private ordering.

This could be considered as paracopyright to the extent it relies on a combination of technological measures, business models, contractual schemes and acceptance of users, which are substitutes for

[53] G. Deleuze, "Post-scriptum sur les sociétés de contrôle," in *Pourparlers – 1972–1990*, (Les Editions de Minuit, Paris, 1990), at 242 (my translation).

the definition in copyright law of the rights of the copyright owners and their proper boundaries.

What makes this transformation more difficult to resist is its apparent plasticity and adaptation to new digital needs and practices. Regulating a number of copies and uses within a device-based individual sphere might not exactly conform to copyright legal exceptions but at least it meets the needs of the consumer and enables the provision of legal downloading of creative content. And, importantly, regulating freedoms of use allowed to the user in that way is more flexible than the current regulatory framework.

What has been lost in this shift is the legitimacy of copyright law to draw the proper boundaries of its scope of protection. Initially, copyright is about entitling the author to control the public exploitation of her works and to decide in what ways her works will be made available to the public. For that purpose, copyright grants the author the right to authorize the making of copies of her work (right of reproduction) and the right to authorize the diffusion of her work to the public (that could encompass, according to the country, rights of public communication, making available, display, performance, or distribution).

The "public" element of such rights is crucial. The core of the copyright monopoly is the public diffusion of the work, either directly by acts of communication or indirectly by the making of copies that could be distributed or perceived by the public. What copyright encompasses is the making available of the work to the public; it is not the reception or enjoyment of the work by an individual, member of that public.[54] This "publicity" of the copyright monopoly is rooted in the history and justifications of literary and artistic property. What technological protection measures, and their offspring, the anti-circumvention laws, do is to shift copyright from a control of public exploitation to the securing of business models and users' reception of works. This is a new direction that copyright takes. It could be deemed legitimate to turn the attention of the copyright law to individual access to works that now constitute the relevant exploitation in digital networks. However, this evolution, namely brought in by anti-circumvention provisions, would certainly merit further discussion. The judicial application of those provisions in EU Member States reveals that the scope of this new copyright still contains many uncertainties. The recent questions that have been referred to the CJEU will, I hope, clarify the matter.

[54] CJEU, October 4, 2011, *Football Association Premier League*, C-403/08 & C-429/08, at 171.

Part VII

Trade secrets

13 A legal tangle of secrets and disclosures in trade: *Tabor v. Hoffman* and beyond

*Jeanne C. Fromer**

State courts in the United States began protecting trade secrets in the mid-nineteenth century as a matter of common law, beginning with the Supreme Judicial Court of Massachusetts's upholding in 1837 of a contract to maintain the secrecy of a chocolate-making process against a claim that it was void for restraining trade.[1] Later in the century, American courts began to elaborate on the basis for and extent of trade secrecy protection.

In this chapter, I explore one such early case from New York, *Tabor v. Hoffman*, decided in 1889.[2] A study of this case indicates that many present-day concerns about overlapping edges between trade secrecy and patent laws – and their interaction and interference with one another's aims – were latent, if not overtly raised, when American courts were just beginning to articulate the common law right of trade secrecy. After telling *Tabor*'s tale, I investigate some of the longstanding interactions and tensions between trade secrecy and patent laws through the lens of the regime's encouragements of disclosure in some ways and secrecy in others. Moreover, even though trade secrecy law is predominantly focused on secrecy, in some ways it enables disclosure. By contrast, although patent law is preoccupied with disclosure, in some ways, it permits and encourages secrecy. In all, patent law and trade secrecy together create a legal tangle of secrets and disclosures in trade. A full review of the *Tabor* case suggests that the innovator there was able to take advantage both of trade secrecy's disclosures and patent law's secrets.

* For their revealing comments, I am grateful to Arnaud Ajdler, Lionel Bently, Stacey Dogan, Rochelle Dreyfuss, Jane Ginsburg, John Goldberg, Scott Hemphill, Ted Sichelman, Henry Smith, and Katherine Strandburg, as well as participants at the IP at the Edge Workshop and the Harvard Law School Private Law Workshop. I thank Todd Melnick for extraordinary library support.

[1] *Vickery v. Welch*, 36 Mass. 523, 527 (1837) (citing *Bryson v. Whitehead*, 1 Sim. & S. 74, 57 Eng. Rep. 29 (1822)).

[2] 118 N.Y. 30.

The court did not appreciate this possibility, instead focusing on the unfairness to the plaintiff of the defendant's appropriation.

Benjamin Tabor invented a 325-pound iron and brass pump known as "Tabor's Rotary Pump," which "[wa]s designed for pumping tan-bark and the liquor with it, and other thick liquids."[3] The pump was very successful in the marketplace.[4] So as to mass produce the pump, Tabor made thirty-six pieces of patterns for the pump's parts, from which the pump could be manufactured.[5] Making these patterns for the pump correctly, according to Tabor, "required a good deal of time, study, thought, labor and money."[6] As per Tabor, the reason for this significant expenditure of time and money to translate the pumps into corresponding patterns is because the patterns do not match up precisely to the pump's pieces because there are both shrinkages and expansions of the pump's metals under different conditions of hot or cold liquid being pumped through it.[7] Getting the patterns right, on Tabor's account, requires a "series of experiments," rather than simple calculations as to shrinkage and expansions.[8] Tabor insisted that he kept these patterns secret and in his possession.[9] Yet he admittedly gave the patterns to Frank Collingnon, a machinist, for the sole purpose that he make pump castings for Tabor.[10]

According to Tabor, without Tabor's or Collingnon's permission or knowledge, Francis Walz, a pattern maker, measured Tabor's patterns to make a copy.[11] Walz got Tabor's patterns from Collingnon's possession.[12] He was able to do so due to his access to Collingnon's working space: Walz had a shop in Collingnon's building and Collingnon sometimes gave him permission to take other patterns.[13] Tabor claimed that William Hoffman had paid Walz to take these patterns and then Hoffman

[3] Supreme Court Findings of Fact and Conclusions of Law at 7, *Tabor v. Hoffman*, 118 N.Y. 30 (1889) [hereinafter Supreme Court Findings]; Trial Transcript at 16–17, *Tabor v. Hoffman*, 118 N.Y. 30 (1889) [hereinafter Trial Transcript]. The case record is on file with the author. An apparent picture and description of a variation on Tabor's pump can be found in International Textbook Company, *International Library of Technology* 24 & fig. 7 (Textbook Company, Scranton, 1902).

[4] Supreme Court Findings, *supra* note 3, at 8.

[5] *Ibid.* at 7; Respondent's Points at 7, *Tabor v. Hoffman*, 118 N.Y. 30 (1889) [hereinafter Respondent's Points].

[6] Supreme Court Findings, *supra* note 3, at 7. Tabor estimated that he spent more than $1,000 on making the patterns here. Trial Transcript, *supra* note 3, at 16.

[7] Trial Transcript, *supra* note 3, at 16–17.

[8] Supreme Court Findings, *supra* note 3, at 7; Trial Transcript, *supra* note 3, at 16–17.

[9] Supreme Court Findings, *supra* note 3, at 7; Trial Transcript, *supra* note 3, at 17–18.

[10] Trial Transcript, *supra* note 3, at 17–18, 32.

[11] Supreme Court Findings, *supra* note 3, at 7–8; Trial Transcript, *supra* note 3, at 33.

[12] Supreme Court Findings, *supra* note 3, at 7; Trial Transcript, *supra* note 3, at 32–33.

[13] Trial Transcript, *supra* note 3, at 32–33.

used a copy of them to produce pumps.[14] In Tabor's view, Walz and Hoffman had copied his patterns to avoid the significant expenditure required to use the pumps themselves to derive corresponding patterns.[15] Tabor professed that owing both to the shrinkages and expansions of the pump's metal and brass castings hiding from view parts of the pump, "[a] perfect set of patterns could not be made from seeing a finished pump."[16]

Hoffman told a different story. He claimed that he had "employed ... Walz to make a set of patterns for castings for pumps, like the one manufactured by [Tabor], ... but there was no agreement or arrangement between ... Walz and [Hoffman] that ... Walz should take any measurements from [Tabor's] patterns."[17] According to Hoffman, Walz got hold of Tabor's patterns when they were in his possession for repairs.[18] Walz used them on Hoffman's behalf but without Hoffman's knowledge until Tabor complained, at which point he stopped and "took all his measurements from a pump which [Tabor] had sold to a third party."[19] Hoffman maintained that using the pumps to come up with patterns necessitated "little more expense and trouble than [to do so] from measurements taken from [Tabor's] patterns."[20] Similarly, Walz indicated that he had used Tabor's patterns only because "it was [just] a little less trouble than to go outside and measure a machine."[21]

In 1885, Tabor sued Hoffman seeking $1,000 in damages, interest, and an injunction restraining Hoffman from making, selling, or otherwise disposing of any pumps made from Tabor's patterns.[22] After Hoffman denied all of the allegations,[23] the case proceeded to a bench trial in the Erie County division of the Supreme Court of the State of New York.

Hoffman attempted to use patent law to shield himself from liability for misappropriating Tabor's trade secrets. He maintained that Tabor's pump was a mere improvement on a previous pump invented by Tabor,

[14] Supreme Court Findings, *supra* note 3, at 8.

[15] Complaint at 4, *Tabor v. Hoffman*, 118 N.Y. 30 (1889) [hereinafter Complaint].

[16] Trial Transcript, *supra* note 3, at 20, 22.

[17] Defendant's Requested Findings of Fact and Conclusions of Law at 11, *Tabor v. Hoffman*, 118 N.Y. 30 (1889) [hereinafter Defendant's Requested Findings]; *accord* Trial Transcript, *supra* note 3, at 52–53.

[18] Defendant's Requested Findings, *supra* note 17, at 11–12.

[19] *Ibid.* at 12. Tabor insisted that Walz copied thirty-five of his thirty-six patterns and ascertained the last one, for a stand, easily only because it was "a perfectly *immaterial piece*, as any kind of a *stand* would answer the purpose." Respondent's Points, *supra* note 5, at 7 (emphasis in original).

[20] Defendant's Requested Findings, *supra* note 17, at 12.

[21] Trial Transcript, *supra* note 3, at 41.

[22] Complaint, *supra* note 15, at 4.

[23] Answer to the Complaint, *Tabor v. Hoffman*, 118 N.Y. 30 (1889).

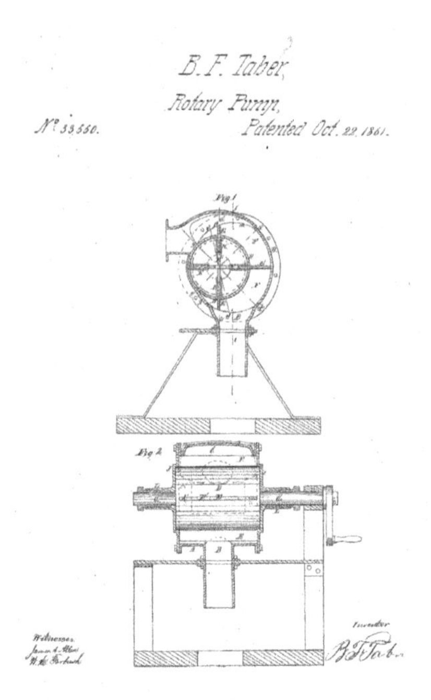

Figure 13.1: Drawing of Tabor's Patented Pump

for which he had received a patent in 1861.[24] Figure 13.1 shows a drawing of the patented pump. Walz testified to that effect.[25] The patent had expired in 1878, several years before the events at issue.[26] Hoffman argued on that basis that "[t]he invention which [Tabor] had patented became, after the expiration of the patent, public property, so that thereafter [Hoffman] had the right to make pumps just like those made by [Tabor] under his patent and to sell them in the market," including from Tabor's patterns based on these pumps.[27] Tabor, however, testified

[24] Defendant's Requested Findings, *supra* note 17, at 10–11; Trial Transcript, *supra* note 3, at 56–57. Although not identified in the trial record, that patent is apparently US Patent No. 33,550 (patented Oct. 22, 1861) (Improvement in Rotary Pumps).

[25] Trial Transcript, *supra* note 3, at 40.

[26] Defendant's Requested Findings, *supra* note 17, at 11; Trial Transcript, *supra* note 3, at 25.

[27] Defendant's Requested Findings, *supra* note 17, at 13. On subsequent appeal to the New York Court of Appeals, Hoffman additionally argued that after the patent's expiration, Tabor "sought to impress the public with the belief that these pumps were still protected by patent by casting upon each the well-known abbreviation 'Pat.,' in violation of [the law]." Appellant's Points, *Tabor v. Hoffman*, 118 N.Y. 30 (1889) [hereinafter Appellant's Points], at 2. Tabor disputed this possibility, maintaining that his pumps were marked "Special Pat. 8 x 8" with a date, with "Pat." standing for "pattern" and not

at trial that the patented pump was an entirely distinct invention from the one at issue in this case.[28] He maintained that the patented pump was "not a pump for pumping liquids in the proper sense of the term; it was a pump for pumping solids, liquids and solids combined."[29] Moreover, Tabor claimed never to have sold the patented pump or used the patterns corresponding to that pump after the patent had expired.[30]

The trial court sided with Tabor on this issue. It declined to find that the pump at issue here involved "substantially the same principle and improvement as the pumps so manufactured under said letters patent, and being substantially the same pump with some changes in some parts of it."[31] The court stated that it was unnecessary to issue a finding on the differences between the patented invention and the pump at issue in the suit, "because both parties agree that it was necessary to have patterns and castings to manufacture the new pump."[32] In so doing, it rejected Hoffman's defense. The court's reasoning is cryptic, but it seems the judge thought that the current pump was different from the patented pump because one needed patterns to make the current pump. Implicitly, the court seems to be linking the premise to the conclusion on the basis that were the pumps the same invention, the patent would have disclosed the current pump's pattern and there would therefore be no need for a new set of patterns.

The Supreme Court proceeded to rule in Tabor's favor on his claim.[33] It credited Tabor's account of why and how Walz used Tabor's patterns for Hoffman.[34] The court then determined that even though Hoffman had every right to make pumps like Tabor's using Hoffman's own patterns, Hoffman "has no right to manufacture pumps from [the] patterns made from measurements taken by Francis Walz from [Tabor's] patterns," reasoning that Tabor "has an exclusive right of property in said patterns."[35] Accordingly, the court enjoined Hoffman from making, selling, or otherwise disposing of both the purloined patterns and any pumps made from the patterns.[36]

In coming to its conclusion, the Supreme Court ruled that "the evidence shows that [Tabor] prepared patterns and spent much time

"patent." Respondent's Points, *supra* note 5, at 14. The Court of Appeals did not take up this particular issue.

[28] Trial Transcript, *supra* note 3, at 26. [29] *Ibid.* at 25. [30] *Ibid.* at 25–26.

[31] Defendant's Requested Findings, *supra* note 17, at 13.

[32] Supreme Court Opinion, *Tabor v. Hoffman*, 118 N.Y. 30 (1889) [hereinafter Supreme Court Opinion], at 67.

[33] Supreme Court Findings, *supra* note 3, at 9. [34] *Ibid.* at 7–8.

[35] *Ibid.* at 8; Supreme Court Opinion, *supra* note 32, at 68.

[36] Supreme Court Findings, *supra* note 3, at 9.

and labor in their production, and also incurred considerable expense."[37] Interestingly, the trial court relied merely on Tabor's own difficulty in making patterns from the pump to conclude both that "the[] patterns were the property of [Tabor], the product and creation of his own reflections, investigations and industry," and that Walz and Hoffman's unauthorized taking was wrongful.[38] There had been ample testimony at trial from six pattern makers and one molder that a pattern maker like Walz could, without much effort, estimate shrinkages and expansions in pump metals based on certain known rules.[39] Moreover, Tabor himself testified that "there is a rule I believe, known to pattern makers by which they estimate shrinkage; I don't know anything about the rule; I never tried it; I didn't use any rule of that description when I made patterns; I used my judgment in the matter."[40] Even though the court explicitly found that "[s]uch patterns can be made from measurements taken ... from the original patterns ... and that a competent pattern maker can make a set of patterns from measurements taken from the pump itself without the aid of plaintiff's patterns,"[41] the court gave that finding no legal weight. The court maintained that such evidence was irrelevant because "[i]t is certainly unjust and inequitable that [Hoffman] should, without [Tabor's] consent, be allowed to use duplicates and measurements from the creations and inventions of [Tabor] – his property, and never intended for public use, to compete with him in manufacturing the same kind of pumps."[42] The court concluded that if Hoffman is correct that it is easy to reverse engineer the pump's patterns from the pump itself, "he will not suffer seriously [from the court's imposition of an injunction], for he can manufacture [patterns] from [Tabor's] pumps."[43]

Hoffman appealed to the General Term of the Supreme Court, Erie County, which affirmed the trial court's judgment. The panel reasoned that:

> [T]he manufacture and sale of the pump in question was not a publication of the plans, specifications and patterns from which the pumps were manufactured. That so as far [as] the improved pump was concerned [Tabor] had the right to

[37] Supreme Court Opinion, *supra* note 32, at 67.

[38] *Ibid.* at 68–69. That said, the court did ambiguously find that "the plaintiff spent, and it required a good deal of time, study, thought, labor and money, to make and perfect said patterns." Supreme Court Findings, *supra* note 3, at 7.

[39] Trial Transcript, *supra* note 3, at 31, 37, 39–40, 45, 48–50, 52, 63. But *cf. ibid.* at 31 (testimony by a molder that different pattern makers have different rules that produce varying patterns from the same pump pieces).

[40] *Ibid.* at 26.

[41] Defendant's Requested Findings, *supra* note 17, at 12.

[42] Supreme Court Opinion, *supra* note 32, at 70–71.

[43] *Ibid.* at 70.

keep the plans, specifications and patterns from the public, and thus secure to himself the benefit of the business in which he was engaged, that [Hoffman] had no right to procure copies surreptitiously without the knowledge of [Tabor] by employing one of his pattern-makers or repairers to so make them, and that the Court has power to restrain the use of the pattern so acquired.[44]

The General Term also affirmed the trial court's rejection of Hoffman's patent-law defense. It reasoned that "[s]o far as the patented pump is concerned, [Tabor] has doubtless no further exclusive property in the invention." For that pump, the court asserted that "[t]he plans and specifications from which the machine was constructed were placed on file in the patent office where they became the property of the public, and all persons desiring may have copies thereof."[45] By contrast, the court continued, "[A]s to the improved machine, the subsequent inventions, a different question is presented. These improvements have never been patented, and consequently [Tabor] is unable to claim any protection through the patent laws. He has invented and constructed patterns from which he has manufactured the improved pump."[46] To the court, there was no requirement – grounded in patent law – that Tabor reveal the patterns, even if he had made the pump commercially available.[47]

Hoffman appealed again, to the New York Court of Appeals, therein pressing the argument that it does not make sense to provide a legal remedy for any competitive injury to Tabor's business, because the same injury would result from selling pumps made from reverse engineering the pumps themselves, a situation which is legally permissible.[48] Moreover, Hoffman insisted that the patterns were not truly secret because pattern makers could readily construct the commercially available pump's patterns by applying known rules to the pump's measurements. To confer legal protection here would, in Hoffman's view, "protect a secret when there is no secret."[49] Tabor disputed this understanding, replying that it was difficult to use the pumps to make patterns. Moreover, Tabor argued that "[t]he fact that Hoffman *could* have made a set of patterns from a finished pump does not by any means give him the right to have a duplicate set made from [Tabor's] patterns while in the hands of [Tabor's] employees for repairs, or to make use of such duplicates."[50]

[44] General Term of the Supreme Court Opinion, *Tabor v. Hoffman*, 118 N.Y. 30 (1889), at 76.
[45] *Ibid.* at 74. [46] *Ibid.* at 75. [47] *Ibid.*
[48] Appellant's Points, *supra* note 27, at 13.
[49] Appellant's Supplemental Points, *Tabor v. Hoffman*, 118 N.Y. 30 (1889), at 18–22.
[50] Respondent's Points, *supra* note 5, at 4, 9.

The New York Court of Appeals affirmed the General Term.[51] The court emphasized that once Tabor made his pumps publicly available by marketing them, without securing patent protection, he relinquished any exclusive property to them. Nonetheless, the court continued, Tabor had kept secret the patterns, "which greatly aided, if they were not indispensable, in the manufacture of the pumps." To the court, the relevant legal question was whether by making public the pumps, Tabor thereby constructively also made public the patterns.[52] If not, Tabor had a valid claim for misappropriation of trade secrets against Hoffman.

The court answered this question in the negative. Because of the discrepancies between the pump and its patterns, for the reasons discussed by the trial court, the patterns' sizes could not be discovered by merely investigating the different pump pieces. The court credited Tabor's account of how much work it took to yield a set of patterns from a pump. Therefore, the court concluded that the pumps' public availability did not undermine the patterns' status as a secret that belonged to Tabor, unless Tabor were to publish the patterns or someone else were to reverse engineer them from the pumps.[53]

Moreover, the possibility that someone might undertake the experimentation necessary to reverse engineer the pumps to derive their patterns – something the court termed "discovery ... by fair means" – does not imply that someone like Hoffman could take Tabor's patterns for his use – what the court calls "discovery by unfair means, such as bribery of a [secretholder]."[54] The court therefore concluded that "[w]hile [Hoffman] could lawfully copy the pump, because it had been published to the world, he could not lawfully copy the patterns, because they had not been published, but were still, in every sense, the property of [Tabor], who owned not only the material substance, but also the discovery which they embodied."[55]

Chief Judge Follett dissented from the Court of Appeals' decision and would have reversed the trial court's judgment. Unlike the majority, he focused on Tabor's expired patent:

> The patent on the original invention having expired, and the plaintiff having voluntarily made the subsequent improvements public by selling the improved article, he lost his right to their exclusive use ... The invention was not the patterns, but the idea represented by them, to which the plaintiff had lost his exclusive right.[56]

[51] *Tabor v. Hoffman*, 118 N.Y. 30 (1889). [52] *Ibid.* at 34–35.
[53] *Ibid.* at 35–36. [54] *Ibid.* at 35–37. [55] *Ibid.* at 37.
[56] *Ibid.* at 37–38 (Follett C.J. dissenting).

At the core of the *Tabor* case are important ways in which trade secrecy intersects and sometimes falls into tension with patent law, particularly with regard to the disclosure and secrecy aims of each. After outlining contemporary trade secrecy and patent laws, I turn to a general discussion of those intersections and tensions.

Current trade secrecy protection looks much like the protection conferred long ago in *Tabor*. Pertinently, the Uniform Trade Secrets Act, adopted in forty-eight states and the District of Columbia, shields, as a trade secret, from certain types of misappropriation information that "derives independent economic value, actual or potential, from not being generally known to, and not being readily ascertainable by proper means by, other persons" and is "the subject of efforts that are reasonable under the circumstances to maintain its secrecy."[57] Misappropriation occurs principally when the acquirer of another's trade secret contravenes a pre-existing contractual or other obligation to the secret holder not to disclose the secret, or commits an improper act of industrial espionage (often quasi-tortious, if not tortious) to get it.[58] So long as a secret remains unrevealed, legal protection is everlasting.[59] Of course, the information comprising the secret might always be properly revealed through acts that do not constitute misappropriation, principally independent discovery or reverse engineering of an available product.[60] With this avenue of sanctioned uses of secrets, so long as they are independently found, as Rochelle Dreyfuss explains, "trade secrecy laws ... safeguard public access."[61]

As the Supreme Court has reasoned, there are thought to be two key purposes to trade secrecy laws: "maintenance of standards of commercial ethics" and "the encouragement of invention."[62] With regard to

[57] Uniform Trade Secrets Act § 1(4) (amended 1985).

[58] Mark A. Lemley, "The Surprising Virtues of Treating Trade Secrets as IP Rights," 61 *Stan. L. Rev.* 311, 317–18 (2008) (citing cases).

[59] David S. Levine, "Secrecy and Unaccountability: Trade Secrets in our Public Infrastructure," 59 *Fla. L. Rev.* 135, 145 (2007).

[60] *Kewanee Oil Co. v. Bicron Corp.*, 416 U.S. 470, 476 (1974) (independent discovery); Cal. Civ. Code § 3426.1(a) (West 2006) (reverse engineering).

[61] Rochelle Cooper Dreyfuss, "UCITA in the International Marketplace: Are We About to Export Bad Innovation Policy?," 26 *Brook. J. Int'l L.* 49, 52 (2000). Contractual prohibitions against reverse engineering trade secrets are typically upheld. *Davidson & Assocs. v. Jung*, 422 F.3d 630 (8th Cir. 2005); *Bowers v. Baystate Tech., Inc.*, 302 F.3d 1334, 1341–45 (Fed. Cir. 2002); *Atari Games Corp. v. Nintendo of America, Inc.*, 975 F.2d 832 (Fed. Cir. 1992); *Balboa Ins. Co. v. Trans Global Equities*, 218 Cal. App. 3d 1327, 267 Cal. Rptr. 787, 795–801 (1990). As such, reverse engineering as protection for the public is often illusory. *See generally* John E. Mauk, "Note, The Slippery Slope of Secrecy: Why Patent Law Preempts Reverse-Engineering Clauses in Shrink-Wrap Licenses," 43 *Wm. & Mary L. Rev.* 819 (2001).

[62] *Kewanee Oil Co. v. Bicron Corp.*, 416 U.S. (1974), at 481; *accord* Lemley, "The Surprising Virtues," *supra* note 58, at 329–32.

commercial ethics, the general idea is that trade secrecy liability will deter people from carrying out certain illicit forms of commercial behavior.[63] Additionally, trade secrecy protection encourages investment in scientific and technological research, according to Mark Lemley, by "giv[ing] the developer of new and valuable information the right to restrict others from using it, and therefore the prospect of deriving supracompetitive profits from the information."[64] Both motivations have served to protect trade and innovation,[65] particularly in an era of mass production, in which commercialization of innovation depends on access to trade secrets by a large number of employees and third parties.[66]

Now consider patent law. Utilitarianism is the dominant purpose of American patent law.[67] According to utilitarian theory, patent law provides the incentive of exclusive rights for a limited duration to inventors to motivate them to create technologically or scientifically valuable inventions. In exchange for this incentive, patent law also requires patentees to disclose their inventions to the public.[68] Without the patent incentive, the theory goes, inventors might not invest the time, energy, or money necessary to create the works because such works might be copied cheaply and easily by free riders, thereby eliminating inventors' ability to profit from their labors. According to utilitarian thinking, public benefits accrue by rewarding inventors for taking two steps they likely would not otherwise have taken: first, to invent, and possibly commercialize; and second, to reveal information to the public about their inventions that serves to stimulate further innovation.[69]

Consistent with utilitarianism, the rights conferred by patent laws are designed to be limited in time and scope.[70] The reason for providing patent protection to creators is to encourage them to produce socially valuable works, thereby maximizing social welfare.[71] If the provided rights were exceedingly extensive, society would be hurt and social welfare diminished.[72] Exclusive rights in patent law prevent competition

[63] *See* Lemley, "The Surprising Virtues," *supra* note 58, at 319 (criticizing this theory for "presuppos[ing] a wrong without offering any substantive definition of what that wrong is").

[64] *Ibid.* at 330. [65] *Ibid.* at 319–20.

[66] James Pooley, *Trade Secrets* § 1.03[1] (Law Journal Press, New York, 2011).

[67] *E.g., Diamond v. Chakrabarty*, 447 U.S. 303, 307 (1980); Dan L. Burk & Mark A. Lemley, "Policy Levers in Patent Law," 89 *Va. L. Rev.* 1575, 1597–99 (2003).

[68] Jeanne C. Fromer, "Patent Disclosure," 94 *Iowa L. Rev.* 539, 545–47 (2009).

[69] *Ibid.* at 547–54.

[70] Mark A. Lemley, "The Economics of Improvement in Intellectual Property Law," 75 *Tex. L. Rev.* 989, 997 (1997).

[71] Ralph S. Brown, "Eligibility for Copyright Protection: A Search for Principled Standards," 70 *Minn. L. Rev.* 579, 592–96 (1985).

[72] Lemley, "The Economics of Improvement," *supra* note 70, at 996–97.

in protected works, allowing the patent holder to charge a premium for access and ultimately limiting these valuable works' diffusion into society.[73] Moreover, given that knowledge is frequently cumulative, society benefits when subsequent creators are not prevented from building on previous scientific and technological creations to generate new works.[74] Therefore, patent law ensures both that the works that it protects will fall into the public domain in due course and that third parties will be free to use the protected works for certain socially valuable purposes.[75]

Moreover, as I have previously explored, patent law's requirement of disclosure of information about inventions can stimulate productivity in two ways:

> First, it permits society at large to apply the information by freely making or using the patented invention after the expiration of the patent. Second, the disclosure can stimulate others to design around the invention or conceive of new inventions – either by improving upon the invention or by being inspired by it – even during the patent term. Otherwise, the patent system would not require disclosure earlier than the expiration of the patent term, as it does here by requiring disclosure at the time of the patent grant, at the latest, and typically much sooner.
>
> ... Disclosure of an invention sets out what others have already accomplished, thereby both revealing information about those discoveries – enabling the avoidance of wasteful duplication of the original inventor's research – and noting, usually implicitly by omission, what has yet to be done. Patent disclosures act, as one commentator labels it, as an "invisible college of technology." Use of these disclosures, in turn, speeds the rate of innovation in society, which is central to economic growth.[76]

There are a number of reasons an innovator might prefer trade secrecy protection to patent protection. First, protection vests without any need for government approval, which is typically time-consuming and expensive to obtain.[77] Second, because trade secrecy laws protect all economically valuable information from misappropriation, they cover inventions that are either unpatentable or of dubious patentability.[78]

[73] *Ibid.* [74] *Ibid.* at 997–98.

[75] As one example of socially valuable uses of patented works, patent law excuses doctors from infringement liability for performing patented medical activity. *See* 35 U.S.C. § 287(c); Katherine J. Strandburg, Chapter 15 in this volume.

[76] Fromer, "Patent Disclosure," *supra* note 68, at 548–50 (some internal quotation marks omitted; quoting Carolyn C. Cooper, "Nineteenth-Century American Patent Management as an Invisible College of Technology," in *Learning and Technological Change* 40 (Ross Thompson ed., Palgrave Macmillan, New York, 1993)).

[77] Lemley, "The Surprising Virtues," *supra* note 58, at 313.

[78] Jeanne C. Fromer, "Trade Secrecy in Willy Wonka's Chocolate Factory," in *The Law and Theory of Trade Secrecy: A Handbook of Contemporary Research* 3, 16–17 (Rochelle C.

Third, protection can last for a longer time, and potentially forever, if the chances are great that the invention will not be independently discovered by a third party for a time exceeding patent duration (or the time in which the invention is commercially important).[79] That is, trade secrecy protection is particularly attractive for inventions that are likely to stay secret, such as chemical or mechanical processes, as they can be shielded from public view and are hard to reverse engineer even as the products they produce are commercialized.[80]

When those conditions do not hold, patent protection is likely to be favored over trade secrecy. An inventor is likely to be happy to forgo trade secrecy protection in exchange for the more certain but time-limited protection that patent law confers if he is willing and able to spend the money and time to obtain patent protection for a patentable invention that is likely to be independently discoverable or reverse engineered once it is commercialized.[81] More extremely, the Supreme Court, in ruling that the federal patent laws do not preempt Ohio's trade secrecy laws, thought that patent protection would always be preferred to trade secrecy when an invention is patentable.[82] Reasoning that trade secrets are at risk of honest discovery and failed lawsuits even when misappropriated, the court stated that "[t]he possibility that an inventor who believes his invention meets the standards of patentability will sit back, rely on trade secret law, and . . . forfeit any right to patent protection is remote indeed."[83] Empirical evidence shows that the Supreme Court's conclusion is categorically wrong,[84] but there is a reasonable set of situations in which patent protection is preferable.

From this comparative description, it might seem that trade secrecy is focused heavily on keeping inventions secret from others for as long as possible, while patent law is centered on ensuring that inventions are

Dreyfuss & Katherine J. Strandburg, eds., Edward Elgar, Cheltenham, 2011); Lemley, "The Surprising Virtues," *supra* note 58, at 313.

[79] Fromer, "Trade Secrecy in Willy Wonka's Chocolate Factory," *supra* note 78, at 16–17; Michael J. Meurer & Katherine J. Strandburg, "Patent Carrots and Sticks: A Model of Nonobviousness," 12 *Lewis & Clark L. Rev.* 547, 577–78 (2008).

[80] *See generally* Fromer, "Trade Secrecy in Willy Wonka's Chocolate Factory," *supra* note 78 (discussing the chocolate industry's preference for trade secrecy over patent protection for its processes).

[81] *Ibid.*

[82] *Kewanee Oil Co. v. Bicron Corp.*, 416 U.S. 470, 484–91 (1974).

[83] *Ibid.* at 490 (citation omitted).

[84] Fromer, "Trade Secrecy in Willy Wonka's Chocolate Factory," *supra* note 78; Lemley, "The Surprising Virtues," *supra* note 58, at 338–41; Sharon K. Sandeen, "*Kewanee* Revisited: Returning to First Principles of Intellectual Property Law to Determine the Issue of Federal Preemption," 12 *Marq. Intell. Prop. L. Rev.* 299, 345–46 (2008).

disclosed widely to the public.[85] In broad strokes, that is true.[86] But it neglects the disclosures about inventions that trade secrecy enables and the secrets about inventions that patent law permits, sometimes in conflicting ways. I turn now to explore the legal tangle of disclosures and secrets in trade secrecy and patent laws, and in particular, the many ways these issues lay under-explored in *Tabor*.

For one thing, *Tabor* suggests that a trade secret can be much less than a true secret, in that it can be something relatively publicly accessible to third parties. The lynchpin for a conclusion that there was misappropriation of a trade secret in *Tabor* was that Hoffman, through Walz, used Tabor's secret and laboriously created patterns to make pump patterns, even though Walz might have used his pattern-making rules to reverse engineer patterns solely from Tabor's commercially available pump. The courts considering Tabor's case apparently situated their ruling in the unfairness to Tabor of using his secret patterns without permission, patterns on which Tabor spent heavily in time and money. In focusing on how hard it had been for Tabor to make the pump's patterns, the courts disregarded the significant, and uncontradicted, trial testimony that pattern makers could have devised patterns corresponding to Tabor's pump using pattern-making rules to account for shrinkages and expansions with significantly greater ease and lesser expense than it took Tabor himself to design the patterns for his pump, as he did so using a less rigorous system of trial and error. For this reason, although nothing of the sort was decided, the full record of the *Tabor* case exposes the possibly erroneous widespread understanding that this case represents the factual situation of the impracticality of reverse engineering a commercially available product to derive otherwise secret information.[87]

[85] In fact, courts hold that information contained in a published patent application destroys the possibility of trade secrecy because there is no longer a secret. *E.g.*, *Tewari De-Ox Sys., Inc. v. Mountain States/Rosen, L.L.C.*, 637 F.3d 604, 611–12 (5th Cir. 2011).

[86] This analysis leaves aside the dissemination effects of inventions protected under each regime. As Katherine Strandburg describes: "Trade secrecy effectively ties disclosure and dissemination together because it permits reverse-engineering and independent invention. When an invention is reverse-engineered or independently invented, it becomes known to others (disclosed) at the same time that it becomes available to others to use (disseminated). Patenting is different, however. Where an inventor seeks to use an invention exclusively rather than to sell embodiments of it, patenting not only raises consumer prices during the patent term, but also separates disclosure (which occurs at the time the patent or application is published) from dissemination (which occurs only when the patent expires at the end of its twenty-year term)." Katherine J. Strandburg, "What if there Were a Business Method Use Exemption to Patent Infringement?," *Mich. St. L. Rev.* 245, 271 (2008).

[87] For a sample of sources embodying this characterization, see Roger M. Milgrim, "Commission Proposed Capital Punishment – By Definition – for Trade Secrets, a Uniquely Valuable IP Right," 88 *J. Pat. & Trademark Off. Soc'y* 919, 936 n.72 (2006),

The implication of *Tabor* is that secret information cannot be used directly by an unauthorized third party, even if it can be discovered by third parties via reverse engineering of public information or products, whether with as much ease as using the secret information directly or with some greater hardship. This observation exposes a puzzle in trade secrecy law: How can information be considered secret, and thus qualify for protection in the first place, if it is reverse-engineerable? *Tabor* suggests that it can be considered to be a secret until it is actually reverse engineered, even if it is beforehand conceivable that the information could be obtained through reverse engineering. The 1939 Restatement of Torts is consistent with this view.[88]

By contrast, most states' current laws – modeled on the more recent Uniform Trade Secrets Act – take a different approach by considering as secret only information that is "not being generally known to, and not being readily ascertainable by proper means by, other persons."[89] These laws thus make it harder for information to qualify as secret. They raise the question whether information that might be obtained through plausible and established techniques of reverse engineering is truly secret (no matter the significant efforts the secret holder put into getting that information and keeping it directly from the public). Just as one must use one's senses to comprehend the observable aspects of a publicly available product, one must comparatively use more abstract "senses" to reverse engineer less readily observed aspects of a publicly available product, as with the patterns in Tabor's pump. The information derived from the former form of perception is not considered to be a trade secret, while the latter might be.[90] Is this difference between the two forms of perception one in degree or in kind? Trade secrecy law presumes without much analysis that it is a difference in kind by making protection hinge on whether reverse engineering to derive the relevant information is hard to

and Laura Wheeler, "Trade Secrets and the Skilled Employee in the Computer Industry," 61 *Wash. U. L.Q.* 823, 831 & n.54 (1983).

[88] Restatement (First) of Torts § 757 cmt. b ("[A] substantial element of secrecy must exist, so that, except by the use of improper means, there would be difficulty in acquiring the information."); *accord Sinclair v. Aquarius Elecs.*, Inc., 42 Cal. App. 3d 216, 226, 116 Cal. Rptr. 654, 661 (1974); *ILG Indus., Inc. v. Scott*, 49 Ill. 2d 88, 94, 273 N.E.2d 393, 396 (1971).

[89] *Supra* p. 279.

[90] *See, e.g., Data Gen. Corp. v. Grumman Sys. Support Corp.*, 825 F. Supp. 340, 359 (D. Mass. 1993) (holding that software distributed only in object code does not destroy the secrecy of the information contained in the corresponding source code); *cf.* Robert G. Bone, "A New Look at Trade Secret Law: Doctrine in Search of Justification," 86 *Cal. L. Rev.* 241, 257 n.81 (1998) ("[H]ow was it possible for anyone to have a secret in information that was part of a publicly marketed product?" (citing *Tabor*)).

accomplish.[91] As *Tabor* attests, trade secrecy protection can vest even in information that is reverse-engineerable if it was wrongfully obtained. That said, the possible philosophical oddness of distinguishing the two situations not infrequently gives some courts pause, and they will not enforce a trade secret that is reverse-engineerable, on the ground that it is not a true secret in the first place. One such court reasoned:

> The unrestricted sale of a product embodying a trade secret places the secret in the public domain. This rule applies even where the defendant acquired the secret in confidence. The rule also applies even though the product would have to be rendered inoperative and studied for 3 or 4 weeks to divine the "secret." The plaintiff in the instant case has sold and leased cameras embodying its alleged secrets without any attempt to restrict customers' use of the product, and the cameras could be fully understood by an engineer in a couple of days of study. The antiquity of the comparable rule in patent law is illustrated by ... *Egbert v. Lippmann*, 104 U.S. 333 (1881), as holding that a "public use" was effective even if the product had to be taken apart. The trade secret owner should not be held to a lower standard of proof than the patent owner.[92]

As another example, some courts find that the chemical analysis of publicly available products is not a trade secret, even though such analysis might be expensive to undertake, because it is common.[93]

Query further the efficiency of trade secrecy's rule treating information that can plausibly be derived through reverse engineering of a publicly available product as a trade secret until reverse engineering happens. This rule forces a trade secret holder's competitors to expend resources to derive independently what might sometimes be procured more cheaply by using the secret directly.[94] Viewed alone, this expenditure is wasteful and might be better directed elsewhere. On the other hand, it diminishes any first-mover advantage the secret holder might otherwise have, thereby muting the secret holder's incentive to innovate in the first

[91] *See* 2 Louis Altman & Malla Pollack, *Callman on Unfair Competition, Trademarks and Monopolies* § 14:28 (citing cases) (4th edn., Thompson Reuters, Eagan, 2011).

[92] *Wesley-Jessen Inc. v. Reynolds*, 182 U.S.P.Q. 135, 144–45 (N.D. Ill. 1974); *accord Cryogenic Assocs. Div. of Beatrice Foods Co. v. Johnston*, 188 U.S.P.Q. 273, 276 (S.D. Ind. 1975).

[93] 2 Altman & Pollack, *Callman on Unfair Competition*, *supra* note 91, at § 14:28 (citing cases).

[94] *Cf. Sony Computer Ent., Inc. v. Connectix Corp.*, 203 F.3d 596, 605 (9th Cir. 2000) (reasoning similarly in permitting as a fair use under copyright law the reverse engineering of copyrighted software to learn how to make interoperable software); Pamela Samuelson & Suzanne Scotchmer, "The Law and Economics of Reverse Engineering," 111 *Yale L. J.* 1575, 1586 (2002) ("Costliness may prevent reverse engineering entirely, especially if the innovator licenses others as a strategy for preventing unlicensed entry.").

place.[95] Additionally, requiring third parties to reverse engineer – rather than use the secret directly – might also be helpful to the third parties (and society at large) by teaching them more about the information, its uses, and further refinements.[96]

The *Tabor* courts did not much emphasize this sort of analysis, instead focusing on the unfairness – and therefore the illegality – of Hoffman's appropriation.

There is another way in which trade secrecy protects already disclosed information. As is clear from *Tabor*, Tabor's trade secrecy right was not destroyed by virtue of him sharing his patterns with the machinist, Collingnon. Generally speaking, trade secrecy protection is not lost if a secret holder discloses the secret confidentially to third parties "to profit from its secrets in its business dealings, not to reveal its secrets to the public."[97] That is, a trade secret holder need not maintain perfect secrecy to retain protection. Unless more widely disseminated, information can qualify for trade secrecy protection even if shared with third parties, such as employees, independent contractors, or others, so long as they hold themselves to a confidential relationship.[98] The reason for permitting such disclosures is that without the help of others, a secret holder typically cannot fully effectuate the information's commercial value.[99] In that sense, a trade secret holder can decide to share his or her secret with select others confidentially, all the while still maintaining secrecy legally.

The trade secret holder is likely to choose to share that information confidentially with a small circle that he or she already trusts – such as trusted employees, those with whom the secret holder has done business, and established companies – so that they can help the secret holder employ the information to commercial advantage without destroying the secrecy.[100] These are precisely the set of people and

[95] *See* Rochelle Cooper Dreyfuss, "Trade Secrets: How Well Should We Be Allowed to Hide Them?: The Economic Espionage Act of 1996," 9 *Fordham Intell. Prop. Media & Ent. L. J.* 1, 31 (1998); Samuelson & Scotchmer, "The Law and Economics of Reverse Engineering," *supra* note 94, at 1586.

[96] *See, e.g.*, Mathew Schwartz, "Reverse-Engineering," *Computerworld*, Nov. 12, 2001, *available at* www.computerworld.com/s/article/print/65532/Reverse_Engineering.

[97] *Metallurgical Indus. Inc. v. Fourtek, Inc.*, 790 F.2d 1195, 1200–01 (5th Cir. 1986).

[98] *Peabody v. Norfolk*, 98 Mass. 452, 461 (1868); Roger M. Milgrim, *Milgrim on Trade Secrets* § 1.04 (Matthew Bender, Albany, NY, 2011); Pooley, *Trade Secrets*, *supra* note 66, at § 4.04[2][a].

[99] *Peabody v. Norfolk*, 98 Mass. at 461; *supra* p. 280.

[100] *Cf.* Sandeen, "*Kewanee* Revisited," *supra* note 84, at 344 (observing that "[t]he sharing and licensing of trade secret information" will likely be targeted at "faithful employees" and trusted "vendors, contractors, business partners, or licensees"); Katherine J. Strandburg, "User Innovation Community Norms: At the Boundary Between Academic and Industry Research," 77 *Fordham L. Rev.* 2237, 2261 (2009) ("Industry

entities that already have a competitive advantage, thus making the rich that much informationally richer.

Trade secrecy's allowance of targeted disclosures is less democratic in sharing the informational wealth than is patent law's disclosure regime. Requiring patentees to disclose their inventions to the public at large in the patent document in exchange for the patent right democratizes innovation. As I have written elsewhere in describing how an effective patent disclosure regime compares with one that is ineffective:

> effective disclosure in a patent system should tend to equalize the positions of the initial innovator and potential competitors by granting the latter the information needed to innovate subsequently in the field. Without successful disclosure, the same inventor will be more likely to continue building up on his original invention because he will be the one with the best information to do so. In fact, inventors appear to innovate based only on the information they already have when other information is difficult to acquire. Ineffective disclosure, by extension, can also prolong the patent right beyond its stated expiration because more of the useful information about an invention remains only in the patentee's hands. Innovative rivalry, despite creating some inefficiencies, is more beneficial to society – both economically speaking and as a matter of distributive justice – than a prospecting system that fully concentrates the investment in a technological area in the hands of the initial innovator. History has shown that "most technological change ... comes through the small contributions of ordinary, anonymous workers and tinkerers." That is, more minds are able to effect that much more technological progress – both in quantitative terms and in terms of the breadth of creativity – which benefits both society and a broader set of innovators, including newcomers and those in the developing world.[101]

Trade secrecy – even with its allowance of targeted disclosures – is much like an ineffective patent disclosure regime, in that those not among the chosen few to whom innovation details have been disclosed have less of a chance to contribute further to innovation. Not only is this harmful to those not in the circle of secrecy, but it is likely detrimental to the public at large, due to a tapered path of innovation, constricted economic growth, and diminished human flourishing.[102]

groups that have developed sharing norms historically seemingly have relied on personal relationships, opening their facilities to visits from competitors, movement of personnel within the industry, and publications to develop the means to enforce them.").

[101] Fromer, "Patent Disclosure," *supra* note 68, at 551 (quoting Robert Friedel, *A Culture of Improvement: Technology and the Western Millennium* (MIT Press, Cambridge, Mass., 2007) 3).

[102] Nonetheless, as Jonas Anderson points out, because of the "time pressure to maximize the value of an innovation" protected through trade secrecy (as protection can end at any time), "inventors who maintain inventions as trade secrets likely have more incentive to efficiently disclose their inventions to the proper individuals." J. Jonas Anderson, "Secret Inventions," 26 *Berkeley Tech. L. J.* 917, 946 (2011).

Mark Lemley, however, argues that "trade secret law actually encourages broader disclosure and use of information, not secrecy."[103] For one thing, he suggests that trade secrecy protection encourages people not to overinvest in protecting secrets, because the law will do it.[104] Were it not for trade secrecy, secret holders would be less likely to involve third parties or even employees in commercial production of products and services related to their secrets out of fear that the secret will get out in a way that will not be protected by the law.[105] As Lemley puts it, trade secrecy "encourages disclosure of information that companies might otherwise be reluctant to share for fear of losing the competitive advantage it provides."[106] He is correct to observe that this situation is better than the alternative – real secrecy – particularly for inventions that inventors reasonably think can be kept secret and thus prefer secrecy to patent protection and concomitant public disclosure.[107] Yet there is evidence that even with trade secrecy laws, at least in certain industries like the candy business, secret holders will take excessive precautions to protect their secrets because they "are far from indifferent between the legal remedies for trade secrecy misappropriations and avoiding an actual misappropriation in the first instance, in that they are of the opinion that the former under-compensate for misappropriation."[108] Moreover, as Lemley recognizes, there is a non-negligible class of inventions – those that are neither inherently self-disclosing nor completely obscured, such as computer software – for which inventors might reasonably choose either trade secrecy or patent protection.[109] For these inventions,

[103] Lemley, "The Surprising Virtues," *supra* note 58, at 333.
[104] *Ibid.* at 333–36. [105] *Ibid.* at 334–36.
[106] *Ibid.* at 335–36. Lemley also maintains that trade secrecy protection provides a semi-solution to Arrow's Information Principle, by enabling bargaining over information without worry that it will lose its secrecy. *Ibid.* at 336–37.
[107] *See supra* p. 288 (suggesting conditions under which inventors might prefer trade secrecy to patent protection). Lemley reasons further that the secrecy requirement the law imposes acts to channel to trade secrecy protection those whose inventions are not self-disclosing, with the rest being channeled to patent protection, if anything. Lemley, "The Surprising Virtues," *supra* note 58, at 335–36. As Lemley sees it, "[t]he traditional conception of the trade-off between patents and trade secrets views the disclosure function of the patent system as one of its great advantages over trade secret law. And indeed the law operates in various ways to encourage inventors to choose patent over trade secret protection where both are possible. But for certain types of inventions we may actually get more useful 'disclosure' at less cost from trade secret than from patent law." *Ibid.* at 314; *cf.* Katherine J. Strandburg, "What Does the Public Get? Experimental Use and the Patent Bargain," *Wis. L. Rev.* 81, 105, 111, 119 (2004) (proposing that patent disclosure is relatively unhelpful for the many inventions that are self-disclosing, as they are best divulged by the commercialization of the invention, but suggesting that energy should be focused on permitting experimental use on patented inventions to effectuate the disclosure function for non-self-disclosing inventions).
[108] Fromer, "Trade Secrecy in Willy Wonka's Chocolate Factory," *supra* note 78, at 15–16.

opting for trade secrecy over patent law is inferior with regard to effectuation of disclosure. Despite Lemley's helpful analysis, there is nonetheless an important tension between the limited disclosures that trade secrecy permits and the thicker public disclosures that patent law requires.[110]

There is another important tension between trade secrecy and patent law with regard to disclosure. Patent law, in its current instantiation, requires patentees to enable their inventions. To satisfy the enablement requirement and be granted a valid patent, the patent applicant must provide a description of "the manner and process of making and using [the invention], in such full, clear, concise, and exact terms as to enable any person skilled in the [relevant] art [how]... to make and use the [invention]."[111] This standard requires patentees to reveal plenty of information about how to make use of their invention, but it need not be more than a person, having ordinary skill in the art, needs to do so without undue experimentation.[112] That means that even though patent law is tasked with promoting disclosure, it permits the patent holder to keep secret any information short of undue experimentation for a person having ordinary skill in the art to make and use the invention. This information is then construed as being a complete disclosure of the invention, even though not all relevant information was spelled out. In that sense, patent law permits the keeping of some secrets related to a patented invention.

Compare patent law's enablement standard with trade secrecy's standard of relative secrecy. Patent law seeks to provide the public – in particular, the person having ordinary skill in the art – with enough information to make and use the invention, all the while conferring the protection of patent law's exclusive rights to the inventor. By comparison, trade secrecy laws provide that if an innovator provides the public with enough material to derive protected information (be it a publicly available product that can be reverse engineered or leakages of the protected information itself), the innovator will lose the shelter of trade

[109] Lemley, "The Surprising Virtues," *supra* note 58, at 338–40.

[110] *Cf.* Sandeen, "*Kewanee* Revisited," *supra* note 84, at 343–45. Interestingly, both patent and trade secrecy laws provide protection to inventors against misuse by the class of people to whom the relevant invention has been disclosed. Patent law requires disclosures to the public at large, and thus, the public is on constructive notice not to make use of the patented invention. Trade secrecy law principally counts as misappropriations unauthorized use of the secret information by the limited class to whom the information has been disclosed.

[111] 35 U.S.C. § 112(a).

[112] *Monsanto Co. v. Syngenta Seeds, Inc.*, 503 F.3d 1352, 1360 (Fed. Cir. 2007) (citing 35 U.S.C. § 112).

secrecy protection.[113] The incentives to disclose are thus different: Inventors naturally want to disclose as little as possible about their creations, but patent law's enablement requirement will push them to disclose a minimally sufficient amount.[114] Choosing trade secrecy's protection, on the other hand, will lead inventors to disclose as little as possible about their creation and to make whatever is publicly available hard to reverse engineer, because once the cat is out of the bag, trade secrecy protection evaporates.

What happens, then, when the worlds of trade secrecy and patent laws collide, as they might have in *Tabor*? We do not have enough information about the pump at issue in the litigation to evaluate whether Hoffman was right that it fell within the scope of Tabor's expired patent. However, suppose for the moment that Hoffman was correct. Recall that Tabor asserted in the context of litigation that it was not possible to derive the patterns corresponding to the pump's pieces without heavy and costly experimentation.[115] Holding Tabor to that claim suggests that the failure to disclose his pump's patterns in the patent – something it seems he did not do, at least completely, in his patent[116] – would contravene today's enablement standard[117] because a person having ordinary skill in the art would have to undertake undue experimentation to make the pumps without also having the patterns, just as Tabor did. Yet if Tabor gravely overestimated how much experimentation it would take a pattern maker to derive patterns for his pump, his patent would be sufficiently enabled

[113] *See supra* p. 286.

[114] Fromer, "Patent Disclosure," *supra* note 68, at 552–53.

[115] *Supra* p. 272.

[116] A perusal of Tabor's patent, US Patent No. 33,550 (patented Oct. 22, 1861) (Improvement in Rotary Pumps), reveals that he provided no express patterns for his invention. However, Tabor did disclose some relative measurements for some, but not all, of the patented pump's parts. *E.g.*, *ibid.* ("A part of the shell on the side of the discharge-orifice is the quadrant of a circle concentric with the valve-cylinder and of equal radius."). Nonetheless, it is unclear whether those relative measurements specify how the pump ought to be constructed or an approximation of how it ought to be should the pump parts expand or contract in use.

[117] When Tabor secured his patent in 1861, an earlier version of patent law's current enablement standard was securely in place. For example, in 1832, the Supreme Court observed that patent law's requirement that "a correct specification and description of the thing discovered" be filed in a patent "is necessary in order to give the public, after the privilege shall expire, the advantage for which the privilege is allowed, and is the foundation of the power to issue the patent." *Grant v. Raymond*, 31 U.S. 218, 247 (1832). And in the Supreme Court's 1854 resolution of the validity of Samuel Morse's patent related to his invention of the telegraph, the Court held that Morse could not claim a broader invention than that which he discovered, and thus, enabled in the patent. *O'Reilly v. Morse*, 56 U.S. 62, 117 (1854).

absent the patterns but his trade secrecy claim would be on shaky ground given the ease of reverse engineering.[118]

All in all, it is hard to see why Tabor ought to be able to have it both ways: having an enabled patent without disclosing the pump's patterns, while having a valid trade secret in the secret patterns because they are difficult to reverse engineer from the commercially available pump. Modern case law makes much the same point.[119] For example, in *Christianson v. Colt Industries Operating Corp.*, the litigants quarreled over whether information alleged to be a trade secret was required to have been disclosed in a patent to satisfy the enablement requirement.[120] Although the Seventh Circuit held that the information was outside the patent's scope and therefore did not have to be revealed,[121] the opposite conclusion on patent scope would have likely necessitated application of the rule that the district court had invoked: "[A] patentee cannot, in equity, claim trade secrecy for conventional information which could readily have been discovered had the required disclosures been made in its patent."[122] Although there are difficulties applying this rule in the context of contemporary patent law,[123] it was that much harder in Tabor and Hoffman's time because then peripheral patent claims were not well established.[124] As is evidenced by Tabor's patent itself, his patent claims were not peripheral but principally and loosely referred to the patent specification.[125] This central claiming in his patent made it hard to ascertain readily whether the current pump was the same, a question the *Tabor* courts never expressly engaged.

There is a further possible collision between trade secrecy and patent laws in *Tabor*. Suppose that Hoffman was right that the pump being

[118] *See supra* p. 283.

[119] *E.g.*, *Rototron Corp. v. Lake Shore Burial Vault Co.*, 712 F.2d 1214, 1215 (7th Cir. 1983); *Dow Chem. Co. v. Am. Bromine Co.*, 210 Mich. 262, 293–94, 17 N.W. 996, 1007 (1920).

[120] 870 F.2d 1292, 1299 (7th Cir. 1989). [121] *Ibid.* at 1301–03.

[122] *Christianson v. Colt Indus. Operating Corp.*, 609 F. Supp. 1174, 1184 (C.D. Ill. 1985). That said, courts allow patentees to retain trade secrecy protection in information related to a patented invention if it was developed after the patent application was filed. *Richardson v. Suzuki Motor Co.*, 868 F.2d 1226, 1244 (Fed. Cir. 1989).

[123] Dan L. Burk & Mark A. Lemley, "Fence Posts or Sign Posts?: Rethinking Patent Claim Construction?," 157 *U. Pa. L. Rev.* 1743 (2009); Jeanne C. Fromer, "Claiming Intellectual Property," 76 *U. Chi. L. Rev.*719 (2009).

[124] Fromer, "Claiming Intellectual Property," *supra* note 123, at 731–35.

[125] Tabor's patent has two claims: (1) "The formation of the shell with the concentric parts *e g* and *f h* and eccentric parts *e h* and *g f*, as and for the purposes described," and (2) "So constructing and arranging the valves, valve-cylinder, and shell as that the valves will not be subjected to a transverse movement while doing their work, for the purposes and substantially as set forth." US Patent No. 33,550 (patented Oct. 22, 1861).

litigated ought to have been in the public domain by virtue of its falling within the scope of the expired patent and not being a significant enough improvement to constitute a new and separate invention. Should the patterns for that pump have landed in the public domain, capable of being copied so long as they are not obtained in a prohibited way, such as through theft? That is, are a pump and its corresponding patterns part and parcel of a single invention?[126] If the pumps and their patterns constitute a single invention, allowing the pump's patterns to be protected by trade secrecy when the pump is in the public domain (both through expiration of the patent, if Hoffman was correct, and even if not, through commercial sale of the pump without patent protection) might constitute an impermissible conflict between the trade secrecy and patent laws. Although its reasoning is hard to parse, it seems the *Tabor* trial court disagreed with this assessment when it stated that it was unnecessary to issue a finding on the differences between the patented invention and the pump at issue in the suit, "because both parties agree that it was necessary to have patterns and castings to manufacture the new pump."[127] If so, the court's unspoken assumption that the pump and its pattern are distinct inventions is unjustified without more firm reasoning.

Given these multiple possible clashes between trade secrecy and patent laws in *Tabor*, perhaps it is not inconceivable to read sympathy with these concerns into Chief Judge Follett's succinct dissent in the Court of Appeals.

The same issues that occupy a robust understanding of *Tabor* and trade secrecy law – the secrecy of information that is reverse-engineerable and how much disclosure of trade secrets is permissible before protection dissolves – is one that will likely arise anew in patent law. Until recently, the effect of maintaining a trade secret would have had a relatively clear effect on the possibility of obtaining patent protection. Under the patent law in effect until March 16, 2013, a patent was statutorily barred if, among other things, "the invention was ... in public use ... in this country, more than one year prior to the date of the application for patent in the United States."[128] A patent applicant's sale of a product produced by a secret method would have constituted a "public use" of the method, possibly barring the patentability of the method depending on whether

[126] The reasoning would go that they are essentially linked, in a way similar to the secrecy (or lack thereof) of private information about a publicly available product that is reverse-engineerable but has not yet been reverse engineered. *See supra* pp. 286–287.
[127] Supreme Court Opinion, *supra* note 32, at 67; *see supra* p. 275.
[128] 35 U.S.C. § 102(b).

the statutory-bar period had passed.[129] By contrast, a third party that had independently discovered that method could have patented it – assuming it had met the other patentability requirements – in spite of the other's prior secret use of that method, which would not have constituted a "public use" as against the third party.[130] The different treatment seemed to have been driven by the policy of encouraging patent applicants to file early rather than sit on their rights to extend their potential term of patent protection.[131] Since March 16, 2013, patent law is different: A patent is, instead, now statutorily barred if, among other things, "the claimed invention was in public use . . . or otherwise available to the public" more than one year before the patent's filing date.[132] It is an open question whether a third party's trade secret linked to a commercially available product, like in *Tabor*, would be "otherwise available to the public," even if not "in public use." Are Tabor's patterns "available to the public" if they are theoretically reverse-engineerable by pattern makers? Or must the patterns be more immediately accessible to the public to qualify? These are principally reformulations of the issues posed above about secrecies and disclosures in trade secrecy law. Are the disclosures that invalidate a patent the same as the disclosures that render a trade secret public?[133]

In sum, a review of the record in *Tabor* provides a helpful specimen with which to explore the tangle of disclosures and secrecies that trade secrecy and patent laws each promote, or at least tolerate. This examination chips away at the case's usual reading, that the pump's patterns were protectable as a trade secret because it was significantly hard to reverse engineer them. This evidence impels the questions of how secret information must truly be to qualify as a trade secret, both with regard to reverse-engineerability and disclosures to third parties. The law tends to cut a good deal of slack for trade secrets to not be truly secret in this regard. On this metric, by comparison, patent law does a better job at disclosing inventions more widely. Yet there are ways in which patent law permits secret-keeping, with regard to the enablement standard and its statutory bars, in ways that come into tension with

[129] *Metallizing Engineering Co. v. Kenyon Bearing & Auto Parts Co.*, 153 F.2d 516 (2d Cir. 1946).

[130] *W.L. Gore v. Garlock*, 721 F.2d 1540 (Fed. Cir. 1983).

[131] Jonathan R. Siegel, "The Polymorphic Principle and the Judicial Role in Statutory Interpretation," 84 *Tex. L. Rev.* 339, 363 n.131 (2005); *see also* Michael J. Meurer & Katherine J. Strandburg, "Patent Carrots and Sticks," *supra* note 79, at 569.

[132] Leahy-Smith America Invents Act, Pub. L. No. 112-29, §§ 3(b)(1), (n), 125 Stat. 284 (2011) (codified in 35 U.S.C. § 102).

[133] *Cf.* Dreyfuss, "Trade Secrets," *supra* note 95, at 11.

trade secrecy provisions. Moreover, there are important questions about what the patent law puts into the public domain that cannot later be maintained as a trade secret. All in all, there is an interconnected jumble of disclosures and secrets in trade secrecy and patent laws, sometimes moving in the same direction and sometimes cutting against one another. These tensions have been long present and still remain mostly unresolved.

14 Patents and trade secrets in England: the case of *Newbery v James* (1817)

Lionel Bently[*]

Just as in the United States, where inventors are confronted with a choice between protecting their inventions by taking out patents or relying on the law of trade secrets, so in the United Kingdom a similar choice exists between patents and reliance on the law of breach of confidence.[1]

The choice arises because in modern patent law, a patent will only be granted where the invention is disclosed in a specification,[2] and that disclosure is published before the patent grant.[3] As the law of confidentiality will only protect information that possesses the key quality of 'relative secrecy',[4] the act of taking out a patent means that the law of confidentiality is no longer available: once 'published' in the specification, the secret ceases to exist.[5] Of course, the patentee may retain other information (so-called 'know-how') that is secret and can be exploited distinctly from the patent, but as regards the invention itself, patenting and protection through confidence are necessarily alternatives.

* This chapter draws on and develops material from: T. Aplin, L. Bently, P. Johnson & S. Malynicz, *Gurry on Confidence: The Law of Confidentiality* (Oxford University Press, 2012) Ch. 2. Thanks to my co-authors as well as the editors and publishers for permitting me to re-use material. I am also grateful to Jeanne Fromer, Robert Burrell, Astron Douglas, Sean Bottomley, Cate Kelly and Tomas Gomes-Arostegui for comments, insights and other assistance.

1 See, L. Bently, 'Trade Secrets and Patents' in Neil Wilkof and Shamnad Basheer (eds), *Overlapping Intellectual Property Rights* (Oxford University Press, 2012).

2 European Patent Convention, Art 83; Patents Act 1977, s. 14(3).

3 There are exceptional circumstances where publication is prohibited in the interests of national security (e.g. Patents Act 1977, s. 22).

4 *Coco v A.N. Clark (Engineers)* [1969] RPC 41, 48 ('necessary quality of confidence'); *Franchi v Franchi* [1967] RPC 149, 153 (Cross J); *Stephens v Avery* [1988] Ch 449, 454H; *Attorney General v Guardian (No. 2)* [1990] 1 AC 109, 177C-E and 282C-D.

5 *Mustad v Allcock and Dosen* (1928) [1964] 1 WLR 109, 111 (HL), where Lord Buckmaster explained that: '[T]he important point about the patent is not whether it was valid or invalid, but what it was that it disclosed, because after the disclosure had been made by the appellants to the world, it was impossible for them to get an injunction restraining the respondents from disclosing what was common knowledge. The secret, as a secret, had ceased to exist.' Publication in foreign patents will not, ipso facto, deprive the contents of the foreign specification of the quality of confidence in England: see *Franchi v Franchi* [1967] RPC 149.

This 'edge' between patents and trade secrecy/confidentiality was not always so stark.[6] Although English patent law is often represented as originating in the early modern period, in particular with the Statute of Monopolies 1623, in fact most of its key features were only conceived and adopted in more recent times. The introduction of a Patent Office did not occur until 1852, the requirement of 'claims' appeared only in 1883, a substantive non-obviousness requirement dates to the late nineteenth century, and examination for novelty was a twentieth-century innovation. The requirement that an applicant submit a specification – that is a written description – was an eighteenth-century innovation, and the question of precisely when, and why, this became a requirement is the subject of some debate.[7]

The requirement that an applicant submit a specification emerged in a period in which the use of secrecy as a mechanism of protection was the norm. In the eighteenth and early nineteenth centuries, businesses restricted access to their premises (and thus their practices) and in some cases processes were deliberately divided up so that no one had access to the whole process.[8] Of course, the capacity to rely on secrecy was greater in certain fields than others: the security offered by secrecy very much depended on the particular state of knowledge (and knowledge-acquisition) at a particular time and place. In the eighteenth century, the protection of medicines was particularly secure because there was as yet no periodic table, and only limited ability to 'reverse engineer' marketed medicines so as to deduce their constituents. As a result commercial agreements relating to secrets became common, many for astonishing sums and many lasting decades.

But while the use of secrecy was common practice in the eighteenth century, the legal underpinnings of such protection remained unarticulated. Certainly, there were standard obligations of secrecy imposed on apprentices and servants, and local, criminal mechanisms for enforcing such contracts. Moreover, commercial arrangements for the exploitation

[6] Christine Macleod, *Inventing the Industrial Revolution: The English Patent System, 1660–1800* (Cambridge University Press, 1988) 52.

[7] See pp. 312–314, *infra*.

[8] J.W. Hall, 'Joshua Field's Diary of a Tour in 1821 through The Midlands', (1924–26) 6 *Transactions of the Newcomen Society* 1, 10 ('The Soho works are never shewn, no person can obtain leave or an order to see them but without professing to shew them they are to be seen.'); H.W. Dickinson, *Matthew Boulton* (Cambridge University Press, 1937) 74. Other businesses sent out spies: J.R. Harris, *Industrial Espionage and Technology Transfer* (Aldershot: Ashgate, 1998); Trevor Ashton, *Iron and Steel in the Industrial Revolution* (Manchester University Press, 1924), 200–05; M.W. Flinn, 'Travel Diaries of Swedish Engineers of the Eighteenth Century', (1957–58) 31 *Transactions of the Newcomen Society* 95; Dickinson, *Matthew Boulton*, 49.

of secrets were the subject of sophisticated contractual arrangements, often accompanied by provisions on arbitration and underpinned by penalties. A late seventeenth-century case had indicated that the Chancery courts were hesitant in their dealings with secrets in the context of inheritance,[9] though cases later in the eighteenth century seemed to indicate a reversal.[10] However, whether Court of Chancery would award injunctive relief to prevent disclosure or misuse of secrets in breach of employment, contractual or other arrangements, was, perhaps surprisingly, untested. When, in the first decades of the nineteenth century the question of protecting secrecy through injunctive relief was first put to the Chancery courts, the question arose as to the relationship between any such protection and the relatively recently developed rules on the patent specification. Could an invention be patented and protected as a trade secret?

The question arose in *Newbery v James*,[11] in the context of the protection of medical remedies, at a time when these constituted one of the most valuable of consumer goods. More importantly, it arose in a period where scientific understanding of disease and of chemistry was quite different from today. As already noted, mere public exposure of a remedy would rarely enable its reverse engineering and replication. As we will see, Lord Eldon LC, in refusing injunctive relief to Newbery to prevent James from disclosing the way of making a remedy, seems to have been motivated by several concerns, one of which was the interaction between trade secrecy and patenting. In particular, he seems to have taken the view that whatever in fact could have been learned from the patent specification, a person could not thereafter ask the court to protect secrets which ought to have been disclosed by the patent.

James' Fever Powders

The case concerned a best-selling medicine, Dr James' Fever Powders,[12] a supposed cure for gout, fever, rheumatism, pleurisy, inflammation, scurvy, chronic distemper and other ailments including small-pox, yellow fever and slow fever.[13] The medicine was said to have been

[9] *Jenks v Holford* (1682) 1 Vern 61; 23 ER 311.

[10] *Tipping v Tipping* (1721) 11 Vin Abr 244 p. 15; *A General Abridgment of Cases in Equity by a Gentleman of the Middle Temple* (Dublin: John Rice, 1792); 2 Eq. Ca. Abr. 468, para. 14 reprinted in 22 ER 398. See also *Gibblett v Read* (1795) 9 Mod 459, 88 ER 573.

[11] (1817) 2 Mer 446; 35 ER 1011.

[12] J.K. Crellin, 'A Note on Dr James's Fever Powder', (1970–77) 1 *Transactions of the British Society for the History of Pharmacy* 136–43.

[13] The Patent refers to 'fevers, rheumatisms, pleurisies, inflammations, gout, scurvy and chronic distempers'; Robert James, *A Dissertation on Fevers and Inflammatory Distempers* (3rd edn, London: J. Newbery, 1755) title page (small-pox, yellow fever and slow fever);

invented by Robert James, MD,[14] a doctor and a prolific author, whose publications included *A Medicinal Dictionary, with a History of Drugs* (1743), *A Treatise on the Gout and Rheumatism* (1745) and a 'universal pharmacopeia' in 1747.[15] It seems James first compounded the medicine – a derivative of antimony (a poison that has virtually no medical application today, but was one of the most widely used elements in medicines in this period) – in 1743, and his later works describe his prescribing of the remedy from this time and its positive effects.[16] The effect of the substance was to make patients sweat and vomit, so it would at least have given the impression of doing something.

In 1746, Robert James entered an agreement to distribute the remedy with the publisher, John Newbery,[17] of the Bible and Sun at 65 St Pauls Churchyard.[18] At the time Newbery was relatively newly established in London, his publications were diverse,[19] and he traded as much in medicines as books.[20] The choice of a publisher as a distributor of medicine might seem rather odd today, but publishers had distribution networks and could use print as a vehicle to promote the product.[21] Newbery published a series of pamphlets by James designed to

Bill of Complaint, The National Archive (hereinafter 'TNA'): PRO C13/198/29 (refers to certain pills for the Gout, Rheumatism, King's Evil, Scurvy and Leprosy and also of a powder for the cure of certain fevers and injection for the whites).

14 MD, *Comitiis Regiis*, 1728.

15 *Pharmacopoeia Universalis: or, a New Universal English Dispensatory* (London, 1747).

16 R. James, *A Dissertation on Fevers* (London: Newbery, 1748).

17 J. Rose, 'John Newbery' in J.K. Bracken and J. Silver (eds), *The British Literary Book Trade, 1700–1820*, (1995) 154 D Lit B 216; S. Roscoe, *John Newbery and his Successors, 1740–1814: A Bibliography* (Wormley: Five Owls Press, 1973); C. Welsh, *A Bookseller of the Last Century: Being Some Account of the Life of John Newbery, and of the Books He Published, with a Notice of the Later Newberys* (1885) (Cambridge University Press, 2010) (reproducing much of the Welsh volume); J.R. Townsend (ed.), *Trade and Plumb-Cake for Ever, Huzza!: The Life and Work of John Newbery 1713–1767* (Cambridge: Colt Books, 1994); W. Noblett, 'John Newbery: Publisher Extraordinary', (1972) 22 *History Today* 265; I. Maxted, 'Newbery, John (*bap.* 1713, *d.* 1767)' in *Oxford Dictionary of National Biography* (Oxford University Press, 2004), online edn, Oct 2008 (www.oxforddnb.com/view/article/19978, accessed 7 April 2012).

18 *Penny London Post or The Morning Advertiser*, 2 October 1745 (announcing the move, but earlier advertisements identify him as already selling from the Bible and Sun).

19 Though they included some on medicine, such as S. Mihles's *Medical Essays and Observations Relating to the Practice of Physic and Surgery* (London: S. Birt and J. Newbery, 1745).

20 Roscoe, *John Newbery and his Successors*, 4 ('so far as money-making was concerned, medicines were at all times John Newbery's chief concern, though his heart may have been in his books.')

21 Rose, 'John Newbery' ('Seventeenth and Eighteenth Century booksellers commonly purveyed nostrums as a sideline, and Newbery was able to sell books and pills through the same national marketing networks'); J. Alden, 'Pills and publishing', (1952) 7 *The Library* (5th ser) 21–37; P. Isaac, 'Pills and Print' in R. Myers and M. Harris (eds), *Medicine, Mortality and the Book Trade* (New Castle, Delaware: Oak Knoll Press, 1998)

accompany the fever remedies, and selling for the price of six pence, when two doses were sold for two shillings and six pence.[22] *A Dissertation on Fevers*, which went into eight editions, described conventional ways of treating fever before cataloguing the successes he had already had with his powders (while recognising a few cases of failure, as where a person was already hindered by prior addiction to gin).[23] The pamphlet also provided an opportunity for James to defend himself from criticism.[24]

James and Newbery went into business early in 1746. In the contract, dated 23 February 1746, James undertook for twenty-one years to make the pills and deliver them to Newbery at the price of eight pence per box of two pills, with similar terms for the powders and injections.[25] In turn, James undertook not to sell the medicines or cause them to be sold (except through his own private practice as a physician, and even then not in such a way as to undercut Newbery). James was, however, left the freedom to sell the medicine abroad as long as he paid Newbery six pence for every box. Newbery undertook to make certain efforts in marketing the remedy, including advertising it in the London and country papers. He also agreed not to use Robert James's name 'in any manner than what the said Robert James should consent to'. James also agreed to instruct Newbery as to how to make the medicines (in order to prevent the secret being lost), and that Newbery 'might have an account in writing sealed up how to make or prepare all or any of the said medicines to be opened by his [Newbery's] representatives after his death in order to inform and instruct him her or them therein'. In turn, Newbery agreed 'not to discover or make known to any person or persons the secret, art or mystery' of making the medicines. The agreement also provided that Newbery contribute half of the expense with James 'in getting and obtaining Letters Patent from his then present Majesty his heirs and successors for the preparing and vending of all or any of the said medicines'. The contract foresaw the need for extension, including a clause allowing renewal of the agreement for seven or eleven years. Finally, it provided that, in the case of any dispute, each party binding himself to the other for the sum of £5,000. On 13 November 1747, when the patent

25. Newbery famously exploited the links between the trades to the full, using fiction to promote his medicine.

[22] R. James, *A Dissertation on Fevers and Inflammatory Distempers. Wherein an Expeditious Method is Proposed of Curing those Dangerous Disorders* (5th edn, London: Newbery 1761).

[23] R. James, *A Dissertation on Fevers* (1748) 1–8 (describing conventional treatments), 9–39 (cataloguing successes).

[24] R. James, *A Dissertation on Fevers* (1748) 41.

[25] Bill of Complaint by Francis Newbery Against Robert G. G. James and Others, 9 February 1816, TNA: C13/198/29.

was granted, a further deed was entered, recognising that Newbery had paid £40 and that James assigned a half share in the patent to Newbery.[26]

The patent

In accordance with the agreement, James applied for a patent. Applications for medicines were increasing in frequency in the middle of the eighteenth century. While Nehemiah Grew's 1698 'Epsom Salts' is frequently cited as the first pharmaceutical patent,[27] and there were five more between the turn of the century and 1740,[28] the 1740s saw fourteen such applications,[29] and the 1750s twenty-two patent grants for medicines.[30] James was thus part of an emerging trend.[31] In applying for a patent, James was conscious that some might see the cure as 'downright quackery', but he asserted that the fact that some spurious patents had previously been granted was no reason why he should not benefit from the legislative policy of inciting industry and rewarding those 'who discover anything for the public Emolument'.[32]

The patent was granted on 13 November 1747.[33] The title of the patent was 'Powder and Pill for the Cure of Fevers and Other Distempers' (and, when Letters Patent came to be numbered by Bennett Woodcroft in his Index of 1862, the patent would be number 626). The patent purported to confer upon James, for fourteen years, the exclusive right to make and sell:

> A powder ... which in a few hours, and with a very few doses, most effectually cured acute fevers of all kinds, rheumatisms, pleurisies and inflammations,

[26] *Ibid.*

[27] A. Johns, *Piracy: The Intellectual Property Wars from Gutenberg to Gates* (Chicago University Press, 2009), 86, 98. See also F.H. Rawlings, 'Old Proprietary Medicine', (1996) 26 *Pharmaceutical Historian* 4–8.

[28] No. 388 (Thomas Byfield, 1711); No. 390 (Richard Stoughton, 1712); No. 442 (Benjamin Okell, 1726); No. 533 (Edward Lovel, 1731); see *Patents for Invention. Abridgments of Specifications Relating to Medicine, Surgery and Dentistry* (2nd edn, London: Eyre and Spottiswoode, 1872).

[29] No. 584 (Robert Hayward, 1742), 587 (Michael and Thomas Betton, 1742), No. 592 (Hooper, 1743), No. 596 (Robert Turlington, 1744), No. 597 (Francis Tanner, 1744), No. 599 (Thomas Greenough, 1744), No. 600 (Joseph Collett, 1744), No. 601 (Peter Henry, 1744), No. 603 (Nicholas Cerreti, 1744), No. 617 (Edmund Neeler, 1746), No. 626 (Robert James, 1747); No. 627 (Thomas Jackson, 1747); No. 633 (Walter Baker, 1748); No. 641 (William Sedgwick, 1749).

[30] Nos 650, 661, 665, 666, 667, 672, 673, 677, 680, 684, 694, 695, 700, 705, 706, 711, 718, 719, 728, 729, 736, 742.

[31] Possibly James valued the benefit it would provide in terms of publicity. See R. Porter, *Quacks: Fakers and Charlatans in English Medicine* (Stroud: Tempus, 2000) xx.

[32] R. James, *A Dissertation on Fevers* (1748), 44. [33] 21 Geo II.

and eminently relieved the gout, scurvy, and other chronical distemper, in a safe, effectual and agreeable manner.

As was becoming routine by then, the grant of the patent was made conditional on the provision of a written specification.[34] In James's case, the specification that was enrolled directed the reader as follows:

THE POWDER. Take Antimony, calcine it with a continued protracted heat, in a flat, unglazed, earthen vessel, adding to it, from time to time, a sufficient quantity of any animal Oil; and Salt, well phlegmated; then boil it in a melted Nitre for a considerable time, and separate the powder from the Nitre by dissolving it in Water.

THE PILL. Take quicksilver, make an amalgama with equal parts of the martial regulus of antimony and pure silver, adding a proportionable quantity of sal ammoniac; distil off the mercury by a retort in a glass receiver; then with this quicksilver make a fresh amalgama with the same ingredients. Distil again, and repeat this operation nine or ten times; then dissolve this mercury in spirit of nitre; put it into a glass retort, and distil to dryness; calcine the caput mortuum till it becomes of a gold colour; burn spirits of wine upon it, and keep it for use.

It is impossible for any one that does not see or attend to the process, to specify the precise dose, because the medicines will be stronger or weaker according as the process is conducted. In general, thirty grains of antimonial powder, and one grain of the mercurial powder is a moderate dose; though sometimes more, sometimes less is required.[35]

On its face, these appear to be two different products encompassed within a single grant.

The medicine was widely advertised from 1748,[36] and, according to James, 'gained a reputation' in 1750.[37] Thereafter the fame of the Fever Powders grew, so that in 1764 James asserted that 1.6 million doses had been sold by Newbery since 1746 (and that he himself had given an

[34] Seaborne Davies pinpoints the key date as 1734: D.S. Davies, 'Early History of the Patent Specification', (1934) 50 *LQR* 86, 90.

[35] The specification is quoted in Anon, *Thoughts and observations on the nature and use of Dr. James's powder, in the prevention and cure of diseases. Addressed to every one who wishes ...* (Colchester, 1790), 1; 32 *Repertory of Arts and Manufactures* (2nd ser) 327. Much of the language of the patent is unfamiliar. To 'calcine' meant 'to burn in the fire to a calx or friable substance' (Johnson, quoted in the *Oxford English Dictionary* (OED)). It was widely assumed that the effect was to produce pure antimony, but it probably made antimony trioxide (or possibly, if nitric acid was used, antimony pentoxide). 'Nitre' was potassium nitrate or saltpetre. It is not clear when salt was 'phlegmated'. A 'regulus' referred to the metallic form. 'Martial' normally suggested a relationship with iron. 'Sal ammoniac' is ammonium nitrate. The 'caput mortuum' refers to the residue. 'Spirit of wine' refers to alcohol.

[36] 'Dr James' Powder for Fevers', *General Advertiser*, 19 March 1748.

[37] R. James, *A Dissertation on Fevers* (6th edn, London: Newbery, 1764) iv ('1750, about which time the Powder began to be in Reputation').

equivalent amount to the poor).[38] During this time, James's patent survived a challenge made to the patent by the administrator of Baron Schwanberg, Walter Baker.[39] Baker claimed James had purchased the secret from Schwanberg, while James claimed that he had developed the medicine himself (before he had ever met Schwanberg) and that the Fever Powder was different from Schwanberg's.[40] On 18 February 1752, the Privy Council referred the issue to the Law Officers,[41] and on 9 December the Law Officers dismissed the application for revocation. In the end, it seems, the Law Officers decided against Schwanberg in a rather formalistic manner by drawing a distinction between Schwanberg's product and that which was the subject of the patent. According to the Law Officers, Schwanberg had disclosed a powder whereas James's patent related to an invention 'compounded of a powder and a pill'.[42] Even assuming that James learned about the powder from Schwanberg, and that James used the powder, the Law Officers regarded the invention in James's patent as something different. They therefore recommended that the Privy Council dismiss the petition for revocation.[43]

The patent lapses: secrecy

In 1761, the year in which the initial patent lapsed, a number of other chemists purported to make James's Fever Powders.[44] James viewed these operators as counterfeiters, (and their remedies as 'Counterfeits and Succedanea') and characterised their claims that their 'adulterations [are] equally effectual' as 'avarice and knavery'.[45] At this point, it became particularly important for James to assert the secrecy of the recipe (and, in turn, the inadequacy of the specification in the patent). In the introduction

[38] R. James, *A Dissertation on Fevers* (6th edn, 1764) iii (1,612,800 doses). According to T.A. Corley, 'James, Robert (*bap.* 1703, *d.* 1776)', *Oxford Dictionary of National Biography*, Oxford University Press, 2004 (www.oxforddnb.com/view/article/14618, accessed 18 Oct 2013), Newbery's own accounts show that in 1768/9 sales were just under 20,000 packages (valued wholesale at £822), and in 1775 some 38,000 packages, worth about £1,600.

[39] The proceedings are described in Walter Baker, *The affidavits and proceedings of Walter Baker, administrator to the late Baron Schwanberg, upon his petition presented to the King in Council* (London: 1754). See also E.W. Hulme, 'Privy Council Law and Practice of Letters Patent for Invention from the Restoration to 1794', Part II (1917) 33 *LQR* 180, 189–91.

[40] Anon, *An Answer to a Late scurrilous Pamphlet Published by One Baker and His accomplices Respecting Dr James' Powder* (London: Printed by J. Bouquet of 6 Paternoster Row, 1754?).

[41] Baker, *The affidavits*, 8. [42] Baker, *The affidavits*, xx.

[43] The report dated 9 December 1752 is reproduced in Baker, *The affidavits*, 95–96.

[44] *London Chronicle*, 27 April 1762; *St James' Chronicle*, 6 May 1762; *Lloyds*, 7 January 1763.

[45] R. James, *A Dissertation on Fevers* (6th edn, 1764) v.

to the 1764 edition of his *Dissertation on Fevers*, he does precisely this by telling the story of an Edinburgh Physician 'of greatest eminence' who did not recommend use of the Fever Powders. James recounts a conversation between the Physician and a Lord, where the cause of the Physician's lack of success with the Fever Powders became clear: he had made up his own version of the powders based on the patent specification, rather than using powders bought from James (and Newbery). The lesson was clear: despite the publication of details in the specification, only James could make up the remedy so that its efficacy could be assured.

John Newbery, and his son Francis, took special care over the possibility of the secret getting out.[46] An example is provided by the manner in which Newbery stymied the plans of a former employee of James, John Hawes, to set up in competition. Hawes, a chemist, had worked at James's manufactory in Lambeth.[47] Newbery obtained from Robert James an affidavit (dated 15 November 1774) 'that the chemist [Hawes] had never compounded the remedy and had no knowledge of the secret'. When James's former employee claimed to be the only possessor of the true formula,[48] Newbery produced the affidavit (along with further affidavits from chemists to the effect that Hawes's powder and James's were not the same).[49] There seems to have been no attempt to use legal means to stifle Hawes, investment instead being spent on convincing consumers that Newbery alone should continue to enjoy their patronage.[50]

Nor could details of the remedy be obtained by reverse engineering.[51] In 1788, the College of Physicians approved a 'generic' equivalent, 'antimonial powder'. Later, Newbery would advertise that following trial even the College acknowledged in its *Pharmacopeia* that James's powders was milder and 'more certain in its operation'.[52] Not long after, in 1791, George Pearson published a paper in the *Transactions of the Royal Society* which discussed the composition of James's powders.[53] Much of the Pearson paper is given over to examining the characteristics of

[46] G. Hussey, *A Physical Inquiry into the Cause and Cure of Fevers* (Dublin: Samuel Watson, 1779) 157 ('so much industry used in keeping these powders a profound secret').

[47] J. Hawes, letter, *Morning Post and Daily Advertiser*, 10 October 1776.

[48] Letter, *Morning Post and Daily Advertiser*, 14 September 1776.

[49] Advert, 'Dr James' Genuine Powders', *London Chronicle*, 19 October 1776; *London Chronicle*, 20 February 1777. Allen Hazen has argued that the text of the advertisement was written by Dr Samuel Johnson: A.T. Hazen, 'Samuel Johnson and Dr Robert James', (1936) 4 *Bull. Hist. Med.* 455, 464–65.

[50] L. Stine, 'Dr Robert James', (1941) 29 *Bulletin of the Medical Library Association* 187, 194.

[51] W.A. Campbell, 'Some Early Chemical Analyses of Proprietary Medicines', (1978) 69(2) *Isis* 226–33.

[52] *The Times*, 1 August 1814, p. 4a (advert).

[53] G. Pearson, 'Experiments and Observations to Investigate the Composition of James' Powder', (1791) 81 *Philosophical Transactions* 317–67.

the remedy, and its reactions and behaviour when mixed with other substances. In 1801, Chevenix attempted to locate an improved process for producing the medicine.[54] Although these serious investigations ought to have worried Francis Newbery in so far as they sought to reveal the secret, they also represent significant signs of approval from those who were experts in the field. Indeed, Chevenix noted that:

> Dr James's Powder is a medicine which has been so long in use, and is so deservedly ranked among the most valuable we possess, that every attempt to render the process for preparing it more simple and more certain, must be of some importance.[55]

The succession

The agreement between Newbery and James, initially for twenty-one years, was extended indefinitely in 1755. When John Newbery died in 1767, his interest was bequeathed[56] to his son, Francis Newbery,[57] who, fifty years later, was to be the plaintiff in *Newbery v James.* Francis Newbery immediately gave up the publishing branch of his father's activities, concentrating on the medicine business. Around the same time, James invented another, related remedy, so-called 'Analeptic pills', and a contract was entered between Francis Newbery and Robert James on the model that had been agreed with John Newbery. As with the powders, Newbery was to assist in obtaining a patent, of which both parties were to become joint owners. James obtained this, his second patent, on 25 November 1774.[58]

When Robert James died in 1776, his son Robert Harcourt James became entitled to his father's interest in the medicine. He continued to comply with the agreement, though some variations were made with respect to payment for advertising and for tax stamps.[59] On Robert

54 R. Chevenix, 'Observations and Experiments upon Dr James's Powders with a Method of Preparing, in the humid Way, a similar substance', (1801) *Philosophical Transactions* 375.

55 R. Chevenix, 'Observations and Experiments', 380.

56 The will is transcribed in Welsh, *A Bookseller of the Last Century*, 160. Rose, 'John Newbery', says, at 224, that the bequest included thirty other patent cures, though the will refers only to Hooper's female pills and Greenough's tincture for teethy.

57 Ian Maxted, 'Newbery, Francis (1743–1818)', *Oxford Dictionary of National Biography*, (Oxford University Press, 2004) (www.oxforddnb.com/view/article/19977, accessed 7 April 2012).

58 The patent was for 'Analeptic pills for the cure of rheumatism, also the loss of appetite, and for the cure of costiveness, giddiness, flatulency, and also disorders occasioned by a sedentary life'. The patent was given the number 1089 in Bennett Woodcroft's Index.

59 Bill of Complaint, 9 February 1816; Answer of George Smith, Pinkstan James, Robert George Gordon James, Rebecca James, Elizabeth Susan James, 1 July 1816.

Harcourt James's death in 1801, the rights in the medicines passed to George Smith, to be held on trust until Robert Harcourt James's son, Robert George Gordon James, was twenty-four years of age (in 1813). It seems to have been as RGG James came to majority that tensions developed between the two parties. In various advertisements, RGG James stated that when he came of age it had been 'found advisable' to remove sales from Newbery;[60] and elsewhere he attributed the decision to Newbery's 'conduct towards my family'.[61] It seems that he was particularly aggrieved over the manner in which Francis had treated his father, particularly when modifying the terms of the agreement in relation to advertising at a time when Robert Harcourt James had been in financial need and thus unable to bargain properly. Whatever the precise cause, it is clear that RGG James thought Newbery was getting too big a cut and he could renegotiate a better deal, or if necessary go elsewhere.[62] The breakdown was gradual: initially, for 1812, 1813, and 1814 RGG James simply instructed George Smith not to settle the accounts with Newbery.[63] Then, when finally he reached the age of twenty-four, he instructed the Jameses' family solicitor, Mr Dyneley, to give notice that they would no longer supply Newbery on existing terms, proposing an alternative arrangement in which Newbery would gain 40 per cent on the wholesale price.[64] Newbery's solicitor, Tyrrell, responded that the existing agreement was binding, that the parties had always co-operated on a basis of roughly equal profit (and remonstrated against the suggestion that James had made that Newbery himself was not privy to the secret).[65] Newbery, in turn, grumbled that the Jameses had mismanaged the manufacturing, such that pills were of different sizes and in different colours.[66]

The litigation

Newbery responded to the threats by instituting proceedings in Chancery.[67] The Bill, issued on Friday 9 February 1816, signed by

[60] *The Morning Post*, 4 July 1818; *Morning Chronicle*, 7 July 1818; *Morning Post*, 21 July 1818.
[61] *The Times*, 18 January 1818, p. 4a.
[62] In one advertisement James alleged Newbery had made over £100,000 from the sale of the Fever Powders and analeptic pills: *The Times*, 1 January 1818, p. 4B. Roscoe, *John Newbery and his Successors*, 17, recounted that Francis Newbery was reputed to have died almost a millionaire.
[63] Bill of Complaint, 9 February 1816.
[64] The letter was dated 29 December 1815: see Bill of Complaint, 9 February 1816.
[65] Bill of Complaint, 9 February 1816. [66] *The Times*, 14 January 1818, p. 4a.
[67] The proceedings were assigned to one of the Six Clerks, Sewell: TNA: IND 1/4158 f. 531.

Chancery barrister James Trower,[68] sets out the background in typical detail, and is supported by an affidavit signed by Newbery.[69] In brief, Newbery relied on the 1755 agreement, which was indefinite in its terms and applied not just to the parties, but their executors, administrators and assigns. On Newbery's understanding, as long as either party wished to persist with the arrangement, he was entitled to do so. Moreover, the agreement indicated an intention to treat the secret as joint property. Consequently, Newbery sought injunctive relief to prevent James from supplying others (as he was threatening to do) and from disclosing the secret to any third party. James's answer, dated 1 July 1816, is briefer, admitting much of the factual background, but emphasising that it was Newbery who had first deviated from the terms of the 1755 agreement when he exacted concessions from Robert Harcourt James in 1776.[70] From that time, the answer alleged, Robert Harcourt James had no longer felt bound by the terms of an agreement that Newbery had abandoned or waived. In short, as successor to the inventor, Dr Robert James, RGG James claimed he was free to do precisely as he wished.

Newbery sought interim relief to prevent James from supplying others with the medicines referred to in the Bill, and Trower appeared for Newbery before Lord Eldon on 10 February 1816.[71] Lord Eldon LC granted a temporary restraining order, which was stated to remain in force until the defendants filed an answer.[72] The defendants finally answered on 1 July 1816, following it with the first motion to dissolve the injunction, which was heard on 18 July 1816. Two formidable teams of Chancery lawyers confronted one another: Newbery had no lesser counsel than Sir Samuel Romilly KC,[73] Sir John Leach,[74] and James Trower, while James was represented by John Bell KC and William Courtenay.[75] There is a brief report of the proceedings on 18 July 1816 in *The Times*, which elaborates upon the arguments of the parties (and

[68] (1756?–1836). Trower was made King's Counsel and from 3 March 1823 to June 1836 was a Master in Chancery.

[69] The affidavit is at TNA: C31/364, First Part (where affidavits for Hilary Term 1816 are collected and ordered by date).

[70] Answer, 1 July 1816.

[71] The Minutes are in Registrar Walker's Minute Books, TNA: C37/2718.

[72] The Order can be found at TNA: C33/626/353–356 (along with a lengthy summary of the Bill and Newbery's affidavit).

[73] (1757–1818).

[74] (1710–1834). Leach was made Vice-Chancellor in 1818.

[75] Eldon was said to have considered Bell to be the best lawyer then at the Equity bar: J.M. Rigg, 'Bell, John (1764–1836)', rev. Beth F. Wood, *Oxford Dictionary of National Biography*, (Oxford University Press, 2004) (www.oxforddnb.com/view/article/2015, accessed 8 April 2012). Only months after the decision in *Newbery*, William Courtenay became a Master in Chancery.

indicates that essentially the same arguments were made at the initial motion).[76] According to the report, Bell (for James) made five points: first, that the contract was not of its nature capable of specific performance; second, that a contract could bind a person for his or her lifetime, but could not operate for posterity; third, that the contract was unenforceable as a restraint on trade; fourth, that because the patent had lapsed, everyone had a right to make the invention; and fifth, that as Newbery had departed from the contract, in the variations effected in the late 1770s, so James was no longer bound. Newbery's team replied that all these arguments had already been made and refuted when the initial motion for an injunction was heard. In any case, they argued that this agreement was no more a restraint of trade than any partnership agreement, and no more problematic for lasting in perpetuity than would be any lengthy contract, such as one for ninety-nine years. Finally they observed that the questions over whether there had been a variation or breach of the contract by Newbery required detailed consideration of the court and that in the meantime the injunction should be maintained.

Rather helpfully, Lord Eldon LC ended the hearing of 18 July with some 'hints to the parties'. He intimated that it was necessary to consider whether what was being made was the same as what had been the subject of the 1755 agreement. If they were the same, he said the composition must tally with the patent (seemingly thereby implying that there was no secret). If they were not the same, specific performance of the agreement could not ensure that no further variations were made by James. Consequently, the question of whether they were the same would need to be tried 'in open court', and he suggested that the parties carefully consider whether that would be in their mutual interests, for if there really were a secret it would inevitably be disclosed. He explained that he offered these hints because he really believed that Newbery and James had been 'benefactors to the public'.[77]

Nothing further seems to have happened until the following spring when James brought a further motion to dissolve the injunction, and, on 27 March 1817, Lord Eldon LC dissolved the *ex parte* injunction, leaving the plaintiff to enforce any contractual rights in the common law courts. As far as I have been able to discover, Newbery did not pursue the action at law, or appeal the Lord Chancellor's decision,[78]

[76] *The Times*, 19 July 1816, p. 3b.

[77] TNA: C 37/2722 (Registrar Walker's Minute Book for Trinity Term, 1816) (Saturday 20 July, 1816. 'Motion part heard last Seal. Mr Trower for Plaintiffs. Mr Bell for Defendants. Cur. Let this motion stand till next Seal.').

[78] TNA: IND1/15029 (index of petitions to appeal decisions in Chancery).

and both parties were forced into competition. James found a replacement distributor, Butler and Sons, a druggist at 4 Cheapside, and asserted that he was the only person who knew how to manufacture the real powders and pills. Newbery continued to use the name 'Dr James' on his products, claiming that he had access to the genuine recipe, in Dr James's hand, and was the only living person to whom the inventor had demonstrated how to make it (and had prior to the case been forced to accept supply from the Jameses).[79] A heated contest flared up in the press, both parties setting out their claims to be the 'genuine maker' of the Fever Powders,[80] sometimes in the very same paper,[81] sometimes in a tit-for-tat battle.[82] Although Newbery, who was seventy-four when the case was fought, died the year after,[83] the firm continued, now styled 'F. Newbery and Sons'. Perhaps surprisingly,[84] the matter of who had the right to use the *name* 'Dr James' stayed out of the courts, and both Butler and Sons and Newbery and Sons continued to trade in 'James' Fever Powders' for the next few decades – on 8 January 1842 two advertisements appearing side by side in the journal *John Bull.*[85]

The reasoning

The only report of Lord Eldon LC's reasons is that of John Harman Merivale, and it is brief, and in it the Lord Chancellor seems to reiterate some of the concerns that he had expressed at the hearing the previous July.[86] However, in the following years of his Chancellorship Lord Eldon LC gave at least three further judgments (in *Williams v Williams*,[87] *Yovatt v Winyard*,[88] and *Abernethy v Hutchinson*[89]), and in the light of the reports

79 *The Times*, 1 January 1818, p. 4B; *The Times*, 20 March 1818.
80 For example, Newbery in *The Morning Post*, 2 August 1817 and James in *The Morning Post*, 9 August 1817.
81 *Bury and Norwich Post*, 6 August 1817; *Caledonian Mercury*, 7 August 1817; *The Times*, 13 February 1818 (papers featuring advertisements by each of the parties).
82 *The Times*, 19 March 1818 (James); 20 March 1818 (Newbery); 21 March 1818 (James); 26 March 1818 (Newbery).
83 Friday 7 August 1818: see *The Times*, 8 August 1818, p. 3f.
84 Although there were damages awards made in the eighteenth century in relation to use of the names of medicines, Chancery's jurisdiction to award injunctive relief was embryonic at this point: see R.H. Eden, *A Treatise on the Law of Injunctions* (London: Butterworth, 1821) 314, referring to *Day v Day* (1816), which appears to be the first such case.
85 *John Bull*, 8 January 1842, 14.
86 (1817) 2 Mer 446; 35 ER 1011.
87 (1817) 3 Mer 157; 36 ER 61.
88 (1820) 1 Jac & W 394; 37 ER 425.
89 (1824–25) 3 LJ OS Ch 2009; 1 H & Tw 28; 47 ER 1313. The decision is more fully reported in *The Lancet*, 26 June 1825.

on those cases we can start to understand some of Lord Eldon's reasons for refusing Newbery the relief he sought.

Let me begin by considering an explanation of *Newbery v James* that gained some credibility later in the century: that the Lord Chancellor was reluctant to protect 'quack medicines'.[90] There is some evidence to support this. In *Williams*, Lord Eldon began by saying he did not think that 'the Court ought to struggle to protect this sort of secrets [*sic*] in medicine'.[91] Moreover, in *Abernethy v Hutchison*, he suggested that *Newbery* 'proceeded upon the utility of the medicines'.[92] It may be that, whatever he thought about the law protecting trade secrets, it should not be developed to protect 'quack' cures.

However, there are good reasons to doubt this explanation. If Lord Eldon LC was seriously contemplating withholding protection from medicines of dubious utility, the court would ultimately have found itself in the embarrassing position of having to decide which medicines were 'quack' and which 'genuine'. It is certainly not obvious why Lord Eldon LC would have regarded the veterinary preparation that featured in *Yovatt v Winyard*,[93] with more favour than James's powders or Williams's eye ointment.[94] In this period, as Mark Jenner has said, the quack 'was above all an imaginative construct, a label which you applied to others, a phantasm which haunted medical jeremiads'.[95] The question

[90] See L.B. Sebastian, *The Law of Trade Marks and their Registration* (London: Stevens and Sons, 1878) 179 ('a quack medicine, or an article intended to deceive the public, the Court will not struggle to protect the secret or to punish those who invade it'); J.H. Slater, *The Law Relating to Copyright and Trade Marks* (London: Stevens and Sons, 1884) 290.

[91] (1817) 3 Mer 157, 160; 36 ER 61, 62.

[92] (25 June 1825) 7 (91) *The Lancet* 377, 378.

[93] (1820) 1 Jac & W 394; 37 ER 425.

[94] Contemporaries struggled to reconcile the cases. See *Morison v Moat* (1851) 9 Hare 241, 255–59; 68 ER 492, 498–500 (Turner V-C). As late as 1841, C.S. Drewry, *The Law and Practice of Injunctions* (London: S. Sweet, 1841) 228–29, stated that cases such as *Newbery v James* and *Williams v Williams* were 'to be distinguished from cases where knowledge of a secret invention is fraudulently obtained'.

[95] M. Jenner, 'Quackery and Enthusiasm, or Why Drinking Water Cured the Plague' in O.P. Grell and A. Cunningham (eds), *Religio Medici: Medicine and Religion in Seventeenth-Century England* (Aldershot: Scolar Press, 1996) 327. See, more generally, W.F. Bynum and R. Porter (eds), *Medical Fringe and Medical Orthodoxy, 1750–1850* (London: Croom Helm, 1987) and R. Porter, *Quacks: Fakers and Charlatans* (the illustrated reissue of *Health For Sale: Quackery in England, 1650–1850* (Manchester: Manchester University Press, 1989). This is not, of course to suggest that the question of whether a pharmaceutical is 'efficacious' or 'safe' is not still to some degree socially constructed. For example, medical historians have pointed out that the fact that the oral contraceptive pill was allowed to remain on the market even after the discovery of potentially dangerous side effects (and this in the post Thalidomide era) says much about the influence of politics on the outcome of regulatory processes. See S. Junod and L. Marks, 'Women's Trials: The Approval of the First Oral Contraceptive Pill in the United States and Great Britain', (2002) 57 *Journal of the History of Medicine and Allied Sciences* 117.

of who was to be regarded as 'quack', and what was a 'quack remedy', was a complex one – caught up within contests between practitioner groups (those of physician, apothecary and druggist), as well as broader views of medicine, religion and economy.[96] Thus the designation of a remedy as a 'quack' was based sometimes on the supposed lack of expertise of the inventor or vendor, sometimes on claims to universality in application (rather than a careful diagnosis of the characteristics of the patient), sometimes on the empirical as opposed to theoretical basis for claims to effectiveness, sometimes on the mode of promotion, sometimes on the fact that the ingredients were unknown, and so on. James's powders could be regarded as a quack remedy by reference to some of those criteria, but by no means all – it was, after all, the invention of a licensed doctor. Moreover, it seems unlikely that these considerations influenced Lord Eldon LC:[97] as of 1817, James's powders had not yet been discredited,[98] and in his 'hints' to the parties at the hearing to dissolve Newbery's interim injunction in July 1816, Lord Eldon LC commended the parties for their contribution to the public good.

Instead, there seem to have been three concerns that informed the denial of injunctive relief:[99] first, the Chancellor doubted whether this was the sort of case in which 'specific performance' could be ordered; second, he had more general doubts about whether (and if so how) a court could deal with cases of secrets; and third, he was concerned with how the information policy that underpinned patent law could be reconciled with Chancery's protection of secrecy.

With respect to the question of whether the court could order specific performance of James's obligation to supply Newbery with the remedies, courts of Equity had already recognised that they could not

[96] For discussion of the role of religion in the framing of what constituted 'quack' remedies, albeit in the early eighteenth century, see M. Jenner, 'Quackery and Enthusiasm', 327.

[97] Cf., in the context of copyright Lord Eldon LC developed rules that meant that immoral works were unprotected: see I. Alexander, *Copyright Law and the Public Interest in the Nineteenth Century* (Oxford: Hart, 2010) 68 ff.

[98] The dubious value of James's powders had still not been determined forty years later when the merits of James's powders and the alternatives to them were the further subject of a paper before the Pharmaceutical Society, published in *The Lancet*.

[99] To a lawyer today, it might look odd that the descendant of James, the developer of the recipe and 'confider' was being sued by the exploiter or 'confidant', especially given that the contract only contains an express obligation of secrecy on Newbery and not James. The circumstances in which a person to whom information has been disclosed can claim an enforceable interest in it was one of the issues in *Douglas v Hello!* [2008] AC 1, but in that case their Lordships only went as far as to recognise an interest of the recipient of the information, *OK! Magazine*, against a third party, leaving open the question of whether it could have enforced an obligation against Douglas and Zeta-Jones. The explanation for the claim in Newbery, implicit in the pleadings, is that Newbery's claim was to 'joint ownership', necessarily carrying obligations of non-disclosure on both parties.

enforce agreements that required supervision.[100] At this time, it was also thought that if it was not appropriate to enforce the contract in full, it was inappropriate to enforce one part of it by way of injunction: the whole matter should be one for a court of law.[101] Moreover, the facts of *Newbery* seem to implicate the principle that specific performance will not be ordered to enforce a contract for personal services.[102] This rule was still developing in the early nineteenth century – indeed, Lord Eldon's decision in *Clarke v Price*[103] would later be viewed as an early authority supporting the rule.[104] Similar concerns may have operated in *Williams v Williams*, which was put in terms of specific performance.[105]

The second concern was whether the processes of the legal system could offer protection for agreements relating to secrets without jeopardising the very matter that it was sought to protect. The problem was that, in order for a court to adjudicate on whether a secret was a secret, or whether a person violated an injunction to keep it secret, it needed to have access to the information: were it to be given such access, there were doubts about whether the secret would still exist. And, according to *The Times'* report of the July 1816 hearing, Lord Eldon had stated the question 'must be tried in open court'. Reflecting on these problems in *Abernerthy*, Lord Eldon LC explained his concern with a secret being revealed in court and later 'finding its way out of the doors at the bottom of the hall'.[106] If this was really the justification for *Newbery*, the implications were potentially significant: the court would never be able to enforce a secrecy or confidentiality agreement, whether between

[100] Note also Lord Eldon's refusal in *Clarke v Price* (1819) 2 Wils Ch 157, 164, 37 ER 270, 272–73 to order specific performance refused in relation to a writing contract: 'I have no jurisdiction to compel Mr Price to write reports for the plaintiffs.' He explained, 'I cannot, as in [*Morris v Colman* (1812) 18 Ves Jr 437; 34 ER 382], say, that I will induce him to write for the plaintiffs, by preventing him from writing for any other person, for that is not the nature of the agreement. The only means of enforcing the execution of this agreement would be to make an order compelling Mr Price to write reports for the plaintiffs; which I have not the means of doing. If there be any remedy in this case, it is at law.'

[101] As a general proposition, this was rejected by Lord Cottenham LC in *Dietrichsen v Cabburn* (1846) 2 Ph 52; 41 ER 861.

[102] *De Francesco v Barnum* (1890) 45 Ch D 430, 438.

[103] (1819) 2 Wils Ch 157; 37 ER 270.

[104] See *Lumley v Wagner* (1852) 1 De GM & G 604, 619–24; 42 ER 687, 693–95 (Lord St Leonards LC, reviewing the authorities) by which time the rule seemingly is well-established. For the policy-based nature of the rule, see *Johnson v Shrewsbury and Birmingham Railway Company* (1853) 3 De GM & G 914; 43 ER 358.

[105] W. Joyce, *The Law and Practice of Injunctions in Equity and at Common Law*, vol 1 (London: Stevens and Haynes, 1872) 218.

[106] *Abernethy v Hutchison* (1825) 7(91) *The Lancet* 377, 378 (Lord Eldon LC).

a vendor and purchaser, trustee and beneficiary, a business and employee or an inventor and a patent agent.

The third possible explanation for Lord Eldon LC's conclusion in *Newbery* is that he was concerned with the relationship between patenting and secrecy. The tension between the two forms of protection had been raised four years earlier in *Canham v Jones*.[107] There, Isaac Swainson had bequeathed to Canham the recipe for a medicine, sold as 'Velno's Vegetable Syrup', and the defendant, Robert Jones, a former servant of Swainson, was alleged to have sold a medicine under the description 'Velno's' or 'de Velno's'. The Vice-Chancellor, Sir Thomas Plumer, rejected the claim, stating that the Bill:

> proceeds upon an erroneous Notion of exclusive Property now subsisting in this Medicine ... If this Claim of Monopoly can be maintained, without any Limitation of Time, it is a much better Right than that of a patentee ... If any exclusive Right in this Medicine ever existed, it has long expired.[108]

In *Newbery*, the concern could have been the same – after all, the parties had behaved as if the secret of how to make the medicine was 'property' that could be maintained for decades and passed down over generations. Indeed, Newbery's claim was that the contract made him not just co-owner of the patents (which had long since expired), but co-owner of the invention and secret itself.

But in *Newbery* the point was not just that the secrecy appeared to give *better* protection than patents, but that it had given *additional* protection. For Lord Eldon LC, this seemed to fly in the face of the policy of disclosure that had come to inform patent law.[109] According to the Merivale report, Lord Eldon LC observed that 'in order to support a patent, the specification should be so clear, as to enable all the world to use the invention as soon as the term for which it has been granted is at an end'.[110] The implication was that the proprietor of a patent could not contend, in his favour, that the specification was inadequate.

The idea that the patentee was bound to disclose the secret to the public was, in fact, a relatively recent innovation in English patent law

107 (1813) 2 Ves & B 218; 35 ER 302.

108 (1813) 2 Ves & B 218, 221; 35 ER 302, 303.

109 See further the report of *Abernethy v Hutchison* (25 June 1825) 7 (91) *The Lancet* 377, 378 (Lord Eldon LC).

110 2 Mer 446, 35 ER 1011. In the same year, in *Williams v Williams*, (1817) 3 Mer 157, 160; 36 ER 61, 62. Eldon LC reiterated that: 'The Court is bound indeed to protect [these sorts of inventions] in cases of patents, to the full extent of what was intended by the grant of the patent, because the patentee is a purchaser from the public, and bound to communicate his secret to the public at the expiration of the patent.'

and a critical shift in thinking about the function of the specification.[111] In 1778, in *Liardet v Johnson*,[112] Lord Mansfield effectively made the completion of the specification obligatory in all cases, and laid down standards which the specification had to meet (the precursor of what patent lawyers refer to as 'sufficiency'). According to counsel's notes, Lord Mansfield instructed the jury:

> The meaning of the Specification is that others may be taught to do a thing for which the Patent is granted, & if the Specification [is] false, the patent is void, for the meaning of the Specification is that after the term [of the Patent] the public shall have the benefit of the discovery.[113]

Although some have disputed the seminal importance of *Liardet v Johnson*,[114] it is clear that by the final decades of the eighteenth century a patent could be invalidated if there was no adequate specification. In *R v Arkwright*,[115] in the Court of King's Bench, the Arkwright patent was revoked. Buller J outlined the rationale of the requirement of enablement and the addressee:

> Upon this point it is clearly settled as law, that a man, to entitle himself to the benefit of a patent for a monopoly, must disclose his secret, and specify his invention in such a way, that others may be taught by it to do the thing for which the patent is granted; for the end and meaning of the specification is, to teach the public, after the term for which the patent is granted, what the art is, and it must put the public in possession of the secret, in as ample and beneficial a way as the patentee himself uses it ... It has been truly said by the counsel, that if the specification be such, that mechanical men of common understanding can comprehend it, to make a machine by it, it is sufficient; but then it must be such,

[111] E.W. Hulme, 'On the Consideration of the Patent Grant, Past and Present', (1897) 13 *LQR* 313, 317–18.

[112] (1778) 1 Web Pat Cas 53; 1 Carp Pat Cas 35. More fully reported in J. Oldham, *The Mansfield Manuscripts and the Growth of English Law in the Eighteenth Century*, vol 1 (Chapel Hill: University of North Carolina Press, 1992) 748.

[113] Quoted in Oldham, *The Mansfield Manuscripts*, 754. See E.W. Hulme, 'On the History of Patent Law in the Seventeenth and Eighteenth Centuries' (1902) 18 *LQR* 280, 285 (drawing on a manuscript copy of the summing up).

[114] J. Adams and G. Averley, 'The Patent Specification: The Role of *Liardet v Johnson*', (1986) 7 *Journal of Legal History* 156. Indeed, elsewhere Hulme speculates that Lord Mansfield first applied the requirement of sufficiency of disclosure in the 1771 case concerning *Brand's Patent*: E.W. Hulme, 'Privy Council Law and Practice of Letters Patent', 192.

[115] (1785) Dav Pat Cas 61; 1 Web Pat Cas 64; 1 Carp Pat Cas 53 (KB, Buller J). See also *Arkwright v Nightingale* (1785) Dav Pat Cas 37, 55–56; 1 Web Pat Cas 60, 61–62; 1 Carp Pat Cas 38, 49–50 (CP, Lord Loughborough CJ); *Turner v Winter* (1787) 1 TR 602, 605 (Ashurst J), 606–07 (Buller J); 99 ER 1274, 1276, 1277; *Boulton and Watt v Bull* (1795) 2 H Bl 463, 478 (Rooke J), 484–85 (Buller J), 496–97 (Eyre CJ); 126 ER 651, 659, 662, 668.

that mechanics may be able to make the machine by following the directions of the specification, without any new inventions or additions of their own.[116]

Although the importance of this development has been widely recognised,[117] there has been virtually no discussion of the broader epistemic conditions that rendered the specification itself a possibility. The requirement that a patent applicant submit a specification which would make the invention 'replicable' or repeatable depended critically on the existence of numerous codes that would make possible the description of the scientific 'arts' and the 'mysteries' of trade. This 'textualisation' of an invention was dependent not just on growth in literacy, but in literacy of a particular sort or sorts (for example, in mechanics, a visual literacy); on the standardisation of terminology, for example in measurement of weight, heat, time, as well as nomenclature for chemicals, processes and instruments; and a level of consistency in the quality of commercially available starting materials.[118] The specification was thus only made possible by key developments in the so-called 'scientific revolution'. These conditions did not simply pre-exist but were, of course, themselves changing and developing, and, at any given time were at different stages for different sectors. In such an environment, the standard in *Liardet* and *Arkwright* would not necessarily have been as easily complied with in these differing sectors.

In *Newbery v James*, the secrets at issue had been patented, and for that patent to be valid the specification would (following *Liardet*) have had to disclose how to make the medicine. However, James's 1747 patent was widely regarded as not enabling the manufacture of the remedy. In a 1791 paper before the Royal Society, George Pearson stated that while James's powders had been patented 'it is well-known that it cannot be prepared by following the directions of the specification in the Court of Chancery'.[119] In fact, in *Liardet* itself, Mansfield offered up the Jameses'

[116] (1785) Dav Pat Cas 61, 106; 1 Web Pat Cas 64, 66; 1 Carp Pat Cas 53, 78–79.

[117] M. Biagioli, 'Patent Republic: Representing Inventions, Constructing Rights and Authors', (2006) 73 *Social Research* 1129, 1160. Also, M. Biagioli, 'Patent Specification and Political Representation: How Patents Became Rights' in M. Biagioli, P. Jaszi, M. Woodmansee, *Making and Unmaking Intellectual Property* (Chicago University Press, 2011), Ch. 1.

[118] Indeed, these 'codes' continue to change: one need only think of developments in genetics over the last thirty years to be reminded that breakthroughs often occur before science has developed the language, concepts, techniques and practices by which those breakthroughs come to be understood. On mechanical representations, see W.J. Rankin, 'The "Person Skilled in the Art" Is Really Quite Conventional: US Patent Drawings and the Persona of the Inventor, 1870–2005', in Biagioli et al., *Making and Unmaking Intellectual Property*, Ch. 3.

[119] Pearson, 'Experiments and Observations', 317–67.

1747 patent as a situation in which a specification was inadequate. Hulme reports Lord Mansfield thus:

'In 1778 Lord Mansfield attacked Dr. James's specification on the ground of insufficiency. He said to have determined in several cases here [i. e. in the King's Bench] that the Specification must state, where there is a composition, the proportions', and he refers to Dr. James's specification as giving no proportions.[120]

Mansfield was right – the James specification, apart from referring to a 'sufficient' quantity of animal oil, a 'protracted' heat, and boiling for a 'considerable' time, said virtually nothing about the proportions of antimony, salt or nitre, let alone the temperature of the 'calcination'. Contemporaries, some of whom were supporters of James in his dispute with Walter Baker as to whether James had stolen the remedy from Schwanberg, had highlighted the critical importance of these matters:

I must inform the Readers who are unacquainted with Chemical Matters, that 'tis very remarkable, in Antimony in particular, that only different Proportions of the Principles or Materials, mix'd with it, or a greater or less Degree of Heat with the same proportions of Ingredients, will make such a Difference in the Preparations thereof, that one shall be a virulent poison, and another a very mild Medicine.[121]

In some ways, James's failure is not all that surprising: the specifications in both patents were provided before the requirement of 'sufficiency of disclosure' had been elaborated by Lord Mansfield in *Liardet*, and it is unclear quite how far these requirements (and the consequences of failure to comply) had been anticipated.[122] Moreover, James himself indicated in the patent that merely carrying out the process specified would not reliably produce the same strength of medicine. The patent stated that it was 'impossible for any one that does not see or attend to the process, to specify the precise dose, because the medicines will be stronger or weaker according as the process is conducted'. In some respects, then, he seems at that stage to have considered the process more of an 'art', for which he should receive recognition of a patent,

[120] E.W. Hulme, 'Privy Council Law and Practice of Letters Patent', 192. See Oldham, *The Mansfield Manuscripts*, 754, discussed in E.W. Hulme, 'On the History of Patent Law', 285. Hulme says: 'It is clear that in 1753 Lord Mansfield formed an unfavourable opinion of the validity of James's patent – probably on good grounds; for the doctor's reputation was not of the highest. But James's specification lends no support to the new legal doctrine, and it is probable Lord Mansfield antedated his own law by some twenty years.'

[121] Anon, *An Answer to a Late Scurrilous Pamphlet*, 38. See also the affidavit of Thomas Greenough, *ibid.* at 41.

[122] Adams and Averley, 'The Patent Specification', 160; MacLeod, *Inventing the Industrial Revolution*, 50.

rather than something that could be taught to others. Of course, the subsequent practices of Newbery in selling the remedy as a commodity somewhat contradicts James's initial claim that only those who had witnessed the production of the cure could safely and effectively administer it.

These 'defects' in the 1747 specification paradoxically buttressed Newbery's claim to the secrecy of the recipe. The fact that the skilled person could not make James's powders by following the specification meant that James and Newbery possessed (at least for a time) information that was not in the public domain. At the same time, it would no doubt have seemed perverse to protect as a trade secret any information which ought to have been disclosed by James in the patent. One possibility is that Lord Eldon LC embraced an 'election' theory – that a person who elected to obtain a patent thereby abandoned any other claim to protect the invention. However, there is nothing to suggest this, and it might have proved difficult to deploy on the facts of the case, given that it was Newbery who wanted to enjoin James, rather than vice versa. James (and his descendants) might have 'elected' to patent, but Newbery was not the original patentee. Another possibility is that Lord Eldon LC treated Newbery as 'estopped' from denying the effectiveness of the disclosure. The estoppels could be said to have derived from his ownership and reliance on the patent: Francis Newbery's father had contributed to the cost of the 1747 patent, as Francis had to the 1774 patent for analeptic pills, and each had been the assignee of a half share. Moreover, although the Merivale report suggests the *Newbery* court proceeded on the basis that the recipe for the analeptic pills had not been patented,[123] when in fact it had been, one commentator suggested that the specification there was also defective,[124] so that the reasoning might have applied *mutatis mutandis*.

Conclusion

Newbery v James represents a moment of hesitation in the development of the law of trade secrecy. Lord Eldon LC was asked to make a decision about an extremely valuable asset that had formed the basis of a commercial relationship that had lasted seventy years in an environment

[123] Given that Newbery's Bill referred to the patent over analeptic pills, it may well be that the Merivale report is mistaken on this point.

[124] *Report from the Select Committee on the Law Relative to Patents for Inventions*, Parl Papers, 1829 (332) III.415, pp. 201–02 ('It was a misstatement to the court, that there had been no patent obtained for the Analeptic Pills; Dr James had a patent for that in 1774; but the specification is not intelligibly worded').

where secrecy afforded strong, potentially perpetual protection (because reverse engineering remained ineffective), but where the emergent policy norms associated with patenting favoured disclosure. His decision raised doubts about whether Chancery courts could protect secrets at all, and specifically about whether they should do so in the face of a lapsed patent for the same invention. In due course, the Chancery courts developed mechanisms for making adjudications on secrets without risking their exposure in open court, elaborating obligations of confidentiality in relation to disclosure and the holding of proceedings *in camera*. The judiciary went on to accept secrecy as an alternative to patenting (and, indeed, as a necessary complement to it in the pre-patenting period). The tension between a policy of supporting secrecy and a policy of promoting openness was resolved through a set of more nuanced rules that, as Jeanne Fromer explains in Chapter 13, gave rise to patent law's secrets and trade secrecy's disclosures.

Part VIII

Open innovation

15 Legal but unacceptable: *Pallin v. Singer* and physician patenting norms

*Katherine J. Strandburg**

In intellectual property discourse, the edge tends to be defined by disputes between producers and consumers or between upstream and downstream innovators. This chapter tells a different kind of story, about the edge between the patent-based innovation system and a user innovator community governed by norms of reputation and sharing.[1] In this story, the user innovator community is the medical profession.

In the mid-1990s, at the height of a period of expansive patent rights, Dr. Samuel Pallin patented an improvement to cataract surgery procedure and sought to license it to other eye surgeons in return for royalty payments. One of those eye surgeons was Dr. Jack Singer. Singer responded to the royalty demand not only by refusing to pay it, but by spearheading what eventually became a political movement against medical procedure patents. Beginning in 1994, physicians lobbied Congress to redraw the line around patentable subject matter so as to exclude medical procedures. Though they did not achieve that objective, they succeeded in convincing Congress to pass 35 U.S.C. § 287(c) in 1997. § 287(c) eliminates remedies against physicians for infringement of many medical procedure patent claims.

Though physician inventors routinely patent medical devices, opposition to patents on medical procedures and medical diagnostic methods

* Note that the author served as counsel for amici medical associations in briefing in *Mayo v. Prometheus*. The analysis described in this chapter is this author's alone and does not purport to represent the views of those clients. This chapter reflects the truly excellent research assistance of Zachary King, Elizabeth Kimmel, and Chris Han. The generous support of the Filomen D. Agostino and Max E. Greenberg Research Fund is also gratefully acknowledged.

[1] See, e.g. Eric von Hippel, *Democratizing Innovation* (MIT Press, Cambridge Mass., 2005); E. von Hippel and G. von Krogh, "Open Source Software and the 'Private-Collective' Innovation Model: Issues for Organization Science," 14 *Org. Sci.* 208 (2003); Katherine J. Strandburg, "User Innovator Community Norms at the Boundary Between Academic and Industrial Research," 77 *Fordham L. Rev.* 2237 (2009); Katherine J. Strandburg, "Norms and the Sharing of Research Materials and Tacit Knowledge" in *Working Within the Boundaries of Intellectual Property*, Rochelle C. Dreyfuss, Harry First, and Diane L. Zimmerman, eds. (Oxford University Press, USA, 2010).

holds strong. This chapter examines that opposition through the lens of user innovation.[2] User innovators invent and improve technologies for their own use, rather than to license or sell them to others. Examples of user innovations include improved manufacturing processes, certain types of software, sports equipment, scientific research tools, and many business methods and service improvements.[3] User innovation succeeds because it depend on users' superior, and "sticky," knowledge of unmet needs and the ways that technologies perform on the ground.[4] Because of their shared interests, users of a particular type of technology often form communities in which the norm is to share information about problems with current technology, suggestions for improvements, innovations they have made, and critiques of those innovations.[5] Patenting is generally eschewed by these communities and innovation is rewarded with reputation. Physicians who devise new medical procedures, diagnostic tests, medical devices, surgical instruments, and the like are also user innovators.[6] This chapter views the story of *Pallin v. Singer* and the

[2] Elsewhere, I undertake a more detailed exploration of these issues. Katherine J. Strandburg, "Derogatory to Professional Character? Physician Innovation and Patents as Boundary-Spanning Mechanisims" (2013), available at http://ssrn.com/abstract=2324003.

[3] See, e.g., von Hippel, *Democratizing Innovation*; K. R. Lakhani and B. Wolf, "Why Hackers Do What They Do: Understanding Motivation and Effort in Free/Open Source Software Projects" in *Perspectives on Free and Open Source Software*, J. Feller et al., eds. (MIT Press, Cambridge Mass., 2005) at 3; C. Lüthje et al., "User-Innovators and 'Local' Information: The Case of Mountain Biking," 34 *Res. Pol'y* 951 (2005); *ibid.* at 8; see Sonali K. Shah, "From Innovation to Firm Formation in the Windsurfing, Skateboarding, and Snowboarding Industries" in *Proc. Sixth Ann. Mtg. Int'l Sports Engineering Ass'n* (2006) available at http://link.springer.com/chapter/10.1007%2F978-0-387-45951-6_6#page-1; Sonali Shah, "Open Beyond Software" in *Open Sources 2.0*, Chris Dibona et al., eds. (O'Reilly Media, Sebastopol CA, 2005) at 339; Katherine J. Strandburg, "What If There Were a Business Method Use Exemption to Patent Infringement?," *Mich. St. L. Rev.* 245 (2008).

[4] See, e.g., von Hippel, *Democratizing Innovation* at 8; Susumu Ogawa, "Does Sticky Information Affect the Locus of Innovation? Evidence from the Japanese Convenience-Store Industry," 26 *Res. Pol'y* 777 (1998).

[5] See, e.g., N. Franke and S. Shah, "How Communities Support Innovative Activities: An Exploration of Assistance and Sharing among End-Users," 32 *Res. Pol'y* 157 (2003); D. Harhoff et al., "Profiting from Voluntary Information Spillovers: How Users Benefit by Freely Revealing their Innovations," 32 *Res. Pol'y* 1753 (2003); L. Janzik et al., "Motivation in Innovative Online Communities: Why Join, Why Innovate, Why Share?," 15 *Int'l J. Innovation Mgmt.* 797 (2011); C. Raasch et al., "The Dynamics of User Innovation: Drivers and Impediments of Innovation Activities," 12 *Int'l J. Innovation Mgmt.* 377 (2008); W. Riggs and E. von Hippel, "Incentives to Innovate and the Sources of Innovation: The Case of Scientific Instruments," 23 *Res. Pol'y* 459 (1994); Karim Lakhani and Eric von Hippel, "How Open Source Software Works: 'Free' User-to-User Assistance?," 32 *Res. Pol'y* 923 (2003).

[6] See, e.g., Aaron K. Chatterji et al., "Physician–Industry Cooperation in the Medical Device Industry," 27 *Health Aff.* 1532, 1533 (2008) ("Physicians may contribute

physician movement that led to the passage of § 287(c) as a narrative of user innovator community norms.

Setting the stage

During the nineteenth and early twentieth centuries, the medical profession and the Patent Office agreed that medical procedures should not be patented. The American Medical Association's (AMA's) first Code of Ethics, adopted in 1847, deemed it "derogatory to professional character" for a physician to hold a patent.[7] The absolute ban on patenting was softened only slightly in 1940, when it was revised to state that it was "unprofessional to receive remuneration from patents or copyrights on surgical instruments, appliances, medicines, foods, methods or procedures."[8] Only in 1955 was the ethical principle revised to permit physicians to patent "surgical instruments, appliances, and medicines" as long as the receipt of remuneration did not "retard [] or inhibit[] research or restrict[] the benefits derivable therefrom."[9] The ban on patenting medical procedures remained in place, though physicians were permitted to obtain copyrights associated with procedures.[10] In 1957, the AMA overhauled and shortened its Principles of Ethics, removing explicit reference to patenting. The 1955 approach to patenting was, however, incorporated by reference as part of a compilation of sections said to be "included within the spirit and intent of the language of the 1957 edition."[11]

directly to the innovation process by inventing medical devices themselves. This kind of 'user innovation' has been documented in diverse settings . . ."); Eric von Hippel, "The Dominant Role of Users in the Scientific Instrument Innovation Process," 5 *Res Pol'y* 212, 231 (1976) (suggesting that user innovation is responsible for "medical and dental innovations (e.g. new dental equipment is usually invented, first used and perhaps discussed in journals by dentists prior to commercial manufacture being undertaken by a dental equipment firm)"); Harold J. Demonaco et al., "The Major Role of Clinicians in the Discovery of Off-Label Drug Therapies," 26 *Pharmacotherapy* 323 (2006); Sheryl Winston-Smith and Sonali Shah, "Do Innovative Users Generate More Useful Insights? An Analysis of Corporate Venture Capital Investments in the Medical Device Industry," 7 *Strategic Entrepreneurship J.* (2013) 151–67; Sheryl Winston-Smith and Andrew Sfekas, How Much Do Physician Entrepreneurs Contribute to New Medical Devices? (working paper), available at www.ncbi.nlm.nih.gov/pubmed/23358387.

[7] Am. Med. Ass'n, Code of Medical Ethics § 4 (1847).

[8] "Organizational Section Proceedings of the New York Session," 114 *JAMA* 2557, 2567 (1940), available at http://jama.jamanetwork.com/data/Journals/JAMA/7654/jama_114_26_014.pdf.

[9] American Medical Association, "Report of Council on Constitution and Bylaws," *Proc. Am. Med. Ass'n Clinical Meeting* 111 (1955), available at www.ama-assn.org/ama/pub/about-ama/our-history/ama-historical-archives/the-digital-collection-historical-ama-documents.page.

[10] *Ibid.*

[11] Am. Med. Ass'n, Principles of Medical Ethics 1957 (1958), available at www.ama-assn.org/resources/doc/ethics/1957_principles.pdf.

A later ethical opinion adopted sometime before 1977 took an even more positive view of patents on medical instruments: "A physician may patent a surgical or diagnostic instrument he or she has discovered or developed. The laws governing patents are based on the sound doctrine that one is entitled to protect one's discovery."[12] There was no such evolution in the AMA's opinions on medical procedures, however. Instead, a 1984 ethics opinion emphasized that, like medical knowledge, skills and techniques were not to be withheld from the community for reasons of personal gain.[13]

Until the middle of the twentieth century, the few judicial and Patent Office opinions involving medical procedure patents were in line with the medical profession's view. In 1862, in *Morton v. New York Eye Infirmary*,[14] a case still cited for its discussion of the patentability of natural phenomena, the court invalidated a patent on the use of ether for anesthesia. In 1883, *Ex Parte Brinkerhoff* denied a patent on the grounds that "[t]he methods or modes of treatment of physicians of certain diseases are not patentable."[15] As late as 1951, a district court opinion in *Martin v. Wyeth Inc.* noted that "[i]nstances of valid patents for a method of medical or surgical treatment have been rare indeed, although a few cases may be found in which therapeutic agents, such as aspirin, have been held patentable."[16] In 1954, however, the Patent Office, in *Ex Parte Scherer*, expressly overruled *Brinkerhoff*, allowing a claim to a method of "injecting fluids into the human body" by a pressure jet.[17] From that point on, medical procedure patents were available in principle, though they seem to have been rare (or at least not salient to physicians) during the next few decades.[18]

The seeds of controversy over medical procedure patents began to be sown in the 1980s. At that time, optimism about the potential for patents to facilitate medical advances, particularly through the newly emerging field of biotechnology, was high. The Bayh-Dole Act[19] reflected an

[12] "Council on Ethics & Judicial Affairs, Am. Med. Ass'n, Opinions on Professional Rights and Responsibilities" in *Code of Medical Ethics: Current Opinions with Annotations* 136, 150 (American Medical Association, USA, 1996–1997, edn. 1996).

[13] AMA Code of Medical Ethics, Opinion 9.08, New Medical Procedures (1984, 1994), available at www.ama-assn.org/ama/pub/physician-resources/medical-ethics/code-medical-ethics/opinion908.page (last visited October 8, 2012).

[14] *Morton v. New York Eye Infirmary*, 17 F. Cas. 879 (C.C.S.D.N.Y. 1862).

[15] 24 Dec. Comm'r 349 (1883), reprinted in *New Decisions*, 27 *J. Pat. & Trademark Off. Soc'y* 793, 798 (1945).

[16] 96 F. Supp. 689, 694–95 (D. Md. 1951), *aff'd*, 193 F.2d 58 (4th Cir. 1951).

[17] *Ex Parte Scherer*, 103 U.S.P.Q. (BNA) 107 (B.P.A.I. July 23, 1954).

[18] See, e.g., "AMA Speaks Out on Managed Care," *UPI*, June 14, 1994 (AMA general counsel states that "methods patents" are a new phenomenon in medicine).

[19] P.L. 96-517, Patent and Trademark Act Amendments of 1980, codified at 35 U.S.C. § 200-12.

assumption that patents would facilitate the commercialization of the neglected fruits of academic research, particularly in the biomedical sciences. The Supreme Court's approval of the patenting of living organisms in *Diamond v. Chakrabarty*[20] gave the green light to biotechnology patenting. The Federal Circuit Court of Appeals was established in 1982, centralizing patent appeals in a single forum, largely because of Congress's sense that courts were unfriendly to patenting.[21] The pro-patent mood continued throughout the 1990s when, for example, the 1994 World Trade Organization (WTO)-based TRIPS Agreement[22] established robust minimum requirements for intellectual property protection internationally and the Federal Circuit expanded patentable subject matter to the point that any method producing a "useful, concrete, and tangible" result was deemed patentable.[23]

The story of *Pallin v. Singer*

Given the generally pro-patent mood of the time and the fact that medical device patenting by physicians had become commonplace, it is perhaps unsurprising that in 1990, when our story begins, Dr. Samuel Pallin was tempted to catch the wave by patenting an improvement in cataract surgery technique. His attempt to enforce that patent against Dr. Jack Singer unleashed the storm of physician opposition to medical procedure patents that led Congress to enact § 287(c).[24]

Sutureless cataract surgery

Human beings have suffered from, and treated, cataracts (opacity of the optic lens) for millennia.[25] Treatment methods have involved breaking up the clouded lens, pushing it away from the line of vision ("couching") and removing the lens entirely. During the early twentieth century, lens

[20] 447 U.S. 303 (1980). [21] See, e.g., S. Rep. No. 97-275, at 2, 5–6 (1981).
[22] Agreement on Trade-Related Aspects of Intellectual Property Rights (1994), available at www.wto.org/english/tratop_e/trips_e/t_agm0_e.htm.
[23] *State Street Bank & Trust Co. v. Signature Financial Group Inc.*, 149 F.3d 1368, 1373–75 (Fed. Cir. 1998).
[24] There had been some controversy about method patents brewing before Pallin filed his patent application, but it was concentrated in the reproductive technology arena. See e.g., U.S. Patent No. 4,009,260 (1977) (method for sex selection); U.S. Patent No. 4,339,434 (1982) (same); U.S. Patent No. 4,874,693 (1989) (method for prenatal testing for Down's syndrome); U.S. Patent No. 4,127,118 (1978) (method for enhancing an erection); U.S. Patent No. 4,816,257 (1989) (surrogate embryo transfer); U.S. Patent No. 4,986,274 (1991) (method for determining fetal gender).
[25] See Thomas V. DiBacco, "The Long View of Cataract Surgery," *Wash. Post*, July 11, 1995, at F9.

removal methods improved greatly, yet removal left patients with better, but still poor vision. In the 1940s, physician Harold Ridley revolutionized treatment by developing the intraocular lens – an artificial replacement lens permanently implanted in the eye. When improved removal methods permitted smaller incisions, flexible lenses, which could be folded for insertion, were developed.

Surgeons also sought to minimize trauma to their patients' eyes by improving their incision techniques. By 1989, cutting-edge surgeons used a "scleral tunnel" technique. The lens of the eye sits behind an outer layer consisting of three parts: the sclera, or "white" of the eye; the cornea, or outer lens; and the limbus, a ring of tissue connecting the cornea and sclera. An "anterior chamber" lies between the cornea and inner lens. In the scleral tunnel technique, the surgeon would make an incision partway through the sclera at some distance from the cornea, "tunnel" through the sclera to reach the anterior chamber, remove the defective natural lens and insert the artificial replacement through the tunnel, and suture the wound. Sutures were problematic, however, because they could induce astigmatism as the wound healed. In the late 1980s, Dr. John Shepherd introduced a technique for closing the wound with a single, loose stitch, thus avoiding some of the problems previously caused by suturing. Some, including the well-known Florida ophthalmologist James Gills, began to suggest the possibility of sutureless surgery.[26]

On March 1, 1990, the trade journal *Ocular Surgery News* (*OSN*) reported sutureless cataract surgery by Dr. Michael McFarland, an Arizona ophthalmologist.[27] *OSN* was the typical forum for early reporting of new surgical techniques. As Dr. Howard Fine later explained in deposition testimony, *OSN* is "part of the medical press rather than a peer-review journal, but it has become the single most important source of new technology for ophthalmologists in the world today because it is accurate, it is timely, and it allows information out years before it would become available in peer-review journals."[28] McFarland had performed his first sutureless surgery in January 1990. By the time the *OSN* report went to press, he had performed twenty-five more sutureless procedures. Shortly after his initial success, McFarland phoned Dr. Paul Ernest, a clinical professor of medicine at Wayne State

[26] Declaration of Samuel L. Pallin, M.D. in Support of Plaintiff's Opposition to Defendants' Motion for Summary Judgment at ¶ 14. Note that all court documents cited in this chapter are found in the record of *Pallin v. Singer*, No. 2:93-cv-202 (D. Vt. March 28, 1996) ("*Pallin v. Singer*").

[27] "Surgeon Undertakes Phaco, Foldable IOL Series Sans Sutures," *Ocular Surgery News*, March 1, 1990, at 1.

[28] *Pallin v. Singer*, Deposition of I. Howard Fine, M.D. at 40.

University, to discuss his procedure. Ernest replicated McFarland's technique in February 1990, then adapted it by extending the scleral tunnel a small distance through the limbus into the cornea before it emerged into the anterior chamber. Ernest believed that such a "corneal lip" was critical to safe sutureless surgery.

At around the same time, Dr. Steven Siepser, a Pennsylvania ophthalmologist, developed his own sutureless technique, which he reported at the March 1990 meeting of the American Society of Cataract and Refractive Surgery (ASCRS). At its meetings, the ASCRS holds "film festivals," at which videos of eye surgeries are screened. Siepser's film of his sutureless surgery received an award.

Siepser's film and *OSN*'s report of McFarland's technique generated both excitement and skepticism among cataract surgeons, inspiring many efforts to replicate and improve upon their techniques. At least three of those so inspired, James Gills, Samuel Pallin, and Jack Singer, believed that the shape of the initial incision might be important for safe sealing of the wound. All three developed similarly shaped incisions. As a result, all three played important roles in the *Pallin v. Singer* lawsuit – Pallin as patentee, Singer as accused infringer, and Gills as creator of the most significant prior art.

Gills, who had specialized almost exclusively in cataract surgery for nearly twenty years, described his proposed incision shape, which he first tested on March 19, 1990, as an "inverted V."[29] He published a photo of the healed wound from that surgery in the August 1990 volume, *Small-Incision Cataract Surgery*.[30]

Singer first tried what he called a "frown incision" on March 20, 1990.[31] Singer, who was particularly noted for his films, published a videotape of that surgery in the *Audiovisual Journal of Cataract and Implant Surgery*.[32] Singer's 1990 surgery was not sutureless; he used Shepherd's single suture technique. Singer began performing sutureless surgeries in February 1991, adopting Ernest's corneal lip seal in conjunction with his frown incision.[33]

[29] *Pallin v. Singer*, Declaration of James P. Gills, M.D. at ¶ 7; Deposition of Dr. James P. Gills at 9.

[30] James P. Gills, "Sutureless Cataract Surgery: From 3 to 3.5mm Incision with Foldable Lens to 6mm Incision with Phacoemulsification and Standard PMMA Lens" in *Small-Incision Cataract Surgery*, James P. Gills and Donald R. Sanders, eds. (Slack, Inc., Thorofare, NJ, 1990) at p. 129.

[31] *Pallin v. Singer*, Declaration of Jack A. Singer, M.D. in Support of Motion for Summary Judgment of Invalidity at ¶ 8.

[32] This appeared in the third issue of the journal's sixth volume in 1990. *Ibid.* at ¶ 9.

[33] *Ibid.* at ¶ 18.

Dr. Samuel Pallin's chevron incision patent

Pallin developed his method, later patented as "Method of Making Self-Sealing Episcleral Incision"[34] after he saw the McFarland and Siepser reports, in an attempt to devise an incision that would permit the sutureless insertion of a hard, rather than folding, intraocular lens. Because Pallin found McFarland's and Siepser's techniques unworkable for hard lenses, he conceived the idea of a "chevron" incision on April 16, 1990. He performed his first sutureless chevron incision surgery the next day. The obese diabetic patient suffered congestive heart failure during the surgery and had to be hospitalized, giving Pallin "no opportunity to place sutures." When the patient returned a week later "the wound had self-sealed."[35]

Having successfully performed sutureless cataract surgery, Pallin immediately sought to publish his results. His April 1990 submission to the peer-reviewed *Journal of Cataract and Refractive Surgery* (*JCRS*) was rejected in July 1990.[36] Pallin's work was, however, reported by *OSN* on August 15, 1990[37] and described in detail in a letter to the editor published in *JCRS* in November 1990.[38] In April 1991, Pallin presented a paper and film entitled "Chevron Sutureless Closure for Rigid Lenses: A Preliminary Report" at an ASCRS symposium.[39] He eventually published a report of much more extensive work (700 surgeries)[40] in *JCRS* as part of an October 1991 special volume devoted to sutureless cataract surgery. This special volume included articles by Pallin, Siepser, Gills, Ernest, Singer, and at least thirteen others.[41]

While pursuing publication, Pallin also took the unusual step of applying for a patent. By April 29, 1990, he had obtained patent counsel.[42] His attorney filed an application on June 28, 1990, and Pallin's patent was issued on January 14, 1992.[43] Claims 1 and 7 are representative.

[34] U.S. Patent No. 5,080,111 (1992).

[35] *Pallin v. Singer*, Declaration of Samuel L. Pallin, M.D. in Support of Plaintiff's Opposition to Defendants' Motion for Summary Judgment at ¶¶ 18–21.

[36] *Pallin v. Singer*, Declaration of Samuel L. Pallin, M.D. in Support of Plaintiff's Opposition to Defendants' Motion for Summary Judgment at ¶ 27.

[37] See *Pallin v. Singer*, Deposition of Samuel L. Pallin, M.D. Volume II at 210–12.

[38] Samuel L. Pallin, "Chevron Incision for Cataract Surgery," 16 *J. Cataract Refract. Surg.* 779 (November 1990).

[39] *Pallin v. Singer*, Curriculum Vitae Samuel Lear Pallin, M.D., F.A.C.S. at 5, Entry No. 42, App. D, Exhibit 1.

[40] Samuel L. Pallin, "Chevron Sutureless Closure: A Preliminary Report," 17S *J. Cataract & Refractive Surgery* 706, 707 (1991).

[41] "Small Incision Surgery: Wound Construction and Closure," 17S *J. Cataract & Refractive Surgery* 659 (1991).

[42] *Pallin v. Singer*, Declaration of Samuel L. Pallin, M.D. in Support of Plaintiff's Opposition to Defendants' Motion for Summary Judgment at ¶ 26.

[43] U.S. Patent No. 5,080,111 (filed June 28, 1990).

Though there was, as we have seen, no lack of relevant professional literature about cataract surgery, the patent examiner considered only seven prior art references, each of which was a patent directed to a *device* for ophthalmic surgery.

1. A method of making a substantially self-sealing episcleral incision comprising;

providing incision making means;

making an incision in the sclera with said means; and

said incision having an appropriate central point 1.5 to 3.0 millimeters posterior to the limbus

wherein portions of said incision extend away from said approximate central point and extend laterally away from the curvature of said limbus.

7. The method of claim 1 further including making an incision having a curvilinear configuration.

Pallin seeks royalties and Singer resists

On June 4, 1993, Pallin's attorneys sent a cease and desist letter to Singer and the Hitchcock Associates clinic where he practiced, alleging that Singer's frown incision technique infringed Pallin's patent. (The clinic is associated with Dartmouth Medical College, where Singer was a clinical professor.) The letter offered Singer a license in return for what it termed a "reasonable royalty" and Singer's agreement to reference the patent when promoting the frown incision technique.[44] A month later, after Pallin and Singer failed to come to terms, Pallin sued Singer and the Hitchcock Clinic for patent infringement. Settlement negotiations ensued, during which, according to Singer, a "graduated royalty of $2,500 – $10,000 per year, which can be increased annually at Dr. Pallin's discretion" was proposed.[45] No settlement was reached during the fall of 1993.

Following the failure of the initial settlement negotiations, Singer made an unanticipated move. He decided to use the lawsuit as a vehicle for fighting what he believed was a dangerous trend toward medical procedure patenting. In February 1994, he sent a mass mailing to fellow ophthalmologists soliciting contributions to a litigation defense fund:

The Clinic and Dr. Singer are vigorously defending this action. We see no merit in the specific allegations, nor do we agree with the underlying premises of Dr. Pallin's suit, i.e., that surgeons can or should patent the shape of incisions, or that giving reports on your own surgical experiences at professional meetings

[44] *Pallin v. Singer*, Complaint at ¶ 15, Letter from John M. White to Jack L. Singer, Entry No. 1, Exhibit B.

[45] *Pallin v. Singer*, Singer February 17, 1994 Letter to Fellow Ophthalmologists, at 1, Entry No. 24, Exhibit B.

can constitute inducement of infringement. We believe that such patenting and such interpretation of what constitutes infringement is inconsistent with the applicable code of professional conduct and the advancement of medical science through the free and open exchange of ideas.[46]

A similar letter to the editor was published in *OSN* on April 1, 1994.[47]

Recall that, by this time, the AMA no longer had a specific ethical prohibition against medical procedure patenting on the books, though the longstanding prohibition incorporated by reference into the Principles of Medical Ethics in 1957 had never been challenged. The historical trend was toward greater acceptance of physician patenting, as reflected in the rosy view that "laws governing patents are based on the sound doctrine that one is entitled to protect one's discovery" expressed in the AMA ethics opinion on device patenting. In light of the generally pro-patent mood of the times, physician acquiescence in medical procedure patenting might have seemed an inevitable next step. Instead, Singer's call for support galvanized the medical community and catalyzed the political movement against medical procedure patenting that resulted in 35 U.S.C. § 287(c).

In April 1994 Singer received a standing ovation after giving an impassioned speech entitled "Free Exchange of Surgical Knowledge" at a meeting of the American Society of Ocular Surgeons (ASOS).[48] One of Pallin's attorneys, who had attended the speech, immediately sent Singer a settlement offer that was considerably more conciliatory than earlier offers:[49] "[R]ecognizing Dr. Singer's contributions in promoting the incision and its benefits," it proposed a "single one time payment of $5,000" and had "no objections to Dr. Singer continuing to promote the frown incision in whatever way he likes." Noting that Singer's speech made clear that his "fundamental objection is not to the Pallin patent alone, but to the present availability of method patents on surgical techniques," the letter argued that, while Singer had a right to work for legal reform, he had "unearthed no proof of invalidity [of Pallin's claims] sufficient to overcome the presumption of validity."

Unappeased, Singer pressed Pallin to disclaim his patent and to agree not to enforce it against other ophthalmologists. The response of Pallin's

[46] *Pallin v. Singer*, Letter from Jack A. Singer and John C. Collins at 1, Entry No. 24, Exhibit B.

[47] Jack A. Singer & John C. Collins, Letter to the Editor, "Defense Fund," *Ocular Surgery News*, April 1, 1994, at 4.

[48] *Pallin v. Singer*, Physicians [*sic*] Program at 52, Entry No. 24, Exhibit J; "Doctor Implores Principles of Hippocrates to Standing Ovation," *Ophthalmology Times*, May 1, 1994, at 28.

[49] *Pallin v. Singer*, Letters from James R. Longacre to George Neuner, Entry No. 24, Exhibit N.

attorney nicely illustrates the culture clash between the patent system's emphasis on individual entitlements and the medical profession's community-based approach to disseminating and rewarding procedure innovation:

What we do with the patent in the future with respect to others who are not defendants in this law suit is our business and has no proper part in any settlement. However, there is no reason to disclaim the patent and we will not do so. The patent is valid and infringed and you have provided no evidence to the contrary.[50]

Pallin's attorneys seem to have felt that Singer's appeals for support from the physician community, like his attempts to negotiate relief for the entire community, were inappropriate. They moved to compel discovery about those activities, arguing that "[t]he defendants' public allegations of invalidity and unenforceability and activities to organize a national movement against Dr. Pallin are areas in which the plaintiff has a right to inquire."[51] The court summarily denied the request, stating merely that "questions regarding defendants' funding of the litigation [are] not relevant to the pending subject matter."[52] Pallin's attorneys were understandably frustrated by the turn of events. Singer's appeals to the physician community effectively switched the playing field from one governed by patent law to one governed by medical community norms of sharing skills and techniques. While Pallin was the plaintiff in the litigation, he became the defendant in the court of medical profession opinion.

Pallin's attempt to situate medical procedure patents within medical community norms

Though Pallin's attorneys seemed nonplussed by Singer's outreach to the physician community, Pallin's actions grew out of his membership in that community. He consistently argued that he resorted to patent enforcement only in response to the community's failure to award him adequate credit for his contributions. A pleading filed on his behalf in the suit against Singer even implied that his initial decision to apply for a patent was a response to his peers' rejection of his initial submission to *JCRS*:[53]

[50] *Ibid.* at 3. [51] *Pallin v. Singer*, Motion to Compel at 8.
[52] *Pallin v. Singer*, Opinion and Order at 2, Entry No. 29.
[53] *Pallin v. Singer*, Plaintiff's Opposition to Defendants [*sic*] Motion for Leave to Amend at 3. This contention was also widely reported in contemporaneous media and law review reports. See, e.g., William B. Lafferty, "Statutory and Ethical Barriers in the Patenting of Medical and Surgical Procedures," 29 *J. Marshall L. Rev.* 891, 892 (1996); Joseph M. Reisman, "*Comment*, Physicians and Surgeons as Inventors: Reconciling Medical Process Patents and Medical Ethics," 10 *High Tech. L. J.* 355, 366 (1995); Wendy W.

As an experienced and respected surgeon he expected to be published. Amazingly, his article was rejected. His invention was harshly criticized by his colleagues. He then retained counsel and a patent application ... was prepared and filed in June of 1990.[54]

There are reasons to doubt this implication in light of the timing of manuscript submission and patent application preparation.[55] It also appears there would have been little justification for perceiving *JCRS*'s rejection of an early report of a few surgeries as a serious affront. The first peer-reviewed *JCRS* article about sutureless cataract surgery was authored by Gills and appeared in May 1991.[56] Gills had access to a very large patient population, as evidenced by the fact that in 1990 he published a monograph reporting 2,000 sutureless surgeries.[57] JCRS did not publish another article about sutureless cataract surgery until the October 1991 special issue, in which Pallin's article appeared alongside several other articles on the topic. Thus, Pallin certainly was not alone in having to wait for publication while experience with sutureless surgery accumulated.

While Pallin's motivations for filing his patent application remain murky, there is little doubt that his later turn to enforcement was driven by discontent with the community's recognition of his contributions. When the patent issued in January 1992, Pallin did not run out to seek royalties. Instead, he sought community recognition by attempting to donate the patent first to the ASCRS and then to the American Academy of Ophthalmology (AAO).[58] Only after these attempts to deploy the patent to gain recognition from the community were rejected did Pallin begin to demand royalty payments. As Pallin perceived things: "The degree of resistance I encountered when I attempted to share my work

Yang, "*Note*, Patent Policy and Medical Procedure Patents; The Case for Statutory Exclusion from Patentability," 1 *B.U. J. Sci. & Tech. L.* 5, para. 51 n. 146 (1995); Brian McCormick, "Just Reward or Just Plain Wrong? Specter of Royalties from Method Patents Stirs Debate," *Am. Med. News*, Sept. 5, 1994, at 3. See, e.g., Eric M. Lee, "35 U.S.C. § 287(c) – The Physician Immunity Statute," 79 *J. Pat. & Trademark Off. Soc'y* 701, 701–02 (1997).

[54] *Pallin v. Singer*, Plaintiff's Opposition to Defendants [*sic*] Motion for Leave to Amend at 3.

[55] Pallin's Declaration filed in December 1994 makes it clear that he prepared his patent application and submitted his manuscript to *JCRS* at around the same time, in April 1990. *Pallin v. Singer*, Declaration of Samuel L. Pallin, M.D. in Support of Plaintiff's Opposition to Defendants' Motion for Summary Judgment at ¶¶ 26–27.

[56] J.P. Gills and D. Wang, "Sutureless Closure for Exchange Surgery of Intraocular Lenses," 17 *J. Cataract Refract. Surg.* 383 (May 1991).

[57] Gills and Sanders, *Small-Incision Cataract Surgery* at 127.

[58] Samuel L. Pallin, "Method Patents Benefit Information Dissemination," *Ocular Surgery News*, July 15, 1994, at 19.

with the profession at large was astounding. The arrogance with which my work was dismissed by individuals whom I had held in high regard was shocking."[59]

Besides justifying his resort to patent enforcement by alleging a failure of the community's reward system, Pallin also argued repeatedly that his use of his patent was an appropriate extension of community norms. Thus, an April 20, 1994 settlement offer portrayed Pallin's patent enforcement strategy as tempered by the sharing norms of the physician community:

> Dr. Pallin has stated on a number of occasions that he would never seek an injunction or an unreasonable royalty from a surgeon or anyone else so you and Dr. Singer may be assured that no one will be stopped from using this incision in the future. At the most they will be asked to pay a small royalty.[60]

A June 1994 settlement offer focused even more clearly on portraying Pallin's actions as consistent with the sharing norm.[61] It recognized Singer's goal of "ensuring that [] the Frown remain available to everyone" and offered to accommodate the sharing norm by refraining from seeking royalties from those who were teaching the technique and forgoing injunctive relief altogether. Pallin also deferred to community reputational norms by offering to credit Singer for his contributions to "popularizing the frown incision."

Pallin also presented himself as a concerned community member seeking revision of the anti-patenting norm in light of changed circumstances. Thus, the June 1994 settlement letter emphasized that Pallin strongly believed that he was "doing the right thing" and "pioneering the way for others to follow." It also asserted that the United States Patent and Trademark Office (USPTO) Official Gazette reflected increasing numbers of procedure patents in ophthalmology and other surgical specialties so that inventors were "watching this debate." Pallin also acknowledged Singer's "goals of embracing a political debate within the profession" and offered to debate him at a professional meeting. Similarly, in a debate with Singer published in a July 1994 AAO newsletter,[62] Pallin argued that the journal publication process was "too easily corrupted by politics and special interests" and that patents therefore might sometimes be the only way for the true inventor

[59] *Ibid.*
[60] *Pallin v. Singer*, Letters from James R. Longacre to George Neuner at 3, Entry No. 24, Exhibit N.
[61] *Pallin v. Singer*, Letter from James R. Longacre to George Neuner at 2–3, Entry No. 37, Exhibit C.
[62] John Hayes, "The War over Patents," *Argus*, July 1994, at 8.

to be recognized. For his part, Singer distinguished medical procedures from devices and drugs, arguing that procedure innovations are incentivized by "the foundation of good medical practice" and generally do not require substantial financial investments that must be recouped through patents. Pallin contended that the growth of managed care would shrink physicians' intrinsic incentives to invent new procedures, which would have to be replaced by the "recognition and small profit" available from patenting. He also disputed Singer's distinction between devices and procedures, arguing that both device and procedure patents should be ethically acceptable as long as royalties were not too expensive (and thus, by implication, did not interfere with the sharing norm).

In the end, the 1994 settlement negotiations failed for reasons that make sense in light of the ongoing battle over the norms of the physician community. Though Pallin eventually went so far as to offer the defendants a royalty-free license,[63] on top of the concessions discussed above, and even attempted to grant such a license unilaterally, Singer refused to settle.[64] Singer demanded nothing less than dedication of the patent to the public or something of equivalent effect,[65] while Pallin was equally adamant that he would not give up his patent. It was time for the court to weigh in.

Pallin v. Singer *in court*

In October 1994, Singer moved for summary judgment of noninfringement and of invalidity in light of the work of Gills, Singer, and McFarland.[66] The summary judgment motion moved the focus from the terrain of community norms and ethics back to the technical patent law issues, at least temporarily. The arguments centered on whether the preamble term "substantially self-sealing" limited the claims and on how that term and the "wherein" clause describing the incision shape should be construed. On May 1, 1995, the court denied the motion, without resolving any of the claim construction issues, holding that "complex factual

[63] *Pallin v. Singer*, Reply Brief on Behalf of Pallin, February 1996, at 8, Entry No. 81.

[64] *Pallin v. Singer*, Letter from James R. Longacre to George Neuner at 1, Entry No. 37, Exhibit E.

[65] Letter from Peter J. Manus to James R. Longacre, *Pallin v. Singer*, Entry No. 37, Exhibit G; see also Rochelle Nataloni, "Pallin vs. Singer Still at Stalemate; Offer Made, Refused," *Ocular Surgery News*, September 15, 1994, at 23 (explaining some of the inner workings of the settlement negotiations and how they came to an impasse).

[66] See *Pallin v. Singer*, Order, Entry No. 43 (granting Singer's request to submit a summary judgment motion in October, which was after the timeframe allotted in the court's rules).

disputes" existed in the case.[67] At that point, it seemed that the case was on track for trial. Fate intervened, however. Judge Franklin Billings, who had been presiding over the case, had taken senior status in September 1994. In September 1995, he reassigned his pending cases, including *Pallin v. Singer*, to newly appointed Judge William Sessions. Singer's attorneys asked the new judge to resolve the claim construction issues and grant summary judgment in light of intervening changes in the law.[68]

Judge Sessions held the requested hearing on March 26, 1996.[69] The hearing must not have gone well for Pallin. Two days later, the court issued a Consent Order declaring the patent claims invalid and non-infringed and ordering Pallin not to make any further enforcement attempts.[70] The *Pallin v. Singer* litigation thus ended, having resulted in no pathbreaking ruling on the patentability of medical procedures (or anything else, for that matter).

The result was widely reported in the medical and mainstream media as a defeat for medical procedure patenting.[71] Pallin did not acknowledge defeat, stating that "My goal from the beginning of this controversy and in this litigation was to demand and achieve recognition for a contribution, which I made to the profession in early 1990 ... I am

[67] *Pallin v. Singer*, Order and Opinion at 7, Entry No. 57. No one seems to have noticed that the Federal Circuit had just held, in *Markman v. Westview Instruments, Inc.*, 52 F.3d 967 (Fed. Cir. 1995), *aff'd*, 517 U.S. 370 (1996), that claim construction is a matter of law for the court to decide.

[68] The intervening change was the *Markman* decision, which had been a basis for reconsideration by several other district courts by that time. See *Am. Permahedge, Inc. v. Barcana, Inc.*, 901 F. Supp 155 (S.D.N.Y. 1995), *aff'd*, 105 F.3d 1441 (Fed. Cir. 1997), and *Elf Atochem N. Am., Inc. v. Libbey-Owens-Ford Co.*, 894 F. Supp 844 (D. Del. 1995) respectively.

[69] *Pallin v. Singer*, Defendants' Motion for Summary Judgment, Entry No. 74.

[70] Consent Order, *Pallin v. Singer*, 1996 WL 274407 (D. Vt. Mar. 28, 1996). Because the case was resolved by settlement, the order does not reflect any rationale for these declarations. See also "Pallin Patent Claims Invalidated; Physicians free to perform cataract surgery without threat of infringement litigation," *PR Newswire* (March 29, 1996), available at Gale Cengage, OneFile Infotrac database, Reference p329DCF020.

[71] See, e.g., Carolyn Lederman, "Pallin Patent Is Invalidated," *Ophthalmology Times*, June 1, 1996, at 10; "Court Rules against Patent on Surgical Procedure," *Argus*, May 1996, at 8; Greg Borzo, "Method Patent Fails; Court: Surgeon Doesn't Have to Pay Royalties," *Am. Med. News*, April 15, 1996, at 1; "Eye Surgeon Loses Effort to Enforce his Patent," *N.Y. Times*, April 3, 1996, at D20; "Judge Rejects Patent for Eye Surgery," *Chi. Trib.*, April 2, 1996, at 12; Editorial, "Patently Ridiculous," *Tulsa World*, April 4, 1996, at A12; "Inside the Industry – Surgical Patents: Judge Dismisses Bellwether Case," *Am. Healthline*, April 2, 1996, available at http://newlive.nationaljournal.com/cgi-bin/ifetch4?ENG+AMERICAN_HEALTHLINE-_-POLL_TRACK-_-AD_SPOTLIGHT+7-ahlindex+1405937-REVERSE+0+0+12710+F+6+6+1+bellwether+AND+judge; *Patenting Knowledge* (PBS television broadcast April 23, 1996), available at www.pbs.org/newshour/bb/health/jan-june96/patent_04-23.html (transcribing the broadcast).

satisfied this goal has now been achieved."[72] He also claimed a moral victory, in that his case had made physicians aware that medical procedures are patentable,[73] and continued to defend medical procedure patenting.[74]

Pallin was wrong, however. Singer's view had prevailed in the court of physician community opinion and the norm against medical procedure patenting had, if anything, been reinforced. Indeed, Singer's 1994 speech to ASOS had ignited an assault on medical procedure patents in the halls of Congress, which also came to a head in 1996.

Negotiating the boundary between physician innovation norms and the patent system

The physician movement against medical procedure patents

Even before Singer's ASOS speech, Pallin's attempt to enforce his patent seems not to have gone over well with his fellow eye surgeons. In a March 15, 1994 interview, for example, Michael McFarland dismissed the idea that patents could replace or supplement the medical community's assessment of credit by documenting "originality." He explained that "traditionally in ophthalmology we've always documented innovation of a new procedure, technique or piece of equipment through our literature, so that will continue to be the way that we document who does what first." He also rejected the notion that patent licenses and royalties could be means to share innovations with fellow surgeons. To McFarland, collecting royalties from another physician was "[u]ndoable, if not unthinkable":

> It's hard for me to conceptualize why anybody would want to bring this whole royalty scheme into ophthalmology and to introduce the legalities involved and to bring lawyers into the picture and file lawsuits against our colleagues ... We ought to get back to trying to figure out better ways to fix folks and to share that with our colleagues for the benefit of the patients.[75]

Singer's ASOS speech painted medical procedure patenting as a threat to medical community sharing norms:

> An insidious virus has been threatening to destroy the foundation of good medical care in the United States since 1954. The virus is method patents for

[72] "Court Rules Against Patent on Surgical Procedure," *Argus*, May 1996, at 8.
[73] Greg Borzo, "Method Patent Fails," at 1.
[74] *Patenting Knowledge* (PBS television broadcast April 23, 1996), available at www.pbs.org/newshour/bb/health/jan-june96/patent_04-23.html (transcribing the broadcast).
[75] "Sutureless Takes Firm Hold On Cataract Surgery: Interview with Mike S. McFarland," 12 *Ocular Surgery News*, March 15, 1994, at 1, 21–32.

medical and surgical procedures. If allowed to proliferate this will effectively block the timeless way of sharing medical and surgical knowledge, and perhaps more importantly will inhibit the interdependent free exchange of information that is the foundation of good medical care. Other victims of medical and surgical method patents include physician autonomy, the doctor–patient relationship, openness in medical research, and free exchange of medical and surgical knowledge.[76]

During the spring of 1994, following Singer's letters and speech, the physician movement to oppose medical procedure patenting took on a life of its own, first among ophthalmologists and then throughout the broader medical community.[77] Dr. Herve Byron, an intraocular lens pioneer, fanned the flames of community outrage in a colorfully written *OSN* column in June 1994. Byron depicted the *Pallin v. Singer* case as a "monumental battle," emphasizing that its "ultimate impact" should be determined on ethical, rather than legal, grounds.[78] He described Singer as "the beleaguered general of all of surgery's ethical war," warned of "devastating and mind-boggling consequences" of a loss in court, and questioned why individual ophthalmologists and medical organizations had not reacted more strongly to the threat "of a plane flying overseas with a potential hydrogen bomb ready to explode." Byron also, however, deplored the potential negative consequences for Pallin if he should lose the lawsuit and end up "despised and [] permanently outlawed from the ophthalmic community by his peers." He urged that steps be taken to bring Pallin back into the fold and warned that failure to effect a dignified reconciliation would result in an outcome "similar to the Vietnamese war – no winners and all losers."

[76] "Doctor Implores Principles of Hippocrates to Standing Ovation," *Ophthalmology Times*, May 1, 1994, at 28.

[77] See, e.g., Ely Jay Crary, Letter to the Editor, "Payment and Credit Due to Dr. Pallin," *Argus*, November–December 1996, at 10; Edward Felsenthal, "Medical Patents Trigger Debate Among Doctors," *Wall St. J.*, August 11, 1994, at B1; H. Dunbar Hoskins, Jr., Letter to the Editor, "Doctors Group Opposes Medical Method Patents," *Wall St. J.*, September 6, 1994, at A13; John S. Jarstad, Letter to the Editor, "Shared Guilt," *Ocular Surgery News*, December 1, 1994, at 3; James R. Longacre, "Pallin Action No Indication of Method Patent Avalanche," *Ocular Surgery News*, December 1, 1994, at 4; Brian McCormick, "Just Reward or Just Plain Wrong," at 3; Mike S. McFarland, Letter to the Editor, "McFarland Responds," *Ocular Surgery News*, September 15, 1994, at 3; Rochelle Nataloni, "AAO's Patent Position Made Public in the National Press," *Ocular Surgery News*, December 1, 1994, at 1; Samuel L. Pallin, Letter to the Editor, "An Unethical Objection to my Surgical Patent," *Wall St. J.*, October 24, 1994, at A15; Samuel L. Pallin, Letter to the Editor, "Incision Reference," *Ocular Surgery News*, September 15, 1994, at 3; Samuel L. Pallin, Letter to the Editor, "Pallin Responds," *Ocular Surgery News*, November 15, 1994, at 4; Jack A. Singer, Letter to the Editor, "Patent Suit," *Ocular Surgery News*, November 15, 1994, at 4.

[78] Herve M. Byron, "Is This Déjà Vu?," *Ocular Surgery News*, June 1, 1994, at 13.

Apparently medical organizations were not as blind to the procedure patent issue as Byron had thought. Only two weeks later, the AMA passed a resolution, sponsored by the AAO, to "vigorously condemn the patenting of medical and surgical procedures and work with Congress to outlaw this practice."[79] In 1995, an AMA report on medical procedure patenting concluded that it is unethical for physicians to "seek, secure or enforce patents on medical procedures."[80]

The AAO's executive vice president, H. Dunbar Hoskins, spearheaded efforts to lobby Congress against medical procedure patents.[81] The Medical Procedure Patent Coalition, which eventually included the AMA, the American College of Surgeons, and the Association of American Medical Colleges, along with the ophthalmology associations and others, sought legislation that would render medical procedures and diagnostic methods unpatentable. Eventually, after several bills were introduced and debated, the lobbying efforts resulted in the enactment of 35 U.S.C. § 287(c) in 1996. Senator Frist, himself a physician, introduced the final version of the bill.[82]

In § 287(c), the physicians got some, but not all, of what they had wanted, which was to exclude medical procedures from patentable subject matter. The proposed ban on medical procedure patents was opposed by the biopharmaceutical industry and by the USPTO. The provision that eventually emerged reflects a compromise. Rather than eliminating medical procedure patents, § 287(c) eliminates *remedies, including injunctive relief*, against *medical practitioners and health care entities only* for infringement of pure procedure patents. By eliminating remedies against physicians, the legislation made it pointless to sue them directly for infringing pure medical procedure patents. However, § 287(c) preserved the value of lawsuits against third parties for inducing or contributing to physician infringement, by allowing the USPTO to continue issuing medical procedure patents and subjecting medical practitioners to technical liability for infringing them. Moreover, the § 287(c) remedy exemption does not apply to all medical procedures. Many

[79] American Medical Association, "Resolutions," *Proc. Am. Med. Ass'n Annual Meeting* 388, 390 (1994), available at www.ama-assn.org/ama/pub/about-ama/our-history/ama-historical-archives/the-digital-collection-historical-ama-documents.page.

[80] American Medical Association, "Reports of Council on Ethical and Judicial Affairs," *Proc. Am. Med. Ass'n Annual Meeting* 200 (1995), available at www.ama-assn.org/ama/pub/about-ama/our-history/ama-historical-archives/the-digital-collection-historical-ama-documents.page.

[81] Editorial, "What the Academy Is Doing to Oppose Method Patents ... and What You Can Do," *Argus*, July 1994, at 14.

[82] Pub. L. No. 104-208, § 616, 110 Stat. 3009-67 (codified as amended at 35 U.S.C. § 287(c)).

claims to medical procedures involving patented devices or drugs fall outside of its scope, as do biotechnology patents.

Despite its limitations, the legislation's passage was widely (though sometimes not entirely accurately) celebrated in the medical press.[83] Singer responded to the bill's passage by stating that "this may be the most important contribution to healthcare that I make during my career."[84]

Viewing the physician community's opposition to medical procedure patents through a user innovation lens

No doubt a number of factors have contributed to the changing relationship between physicians and patents. Commentators often attribute the softening of the profession's absolute anti-patent stance to a spiral of increasing healthcare commercialization and decreasing medical professionalism over time.[85] The *Pallin v. Singer* story does not fit into that picture. During the heyday of enthusiasm for the patent system's potential for medical innovation generally, and at a time when the patentability of methods was otherwise expanding, the physician community resoundingly rejected medical procedure patenting. Physicians took this stand despite their support for physician patenting of medical devices. The lens of "user innovation" suggests a possible explanation of the line the physician community has drawn between procedure and device patenting.

Physicians and other medical caregivers are the primary users of medical procedures and also are likely to be the primary innovators. Because they are also users, physician innovators benefit directly from the norm of sharing medical procedure inventions: it gives them access to the collective inventive output of the community for use in treating their patients. The sharing norm also allows physician innovators to build upon and improve one another's innovations. They have strong common interests in effective patient care, which further motivate the community norms of disclosure and sharing. Of course, physicians, like many other types of

[83] See, e.g., Julie Rovner, "Congress Moves to Restrict Medical-Procedure Patents," 348 *Lancet* 1025 (1996); "Legislative Success in '96," *Argus*, November–December 1996, at 30; Greg Borzo, "Royalty Relief: Procedure Patents Not Enforceable," *Am. Med. News*, October 21, 1996, at 3; Chet Scerra, "Medical Patent Bill Gives Doctors New Protections," *Ophthalmology Times*, January 15, 1997, at 28, 30.

[84] *Ibid.*

[85] See, e.g., Jane Applegate, "Surgery: The Mother of Invention," *L.A. Times*, April 5, 1991, at 3; Arnold S. Relman, "Medical Professionalism in a Commercialized Health Care Market," 75 *Clev. Clinic J. Med.* S33 (2008).

user innovators, also compete with one another to some extent and seek rewards for their inventive efforts. This interplay between the drive for credit and the drive for access likely explains why user innovator communities so often eschew the exclusivity and inflexibility of legally defined intellectual property rights in favor of tailored reputation rewards and sharing norms.[86]

The physician community relies on an internally governed system of publication credit and other reputational mechanisms for allocating rewards for procedure inventions and thus sees medical procedure patents as unnecessary, cumbersome, and threatening to the sharing norm. Formal IP rights can threaten such a norms-based governance regime. Exclusive IP rights may allow community members to defect from the community's reward system by insisting on rewards that are excessive in relation to the credit the community has allocated. If the number of such defections begins to rise, these internal governance mechanisms may be destabilized.[87] User innovator community norms against patenting help to stabilize the reputation-based reward system and associated sharing norms. Of course, doing away entirely with the patent rights that provide the tools for defection is an even more effective stabilization mechanism. Physician opposition to medical procedure patents thus makes sense as an attempt to protect the medical community's norms-based innovation system.

Medical device innovation is different. Modern medical device innovation generally requires extensive collaboration with commercial firms. Device development often requires expertise in non-medical fields, such as electrical engineering and materials science, and an understanding of manufacturing processes. Device commercialization demands expertise regarding the regulatory approval process. Internal community norms cannot effectively allocate rewards when physician innovators must find their collaborators on the other side of the boundary between industry and the physician community. For medical device inventions, patents provide a shared currency for allocating rewards across community boundaries, while contracts and licenses, rather than norms, govern collaborative relationships.

The *Pallin v. Singer* story can be read against this user innovator community backdrop. The physician community viewed Pallin as a

[86] For further discussion of this point, see Katherine J. Strandburg, "Intellectual Property at the Boundary" in *Festschrift for Eric von Hippel*, Karim Lakhani and Dietmar Harhoff, eds., Ch. 12 (forthcoming 2013) available at http://ssrn.com/abstract=2323986.

[87] *Ibid.* See also Jonathan Barnett, "The Illusion of the Commons," 25 *Berkeley Tech. L. J.* 1751 (2010).

defector from the anti-patenting norm. Pallin, on the other hand, claimed that he resorted to patent enforcement because the community's reward system failed to give him enough credit for his contributions. Whether or not Pallin was justified in his view, the story highlights the fact that all systems of allocating rewards for invention are imperfect. Reputation systems can turn into old boys' networks that are difficult for outsiders without the right contacts and pedigrees to penetrate. Patent systems impose deadweight loss, while overburdened patent examiners cannot compete with the domain-specific expertise reflected in allocations of credit by expert communities. From society's perspective, whether user innovator community norms are desirable replacements for intellectual property in particular arenas depends on factors such as the way in which community membership is determined, the Patent Office's level of expertise, the relative transaction costs of the IP- and norms-based systems, and the importance of inventive contributions by outsiders to the community.

The aftermath

Since its passage, § 287(c) has been invoked only rarely. It has been the subject of only one published opinion, issued in 2008.[88] The provision's dormant status is puzzling in light of the many statutory interpretation issues that would seem to tempt patentees to test the provision's boundaries. Perhaps this situation reflects the law's effectiveness at deterring suits against physicians for infringing medical procedure patents. Or perhaps the main effect of the *Pallin v. Singer* episode was to clarify and reaffirm the norm against medical procedure patenting. That norm, rather than the technicalities of § 287(c)'s language, sets the boundary of acceptable physician behavior.

While the scope of § 287(c)'s exemption for suits against physicians has not been tested, the issue of medical procedure patenting has come to the fore once again in cases, such as *Mayo v. Prometheus*,[89] involving secondary liability premised on physician infringement of medical diagnostic method claims. The patentees in these cases have sued the laboratories that measure metabolite blood levels, sequence and interpret DNA samples, and so forth. Physicians have argued, and the Supreme Court

[88] *Emtel, Inc. v. Lipidlabs, Inc.*, 583 F. Supp. 2d 811 (S.D. Tex. 2008).
[89] *Mayo Collaborative Servs. v. Prometheus Labs, Inc.*, 132 S. Ct. 1289 (2012) (invalidating diagnostic procedure claims as drawn to unpatentable natural phenomena in suit against laboratory for inducing physician infringement).

has agreed, that these patents cover unpatentable subject matter.[90] Many of their arguments about the dangers such patents pose to the medical community are similar to those made by physicians during the *Pallin v. Singer* controversy. As both medical science and medical practice continue to evolve, the boundary between the realm of community-based user innovation norms and the patent system will no doubt continue to be contested. In medical innovation, intellectual property truly does live "at the edge."

[90] See, e.g., *Mayo Collaborative Servs. v. Prometheus Labs., Inc.*, 132 S. Ct. 1289, 1304–05 (2012) (quoting amicus brief of numerous medical associations opposing patentability of certain medical diagnostic procedures); Brief of Amici Curiae American Medical Association et al. in Support of Petitioners, *Ass'n for Molecular Pathology v. Myriad Genetics, Inc.*, No. 12-398 (U.S. S. Ct. 2013) (opposing patents on human genes and genetic tests); Brief of American Medical Association et al. in Support of Petitioner, *Lab. Corp. v. Metabolite Labs., Inc.*, No. 04-607 (U.S. S. Ct. 2004) (opposing patentability of certain medical diagnostic procedures); Opinion 9.095, Code of Medical Ethics of the AMA (1996, 2008), available at www.ama-assn.org/ama/pub/physician-resources/medical-ethics/code-medical-ethics/opinion9095.page (last visited February 21, 2013) ("The use of patents, trade secrets, confidentiality agreements, or other means to limit the availability of medical procedures places significant limitation on the dissemination of medical knowledge, and is therefore unethical."). Note that this author represented the amici medical associations in *Mayo v. Prometheus*.

16 Physicians as user innovators

*Stefan Bechtold**

Introduction

Innovation law paints with a broad brush. Property rights are granted under patent and copyright law in order to encourage innovation. Generally speaking, these rights do not distinguish between different technologies and areas of application. While there is an ongoing debate on where the "edge" in intellectual property law lies – that is, whether it should become more tailored to specific industries, and whether courts have, in fact, already assumed this task[1] – statutory differentiations for different technologies are still relatively rare.

One of these rare exceptions concerns medical treatment methods. The patent systems in Europe, the US and many other countries either exempt medical treatment methods from patentability or shield physicians from the enforcement of such patents. While various policy reasons for such exceptions can be traced back decades and even centuries, today the exceptions are usually justified on ethical and moral grounds.

In her chapter in this volume (Chapter 15), Katherine Strandburg describes the evolution of the medical treatment exception in the US and analyzes it through the lens of user innovation scholarship. The second section of this companion chapter will point out similarities and differences in the evolution of the medical treatment exception in Europe. The third section will complement Katherine Strandburg's historical account by pointing to some empirical evidence of medical progress in user innovation communities and by considering how well

* The author would like to thank Rochelle Dreyfuss for excellent comments, as well as Linus Hug and Rudolf Hug for very helpful research assistance in identifying literature and case law for this chapter.

[1] *See* Dan L. Burk & Mark A. Lemley, "Policy Levers in Patent Law," 89 *Va. L. Rev.* 1575 (2003); Michael W. Carroll, "One for All: The Problem of Uniformity Cost in Intellectual Property Law," 55 *Am. U. L. Rev.* 845 (2006); Geertrui van Overwalle, "Policy Levers Tailoring Patent Law to Biotechnology: Comparing U.S. and European Approaches," 1 *U. C. Irvine L. Rev.* 435 (2011).

the European experience supports an understanding of physicians as user innovators. This section will also describe the implications of this framing for patent policy. The final section will provide some concluding thoughts.

Evolution of medical treatment exceptions in Europe

In 1569, a French Huguenot family of surgeons called Chamberlen emigrated from Paris to England to escape religious persecution. At that time, many women and babies died in childbirth. Members of the Chamberlen family invented the obstetric forceps, which would revolutionize childbirth and significantly reduce the number of infant deaths. For a long time, the Chamberlen family made great efforts to keep their invention secret. In fact, the surgeon would carry the forceps in a lined box, would only use them once everyone had left the room and the mother was blindfolded, and would make sinister noises as the "secret" was applied. The Chamberlen family succeeded in keeping their invention secret within the boundaries of their family for more than one hundred years, with alternative sets of forceps becoming widely used only in the early eighteenth century and fully described only in 1733.[2]

As this example demonstrates, the tension between medical progress, sharing norms within the medical community, private interests, and public policy dates back several centuries in Europe. It was only in the nineteenth and twentieth centuries, however, that this tension manifested itself in the patent systems of European countries. In the United Kingdom, physicians had developed informal social norms against patenting medical technologies in the late nineteenth and early twentieth centuries.[3] In 1914, the Solicitor General held that medical treatment methods were not patentable, because they lay outside the sphere of economic activity, resulted in no "vendible product,"[4] and did not amount to a "manner of manufacture."[5] Later court decisions followed

[2] James H. Aveling, *The Chamberlens and the Midwifery Forceps* 217–18 (J. & A. Churchill, London, 1882); Peter M. Dunn, "The Chamberlen Family (1560–1728) and Obstetric Forceps," 81 *Arch. Disease in Childhood: Fetal & Neonatal Ed.* F232 (1999); Maurice Adrian, *Les Chamberlen* 32–40 (Ph.D. thesis, Faculté de Médecine de Paris, 1923); M. Dumont, "Histoire et Petite Histoire du Forceps," 13 *J. de Gynécologie Obstétrique & Biologie de la Reproduction* 743, 745–47 (1984).

[3] Stamatia T. Piper, *The Emergence of a Medical Exception from Patentability in the 20th Century* 122–84 (D.Phil thesis, University of Oxford, 2008).

[4] In the Matter of C. & W's Application for a Patent, (1914) 31 R.P.C. 235 (S-G); *see also* Re Calmic Engineering Co.'s App., [1973] R.P.C. 684.

[5] Eddy Ventose, *Medical Patent Law: The Challenges of Medical Treatment* 289, 297–98 (Edward Elgar, Cheltenham, 2011).

this reasoning and ruled that medical treatment methods were not patentable due to a lack of industrial applicability. Between the two world wars, a broad medical exception was considered, but never adopted.[6] Thereafter, the judicially created exemption of medical treatment methods from patentability endured, although on different grounds. After the High Court of Australia had rejected the "manner of manufacture" test in 1959,[7] English courts gradually dropped justifications based on a lack of industrial applicability and adopted different rationales for medical treatment exceptions, in the form of public health and ethical concerns.[8]

In the very early twentieth century, the German Imperial Patent Office granted several patents on medical treatment methods.[9] From 1904, however, the Office increasingly refused to grant such patents on industrial applicability grounds.[10] As in the United Kingdom, over the subsequent decades, the discussion on exceptions for medical treatment methods shifted from questions of industrial applicability to ethical and moral concerns. In an important decision in 1967, the German Federal Court of Justice held that a cosmetic-surgical method was not patentable, citing both rationales. Among other arguments, the court stated that it was commonly understood that physicians should not carry out their profession in a profit-maximizing manner and that they had special obligations toward public health and society.[11] The patent systems of other European countries developed in a similar fashion. In countries such as Belgium, France, and Italy, the patent requirement of industrial applicability was likewise the largest obstacle to medical treatment patents.[12]

While the patent systems of many European countries had long exempted medical treatment methods from patentability in one way or another, the opening of negotiations for the European Patent Convention (EPC) brought the issue to the fore in Europe. Because similar

[6] Piper, *supra* note 3, at 185–243.
[7] National Research Development Corporation (NRDC) v. Commissioner of Patents, (1959) 102 C.L.R. 252 (Austl.).
[8] Ventose, *supra* note 5, at 304, 330.
[9] *See* Reiner Moufang, "Methods of Medical Treatment under Patent Law," 24 *Intern. Rev. Ind. Prop. & Copyright L.* 18, 22 note 13 (1993) (citing, e.g., German patent No. 150666 (1903) for a method of removing deeper stitches from wounds or German patent No. 150699 (1903) for treating curvature of the human spine).
[10] Decision of the Board of Appeal II of the Imperial Patent Office of December 30, 1904, 1905 Bl. f. PMZ 4 – *Badewasser*; *see* Matthias A. Bosch, *Medizinisch-technische Verfahren und Vorrichtungen im deutschen, europäischen und amerikanischen Patentrecht* 45–48 (1999); Moufang, *supra* note 9, at 22.
[11] Bundesgerichtshof, BGHZ 48, 313 – *Glatzenoperation*. For a detailed analysis of medical treatment methods under German patent law, *see* Bosch, *supra* note 10.
[12] Moufang, *supra* note 9, at 26–27.

exceptions were recognized in various European patent systems, there was little policy debate on whether medical treatment methods should generally receive special status in patent law during the drafting of the EPC in the late 1960s and early 1970s.[13] Rather, discussions focused on the specific wording of the exception. Exceptions concerning therapeutic and diagnostic methods were introduced in drafts starting in 1964 and 1965,[14] but it took four more years for the draft exception to be extended to surgical methods.[15] In the end, the drafters decided to adopt a rather broad exception and to leave the definition of its boundaries to the courts.[16] Consistent with Article 27.3(a) of the Agreement on Trade-Related Aspects of Intellectual Property Rights (TRIPS Agreement), Article 53(c) EPC 2000[17] reads:

> European patents shall not be granted in respect of . . . methods for treatment of the human or animal body by surgery or therapy and diagnostic methods practised on the human or animal body; this provision shall not apply to products, in particular substances or compositions, for use in any of these methods.

As Katherine Strandburg recounts, medical treatment methods are patentable in the US. However, § 287 (c) of the Patent Act provides immunity against enforcement of such patent claims for physicians and "related health care entities." This immunity applies to "medical or surgical procedure(s) on a body";[18] it is debatable to what extent it applies to diagnostic methods as well. The EPC thus differs from the US approach in at least two important ways.[19] First, the EPC does not only limit enforcement of medical treatment patents against physicians; it excludes such methods from patentability altogether. Second, this exclusion covers not only therapeutic and surgical, but certain diagnostic methods as well. As a result, the EPC exception is significantly broader in scope and depth than 35 U.S.C. § 287 (c).

[13] Ventose, *supra* note 5, at 9.

[14] European Patent Office, Enl. Bd. App., Medi-Physics/Treatment by surgery (G 1/07), [2010] E.P.O.R. 25, 225, 227; Ventose, *supra* note 5, at 187; Moufang, *supra* note 9, at 28.

[15] On the historical development of the European Patent Convention, *see* Ventose, *supra* note 5, at 119; Moufang, *supra* note 9, at 28–31.

[16] Ventose, *supra* note 5, at 73–75.

[17] In the EPC 1973, the relevant provision was Article 52(4) EPC 1973. It had the same effect as Article 53(c) EPC 2000.

[18] 35 U.S.C. § 287(c)(2)(A).

[19] For a comparison between medical treatment exceptions in US and European patent law, *see* Todd Martin, "Patentability of Methods of Medical Treatment: A Comparative Study," 82 *J. Pat. & Trademark Off. Soc'y* 381 (2000); Anne S. Wolfrum, *Patentschutz für medizinische Verfahrenserfindungen im Europäischen Patentsystem und im US-Recht* (Mohr Siebeck, Tübingen, 2008). The European exception also applies to medical treatment on the animal body. This dimension will not be explored in this chapter.

As the EPC exception is broader than its US counterpart, it is not surprising that a considerable amount of the case law of the Boards of Appeal of the European Patent Office[20] has focused on defining the boundaries of the exception. Concerning therapeutic methods, the exception includes both curative and prophylactic treatments;[21] cosmetic methods are not covered even if they have some accidental therapeutic effect.[22] As the exception does not apply to "products, in particular substances or compositions, for use in any of these methods," the combination of a device with a method raises complex legal problems.[23] With respect to diagnostic methods, the Enlarged Board of Appeal of the European Patent Office has held that they fall under the exception only if they include all the steps necessary for diagnosis and if these steps are practiced directly on the human body.[24]

Various policy rationales have been used to justify the broad exception for medical treatment methods under the EPC. Similar to the evolving debate in individual European countries, legislators and courts argued for a long time, under the EPC 1973, that medical treatment methods were not subject to industrial application and therefore not patentable. During the reform of the EPC in 2000, it was made clear that the alleged lack of industrial applicability was a fiction[25] and that "methods of treatment and diagnostic methods are excluded from patentability in the interests of public health."[26]

[20] On the appeal procedure before the European Patent Office, *see* Andrea Veronese, "Appeal Procedure before the European Patent Office," in *Patent Law and Theory: A Handbook of Contemporary Research* 227 (Toshiko Takenaka ed., Edward Elgar, Cheltenham, 2008). Empirical data on the opposition procedure is provided by Dietmar Harhoff & Markus Reitzig, "Determinants of Opposition Against EPO Patent Grants: The Case of Biotechnology and Pharmaceuticals," 22 *Intern. J. Indus. Organ.* 443 (2004).

[21] European Patent Office, Tech. Bd. App., Duphar/Pigs II (T 19/86), [1988] E.P.O.R. 10, 13; ICI/Cleaning plague (T 290/86), [1991] E.P.O.R. 157, 162; General Hospital/ Contraceptive method (T 820/92), [1995] E.P.O.R. 446, 451.

[22] Ventose, *supra* note 5, at 89–96.

[23] On the one hand, e.g., a transcutaneous electrical nerve stimulation (TENS) apparatus with an anaesthetic agent can be patented; *see* European Patent Office, Tech. Bd. App., Stimtech/Transcutaneous electrical nerve stimulation (T 94/83), [1979–85] E.P.O.R. C811. On the other hand, problems still arise in case of hybrid claims such as the use of implantable devices to obtain therapeutic effects: *see* Ventose, *supra* note 5, at 80–88.

[24] European Patent Office, Enl. Bd. App., Cygnus/Diagnostic methods (G 1/04), [2006] E.P.O.R. 15, 161. For a detailed analysis of medical treatment methods under European patent law, *see* Ventose, *supra* note 5; Wolfrum, *supra* note 19.

[25] *See*, e.g., European Patent Office, Enl. Bd. App., Cygnus/Diagnostic methods (G 1/04), [2006] E.P.O.R. 15, 161, 171.

[26] European Patent Convention, Basic Proposal for the Revision of the European Patent Convention, Document MR/2/00, at 45 (2000); *see also* European Patent Office, Enl. Bd. App., Medi-Physics/Treatment by surgery (G 1/07), [2010] E.P.O.R. 25, 225, 231–32.

Since then, courts have adopted ethical, moral and public health considerations to justify the EPC medical treatment methods exception. They have held, for example, that patent law should not interfere with the saving of human life or the alleviation of human suffering.[27] And they have insisted that physicians should be free to choose the best medical treatment for a patient without being prevented by exclusive patent rights.[28] This argument relates to a "right to health," the notion of which can be observed in various European countries, which includes a right of access to a decent minimum of health care[29] and which is largely unrecognized in US law.[30]

It is now widely accepted that the exception of Article 53(c) EPC is primarily driven by ethical, moral and public health concerns.[31] Still, the exception has not been accepted without criticism. The Enlarged Board of Appeal of the European Patent Office has expressed some sympathy for a more limited exception similar to 35 U.S.C. § 287 (c). Under such an exception, medical treatment methods would be patentable in Europe, but country-level rules on patent infringement would exempt

[27] Wellcome Foundation Ltd v. Plantex, [1979] RPC 514, 540 (Eng.); European Patent Office, Enl. Bd. App., Medi-Physics/Treatment by surgery (G 1/07), [2010] E.P.O.R. 25, 225, 232.

[28] European Patent Office, Tech. Bd. App., University of Manitoba/Lung ventilator device (T 0592/98), at ¶ 2 (2001), www.epo.org/law-practice/case-law-appeals/advanced-search.html; Enl. Bd. App., Cygnus/Diagnostic methods (G 1/04), [2006] E.P.O.R. 15, 161, 171; Enl. Bd. App., Medi-Physics/Treatment by surgery (G 1/07), [2010] E.P.O.R. 25, 225, 227; Tech. Bd. App., Wellcome/Pigs 1 (T 116/85), [1988] E.P.O.R. 1, 5; *see also* Bristol-Myers Squibb Co. v. Baker Norton Pharmaceuticals Inc., [1999] R.P.C. 253, 274 (Eng.).

[29] Ventose, *supra* note 5, at 47–50; Christopher A. Sims, "But Economics Is Not an Experimental Science," 24 *J. Econ. Persp.* 59, 49 (2010); *see also* American Medical Association, Council on Ethical and Judicial Affairs, "Ethical Issues in the Patenting of Medical Procedures," 53 *Food & Drug L .J.* 341, 344–45 (1998).

[30] Alicia Ely Yamin, "The Right to Health under International Law and its Relevance to the United States," 95 *Am. J. Pub. Health* 1156 (2005); Richard A. Epstein, *Mortal Peril: Our Inalienable Right to Health Care?* (Addison-Wesley, Cambridge, Mass., 1997); Cass R. Sunstein, "Why Does the American Constitution Lack Social and Economic Guaranties?," in *American Exceptionalism and Human Rights* (Michael Ignatieff ed., Princeton University Press, Princeton, NJ, 2005); David S. Law & Mila Versteeg, "The Declining Influence of the United States Constitution," 87 *N.Y.U. L. Rev.* 762, 774–75, 806 (2012); Eleanor D. Kinney & Brian A. Clark, "Provisions for Health and Health Care in the Constitutions of the Countries of the World," 37 *Cornell Int'l L. J.* 285 (2004); Puneet K. Sandhu, "A Legal Right to Health Care: What Can the United States Learn from Foreign Models of Health Rights Jurisprudence?," 95 *Cal. L. Rev.* 1151 (2007); Jennifer P. Ruger, "Toward a Theory of a Right to Health: Capability and Incompletely Theorized Agreements," 18 *Yale J. L. & Humanities* 273 (2006).

[31] European Patent Office, Enl. Bd. App., Medi-Physics/Treatment by surgery (G 1/07), [2010] E.P.O.R. 25, 225, 232.

physicians from liability.[32] Some European courts have gone even further and questioned whether there should be any exception for medical treatment methods at all.[33]

Physicians as user innovators

While ethical concerns are widely used on both sides of the Atlantic to justify exceptions for medical treatment methods in patent law, Katherine Strandburg points to a complementary justification which has received less attention: Physicians may be user innovators, and medical treatment exceptions may preserve some space for user innovation.[34] This section will complement Katherine Strandburg's analysis by pointing to some empirical evidence, by analyzing to what extent the European experience supports her framing of physicians as user innovators, and by describing the implications this has for patent policy.

Social norms in the medical profession

User innovation communities rarely rely on formal intellectual property protection. Rather, they often establish informal norms to provide rewards and punish free riders. The physicians' community is one which is heavily shaped by social norms. The medical profession adheres to a code of ethics which includes a strong sharing norm. The Hippocratic Oath includes such a norm,[35] and the Code of Medical

[32] *Ibid.* at 225, 230; European Patent Office, Enl. Bd. App., Cygnus/Diagnostic methods (G 1/04), [2006] E.P.O.R. 15, 161, 173.

[33] In a case involving a Swiss-type claim on specific dosage instructions for a cancer medication, then Judge Jacobs wrote: "The thinking behind the exception is not particularly rational: if one accepts that a patent monopoly is a fair price to pay for the extra research incentive, then there is no reason to suppose that that would not apply also to methods of treatment," Bristol-Myers Squibb Co. v. Baker Norton Pharmaceuticals Inc., [1999] R.P.C. 253, 274 (Eng.); similarly, Judge Whitford held in Schering A.G.'s Application: "Although it is difficult to see any logical justification for the practice in relation to processes for medical treatment, if the object of the system is in truth to give hope of a reward to people whose research and industry results in valuable products or processes . . . " [1971] 1 W.L.R. 1715, 1720 (Eng.).

[34] On the general concept of user innovation, *see* Eric von Hippel, *Democratizing Innovation* (MIT Press, Cambridge, Mass., 2005).

[35] Stavros Antoniou et al., "Reflections of the Hippocratic Oath in Modern Medicine," 34 *World J. Surgery* 3075, 3076 (2010) (citing the original Hippocratic Oath as follows: "To hold him who has taught me this art as equal to my parents . . . and to . . . teach [his offspring] this art – if they desire to learn it – without fee and covenant; to give a share of precepts and oral instruction and all the other learning to my sons and to the sons of him who has instructed me and to pupils who have signed the covenant and have taken an oath according to the medical law, but no one else"); Steven Miles, *The Hippocratic Oath and the Ethics of Medicine* 8 (Oxford University Press, New York, 2005).

Ethics of the American Medical Association reads: "A physician shall ... make relevant information available to patients, colleagues, and the public, obtain consultation, and use the talents of other health professionals when indicated."[36] The Council on Ethical and Judicial Affairs of that association has pointed out that, "[s]ince the time of Hippocrates, physicians have relied on the open exchange of information without the expectation of financial reward for advancing medical science"[37] and has condemned medical treatment patents as unethical.[38] The World Medical Association has stated that "physicians have an ethical responsibility to make relevant scientific information available to colleagues and the public, when possible" and considers the patenting of medical procedures "unethical and contrary to the values of the medical profession."[39]

While the sharing norm has come under increasing attack in recent years in many fields of medical and biotechnological research,[40] it is still relatively intact among physicians.[41] In addition, medical professionals, like research scientists,[42] have created effective reward structures for physicians that do not rely on patent protection and may make it superfluous or even counterproductive. New medical treatment methods are published in peer-reviewed journals, which can provide substantial incentives: The reputation and career of a physician can depend on publications.[43] University tenure and research grants provide further incentives.[44]

[36] American Medical Association, Principles of Medical Ethics, Section V (2001), www.ama-assn.org/ama/pub/physician-resources/medical-ethics/code-medical-ethics/principles-medical-ethics.page; *see also* American Medical Association, Code of Medical Ethics, Opinion 9.08 (1994), www.ama-assn.org/ama/pub/physician-resources/medical-ethics/code-medical-ethics/opinion908.page: "Physicians have an obligation to share their knowledge and skills and to report the results of clinical and laboratory research ... The intentional withholding of new medical knowledge, skills, and techniques from colleagues for reasons of personal gain is detrimental to the medical profession and to society and is to be condemned"; *see also* American Medical Association, *supra* note 29.

[37] American Medical Association, *supra* note 29, at 343. [38] *Ibid.* at 351.

[39] World Medical Association, Statement on Patenting Medical Procedures (2009), www.wma.net/en/30publications/10policies/m30/index.html.

[40] *See only* Rebecca S. Eisenberg, "Proprietary Rights and the Norms of Science in Biotechnology Research," 97 *Yale L. J.* 177 (1987).

[41] Ventose, *supra* note 5, at 63; Alexandra Sims, "The Case Against Patenting Methods of Medical Treatment," 29 *Eur. Intell. Prop. Rev.* 43, 45 (2007).

[42] Eisenberg, *supra* note 40.

[43] American Medical Association, *supra* note 29, at 349; World Medical Association, *supra* note 39; Ventose, *supra* note 5, at 64–65.

[44] Ventose, *supra* note 5, at 66.

Empirical evidence

While the importance of social norms in the medical profession may indicate that physicians act as user innovators, there is some empirical evidence, over and above Katherine Strandburg's historical analysis, that supports this hypothesis. The most interesting evidence comes from management science literature focusing on medical progress and the health sector.

Recent research in management science has raised some doubts about the general perception of how medicine progresses. The orthodox view has been that progress in medicine is achieved by scientific research that increases our understanding of how the body works. Under this paradigm, good research policy involves investing in basic research, funding biomedical and healthcare research, and providing strong intellectual property rights as incentive mechanisms.[45] However, this policy may underestimate the extent to which medical progress is driven by learning in medical practice.[46]

In an interview-based case study on a novel treatment for heart failure (using a "Left Ventricular Assist Device" or LVAD),[47] Piera Morlacchi and Richard Nelson have demonstrated that learning within and across organizations was at least as important for the development of this novel method as the increased scientific understanding of heart failure.[48] The *development process* in the field was driven by ad hoc collaboration among surgeons, engineers, and researchers from related disciplines. Many of the surgeons had known each other since medical school. Informal cooperation led to close personal relationships. A limited number of

[45] On this view, *see Measuring the Gains from Medical Research: An Economic Approach* (Kevin M. Murphy & Robert E. Topel eds., University of Chicago Press, 2003).

[46] Piera Morlacchi & Richard R. Nelson, "How Medical Practice Evolves: Learning to Treat Failing Hearts with an Implantable Device," 40 *Res. Pol'y* 511 (2011); Richard R. Nelson et al., "How Medical Know-How Progresses," 40 *Res. Pol'y* 1339 (2011); Annetine Gelijns & Nathan Rosenberg, "The Dynamics of Technological Change in Medicine," 13 *Health Aff.* 28, 30–31 (1994); Annetine C. Gelijns & Nathan Rosenberg, "From the Scalpel to the Scope: Endoscopic Innovations in Gastroenterology, Gynecology, and Surgery," in *Sources of Medical Technology: Universities and Industry* 67 (Nathan Rosenberg et al. eds., National Academies Press, Washington DC, 1995).

[47] An LVAD is a mechanical circulatory device that partially or completely takes over the functions of a failing heart. While LVADs have improved significantly with respect to survival rates and quality of life, they are still not widely adopted for various medical reasons.

[48] Morlacchi & Nelson, *supra* note 46, note on page 521 that "[t]he efforts that led to today's LVADs were not induced by any advance in understanding of heart disease"; *see also* Nelson et al., *supra* note 46, at 1340: "There are many cases where ability to treat a disease has increased dramatically, without any dramatic improvement in basic scientific understanding of that disease."

leading cardiac centers served as hubs of this informal network. *Collective and cumulative learning* through the actual use of the innovation, in particular by physicians and medical teams, was of paramount importance for the cumulative innovation process.[49] *Information transmission* within the community was achieved at meetings during medical conferences and in committees, laboratories, and federal agencies. It was common practice to openly discuss new ideas and methods at such meetings. Information on new surgical techniques and devices spread across the community by word of mouth. An *open environment* for the exchange of ideas enabled the kind of interactions that were critical for this community. The *social norms* of the surgeon community were shaped and transmitted at the various meetings mentioned.[50] *Incentives* were provided by publication in peer-reviewed journals and by peer recognition. Supported and sometimes initiated by public funding agencies, novel devices were built in *collaboration* between academic medical centers and research groups in commercial laboratories or companies.[51] *Feedback loops* between device users as well as device designers and manufacturers ensured that the latter would learn from the former about strong and weak aspects of the devices as well as urgent and desirable design changes.[52]

In another case study, this one on the development of the intraocular lens which is now a standard treatment for cataract, Stan Metcalfe, Andrew James, and Andrea Mina pointed out that progress in cataract surgery is not well grounded in science, but was advanced by the experience of practitioners.[53] The development and success of this surgical method was the result of a limited number of so-called "lead users" experimenting with various versions of the method and communicating with each other in scientific literature, at conferences, and through personal visits.[54] This surgical innovation depended heavily on the communication of tacit knowledge across informal networks. Such communication led to shared understanding, the development of standards, and accepted norms of practice.[55]

[49] On collective and organizational learning in hospitals, *see also* Gary P. Pisano et al., "Organizational Differences in Rates of Learning: Evidence from the Adoption of Minimally Invasive Cardiac Surgery," 47 *Mgmt. Sci.* 752 (2001).

[50] Morlacchi & Nelson, *supra* note 46, at 516, 521. [51] *Ibid.* at 517.

[52] *Ibid.* at 521; Nelson et al., *supra* note 46, at 1342; Gelijns & Rosenberg, *supra* note 46, at 31.

[53] J. Stan Metcalfe et al., "Emergent Innovation Systems and the Delivery of Clinical Services: The Case of Intra-Ocular Lenses," 34 *Res. Pol'y* 1283, 1287 (2005).

[54] Metcalfe et al., *supra* note 53, at 1288–93; *see also* Gelijns & Rosenberg, *supra* note 46, at 31.

[55] Metcalfe et al., *supra* note 53, at 1289, 1299–1300; *see also* Dan L. Burk, "The Role of Patent Law in Knowledge Codification," 23 *Berkeley Tech. L. J.* 1009, 1015 (2008).

Other similar studies and anecdotal evidence point in the same direction. Feedback from medical practitioners has been essential in the history of treating HIV.[56] Physicians contributed to nearly 20 percent of the 26,000 medical device patents filed in the US between 1990 and 1996, and the advances covered in these patents were more influential than patented medical devices invented without physician involvement.[57] In one study, 57 percent of the off-label drug therapy innovations analyzed were discovered by practicing clinicians independent of pharmaceutical companies or university research.[58] According to a German industry report, the ideas behind 52 percent of all new medical products originate from users of these products.[59]

Care is necessary when generalizing from the results of such studies. Some of them relate to medical devices, some to medical treatment methods, and some to both. In general, there is limited empirical evidence on the relationship between incentives created by the patent system and innovation in medical treatment methods.[60] Still, some tentative observations seem possible. As medical lead users, physicians play an important role in health care innovation.[61] Due to the complexity of the human body and the heterogeneity of the patient population, feedback from adopters to developers is highly important.[62] As a result, "many medical technologies develop as they diffuse, in a dynamic

[56] Monica Merito & Andrea Bonaccorsi, "Co-evolution of Physical and Social Technologies in Clinical Practice: The Case of HIV Treatments," 36 *Res. Pol'y* 1070, 1071 (2007).

[57] Aaron K. Chatterji et al., "Physician–Industry Cooperation in the Medical Device Industry," 27 *Health Aff.* 1532 (2008). The influence of a patent was measured by patent citations and an analysis of patent breadth. The study focuses on the market for medical devices, which are patentable both in the United States and in Europe. *See also* Edward B. Roberts, "Technological Innovation and Medical Devices," in *New Medical Devices: Invention, Development, and Use* 35 (Karen B. Ekelman ed., National Academies Press, Washington DC, 1988).

[58] Harold J. DeMonaco et al., "The Major Role of Clinicians in the Discovery of Off-Label Drug Therapy," 26 *Pharmacotherapy* 323 (2006).

[59] The report by the German Medical Technology Association does not provide a citation for this number, *Bundesverband Medizintechnologie, Branchenbericht Medizintechnologien* 16 (2011), www.bvmed.de/stepone/data/downloads/7c/e4/00/bvmed-annrep1112.pdf.

[60] Ventose, *supra* note 5, at 18–20, cites the patent on the Surrogate Embryo Transfer (SET) (treating infertility in women) as an anecdotal example where patent protection was necessary to secure financing for a costly medical treatment, but acknowledges that no comprehensive empirical research exists; *see also* American Medical Association, *supra* note 29, at 349; Ventose, *supra* note 5, at 445–47.

[61] Jérôme Galbrun & Kyoichi J. Kijima, "A Co-evolutionary Perspective in Medical Technology: Clinical Innovation Systems in Europe and in Japan," 17 *Asian J. Tech. Innov.* 195, 207 (2009); Metcalfe et al., *supra* note 53, at 1297–98.

[62] Annetine C. Gelijns et al., "Capturing the Unexpected Benefits of Medical Research," 339 *New Eng. J. Med.* 693, 694 (1998); Merito & Bonaccorsi, *supra* note 56, at 1072; Metcalfe et al., *supra* note 53, at 1284.

manner."[63] Medical progress is achieved by physicians combining scientific and explicit knowledge with practical experience from working with patients and talking to colleagues.[64] This discussion demonstrates that, in addition to Katherine Strandburg's historical analysis, some (limited) contemporary empirical evidence exists that the physician community is a user innovation community.

Implications for patent policy

If the idea that physicians are user innovators is correct, it has various implications for patent policy. In general, if an innovation community is characterized by strong cumulative and collective learning and has developed institutions to encourage such learning, the interaction between the learning process, the institutions, and the patent regime must be scrutinized carefully, as the patent regime may support, inhibit, or disrupt the learning process.[65] A close connection exists between social norms in a research community, the surrounding intellectual property framework, and the resulting patenting activity of this community.[66] In particular, a linear innovation model which assumes that property rights are necessary to incentivize scientific research and, thereby, medical progress may be too simplistic. Such a model may underestimate the importance of collective learning, feedback loops, and institutional regimes which complement and sometimes even substitute for property rights.

In the context of biotechnology research, Rebecca Eisenberg and Arti Rai have argued that social norms on sharing and collaboration within the scientific community may be threatened by the increasing availability of patent rights on research results and tools.[67] Similarly, changing or repealing medical treatment exceptions in patent law could lead to a breakdown of social norms concerning sharing, learning, and collaboration among physicians.[68] At the same time, an existing

[63] Merito & Bonaccorsi, *supra* note 56, at 1072.

[64] *Ibid.* at 1073; *see also* Jérôme Galbrun & Kyoichi J. Kijima, "Fostering Innovation in Medical Technology with Hierarchy Theory: Narratives on Emergent Clinical Solutions," 27 *Sys. Res. & Beh. Sci.* 523, 533 (2010); Galbrun & Kijima, *supra* note 61.

[65] Morlacchi & Nelson, *supra* note 46, at 522.

[66] Eisenberg, *supra* note 40.

[67] *Ibid.* at 230–31; Arti Rai, "Regulating Scientific Research: Intellectual Property Rights and the Norms of Science," 94 *Nw. U. L. Rev.* 77, 109–11 (1999).

[68] On the general role of expressive law in influencing preferences and affecting equilibrium selection, *see* Robert D. Cooter, "Expressive Law and Economics," 27 *J. Legal Stud.* 585 (1998); Cass R. Sunstein, "On the Expressive Function of Law," 144 *U. Penn. L. Rev.* 2021 (1996); Richard H. McAdams, "The Origin, Development, and Regulation of Norms," 96 *Mich. L. Rev.* 338 (1997); Richard H. McAdams, "A Focal Point Theory of

medical treatment exception may contribute to the stability of the physician innovation community.

Interestingly, the EPC exclusion appears to be well crafted to take account of these observations. The exception is narrow. It mainly covers medical treatment of patients by a physician. Products, substances, and compositions that are used in surgical, therapeutic, or diagnostic methods do not fall under the exception (Article 53(c)(2) EPC). Thereby, products used in medical treatments, genetic therapies and other capital-intensive, high-tech methods are not affected and can often be patented.[69] Instead, the European medical treatment exception focuses primarily on methods whose development is not particularly costly.[70] As a result, inventions that require heavy upfront investment are eligible for patents while inventions to which users are more likely to contribute are not subject to protection.

In addition, the Enlarged Board of Appeal of the European Patent Office often adopts a narrow interpretation of Article 53(c) EPC.[71] In general, the narrow interpretation restricts the scope of the exception to the actual medical treatment of patients by a physician. If physicians do form a user innovation community, the scope of Article 53(c) EPC corresponds rather well to the scope of that community. By restricting the scope of the exception to physicians and by defining the interaction with related methods that fall outside the scope of the exception,[72] the European exception contributes to preserving the insularity of the innovation ecosystem for medical treatment methods. This corresponds with the observation that the number of cases in which individual physicians have attempted to seek patent protection for medical treatment methods is relatively small in Europe.[73]

Expressive Law," 86 *Va. L. Rev.* 1649 (2000). For an explicit analysis in the context of research results and tools, *see* Katherine Strandburg, "Norms and the Sharing of Research Materials and Tactic Knowledge," in *Working within the Boundaries of Intellectual Property: Innovation Policy for the Knowledge Society* 85 (Rochelle C. Dreyfuss et al. eds., Oxford University Press, 2010).

[69] Ventose, *supra* note 5, at 16–17.

[70] *See also* American Medical Association, *supra* note 29, at 349; World Medical Association, *supra* note 39.

[71] *See*, e.g., European Patent Office, Enl. Bd. App., Cygnus/Diagnostic methods (G 1/04), [2006] E.P.O.R. 15, 161, 177.

[72] On hybrid methods, *see supra* note 23.

[73] An analysis of the case law of the Technical Boards of Appeal of the European Patent Office (as available through the search engine www.epo.org/law-practice/case-law-appeals.html and analyzed in Ventose, *supra* note 5) reveals the following patterns. About 220 decisions have dealt with questions of Article 53(c) EPC 2000 or Article 52(4) EPC 1973 in one way or the other. Of the decisions which deal with medical treatment methods on the human body in a substantive matter, twelve decisions involve individuals on either side of the appeal procedure. Four of these decisions are cases in

All this is not to say that patents cannot contribute to the progress of medical treatment methods. As a field becomes more stable, knowledge more codifiable and tacit knowledge less important, the importance of patenting may increase.[74] In fact, the study on the intraocular lens mentioned above highlights the importance of patents on lens design and lens material, as well as on surgical methods and tools.[75] Therefore, the argument is not that medical treatment would not progress under any circumstances in the presence of more elaborate patent protection. Rather, the argument is that a fairly stable system of developing and sharing explicit and tacit knowledge among physicians has emerged; that this community has created the necessary institutions to incentivize innovative behavior; and that the legislators should think twice before interfering with this ecosystem. It is an argument not about how to achieve a Pareto-optimal innovation regime, but about how to preserve a stable innovation regime given the lack of knowledge about what a Pareto-optimal innovation regime would look like. Such argument may not only justify exceptions for medical treatment methods in patent law. It may also justify limiting such exceptions to physicians, as they form the immediate user innovation community, while pharmaceutical or biomedical companies that develop products for use in medical treatments do not.[76]

Conclusion

Initially, the European exceptions for medical treatment methods were justified on the grounds that there was no industrial application for such methods. Over the last few decades, such justifications have been replaced by ethical, moral and public health considerations. The chapter by Katherine Strandburg and this companion chapter have pointed to a complementary justification which has not hitherto been part of the medical treatment debate. Physicians show many features of user innovation communities. Patent law exceptions for medical treatment methods may exist to preserve the innovation ecosystem within such a community and to structure boundary-spanning interactions with other

which a Technical Board of Appeal denied patent protection because of the medical treatment methods exception. A more detailed analysis of the case law is beyond the scope of this chapter.

[74] Metcalfe et al., *supra* note 53, at 1293. On the general relationship between knowledge codification and patent law and the danger that patent incentives may encourage codification rather than invention, *see* Burk, *supra* note 55, at 1020.

[75] Metcalfe et al., *supra* note 53, at 1290, 1293–97.

[76] *See also supra* p. 355.

communities. From a normative perspective, this does not necessarily mean that the current exceptions for medical treatment methods are the optimal solution. Rather, the focus on the user innovation dimension should be understood as an attempt to better understand the dynamic relationship between social norms and innovation regimes that we see at the "edge."

Part IX

Limitations: Patent subject matter and scope

17 *Funk* forward

Ted Sichelman[*]

In 1948, the US Supreme Court decided *Funk Brothers Seed Company v. Kalo Inoculant Company*,[1] a case involving the patent eligibility of a mixture of bacteria used to inoculate leguminous plants (like alfalfa sprouts and string beans). Perhaps the immediate question is why a 1948 case involving sprouts and string beans is relevant in 2013. Indeed, the *Funk Brothers* opinion had lain relatively dormant, with no citations to it in the Supreme Court and a relatively meager thirty-three citations in the lower courts over the next quarter century.[2] However, in 1972, for the first time since *Funk Brothers*, the Supreme Court addressed subject matter eligibility in *Gottschalk v. Benson*,[3] setting off a series of three more eligibility cases in the Court over the next ten years.[4] All cited *Funk Brothers*. Of greatest note in this vein, when the Supreme Court was confronted with the patentability of a genetically modified bacterium in its landmark 1980 case *Diamond v. Chakrabarty*, it turned to *Funk Brothers* to help it set the boundaries between unpatentable "nature's handiwork" and patentable human handiwork. Fast forward to 2013 and *Funk Brothers* is yet again a touchpoint for patent eligibility, featuring prominently in the *Myriad*[5] and *Mayo v. Prometheus*[6] line of opinions,

* I thank Rochelle Dreyfuss, Jane Ginsburg, Justine Pila, and Kathy Strandburg, as well as attendees at the Intellectual Property at the Edge: The Contested Contours of IP workshop at Columbia Law School, for their helpful comments and discussions.

1 *Funk Bros. Seed Co. v. Kalo Inoculant Co.*, 333 U.S. 127 (1948).

2 The number of citations was calculated with Westlaw's Keycite feature.

3 409 U.S. 63, 65, 71–72 (1972)

4 *Parker v. Flook*, 437 U.S. 584 (1978); *Diamond v. Chakrabarty*, 447 U.S. 303 (1980); *Diamond v. Diehr*, 450 U.S. 175 (1981).

5 *Association for Molecular Pathology v. Myriad Genetics, Inc.*, 133 S. Ct. 2107, 2013 WL 2631062 (2013); *Ass'n for Molecular Pathology v. U.S. Patent & Trademark Office and Myriad Genetics, Inc.*, 689 F.3d 1303 (Fed. Cir. 2012); *Ass'n for Molecular Pathology v. U.S. Patent & Trademark Office*, 669 F. Supp.2d 365 (S.D.N.Y. 2009).

6 *Mayo Collaborative Services v. Prometheus Laboratories, Inc.*, 132 S. Ct. 1289 (2012); *Prometheus Laboratories, Inc. v. Mayo Collaborative Services*, 628 F. 3d 1347 (Fed. Cir. 2010); *Prometheus Laboratories, Inc. v. Mayo Collaborative Services*, 86 U.S.P.Q. 2d 1705 (S.D. Cal. 2008). Although the Supreme Court explicitly cited *Funk Brothers* just a few

involving the patentability of medical diagnostic tests and genes, respectively. *Funk Brothers* even turned up in the Supreme Court's opinion in *Bilski v. Kappos*, concerning business methods.[7] Given the resurgence of this once-forgotten case, its re-examination is surely justified.

Of course, this conclusion does little to answer the question of just how to re-examine the opinion. One way would be to begin with the opinion itself, tracing its effects at least starting at *Benson*, through *Chakrabarty*, to *Bilski*, *Mayo*, and *Myriad*. Yet, *Funk Brothers* has resulted in much ink in the academic literature, and by stringing together several excellent pieces, one achieves such a historical analysis.[8] As such, in this chapter, I start from *Myriad*, *Mayo*, and *Bilski*, tracing the path to *Funk Brothers* in reverse.[9] By doing so, I illuminate how thorny and problematic legal issues in today's case law are reflected by the *Funk Brothers* decision itself. Indeed, I argue that the misguided reasoning of the *Funk Brothers* majority opinion – which declared the bacteria mixture ineligible for patenting – continues to plague patentable subject matter jurisprudence. Thus, by considering the mistakes of the *Funk Brothers* Court, we can hope to (someday) remedy the missteps by today's courts.

In concert with the theme of this book, the first section of this chapter discusses the difficulties involved in drawing lines at "the edge" of patentability – specifically, in distinguishing unpatentable "laws of nature" from patentable "applications of laws of nature." In so doing, I criticize the *Funk Brothers* majority opinion – and recent affirmation of such an approach in *Mayo* – for improperly importing concepts of novelty and obviousness into patent eligibility determinations. The second section investigates further why courts and commentators so often import doctrines from beyond Section 101 of the Patent Act – the eligibility section – in order to decide subject matter issues. I conclude that the "point of novelty" and gatekeeper approaches to patentable subject matter – which provide a rationale for this importation of doctrines – do not optimally serve the aims of patent law. In the third section, I use Justice Frankfurter's concurrence in *Funk Brothers* as a starting point to describe a better theory of patentable subject matter

times in *Mayo*, as I describe herein, the core principles of *Funk Brothers* animated the opinion. See below pp. 368–69.

7 *Bilski v. Kappos*, 130 S. Ct. 3218 (2011).

8 See, e.g., Donald Chisum, *Chisum on Patents* §1.02 (2012); Michael Risch, "Everything is Patentable," 75 *Tenn. L. Rev.* 591 (2008); Linda Demaine & Aaron Fellmeth, "Reinventing the Double Helix: A Novel and Nonobvious Reconceptualization of the Biotechnology Patent," 55 *Stanford L. Rev.* 303 (2002).

9 Unfortunately, the Supreme Court decided *Myriad* just a few days before this volume went to press, necessitating a briefer treatment of that opinion.

devised by Professors Mark Lemley, Michael Risch, Polk Wagner, and myself. Our approach focuses on patent scope – but not the sort that tends to drive decisions under traditional disclosure doctrines. Rather, patent eligibility scope examines the extent to which a patent claim forecloses future innovation, weighing those costs against the benefits of the practical application actually invented and disclosed by the inventor. Although the Supreme Court in *Mayo* relied upon our theory in part to justify its "inventive concept" approach to patentable subject matter, I explain why our theory ultimately points in quite an opposite direction from the Court's decision. The chapter concludes by describing what we believe is a superior test.

Discerning laws of nature from "applications" of laws of nature

In the Supreme Court's decision in *Bilski*, quoting from *Diamond v. Diehr* 450 U.S. 175 (1981), the Court affirmed "that while an abstract idea, law of nature, or mathematical formula could not be patented, an application of a law of nature or mathematical formula to a known structure or process may well be deserving of patent protection."[10] The Court echoed this language in *Mayo*.[11] Of note here, the Court derived this prescription from *Funk Brothers*, in which it was stated: "He who discovers a hitherto unknown phenomenon of nature has no claim to a monopoly of it which the law recognizes. If there is to be invention from such a discovery, it must come from the application of the law of nature to a new and useful end."[12]

Yet, discerning the line between a law of nature and an "application" of such can be tricky in practice. In *Bilski*, in addition to quoting *Diehr*'s *Funk Brothers*'-derived mantra that an "application of law of nature" is potentially patentable, the Court noted that "*Diehr* emphasized the need to consider the invention as a whole, rather than 'dissect[ing] the claims into old and new elements and then . . . ignor[ing] the presence of the old elements in the analysis.'"[13] Yet, just three sentences later, the Court began its analysis that rejects Bilski's claims with the remark that "Claims 1 and 4 in petitioners' application explain the basic concept of hedging, or protecting against risk: 'Hedging is a fundamental economic practice long prevalent in our system of commerce and taught in any introductory finance class.'" As an initial matter, if hedging is an "economic *practice*," it seems that a claim covering it in a specific context could very well

[10] *Bilski*, 130 S. Ct. at 3230.
[11] *Mayo*, 132 S. Ct. at 1293–94 (quoting same).
[12] *Funk Bros.*, 333 U.S. at 130.
[13] *Bilski*, 130 S. Ct. at 3230.

qualify as a "*practical* application" of an abstract idea. Rather, as Justice Stevens' dissent rightly recognizes, the Court makes the conclusory assertion that the claims cover merely an unpatentable "abstract idea." Moreover, whether the "practice" had been "long prevalent . . . and taught in any introductory finance class" is irrelevant to an eligibility determination – at least under the *Diehr* model that precludes "ignor[ing] the . . . old elements in the analysis," otherwise supported by the Court in *Bilski*. Under such an approach, the issue should not merely be one of whether the novel or non-obviousness elements are the sort eligible for patenting, but rather whether the subject matter *as a whole* is eligible. In other words, what we should "ignore" when making our subject matter eligibility determination is whether any given claim element is novel or non-obvious. Unfortunately, in *Mayo*, the Court (albeit, implicitly) laid to rest *Diehr*'s whole claim approach in favor of an "inventive concept" approach that focuses on whether the inventive elements of the claimed invention are eligible subject matter,[14] effectively importing novelty and non-obviousness back into the eligibility analysis. In essence, the inventive concept test is a variant of the "point of novelty" approach that the Court had endorsed in *Flook*, but (again, implicitly) rejected in *Diehr*.[15]

Even earlier in this spectrum of confusion is the *Funk Brothers* opinion itself. As noted above, the patent in *Funk Brothers* contained claims-at-issue covering inoculants for leguminous plants made up of multiple strains of bacteria, which, when delivered to the plant, allows it to fix nitrogen from the soil, which helps the plant grow.[16] Each species of bacteria only works with select groups of the leguminous plants. For instance, *rhizobium trifolii* can be used to inoculate red, crimson, mammoth, and alsike clover, but *not* alfalfa, white, or yellow sweet clover. Prior to the invention at issue in *Funk Brothers*, farmers could purchase packages of single-strain bacteria that promoted growth in the

[14] Additionally, the *Mayo* court appeared to leave open the possibility that the inventive "combination" of otherwise non-inventive elements could support an eligibility finding. *Mayo*, 132 S. Ct. at 1294. For an in-depth and insightful discussion of the Court's inventive concept approach, see Katherine J. Strandburg, "Much Ado About Preemption," 50 *Hous. L. Rev.* 563 (2012).

[15] To the extent the inventive combination of non-inventive elements supports a finding of "inventive concept," see *supra* note 14, the inventive concept test is somewhat broader than the point of novelty test of *Flook*.

[16] Claim 4 was cited by the Court as illustrative: "An inoculant for leguminous plants comprising a plurality of selected mutually non-inhibitive strains of different species of bacteria of the genus Rhizobium, said strains being unaffected by each other in respect to their ability to fix nitrogen in the leguminous plant for which they are specific." *Funk Bros.*, 333 U.S. at 128 n. 1.

matching groups of plants. Of course, this meant that if farmers grew both red clover and alfalfa clover, they would need to purchase two separate packages of bacteria – one strain for the red clover and another for the alfalfa. When the bacteria were mixed with a common base, they generally had an inhibitory effect upon one another, reducing their efficiency in promoting plant growth. The inventor in *Funk Brothers* discovered how to isolate and mix different strains of bacteria so that they would *not* have inhibitory effects on one another. This allowed multiple strains to be sold in one package, which presumably decreased manufacturing costs and made application of the inoculants less time-consuming for farmers.

The Court did not confront the patent eligibility of the methods used to select and test the non-inhibitive strains. Rather, it considered product claims for the end mixture of the non-inhibitory strains. It was not contested that the effect of the mixed strains on a plant was essentially the same as if the plant had solely been inoculated with the single strain that promoted growth in that type of plant. Thus, the mixing of the bacteria led to no new properties or results when compared with an effective single-strain inoculation. Indeed, the novel – and commercially valuable – property was that the mixed-strain inoculant *produced the same results* as the single-strain inoculant.

Yet, focusing on this same output, rather than the very different input, the Court in *Funk Brothers* held that the claimed mixtures were not patentable, because:

> [T]hese bacteria, like the heat of the sun, electricity, or the qualities of metals, are part of the storehouse of knowledge of all men. They are manifestations of laws of nature, free to all men and reserved exclusively to none. He who discovers a hitherto unknown phenomenon of nature has no claim to a monopoly of it which the law recognizes. If there is to be invention from such a discovery, it must come from the application of the law of nature to a new and useful end.[17]

The Court's reasoning here shows the confusion that can easily arise when trying to distinguish natural phenomena from applications of such. As an initial matter, the claims-at-issue did not merely cover single strains of bacteria that exist in nature but various mixtures of strains that do not. Thus, the claims covered compositions that are not natural phenomena. Indeed, the Circuit Court of Appeals hearing the case below recognized as much, finding that the claimed mixtures were "new and different composition[s]" from what existed in nature.

[17] *Ibid.* at 130.

Instead of contesting the Appeals Court's holding directly, the Court instead held that the claims essentially covered a "law of nature": "Discovery of the fact that certain strains of each species of these bacteria can be mixed without harmful effect to the properties of either is a discovery of their qualities of non-inhibition. It is no more than the discovery of some of the handiwork of nature and hence is not patentable."[18] To be certain, the Court recognized that the claims did not solely cover a law of nature – rather they were "an application of that newly-discovered natural principle."

At this point, the Court should have ended its analysis, which would have resulted in a finding of patent eligibility. Instead, the Court proceeded to add another requirement – namely, that *the application* of the newly discovered principle *itself* be novel: "But however ingenious the discovery of that natural principle may have been, the application of it is hardly more than an advance in the packaging of the inoculants."[19] The packaging of the inoculants was clearly well within the prior art, and the resulting mixture did not achieve effects any different from the way individual strains would inoculate the plants. In the Court's words, "They serve the ends nature originally provided and act quite independently of any effort of the patentee."[20]

Yet, such a rule could easily be used to defeat all sorts of patents for which protection serves a valuable role, and which have been granted as a matter of course historically. As Justice Frankfurter articulately explained in his concurrence in *Funk Brothers*:

> Everything that happens may be deemed "the work of nature," and any patentable composite exemplifies in its properties "the laws of nature." Arguments drawn from such terms for ascertaining patentability could fairly be employed to challenge almost every patent. On the other hand, the suggestion that "if there is to be invention from such a discovery, it must come from the application of the law of nature to a new and useful end" may readily validate [the inventor's] claim. Nor can it be contended that there was no invention because the composite has no new properties other than its ingredients in isolation. [The inventor's] mixture does in fact have the new property of multi-service applicability. Multi-purpose tools, multivalent vaccines, vitamin complex composites, are examples of complexes whose sole new property is the conjunction of the properties of their components. Surely the Court does not mean unwittingly to pass on the patentability of such products by formulating criteria by which future issues of patentability may be prejudged.[21]

Justice Frankfurter's concurrence is a useful starting point for describing a novel theory of patentable subject matter that I – along with Mark

[18] *Ibid.* at 131. [19] *Ibid.* [20] *Ibid.* [21] *Ibid.* at 135.

Lemley, Michael Risch, and Polk Wagner – have formulated. Our approach centers not on the concern as to whether the application of a law of nature or abstract idea is itself novel, but simply asks whether there is a practical application at all, leaving novelty to the realm of the remainder of the Patent Act. However, before embarking on this discussion, it is useful to ask how and why the concept of novelty (as well as other patent law concepts) elsewhere in the Act became wrapped up in patent eligibility at all.

From mixing bacteria to mixing (up) doctrines

The *Funk Brothers* majority opinion rather conclusorily holds that the application of a law of nature in a tangible product must itself be novel and non-obvious, regardless of whether the discovery of the law itself was novel and non-obvious. Some judges and commentators have relied upon this distinction to treat *Funk Brothers* as an obviousness decision, rather than one concerning patentable subject matter.[22] In Professor Chris Holman's view, for instance, "if *Funk Brothers* was really decided based on obviousness rather than patent eligibility ... the two decisions [*Funk Brothers* and *Chakrabarty*] are easily reconciled."[23]

Yet, such a view is unsatisfying, because the Justices in the *Funk Brothers* majority did not contest that the discovery itself was novel and non-obvious.[24] More broadly, from a policy perspective, if certain discoveries of laws of nature result in practical applications that would not have been manufactured and sold absent patent protection, then a rule like *Funk Brothers* – whether styled as one of eligibility or obviousness – would unduly dampen innovation.

Perhaps not unsurprisingly, commentators and the courts have articulated other rationales for the *Funk Brothers* rule. First, some argue that by

[22] See *Association for Molecular Pathology v. U.S. Patent and Trademark Office ("Myriad II"), Ass'n for Molecular Pathology v. U.S. Patent & Trademark Office and Myriad Genetics, Inc.*, 689 F.3d 1303, 1327 (Fed. Cir. 2012) (Lourie J.) ("To underscore the point, the [Supreme] Court compared Chakrabarty's engineered bacteria with the mixed bacterial cultures found unpatentable in Funk Brothers, again casting this case, more relating to obviousness, in terms of § 101.").

[23] Christopher Holman, "Amicus Brief Filed by Alnylam Pharmaceuticals Argues that Funk Bros. Is About Obviousness, Not Patent Eligibility," Holman's Biotech IP Blog, November 10, 2010, http://holmansbiotechipblog.blogspot.com/2010/11/amicus-brief-filed-by-alynlam.html.

[24] To be fair to Professor Holman, he does not take a position one way or the other on whether *Funk Brothers* was actually decided on obviousness grounds. Rather, assuming that *Funk Brothers* was so decided, he contends that its holding is reconcilable with *Chakrabarty*. For reasons I discuss below, I contend that the cases are reconcilable regardless of such an assumption.

ignoring whether any of the elements of the claimed invention are novel and non-obvious, clever patent prosecutions could transform what is essentially a claim to a law of nature or natural phenomenon into a patentable "practical application." Such word games could tie up laws of nature for use only by the patentee, hindering others from using these "building blocks" of science and technology.

Justice Breyer first expressed such a view in his dissent from the Court's order dismissing its grant of certiorari in *Laboratory Corp. v. Metabolite*, in which he stated that "Why should it matter if the test results themselves were obtained through an *unpatented* procedure that involved the transformation of blood? ... Indeed, to use virtually any natural phenomenon for virtually any useful purpose could well involve the use of empirical information obtained through an *unpatented* means ..."[25] In *Mayo*, Justice Breyer more fully developed this view, relying on the Court's earlier concerns in *Flook*, *Morse*, and *Benson*:

> Those cases warn us against interpreting patent statutes in ways that make patent eligibility "depend simply on the draftsman's art" without reference to the "principles underlying the prohibition against patents for [natural laws]." They warn us against upholding patents that claim processes that too broadly preempt the use of a natural law. And they insist that a process that focuses upon the use of a natural law also contain other elements or a combination of elements, sometimes referred to as an "inventive concept," sufficient to ensure that the patent in practice amounts to significantly more than a patent upon the natural law itself.[26]

Second, some view the incorporation of novelty and non-obviousness concepts into patentable subject matter as serving an important "gatekeeper" function for patents of suspect validity. Here, the fear is that some patent claims might very well pass muster under the novelty and non-obviousness requirements, at least at the Patent Office, because their subject matter is so abstract that it is difficult as a *practical matter* to find prior art and apply that prior art to prevent those claims from issuing. An expansive patentable subject matter rule acts a prophylactic measure to keep such claims unpatentable by obviating the need to resort to a traditional novelty and non-obviousness review.

However, neither of these justifications is particularly persuasive. As for Justice Breyer's view – which, apparently, is now the unanimous

[25] *Laboratory Corp. of America Holdings v. Metabolite Laboratories, Inc.*, 548 U.S. 124, 136 (2006) (Breyer J., dissenting from dismissal of *certiorari* as improvidently granted) (emphasis added).

[26] *Ibid.* (citing *Flook*, 437 U.S. at 593; *Benson*, 409 U.S. at 71–72; *O'Reilly v. Morse*, 15 How. 62, 112–20 (1854)).

Court's view following *Mayo*[27] – the issue boils down to whether an "inventive concept" approach to patentable subject matter tends to eliminate from patentability those inventions that would be a net cost to society, yet retains those inventions that would be a net benefit. The crux of the inventive concept view – arguably an adaptation of the earlier point of novelty approach – is that inventions that are merely an obvious application of what is essentially a law of nature, natural phenomenon, or abstract idea tend to remove from the "storehouse of knowledge" those ideas that, in the words of the *Funk Brothers*' Court, should be "free to all men and reserved exclusively to none." In other words, these inventions are so fundamental to society – particularly, as building blocks for future innovation – that *even if they would not have resulted absent a patent*, they should still be precluded from patentability.

Here, it is essential to recognize that an implicit assumption in this argument is that these inventions would pass muster under the separate novelty and obviousness prongs of the Patent Act, even if examined perfectly by the Patent Office. In a well-functioning patent system, such an assumption generally implies that absent the patent system, such invention would typically not have been made (or perhaps commercially made) during the twenty-year period for which the inventor enjoys exclusionary rights, or at least would have been substantially accelerated by the promise of a patent.[28] Of course, there are boundary cases, but the general thrust here is that despite the substantial influence of the patent system on the genesis of the discovery, the discovery is so fundamental that no matter how "practical" the application, as long as the application itself is routine or conventional, then patentability should be negated. For reasons presented earlier, the downside of such an approach is to exclude numerous *practical* inventions that are of great benefit to society. One particularly important set of examples are medical diagnostic tests. In both the *Mayo* and *Myriad* cases, few seem to doubt that the medical tests at issue – one for determining the appropriate dosage of a particular drug and another that screens for breast cancer – have significant social value.

[27] Although the Court did not revisit the inventive concept approach in *Myriad*, it did nothing to disturb it. Indeed, the Court's holding did not necessitate discussing this approach. See *Myriad*, 133 S. Ct. at 2116–17. Importantly, the "inventive concept" comes into play only when there is an initial finding of a law of nature, natural product, or abstract idea, and a further "application" of such through additional elements. See *Mayo*, 132 S. Ct. at 1290, 1292. Thus, the Court's finding that claimed cDNA was sufficiently man-made was sufficient to remove it from inventive concept analysis. See *Myriad*, 133 St. Ct. at 2117–19. Nor would such an analysis apply to the claimed genomic DNA, since there was no application involved in such a claim. See *ibid.* at 2116–17.

[28] See Michael Abramowicz & John F. Duffy, "The Inducement Standard of Patentability," 120 *Yale L. J.* 1590 (2011).

The concerns that ordinary medical tests in essence embody fundamental "laws of nature" such that a patent on the test is equivalent to a patent on the underlying biochemical relationship (e.g., between a particular genetic mutation and breast cancer) or impinge upon the freedom of thought of the user (e.g., that merely thinking about the relationship between a measured metabolite and optimal dosage regime may constitute infringement) are certainly ones that should be taken seriously. Yet, like immorality concerns – for example, that gene patents should not be granted because they are fundamentally immoral – patentable subject matter does not seem the best approach for addressing them. Rather, a broad experimental use exception, compulsory licensing, limitations on indirect infringement, and other mechanisms that allow researchers to perform basic research and improve the underlying inventions – as well as allow third parties to verify independently the results of diagnostic tests[29] – seem more appropriate. In other words, one need not eliminate conventional applications of laws of nature from patentability to ensure that future innovation involving those laws is not unduly retarded. Assuming my intuition is correct – and there has been little empirical analysis to conclusively support or refute either view – then patent eligibility denials would be limited only to those relatively "pure" abstract ideas, natural laws, and natural phenomena. Although there would be gray areas in determining what is "pure," since relatively few claims under such a test would possibly constitute unpatentable subject matter, there would be few "hard cases" to resolve.

If my intuition that the benefits of patenting conventional – but novel, non-obvious and properly disclosed – applications of natural laws and phenomena generally outweigh the costs is wrong, then my previous arguments do not hold. In this vein, the gatekeeper theory turns on the belief that Congress and the Patent Office tend to make mistakes – explicitly and implicitly – in allocating patent rights to inventions that do not deserve them. In other words, they afford twenty-year exclusive rights of relatively broad scope to inventions that either would have been made at roughly the same time without such expansive protection or impose such large social costs that they are not worth the "embarrassment of an exclusive patent."[30]

Of course, the courts cannot override Congress per se, but Congress's lack of substantive delineation on exactly what does and does not count

[29] See Brenda Simon, "Patent Cover-Up," 47 *Hous. L. Rev.* 1299 (2011).

[30] Letter from Thomas Jefferson to Isaac McPherson (August 13, 1813), in 6 *The Writings of Thomas Jefferson: Being his Autobiography, Correspondence, Reports, Messages, Addresses, and Other Writings, Official and Private* 175, 181 (H.A. Washington ed., Taylor & Maury, Washington DC, 1854).

for patenting provides the courts leeway to foreclose protection in particular areas. For instance, the natural law, natural phenomena and abstract ideas exceptions to patentability are wholly creatures of judicial making. The theory here is that only certain types of invention should enjoy the broad protection afforded by a patent. As such, the courts and the Patent Office should act as gatekeepers, excluding those classes of inventions that Congress did not clearly contemplate as patent eligible and that do not justify such broad protection (e.g., software).[31] Moreover, in other classes of inventions, the gatekeeping theory asserts that the Patent Office often has a difficult time performing a suitable level of examination, which results in patents being granted that otherwise should not have issued. For instance, in business methods, some commentators contend that the Patent Office does not have sufficient access to prior art in this area to appropriately invalidate applications lacking novelty or that are obvious.[32] An expansive gatekeeping approach to patentable subject matter would prevent these sorts of costly Type 1 (false positive) errors from occurring by removing certain classes of invention from patent eligibility entirely.

In *Myriad*, the Supreme Court basically adopted a gatekeeper approach, by purporting to draw a boundary between unpatentable, "naturally occurring" products and patentable, "synthetic" products altered by humans.[33] Indeed, the *Myriad* Court read *Funk Brothers* as supporting its approach, finding that the mixture of non-inhibitory strains of bacteria was effectively "naturally occurring," in contrast to the genetically altered strains in *Chakrabarty*.[34] Yet, like my views on Justice Breyer's inventive concept approach, I generally find the gatekeeper approaches unpersuasive, at least in the expansive form in which they commonly appear. First, as I explained earlier, separating the "natural" from the "synthetic" is not so simple a task. In this regard, the court generally relies on unstated, ill-formed views of what constitute "natural laws" and "products of nature," failing to take heed of the rich body of contemporary philosophical literature debunking the naïve view that there is a principled way to discern "true" laws of

[31] See, e.g., Kevin Emerson Collins, "Propertizing Thought," 60 *SMU L. Rev.* 317 (2007); Pamela Samuelson, "*Benson* Revisited: The Case Against Patent Protection for Algorithms and Other Computer Program-Related Inventions," 39 *Emory L. J.* 1025, 1042–43 (1990); Joshua D. Sarnoff, *Patent Eligible Inventions after* Bilski*: History and Theory* (February 7, 2011) (unpublished manuscript), *available at* http://papers.ssrn.com/sol3/papers.cfm?abstract_id=1757272.

[32] See, e.g., Michael J. Meurer, "Controlling Opportunistic and Anti-Competitive Intellectual Property Litigation," 44 *B. C. L. Rev.* 509 (2003).

[33] *Myriad*, 133 S. Ct. at 2116–19. [34] *Ibid.* at 2116–17.

nature.[35] Rather, on these accounts, so-called "scientific law" is merely a man-made, synthetic "model" that proves useful in explaining experimental outcomes and as a framework in applied domains.[36] Although these models may exhibit different properties from their practical applications, this distinction does not turn on one between the "natural" and "synthetic." Second, gatekeeper theories tend to preference older technologies, because newer technologies are the ones hardest to examine properly. Yet, the point of patent law is precisely to spur new technologies. Hence, there is a fundamental tension between gatekeeping – at least in practice – and the goals of the patent system. This tension is exacerbated by current judicial and Patent Office practice, which – in order to keep the administrative costs of gatekeeping low – tend to draw bright lines to demarcate areas of patentable subject matter from non-patentable subject matter. These practices remove the flexibility that a more policy-driven approach requires, and introduce more than a modicum of arbitrariness in many cases. Of course, these concerns raise the specter of the old rules–standards debate – which is often difficult to answer without concerted empirical analysis – but in a legal field with rapid change, rigid rules often seem out of place. Third, gatekeeping rules often take on a life of their own, continually removing themselves with each additional judicial opinion or agency interpretation from their fundamental purposes. Thus, instead of viewing the "transformation of matter" through the lens of appropriate innovation incentives, the courts' reasoning often takes on a "hyperreal" self-referentiality, resulting in scholastic ruminations significantly lacking coherence in the policy sense. The Federal Circuit's ongoing application of its "machine-or-transformation" test for patentability is a clear case in point.

Another line of argument in the patentable subject matter debate relies upon moral concerns to cabin patentability. Advocates here believe that ethics should sometimes override pure utilitarian concerns to prevent certain types of subject matter from being patented. In the US, these views are relatively rare, because the premise of the Intellectual Property Clause in the Constitution is a decidedly utilitarian one: "To promote the Progress of Science and useful Arts . . ."[37] Nonetheless, there are exceptions, such as the prohibition on patenting human organisms.

[35] See generally Jacob Sherkow, "The Natural Complexity of Patent Eligibility," 99 *Iowa L. Rev.* (forthcoming 2014) (explaining a variety of these contemporary philosophical approaches to understanding so-called "scientific law").

[36] See *ibid.*

[37] U.S. Const. art. I, § 8, cl. 8; *see also* Peter S. Menell, "Intellectual Property: General Theories," in 2 *Encyclopedia of Law and Economics* 129, 130–48, 155–56 (Boudewijn Bouckaert & Gerrit De Geest eds., Edward Elgar, Cheltenham, UK, 2000)

In Europe, such views are more prevalent. For instance, one of the major patent law conventions contains a clause that allows Member States to create exceptions (with some caveats) to patentability for "inventions the publication or exploitation of which would be contrary to *ordre public* or morality" and "plant or animal varieties or essentially biological processes for the production of plants or animals."[38] As Professor Justine Pila explains in Chapter 18, patent eligibility in Europe is frequently confused with public policy exclusions.

Like novelty and obviousness, even setting the US Intellectual Property Clause aside, it seems unwise to mix up issues of morality with those of patentable subject matter. The patent offices around the world are not particularly well suited to consider ethical concerns. Rather, their expertise lies in the technological realm, and any fine distinctions made to distinguish patentable from unpatentable subject matter along ethical lines will tend to adopt technological heuristics that are very likely to be poor means of sorting moral from immoral. Rather, concerns about negative social effects of technology are better left to the "regulators" – those agencies that actively enforce laws that prohibit particular technologies and behavior related to them. For instance, instead of removing "human chimeras" – that is human–non-human genetic mixes from patentability – it would be more sensible simply to ban such organisms via regulatory laws, with enforcement by the appropriate agency. Of course, for some inventions, the mere disclosure of information relating to the invention may be a serious concern. Even so, a general ban on publication of such material (be it in a patent, journal article, or otherwise) – consistent with the constraints of the First Amendment, of course – seems a more direct approach than trying to regulate disclosure via a ban on patentability.

Patentable subject matter as a matter of (future) patent scope

Some commentators and judges mix doctrines other than novelty and non-obviousness into the patentable subject matter inquiry.[39] One line of

("The United States Constitution expressly conditions the grant of power to Congress to create patent and copyright laws upon a utilitarian foundation.").

[38] Convention on the Unification of Certain Points of Substantive Law on Patents for Inventions, Article 2.

[39] See Tun-Jen Chiang, "The Rules and Standards of Patentable Subject Matter," 2010 *Wis. L. Rev.* 1353, 1363, 1381; Efthimios Parasidis, "A Uniform Framework for Patent Eligibility," 85 *Tul. L. Rev.* 323, 387–89 (2010); Bryan Treglia, "Separating Abstract Ideas and Laws of Nature from Patentable Subject Matter," 48 *Jurimetrics J.* 427,

doctrines involves enablement and related disclosure requirements, which I avoided discussing in the previous section, as it serves as a starting point for my and my co-authors' theory of patentable subject matter. In short, our theory is that patent eligibility plays a role when the scope of the claim is much greater than the practical application actually invented.[40] However, unlike previous theoretical approaches, we believe this is so even if the traditional disclosure requirements of enablement and written description are met under Section 112 of the Patent Act. Rather, scope issues for patent eligibility concern whether the claim unduly forecloses improvements and modifications to the original invention. A scope theory of patent eligibility is attractive on both descriptive and normative grounds. In our earlier paper, we explained how our theory rationalized Supreme Court and Federal Circuit cases from *Benson* onward.[41] However, we did not do so for *Funk Brothers*. Interestingly, *Funk Brothers* – particularly Justice Frankfurter's concurrence – is perhaps the best example of the theory at work, so it is here that I begin my explication.

Justice Frankfurter's presaging of the scope theory of patentable subject matter

Consistent with the scope theory's premise, in *Funk Brothers* Justice Frankfurter concurred on the grounds that the claim-at-issue was much broader than what the inventor had actually invented. As noted earlier, Justice Frankfurter did not believe the *subject matter* – a non-inhibitory mixture of inoculants – was ineligible for patenting per se. Rather, in his view:

> [The inventor] appears to claim that since he was the originator of the idea that there might be mutually compatible strains and had practically demonstrated that some such strains exist, everyone else is forbidden to use a combination of strains whether they are or are not identical with the combinations that [the inventor] selected and packaged together ... Its acceptance would require, for instance in the field of alloys, that if one discovered a particular mixture of metals, which when alloyed had some particular desirable properties, he could patent not merely this particular mixture but the idea of alloying metals for this purpose, and thus *exclude everyone else from contriving some other combination of metals* which, when alloyed, had the same desirable properties ... It only confuses the issue, however, to introduce such terms

434–37 (2008); Donald S. Chisum, "Weeds and Seeds in the Supreme Court's Business Method Patents Decision: New Directions for Regulating Patent Scope," 15 *Lewis & Clark L. Rev.* 11 (2011).

[40] Our theory was primarily directed to abstract ideas and natural phenomena, but here I apply it to laws of nature.

[41] Mark A. Lemley, Michael Risch, Ted Sichelman & Polk Wagner, "Life After Bilski," 63 *Stan. L. Rev.* 1315, 1328 (2011).

as "the work of nature" and the "laws of nature." For these are vague and malleable terms infected with too much ambiguity and equivocation.[42]

Justice Frankfurter's formulation aligns with our theory of patentable subject matter. Under our view, patentable subject matter "operates where a patent claim is 'too broad' in the sense that it encroaches upon society's right to unfettered access to scientific truths, fundamental principles, and the like; these properly belong in the commons upon which future innovations can be built, 'free to all men and reserved exclusively to none.'"[43] Nonetheless, Justice Frankfurter's approach does not fully distinguish between issues of enablement – whether the inventor has disclosed enough material so that a person having ordinary skill in the art could make and build the invention *at the time of filing* – and whether the inventor has simply foreclosed too many avenues of *future* research. Indeed, focusing on the enablement requirement of the Patent Act, Justices Burton and Jackson dissented in *Funk Brothers*, contending:

The record thus indicates that the description is sufficiently full, clear, concise and exact to enable persons skilled in the art or science to which this discovery appertains or with which it is most nearly connected to make, construct, compound and use the same. There is no suggestion as to how it would be reasonably possible to describe the patented product more completely. The patent covers all composite cultures of bacterial strains of the species described which do not inhibit each other's ability to fix nitrogen. Bacteriologists, skilled in the applicable art, will not have difficulty in selecting the non-inhibitive strains by employing such standard and recognized laboratory tests as are described in the application for this patent.[44]

Justice Frankfurter did not directly respond to Justice Burton's dissent, but he could have argued that *even if* the patent claim were enabled, because the inventor actually invented only a narrow set of practical applications of the general idea of combining non-inhibitory strains of inoculants, the claim would have foreclosed far too much follow-on research and development to be eligible subject matter. Such a distinction between "enablement" scope and "eligibility" scope forms the foundation of our approach to patentable subject matter.

Like Justice Frankfurter's concurrence, we jettison conceptual line-drawing among various types of innovations in favor of a more policy-driven approach. As we stated in our earlier article:

Understood in this way, the abstract ideas doctrine is not about finding a conceptual category of inventions that is entitled to no protection at all, nor

[42] *Funk Bros.*, 333 U.S., at 135. [43] Lemley et al. *supra* note 41 at 1328.
[44] *Funk Bros.*, 333 U.S., at 137.

about determining the quality of the disclosure. Instead, it is about encouraging cumulative innovation and furthering societal norms regarding access to knowledge by preventing patentees from claiming broad ownership over fields of exploration rather than specific applications of those fields.[45]

Interestingly, Justice Breyer in *Mayo* attempted to ground the Court's opinion in part upon our theory:

> [E]ven though rewarding with patents those who discover new laws of nature and the like might well encourage their discovery, those laws and principles, considered generally, are "the basic tools of scientific and technological work." ... And so there is a danger that the grant of patents that tie up their use will inhibit future innovation premised upon them, a danger that becomes acute when a patented process amounts to no more than an instruction to "apply the natural law," or otherwise forecloses more future invention than the underlying discovery could reasonably justify.[46]

Yet, in actually examining the *Mayo* patent, Justice Breyer and the Court undertook a very simplistic comparison of the underlying discovery and the claimed invention. Rather than asking whether the discovery was likely to foreclose substantial amounts of potential future research, the Court reasoned that whether the natural law was broad or narrow was irrelevant, so long as the claimed invention "inhibit[ed] future research." Justice Breyer grounded this categorical approach on the inability of judges to gauge just how much future research a given claim would foreclose. However, judges routinely examine patent scope issues in the context of enablement. Granted, such enablement determinations are backward-looking and judges use the patent document as evidence to make an assessment. However, enablement assessments inevitably involve the introduction of extrinsic evidence and ultimately turn on technologically grounded judgments. Similarly, in cases involving eligibility scope determinations, parties can introduce evidence regarding future research,[47] and, like enablement determinations, judges can suitably assess whether the scope of the claim is justified.[48]

[45] Lemley et al. *supra* note 41, at 1329.

[46] *Mayo*, 132 S. Ct. at 1301–02 (citing Lemley et al., *supra* note 41). The Court reaffirmed this principle in *Myriad*. See *Myriad*, 133 S. Ct. at 2115–16.

[47] In some cases, the follow-on research will have begun by the time the patentee winds up in court, allowing the judge direct access to evidence regarding the extent to which the claims foreclose such research. See Rochelle C. Dreyfuss & James P. Evans, "From Bilski Back to Benson: Preemption, Inventing Around, and the Case of Genetic Diagnostics," 63 *Stan. L. Rev.* 1349, 1370–71 (2011).

[48] If it truly is the case that judges are ill-equipped to make such determinations, the same would hold true not only for enablement scope determinations, but also several other recurring judicial assessments in patent law cases (e.g., obviousness, claim construction). Perhaps judges are ill-equipped across the board, but until a

The larger problem with Justice Breyer's approach is that it ignores – as Justice Frankfurter warned – that at some level of generality, nearly all inventions can be viewed as embodying natural laws, natural phenomena, or abstract ideas: "Everything that happens may be deemed 'the work of nature.'"[49] Moreover, all claimed inventions will tend to "inhibit" at least some non-trivial amount of "future research," because nearly all inventions can be improved. In this sense, Justice Breyer's approach broadly interpreted could be used to invalidate scores of patents. Indeed, it ignores the well-settled case law that patent claims typically cover after-arising technology, even if that technology is separately patented, yielding returns to both original and follow-on inventors. By failing to account for the specific amount of future innovation foreclosed, the *Mayo* test could wreak substantial havoc.

A multi-factored, policy-driven test for patentable subject matter

The alternative to Justice Breyer's test is not, as he proclaims, making patentable subject matter doctrine a "dead letter." In our original article, we identified five factors that can be used to test the patent eligibility of abstract ideas.[50] In my view, these factors also apply quite well to analyzing laws of nature and natural phenomena. First, one should consider "the generative nature of the new technology." In terms of natural laws, perhaps the better question is whether the practical application of the natural law is one of a small number of ways of applying the law, or whether the law is so fundamental that it is likely to lead to a long chain of practical applications.

In *Funk Brothers*, the discovery that there were at least some strains of non-inhibitory bacteria that could be mixed together seems fairly generative when compared to the narrow set of practical applications disclosed in the application. In this sense, Justice Frankfurter's analogy – that the claim-at-issue was akin to claiming the ability to alloy metals – is probably apt. On the other hand, if all the various permutations of bacteria mixtures were easily obtainable from the narrow set actually disclosed, then perhaps Justices Burton and Jackson were more correct. The facts presented in the *Funk Brothers* opinion do not decisively resolve the issue.

congressional determination otherwise, we are stuck with the assumption that judges are not so incompetent. There is no apparent reason why such an assumption should apply to some technologically oriented judicial determinations but not to others.

[49] *Funk Bros.*, 333 U.S., at 135. [50] *Mayo*, 132 S. Ct. at 1303.

In *Mayo* and *Myriad*, the results on this factor seem clearer. In *Mayo*, the natural law at issue – if there was one at all – was a specific correlation between a metabolite and the optimal amount of drug to administer, and hence was relatively narrow. Thus, allowing a claim over all practical applications would not seem to foreclose much beyond what was actually invented. Indeed, the accused infringer, Mayo's test – which Justice Breyer used as an example of a "refinement" of the original invention – was a minor, almost trivial, variation on the original disclosure. Although Justice Breyer also mentioned the potential inhibition on "more refined treatment recommendations ... [based on] later discovered features of metabolites, human physiology or individual patient characteristics,"[51] these sorts of downstream effects are not materially different from those created by patents covering other kinds of biomedical inventions. In contrast, in *Myriad*, a claim to a gene could very well foreclose many avenues of research not embodied in one type of diagnostic test designed to measure the likelihood of breast cancer. If this is so, then the Supreme Court's distinction in *Myriad* between unpatentable, "naturally occurring" genomic DNA and patentable, "synthetic" complementary DNA seems one without much of a meaningful difference.[52]

A second factor in the analysis concerns the nature of innovation in the applicable industry. In *Funk Brothers*, the industry was primarily agricultural, which involves a fair share of cumulative innovation,[53] again supporting Justice Frankfurter's determination. In other industries, like pharmaceuticals, innovation is more "discrete," and applications of particular natural laws are more of a one-time occurrence. And in some industries, like biotechnology, inventions tend to contain a mixture of discrete and cumulative elements. Of course, deviations from industry generalizations occur regularly, and one must be careful to examine the particular facts of each patent claim-at-issue. For instance, while the metabolite-based diagnostic test in *Mayo* seems unlikely to be improved significantly, the gene-based one in *Myriad* could very well be.

A third factor examines how quickly the value of a typical invention dissipates in a given industry and the speed with which inventions are made. In *Funk Brothers*, the mixed inoculants have long-term value and innovation appears to move slowly – indeed, essentially the same mixtures are still sold today.[54] When innovation progresses slowly and

[51] *Ibid.*, at 1302. [52] *Myriad*, 133 S. Ct., at 2116–19.

[53] See, e.g., Katherine J. Strandburg, "Evolving Innovation Paradigms and the Global Intellectual Property Regime," 41 *Conn. L. Rev.* 861, 865 (2009).

[54] See Fix-N-Grow Legume Inoculant, www.oldsgardenseed.com/products/fixngrow.html (last visited April 4, 2012).

inventions have long shelf lives, the costs of granting overly broad claims are less, because those claims will expire in twenty years, and the practical application is still likely to have substantial value. Conversely, when the pace of innovation is quick and there is rapid turnover – for instance, in the mobile phone industry – broad patent claims may hold up innovation, especially in the presence of high transaction costs. In the biotech and pharmaceutical industries, which tend to have longer time horizons and slower innovation curves, this factor would counsel in favor of more expansive patentable subject matter.

The fourth factor is similar to enablement in that it examines the number of specific practical applications disclosed in a patent application. When a patent applicant discloses one specific application, but claims broadly, then the cost to future innovation is likely to be higher. Unlike the enablement inquiry, however, such an examination would not be tied to the filing date of the application. Indeed, under current enablement doctrine, one or just a few disclosed embodiments are often found by courts to enable relatively broad claims. For eligibility considerations, the issue would not concern whether those embodiments are a sufficient disclosure of how a natural law can be applied today, but rather how it might be applied for at least the next twenty years. Again, this factor dovetails with Justice Frankfurter's concurrence, which relied heavily on the fact that the inventor disclosed quite a narrow application of the general principle claimed.[55] In *Mayo*, the claim-at-issue – which is relatively narrow – seems fairly consonant with the disclosure. In *Myriad*, the issue is more difficult. The disclosure involves specific tests using the claimed genes, BRCA1 and BRCA2, for breast cancer – but at least some of the claims are for the genes themselves.[56] Although the patent disclosure identifies these gene sequences in full, the claim to a gene sequence broadly bars the use of the gene for any practical purpose. Thus, in a sense, the *Myriad* gene claims cover the "abstract idea" of using the BRCA1 and BRCA2 genes for *any* known and *unknown* application. Whether these genes are likely to have other important practical applications over the next twenty years seems difficult to answer, at least based on the facts proffered in the case. And it is important to recognize that "research" itself is not a practical application in this instance, because the claimed genes are not "research tools" per se. In any event, to the extent that gene patents discourage fundamental research – in a university or even commercial setting – a

[55] In contrast, in *Chakrabarty*, the claim to the combination of plasmids into a single microorganism that could be used to break down crude oil was much more consonant with what Dr. Chakrabarty actually disclosed.

[56] See, e.g., U.S. Pat. No. 5,747,282 (issued May 5, 1998).

broad research exemption to infringement and meaningful obviousness and disclosure requirements seem a wiser course to follow than eliminating patentability for genomic DNA, as the Supreme Court did in *Myriad*.

The last factor of our test examines whether the inventor's contribution is pioneering or merely incremental in nature. This factor is important, because none of the previous factors takes directly into account the importance of the incentives the patent system offers for the invention to be invented in the first place. As we stated previously, "Truly groundbreaking patents may require broader protection for the simple reason that an inventor who opens up a new field may have less idea how her invention will be used by others."[57] Of course, such a sentiment cuts against the grain of our policy thrust – protecting future innovation. Thus, in my personal view, this factor should be viewed more as a safety valve to protect only the most important inventions that would not have been made, or at least would have been substantially delayed, in the absence of patent protection. In *Funk Brothers*, arguably the invention was not terribly important, as the base inoculants were still available, albeit in separate packages. In *Mayo* and *Myriad*, this question is much more difficult, and turns on a factual inquiry of more depth than I can offer in this short chapter.

Conclusion

Justice Frankfurter had the right intuitions when he relied on scope to reject the broad claim-at-issue in *Funk Brothers*. Instead of making conceptual distinctions between patent claims that impermissibly cover "natural laws" and those that do not – like the majority did – he compared the scope of the claim-at-issue to what the inventor actually invented. Unlike the dissenting Justices, who merely examined whether the claim met the enablement requirement, Justice Frankfurter went beyond this near-term concern to investigate the longer-term concern of whether the claim unduly foreclosed future innovation.

This sort of forward-looking inquiry into patent scope is the appropriate vehicle for determinations of patent eligibility. Unlike Justice Breyer's reliance on patent scope as a policy driver of eligibility in *Mayo* to support a bright-line test that could potentially invalidate numerous issued and pending patents, an appropriate test should take into account a variety of factors to determine whether a claim-at-issue unduly forecloses future innovation.[58] As Mark Lemley, Michael Risch, Polk Wagner, and

[57] Lemley, *supra* note 41, at 1340.

[58] See generally Tun-Jen Chiang, *supra* note 39, at 1353 (examining the well-known trade-offs of rules and standards in the context of patentable subject matter).

I have argued similarly elsewhere,[59] such an approach should focus at least on the following factors:

- whether the claimed invention is likely to be generative of future innovation;
- whether the industry of concern relies heavily on cumulative innovation;
- whether the technological field at issue is fast-moving and whether the value of the innovation is likely to dissipate rapidly;
- whether the patent has disclosed a small number of embodiments but claimed a broad inventive principle;
- whether the patentee has made an important contribution relative to the prior art.

A forward-looking, policy-driven inquiry based on these factors overcomes the problems of bright-line gatekeeping approaches, while properly cabining the scope of patentable subject matter. In so doing, it can help rationalize the case law and resolve fundamental problems with the dominant "machine-or-transformation" test for patentability and the more recent pronouncements of the Supreme Court in *Myriad* and *Mayo*. Hopefully, instead of continuing to follow the *Funk Brothers* majority's misguided approach, the Court will one day resurrect Justice Frankfurter's more principled reasoning.

[59] See Lemley et al., *supra* note 41, at 1341.

18 Patent eligibility and scope revisited in light of *Schütz* v. *Werit*, European law, and copyright jurisprudence

*Justine Pila**

Introduction

In recent work I have argued that when properly construed, the requirement for an invention in patent law – denoted also as 'patent eligibility' and 'inherent patentability' – sets the 'edges' of the patent system in two ways.[1] The first is by defining the categories of subject matter capable of supporting a patent, and the second is by restricting the protection conferred by a patent to individual subject matter conceived qua invention. It is in serving these functions that the requirement for an invention helps to fulfil the public benefit objectives of the patent system by mediating the balance struck by patents between individual patentees and the public.[2]

In Chapter 17, Professor Ted Sichelman considers the role of eligibility in US patent law. He contends that in its first ('gatekeeper') role, eligibility ought to be understood expansively, to permit the protection of any 'practical application'. This leaves eligibility in its second role, as a post-patent determinant of patent scope. It is this to which Sichelman directs his main attention, proposing a theory of 'patent eligibility scope' according to which judicial constructions of patent claims depend on

* My thanks to the editors for their valuable comments on earlier drafts.

[1] This is a central theme and the opening paragraph of the Preface to my 2010 monograph on eligibility, J. Pila, *The Requirement for an Invention in Patent Law* (Oxford University Press, 2010); see at p. vii. It is also central to (and discussed in) various other of my works, including J. Pila, 'Chemical Products and Proportionate Patents Before and After *Generics* v. *Lundbeck*', *King's Law Journal*, 20 (2009) 489–521; J. Pila, 'On the European Requirement for an Invention', *IIC: International Review of Intellectual Property and Competition Law*, 41 (2010) 906–26, republished in an extended form in J. Pila, 'The Future of the Requirement for an Invention: Inherent Patentability as a Pre- and Post-Patent Determinant', in G. Ghidini & E. Arezzo (eds), *Biotechnology and Software Patent Law: A Comparative Review on New Developments* (Edward Elgar, Cheltenham, 2011) 55–90; J. Pila, 'Patents for Genes and Methods of Analysis and Comparison', *Law Quarterly Review*, 126 (2010) 534–38; J. Pila, 'Chemical Product Patents and Biogen Insufficiency Before the House of Lords', *Law Quarterly Review*, 125 (2009) 573–78.

[2] Pila, *The Requirement for an Invention in Patent Law*, vii.

weighing the costs of foreclosing use of the specified subject matter against the benefits of its disclosure to innovation, technology, and industry.[3]

In this response to Sichelman's chapter I consider his argument from the perspective of UK and European law. Given our agreement regarding the role of eligibility as a post-patent determinant, my focus is confined to the details of his approach. In the suggestion made, that approach runs against the grain of UK patent jurisprudence by virtue of its 'fuzzy and uncertain' nature, and is therefore unlikely to be accepted by the UK courts.[4] On the other hand, recent UK cases can be read as going to the other extreme by eschewing regard to any policy considerations that might limit the protection of the patentee. Such cases invite reconsideration of the UK courts' method of determining patent scope. Hence the aim of this chapter, which is to undertake such a reconsideration drawing on Court of Justice of the European Union (CJEU) and copyright jurisprudence. In a postscript at the end I consider the implications for my analysis of the Supreme Court's opinion in *Schütz (UK) Ltd* v. *Werit (UK) Ltd*,[5] published after this chapter was completed but before it went to press. In the argument I make, that case supports my analysis and argument by adopting a new approach to patent infringement which falls between the two extremes of Sichelman and recent UK cases, is consistent with CJEU jurisprudence, and is akin to the approach adopted in copyright.

Judicial approaches to patent scope in the UK

Under the Patents Act 1977 (UK), the scope of protection conferred by a patent is defined in section 60 according to the type of invention in question. Where the invention is a product, section 60(1)(a) applies, and the patent is infringed by any person who, while the patent is in force, 'makes, disposes of, offers to dispose of, uses or imports the product or keeps it whether for disposal or otherwise' in the UK without the consent of the patentee.

Of central importance in section 60 is 'the invention' to which the patent and its protection relate. Under section 125(1), 'the invention' for these purposes: 'shall . . . be taken to be that specified in [the patent] claim . . . as interpreted by the description and any drawings contained in that specification, and the extent of the protection conferred by a

[3] See *ibid.* p. 2; also Sichelman, Chapter 17 (at pp. 374–375).
[4] [2011] EWCA Civ 303, [2011] F.S.R. 19 at [72].
[5] *Schütz* v. *Werit* [2013] UKSC 16.

patent...shall be determined accordingly'. By further provision of section 125(3), the Protocol on the Interpretation of Article 69 of the European Patent Convention (EPC)[6] applies for the purpose of section 125(1), so as to require that the claims be interpreted in a way that ensures 'that the extent of the protection conferred by a [UK] patent...combines a fair protection for the patent proprietor with a reasonable degree of legal certainty for third parties'. Hence the central question, what exactly do section 125 and the Protocol require and permit of the courts when identifying the invention specified in the claims, and thereby determining the scope of protection conferred by the patent monopoly? Clearly they neither require nor permit the courts to give carte blanche to the patentee in defining that scope. Among other things, as formal legal documents equivalent to contracts and statutes, patent claims are required to be interpreted 'purposively'. This has been accepted in the UK since *Kirin-Amgen Inc.* v. *Hoescht Marion Roussel Ltd*,[7] where Lord Hoffmann (for the House of Lords) stated as follows:

> The determination of the extent of protection conferred by a European patent is an examination in which there is only one compulsory question, namely that set by art 69 and its Protocol: what would a person skilled in the art have understood the patentee to have used the language of the claim to mean? Everything else ... is only guidance to a judge trying to answer that question.[8]

On the other hand, as the courts' interpretive task does not take place in a legal vacuum, the purpose of the claimant cannot be the only consideration when construing patent claims. This is consistent with the further principle, recognized in *Kirin-Amgen*, that the purposive approach to claim construction requires that claims be read *contextually*.[9] In *Kirin-Amgen* contextualism was explained primarily as a means of avoiding the dangers of literalism.[10] In *Virgin Atlantic Airways Ltd* v. *Premium Aircraft Interiors UK Ltd*,[11] however, the Court of Appeal confirmed that it also requires that the claims be construed in their statutory context. Hence its decision that for the purpose of such construction, the notional skilled reader must be taken to assume that the claims were drafted with

[6] Convention on the Grant of European Patents (1973) 13 I.L.M. 268, as amended (EPC).
[7] [2004] UKHL 46, [2005] R.P.C. 9 (*Kirin-Amgen*). See especially at [32], [48].
[8] See *Kirin-Amgen* at [69]. The reference to 'purposive construction' is from Lord Diplock's opinion in *Catnic Components Ltd* v. *Hill & Smith Ltd* [1982] R.P.C. 183 at 243, which Lord Hoffmann affirmed in *Kirin-Amgen* as the approach required by the Protocol. See *Kirin-Amgen* at [48].
[9] See *Kirin-Amgen* at [29], [32], [48].
[10] See *ibid.* [41]. The Protocol expressly prohibits 'strict, literal' interpretations of claims.
[11] [2009] EWCA Civ 1062, [2010] R.P.C. 8.

knowledge of patent law and associated conventions of claim drafting.[12] The decision is important in confirming the central premise of section 125, that a subject matter specified in a claim is only protected on the basis that it is a 'patentable invention' within the meaning of section 1, and in its proper conception as the same.[13]

There remains the difficult question of whether the courts' recognition of the importance of context permits or requires that they consider the patent system's underlying policy aims, in addition to its rules and associated practices. A compelling argument can be made that it does, on two grounds. First, it is only with regard to those aims that the meaning of 'fair protection' for the patentee can be determined, and the requirements of the Protocol satisfied. And second, one cannot answer any legal question in a principled way without regard to the consequences of the answer and the initial reason for asking the question. The second of these points was well expressed by Lord Hoffmann in *Merrell Dow*, in his following remarks regarding the requirement of novelty:

> There is an infinite variety of descriptions under which the same thing may be known. Things may be described according to what they look like, how they are made, what they do and in many other ways. Under what description must it be known in order to justify the statement that one knows that it exists? *This depends entirely upon the purpose for which the question is being asked.*[14]

Why, then, it seems important to ask, are the courts required to interpret patent claims? The main reasons are twofold: first, to identify the object of the patentability enquiry for the purpose of determining whether a patent may be (or has been) validly granted; and second, to identify the object of the infringement enquiry, and thereby to decide what commercial and industrial activities are foreclosed for the period of the patent monopoly, having regard to the nature of the patent's contribution, and notwithstanding the cost of such foreclosure to society.

Of all of the possible factors bearing upon claim construction, this is the most controversial and difficult to unravel. Among other things, to

[12] *Ibid.* [13]–[15].

[13] See *Kirin-Amgen* at [33]–[34]; *ibid.* [12]–[13]. See also *Merrell Dow Pharmaceuticals Inc.* v. *H.B. Norton & Co. Ltd* [1995] UKHL 14, [1996] R.P.C. 76 at [36], [40]–[42] (Lord Hoffmann, emphasizing the restriction of protection to individual subject matter when conceived 'under the description' of the invention). For a fuller discussion see J. Pila, 'On the European Requirement for an Invention', note 1 above.

[14] See *Merrell Dow Pharmaceuticals Inc.* v. *H. B. Norton & Co. Ltd* [1995] UKHL 14, [1996] R.P.C. 76 at [36] (considering the meaning of 'novelty') (emphasis added).

say that the impact of patent scope ought to inform its determination is to suggest that the process of claim interpretation ought to be an explicitly normative one. In this regard, the terminology of 'normative characterization' might be usefully adopted. That terminology has been proposed by Professors Mark Freedland and Nicola Kountouris to express the idea of the essential and integral link which exists between the legal classification of personal work relations and its consequences. '[I]t is a terminology', they explain, 'which seeks to capture the essential connectedness between identifying the legal character of a given personal work relation and making normative propositions about that relation.'[15] So too here, the terminology of 'normative characterization' (or 'normative interpretation') captures well the idea that judicial interpretations of the invention specified in the claims are essentially and integrally connected to the legal consequences of the same, including the scope and impact of the patentee's monopoly.

To say that the impact of patent scope ought to inform its determination is also to suggest that the courts and appropriate institutions are equipped to identify and assess such impact; that 'normative interpretation' is an appropriate task for the courts. Before the introduction of the EPC in 1977, when the UK patent system was still largely a creature of the common law informed by section 6 of the English Statute of Monopolies 1623,[16] such a suggestion might have stood on firmer ground. On the other hand, and as pointed out above, even under the EPC it is difficult to see how the 'fair protection' which the Protocol requires can be ensured to a patentee without regard to the impact of the patent on society.

Until recently, this seems also to have been the view of the courts. For example, in *Biogen Inc.* v. *Medeva plc*[17] Lord Hoffmann (for the House of Lords) relied on the need to prevent 'research and healthy competition' from being stifled to support his conception of the claimed invention, and through it of the patentee's monopoly.[18] So too in *Kirin-Amgen*, his Lordship (again for the House of Lords) invoked the 'social contract between the state and the inventor which underlies patent law' – by which '[t]he state gives the inventor a monopoly in return for an immediate disclosure of all the information necessary to enable performance of the invention' – to support his conception of the claimed invention, and through it of the patentee's monopoly.[19] On the other hand, more

[15] M.R. Freedland & N. Kountouris, *The Legal Construction of Personal Work Relations* (Oxford University Press, 2011) 6.
[16] 21 Jac. 1 c. 3. [17] [1996] UKHL 18, [1997] R.P.C. 1 (HL). [18] *Ibid.* 52.
[19] *Kirin-Amgen* at [77].

recently in *Generics Inc.* v. *Lundbeck A/S*[20] the House of Lords – following decisions of Lord Hoffmann and Jacob LJ in the Court of Appeal – eschewed such explicit resort to policy in conceiving the claimed invention with a view to maximizing protection for the patentee in the belief that section 60(1)(a) guaranteed the same.[21] Their reasoning suggests a disinclination to permit considerations of policy expressly to limit the extent of protection conferred by individual patents – notwithstanding the need to interpret claims contextually, and the UK courts' continued invocation of policy to support expansive interpretations of the requirements of patentability.[22] The same effort to avoid explicit policy reasoning can also be seen in a very different context: the Court of Appeal's decision in *Schütz* v. *Werit*.[23]

Eschewing policy limits on patent scope to maximize protection (for products at least): *Schütz* v. *Werit*

Schütz v. *Werit* involved a patent for a container used for transporting liquids which comprised a cage and a plastic bottle. The dispute arose from the defendant's reconditioning of the containers, which the plaintiff argued infringed its exclusive right to make the invention under section 60(1)(a).

The main authority relied on by both parties was *United Wire Ltd* v. *Screen Repair Services (Scotland) Ltd*.[24] That case involved an invention which had been described in the claims as 'a shifting screen assembly... comprising a frame and two screens superimposed one on the other and adhesively secured...', and which the defendants had resold after reconditioning. According to the trial judge, by reconditioning the screens the defendants had merely prolonged their life, which involved a repair of the invention permitted under the implied licence which the defendants had acquired from the patentee on purchasing the product. The Court of Appeal and House of Lords disagreed. Accepting the statement of Lord

[20] [2009] UKHL 12, [2009] R.P.C. 13 (HL).

[21] For a discussion see Pila, *The Requirement for an Invention in Patent Law*, note 1 above, pp. 303–08; also Pila, 'Chemical Products and Proportionate Patents', note 1 above; Pila, 'Chemical Product Patents and Biogen Insufficiency Before the House of Lords', note 1 above.

[22] See, e.g., *Human Genome Sciences Inc.* v. *Eli Lilly and Co.* [2011] UKSC 51 at [99] (Lord Neuberger). For a discussion see J. Pila, 'Some Reflections on Method and Policy in the Crowded House of European Patent Law and their Implications for India', *National Law School of India Review*, 24 (2012) 54–74.

[23] [2011] EWCA Civ 303, [2011] F.S.R. 19 (CA). On the Supreme Court's decision see the Postscript below.

[24] [2001] R.P.C. 24 (CA, HL).

Hoffmann in *Canon Kabushiki Kaisha* v. *Green Cartridge Co. (Hong Kong) Ltd*: 'that the concept of a licence ... is not really applicable to the repair of a patented article [b]ecause repair is by definition something which does not amount to the manufacture of the patented article [and therefore] is not an infringement of the monopoly conferred by the patent',[25] Aldous LJ in the Court of Appeal identified the sole question to be decided as 'whether the acts of [the] defendant amount to manufacture of the product [having regard to] the nature of the invention as claimed and what was done by the defendant'.[26] He held that it did: by preparing a frame obtained from an assembly made by the plaintiff, and adding two meshes and tension to give it the features of the claim, the defendants had made the patented product in contravention of the plaintiff's monopoly.

The House of Lords affirmed this decision. In the opinion of Lord Bingham, that decision was consistent with 'the crucial underlying question' in any patent infringement action – 'whether what the defendant is shown to have done has deprived the patentee of the full rights to which his patent entitled him'.[27] Lord Hoffmann shared this view, and emphasized the importance when answering the relevant 'crucial question' of properly identifying the invention specified in the claims:

> [I]n this case the Court of Appeal was in my opinion entitled to substitute its own evaluation because I think, with great respect to the judge, that he did not correctly identify the patented product. He said that the frame was an important part of the assembly and that the defendants had prolonged 'the screen's useful life'. It is quite true that the defendants prolonged the useful life of the *frame*. It would otherwise presumably have been scrapped. But the *screen* was the combination of frame and meshes pre-tensioned by attachment with adhesive according to the invention. That product ceased to exist when the meshes were removed and the frame stripped down to the bare metal. What remained at that stage was merely an important component, a skeleton or chassis, from which a new screen could be made.[28]

In *Schütz* v. *Werit*, the difficulty facing the courts was what answer could be extracted from *United Wire* to the central question of when replacing part of an invention constitutes a making of that invention within the meaning of section 60(1)(a). According to the trial judge, the answer is when the part replaced does not embody any part of the inventive concept of the claim.[29] It followed, he decided, that the defendant's reconditioning of the container did not infringe the patent, for its inventive concept was

[25] [1997] A.C. 728 (H.L.) 735, cited in *United Wire* [2001] R.P.C. 24 at [24] (Aldous LJ), [55] (Lord Bingham), [71]–[72] (Lord Hoffmann).
[26] [2001] R.P.C. 24 at [30] (Aldous LJ). [27] *Ibid.* [54]. [28] *Ibid.* [73].
[29] [2010] EWHC 660 (Pat.), [2010] F.S.R. 22 at [197]–[98].

'wholly embodied in the ... cage', and the defendant's reconditioning activities were confined to replacing the plastic bottle.[30]

The Court of Appeal disagreed with this finding and its basis. In the view of Jacob LJ, the 'whole of the inventive concept' test which the trial judge supported is 'fuzzy and uncertain',[31] unsupported by law,[32] and inappropriately motivated by a policy concern to limit the economic impact of the plaintiff's monopoly.[33] Regarding the last of these, Jacob LJ referred to the House of Lords' rejection of a spare parts exception to copyright infringement in *Canon* v. *Green Cartridge*, notwithstanding the consequences of doing so for the market and competition, and cited with approval the statement of Lord Hoffmann in that case that '[t]he courts are ill-equipped to pronounce upon ... questions of economic policy [which] are generally left to specialized bodies such as the Monopolies and Mergers Commission'.[34]

The Court of Appeal's decision in *Schütz* v. *Werit* reflects the same concern as the Court of Appeal and House of Lords in *Generics* v. *Lundbeck* to ensure full protection for proprietors of product patents. It also reflects the restricted role of domestic courts since the introduction of the EPC. For example, under the pre-EPC regime inherent patentability was defined with reference to section 6 of the Statute of Monopolies, which restricted protection to subject matter 'not contrary to the law, nor mischievous to the state, by raising prices of commodities at home, or hurt of trade, or generally inconvenient'; a restriction which the courts were entrusted to interpret.[35] Given this, it may be truer to say that the EPC has altered the constitutional remit of domestic courts than that they are ill-equipped to consider questions of (social or) economic policy; a suggestion which receives some support from the following statement of Aldous LJ in *United Wire*:

> The concept of implied licence [to repair an invention] in patent cases does not seem apt now infringement has been defined in the Patents Act 1977 which was an Act giving effect to European obligations.[36]

Overall, the Court of Appeal's criticism of the trial judge in *Schütz* v. *Werit* for his 'fuzzy and uncertain' reasoning, and his alleged concern

[30] *Ibid.* [206]. [31] [2011] EWCA Civ 303, [2011] F.S.R. 19 at [72].
[32] *Ibid.* [73]–[76]. [33] *Ibid.* [78]–[79].
[34] *Ibid.* [79] (quoting from *Canon* [1997] A.C. 728, 738 (Lord Hoffmann)).
[35] On the courts' application of this exclusion before 1977 see Pila, *The Requirement for an Invention in Patent Law*, note 1 above, ch. 3, especially pp. 72–73, 98–101.
[36] [2001] R.P.C. 24 at [25]. On the inappropriateness of the courts deciding matters of social or economic policy generally see, e.g., *In re P* [2008] UKHL 38, [2009] 1 A.C. 173 at [48] (Lord Walker).

with economic policy, seems unfair for two reasons. The first is the trial judge's concern to contain the role of judicial policy reasoning in determining patent scope. That concern is apparent from his rejection of both the 'implied licence to repair' theory, and the approach of German courts to determining infringement, on the ground that each 'force[s] backward' and renders uncertain the boundaries of the patent monopoly.[37] This leaves the second reason, which is that all patent decisions involve economic policy, whether or not they are acknowledged to do so. Thus, the point is not whether the patentee is entitled to full protection for his claimed invention, but what exactly 'full protection' means. In the remainder of this chapter I draw on CJEU and copyright jurisprudence to consider this, before returning to consider the Supreme Court's decision in *Schütz* v. *Werit*, and its implications for my analysis, in a postscript.

Subject matter-based constraints on patent scope: insights from CJEU and copyright jurisprudence

In the UK, the scope of protection conferred by copyright is defined in section 16 of the Copyright, Designs and Patents Act 1988 (UK). Under that section, copyright in a work is infringed by any person who, without the licence of the copyright owner, does or authorizes another to do any of the acts restricted by the copyright, directly or indirectly, in relation to the work as a whole or any substantial part of it. The effect of this definition is to restrict the scope of copyright protection to 'substantial parts' of individual works.

The leading authorities on 'substantial part' are *Designers Guild Ltd* v. *Russell Williams (Textiles) Ltd*[38] and *Newspaper Licensing Agency* v. *Marks & Spencer plc* (*NLA*).[39] According to Lord Hoffmann in both cases, whether part of a work is a substantial part depends on whether it reflects sufficient of the constitutive features of the relevant work, properly conceived.[40] Those features differ according to the particular work in question. For example, what constitutes a poem as a copyright work is

[37] See [2010] EWHC 660 at [199], [194]–[95]. As described by the trial judge, the German approach involves a multi-factor test that requires the courts, in certain contexts at least, to balance the interests of the patentee against those of the user.

[38] [2000] UKHL 58, [2000] 1 W.L.R. 2416 (HL).

[39] [2001] UKHL 38, [2002] R.P.C. 225 (HL).

[40] For a detailed discussion see J. Pila. 'An Australian Copyright Revolution and its Relevance for UK Jurisprudence: *IceTV* in the Light of *Infopaq* v. *Danske*', *Oxford University Commonwealth Law Journal*, 9 (2010) 77–93; J. Pila, 'Copyright and its Categories of Original Works', *Oxford Journal of Legal Studies*, 30 (2010) 229–54.

different from what constitutes a compilation or typographical arrangement as a copyright work, and it is different in ways that affect judicial determinations of 'substantial part', and thus of the scope of protection which each work's copyright confers.

It seems natural to ask why an equivalent 'substantial part' test does not exist in patent law, and whether such a test might be adopted by the courts notwithstanding its omission from section 60 (and the EPC). That it might and even ought to be adopted is consistent with the courts' statutory obligation to interpret the claims contextually, including in the light of the patentability requirements. The effect of that obligation, as explained above, is to limit the protection conferred by a patent to the claimed subject matter in its capacity as a section 1 invention, consistent with the restricted protection conferred by copyright.

Two examples may be useful to demonstrate further the implications of this analysis for patent scope. The first is provided by the European law of copyright infringement. Under Article 2(a) of the Information Society Directive,[41] EU Member States are required to 'provide for the exclusive right to authorize or prohibit direct or indirect, temporary or permanent reproduction by any means and in any form, in whole or in part . . . for authors, of their works'. Thus, copyright in an authorial work is infringed under European law by any unauthorized reproduction of the work 'in part'. On its face, this might be thought to support an expansive test of infringement, similar to that supported by the Court of Appeal in *Schütz* v. *Werit*, and in contrast to the approach of Lord Hoffmann in *Designers Guild* and *NLA*. According to the CJEU and the Court of Appeal, however, this is not the case.[42] Rather, Article 2(a) only prohibits reproductions of parts of a work that express its author's own intellectual creation (according to the CJEU),[43] or that are qualitatively substantial within the meaning of *Designers Guild* (according to the Court of Appeal).[44] In this way, the European and UK conceptions of copyright works as expressive creations of a particular category constrain the scope of protection conferred by copyright by limiting it to works conceived in their capacity as the same.[45]

[41] Directive 2001/29/EC on the harmonisation of certain aspects of copyright and related rights in the information society [2001] O.J. L. 167/10.
[42] See (C-5/98) *Infopaq International A/S* v. *Danske Dagblades Forening* [2009] E.C.D.R. 16 (CJEU); *The Newspaper Licensing Agency Ltd* v. *Meltwater Holding BV* [2011] EWCA Civ 890.
[43] See *Infopaq* [2009] E.C.D.R. 16 at [37]–[39].
[44] See *The Newspaper Licensing Agency Ltd* [2010] EWHC 3099 at [81]; [2011] EWCA Civ 890 at [23–[24].
[45] See *Infopaq* [2009] E.C.D.R. 16 at [51].

This leads to my second example, which is of the similar subject matter-based constraint imposed by the CJEU in the context of genetic product patents. According to Article 3 of the Biotech Directive,[46] EU Member States must ensure patent protection for 'inventions which are new, which involve an inventive step and which are susceptible of industrial application'. Under Article 5(3), where the invention is an isolated gene sequence, '[t]he industrial application of [the] sequence or [the] partial sequence of [the] gene must be disclosed in the patent application'. This requirement is further supported by recitals (23) and (24) of the Directive, which provide that 'a mere DNA sequence without indication of a function does not contain any technical information and is therefore not a patentable invention', and that 'in order to comply with the industrial application criterion it is necessary in cases where a sequence or partial sequence of a gene is used to produce a protein or part of a protein, to specify which protein or part of a protein is produced or what function it performs'. In *Monsanto Technology LLC* v. *Cefetra BV et al.*,[47] the question arose for the CJEU whether these provisions of the Biotech Directive permit claims for the protection of isolated DNA sequences as such, so as to ensure the expansive scope of protection recognized for product claims by the House of Lords in *Generics* v. *Lundbeck*. The Court held that it does not. In its decision,

> ... the import of recitals 23 and 24 in the preamble to, and Article 5(3) of the Directive is that a DNA sequence does not enjoy any protection under patent law when the function performed by that sequence is not specified.
>
> Since the Directive thus makes the patentability of a DNA sequence subject to indication of the function it performs, it must be regarded as not according any protection to a patented DNA sequence which is not able to perform the specific function for which it was patented.[48]

It is submitted that the principle underlying this reasoning is the same as that underlying the Court's interpretation of Article 2(a) of the Information Society Directive and Lord Hoffmann's reasoning in *Designers Guild* and *NLA*, namely, that the protection conferred by European patent law is confined to inventions which satisfy the requirements of patentability, and that the scope of such protection must be defined in a way which properly reflects this. This submission supports my wider argument, that the Patents Act properly interpreted requires that the

[46] Directive 98/44/EC on the legal protection of biotechnological inventions O.J. L. 213 (30 July 1998) 13–21.

[47] [2010] E.U. E.C.J. C-428/08, [2011] F.S.R. 6 (CJEU).

[48] *Ibid.* [44]–[45].

scope of protection be limited with reference to the requirements of patentability so as to ensure that the subject matter specified in the claim is protected qua invention; and that the concepts of 'full' and 'fair' protection are understood accordingly.[49] The 'whole of the inventive concept' test which the trial judge supported in *Schütz* v. *Werit* may be consistent with this: the inventive concept of an invention being analogous to the original expressive aspects of an authorial work. By contrast Sichelman's theory is not, for while it purports to treat 'eligibility' as the central mechanism for determining patent scope, the test it advocates does not depend on an assessment of the constitutive aspects of patentable subject matter per se, but rather on the impact of the patent on society. In saying this I do not deny that eligibility ought to be conceived with that impact in mind – which indeed it ought to be[50] – but rather draw attention to the absence of any conception of eligible subject matter in Sichelman's theory (beyond that which can be inferred from his references to 'practical application' and 'technology'). For example, applying his theory in the analogous setting of copyright would require the courts to determine 'substantial part' having regard to the costs of foreclosing use of the work as against its benefits to society. In fact, this is very similar to the theory proposed for copyright by Spence and Endicott in their 2005 article 'Vagueness in the Scope of Copyright'.[51] There the authors criticized Lord Hoffmann's approach to 'substantial part' in *Designers Guild* and *NLA* for its 'vagueness', and argued that it ought to be replaced with a test better tailored to the (alleged) purpose of copyright in incentivizing 'the creation, dissemination and efficient exploitation of protected works', and promoting authors' 'expressive autonomy'.[52] The particular test which they supported involved a balancing of the economic and expressive interests in permitting and foreclosing use of the protected work.[53] Remove the reference to 'expressive autonomy' and one is left with an approach similar to Sichelman's 'patent eligibility scope' approach.[54]

[49] For a fuller discussion see the works cited in note 1 above.

[50] See Pila, *The Requirement for an Invention in Patent Law*, note 1 above, p. 338.

[51] M. Spence & T. Endicott, 'Vagueness in the Scope of Copyright', *Law Quarterly Review*, 121 (2005) 657–80.

[52] See *ibid.* 672–73.

[53] See *ibid.* 673–74 (proposing that courts determine substantial part having regard to: '(i) the impact of the taking on the market for the original work; (ii) the effect of precluding the taking on the market for substitutes for the work; (iii) the importance of the part taken to the expressive effect of the original work; and (iv) the effect of precluding the taking on the normal conduct of expressive exchange').

[54] Compare, for example, the Spence & Endicott factors (*ibid.*) with those proposed by Sichelman (Chapter 17).

As with Lord Hoffmann's opinion in *Biogen* v. *Medeva*, it is possible to read Spence and Endicott's 2005 proposal as born of despair at the absence of clear and sufficient limits on the scope of intellectual property protection, in addition, perhaps, to disagreement over the policies reflected in its development.[55] According to Lord Hoffmann in *Kirin-Amgen*, the doctrine of equivalents owes its origins to a similar sense of despair; the courts' having 'felt unable to escape from interpretations which "unsparing logic" appeared to require and which prevented them from according the patentee the full extent of the monopoly which the person skilled in the art would reasonably have thought he was claiming'.[56] However, just as the doctrine of equivalents has been criticized for having 'taken on a life of its own, unbounded by the claims',[57] so the Sichelman and Spence and Endicott proposals seem susceptible to this complaint. The point underlines the central difficulty in this area, which is how to ensure an approach to determining patent scope which takes proper account of (legislative) policy while also remaining sufficiently grounded in the patent claims.

It is submitted that the answer to this is to ensure that determinations of patent scope are properly linked to that which merits a subject matter its protection, as occurs in copyright.[58] This is consistent with the principle affirmed in *Generics* v. *Lundbeck*, that the contribution for which a patent is granted, and with reference to which its scope of protection must consequently be defined, is *the invention*; a principle which the Court of Appeal in *Schütz* v. *Werit* seems to have been concerned to respect. If this is true, I have elsewhere argued, we need a robust and meaningful definition of what constitutes an invention, and an understanding of how individual subject matters are properly conceived 'under the [same] description'.[59] My own view is that any such conception ought properly to reflect the utilitarian purpose of the patent system in promoting the industrial arts, and thus go beyond the technical features

[55] Central to Spence & Endicott's criticism of the *Designers Guild* approach was its failure fully to recognize and give effect to the so-called 'idea/expression distinction' by limiting copyright protection to works' expressive form. That this criticism is of a policy nature is underlined by the absence of any such distinction in UK law other than via (indirectly applicable) European copyright directives and in the context of certain specific subject matter categories. On the status of that distinction see further Pila, 'An Australian Copyright Revolution and its Relevance for UK Jurisprudence', note 42 above, at 90–91.

[56] *Kirin-Amgen* at [41].

[57] See *Warner-Jenkinson Co. Inc.* v. *Hilton Davis Chemical Co.* (1997) 520 U.S. 17 at 28–29, discussed in *Kirin-Amgen* at [39].

[58] For a fuller discussion see the works cited in note 1 above.

[59] See, e.g., Pila, *The Requirement for an Invention in Patent* Law (note 1 above); Pila, "Patents for Genes and Methods of Analysis and Comparison" (note 1 above), and the other works cited at note 1.

of a subject matter to include the advance which it is purported to represent.[60] Hence my proposed conception of the requirement for an invention, as a requirement for a purposive human method of working upon the physical world to produce an objectively discernible (material) result directed to advancing the industrial arts;[61] a conception the first part of which has recently been accepted by the Enlarged Board of Appeal of the European Patent Office.[62]

Conclusion

Patent eligibility is a widely contested and misunderstood aspect of patent law. It is frequently confused with the secondary patentability requirements, including those of novelty and inventive step, as well as with the public policy exclusions in respect of methods of medical treatment, plant and animal varieties, and inventions the commercial exploitation of which would be contrary to *ordre public* or morality. At the heart of its contestation is whether it can be completely separated from these requirements and exclusions. As the discussion above makes clear, my own view is that it cannot be;[63] a view with which Sichelman disagrees. Indeed, it is the 'importation' of eligibility into the secondary requirements of patentability which he particularly decries, and which he sees in the US Supreme Court's reasoning in *Funk Brothers Seed Co* v. *Kalo Inoculant Co*,[64] as well as in subsequent applications of the natural phenomena exclusion which *Funk Bros.* explicates.[65] His response is to reject that explication, the natural phenomenon exclusion, and the understanding of eligibility on which each of them is based. According to that understanding, one role of inherent patentability is to limit the operation of the patent system by defining the types of subject matter capable of supporting a patent grant. In Sichelman's argument, such 'gatekeeper' accounts of eligibility are problematic in their discrimination against newer technologies in obstruction of the aim of the US patent system 'to spur new technologies'.[66] What the law needs instead, he suggests, is a 'forward-looking inquiry into patent scope'.[67]

[60] See Pila, *The Requirement for an Invention in Patent Law*, note 1 above, p. 338.
[61] See *ibid.*
[62] See (G2/07 & G1/08) *Essentially Biological Processes* [2011] EPOR 27, [128]–[132] (E.B.A.).
[63] See *ibid.* p. vii, Pila, 'On the European Requirement for an Invention', note 1 above.
[64] 333 U.S. 127 (1948).
[65] See Sichelman, Chapter 17 (at pp. 361, 367–372).
[66] See *ibid.* p. 372. [67] See *ibid.* p. 380.

The main burden of Sichelman's argument seems clear: to maximize the range of subject matter capable of supporting a patent while ensuring that the scope of protection which the patent confers is proportionate to the contribution made by the patentee. Hence his argument that inherent patentability ought to be given little rein as a pre-patent determinant of patent availability, and substantial rein as a post-patent determinant of US patent scope.

The latter part of this statement is one with which I agree, and have argued for previously. However, in the arguments I have made, for eligibility to serve its post-patent role effectively, it must be conceived in more than *de minimis* terms.[68] The reason is that only then will it be capable of supporting the process of claim interpretation above[69] by anchoring it to both 'technology', and the purpose of the patent system in rewarding contributions to the industrial arts. It is submitted that only once such a conception of eligibility is accepted, along with the need to limit patent protection accordingly by conceiving claimed subject matter with reference to the same, will the existing tension between defining patent scope with reference to the subject matter specified in the claims, and ensuring that such scope is proportionate having regard to the contribution which the patent makes, be satisfactorily resolved.[70] As I have tried to show above, this is a conclusion which finds support in CJEU and copyright jurisprudence.

It will be apparent from this discussion that my disagreement with Sichelman is in part substantive and in part methodological. Substantively, I reject his view of the patent system as existing 'to spur new technologies' by protecting any 'practical application', much as I reject a view of the copyright system as existing to encourage the creation of new works. One reason is that the concepts of 'practical application' and 'technology' are too vague and unstable to support principled law-making in the patent field. Another is the need to engage with the reason for seeking to spur new technologies, and to ensure that that reason informs the manner of its pursuit.[71]

[68] Pila, 'On the European Requirement for an Invention', note 1 above, 925–26.

[69] See pp. 386–387 above.

[70] Pila, 'On the European Requirement for an Invention', note 1 above, 925–26; Pila, *The Requirement for an Invention in Patent Law*, note 1 above, p. 338.

[71] On the relevance of the purpose of patent protection for the scope of patent eligibility generally see *Association for Molecular Pathology* v. *Myriad Genetics Inc.* 569 U.S. 12-398 (2013) (deciding that the patentability of isolated genes could not be determined without regard to the purpose of the US patent system, and that as that purpose is to promote creation, and the act of isolating a gene from its natural environment does not involve the creation of anything, isolated genes are not patentable under US law).

Perhaps more interesting is our methodological disagreement, regarding the best manner of determining patent scope. In this chapter I have defended my earlier writings on that issue, drawing on UK and European jurisprudence to that end. In taking this approach, however, I do not mean to deny the existence of alternative methods of determining patent scope, which may be feasible and desirable in the UK and Europe. In the space that remains I will mention one such method: a proportionality-based test derived from general principles of European law.[72]

According to the principle of proportionality, limitations on constitutional rights and freedoms must be necessary, suitable and proportionate *sensu stricto* having regard to their legitimate purpose. Adapting this principle for current purposes, we might define the proper scope of a patent monopoly as that which is necessary, suitable and proportionate having regard to the legitimate purpose it seeks to serve, and the impact of granting it on other (legitimate) interests. In the European context, and reflecting the public law origins of proportionality, such purpose and interests tend to be derived from constitutional rights and values. For example, and taking the very different case of peer-to-peer sharing of copyright material (P2P), the legitimate purpose to be served by an order seeking the disclosure of internet users' identities will be that of enabling a claimant to protect his or her copyright, and the (legitimate) interests affected by such an order will include the privacy and data protection interests of internet users, and the defendant's freedom to conduct the business of an internet service provider. While the reconciliation of these four competing interests (drawn from the Charter of Fundamental Rights[73]) will differ in the hands of different courts, the need to identify them expressly ensures a degree of discipline and transparency in their decision-making, as well as grounding P2P jurisprudence in the constitutional values of the general (European) legal order.

As I have argued elsewhere, proportionality has an important role to play – and is playing an increasingly important role – in the European and UK IP fields because of its support for a model of harmonization focused on convergence around general legal principles. An important by-product of that model is the constitutionalization of intellectual property,

[72] For a full discussion see J. Pila, 'A Constitutionalized Doctrine of Precedent and the *Marleasing* Principle as Bases for a European Legal Methodology', in A. Ohly & J. Pila (eds), *The Europeanization of Intellectual Property Law: Towards a European Legal Methodology* (Oxford University Press, 2013) ch. 13, from which the ensuing discussion is drawn.

[73] Charter on Fundamental Rights of the European Union (Charter) O.J. C 364/1 (18 December 2000).

and of common law judicial decision-making. Hence its relevance for the current discussion, which lies in its value as a means of supporting judicial policy-based reasoning. Borrowing again from copyright jurisprudence, we find a good example of this value in the law of fair dealing.

According to the UK fair dealing defences, the unauthorized use of a copyright work for the statutory purposes of criticism or review, reporting current events, or research or private study, is permitted provided it is 'fair'.[74] Central, therefore, is the concept of 'fairness', and how it is determined by courts in a particular case. In the UK, the established approach to fairness is to consider a list of judicially formulated factors – factors which, significantly, map closely to the Spence and Endicott test of copyright scope discussed above,[75] as well as to the US copyright law of fair use – including the purpose and extent of the use, the impact of the use on the copyright owner's market, and the extent of the work's prior circulation to the public.[76] In addition, however, UK courts have sometimes expressed their conclusions on fair dealing in language reminiscent of the European proportionality test. An example is the case of *Ashdown* v. *Telegraph Group Ltd*, where the Court of Appeal summarized its decision in the following terms:

> We do not ... consider that it is arguable that there was any justification for the extent of the reproduction of [the copyright work]. It appears to us that the [work] was deliberately filleted in order to extract colourful passages that were most likely to add flavour to the article and thus to appeal to the readership of the newspaper. Mr Ashdown's work product was deployed in the way that it was for reasons that were essentially journalistic in furtherance of the commercial interests of the Telegraph Group. We do not consider it arguable that Article 10 requires that the Group should be able to profit from this use of Mr Ashdown's copyright without paying compensation.[77]

In effect, the Court's reasoning here is that the use of the work was excessive having regard to the legitimate (freedom of expression) purpose which it allegedly served.[78] This is consistent with a proportionality-based analysis. By alluding to such analysis, however, the Court inadvertently exposed the incoherence of its traditional 'judicial factors' approach to fairness by drawing attention to their focus on the private interests and motivations of the litigating parties

[74] See Copyright, Designs and Patents Act 1988 (UK), ss. 29, 30.
[75] And hence Sichelman's test of patent scope; see note 55 above.
[76] See, e.g., *Ashdown* v. *Telegraph Group Ltd* [2002] QB 546 (CA); *N.L.A. Ltd* v. *Meltwater Holding BV* [2011] EWCA Civ 890.
[77] [2002] QB 546 at [82].
[78] See Charter on Fundamental Rights of the European Union, Article 16.

at the expense of the legitimate (freedom of expression) purpose of the dealing itself. In so doing it exposed a disjuncture between the statutorily expressed purposes of the fair dealing defences and the courts' method of applying them, and between the UK law of copyright and the constitutional values of the general European and UK legal orders themselves; the courts' construction of fair dealing reflecting an a priori prioritization of IP owners' property rights above other fundamental rights, such as freedom of expression.[79] Hence my suggestion, that quite apart from its methodological value for Europe in supporting a particular form of legal integration, proportionality has an important role to play in supporting coherent and democratic decision-making more generally by ensuring that IP and other private law systems are fully integrated into the general legal orders of which they form part, and – most importantly for this chapter – by imposing a normative and doctrinal discipline on courts when reasoning from the law to decisions in individual cases.

Would the European principle of proportionality provide a feasible and desirable alternative to the approaches to claim construction considered above? As noted, its adoption as the basis for a common European test of patent scope would certainly be in keeping with wider trends within the EU and the UK. On the other hand, it would be open to the same criticisms as Sichelman's approach, including that it gives undue respectability and credibility to discretionary decision-making, subverts democratic policy- and law-making,[80] and generally assigns too much power to the courts.[81] It also presumes that different interests *can* be weighed and balanced, which is widely contested by EU and public lawyers and legal theorists alike.[82] Nonetheless, it offers another, and specifically European, methodological tool for resolving the central challenge which all patent jurisdictions face, of ensuring that the protection conferred by a monopoly grant is proportionate to the contribution which the monopolized invention makes.

[79] That fundamental rights have a prior equal weight is a central tenet of proportionality-based reasoning, and has been expressly recognized by the UK courts in the P2P and privacy contexts. See, e.g., *Campbell* v. *M.G.N. Ltd* [2004] UKHRR 648, [2004] UKHL 22, [55]–[56] (Lord Hoffmann).

[80] By, for example, preventing the legislature from deciding how different constitutional values ought to be reconciled.

[81] See T. Harbo, 'The Function of the Proportionality Principle in EU Law', *European Law Journal*, 16 (2010) 158–85.

[82] See, e.g., Harbo (*ibid.*); L. Alexander & K. Kress, 'Against Legal Principles', *Iowa Law Review*, 82 (1996–1997) 739–86; T.A.O Endicott. 'Proportionality and Incommensurability', (2012), University of Oxford Legal Research Paper No. 40/2012, http://ssrn.com/abstract=2086622.

Postscript: the Supreme Court's decision in Schütz *v.* Werit

As noted in the Introduction, the Supreme Court beat this volume to press with its judgment in the *Schütz* v. *Werit* appeal.[83] Adopting a 'somewhat more nuanced' version of the trial judge's 'whole inventive concept' test,[84] Lord Neuberger (writing for the Court) overturned the Court of Appeal's decision of patent infringement, along with the reasoning on which that decision was based. The starting point for his decision was the need to interpret patent rights 'contextually', and having regard to the following considerations: (a) the terms of the rights' legislative expression; (b) the need for legal 'clarity and certainty', and to 'protect the patentee's monopoly while not stifling reasonable competition'; (c) the 'happenstance' nature of patent claims, and the (potentially irrational) legal and strategic aims which their drafting reflects; and (d) the need to respect precedent while also acknowledging the 'European patent scheme',[85] including both the EPC and the 1975 Community Patent Convention.[86] According to Lord Neuberger, the specific question to be asked in deciding infringement was whether the replaced part of the patented container was sufficiently important to be more than 'a subsidiary part' of it.[87] The Court decided it was not. Thus, in replacing the bottle the appellants had not infringed the respondents' right to make the container.[88]

It is submitted that this reasoning provides a strong endorsement of the analysis above. Above all, it derives from the need to interpret patent rights contextually a test of infringement which takes explicit account of patent policy, while also remaining firmly anchored in the patent claims. It also involves a test of infringement which is virtually identical to that adopted in copyright – the main difference being its reference to 'subsidiary' rather than 'substantial' part – and which similarly ties the scope of rights to those qualitative aspects of the subject matter which merit it a patent monopoly.[89] Given this, and for the reasons discussed at length

[83] [2013] UKSC 16. [84] *Ibid.* [77]. [85] *Ibid.* [26]–[28].

[86] Convention for the European Patent for the Common Market 76/76/EEC (15 December 1975). This Convention never received the ratifications required to take effect. In substance however it has much in common with the current European unitary patent regulation (Regulation (EU) 1257/2012 of the European Parliament and of the Council of 17 December 2012 implementing enhanced cooperation in the area of the creation of unitary patent protection). For a discussion see J. Pila, 'The European Patent: An Old and Vexing Problem', *International & Comparative Law Quarterly*, 62 (2013) 917–40.

[87] [2013] UKSC 16 at [61].

[88] *Ibid.* [78]. Important were the bottle's freestanding and replaceable nature, its lack of connection to the article's inventive concept, and its much shorter life expectancy than the article's other component.

[89] *Ibid.* [77].

above, the Supreme Court's decision is to be welcomed. By adopting a test of infringement akin to that adopted in copyright, it eschews the extremes of both Sichelman and the *Schütz* v. *Werit* Court of Appeal, and ensures that patent scope is limited with reference to the patented subject matter properly conceived.

Before concluding, it is worth highlighting a further aspect of the Supreme Court's reasoning in *Schütz* v. *Werit*, which is its explicit reference to the Community Patent Convention in support of its reasoning. The importance of that reference derives from the very different values of the EPC and EU patent systems, and the different impact of each on European and UK jurisprudence.

As has been seen, the EPC is at least partly to blame for the tendency of UK courts post-*Lundbeck* to eschew explicit resort to policy with a view to maximizing protection for patentees. As has also been seen, EU law is having a rather different impact as a result of its constitutionalization of IP, and its support of judicial policy-based reasoning. Indeed, this could be said to account for the CJEU's approach to infringement in *Monsanto*, mirroring its approach to infringement in the neighbouring field of copyright. Read in that light, the importance of the Supreme Court's reference to the EU patent system in *Schütz* becomes apparent: it served to check (what I have previously referred to as) the expansionist and insular tendencies of the European Patent Organization, including its technophile view of patentability,[90] and to pave the way for an alternative approach more akin to that of the CJEU, reflecting the same middle ground position described above.

[90] See Pila, 'A Constitutionalized Doctrine of Precedent', note 72 above.

Part X

Limitations: Copyright and trademark defenses

19 Make me walk, make me talk, do whatever you please: Barbie and exceptions

*Rebecca Tushnet**

Barbie® is a symbol of America – down to the ®, representing Mattel's claim of exclusivity. The Barbie brand is capacious, covering products of every kind. You and your Barbie can even wear matching jewelry. The doll represents an aspiration to an ideal and also a never-ending mutability. One basic body has been changed over time and reworked into multiple ethnicities, dressed in a seemingly infinite selection of outfits, themselves representing a wide range of hobbies and careers (getting married might be one or the other), though almost always with feet arched to wear high heels, even for Army Medic Barbie.[1]

Barbie is the perfect woman, and she is also grotesque, plasticized hyperreality, presenting a femininity exaggerated to the point of caricature.

Barbie's marketplace success, combined with (and likely related to) her overlapping and contradictory meanings, also allows her to embody some key exceptions to copyright and trademark law. Though Mattel's lawsuits were not responsible for the initial recognition of those exceptions, they illuminate key principles and contrasts in American law. Mattel attempted to use both copyright and trademark to control the meaning of Barbie, reflecting a trend towards such overlapping claims: Creative material becomes a brand, and brands have so many creative elements that copyright's low originality standard recognizes copyrightable subject matter therein. Trademark can thus be asserted as a means to provide copyright owners with potentially perpetual rights, and copyright can be asserted as a means for trademark owners to evade limits designed for commercial transactions.

In order to ensure that their combined scope is no greater than the sum of their parts, both trademark and copyright defenses ought to be considered together. The Barbie cases highlight the problem that overlaps

* Julie Cohen provided valuable feedback, as did participants at the roundtable organized around this volume.

[1] As a result, I can report, her flat-footed boots rarely stay on.

between the two regimes can challenge the very idea of IP boundaries, unless robust defenses exist against overclaiming. More broadly, there is an international debate over whether US copyright fair use, with its focus on transformativeness and flexibility in response to new situations, is a good model for other nations as they consider modernizing their own copyright exemptions and limitations. Fair use has been attacked as notoriously vague and unpredictable. On the other hand, America has produced a number of powerhouse industries, many of them (such as search engines) successfully reliant on fair use even in America's notoriously litigious environment. International comparisons are fraught with danger, but perhaps something about the boundaries of IP can be learned from comparing two American versions of fair use, both of which have been employed to defend unauthorized uses of the famous Barbie doll.

American copyright law has a number of highly detailed and even baroque statutory limitations allowing particular types of uses, and then a general fair use defense, which has often been decried for its uncertainty. American trademark law, by contrast, has historically been mostly judge-made, with the occasional statutory defense or limitation. Every circuit now uses a multifactor test to identify infringement, though some courts modify the test in certain circumstances, such as use of a trademark as a search keyword to trigger competitive advertising, or in cases of "nominative fair use." While the initial ban on confusion was generally worded, more recent legislative changes to trademark law have been more likely to follow the same complex and reticulated model as copyright's non-fair-use-based exclusions. The federal trademark dilution law and its subsequent revision added a number of multifactor tests and multi-step exemptions, and anti-cybersquatting law is similar in this regard. This tendency of the law to become more complex over time has significant costs, especially for defendants who find their potential defenses turned into a confusing maze of overlapping but differently defined concepts.[2]

When contrasted to current trademark defenses, copyright's vagueness starts to look a little better.[3] Perhaps because of the four-factor fair use test codified in the 1976 Copyright Act, courts have been less likely to add new elements defendants must satisfy in order to qualify for fair use

[2] *See* W. McGeveran, "Rethinking Trademark Fair Use," 94 *Iowa L. Rev.* 49 (2008).

[3] A robust literature on predicting fair use has developed, and though it does differ in the details, the commentators suggest that fair use is not much worse in terms of predictability than any other concept in America's highly litigious culture. *See* B. Beebe, "An Empirical Study of U.S. Copyright Fair Use Opinions, 1978–2005," 156 *Penn. L. Rev.* 549 (2008); M. Sag, "Predicting Fair Use," 73 *Ohio St. L. J.* 47 (2012); P. Samuelson, "Unbundling Fair Uses," 77 *Fordham L. Rev.* 2537 (2009).

(though at the same time each individual factor can be weighed to accord with a judge's view of the equities).

This chapter examines several Barbie cases – all involving defense wins on the part of a creative refashioner of Barbie's image – that illustrate how courts have responded to attempts to suppress criticism, parody, and playfulness using existing works. I conclude that copyright's flexible fair use defense is easier to understand and implement than the current set of overlapping and yet often rigid defenses courts have cobbled together in trademark cases. Trademark could benefit from clearer identification of nonactionable categories of use. The full set of protected uses might not be the same as the set of copyright fair uses, but at the very least a creative commentary should as clearly be beyond the trademark owner's power to suppress as it is beyond a copyright owner's reach.

Barbie

Barbie means many things to many people.[4] Yochai Benkler used her as an example of the heterogeneity of meaning that, while it always existed, was exposed in new and more salient ways by the rise of the Internet and, in particular, search engines. The top results from his Google search, as reported in his 2006 book, in order, were: Mattel's official site; the official collectors' site; AdiosBarbie.com (a critical site); a Barbie-collectible magazine; a quiz, *If You Were a Barbie, Which Messed Up Version Would You Be?*; the Visible Barbie Project (discussed below); "Barbie: The Image of Us All" (an undergraduate paper on the cultural history of Barbie); a Barbie and Ken sex animation; a Barbie dressed as a suicide bomber; and Barbies dressed and painted as countercultural

[4] *See, e.g.*, *Mattel, Inc.* v. *3894207 Canada Inc.*, [2006] 1 S.C.R. 772, 2006 SCC 22 para. 79 (noting that Barbie's meanings are not all positive and that "the association of the BARBIE doll with food might be taken as a warning of blandness"); J.B. Thomas, *Naked Barbies, Warrior Joes, and Other Forms of Visible Gender* (University of Illinois Press, 2003), 6 ("Barbie's adult female body makes her appear as a sort of Everywoman, and because most women's bodies do not look like Barbie's, that quality often generates controversy. Currently, Barbie's biggest public relations problem is her overly perfect physique. Balancing that is her greatest strength – the idiosyncratic uses people make of her . . ."); T. Kelly, "Sarah Haney, Photographer, Captures the Darker Side of Barbie," 19 March 2012, at 11:48 am, www.huffingtonpost.com/2012/03/19/sarah-haney-barbie-photos_n_1354425.html?ncid=edlinkusaolp00000003 ("I was able to expand it so much beyond the initial joke in large part because the doll herself embodies such a contradiction," Haney said in an email to the Huffington Post. "She's marketed as this wholesome, all-American Madonna to little girls, but if you look at her as an adult, particularly at her body and clothes, she's a pretty clear embodiment of the whore." "Still," Haney said "Barbie is the perfect icon to poke fun at.").

images.[5] Benkler celebrates these juxtapositions, arguing that a search for "Barbie" will now immediately foreground Barbie's culturally contested status because Google's algorithms prize individual, nonmarket judgments of relevance as well as dollars spent on advertising. "It is easier for the little girl to see that the doll is not only a toy, not only a symbol of beauty and glamour, but also a symbol of how norms of female beauty in our society can be oppressive to women and girls ... [The search results show] that Barbie can have multiple meanings ..."[6] (Notably, this is perhaps the only time that little girls are imagined in the scholarly discourse to be standard or normative internet searchers.)

Michael G. Cornelius articulates one aspect of Barbie's success, her role embodying the mass marketing of culture, displaying clothes and therefore suggesting identities:

> Collectors will easily purchase dozens and dozens of the same doll – of the same form, the same plastic structure – in order to amass the paraphernalia associated with the particular look packaged onto the doll ... Barbie herself is not her physique, not her plastic curves and molded-over vagina; rather, she is the hair and clothing that cover these aspects of her personage. Her names suggest as much, since Barbie alters identity every time she switches wardrobe: differing personas like Ballerina Barbie, Western Barbie, and Pan Am Stewardess Barbie are differentiated only by raiment, hairstyle, and accoutrement. Her identity is designed to be discerned by how her form is both covered and represented by these accessories.[7]

As it turns out, reworkings of Barbie – like children's play with Barbie – often challenge this body/clothing dichotomy by focusing on the plastic, exaggerated body itself, stripping away the variations.[8] The Visible Barbie Project,[9] for example, represents a standard childhood Barbie torture, featuring pictures of Barbie in various stages of dismemberment.

[5] Y. Benkler, *The Wealth of Networks* (Yale University Press, 2006), 286 tbl.8.1. *But see* T. Slee, "Googling Barbie Again," whimsley.typepad.com/whimsley/2009/07/googling-barbie-again.html ("[T]he little girl who searches for Barbie on Google will now encounter a commodity toy ... [T]he remaining countercultural site from 2008 has now been pushed over the edge to page 2 of the search results, displaced by two Google-owned collections of links (News and Videos) ... [T]he remaining link is to Wikipedia, now the only non-commercial site on the front page.").

[6] Benkler, *supra* note 5, at 287.

[7] M.G. Cornelius, "Beefy Guys and Brawny Dolls: He-Man, the Masters of the Universe, and Gay Clone Culture," in M.G. Cornelius (ed.), *Of Muscles and Men: Essays on the Sword and Sandal Film* (Jefferson, NC: Mcfarland, 2011), 154–55.

[8] Thomas, *supra* note 4, at 6 (suggesting that adult responses to Barbie are often similar to children's transformative play, placing Barbie "into what both groups deem 'real-life' situations").

[9] www.trygve.com/visible_barbie.html.

Barbie's literal malleability allows her to stand in for a range of anxieties. Amy Richards and Jennifer Baumgartner wrote of their childhood experiences with the doll:

> Barbie didn't so much influence us as she was a blank screen on which to project what was happening in our heads ... The traditional feminist distaste for Barbie has also kept many young women closeted about their dolly-loving past. They fear that loving Barbie will water down or jeopardize their feminism.[10]

Richards and Baumgartner bring out a theme that often underlies the kinds of critiques that get challenged on trademark and copyright grounds: Very few people bother to devote substantial attention to destroying, criticizing, or re-envisioning something to which they are indifferent. A strong critical response usually indicates emotional involvement, which can have significant elements of love as well as hate.[11] And the idea of the "blank screen" also raises an issue with legal consequence: If the law favors critique, then it may be important to know what the meaning of an original work is. Can a "blank screen" have a meaning to which a second-coming artist might oppose herself?

Barbie girls

Mattel *v.* Pitt

Though the most well-known and doctrinally significant Barbie cases come from the Ninth Circuit, I begin with *Mattel* v. *Pitt*,[12] a Barbie decision from the Southern District of New York. *Pitt* involved bullying, which may well have influenced the fair use outcome: pro se defendant Susanne Pitt, a resident of the United Kingdom, agreed to remove the challenged pictures from the internet, but Mattel pursued its case in the United States anyway. Given the lower tolerance for parody in many jurisdictions, being sued in the United States may well have ultimately worked in Pitt's favor once the case got to the point of a judicial resolution – but it is notable that Mattel still chose to sue in the United States, most likely because of the statutory damages provisions that allowed

[10] A. Richards & J. Baumgartner, *Manifesta: Young Women, Feminism, and the Future* (New York, NY: Farrar, Straus and Giroux, 2000) 197.

[11] "A Conversation with Alice Randall," www.houghtonmifflinbooks.com/readers_guides/wind_done_gone/index2.shtml#conversation (explaining that Randall's love for *Gone with the Wind*, as much as her pain at the racist portrayals therein, drove her to create *The Wind Done Gone*, a rewriting of Margaret Mitchell's iconic work to introduce positive and heroic African-American characters and to reveal the racial and sexual stereotypes of the original).

[12] *Mattel, Inc.* v. *Pitt*, 229 F. Supp. 2d 315 (SDNY 2002).

Mattel to *threaten* her with hundreds of thousands of dollars in alleged damages at the outset. Thus, *Pitt* introduces many of the relevant themes, from sexuality to the practical utility of defenses to small producers facing large corporations.

Pitt altered Barbies into "Dungeon Dolls," with added nipples and genitalia,[13] and offered them for sale online. She also posted pictures of her creations, showing dolls sexually torturing and being tortured.[14] Mattel sued for infringement of its copyright in SuperStar Barbie, a doll's head sculpture. Pitt wrote to the court that her work constituted "legitimate freedom of artistic expression" and that "Barbie's origins can be traced to a German 'adult' cartoon and doll called 'Lilli' and that [her] website [was] offered free of charge, 'as entertainment in the same free spirit as the original creator.'"

Construing her letters liberally – including their citation to the *Walking Mountain* district court opinion, to be discussed shortly – the court found them to raise a fair use defense.[15] Section 107 of the Copyright Act provides that fair use is not an infringement of copyright. Though formulated in a way that it could be read as the plaintiff's burden as part of its prima facie case to show that the defendant's use is not fair, American courts have generally treated fair use as an affirmative defense, with the burden on the defendant. Congress provided four factors for courts to consider in determining fair use, along with a preamble listing several types of uses and permission to consider other relevant factors.[16] The four factors, paraphrased, are: (1) the character of the defendant's use, including whether it is commercial (and, more recent case law emphasizes, whether it is transformative in the sense of giving new meaning or purpose to the original); (2) the nature of the

[13] Or perhaps Pitt restored them. *See* Thomas, *supra* note 4, at 116 (Barbie's creator gave a Lilli doll, a German sex doll, to a Mattel engineer who had a prototype made in Japan, but the prototype had nipples, so the engineer filed them off). See "Kidnapped, Page 1," archived 18 October 2000, at web.archive.org/web/20001018155219/http://www.dungeondolls.com/page1.htm.

[14] Again, this may have been reclamation of the cruelty that has always been a part of Barbie, as well as a reconstruction of the often sexualized tortures children have inflicted on Barbies for decades. *See* Thomas, *supra* note 4, at 123 ("The bitch-goddess identity has been with Barbie since her inception . . . During the 1960s she was characterized as a "perfect bitch" and criticized for having a 'predatory' nature. Men worried that she would turn little girls who played with her into a generation of 'independent' and 'viperous' women.") (citations omitted).

[15] *Mattel, Inc.* v. *Pitt* 229 F. Supp. 2d at 319.

[16] Courts have largely ignored the preamble and have certainly not treated its listed categories as presumptively fair, and they rarely consider factors other than the listed four, though those four are so capacious as to allow for almost any consideration a court deems relevant.

plaintiff's work (which includes whether it is factual or fictional and whether it is published or unpublished – the scope of fair use is theoretically narrower for the latter of each); (3) the amount of the work used by the defendant; and (4) the effect of the use on the market for the plaintiff.

The court found Pitt's response sufficient to deny Mattel's motion for summary judgment. Initially, the court found the Dungeon Dolls to be transformative, as evidenced both by "costume and anatomy," as well as context.[17] The dolls' bondage gear was "quite different from that typically appearing on Mattel's products for children." The images of the doll on the website showed her – reworked into Lily the Diva Dominatrix – as "the protagonist in a tale of sexual slavery and torture, the victim of which was another reconfigured Barbie." The court distinguished this type of transformation from a mere substitution of one outfit for another – returning again to the interaction between the physical body of the doll and her clothing. Wryly, the court commented that, to its knowledge, "there is no Mattel line of 'S & M' Barbie." (The court did not have the benefit of Mattel's Catwoman Barbie, created later, which, while lacking nipples and genitalia, at least suggests a gesture towards non-vanilla sensibilities.)[18]

This transformation, the court concluded, sufficiently commented on Barbie herself rather than simply constituting general social criticism. This distinction is typical in fair use cases, even though there is no real historical or market-based justification for distinguishing "parody" from "satire," and even though drawing such a line regularly forces courts into the ill-fitting position of art critic.[19] Here, however, the court was readily persuaded that Barbie was at least in part the target of the transformation. Pitt wanted to resurrect the "original idea of the female figure she claims inspired Barbie," Lilli, who was a character of easy virtue and not a child's toy. As a result of this origin, Pitt suggested, sex was inherent in the doll, and she was "simply revealing this sexual nature by placing Barbie in a 'modern erotic context.'"

This explanation, not incidentally, reveals some of the inherent tensions in transformativeness analysis. In theory, a successful defendant should add meaning that "transforms" the original with new meaning or purpose. Yet courts are more likely to find that the original work is, at

[17] *Mattel, Inc.* v. *Pitt* 229 F. Supp. 2d at 322.

[18] *See also* Tattooed Barbie and pregnant teenage Midge (Barbie's cousin), among other authorized versions: "'Drag Queen' Barbie and 9 other Controversial Barbies," theweek.com/article/slide/232280/drag-queen-barbie-and-9-other-controversial-barbies.

[19] *See* B.P. Keller & R. Tushnet, "Even More Parodic than the Real Thing: Parody Lawsuits Revisited," 94 *Trademark Reporter* 979, 983, 987–88 (2004).

least in part, the "target" of the transformation if they can perceive the seeds of the transformation in the original; otherwise there seems to be no organic and justified connection between the original and the accused work.[20] So transformation regularly means revealing or exaggerating what is already there, rather than adding something that was not previously present, even though one might ordinarily expect the latter to count as "new meaning." Because the images offered an interpretation of Barbie, the court concluded that the accuracy of Pitt's claims about Barbie's genealogy was immaterial to whether the dolls constituted parody. As an attempted commentary on Barbie's sexual nature, Pitt's images were "patently transformative."

After a finding of transformativeness, the other fair use factors favored Pitt, as is typical.[21] The nature of Mattel's work was creative, but this is generally true in transformative use cases and did not help Mattel much. Likewise, though Pitt used the entire work – the doll's head – she changed it substantially by decorating it and the doll body. In transformative use cases, the amount of the work taken can be substantial where that furthers the purpose of creating a new message or meaning. Finally, there was "slim to no" likelihood of market substitution. Mattel was only entitled to markets that creators would in general develop or license others to develop. Here, Dungeon Dolls posed no apparent danger of usurping demand for Barbie dolls, and Mattel was unlikely to develop or license "adult" dolls. The court denied Mattel's motion for summary judgment, and there the case ended.

Mattel *v.* MCA

In the next case, Mattel brought only trademark claims.[22] The legal path of its challenge highlights the problem in trademark of complex and overlapping multifactor defenses. A defendant can have difficulty figuring out which is supposed to apply, and their proliferation may suggest to courts that they should screen out many cases by interpreting each one narrowly, leaving some uses that should be protected essentially homeless.[23]

[20] *See, e.g., Dr. Seuss Enters., L.P.* v. *Penguin Books USA, Inc.*, 109 F.3d 1394 (9th Cir. 1997).

[21] *See* Beebe, *supra* note 3, at 605–06.

[22] *Mattel* v. *MCA* 296 F.3d 894 (9th Cir. 2002), aff'g 28 F. Supp. 2d 1120 (CD Cal. 1998).

[23] *See, e.g.*, J. McCarthy, *McCarthy on Trademarks*, 4th edn. (St. Paul, MN: West Group 1994), § 31.129 ("There is a problem that faces one who … claims that she is merely using another's trademark in a noninfringing manner to convey some social, artistic, entertainment or political expression protected by the First Amendment as free speech.

In 1997, Aqua, a Danish band, released "Barbie Girl," which featured one singer "impersonating" Barbie, "singing in a high-pitched, doll-like voice," while another singer took the role of Ken.[24] The song became a novelty hit, and Mattel sued for trademark infringement and dilution.

The district court conducted a lengthy confusion analysis, using the standard American multifactor test. Though different courts number and name the factors slightly differently, the test considers mainly the strength of the plaintiff's mark; the similarity of the marks; the relatedness of the parties' goods and services or their likely expansion into each other's markets; the parties' marketing channels; any evidence of actual confusion; the degree of care exercised by the relevant consumers; and the defendant's intent. After working its way through all this, the district court concluded that no confusion was likely. The fact that the court felt the need to spend so much time coming to such an obvious conclusion, however, suggests the need for more robust defenses that would preserve courts' and defendants' resources. This is especially true given the expense of a full summary judgment motion, the typical stage at which litigated trademark cases are resolved. A defendant must be prepared to provide evidence on the nature of the parties' markets, the relationship between their advertising channels, the defendant's own intent, evidence of any confusion or lack thereof (with expensive survey evidence prized above anecdotes; in *MCA*, for example, Mattel submitted a 556-person survey in support of its confusion claim), and multiple other factors. For this reason, the threat of a trademark lawsuit is often enough to chill even completely legitimate behavior.

Alongside its confusion analysis, the district court also held that "Barbie Girl" was a parody that neither diluted nor infringed Mattel's rights, because it constituted "nominative fair use," a concept identified by the Ninth Circuit as a type of referential use of a mark that furthers freedom of speech and does not implicate trademark's source-identifying functions. "[N]ominative use of a mark – where the only word reasonably available to describe a particular thing is pressed into service – lies outside the strictures of trademark law."[25] The test requires three elements:

> First, the product or service in question must be one not readily identifiable without use of the trademark; second, only so much of the mark or marks may be

The problem is that there is no easily articulated, clearly defined legal principle that can quickly resolve the conflict. There is no statutory or judge-created safe harbor or affirmative defense that easily resolves such conflicts. Rather, there is a buffet of various legal approaches to choose from. Different courts will choose different approaches and some courts will use more than one.").

[24] *Mattel* v. *MCA*, 296 F.3d at 899.

[25] *New Kids on the Block* v. *News America Publishing*, 971 F.2d 302, 308 (9th Cir. 1992).

used as is reasonably necessary to identify the product or service; and third, the use must do nothing that would, in conjunction with the mark, suggest sponsorship or endorsement by the trademark holder.[26]

"Barbie Girl" satisfied each element. In particular, the repetition of "Barbie" and "Ken" throughout the song were reasonably necessary to the purpose and form of the parody, converting the second factor into a flexible test rather than an "absolute minimum possible" approach.[27] The song's references to Barbie participated in a pre-existing conversation about Barbie's meaning and value; this picks up on the copyright fair use question of transformation as criticism.[28]

Mattel argued that the song flunked the third prong of the nominative fair use test because it provided survey evidence that consumers thought the song was endorsed by Mattel. Though there were serious problems with the survey questions, the district court addressed the issue more directly: In the Ninth Circuit, nominative fair use is "not a likelihood of confusion standard." If the elements of the test are satisfied, a court need not consider evidence of actual confusion (or any of the other standard confusion factors) because the use is not a violation of the Lanham Act as a matter of law.[29] Subsequent Ninth Circuit cases have refined this concept further, holding that nominative fair use is a substitute for the usual confusion test, not a separate defense that can be overcome with sufficient evidence of confusion.[30]

The Court of Appeals affirmed on slightly different grounds, again illustrating how US trademark defenses can cause conceptual confusion

[26] *Ibid.* [27] *Mattel* v. *MCA*, 28 F. Supp. 2d at 1142.

[28] *Ibid.* at 1139 ("Plaintiff dismisses such criticism of its product as simply the view of a 'few extremists,' but this argument only emphasizes the fact that individuals disagree about the meaning and values associated with the doll . . . "); *see also* J.C. Ginsburg, "Of Mutant Copyrights, Mangled Trademarks, and Barbie's Beneficence: The Influence of Copyright on Trademark Law," in G.B. Dinwoodie & M.D. Janis (eds.), *Trademark Law and Theory: A Handbook of Contemporary Research* (Northampton, MA: Edward Elgar Publishing, 2008), 481, available at lsr.nellco.org/columbia/pllt/papers/07138 (arguing that trademark defenses can fruitfully borrow from copyright's free speech-oriented concept of transformative use, as the *Walking Mountain* court did). Ginsburg suggests, and I agree, that a court that has found a use to be fair for copyright's purposes is highly likely to find it fair for trademark's purposes, but why this is remains somewhat underexplained – in other areas, it is not uncommon for conduct that does not violate one law to violate another, especially when the formal justifications for the laws (incentivizing expression and protecting consumers from deception, for example) are different. I suspect that courts may be incorporating concepts of misuse into their fairness analysis – often, cases of overlapping claims should have been brought, if at all, only as copyright claims or only as trademark claims, and a fairness finding on the "wrong" claim recognizes that.

[29] *Mattel* v. *MCA*, 28 F. Supp. 2d at 1143.

[30] *See Toyota Motor Sales, U.S.A., Inc.* v. *Tabari*, 610 F.3d 1171 (9th Cir. 2010).

and wasted litigation energy. Judge Kozinski described Barbie's multiplicity and malleability, treating authorized and unauthorized revisionings as similar in import: "Barbie has been labeled both the ideal American woman and a bimbo. She has survived attacks both psychic (from feminists critical of her fictitious figure) and physical (more than 500 professional makeovers)."[31]

The Court of Appeals posited that the ordinary "likely confusion" test usually strikes a good balance between the trademark owner's property rights and the public's freedom of speech. "But when a trademark owner asserts a right to control how we express ourselves – when we'd find it difficult to describe the product any other way (as in the case of aspirin), or when the mark (like Rolls Royce) has taken on an expressive meaning apart from its source-identifying function – applying the traditional test fails to account for the full weight of the public's interest in free expression."[32]

Aqua's use was both expressive and referential. The title of the song described the song, rather than identifying its producer. The song poked fun at Barbie, and the values Aqua thought she represented, with lyrics such as: "Life in plastic, it's fantastic. You can brush my hair, undress me everywhere/Imagination, life is your creation ... I'm a blond bimbo girl, in a fantasy world/Dress me up, make it tight, I'm your dolly." Distinguishing an earlier case finding that a book about the O.J. Simpson murder trial in the style of Dr. Seuss infringed Dr. Seuss's trademarks,[33] the court emphasized that Barbie herself was the target of the song, not the medium for criticizing some third thing. As a result, traditional confusion analysis was inappropriate, and free speech interests deserved more weight.

The *MCA* court thus adopted the Second Circuit's test from *Rogers* v. *Grimaldi*,[34] which provides that trademark law does not reach titles that are in any way artistically relevant to the underlying work and that do not explicitly mislead as to their source (for example, by a false claim to be an

[31] *Mattel* v. *MCA*, 296 F.3d at 898. The district court, too, referenced Barbie's physicality and the assaults to which she is regularly subjected. *Mattel*, 28 F. Supp. 2d at 1138 ("In the [Barbie Girl] video, the pretend Ken pulls the pretend Barbie's arm off; the singers, playing with a fake-looking arm, appear to be poking fun at the fact that Barbie, like all dolls, can be taken apart by her more adventuresome owners."); *ibid.* at n. 20 ("Indeed, in a book copyrighted by Mattel about Barbie, the introduction states that 'the first thing most children want to do to a doll is take off her clothes.' It further notes that Barbie, a 'buxom fashion queen[,] is often a creature tortured for effect. Her head pops off, fits back on, and does a 360-degree rotation.'") (citation omitted).

[32] *Mattel* v. *MCA*, 296 F.3d at 900.

[33] *Dr. Seuss Enters., L.P.* v. *Penguin Books USA, Inc.*, 109 F.3d 1394 (9th Cir. 1997).

[34] 875 F.2d 994 (2d Cir. 1989).

authorized or official biography). The court's reasoning was both normative – titles are expressively valuable – and empirical – positing that consumers generally do not expect that a title of a book, song, or other expressive work identifies the publisher or producer; instead, it signals something about the content, whether directly or through allusion. "If we see a painting titled 'Campbell's Chicken Noodle Soup,' we are unlikely to believe that Campbell's has branched into the art business. Nor, upon hearing Janis Joplin croon 'Oh Lord, won't you buy me a Mercedes-Benz?,' would we suspect that she and the carmaker had entered into a joint venture."[35]

Notably, after Joplin's death, her stepsister did in fact authorize the use of the song in a Mercedes advertisement,[36] just as Aqua would later license its song to Mattel. Judge Kozinski's claims sound in empirics, but empirics alone are vulnerable to trademark owners' attempts to change consumers' expectations. The normative component of the test discourages them from doing so. Another point about these examples is that Judge Kozinski's quotation of song lyrics, not just titles, foreshadows the expansion of *Rogers*. Framed as a rule about titles, *Rogers* is easily expanded to content, which is good from the point of view of free speech but makes a tautology of the concept of "artistic relevance," since the subject of an expressive work will by definition be artistically relevant to that work. In the event, *Rogers* dictated summary judgment in Aqua's favor. The use of Barbie in the title was clearly relevant to the song itself, and did not explicitly claim that the song was produced by Mattel.

Mattel also claimed dilution under the then-current federal trademark dilution statute. The dilution statute's definition of dilution was somewhat opaque: "[T]he lessening of the capacity of a famous mark to identify and distinguish goods or services" caused by another person's "commercial use in commerce," with some exceptions. The court's statutory analysis is now obsolete, but the basic contours of its reasoning were accepted by the later revision of federal dilution law: because the song was "noncommercial speech" – which meant "not advertising" – it was not a "commercial use in commerce" and was therefore excluded from the scope of dilution law. Nonetheless, the court unequivocally held that use of the mark was (nonactionably) dilutive because, "while a reference to Barbie would previously have brought to mind only Mattel's doll, after the song's popular success, some consumers hearing Barbie's name will think of both the doll and the song, or perhaps of the song

[35] *Mattel* v. *MCA*, 296 F.3d at 902.

[36] J. Doyle, "Selling Janis Joplin, 1995," 10 March 2008, www.pophistorydig.com/?tag=janis-joplin-mercedes-ad.

only."[37] This was a "classic blurring injury" because the distinctiveness of the mark was diminished if the mark "no longer brings to mind the senior user alone."[38]

Whatever the actual likelihood of such changes in consumer reactions, the flexibility (or standardlessness) of dilution as a concept is apparent in the fact that the court saw no contradiction between this holding and its prior holding that the song was about Barbie. Other courts have doubted that a referential use can blur, rather than reinforce, a trademark.[39] The song might be able to change or add to the *meanings* of Barbie, but that is a far different thing than making people think that there is more than one *source* of Barbie (reducing the mark's capacity to *identify and distinguish* Barbie from other products). This very flexibility is why dilution has seemed to need strong categorical defenses. When Congress revised the dilution statute a few years after the *MCA* case, however, it followed the now-common practice of creating a long and detailed exclusion designed to protect freedom of speech.[40] Unfortunately, precisely because of its length and detail, trademark owners can still argue that some commentary is covered by dilution law.[41]

Mattel *v.* Walking Mountain

In the final case, trademark and copyright claims went together. Mattel sued artist Thomas Forsythe for producing seventy-eight "Food Chain Barbie" photos portraying Barbie "in various absurd and often sexualized positions."[42] For example, "Malted Barbie" featured a nude Barbie

[37] *Mattel* v. *MCA*, 296 F.3d at 903–04. [38] *Ibid.* at 904.

[39] *See, e.g.*, *Louis Vuitton Malletier S.A.* v. *Haute Diggity Dog, LLC*, 507 F.3d 252, 267 (4th Cir. 2007) (holding that successful parody is unlikely to dilute a famous mark because it simultaneously communicates that it is a satire of the mark); *Jordache Enterprises, Inc.* v. *Hogg Wyld, Ltd*, 625 F. Supp. 48, 55 (DNM 1985) (quoting with approval McCarthy's conclusion that successful parodies reinforce an association with the trademark owner because the success of the joke depends on continued association of the mark and the owner).

[40] 15 U.S.C. § 1125(c)(3) (excluding "[a]ny fair use, including a nominative or descriptive fair use, or facilitation of such fair use, of a famous mark by another person other than as a designation of source for the person's own goods or services, including use in connection with – (i) advertising or promotion that permits consumers to compare goods or services; or (ii) identifying and parodying, criticizing, or commenting upon the famous mark owner or the goods or services of the famous mark owner," "[a]ll forms of news reporting and news commentary," and "[a]ny noncommercial use of a mark").

[41] *See, e.g.*, *Louis Vuitton*, 507 F.3d at 266 (noting that parodic use as a mark for a parody product fell outside the statutory exemption); *Louis Vuitton Malletier, S.A.* v. *Hyundai Motor America*, 2012 WL 1022247 (SDNY) (finding that dilution law covered a satirical use of Louis Vuitton's mark in an advertisement even though the defendant did not use the mark to refer to its own goods or services).

[42] *Mattel Inc.* v. *Walking Mountain Prods.*, 353 F.3d 792 (9th Cir. 2003).

Figure 19.1: Tom Forsythe, Land of Milk and Barbie (author's collection)

placed on a malt machine, while "Barbie Enchiladas" showed four Barbie dolls wrapped in tortillas and covered with salsa in a casserole dish in an oven, and "Land of Milk and Barbie" showed Barbie bathing in milk (see Figure 19.1). Mattel alleged copyright, trademark and trade dress infringement, along with trademark dilution.

Forsythe stated that the photos were his attempt to critique "the objectification of women associated with [Barbie]," and to attack "the conventional beauty myth and the societal acceptance of women as objects because this is what Barbie embodies." He chose Barbie as his target because "Barbie is the most enduring of those products that feed on the insecurities of our beauty and perfection-obsessed consumer culture." Despite Forsythe's limited market success (he earned well under $4,000 from the series, though his works were displayed in various exhibitions), Mattel sued and thereafter engaged in aggressive litigation tactics, including an incredibly broad subpoena to a nonparty museum that resulted in sanctions.

The courts, both at the district and appellate levels, went through the same fair use analysis as in *Pitt*. One notable difference was that Mattel offered a survey in which it had presented ordinary consumers with color copies of Forsythe's photos and asked them what meaning they perceived. According to Mattel, a reasonable jury could, like many respondents in the survey, fail to perceive a parodic character in the works. The Court of Appeals easily dismissed the survey: For copyright fair use, parody is a question of law, not of "majority opinion." Instead, parody was "an objectively defined rhetorical device." As the Supreme Court had put it, the question was whether parody could "reasonably be perceived,"[43] an inquiry distinct from whether a majority of viewers would primarily perceive a parody. Moreover, parody has First Amendment value, and so even if there is disagreement about the "success or extent" of a parody, "parodic elements in a work will often justify fair use protection." The survey was irrelevant because a majority vote could not be allowed to suppress artistic creativity. The court then quoted Justice Holmes' well-known statement that "it would be a dangerous undertaking for persons trained only to the law to constitute themselves final judges of the worth of [a work],"[44] glossing over the way that Mattel's survey purported to alleviate this danger by having the public judge the worth of a work instead.

Forsythe's use could reasonably be perceived (by the court, implicitly) as a parody of Barbie, given the social context of his work and the actual content of the photos. Mattel had created an image of Barbie as the ideal American woman, associating her with beauty, wealth, and glamour. Forsythe reversed this image "by displaying carefully positioned, nude, and sometimes frazzled looking Barbies in often ridiculous and apparently dangerous situations." He offered "a different set of associations and a different context for this plastic figure." Barbie's smiling obliviousness to the dangers to which the photos showed her exposed – dangers posed by "domestic life in the form of kitchen appliances" – created a "disturbing[]" effect, and in some photos the doll was sexualized by "sexually suggestive contexts." The court concluded that "[i]t is not difficult to see the commentary that Forsythe intended or the harm that he perceived in Barbie's influence on gender roles and the position of women in society." Though the commentary could be *seen*, it apparently could not be *stated*. The court did not and probably could not translate Forsythe's visual message cleanly into words.

[43] *Campbell* v. *Acuff-Rose Music, Inc.*, 510 U.S. 569 (1994).
[44] *Bleistein* v. *Donaldson Lithographing Co.*, 188 U.S. 239, 251 (1903).

This failure to elaborate was not necessarily a weakness. By situating Forsythe's commentary within an existing cultural debate over Barbie's meaning, the court recognized that Barbie was already not entirely under Mattel's control. And this multiplicity of meaning has important implications for how courts should think about transformativeness. Even a defendant-favorable fair use case can fix one meaning to the plaintiff's work, another meaning or purpose to the defendant's work, and then declare them different enough that the defendant's use is transformative and therefore fair. When the defendant loses, the court tends to determine that the meaning of the works is the same, taking a universalist perspective that denies that different observers might generate different meanings from the same work. A court that finds a work nontransformative because it judges that the original already contained the elements highlighted by the defendant's work[45] is mistaking aspects of meaning for the whole.

Interpretation is the condition of expression. *Pitt* and *Walking Mountain* demonstrate that it is the contest among possible meanings of a work, some of which are given greater salience by a second-comer's commentary, that produces the "transformativeness" fair use doctrine seeks. Barbie is already sexual; Barbie is desexualized. Barbie is materialistic and shallow; Barbie encourages girls to run for president. Barbie already covers all the bases. But people still get to make unauthorized uses of her.

Moreover, though Forsythe could have made similar statements without using Barbie, Barbie "conveys these messages in a particular way that is ripe for social comment." The Court of Appeals was unwilling to accept a definition of parody that would require the parodist to show that his parody was impossible without using the copyrighted work. To do so would unacceptably dictate to artists what their subjects could be. Similarly, the Court of Appeals rejected Mattel's argument that Forsythe had simply used too much of Barbie by using her entire body. Significantly for other fair uses, the court pointed out that fair use of a visual or sculptural work may be different from fair use of songs, video, or written works. The latter can be "naturally severable" in that a transformative user can select portions of the original and then add to them. But given his subject (a doll) and his medium (photography, as opposed to, say, painting or prose), Forsythe needed to transform by recontextualizing the doll. Though his medium was different, his use was ultimately no different from that of a musical parodist who took a song's

[45] *Salinger* v. *Colting*, 641 F. Supp. 2d 250, 258 (SDNY 2009), rev'd on other grounds, 607 F.3d 68 (2d Cir. 2010).

"basic melody" and transformed it with other elements. Barbie emerged from his photos "imbued with a different character." Given the transformation, Mattel's argument that Forsythe could have used less of the doll was meritless. Again, artists are not required to use the "absolute minimum" of works they are transforming. Finally, the court pointed out that Mattel was unlikely to license critical uses of Barbie, nor was it sound public policy to allow Mattel to control the market for interpreting Barbie.

Mattel's trademark claims were equally unsuccessful. The Court of Appeals reiterated the free speech value of expression about a cultural icon, then applied the *Rogers* test to Forsythe's use of the term "Barbie" in the names of his pictures. The test was easily satisfied: The use of Barbie was relevant to the content of Forsythe's work, and the titles did not explicitly mislead as to Mattel's sponsorship of the photos. Given those two factors, the public interest in freedom of artistic expression decisively outweighed any interest Mattel asserted in avoiding potential consumer confusion. (Among other things, it is hard to imagine that any consumer confusion would change consumer behavior in any material way. Barbie buyers are likely to keep buying Barbies after seeing Forsythe's photos no matter whether they think the photos are authorized or not.)

The court used a different analysis when assessing Mattel's trade dress claim based on the portrayal of Barbie in the photos. Of the possible tests – a standard multifactor likelihood of confusion test, a version of *Rogers* expanded to expressive content, and nominative fair use – the Court of Appeals chose the last, as a narrower ground for its holding,[46] even as it recognized that Barbie's appearance (trade dress) played a similar role in American culture to the Barbie word mark. Indeed, they are indelibly linked: Barbie, the word mark means what it does because Barbie looks how she looks.

Forsythe's use was nominative. He used the trade dress to refer to or "conjure up" Mattel's product in order to create his own work, and this use was "reasonably necessary," indeed, virtually required, given his choice of medium.[47] Implicit was that Forsythe had every right to choose photography as his medium of commentary. Trademark law could not be used to limit him to words, or even to drawing Barbie

[46] Ultimately, the Ninth Circuit recognized that *Rogers*' First Amendment-protective test could be applied to a work's content, not just its title. *E.S.S. Entertainment 2000, Inc.* v. *Rock Star Videos, Inc.*, 547 F.3d 1095 (9th Cir. 2008).

[47] As Jane Ginsburg has noted, the use of "conjure up" seems borrowed from fair use's third factor, and likewise functions flexibly: a second-comer is allowed to use the amount of the mark (or work) appropriate to the purpose. *See* Ginsburg, *supra* note 28.

freehand. This conclusion also meant that Forsythe had not used more of the trade dress than reasonably necessary. The "necessary" amount is a case-by-case question, so it too was affected by Forsythe's choice of a visual medium: Given that he was creating photos, and given that his goal was to comment on "the social implications of Barbie, including issues of sexuality and body image," his uses were both reasonable and necessary. This conclusion is required to keep the nominative fair use test from discriminating against expressive uses in nontextual media. But it also represents an expansion of the original idea that nominative uses only involve word marks, even though the case that first named the defense expressly distinguished word marks from visual components, such as distinctive fonts.[48]

The court's analysis of the third prong of the nominative fair use test was particularly illuminating of the weaknesses of the test, despite its favorable result for Forsythe. The Ninth Circuit in *New Kids* initially stated this prong as a negative one: "[T]he user must do nothing that would, in conjunction with the mark, suggest sponsorship or endorsement by the trademark holder,"[49] and restated it in those same negative words in *Walking Mountain*. As Forsythe did not do anything to suggest sponsorship, such as calling his series "Official Barbie Food Chain," that would seem to be the end of the matter. But the *Walking Mountain* court called this prong a "closer call" than the other two, even though the court then stated that no explicit disclaimer was required in cases of nominative fair use and even though it is the second prong – reasonable necessity – that seemed to call for the exercise of the most judgment. Indeed, courts applying *New Kids* have often read this third prong as justifying a quick-and-dirty confusion analysis, using much more intuition and much less evidence than the ordinary multifactor confusion test.[50]

While defendants often win when a court has already decided that nominative fair use is the appropriate frame for a particular situation, the half-acknowledged use of affirmative confusion analysis makes this "quick look" potentially quite hazardous to predictable and speech-protective results, as critics have noted.[51] Changing "the defendant must

[48] *New Kids on the Block* v. *News Am. Pub., Inc.*, 971 F.2d 302 (9th Cir. 1992).

[49] *Ibid.* at 308.

[50] As Professor McGeveran has noted, "trademark fair use frequently devolves into a clumsy alternate means of asking the fundamental question of trademark law: whether a defendant's use of a plaintiff's mark is likely to confuse consumers." *See* McGeveran, *supra* note 2, at 51.

[51] *See generally ibid.*; *compare Swarovski Aktiengesellschaft* v. *Building #19, Inc.*, 704 F.3d 44 (1st Cir. 2013) (lifting preliminary injunction based on trial court's holding that a

do nothing else to suggest affiliation other than use the plaintiff's mark" to "the defendant's use must not suggest affiliation" simply restates the dominant confusion test, leaving the point of the rest of nominative fair use somewhat unclear.

In *Walking Mountain*, the court concluded that Forsythe's other materials – making clear his artistic stance towards Barbie – "reduce the likelihood of any consumer confusion as to Mattel's endorsement of Forsythe's work. Any reasonable consumer would realize the critical nature of this work and its lack of affiliation with Mattel. Critical works are much less likely to have a perceived affiliation with the original work." But this is just an on-the-cheap confusion analysis. It has the virtue of avoiding reference to evidence of actual consumer confusion (which is important since surveys can often be constructed to find likely confusion), but it provides regrettably little guidance for the next expressive use case, especially if the next court finds a plaintiff's survey compelling.

Nominative fair use *could* be more than this – it could be a genuine defense precluding inquiry into confusion, the way that the *Rogers* test is. In fact, arguably *Rogers* should completely replace *New Kids* in protecting uses of trademarks in traditional expressive works such as books, movies, and songs, leaving *New Kids* or other doctrines (such as the general American rule that comparative advertising is nonconfusing) to deal with advertising. Or *New Kids*' negative formulation of the third prong could be taken seriously: A defendant's referential use, when reasonably necessary to make the reference communicate the defendant's message, should be conclusively presumed nonconfusing unless the defendant takes some other affirmative step to indicate that its product comes from the plaintiff.

Regardless, having disposed of the infringement claim, the *Walking Mountain* court quickly rejected Mattel's dilution claim, since Forsythe's use as a parody was a noncommercial use explicitly excluded from the scope of federal dilution law. In addition, given how bad Mattel's arguments were, and how Mattel was apparently using its resources to intimidate an ordinary artist, the Court of Appeals remanded the case to the district court for reconsideration of whether to award fees under both the copyright and trademark statutes. Though American law does not ordinarily provide for fee-shifting, both statutes allow it under certain

defendant relying on nominative fair use used more of a mark than necessary because the trial court had failed to make an underlying finding that confusion was likely), *with Tabari*, 610 F.3d at 1181 (apparently holding that using "too much" of a mark in a referential context "might" cause confusion and was therefore enjoinable, without further consideration of likely confusion).

circumstances, including for abusive claims. The remand was a strong suggestion that Mattel ought to be paying Forsythe's fees, which ultimately cost Mattel nearly two million dollars.

Conclusions: Come on, Barbie, let's go party

It is common for lawyers to point to a different field of law to look for a fix to problems in a field under criticism. Judges in trademark cases challenging expressive uses borrow concepts from copyright; reformers in fair dealing jurisdictions suggest learning from fair use's flexibility; reformers in the US look for the greater certainty they hope can be found in narrower but more clearly defined exceptions. But law is fractal and the actual operation of a doctrine may differ from its appearance from the outside. Add to this the interaction between judicial and legislative rule making, which in the US has often meant the creation of new and sometimes baroque multi-step tests from both sources, and it can be extremely hard to figure out what is going on with copyright and trademark defenses.

Still, freedom of expression demands clear protection for certain expressive uses. It is therefore worth noting that every judge, district and appellate engaged in essentially the same copyright analysis in *Pitt* and *Walking Mountain*. By contrast, *MCA* and *Walking Mountain* involved multiple trademark tests, spending a great deal of effort to reach the same simple conclusion – a concern Robin Jacob also raises in Chapter 20 on UK law. More generally, copyright fair use, which has developed general categories that are in practice presumptively free from liability, seems more attractive in comparison to repeated judicial or legislative creation and alteration of multifactor tests hyperspecialized for particular situations. Both copyright fair use's notorious vagueness and the vaunted predictability of narrower exemptions may have been overstated.

Copyright's fair use defense has developed a number of prototypes and clusters that make it a good model for preserving freedom to criticize in an environment – such as the American legal environment – in which intellectual property owners are willing to sue critics and artists.[52] As Joseph Singer has recently explained, standards can be both predictable (when they encounter standard cases) and flexible (when they encounter innovations, either in a defendant's unexpected use or a plaintiff's claim to control something that used to be free):

> Standards are often more predictable than we may think because they are elaborated through the case law system in a way that produces generalizations

[52] *See, e.g.*, Beebe, *supra* note 3; Sag, *supra* note 3; Samuelson, *supra* note 3.

> that approach the form of rules. Both rules and standards operate through explicit or tacit *exemplars*; storytelling defines the contexts in which both rules and standards apply. Exemplars give standards a fair degree of predictability. Standards also often contain implicit *presumptions*. Such default outcomes function as "soft rules" that often approach or exceed the predictability we typically associate with rigid rules. For these reasons, standards are often far more constraining and decision-guiding than the scholars may assume.[53]

Not only does this realization help to rehabilitate copyright fair use against the many criticisms of its unpredictability, it provides some guidance for trademark law. Modern plaintiffs are increasingly likely to bring both copyright and trademark claims against expressive uses. They do not care about the name of the doctrine as long as it suppresses a disfavored use, which is related to the fact that, instead of protecting a traditional trademark or a series of copyrighted works, IP owners now seek to protect a "brand."[54] A working copyright fair use is not enough. We also need working defenses in trademark to protect the same uses: an internal harmonization of boundaries. Given the proliferation of tests, trademark's current defenses lack the supposed benefits of rules (predictability, clarity) while rarely delivering the flexibility of standards.

Norm entrepreneurs like Peter Jaszi and Patricia Aufderheide have vigorously argued that Larry Lessig's famous claim that copyright fair use is "the right to hire a lawyer"[55] is misguided and detrimental. Instead, they suggest, most fair use determinations – certainly most determinations of the kind that an individual creator or an educational institution is likely to be making – can be made by paying attention to context, norms of fair practice, and the statutory fair use factors (primarily the nature of the use).[56] Aufderheide and Jaszi caution that "Exaggerating or misrepresenting the acts of fair users, and their consequences, can unnecessarily deprive people of the agency to accomplish routine acts of cultural expression . . . Fair use does not usually require courage. It should be something that elementary schoolchildren can do without drama."[57] A flexible defense that, over time, develops protected categories of use can provide predictability for ordinary users without

[53] J. Singer, "The Rule of Reason in Property Law," 46 *U.C. Davis L. Rev.* 1369, 1387–88 (2013) (footnote omitted).

[54] *See generally* D.R. Desai, "From Trademarks to Brands," 64 *Fla. L. Rev.* 981 (2012).

[55] L. Lessig, *Free Culture: The Nature and Future of Creativity* (New York, NY: Penguin Books 2005) 187.

[56] P. Aufderheide & P. Jaszi, *Reclaiming Fair Use: How to Put Balance Back in Copyright* (University of Chicago Press, 2011); *cf.* Singer, *supra* note 53, at 11 ("Predictability in property law comes as much from deferring to possession, reliance, custom, and moral norms as it does from formal documents of title.").

[57] Aufderheide & Jaszi, *supra* note 56, at 68.

requiring resort to an increasingly dysfunctional legislative process every time conditions change.

Of course, making a fair use – even a fair use that reasonable people would with near unanimity agree is fair – is no guarantee that a fair use will go unchallenged. America lacks a threats action providing a general remedy for unfounded threats of copyright or trademark infringement,[58] and so there is little deterrent to an intellectual property owner sending a threat letter to shut up a critic, who will rarely be able to secure counsel. Even if an artist does find counsel, the slimmest possibility of statutory damages in copyright, or even the simple burden of litigation, may be enough to force her to capitulate. But at the same time, Mattel's overreaching produced precedents to which creators can now appeal, and a quick search online for Barbie-related art shows that unauthorized creative reuses are flourishing.[59]

A key question for limitations and exceptions to trademark and copyright, then, is how they will shape behavior on the ground. The early critical uses of Barbie, including Dungeon Dolls, often went offline, but they were quickly replaced. A fee award against Mattel (as in *Walking Mountain*) has some deterrent effect, but more significant might be the larger culture that empowers people to create responses to corporate productions, and then at least sometimes to resist threats when they materialize.

[58] *See* 17 U.S.C. § 512(f) (providing limited cause of action for abuse of the notice and takedown system for identifying copyright infringement to online service providers); *cf.* Trade Marks Act, 1994, c. 26, § 21 (Eng. & Wales) (providing cause of action for groundless threat by trademark claimant); L.C. Grinvald, "Shaming Trademark Bullies," 2011 *Wisc. L. Rev.* 625 (canvassing national laws on groundless threats by trademark owners and proposing a similar remedy in the US).

[59] *See, e.g.*, "Altered Barbie," alteredbarbie.com/artwork/all_art (collecting various artists' work); "Debbie Curtis Barbie Art," debbiecurtisart.com/home.html (showcasing work of painter who takes Barbie as her subject); "Margaux Lange," www.margauxlange.com/ (featuring jewelry made from Barbie parts).

20 Parody and IP claims: a defence? – a right to parody?

Rt. Hon. Sir Robin Jacob

> Does the law have a sense of humour? This question is raised whenever the irresistible force of free expression, in the form of parody, meets the immovable object of property rights in the form of trademark protection.[1]

So begins Justice Albie Sachs' glorious assenting judgment in the Constitutional Court of South Africa.[2] The Court reversed the Supreme Court's finding that the slogans on this T-shirt (see Figure 20.1) infringed Carling's famous registered trade mark for its Black Label beer. He asked his question in the context of trade marks,[3] but the same question arises, more frequently, with copyright. Indeed I suppose the Carling registered mark must also be the subject of copyright[4] and the complaint could have included a copyright claim.

What Laugh It Off, the plaintiff in the case, did was offensive. It changed 'Black Label' to 'Black Labour', 'Carling Beer' to 'White Guilt', 'America's Lusty, Lively Beer' to 'Africa's lusty lively exploitation since 1652' and 'enjoyed by men all around the world' to 'No regard given worldwide'. Laugh It Off contended that the T-shirt 'either criticises the way SAB markets its beer by targeting black workers, or generally criticises

[1] *Laugh It Off Promotions CC v South African Breweries (Finance) B.V. t/a Sabmark International*, Constitutional Court of South Africa, Case CCT 42-04, 27 May 2005, per Albie Sachs J.

[2] *Ibid.* This is a must-read for anyone interested in parody and IP.

[3] Very oddly no one in the case seems to have considered whether there was a straightforward defence: that although the attacked use resembled the Carling mark it was not confusingly similar to it. It could have been argued that 'similar' within the meaning of s. 34(1)(c) of the South African Trade Marks Act means 'confusingly similar'. The whole point of the parody would have been missed if Laugh It Off's 'mark' was confusingly similar. South Africa does not need to go down the overprotective European approach to trade marks which treats them as precious icons to be cosseted, venerated and treated like sacred cows.

[4] Unless it was too old. The company is indeed old, but the device marks on which it sued, judging by their date of registration in the early 1990s were probably well in copyright. Device trade marks are regularly updated with a consequent new copyright.

Figure 20.1 The Laugh It Off T-shirt

the exploitation of blacks by whites'.[5] Crude, not particularly funny, slightly unclear in what was being parodied, but a parody nonetheless.[6]

Laugh It Off was a small business and the sales of this T-shirt were very small. But instead of just ignoring it, Carling sued and created a cause célèbre. A wiser course would almost certainly have been to do nothing.[7] Not only can we be grateful to the obdurate and rigid line taken by Carling which gave us the splendid judgments of the Constitutional Court, but there is a lesson from that too. It is not merely that people do not like being parodied (which is hardly surprising) but that some are so touchy they will sue for the slightest 'insult'. There are a significant number of powerful IP owners who definitely do not have a sense of humour.[8]

[5] Media Summary, *Laugh It Off Promotions CC v South African Breweries (Finance) B.V. t/a Sabmark International* CCT 42/04.

[6] I remember a much wittier T-shirt. It had 'Horrids' written in the characteristic script and green colour of Harrods department store. It was duly injuncted on the basis of copyright in the absence of a parody exception (not reported but I was in court at the time, around the mid-1970s).

[7] In the early days of the internet I asked Coca-Cola's chief trade mark counsel what they were going to do about 'Coke sucks' sites. He said, with refreshing realism: 'Nothing – if we sued we'd give publicity and make things worse.'

[8] Sometimes it may be the legal department. I am reminded of part of the correspondence between Warner Bros.' legal department and Groucho Marx when the former (whose film *Casablanca* had recently been a success) threatened legal action against '*A Night in Casablanca*': Groucho wrote: 'I have a hunch that this attempt to prevent us from using the title is the brainchild of some ferret-faced shyster, serving a brief apprenticeship in your legal department. I know the type well – hot out of law school, hungry for success, and too ambitious to follow the natural laws of promotion. This bar sinister probably needled your attorneys, most of whom are fine fellows with curly black hair, double-breasted suits, etc., into attempting to enjoin us. Well, he won't get away with it! We'll fight him to the highest court! No pasty-faced legal adventurer is going to cause bad blood between the Warners and the Marxes. We are all brothers under the skin, and we'll remain friends till the last reel of "A Night in Casablanca" goes tumbling over the spool.' Available at http://archive.org/details/Groucho_Marx_Letter_to_Warner_Brothers.

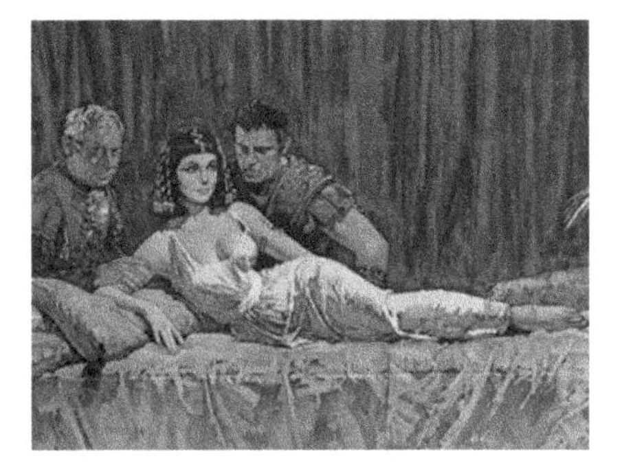

Figure 20.2 *Cleopatra* film poster

Another example of a humourless, but this time successful, plaintiff comes from the time when I was doing my Bar Finals. In 1963 Twentieth Century Fox launched the epic film *Cleopatra*, starring Elizabeth Taylor, Richard Burton and Rex Harrison. A famous poster for the movie is shown in Figure 20.2.

In early 1964 the 'Carry on Team' came out with *Carry on Cleo*, starring Amanda Barrie, Sidney James and Kenneth Williams. To put it into context for Americans and others who do not understand the British psyche,[9] the *Carry On* films were a series of smutty humorous films with absurd plot and characters. The lines were replete with double entendres and dreadful puns.[10] The poster which Twentieth Century got injuncted for copyright infringement is shown in Figure 20.3.[11]

I thought then and think now that was ridiculous.[12] There is a good case for saying this was not an infringement at all.[13] But, assuming it prima facie was, it seems obvious that there should have been a defence of parody. Few really dispute that, and that the defence should apply both to copyright and trade mark infringement.[14] Putting it another way, the right of 'property' – a word which carries with it the automatic implication of the right to exclude – should be circumscribed to allow

[9] Understanding a *Carry On* is a bit like trying to understand not only how cricket is played but why.

[10] E.g., when Caesar is attacked, he cries out: 'Infamy! Infamy! They've all got it in for me!'

[11] *Twentieth Century Fox v Anglo-Amalgamated Film Distributors* (1965) 109 S.J. 107. A short report of the judgment granting an interlocutory injunction. The Judge, amazingly enough, thought that the poster was damaging.

[12] Mr Bumble comes to mind.

[13] The Judge applied the 'so near as to suggest the original' test which is not the same as the statutory test of 'reproduce a substantial part'.

[14] Particularly, as the European cases and *Carling* show, that these days the prima facie scope of trade mark rights extends so far.

Figure 20.3 *Carry On Cleo* film poster

for some sorts of parody. And I think it should not matter what kind of intellectual property is in play.[15]

Unlike in the United States,[16] parody is not currently an exception to copyright in the UK. The Hargreaves Report on Intellectual Property,[17] however, included in its recommendations that such an exemption be created. The problem is what sorts of parody should be allowed? In the EU, which increasingly has legislative power over IP,[18] the position is that each Member State can do its own thing about this as far as copyright is concerned. Article 5(3) of the Information Society Directive (ISD)[19] says: 'Member States may provide for exceptions or limitations to the rights provided for in Articles 2 and 3 [i.e. the reproduction and communication rights] in the following cases: ... (k) use for the purpose of caricature, parody or pastiche.'

The permissibility of parody is clearly an issue which has plagued the courts for some time. By their very nature, parody exceptions contest the scope of protection of intellectual property. They are at the edge of what is permissible and even now many courts have trouble deciding what is permissible and what steps over that precarious edge into infringement.

The French have legislated.[20] Article L122-5 of the French IP code says: '[o]nce a work has been disclosed, the author may not prohibit ... (4) parody, pastiche and caricature, observing the rules of the genre'. I doubt whether this is helpful. For when it comes to parody 'the genre' has no rules, making legislation immensely difficult. Parody ranges from the downright brutally offensive to the respectful *hommage.* I cannot imagine any way of determining the 'rules of genre'. It would be left to the court to make them up – in effect to read these words as if they meant 'fair'. [21]

[15] Copyrights, trade marks, design rights or moral rights can all potentially get in the way of parody.

[16] Where 'fair use' generally allows parody – see Rebecca Tushnet, Chapter 19 in this volume.

[17] Digital Opportunity, A Review of Intellectual Property and Growth, May 2011.

[18] Article 118 of the Lisbon Treaty on the functioning of the EU says so, but what is now called the EU has been making IP laws at least since the Trade Marks Directive 93/89.

[19] The Information Society Directive 2001/29/EC (ISD).

[20] So have a number of others. The current Consultation (see below) wants 'evidence' but does not seem to have had the wit to try to find out how the parody exceptions are actually working in other countries.

[21] French case law has indeed done just that. The courts have articulated some rules. These include that the parody not be confusing; that the parody not intend personally to harm the author and – somewhat uncertainly – that the parody is intended to be funny. See, e.g., Tribunal de Grande Instance de Paris, third chamber, first section, Judgment of 13 February 2002, available at www.legalis.net/spip.php?page=jurisprudence-decision&id_article=57 (reproduction of press photos without significant changes is confusing and not parody); Tribunal de Grande Instance de Paris, third chamber,

As far as trade marks are concerned, there is no provision for parody in current EU legislation.[22] But the recent Max Planck study[23] has recommended that: 'It should also be specified that parodies, as particular form of criticism or comment, also fall into the ambit of the provision [i.e. of a "referential use" defence]. The use would be allowed to the extent that it does not contravene principles of honest practices in industrial and commercial matters.'[24] Any implementing legislation, if it comes to pass, and it probably will, will be EU wide, unlike copyright, where currently Member States may do their own thing. Of course 'honest practices etc.' also probably amounts to a rather fuzzy 'what the court thinks fair'. And, of course, everyone knows the US has 'fair use', leaving it all to the courts. I do not suppose anyone thinks that thereby a clear bright line has been achieved.

Can one do better? Or must one simply leave an appeal to fairness to define a parody exception to IP rights? Well the UK Government thinks one can do better. I suspect it is wrong. Let us examine what it is up to more closely. The December 2006 Gowers Review of Intellectual Property[25] recommended, after consultation, that there should be created an 'exception to copyright for the purpose of caricature, parody or pastiche by 2008'.[26] The UK Government, instead of then just getting on with it, put it out to consultation again, as if Gowers had not already done so. This was by a 'newspeakly' named document called 'Taking Forward the Gowers Review, Proposed Changes to the Copyright Exceptions' published in December 2007 (so much for 'by 2008'). I do not know what happened to that consultation, for the next event, under the new Coalition Government, was another review of IP law by another distinguished journalist, Professor Ian Hargreaves. Like Gowers, he was given just six months to cover the whole of IP. As far as parody and copyright were concerned he said: 'Government should deliver [more newspeak!] copyright exceptions at national level to realise all the

third section, Judgment of 13 February 2001, available at www.legalis.net/spip.php?page=jurisprudence-decision&id_article=77 (parody implies the intention to amuse without gratuitous harm).

22 Hardly surprising. I do not suppose that at the time of the original Trade Marks Directive (1989) anyone ever thought that trade mark right could extend to parody in the first place. And so it shouldn't.

23 Max Planck Institute for Intellectual Property and Competition Law, Munich, Study on the Overall Functioning of the European Trade Mark System, 15 February 2011.

24 *Ibid.*, para. 5.262.

25 Andrew Gowers, an ex-editor of the *Financial Times* was asked to produce a review of the whole of IP law within six months – an obviously impossible task, not least for someone with no IP background.

26 Gowers Review of Intellectual Property, December 2006, recommendation 12; see paras. 4.89–4.90.

opportunities within the EU framework, including format shifting, parody, non-commercial research, and library archiving'.[27] He noted that: 'After two consultations the only concrete action has been the abandonment of efforts to bring in . . . an exception to cover parody.'[28]

The UK Government published a response to Hargreaves in August 2011. It said it would 'bring forward proposals in autumn 2011 for a substantial opening up of the UK's copyright exceptions regime . . . This will include proposals . . . to introduce an exception for parody.' [29] The next step was, the reader will now not be surprised to learn, a document called: 'Consultation on proposals to change the UK's copyright system'.[30]

To that I now turn. Hargreaves said decisions on IP policy should be 'evidence based'. I do not know what he had in mind as to what constitutes 'evidence'. I do not suppose the UK Government knows either but it says it agrees. I rather think 'evidence' is, and can only be, either material put forward by various lobbying groups, or so-called 'economic' evidence based on tenuous or speculative data. As far as parody is concerned, it is impossible to see how there can be any real concrete 'evidence'. The Consultation has four and a half pages on the subject.[31] It consists mainly of statements of the blindingly obvious or questions which cannot possibly be answered either at all or quantitatively.

Here is an example of the blindingly obvious. Under the heading 'Impact on creators of original works' it says:[32]

> Four potential effects of a parody exception on the sales of original works have been identified: 1) lost sales due to confusion between a parody and an original work; 2) increased sales due to greater publicity and awareness for the original; 3) lost sales due to negative reputational effects on the original; 4) increased sales due to positive reputational effects on the original.

But even this is inadequate. Thus it ignores what can be one of the key reasons why some people sue for copyright infringement – damage to *amour propre*, a real matter of concern to touchy – too touchy – copyright owners as I have observed above. And it devotes quite a bit of space (not only here but elsewhere in the Consultation) to 'lost sales due to

[27] Digital Opportunity, A Review of Intellectual Property and Growth, May 2011, para. 5.40.
[28] *Ibid.*, para. 10.5.
[29] The Government Response to the Hargreaves Review of Intellectual Property and Growth, 3 August 2011, p. 7.
[30] Consultation on proposals to change the UK's copyright system, Ref 2011-004.
[31] Consultation Document – Proposals to change the UK copyright system, pp. 83–88, paras. 7.100 to 7.122.
[32] *Ibid.*, para. 7.111

confusion'. That is rather ridiculous for two reasons. A parody which is liable to be taken for the original is an unsuccessful parody; because the whole point of parody is that the audience recognises it for what it is. Secondly, if a work is deceptive, the law has an independent remedy – passing off. For instance in *Clark v Associated Newspapers*[33] a well-known colourful politician successfully sued the London *Evening Standard*, which published a spoof 'Alan Clark Diary'. He proved that a substantial number of people thought the diary was actually his, that they were confused or deceived.[34] No one suggests that a parody which deceives should be allowed. You do not have to consult about such a self-evident matter. So also for parody which is defamatory: defamation has its own causes of action, most relevantly for libel.

Incidentally, it is interesting to observe that the parody in the *Clark* case, a literary parody, did not involve any question of copyright infringement. It is an odd fact that it is much more possible to parody a literary work, or an author's literary style, without substantially reproducing a copyright work, than it is to parody a visual or musical work. The *Oxford Book of Parody*[35] is full of parodies down the ages which could never have amounted to a prima facie copyright infringement which needed a defence. That fact ought to inform the Government. If literary authors have to put up with parody, why not authors of other types of work?

I turn to exemplify some obviously unanswerable questions (or at least not usefully answerable questions) posed by the Consultation:

78. Do you agree that a parody exception could create new opportunities for economic growth?
79. What is the value of the market for parody works in the UK and globally?
80. How might a parody exception impact on creators of original works and creators of parodies? What would be the costs and benefits of such an exception?[36]

And:

82. How should an exception for parody, caricature and pastiche be framed in order to mitigate some of the potential costs described above?
83. Would making this a 'fair dealing' exception sufficiently minimise negative impacts to copyright owners, or would more specific measures need to be taken?
84. Are you able to provide evidence of the costs and benefits of such an exception?[37]

[33] [1998] 1 WLR 1558; [1998] RPC 261.
[34] Or at least the Judge held he proved – many of us doubt he was right on the facts.
[35] J. Gross, (ed.), *The Oxford Book of Parodies* (Oxford University Press, 2012).
[36] Consultation Document, p. 86. [37] Consultation Document, p. 88.

Did those who wrote this, in their desire for 'evidence', seriously expect that anyone could give concrete reliable answers to these questions?[38]

I have another concern about this Consultation. Nowhere does it mention free speech – yet parody often involves just this. The notion that one is concerned solely with market economics mistakenly confines the debate. Article 10(1) of the European Convention on Human Rights says: 'Everyone has the right to freedom of expression.' It is qualified by Article 10(2), which includes 'the protection of the reputation or the rights of others'. But the qualification is not so extensive as to prevent reasonable criticism – which is just what a parody may be. Free speech really matters: it should in some cases trump IP rights, as it did in the *Carling* case.

Further, the Consultation explicitly refused to address another way in which parody may be restricted by IP rights – no qualification of the so-called 'moral right' is proposed. The Consultation says:

> As well as economic rights, the Copyright Act provides certain moral rights to creators, which derive from international law, including the right to be identified as the author of a work and the right to object to derogatory treatment of a work. These rights, deriving from international law, include the right to object to derogatory treatment applies [*sic*] to any use of a work that amounts to distortion or mutilation of the work, or is otherwise prejudicial to the honour or reputation of its creator. Moral rights therefore clearly place limits on the extent of any parody exception. However, many parodies will not constitute derogatory treatment of a work and moral rights and parody exceptions coexist in many other European countries, including those that provide much stronger moral rights than in the UK.[39]

It is not much use providing a defence of parody to copyright infringement if the author has another weapon. The Consultation blithely asserts that 'many parodies will not constitute derogatory treatment of a work'. I doubt that. In particular the so-called 'integrity right' could well get in the way. The Copyright Designs and Patents Act 1988 gives an author a

[38] In a meeting about this book Professor Barton Beebe suggested the questions themselves are parodies. Actually there is a small exercise by Erickson, Kretschmer and Mendis which examines parodies of pop songs on YouTube. (K. Erickson, M. Kretschmer and D. Mendis, Copyright and the Economic Effects of Parody: An empirical study of music videos on the YouTube platform, and an assessment of regulatory options, Parody and Pastiche. Study III. January 2013, IPO 2013/24). It concludes they are harmless and even could help promote the original. Such parodies of course only form a small part of the universe of parodies – and are all essentially non-commercial. The self-evident reality is that the IPO's questions are unanswerable – and in any event parody is self-evidently more about free speech than economics or markets.

[39] Consultation Document – Proposals to change the UK copyright system, para.7.105.

right 'not to have his work subjected to derogatory treatment'.[40] That is defined in section 80(2) (emphasis added):

(2) For the purposes of this section—

(a) 'treatment' of a work means *any addition to, deletion from or alteration to or adaptation of the work*, other than ... [minor exception]

(b) *the treatment of a work is derogatory if it amounts to distortion or mutilation of the work or is otherwise prejudicial to the honour or reputation of the author or director* ...

Consider a parody of an artistic work; say a photograph or a poster. Almost certainly that will involve something by way of *addition to, deletion from or alteration to or adaption of it.* I cannot conceive of a parody which would not amount to at least one of these things. Some courts may consider that enough. A better reading is that there is an overall requirement too: whether the parody *is otherwise prejudicial to the honour or reputation of the author.* Note that the basic test is '*prejudicial to the honour or reputation of the author*'. Is not all adverse criticism prejudicial to the person criticised? Adverse criticism may be entirely justified but harmful to the author's reputation – indeed a justified criticism may be more harmful than one which has no justification.

Remember, as I have said twice before, authors can be ever so touchy. Perhaps the most famous daft example of this in the context of the integrity right comes from Canada. In *Snow v The Eaton Centre*,[41] a sculptor had made some models of Canada Geese to hang in the atrium of the Eaton Centre Shopping Mall like a flight of geese. To jolly up the Mall for Christmas, its owners put red ribbons round the necks of the geese. The sculptor took umbrage, sued and won. He persuaded the court that the sculpture's integrity was 'distorted, mutilated or otherwise modified' and that was 'to the prejudice of the honour or reputation of the author' contrary to section 28.2 of the Canadian Copyright Act. Most people think the decision silly on its facts, but for present purposes it illustrates how powerful the 'moral right' can be.

So I think the Consultation underestimates the potential of moral rights to allow for parody where the author is the subject of it. The real reason why some parodies may escape the integrity right is different: that the parody does not attack the reputation of the author but someone else. Thus Laugh It Off would escape being caught by this provision. It was

[40] Section 80(1). [41] (1982) 70 C.P.R. (2d) 105.

Figure 20.4 Nadia Plesner, "Dafurnica" (2010)

prejudicial to Carling's reputation, not that of the unknown author of the trade mark itself.

The Consultation says nothing can be done about providing a parody exception to moral rights because there is an international obligation to provide for the moral right which does not have any such express exception.[42] Technically this so; the UK Act was copied from Article 6*bis* of the Berne Convention.[43] But it would surely be worth exploring how far the obligation has been 'written down' in the jurisprudence of other countries.

Moreover, Article 10 of the European Convention on Human Rights may itself provide a right of parody where free speech is involved. It did so, for instance, when Louis Vuitton sued the artist Nadia Plesner for depicting a poor African child carrying a chihuahua dog and its 'Audra' handbag. She had used it originally on a T-shirt and agreed to give up after threats by Vuitton. Then she used the same figure again in a picture she called 'Darfurnica', a protest about genocide in Darfur. The painting is shown in Figure 20.4.

Vuitton got an *ex parte* injunction from the Dutch Court to restrain its depiction anywhere in the EU. Plesner retaliated by seeking in effect a declaration that Article 10 trumped Vuitton's right (actually

[42] Ricketson and Ginsburg, argue that parodies do not harm honour or reputation within the meaning of Article 6*bis*; S. Ricketson and J. Ginsberg, *International Copyright and Neighbouring Rights: The Berne Convention and Beyond* (Oxford University Press, 2006), para. 10.29. But one can easily foresee that a powerful offended parody victim might want to argue otherwise, and that, depending on how offensive the parody was, a court might rule otherwise.

[43] Introduced by the Rome Act of 1928.

it was a registered design right, but the type of right should make no difference). Vuitton was equivocal about whether it actually wanted to suppress the whole picture and in the end said it did not – even though it was the picture that provoked the claim. Judge Edgar Brinkman ruled in Plesner's favour irrespective of whether the figure was in the whole picture or not.[44] He held that Article 10 did prevail over Vuitton's 'property'[45] right. Judge Brinkman records that there was a parallel *ex parte* injunction in France. Researches do not show that anything happened after that, so presumably the African boy remains injuncted in France.

A similar use of Article 10 was made by the German Federal Court in a silly trade mark infringement case about a postcard. The card ridiculed Milka chocolate's idyllic advertising theme using cows and mountains with a purple background corresponding to Milka's colour mark registered for, inter alia, chocolate. The Court held it was prima facie an infringement[46] but that free speech and Article 10 rights meant that the use was with 'due cause'.[47] What a convoluted way of reaching the only sensible result!

I do not think anyone could complain if the moral rights legislation were made expressly subject to the provisions of the European Convention on Human Rights, which indeed is probably the legal position under the Human Rights Act 1998 (UK).[48] Indeed I would go further and make all IP rights expressly subject to the Convention.

I turn to what I think the UK Government should do in relation to copyright. I have little to say, for it is not complicated. It should put forward legislation for an additional exception to copyright infringement (of all types of work). This could simply provide:

(1) It is not an infringement of the copyright in any type of work to make a fair parody, caricature or pastiche[49] of it.

[44] 4 May 2011.

[45] Note again the invocation of 'property' as a justification for an oppressive injunction.

[46] Another example of how protective the European trade mark has become; cf. the point I made about the Black labour (Carling) case above.

[47] Case I ZR 159/02, 3 February 2005. Under Art 9(1)(c) of the Community Trade Mark Regulation as amended (2009/207/EC) and national law implementing Article 5(2) of the Trade Marks Directive as amended (08/95/EC), in the case of dissimilar goods the proprietor must show that the use of the defendant's sign is 'without due cause'.

[48] Section 3(1) provides: 'So far as it is possible to do so, primary legislation and subordinate legislation must be read and given effect in a way which is compatible with the Convention rights.'

[49] I use the phrase in the ISD. There can be absolutely no point in trying to define these more. The Consultation asks whether there should be a further definition. That is obviously a pointless question.

I am not sure that any more is worth adding to try to define 'fair'. But if it is, it should be woolly. Something like:

(2) In considering what is 'fair' the court shall take into account all relevant circumstances, including the extent, if at all, to which the work complained of is competitive with that work, the degree, if any, of the offensiveness of the parody, or the degree to which the parody may constitute fair comment on the work, its author or any matter of public interest.

And I would add an express provision:

(3) All rights provided for in this Act and any other intellectual property right are subject to the provisions of the European Convention on Human Rights and in particular any fair parody caricature or pastiche shall be permitted if it is an exercise of the right of freedom of expression provided for by Article 10(1) of that Convention.

Finally the Government should get on with it. No more consulting or wishing for an impossible evidence base.

Postscript

After this chapter was written[50] the UK Intellectual Property Office (IPO) announced that a 'fair dealing' for parody would be provided.[51] It said:

The Government will legislate to allow limited copying on a fair dealing basis for parody, caricature and pastiche, while leaving the existing moral rights regime unchanged. It considers that this permitted act will provide economic and cultural benefits by removing unnecessary restrictions on the activity of some creators, reducing administrative costs, and encouraging creators, without causing any significant economic harm to holders of rights in the parodied content. The requirement that any parody use of a work be 'fair dealing' is an additional restriction which ensures that the exception is not misused, and will preclude the copying of entire works where such taking would not be considered fair (for example if such works are already licensable for a fee). The existing moral rights regime will be maintained unchanged, so that creators will be protected from damage to their reputation or image through the use of works for parody.

In addition to the benefits to parodists outlined above, of allowing easier production of parody works, there are compelling social and cultural benefits such as the development of free speech and the fostering of creative talent. The wider public would also benefit from increased legal clarity and

[50] It was sent to the UK IPO in draft pursuant to the latest round of consultation.

[51] Under the Orwellian title 'Modernising Copyright, A modern robust and flexible framework', 17 December 2012.

opportunities for freedom of expression when creating parody for non-commercial reasons. The Government agrees with the Business, Innovation and Skills Select Committee that genuine political and satirical comment should be protected.

So something should happen. I would be pleased to see they adopted all my proposals include (3) above, but I doubt they will do anything so sensible.

Index

Cambridge Intellectual Property and Information Law

Titles in the series (formerly known as Cambridge Studies in Intellectual Property Rights)

Brad Sherman and Lionel Bently
The Making of Modern Intellectual Property Law
978 0 521 56363 5

Irini A. Stamatoudi
Copyright and Multimedia Products: A Comparative Analysis
978 0 521 80819 4

Pascal Kamina
Film Copyright in the European Union
978 0 521 77053 8

Huw Beverly-Smith
The Commercial Appropriation of Personality
978 0 521 80014 3

Mark J. Davison
The Legal Protection of Databases
978 0 521 80257 4

Robert Burrell and Allison Coleman
Copyright Exceptions: The Digital Impact
978 0 521 84726 1

Huw Beverly-Smith, Ansgar Ohly and Agnès Lucas-Schloetter
Privacy, Property and Personality: Civil Law Perspectives on Commercial Appropriation
978 0 521 82080 6

Philip Leith
Software and Patents in Europe
978 0 521 86839 6

Lionel Bently, Jennifer Davis and Jane C. Ginsburg
Trade Marks and Brands: An Interdisciplinary Critique
978 0 521 88965 0

Geertrui Van Overwalle
Gene Patents and Clearing Models
978 0 521 89673 3

Jonathan Curci
The Protection of Biodiversity and Traditional Knowledge in International Law of Intellectual Property
978 0 521 19944 5

Lionel Bently, Jennifer Davis and Jane C. Ginsburg
Copyright and Piracy: An Interdisciplinary Critique
978 0 521 19343 6

Megan Richardson and Julian Thomas
Framing Intellectual Property: Legal Constructions of Creativity and Appropriation 1840–1940
978 0 521 76756 9

Dev Gangjee
Relocating the Law of Geographical Indications
978 0 521 19202 6

Andrew Kenyon, Megan Richardson and Ng-Loy Wee-Loon
The Law of Reputation and Brands in the Asia Pacific Region
978 1 107 01772 6

Annabelle Lever
New Frontiers in the Philosophy of Intellectual Property
978 1 107 00931 8

Sigrid Sterckx and Julian Cockbain
Exclusions from Patentability: How the European Patent Office Is Eroding Boundaries
978 1 107 00694 2

Sebastian Haunss
Conflicts in the Knowledge Society: The Contentious Politics of Intellectual Property
978 1 107 03642 0

Helena R. Howe and Jonathan Griffiths
Concepts of Property in Intellectual Property Law
978 1 107 04182 0

Rochelle C. Dreyfuss and Jane C. Ginsburg
Intellectual Property at the Edge: The Contested Contours of IP
978 1 107 03400 6